WOMEN AND VALUES

READINGS IN RECENT FEMINIST PHILOSOPHY

Marilyn Pearsall
California State University, Sacramento

Wadsworth Publishing Company
Belmont, California
A Division of Wadsworth, Inc.

Philosophy Editor: Kenneth King
Production: Del Mar Associates
Designer: Gary Head
Copy Editor: Andrea Matyas Olshevsky
Cover Design: John Odam
Cover Illustration: Detail of *Youth*, 1910, by Aristide Maillol,
courtesy Hirshhorn Museum and Sculpture Garden, Smithson-
ian Institution

Printed in the United States of America

1 2 3 4 5 6 7 8 9 10———90 89 88 87 86

0-534-05472-2   *Slatners* 35'906 /14.15. 10.87

Library of Congress Cataloging-in-Publication Data
Main entry under title:

Women and values

  1. Feminism—Philosophy—Addresses, essays, lectures.
2. Feminism—United States—Addresses, essays, lectures.
3. Social values—Addresses, essays, lectures.
4. Feminism—Moral and ethical aspects—United States—
Addresses, essays, lectures. I. Pearsall, Marilyn.
HQ1221.W89 1986   305.4'2'01   85-15254
ISBN 0-534-05472-2

WOMEN
AND
VALUES

For my daughters,
Cornelia and Sabrina

Contents

Preface

Despite the gratifying fact that there are now several good anthologies of feminist philosophic writings, a certain area has yet to be addressed. There is still a need for a text that deals systematically with ethical issues from a feminist perspective. This anthology is designed to fill this need.

To achieve this goal, I have selected articles with several facts in mind. First, feminist writing has achieved a high level of scholarship. This has inclined me to select recent articles from the available literature. It is hoped that this text will have an impact on current thinking and on the present debates in the field. Second, past anthologies have included many selections by male authors. Given today's volume of high-caliber writings by women philosophers and thinkers, there is a substantial corpus of theoretical writings by women. Thus, I have sought only women thinkers.

A third fact has directed my selection. There is a felt need for an anthology that is of a more philosophic (as opposed to primarily political) orientation. So I have chosen feminist writings that fall into traditional philosophic categories: social philosophy, legal philosophy, moral theory, and the like.

But another fact that guided me is that feminist thought has recently turned to applying hard-won feminist insights to traditional academic disciplines. Thus, I have avoided writings by women who concern themselves with the traditional issues only in the traditional manner. Instead, this text offers a woman's voice, that is, feminist writings that take significantly different approaches to traditional issues.

The text has been arranged in such a manner that it will be a flexible teaching instrument. Chapter 1 begins with a discussion of the notion of feminist theory itself. Chapter 2 presents selections that lay the groundwork necessary for later discussions. These selections focus on theories of sex difference and the nature/culture debate. Chapters 3 through 8 then present readings in value theory organized under standard headings. Chapter 3 presents readings dealing with social philosophy, Chapter 4 with political philosophy, and Chapter 5 with philosophy of law. Chapter 6 deals with philosophy of religion and Chapter 7 with philosophy of art.

Thus, Chapters 3 through 7 focus on standard areas of value inquiry. Chapter 8 turns to ethical theory strictly so-called. I have divided Chapter 8 into two sets of readings—the one dealing with theoretical considerations, the other consisting of articles on applied ethics.

As I previously stated, this anthology is meant to be a flexible and useful introductory text for philosophy and women's studies courses. If used for an introductory-level philosophy course, I would suggest covering Chapters 1, 2, 3, 4, and 6 (and if time permits, the first part of Chapter 8). A course in ethical theory should cover the selections in Chapters 1, 2, and both parts of Chapter 8. A course in social/political philosophy should cover Chapters 2, 3, 4, and 5. A women's studies course might well draw on Chapters 1, 5, 6, 7, and the second part of Chapter 8.

Since this is meant to be a text that is useful for philosophy classes and women's studies classes, it does not presuppose previous philosophic training or a detailed knowledge of feminism and feminist theory. Two particular features should help the student who might not have a background in either field. First, after each of the readings there are questions for discussion that should help the student follow the content of the selection. Second, an introductory chapter has been included in which I briefly consider a survey of feminist theory and feminist approaches to moral theory.

Women's moral theory is an expression of the collective efforts of feminist thinkers, past and present. The text itself is an acknowledgment of this fact. However, I would also like to thank those more immediately concerned with this project. Ken King, my editor, believed in this work from the start. I would also like to thank Debbie Fox and Peggy Meehan at Wadsworth. Discussion with Gary Jason, in particular, as well as Michael Carella and Patrick Huckle, colleagues at San Diego State University, were especially helpful. I greatly appreciate the reviews of this book done by Rosemarie Tong, Williams College, and Alison M. Jaggar, Rutgers University. Finally, I thank Cornelia Pearsall for scholarly assistance.

Introduction

Toward a Feminist Transvaluation of Value Theory

Value theory is the systematic theory of values. As such, it is one of the three basic fields of philosophy along with *metaphysics* (the study of the nature of reality) and *epistemology* (the study of knowledge and belief). General value theory, or *axiology*, addresses questions concerning the nature, meaning, and scope of values and value judgments.

Traditional value theory is, of course, *male* value theory, and it has been done as (male) theory-building is characteristically done. The standard approach is to carve out areas for investigation, formulate questions and a methodology for dealing with those questions, and then allow the researchers in a given area to conduct their specialized endeavor.

Thus, traditional value theory has focused on certain domains. Social philosophers discuss which social structure is the best (meaning the best for *man*kind). Similarly, political philosophers ask which political system is the "best." Philosophers of law ask which legal system is the most "just." Other philosophers question the nature of art and artistic endeavor and what is a "good" work of art. Or they examine the basic concepts of religion and inquire about their meaning and function. And ethical theorists investigate the nature of "right" or "good" in respect to human conduct.

Feminist considerations arose quite outside the academic world of traditional (male) value theory. To understand the transvaluation of value theory in feminist thought, we need to understand the revolution in feminist thinking.

Feminism has a complex history as well as a philosophy. To simplify this history somewhat, it is generally said that feminist thought occurred in two waves. The first wave of feminism appeared at the start of the nineteenth century (with anticipations in the seventeenth and eighteenth centuries) with the representative text *A Vindication of the Rights of Woman,* by Mary Wollstonecraft (1792) and later with *The Declaration of Sentiments* of the Seneca Falls Convention (1848). The first wave gave rise to the women's suffrage movement in Europe and the United States and culminated in the United States in women's right to vote (1920). Then came a period of relative dormancy in the political and theoretical activity of women.

The second wave of feminism began shortly after World War II, with the appearance of Simone de Beauvoir's now classic text, *The Second Sex* (1949). De Beauvoir's brilliant work was a turning point in the history of feminist thought. Perhaps the key to understanding the paradigm change wrought by de Beauvoir is to see that she shifted the conceptual framework of feminism from a discussion of *equality* to a discussion of *freedom*. According to de Beauvoir, women could not be equal, could not be anything but "the second sex," until they were *free* to change themselves and their conditions. So with the publication of *The Second Sex*, feminism went beyond a demand for equality—it became a call for liberation.

In *The Second Sex*, de Beauvoir agrees with the existentialist claim that man is his freedom. But, she argues, it follows that woman is her freedom, too. Why then, is woman always and everywhere subordinate to man? De Beauvoir's insightful answer is that woman has been constituted as the Other to man's Self; she has become object to his subject, and he has mediated the world for her.

> What peculiarly signalizes the situation of woman is that she—a free and autonomous being like all human creatures—nevertheless finds herself living in a world where men compel her to assume the status of Other.

De Beauvoir argues that man enslaves woman because he flees from himself (that is, the burden of freedom) "by means of the other, whom he oppresses to that end."

So, de Beauvoir asserts, woman is not now her freedom, which means that she must project herself into the future and must undertake projects. For existential ethics, choice is central to being fully human; to be free to choose *is* to be fully human ("Man is his freedom").

> Every subject plays his part as such specifically through exploits or projects that serve as a mode of transcendence; he achieves liberty only through a continual reaching out toward other liberties. . . . Every individual concerned to justify his existence feels that [it] involves an undefined need to transcend himself, to engage in freely chosen projects.

The corollary to de Beauvoir's exhortation to women to choose their freedom is: Women cannot look to men to grant them freedom. If that were the case, women would not themselves be choosing their freedom; they must seek their own transcendence.

This line of thought forms a dramatic shift from the point of view of first-wave feminism. Whereas earlier feminism was stated as a demand for legal equality, de Beauvoir's response is that, in effect, not only must women be free to choose *not* to be the second sex, but they must choose the act of freedom: They must choose to liberate themselves. Thus the second wave is a women's liberation movement.

Another reason for seeing de Beauvoir's text as a watershed in feminist thought is that she explicitly grapples with two major theoretical systems that had not previously been addressed in feminist thought: Marxism and Freudianism. At the outset of her existentialist text, de Beauvoir rejects both systems as explanations of women's situation. She denies the Freudian claim that "anatomy is destiny," that is, that woman's situation is the outcome of her biology. And she also denies the Marxist view that a woman's identity is determined primarily by "the means of production" (the economics) of the society in which she lives. Feminist theorists of the second wave follow de Beauvoir in paying special attention to the Marxist and Freudian perspectives, utilizing or rejecting many of their concepts.

Although there are several distinct strains of contemporary feminism, they all bear the mark of de Beauvoir's initial theory to some degree. One school of present feminist thought is exemplified by Shulamith Firestone's text, *The Dialectic of Sex* (1970), which is both an amalgam and a critique of preceding lines of thought (existentialist, Marxist, and Freudian). Firestone is one of the first thinkers to have clearly set forth the essential features of what is now called *radical feminism*. She takes up de Beauvoir's existential question, Why have women been constituted as Other, as object? And she answers it by utilizing Marxist and Freudian elements, while creating a new feminist point of view.

In the opening statement of *The Dialectic of Sex,* ''Sex class is so deep as to be invisible,'' Firestone tells us that her view is one of a class analysis, but a class analysis with a difference. Traditional Marxist class analysis holds that there is a class struggle between the owners of the means of production and the workers; the oppressor is the bourgoisie; the oppressed is the proletariat. But the class struggle postulated by Firestone is carried on between women as a class and men as a class: Men are the oppressors, and women are the oppressed. And since the class struggle propounded by Firestone is between sex classes, sexuality in all its aspects is central to her theory. Firestone's thesis is that the origin of women's oppression (as Other, as object) is the sexual, or procreative, function of women, because women were ''at the mercy of their biology.'' This led, she claims, to the first division of labor and to the rise of sex classes. Thus, Firestone sees sexuality as fundamental to feminism *and* Freudianism, but she rejects the idea that there is anything immutable about the nature of sexuality. Specifically, she rejects Freud's thesis that women have masculine envy, and she argues that women envy only men's power, not their anatomy.

Firestone's analysis, therefore, of what she calls ''the dialectical materialism of sex'' employs and yet discards Marxist and Freudian theory. It also incorporates elements of de Beauvoir's existential view in that the dialectic of sex can only be resolved by women themselves. Firestone then adds another crucial element—one reminiscent of the first wave of feminist thought, but now revolutionary rather than reformist: the notion that there must be a collective resolution of the sex class struggle. De Beauvoir proposes the individual solution; but the individual woman, says Firestone, cannot solve the sex class struggle: Only ''sisterhood is powerful.''

Of *radical feminism* we can say then that its method is ''consciousness-raising,'' that is, it raises women's (class) consciousness of their oppression. And its aim is to liberate women from the oppression of men. In other words, the universal domination of men and subordination of women must cease.

''Sexual politics,'' as Kate Millett calls it, must be transformed. The fundamental maxim of radical feminism, ''the personal is political,'' means that everything that happens in the personal lives of women happens to them as a sex class and, therefore, is political. As Alison Jaggar summarizes:

> On this view, there is no distinction between the ''political'' and the ''personal'' realms: every area of life is the sphere of ''sexual politics.'' All relations between women and men are institutionalized relationships of power and so constitute appropriate subjects for political analysis.

So, in consciousness-raising groups women will share their personal experiences and, together, analyze their political condition.

The second wave of feminism has brought forth a number of different ''types'' or ''camps'' of feminism having diverse views on tactics and strategies for change as well as on more fundamental concepts. One way to indicate the variety of current feminist thought is to contrast each with radical feminism.

In contrast with radical feminism (and socialist feminism), liberal feminism is reformist and evolutionary rather than revolutionary. The liberal feminist is heiress to the nineteenth-century liberal tradition of the first wave, which adopts securing the rights of individuals and recognizing the equality of all individuals as its central goals. Liberal feminism, accordingly, emphasizes securing women's rights through legislation, especially through the passage of the Equal Rights Amendment (ERA). It also promotes equal opportunity for women as individuals (affirmative action).

One way to see the difference between liberal feminism and radical feminism is to ask: What is the basis of women's subordinate position? A radical feminist would construct an answer centering on the notion of women as a class—a sex class that faces class oppression and needs to act collectively.

The sex class (radical feminist) analysis indicates a radical solution: overthrow of the oppressor class. By comparison, a liberal feminist would construct an answer based on the notion of the sex roles of males and females and our socialization to them. And since women have been much less favored in their sex roles and socialization, liberal feminists argue for the attenuation of rigid sex roles and an "androgynous" ideal. The sex-role analysis also suggests the institution of meliorative measures such as providing more adequate child care facilities for working mothers, nonsexist school programs and texts, and so on.

Socialist feminists, like radical feminists, propose that meliorative measures are not sufficient, but the socialist feminist does not focus on the notion of women as a sex class. Instead, the socialist feminist adopts and extends the traditional Marxist class analysis to include a discussion of the "means of reproduction" as well as the "means of production." In their view, it is in regard to the means of reproduction that women have been exploited and alienated. Thus socialist feminists are concerned with wages for housework, the psychodynamics of the nuclear family, and motherhood.

Although socialist feminism is concerned with the fight against patriarchy, it views that task as being inseparable from the struggle against capitalism (and racism). Since it draws on the theoretical heritage of traditional Marxism, socialist feminism has perhaps a more theoretical orientation than radical feminism, which arises more directly from women's consciousness-raising (rap) groups. In its commitment to viewing the oppression of women as arising from capitalism, patriarchy, and racism, socialist feminism is characterized by a multicausal, multisystems analysis.

These as well as other types of feminism are represented in the readings that follow, in which women thinkers of all perspectives articulate and transform the various domains of value theory.

The revolution in feminist thought is in the process of transforming traditional academic philosophy. In particular, over the last decade a corpus of theoretical work on values and value theory informed by women's consciousness and feminist imperatives has emerged. The selections in this book have been chosen from this growing body of writings. They speak about women and their values. The issues discussed and the conceptual schemes employed to explore them are the work of women thinkers who are the "daughters of the second wave." This collection of their essays is offered as part of the process of liberating our thinking from masculinist modes and patriarchal ideology.

To better display the profound transvaluation of value inquiry wrought by contemporary feminists, I have selected essays bearing on each of the traditional male value-domains. In these readings, feminist theorists of many persuasions present their values and voice their own felt concerns. The only restriction I imposed in selecting the readings is that these thinkers must speak from a feminist point of view, that is from a stance that recognizes the oppression of women in male-dominated society. There is, however, ample room in this general perspective to allow for interesting and important debates among women.

We cannot predict what feminist ethical theory will eventually look like or what forms it will take, but we know it will be the collective work of many women thinkers. We are now in the process of the feminist "reconstruction of self and society." What can be said is that feminist ethics will have certain features. First, it will be highly *personal*; it will draw on the shared experiences of women's everyday lives. Second, it will have an *emancipatory* promise, for it is founded on a liberationist philosophy. Along with social and political philosophy,

philosophy of art, and philosophy of religion and their concomitant areas of inquiry, moral theory as developed by feminists may be seen as undoing patterns of conceptual dominance that before seemed permanent (what Dale Spender calls "the intellectual double-standard").

Thus it follows that feminist ethics will be highly *critical* of traditional ethics. Moral theory as developed by male philosophers has, according to women theorists, reflected and supported masculinist ideology. The concepts of "person," "equality," "justice," "freedom," "self," "nature," "subject," and many more, as they are used in ethical theory, need to be re-evaluated and re-visioned.

Certain moral issues must be of particular interest to feminist philosophers, because these issues have received little or no attention in the past. Abortion, rape, pornography, prostitution, domestic violence, sex discrimination, and so on must be discussed and debated by feminists and among feminists. These *women's issues* affect women's lives and are of central concern to feminist ethics.

Thus feminist ethics lends new meaning to moral concepts and moral issues as they become part of the feminist critique of existing values. Can we say that women will create their own ethics? In other words, is there a distinctive women's morality? If so, what will it look like? Will it have a different methodology from that of traditional (male) ethical theory? There is evidence to suggest that this might be the case; it may be that women differ from men in the way they experience and formulate moral concepts and moral issues. According to Carol Gilligan, out of "our shared fate," women may speak "in a different voice."

In any case, what we are seeing now is of the utmost significance in that feminist philosophers are engaging in a most radical critique of existing modes of ethical thought and in a most challenging exploration of moral issues. From this circumstance, we can expect profound alteration in the ways women will consider values and value theory.

WOMEN
AND
VALUES

1

Feminist Theory and Practice

Feminist theory is dialectically related to feminist practice and emerges from what Simone de Beauvoir calls "women's concrete situation (as wife, mother, prostitute, lesbian, as young, as old)." The dialectical relationship between feminist theory and practice is exemplified by the central feminist methodological device, consciousness-raising, which is the direct sharing by women of their personal experience.

Feminist theory arises out of the felt abuses that women testify to in consciousness-raising groups and the perceived oppression of women. As Marilyn Frye says, "What 'feminist theory' is about, to a great extent, is identifying those forces . . . which maintain the subordination of women to men." And feminist thinkers develop their theoretical analysis in great measure from looking at issues central to the experiences and lives of women, such as housework, child care, abortion, sex discrimination, sexual harassment in the workplace, prostitution, rape, and pornography.

The close connection between feminist theory and actual feminist practice ensures that feminism does not become monolithic and authoritarian. Feminists choose to strive to represent diversities as well as commonalities among women, especially in regard to the parameters of race and class.

Jane Flax points out that theory has been male theory, which means that men have been doing the theorizing in all fields. By contrast, women have been silenced, or at least muted, in patriarchal discourse. Thus, she says, women must be wary of identifying with past modes of thought. Flax discusses feminist theorizing in terms of shared assumptions: women's oppression as a "given"; the structural and systematic nature of male domination (patriarchy); and the need to understand and confront that oppression. She outlines an agenda of feminist imperatives around three spheres: production, reproduction, and psychodynamics, which, she asserts, mutually support patriarchy.

According to Nancy Hartsock, an agenda for feminist theory must take into account the issues of women in capitalist society as well as in patriarchy. In other words, it must deal with class differences as well as the sex/gender system. She sees a socialist feminist theory arising out of women's everyday lives that addresses the need for collective action for change. In this way, Hartsock holds, feminist theory can ground socialist theory by connecting personal experience and political generality and by showing that capitalism and patriarchy are interlocking systems that oppress women.

Finally, feminist thinkers wish to engage in a discourse that encompasses women of all social, ethnic, and national backgrounds, in order to develop strategies and tactics that speak to the needs and desires of all women. Maria Lugones and Elizabeth Spelman's dialogue represents the point of view of the woman of color as well as of the white/Anglo woman concerning feminist theory. Lugones and Spelman seek a woman's voice that will speak not only for white, middle-class women but will incorporate the ideas and issues of women of color. Since no woman should be silenced, it is a feminist imperative to find ways to articulate our diversity along with our commonality. Women of color must represent their own experience and the meaning of that experience for themselves. Lugones and Spelman's critique of androcentric theory offers some ways for us to speak together that are respectful of all women.

Women Do Theory

Jane Flax

I begin with an overview of feminist theory and a discussion of the activity of theorizing. I then present a theoretical framework that I've developed after trying various theories and finding none of them sufficient to explain the range of things I think a feminist theorist needs to explain.

Let me say a little about how I ended up doing feminist theory. I have been interested in philosophy and political theory for a long time. I am also interested in psychoanalysis, and have practiced as a feminist therapist. So, partly, I've been trying to put together more traditional ideas of theory with those I've learned as a therapist, especially from psychoanalysis.

Very early I began to connect theory with political activity. I chose political science because I thought there I would learn about politics—which was a mistake. Some political scientists seem to consider theory to be something done 3,000 years ago by Aristotle and Plato, unrelated to the present world. And yet, one of my attractions to theory was that through it, I could learn to systematize my experience. Political science was not much help.

Over time, however, I have found traditional theory to be very helpful in recognizing other people's mental processes as they try to understand the structure of the world systematically. That is, much traditional theory is a kind of internal discourse among thinkers—like a 3,000-year conversation in which people take up each others' ideas and reapply them. I'm

From *Quest*, Vol. V, No. 1 (Summer 1979), pp. 20–26. Reprinted by permission of Jane Flax.

interested in many parts of that discourse: what can politics do; what is the ideal political system; what are just relationships; what does "equality" mean?

These issues have been dealt with in the women's movement, but not always in the context of theory. For instance, what it would mean to have a really liberated society is a question of equality and justice that has been debated since the first political theory was attempted. But feminists don't often think of our questions as part of that ongoing political discourse.

In traditional political theory, however, the relationships between men and women, and the status of women, are rarely discussed. They are certainly not generally seen as problems. Some traditional political theorists talk about the family and the role it plays for the state of course; and some have argued for the liberation of women. Plato, for instance, argued that women *could* be philosopher kings since these should be chosen on merit and no inherent proof existed that women were any less intellectually capable than men.[1] Other political theorists, however, have argued that woman cannot think abstractly and has a less developed moral sense. Thus, part of the problem feminist theorists face is taking the general "grammar" and concepts of traditional theory and applying them to women and the issues that affect us.

This brings me to the questions, "what is feminist theory?" and, more generally, "what is theory?" The most important characteristic of theory is that it is a *systematic, analytic* approach to everyday experience. This everybody does unconsciously. To theorize, then, is to bring this unconscious process to a conscious level so it can be developed and refined. All of us operate on theories, though most of them are implicit. We screen out certain things; we allow others to affect us; we make choices and we don't always understand why. Theory, in other words, makes those choices conscious, and enables us to use them more efficiently.

For example, implicit in my choices about the work I could do is an understanding of where power lies, what I'm likely to be able to do, where I'm likely to meet the most frustration, and when I'm likely to be most effective. I might not think through those things consciously, but I make choices on these bases. If you push that explanation, you'll find a series of assumptions about the way the world works, what's available (to me), and what isn't. That's implicit theory-making. The problem is to make it explicit.

Blocks to Explicit Theory

One of the problems with theory is that women aren't supposed to be able to do it; women aren't supposed to be able to think abstractly. So when you say to a woman, "Okay, now let's read theory," she's likely to panic.

In addition, theoretical writing is often so full of jargon that it seems divorced from ordinary experience. Unfortunately, many theorists have an entrepreneurial interest, a territorial mentality, and they encourage everyone else to believe that their work is impossibly complex. This discourages women—and men—from engaging in theory because it seems hostile and unintelligible. I don't think that the issues *are* inherently so difficult or so far removed from ordinary understanding. I think theorists build turfs and *make* it difficult for others to understand that turf—just like any other professional.

Feminist Theory

Feminist theory is based on a series of assumptions. First, it assumes that men and women have different experiences; that the world is not the same for men and women. Some women think the experiences of women should be identical to the experiences of men. Others would like to transform the world so that there are no such dichotomous experiences. Proponents of both views, however, assume that women's experiences differ from men's, and that one task of feminist theory is to explain that difference.

Secondly, feminist theory assumes that women's oppression is not a subset of some other social relationship. Some argue that if the class system were destroyed, then women would not be oppressed—I don't classify that as feminist theory. Feminist theory assumes that women's oppression is a unique constellation of social problems and has to be understood in itself, and not as a subset of class or any other structure.

It also assumes that women's oppression is not merely a case of what the Chinese call "bad attitudes." I have problems with the word "sexism," because the term implies that women's oppression will disappear when men become more enlightened. On the contrary, I think feminist theory assumes that the oppression of women is part of the way the structure of the world is organized, and that one task of feminist theory is to explain how and why this structure evolved.

Feminist theory names this structure "patriarchy," and assumes that it is a historical force that has a material and psychological base. What I mean by "patriarchy" is the system in which men have more power than women, and have more access to whatever society esteems. What society esteems obviously varies from culture to culture; but if you look at the spheres of power, you'll find that all who have it are male. This is a long-term historical fact rooted in real things. It's not a question of bad attitudes; it's not a historical accident—there are real advantages to men in retaining control over women. Feminist theorists want to explain why that's so.

Patriarchy works backwards as well. It affects the way men and women feel about themselves, and is so deeply internalized that we can't imagine a world without gender. As much as we talk about androgyny, or some situation in which gender isn't so significant, I don't think any of us could imagine a world in which gender would not bring with it many special meanings. *We* may still want to attach special meanings to gender, but a feminist theory would argue that the power attached to gender should disappear; it should not determine whether a person is excluded or included in whatever is esteemed by society.

Goals of Feminist Theory

Feminist theory has several purposes. The first is to understand the power differential between men and women. How did it come into being? Why does it exist now? What maintains it? How do the power relations between men and women affect other power relations—for instance, race and class—and how does patriarchy reinforce other oppressive power structures?

Secondly, the purpose is to understand women's oppression—how it evolved, how it changes over time, how it's related to other forms of oppression, and finally, how to change our oppression.

In feminist theory, one issue that emerges consistently is the necessity to understand the family, because it is one of the central mediating structures between all other structures of oppression. The family is where we're internally formed, where we learn about gender, where we experience class and race systems in personal and intimate ways. Therefore, understanding the functions of the family should be one of the crucial goals of feminist theory; yet it remains an area that is particularly undeveloped.

A third purpose of feminist theory is to overcome oppression. Feminist theory is the foundation of action and there is no pretense that theory can be neutral. Within feminist theory is a commitment to change oppressive structures and to connect abstract ideas with concrete problems for political action. It is senseless to study the situation of women without a concomitant commitment to do something about it. The theorist has to draw out the consequences of the theory and use life experience as a part of her basis for understanding, for feeding into the development of theory.

Traditional political theory has always been attached to action. Plato wrote *The Republic* partly because he thought that Athenian democracy was degenerating and he wanted to understand why, and how. It's only contemporary social science theory that claims to be objective, neutral, value-free. I don't think any form of knowledge is neutral, but certainly feminist theory cannot claim neutrality. I think that's one of the problems of women's studies programs. They are too often developed as though they are mere intellectual exercises; some may be, but the study of women is not.

The Evolving Theoretical Framework

I assume that feminist theory must point to a clear and real base for the oppression of women—feminist theory has to be rooted in human experience. I also assume that there are three basic realms of human activity.

The first is production—we need to produce food, clothing and shelter for our survival. (Obviously, different cultures will produce in different ways. Even people who live on tropical islands have to organize the gathering and preparation of coconuts.) Marx called this the material substructure of human life, and I call it the realm of production.

People also need to reproduce. Not only must we produce the next generation biologically, but we also need to reproduce good citizens for the society. We need to inculcate the values, attitudes, and beliefs appropriate to that culture. A good American citizen will have ideas and expectations very different from a good Mesopotamian citizen living 3,000 years ago. But no matter which society, somehow the unformed person must be trained in its values. In our society, acculturation is conducted by a variety of organizations, including the family and later the school, and the state is involved in setting out certain policies which translate into procedures for acculturating individuals.

The third realm of human activity is the individual's internal life. This is what Freud called "the unconscious," and what I call "psychodynamics." The psychodynamic sphere is where our biological and our mental lives meet, and must be organized. One of the most important aspects of this sphere is sexuality. One of the questions feminists must ask is how a basically "polymorphous species"[2] ends up, in most cultures, a genitally-oriented, heterosexual and monogamous species. Though all cultures allow varying degrees and varieties of sexual pleasure, every civilization channels its citizens' eroticism into practices acceptable to the society.

When we talk about the situation of women, we must examine how all three spheres cooperate to produce our oppression. The elimination of an oppressive structure in one sphere only is inadequate because the other spheres will re-emerge as even more oppressive.

For instance, in the Soviet Union, where the class system is supposedly abolished, men *still* retain the power. The upper structure of the Communist Party is almost entirely male. And while women may move into occupations (as in the United States), those occupations lose their prestige when they do.[3]

Why didn't the oppression of women disappear? For one thing, the structure of the family was not altered—no efforts were made to change the reproductive spheres.[4] So, even though one structure of oppression may have been dealt with, the other two remain intact. Hence, we cannot expect women to be fully participating persons, nor that the full range of women's experience will be expressed in social values. This is a material view of women in that it locates oppression within our material lives. And yet it also teaches us to look at each of the three spheres of human activity, to see how each one particularly impinges upon women.

The Intersection of Spheres

One of the most important characteristics of the family is that all three spheres intersect here. In our society, the family is the structure in which we learn to repress and channel our sexuality—where homosexuality is forbidden and where heterosexuality is promoted. It's also the place in which, obviously, external authority is transmitted by and translated in our parents' teachings. It's in the family that the standards of acceptable social behavior are first taught.

Even though most production is no longer done within the family, this is still the structure in which we are taught behaviors appropriate to our class. Lillian Rubin, in *Worlds of Pain*, shows that working-class people become acculturated in the proper expectations of their class and that these expectations are perpetuated from generation to generation. So, the class system impinges upon the family, not only in the obvious ways (such as the kinds of housing or childcare you can afford), but also in more subtle ways.

Other structures influence and are perpetuated by these three spheres. The state, for example, structures and benefits from the ways reproduction and psychodynamics interact in class divisions and modes of production. It also benefits from the lingering effects of the psychodynamic sphere on political and personal action.

Reproduction is obviously segregated on the basis of sex. Women are nurturers, men are authority figures—a very important distinction in terms of the developing person. This means that both acculturation and reproduction are sex-segregated.

Thus, as feminism teaches us, the class system is not the same for men and women. It's a mistake to take traditional class analysis and impose it upon the experience of women when it is clear that women's work is sex-segregated and class-segregated (80% of women work in jobs where more than half the jobs are held by women).

And finally, the psychodynamic sphere so thoroughly remembers that we're either a *male* or a *female* person, that gender becomes part of who we are. Thus, though we succeed in developing an analysis of patriarchy and capitalism, we still find ourselves repeating old, self-defeating patterns. We can't explain how this happens. Rationally, we've got it all worked out, and yet something refuses to change. That's partly because a great deal happens unconsciously, as we act out old patterns that are accessible neither to reason nor to control since the psychodynamic sphere *is* unconscious. It's the realm of dreams and associations. It's the world of sexuality; it's your internal life. But also it's hard for us to grasp because feminists haven't done much work on it.

Conclusion

My assumptions are, then, that these three spheres of life are crucial for everybody, that they're experienced differently by men and women, and that both the experience and the oppression of women are rooted in all three. I believe we must examine each sphere to see how women's and men's experience are different, and how it contributes to that difference. If we would end the oppression of women, we must transform all three spheres; change in one sphere alone will not liberate women.

The psychodynamic sphere can be changed by completely transforming the rearing of children. Dorothy Dinnerstein's book, *The Mermaid and the Minotaur*, is a good reference on the transformation of childrearing. Dinnerstein maintains that both males and females have to be present in the child's life from infancy. It's important that children not be raised by one female person, or a group of female persons. The child also needs peers. In fact, it makes day care and childrearing not something that enables women to work, but locates both right in the center of feminist demands. A feminist revolution must deal with the way children are reared. To create liberated persons requires a transformation in childrearing.

It also means that homosexuality is not just a nicety we support to appease our lesbian sisters. We must recognize that heterosexuality is also part of the structure of the oppression of women. Sexual repression is one of the ways in which women are oppressed and one of the ways in which patriarchy is maintained. On another level, restraining sexuality is a very powerful way of controlling people—as Wilhelm Reich understood in his analysis of the Nazis. Therefore, to fight for a variety of expressions of sexuality has to be part of feminism. It shouldn't be incorporated because lesbians insist, "What about us?" It's absolutely central to feminism. These are two concrete conclusions which grow out of an analysis of the psychodynamic sphere.

Notes

1. An interesting sidelight is that the head of Plato's academy was a woman who was stoned by the Christians—one of the first of the Christians' many acts against women playing an intellectual, active role.
2. Polymorphous means that we can derive erotic pleasure from a wide variety of experiences; not only from experiences between ourselves and other persons, but also between ourselves and all sorts of physical objects.
3. Seventy-five percent of physicians in the Soviet Union are women, but a physician there is like a social worker here.
4. It's not permissible to be a homosexual or to engage in sexual relations with many different persons of either gender in the Soviet Union, China or Cuba.

Study Questions

1. How does Flax define "theory"? What are the difficulties of trying to move from implicit to explicit theory making?
2. What assumptions, according to Flax, are common to all feminist theories? Would all feminists agree?
3. What goals does Flax see for feminist theory?
4. What three realms of human activity does Flax mention? Why does she feel that oppression of women must be fought in all three spheres simultaneously?
5. In what areas do these three spheres overlap?
6. What implications are there for feminist theory in regard to these spheres?

Feminist Theory and the Development of Revolutionary Strategy

Nancy Hartsock

A number of writers have detailed problems of the left in America. They have pointed out that it has remained out of touch with large numbers of people, and that it has been unable to build a unified organization, or even to promote a climate in which to debate socialist issues. The left has been criticized for having a prefabricated theory made up of nineteenth-century leftovers, a strategy built on scorn for innovation in politics or for expanding political issues. Too often leftist groups have held that the working class was incapable of working out its own future and that those who would lead the working class to freedom would be those who had memorized the sacred texts and were equipped with an all-inclusive theory that would help them organize the world.

While such a list of criticisms presents a caricature of the left as a whole, it points to a number of real problems, and overcoming them will require a reorientation. Here I can only deal with one aspect of the task: the role of feminist theory and the political practice of the women's movement as a model for the rest of the left.

I want to suggest that the women's movement can provide the basis for building a new and authentic American socialism. It can provide a model for ways to build revolutionary strategy and ways to develop revolutionary theories which articulate with the realities of advanced capitalism. Developing such a model requires a redefinition of theory in general in the light of a specific examination of the nature of feminist theory and practice, a reanalysis of such fundamental questions as the nature of class, and a working out of the implications of feminist theory for the kinds of organizations we need to build.

Theory and Feminist Theory

Theory is fundamental to any revolutionary movement. Our theory gives us a description of the problems we face, provides an analysis of the forces which maintain social life, defines the problems we should concentrate on, and acts as a set of criteria for evaluating the strategies we develop. Theory has an even broader role, however. As Antonio Gramsci has pointed out, "One can construct, on a specific practice, a theory which, by coinciding and identifying itself with the decisive elements of the practice itself, can accelerate the historical process that is going on, rendering practice more homogeneous, more coherent, more efficient in all its elements, and thus, in other words, developing its potential to the maximum."[1] Thus, theory itself can be a force for change.

At the same time, however, Gramsci proposes that we expand our understanding of theory in a different direction. We must understand that theorizing is not just something done by academic intellectuals but that a theory is always implicit in our activity and goes so deep as to include our very understanding of reality. Not only is theory implicit in our conception of the world, but our conception of the world is itself a political choice.[2] That is, we can either accept the categories given to us by capitalist society or we can begin to develop a critical understanding of our world. If we choose the first alternative, our theory may remain forever implicit. In contrast, to choose the second is to commit ourselves to working out a critical and explicit theory. The political action of feminists over most of the last decade provides a basis for articulating the theory implicit in our practice.[3] Making the theory explicit is difficult but necessary to improve the work feminists are doing.

The Nature of Feminist Theory

Women who call themselves feminists disagree on many things. To talk in such unitary terms about a social movement so diverse in its aims and goals may seem at first to be a mistake. There is a women's movement which appears on television, has national organizations, and is easy for the media to reach and present as representative of feminist thought. But there is a second movement, one harder to find, that is made up of small groups and local organizations whose members work on specific local projects, a movement which came together around the immediate needs of women in a variety of cities, a movement whose energies have gone directly into work for change. It is these groups that form the basis for my discussion of feminist theory. These groups were concerned with practical action—rape crisis centers, women's centers, building women's communities, etc. In coming together as feminists to confront the problems which dominate their lives, women have built a movement profoundly based on practice. Indeed, one of the major tasks for the women's movement is precisely the creation of revolutionary theory out of an examination of our practice.[4]

All these groups share a world view that differs from that of most socialist movements in advanced capitalist countries, and that is at the same time surprisingly close to Marx's world view. It is this mode of analysis, with its own conception of social theory as well as the concrete theories we are developing out of it, that are the sources of feminism's power and the reason I can argue that through our practice, feminists have become the most orthodox of Marxists. As Lukacs argued, orthodoxy in Marxist theory refers exclusively to method.[5]

At bottom, feminism is a mode of analysis, a method of approaching life and politics, a way of asking questions and searching for answers, rather than a set of political conclusions about the oppression of women. Women are applying that method to their own experiences as women in order to transform the social relations which define their existence. Feminists deal directly with their own daily lives—something which accounts for the rapid spread of this movement. Others have argued that socialist feminism must be recognized as a definite tendency within Marxism generally; in contrast, I am suggesting that because feminists have reinvented Marx's method, the women's movement can provide a model for the rest of the left in developing theory and strategy.

The practice of small-group consciousness-raising—with its stress on examining and understanding experience and on connecting personal experience to the structures which define women's lives—is the clearest example of the method basic to feminism. Through this practice women have learned that it was important to build their analysis from the ground up, beginning with their own experiences. They examined their lives not only as thinkers but, as Marx would have suggested, with all their senses. Women drew connections between their personal experiences and political generalities about the oppression of women; indeed they used their personal experience to develop those generalities. We came to understand our experience, our past, in a way that transformed both our experience and ourselves.[6]

The power of the method feminists developed grows out of the fact that it enables women to connect their everyday lives with an analysis of the social institutions which shape them. The institutions of capitalism (including its imperialist aspect), patriarchy, and white supremacy cease to be abstractions; they become lived, real aspects of daily experience and activity. We see the concrete interrelations among them.

All this means that within the feminist movement, an important role for theory has been reemphasized—one in which theorists work out and make "coherent the principles and the problems raised by the masses in their practical activity."[7] Feminism as a mode of analysis, especially when consciousness-raising is understood as basic to that method, requires a redefinition of the concept of intellectual or theorizer, a recasting of this social role in terms of everyday life.

Because each of us is a potential theorist, intellectual, and activist, education comes to have a very different role in the women's movement than it does in the rest of the left today. The kind of political education feminists are doing for themselves differs fundamentally from what I would call instruction, from being taught the "correct political line." Education—as opposed to instruction—is organically connected to everyday life.[8] It both grows out of and contributes to our understanding of it.

Personal and Political Change

"If what we change does not change us/we are playing with blocks."[9]

Feminist emphasis on everyday life leads to a second area of focus: the integration of personal and political change. Since we come to know the world (to change it and be changed by it) through our everyday activity, everyday life must be the basis for our political work. Even the deepest philosophical questions grow out of our need to understand our own lives. Such a focus means that reality for us consists of "sensuous human activity, practice."[10] We recognize that we produce our existence in response to specific problems posed for us by reality. By working out the links between the personal and the political, and by working out the links between daily life and social institutions, we have begun to understand existence as a social process, the product of human activity. Moreover, the realization that we not only create our social world but can change it leads to a sense of our own power and provides energy for action.

Feminism as a method makes us recognize that human activity also changes us. A fundamental redefinition of the self is an integral part of action for political change.

If our selves are social phenomena and take their meaning from the society of which we are a part, developing an independent sense of self necessarily calls other areas of our lives into question. We must ask how our relationships with other people can foster self-definition rather than dependence and can accommodate our new strengths. That is, if our individuality is the ensemble of our social relations, "to create one's personality means to acquire consciousness of them and to modify one's own personality means to modify the *ensemble* of these relations."[11] Clearly, since we do not act to produce and reproduce our lives in a vacuum, changed consciousness and changed definitions of the self can only occur in conjunction with a restructuring of the social (both societal and personal) relations in which each of us is involved.

Thus, feminism leads us to oppose the institutions of capitalism and white supremacy as well as patriarchy. By calling attention to the specific experiences of individuals, feminism calls attention to the totality of social relations, to the social formation as a whole. A feminist mode of analysis makes it clear that patriarchy, capitalism, white supremacy, forms of social interaction, language—all exist for us as historic givens. Our daily lives are the materialization at a personal level of the features of the social formation as a whole. The historical structures that mold our lives pose questions we must respond to and define the immediate possibilities for change.

Although we recognize that human activity *is* the structure of the social world, this structure is imposed not by individuals but by masses of people, building on the work of those who came before. Social life at any point in time depends on a complex of factors, on needs already developed as well as on embryonic needs—needs whose production, shaping, and satisfaction is a historical process. Developing new selves, then, requires that we recognize the importance of large-scale forces for change as well as that the people we are trying to become—fully developed individuals—can only be the products of history and struggle.

This history and struggle necessitates the creation of a new collectivity closely linked to the creation of new individuals, a collectivity which fundamentally opposes the capitalist concept of the individual. The creation of this new collectivity

> presupposes the attainment of a "cultural-social" unity through which a multiplicity of dispersed wills, with heterogeneous aims, are welded together with a single aim, on the basis of an equal and common conception of the world, both general and particular, operating in transitory bursts (in emotional ways) or permanently (where the intellectual base is so well rooted, assimilated, and experienced that it becomes passion).[12]

Clearly, we can only transform ourselves by struggling to transform the social relations which define us: changing selves and changed social institutions are simply two aspects of the same process. Each aspect necessitates the other. To change oneself—if individuality *is* the social relations we are involved in—is to change social institutions. Feminist practice reunites aspects of life separated by capitalism and does so in a way which assimilates the intellectual aspect to passion. As Marx said: "The coincidence of the changing of circumstances and of human activity or self changing can be conceived and rationally understood only as *revolutionary practice*."[13] This process of self-changing and growing in a changed world leads us to a sense that our lives are part of a number of larger processes and that all the aspects of our lives must be connected.

The Importance of Totality

By beginning with everyday life and experience, feminism has been able to develop a politics which incorporates an understanding of process and of the importance of appropriating our past as an essential element of political action. We find that we constantly confront new situations in which we act out of our changed awareness of the world and ourselves and in consequence experience the changed reactions of others. What some socialists have seen as static, feminists grasp as structures of relations in process—a reality constantly in the process of becoming something else. Feminist reasoning "regards every historically developed social form as in fluid movement and therefore takes into account its transient nature no less than its momentary existence."[14] This mode of understanding allows us to see the many ways processes are related and provides a way to understand a world in which events take their significance from the set of relationships which come to a focus in them. Thus, we are led to see that each of the interlocking institutions of capitalism, patriarchy, and white supremacy conditions the others, but each can also be understood as a different expression of the same relations.

Since each phenomenon changes form constantly as the social relations of which it is composed take on different meanings and forms, the possibility of understanding processes as they change depends on our grasp of their role in the social whole. For example, in order to understand the increased amount of wage work by women in the United States we need to understand the relation of their work to the needs of capitalism. But we must also look at the conditions of work and the kind of work prescribed for women by patriarchy and white supremacy as different aspects of the same social system. As feminists, we begin from a position which understands that possibilities for change in any area are tied to change occurring in other areas.

Both capitalism and socialism are more than economic systems. Capitalism does not simply reproduce the physical existence of individuals. "Rather it is a definite form of activity of these individuals, a definite form of expressing their life, a definite *mode of life* on their part . . . [and this coincides with] both *what* they produce and *how* they produce."[15] A mode of life is not divisible. It does not consist of a public part and a private part, a part at the workplace and a part in the community—each of which makes up a certain fraction, and all of which add up to 100 percent. A mode of life, and all the aspects of that mode of life, take meaning from the totality of which they form a part.

In part because of shifts in the boundaries between the economic and the political and because of the increasing interconnections between the state apparatus and the economy (through means as varied as public education and government regulation of industry), it becomes even more necessary to emphasize that one can only understand and penetrate, and transform reality as a totality, and that "only a subject which is itself a totality is capable of this penetration." Only a collective individual, a united group of people "can actively penetrate the reality of society and transform it in its entirety."[16]

Feminism and Revolution

If all that I have said about feminism as a method rooted in dealing with everyday life holds true, what is it that makes this mode of analysis a force for revolution? There are three factors of particular importance: (1) The focus on everyday life and experience makes action a necessity, not a moral choice or an option. We are not fighting other people's battles but our own. (2) The nature of our understanding of theory is altered and theory is brought into an integral and everyday relation with practice. (3) Theory leads directly to a transformation of social relations both in consciousness and in reality because of its close connection to real needs.

First, how does a feminist mode of analysis make revolution necessary? The feminist method of taking up and analyzing experience is a way of appropriating reality. Experience is incorporated in such a way that our life experiences become a part of our humanness. By appropriating our experience and incorporating it into ourselves, we transform what might have been a politics of idealism into a politics of necessity. By appropriating our collective experience, we are creating people who recognize that we cannot be ourselves in a society based on hierarchy, domination, and private property. We are acquiring a consciousness which forces us, as Marx put it, "by an ineluctable, irremediable and imperious *distress*—by practical *necessity*—to revolt against this inhumanity."[17] Incorporating, or making part of ourselves, what we learn is essential to the method of feminism.

Second, I argued that a feminist mode of analysis leads to an integration of theory and practice. For feminists, theory is the articulation of what our practical activity has already appropriated in reality. As Marx argued, as struggle develops, theorists "no longer need to seek science in their minds; they have only to take note of what is happening before their eyes and to become its mouthpiece."[18] If we look more closely at the subject about which Marx was writing on this occasion—the British working class—we find that by the time Marx wrote these words that group had already developed theory out of its practice to a considerable degree. A variety of trends had emerged, and ideas about organization and politics had been diffused over a wide area. Isolation from experienced national leadership, and the overimportance of personalities created problems, but the facility with which English working-class people formed associations is impressive. They used a variety of forms taken over from Methodism, friendly societies, trade unions, etc. By the time Marx wrote, it was clear that most people understood that power came from organization.

In looking at history, one is especially struck with the number of false starts, the hesitancy, the backtracking that went into making what we would today recognize as class consciousness. Forming theory out of practice does not come quickly or easily, and it is rarely clear what direction the theory will finally take.

Feminists, in making theory, take up and examine what we find within ourselves; we attempt to clarify for ourselves and others what we already, at some level, know. Theory itself, then, can be seen as a way of taking up and building on our experience. This is not to say that feminists reject all knowledge that is not firsthand, that we can learn nothing from books or from history. But rather than read a number of sacred texts we make the practical questions posed for us in everyday life the basis of our study. Feminism recognizes that political philosophy and political action do not take place in separate realms. On the contrary, the concepts with which we understand the social world emerge from and are defined by human activity.

For feminists, the unity of theory and practice refers to the use of theory to make coherent the problems and principles expressed in our practical activity. Feminists argue that the role of theory is to take seriously the idea that all of us are theorists. The role of theory, then, is to articulate for us what we know from our practical activity, to bring out and make conscious the philosophy embedded in our lives. Feminists are in fact creating social theory through political action. We need to conceptualize, to take up and specify what we have already done, in order to make the next steps clear. We can start from common sense, but we need to move on to the philosophy systematically elaborated by traditional intellectuals.

A third factor in making feminism a force for revolution is that the mode of analysis I have described leads to a transformation of social relations. This is true first in a logical sense. That is, once social relations are situated within the context of the social formation as a whole, the individual phenomena change their meanings and forms. They become something other than they were. For example, what liberal theory understands as social stratification becomes clearer when understood as class. But this is not simply a logical point. As Lukacs has pointed out, the transformation of each phenomenon through relating it to the social totality ends by conferring "reality on the day to day struggle by manifesting its relation to the whole. Thus it elevates mere existence to reality."[19] This development in mass political consciousness, the transformation of the phenomena of life, is on the one hand a profoundly political act and on the other, a "point of transition."[20] Consciousness must become deed, but the act of becoming conscious is itself a kind of deed.

If we grant that the women's movement has reinvented Marx's method and for that reason can be a force for revolution, we need to ask in what specific sense the women's movement can be a model for the rest of the left. At the beginning I outlined a number of criticisms of the left, all rooted in the fact that it has lost touch with everyday life. The contrast I want to draw is one between what Gramsci recognized as "real action," action "which modifies in an essential way both man and external reality," and "gladiatorial futility, which is self-declared action but modifies only the word, not things, the external gesture and not the [person] inside."[21]

At the beginning of this paper I suggested that education took on a new significance for the women's movement because of the role of personal, everyday experience in constructing theory and transforming reality. Feminists are aware that we face the task of building a collective will, a new common sense, and this requires that we must participate in a process of education in two senses. We must, first, never tire of repeating our own arguments and, second, work to raise the general intellectual level, the consciousness of larger numbers of people in order to produce a new and different understanding of everyday life. The women's movement is working at both these tasks—the first by insisting that every woman can reconstruct the more general feminist arguments on her own, the second by turning to the writings of more traditional intellectuals for whatever guidance we may find there.

Marx applied his method systematically to the study of capital. Feminists have not yet really begun systematic study based on the mode of analysis we have developed. Here I can only mention some of the questions which are currently being debated in the women's movement—issues on which there is not yet a consensus but whose theoretical resolution is inseparable from practical, daily work for change.

Issues for Feminist Theory

The Nature of Class

Marxists have devoted a great deal of attention to the nature of class. Most Marxist theorists agree that there are problems with traditional definitions of class. If to be working class means to have nothing to sell but labor power, then the vast majority of the American population falls within this definition. If to be working class means to contribute directly to the production of surplus value, then far fewer of us fall into that category. A number of modifications of these traditional ideas have been presented. Some writers have argued that there is a "new" working class, that what is important now is the possibility for alliances with sectors of the "new petty bourgeoisie," that knowledge and its possession (science) have become productive forces, or that the working out of the division of mental from manual labor with its attendant ritualization of knowledge is critical to the working out of class boundaries. In this maze of theories about the nature of class under advanced capitalism, a feminist mode of analysis can provide important insights into the nature of class as it structures the concrete existence of groups and individuals.

Because feminists begin from our own experience in a specific advanced capitalist society, we recognize that the lived realities of different segments of society are varied. While it is true that most people have only their labor power to sell (for wages or not), there are real differences in power, privilege, ability to control our lives, and even chances for survival. By focusing on people's daily lives we are learning that our class is not defined by our relationship to the mode of production in the simple sense that if we sell our labor power (for a day or a lifetime) or are part of the family of someone (presumably male) who does, we are working class. Being working class is a way of living life, a mode of life not exclusively defined by the simple fact that we have only our labor power to sell.

Class distinctions in capitalist society are part of a totality, a mode of life which is structured as well by the traditions of patriarchy and white supremacy. Class distinctions in the United States affect the everyday lives of women and men, white and black and Third World people in different ways. A feminist mode of analysis leads us to ask questions which recognize that we already know a great deal about class (in fact, in our daily activity we act on what we know), but need to appropriate what we know to make it into explicit theory.

One's social class is defined by one's place "in the ensemble of social practices, i.e., by [one's] place in the social division of labor as a whole," and for that reason must include political and ideological relations. "Social class, in this sense, is a concept which denotes the effects of the structure within the social division of labor (social relations and social practices)."[22] Feminists writing about class have focused on the structures produced by the interaction of political, ideological, and more strictly economic relations, and have done so from the standpoint of everyday life and activity.

Some of the best descriptions of class and its importance in the women's movement were produced by the Furies, a lesbian/feminist separatist group in Washington, D.C. When the Furies began, many members of the collective knew very little about the nature of class. But the collective included a number of lower- and working-class women who were concerned about ways middle-class women oppressed them. As one middle-class woman wrote:

> Our assumptions, for example, about how to run a meeting were different from theirs, but we assumed ours were correct because they were easiest for us—given our college educations, our ability to use words, our ability to abstract, our inability to make quick decisions, the difficulty we had with direct confrontations. . . . I learned [that] class oppression was . . . a part of my life which I could see and change. And, having seen the manifestations of class in myself, I better understood how class operated generally to divide people and keep them down.[23]

In the context of working for change, it became clear that

> refusal to deal with class behavior in a lesbian/feminist movement is sheer self-indulgence and leads to the downfall of our own struggle. Middle-class women should look first at that scale of worth that is the class system in America. They should examine where they fit on that scale, how it affected them, and what they thought of the people below and above them. . . . Start thinking politically about the class system and all the power systems in this country.[24]

What specifically did the Furies learn when they looked at the way class functioned in daily life? First, they learned the sense in which we have all, no matter what our class background, taken for granted that the "middle class way is *the right way*." Class arrogance is expressed in looking down on the "less articulate," or regarding with "scorn or pity . . . those whose emotions are not repressed or who can't rap out abstract theories in thirty seconds flat." Class supremacy, the Furies found, is also apparent in a kind of passivity often assumed by middle- and especially upper-middle-class women for whom things have come easily. People who are "pushy, dogmatic, hostile, or intolerant" are looked down on. Advocating downward mobility and putting down those who are not as "revolutionary" is another form of middle-class arrogance. What is critical about all of this is that "middle-class women set the standards of what is good (and even the proper style of downward mobility which often takes money to achieve) and act 'more revolutionary than thou' towards those who are concerned about money and the future." Middle-class women retain control over approval. The small, indirect, and dishonest ways of behaving in polite society are also ways of maintaining "the supremacy of the middle class and perpetuating the feelings of inadequacy of the working class."[25]

These accounts of barriers created by class differences within the women's movement lead us toward an understanding of several important points about the nature of class. They lead us to see first that class is a complex of relations, one in which knowledge or know-how is at a premium, and second, at a deeper level, that what is involved in the daily reality of class oppression is the concrete working out of the division between mental and manual labor. Class, especially as it affects the lives of women, is a complex of a number of factors in which political and ideological aspects as well as strictly economic factors play an important role. Theorists have focused too closely on the domination of men by production pure and simple. Looking at the role of class in women's lives highlights the importance of other factors as well, such as the role of family and patriarchal traditions. For both women and men class defines the way we see the world and our place in it, how we were educated and where, and how we act—whether with assurance or uncertainty. The process of production must be seen to include the reproduction of political and ideological relations of domination and subordination. It is these factors that lead to the feelings described as "being out of control," "feeling like you don't know what to do," and feeling that you are incompetent to judge your own performance.[26]

At bottom, people are describing the way it feels to be on the "wrong" side of the division between mental and manual labor. Indeed, the division between mental and manual labor is precisely the concentrated form of class divisions in capitalism. It is critical to recognize that mental labor is the exercise of "political relations legitimized by and articulated to, the monopolization and secrecy of knowledge, i.e., the reproduction of the ideological relations of domination and subordination."[27] Mental labor involves a series of rituals and symbols. And it is always the case that the dominated group either does not know or cannot know the things that are important.

By calling attention to life rather than theory, the women's movement has called attention to cultural domination as a whole—has begun a political analysis that does not take place in isolation from practical activity. By noticing the real differences among women in terms of class—confidence, verbal ability, ease about money, sense of group identity—we are developing new questions about class. While we have barely begun the task of reconstructing the category of class, we are learning that it is important to pay attention to the mechanisms of domination as a whole. By looking at class as a feature of life and struggle, the women's movement has established some of the terms any revolutionary movement must use: Until we confront class as a part of everyday life, until we begin to analyze what we already know about class, we will never be able to build a united and large-scale movement for revolution. In this task, we need to recognize the decisive role of the division between mental and manual labor in all its complexity for the formation of the whole mode of life that is capitalism.

Organizations and Strategies

Feminism, while it does not prescribe an organizational form, leads to a set of questions about organizational priorities. First, a feminist mode of analysis suggests that we need organizations which include the appropriation of experience as a part of the work of the organization itself. We need to systematically analyze what we learn as we work in organizations. While the analysis of our experience in small groups was valuable, we need to develop ways to appropriate our organizational experience and to use it to transform our conception of organization itself. Some feminist organizations are beginning to do this—to raise questions about the process of meetings or about the way work is done and should be done.

Because so many of us reacted to our experience in the organizations of the rest of the left by refusing to build any organizational structures at all, we have only begun to think about the way we should work in organizations with some structure. We need to build the possibilities for change and growth into our organizations rather than rely on small groups. This means that we need to systematically teach and respect different skills and allow our organizations to change and grow in new directions. We need to use our organizations as places where we begin to redefine social relations and to create new ways of working which do not follow the patterns of domination and hierarchy set by the mode of production as a whole.

A feminist mode of analysis has implications for strategy as well. We can begin to make coalitions with other groups who share our approach to politics. We cannot work, however, with people who refuse to face questions in terms of everyday life or with people who will not use their own experience as a fundamental basis for knowledge. We cannot work with those who treat theory as a set of conclusions to be pasted onto reality and who, out of their own moral commitment, make a revolution for the benefit of their inferiors. A feminist mode of analysis suggests that we must work on issues which have real impact on daily life. These issues are varied—housing, public transportation, food prices, etc. The only condition for coalition with other groups is that those groups share our method. So long as those we work with are working for change out of necessity, because they, like us, have no alternative, there is a real basis for common action.

As we work on particular issues, we must continually ask how we can use these issues to build our collective strength. The mode of analysis developed by the women's movement suggests several criteria with which to evaluate particular strategies. First, we must ask how our work will educate ourselves and others politically, how it will help us to see the connections between social institutions. Second, we must ask how a particular strategy materially affects our daily lives. This involves asking: How does it improve our conditions of existence? How will it affect our sense of ourselves and our own power to change the world? How will a particular strategy politicize people, make people aware of problems beyond individual ones? Third, we must ask how our strategies work to build organizations—to build a collective individual which will increase our power to transform social relations as a whole. Fourth, we must ask how our strategies weaken the institutions which control our lives—patriarchy, white supremacy, and capitalism. Our strategies must work not simply to weaken each of these institutions separately but must attack them on the basis of an understanding of the totality of which they form parts.

In all this, however, we must remember that there is no "ready made, pre-established, detailed set of tactics which a central committee can teach its . . . membership as if they were army recruits."[28] In general, the tactics of a mass party cannot be invented. They are "the product of a progressive series of great creative acts in the often rudimentary experiments of the class struggle. Here too, the unconscious comes before the conscious. . . ."[29]

Most important, a feminist mode of analysis makes us recognize that the struggle itself must be seen as a process with all its internal difficulties. We must avoid, on the one hand, developing a narrow sectarian outlook, and, on the other, abandoning our goal of revolution. We must continue to base our work on the necessity for change in our own lives. Our political theorizing can only grow out of appropriating the practical political work we have done. While the answers to our questions come only slowly and with difficulty, we must remember that we are involved in a continuous process of learning what kind of world we want to create as we work for change.

Notes

1. Antonio Gramsci, *Selections from the Prison Notebooks*, trans. Quinton Hoare and Geoffrey Nowell Smith (New York: International Publishers, 1971), p. 365. Gramsci adds that "the identification of theory and practice is a critical act, through which practice is demonstrated rational and necessary and theory realistic and rational."
2. Ibid., p. 327. See also p. 244.
3. I should perhaps note here that I am speaking as a participant as well as a critical observer. The experience I use as a reference point is my own as well as that of many other women.
4. Feminists are beginning to recognize the importance for the movement of conscious theorizing—for critical analysis of what we have been doing for most of the last decade. Among the current issues and problems being reevaluated are the significance of service projects, the importance of leadership, new possibilities for developing organizational structures, and our relationship to the rest of the left.
5. George Lukacs, *History and Class Consciousness* (Cambridge, Mass: M.I.T. Press, 1971). p. 1.
6. This is not to say there have been no problems or that beginning with personal experience always led women to think in larger terms. Some groups have remained apolitical or have never moved beyond the level of personal issues; others have become so opposed to any organizations other than personal organizations that they are immobilized. Problems about the "correct line" are also part of the current debate in the women's movement. On current problems, see Bunch, "Feminist Options."

7. Gramsci, *Selections*, p. 330.
8. Ibid., p. 43.
9. Marge Piercy, "A Shadow Play for Guilt," in *To Be of Use* (Garden City, N.Y.: Doubleday, 1973), p. 17.
10. Karl Marx, "Theses on Feuerbach," in Karl Marx and Friedrich Engels, *The German Ideology*, ed. C.J. Arthur (New York: International Publishers, 1970), p. 121. This method also overcomes the passivity characteristic of much of American life. See, for example, Richard Sennett and Jonathan Cobb, *The Hidden Injuries of Class* (New York: Vintage, 1973), p. 165, and Stanley Aronowitz, *False Promises* (New York: McGraw-Hill, 1973), p. 112.
11. See Gramsci, *Selections*, p. 352.
12. Gramsci, *Selections*, p. 349.
13. Marx, "Theses on Feuerbach," p. 121. See also Gramsci, *Selections*, pp. 352, 360.
14. Karl Marx, *Capital*, vol. 1 (Moscow: Foreign Language Publishing House, 1954), p. 20.
15. Marx and Engels, *German Ideology*, p. 114.
16. Lukacs, *History*, p. 39.
17. Karl Marx, *Selected Writings in Sociology and Social Philosophy*, trans. T. B. Bottomore (New York: McGraw-Hill, 1956), p. 232.
18. Karl Marx, *The Poverty of Philosophy* (New York: International Publishers, 1973), p. 125.
19. Lukacs, *History*, p. 22.
20. Ibid., p. 178. See also Gramsci's contention that "for a mass of people to be led to think coherently and in the same coherent fashion about the real present world, is a 'philosophical' event far more important and 'original' than the discovery by some philosophical 'genius' of a truth which remains the property of small groups of intellectuals" (*Selections*, p. 325).
21. Ibid., pp. 225, 307.
22. Poulantzas, *Classes in Contemporary Capitalism*, p. 14.
23. Ginny Berson, "Only by Association," *The Furies* 1, no. 5 (June/July 1972): 5–7.
24. Nancy Myron, "Class Beginnings," *The Furies* 1, no. 3 (March/April 1972): 3.
25. Charlotte Bunch and Coletta Reid, "Revolution Begins at Home," *The Furies* 1, no. 4 (May 1972): 2–3. See also Dolores Bargowski and Coletta Reid, "Garbage Among the Trash," *The Furies* 1, no. 6 (August 1972) 8–9. Some of the essays from the Furies are collected in *Class and Feminism*, Ed. Nancy Myron and Charlotte Bunch (Baltimore: Diana Press, 1974).
26. These statements come from Sennett and Cobb, *Hidden Injuries of Class*, pp. 97, 115, and 157. One of the most important effects of class is to make working-class people doubt they have a legitimate right to fight back.
27. Poulantzas, *Classes*, p. 240.
28. Rosa Luxemburg, "Organizational Questions of Russian Social Democracy," *Selected Writings of Rosa Luxemburg*. ed. Dick Howard (New York: Monthly Review Press, 1971), p. 289.
29. Ibid., p. 293.

Study Questions

1. Why is theory important to a revolutionary?
2. In what way is feminism a "method"? What is an example of this method? How does this method help women understand their daily lives?
3. In what way does feminism relate personal and social change? What implications does that have for the analysis of social institutions?
4. In what way does feminist reasoning regard social structures as fluid, as opposed to static? In what way is feminist reasoning holistic? How does this make the feminist framework more adequate for understanding social phenomena?
5. What makes the feminist mode of analysis a force for revolution?
6. How have feminists modified the traditional Marxist concept of class? In particular, what did the Furies discover?

Have We Got a Theory for You!
Feminist Theory, Cultural Imperialism and
the Demand for "The Woman's Voice"

Maria C. Lugones and Elizabeth V. Spelman

Prologue

(*In an Hispana voice*) A veces quisiera mezclar en una voz el sonido canyenge, tristón y urbano del porteñismo que llevo adentro con la cadencia apacible, serrana y llena de corage de la hispana nuevo mejicana. Contrastar y unir

> el piolín y la cuerda
> el traé y el pepéname
> el camión y la troca
> la lluvia y el llanto

Pero este querer se me va cuando veo que he confundido la solidaridad con la falta de diferencia. La solidaridad requiere el reconocer, comprender, respetar y amar lo que nos lleva a llorar en distintas cadencias. El imperialismo cultural desea lo contrario, por eso necesitamos muchas voces. Porque una sola voz nos mata a las dos.

No quiero hablar por ti sino contigo. Pero si no aprendo tus modos y tu los mios la conversación es sólo aparente. Y la apariencia se levanta como una barrera sin sentido entre las dos. Sin sentido y sin sentimiento. Por eso no me debes dejar que te dicte tu ser y no me dictes el mio. Porque entonces ya no dialogamos. El diálogo entre nosotras requiere dos voces y no una.

Tal vez un día jugaremos juntas y nos hablaremos no en una lengua universal sino que vos me hablarás mi voz y yo la tuya.

Preface

This paper is the result of our dialogue, of our thinking together about differences among women and how these differences are silenced. (Think, for example, of all the silences there are connected with the fact that this paper is in English—for that is a borrowed tongue for one of us.) In the process of our talking and writing together, we saw that the differences between us did not permit our speaking in one voice. For example, when we agreed we expressed the thought differently; there were some things that both of us thought were true but could not express as true of each of us; sometimes we could not say "we"; and some-

From *Women's Studies International Forum*, Vol. 6, No. 6 (1983), pp. 573–581. Reprinted by permission of Pergamon Press.

times one of us could not express the thought in the first person singular, and to express it in the third person would be to present an outsider's and not an insider's perspective. Thus the use of two voices is central both to the process of constructing this paper and to the substance of it. We are both the authors of this paper and not just sections of it but we write together without presupposing unity of expression or of experience. So when we speak in unison it means just that—there are two voices and not just one.

Introduction

(*In the voice of a white/Anglo woman who has been teaching and writing about feminist theory*) Feminism is, among other things, a response to the fact that women either have been left out of, or included in demeaning and disfiguring ways in what has been an almost exclusively male account of the world. And so while part of what feminists want and demand for women is the right to move and to act in accordance with our own wills and not against them, another part is the desire and insistence that we give our *own* accounts of these movements and actions. For it matters to us what is said about us, who says it, and to whom it is said: having the opportunity to talk about one's life, to give an account of it, to interpret it, is integral to leading that life rather than being led through it; hence our distrust of the male monopoly over accounts of women's lives. To put the same point slightly differently, part of human life, human living, is talking about it, and we can be sure that being silenced in one's own account of one's life is a kind of amputation that signals oppression. Another reason for not divorcing life from the telling of it or talking about it is that as humans our experiences are deeply influenced by what is said about them, by ourselves or powerful (as opposed to significant) others. Indeed, the phenomenon of internalized oppression is only possible because this is so: one experiences her life in terms of the impoverished and degrading concepts others have found it convenient to use to describe her. We can't separate lives from the accounts given of them; the articulation of our experience is part of our experience.

Sometimes feminists have made even stronger claims about the importance of speaking about our own lives and the destructiveness of others presuming to speak about us or for us. First of all, the claim has been made that on the whole men's accounts of women's lives have been at best false, a function of ignorance; and at worst malicious lies, a function of a knowledgeable desire to exploit and oppress. Since it matters to us that falsehood and lies not be told about us, we demand, of those who have been responsible for those falsehoods and lies, or those who continue to transmit them, not just that we speak but that they learn to be able to hear us. It has also been claimed that talking about one's life, telling one's story, in the company of those doing the same (as in consciousness-raising sessions), is constitutive of feminist method.[1]

And so the demand that the woman's voice be heard and attended to has been made for a variety of reasons: not just so as to greatly increase the chances that true accounts of women's lives will be given, but also because the articulation of experience (in myriad ways) is among the hallmarks of a self-determining individual or community. There are not just epistemological, but moral and political reasons for demanding that the woman's voice be heard, after centuries of androcentric din.

But what more exactly is the feminist demand that the woman's voice be heard? There are several crucial notes to make about it. First of all, the demand grows out of a complaint, and in order to understand the scope and focus of the demand we have to look at the scope and focus of the complaint. The complaint does not specify *which* women have been silenced, and in one way this is appropriate to the conditions it is a complaint about: virtually no women have had a voice, whatever their race, class, ethnicity, religion, sexual alliance, whatever place and period in history they lived. And if it is as women that women have been silenced, then of course the demand must be that women as women have a voice. But in another way the complaint is very misleading, insofar as it suggests that it is women as women who have been silenced, and that whether a woman is rich or poor, Black, brown or white, etc., is irrelevant to what it means for her to be a woman. For the demand thus simply made ignores at least two related points: (1) it is only possible for a woman who does not feel highly vulnerable with respect to other parts of her identity, e.g., race, class, ethnicity, religion, sexual alliance, etc., to conceive of her voice simply or essentially as a "woman's voice"; (2) just because not all women are equally vulnerable with respect to race, class, etc., some women's voices are more likely to be heard than others by those who have heretofore been giving—or silencing—the accounts of women's lives. For all these reasons, the women's voices most likely to come forth and the women's voices most likely to be heard are, in the United States anyway, those of white, middle-class, heterosexual Christian (or anyway not self-identified non-Christian) women. Indeed, many Hispanas, Black women, Jewish women—to name a few groups—have felt it an invitation to silence rather than speech to be requested—if they are requested at all—to speak about being "women" (with the plain wrapper—as if there were one) in distinction from speaking about being Hispana, Black, Jewish, working-class, etc., women.

The demand that the "woman's voice" be heard, and the search for the "woman's voice" as central to feminist methodology, reflects nascent feminist theory. It reflects nascent empirical theory insofar as it presupposes that the silencing of women is systematic, shows up in regular, patterned ways, and that there are discoverable causes of this widespread observable phenomenon; the demand reflects nascent political theory insofar as it presupposes that the silencing of women reveals a systematic pattern of power and authority; and it reflects nascent moral theory insofar as it presupposes that the silencing is unjust and that there are particular ways of remedying this injustice. Indeed, whatever else we know feminism to include—e.g., concrete direct political action—theorizing is integral to it: theories about the nature of oppression, the causes of it, the relation of the oppression of women to other forms of oppression. And certainly the concept of the woman's voice is itself a theoretical concept, in the sense that it presupposes a theory according to which our identities as human beings are actually compound identities, a kind of fusion or confusion of our otherwise separate identities as women or men, as Black or brown or white, etc. That is no less a theoretical stance than Plato's division of the person into soul and body or Aristotle's parcelling of the soul into various functions.

The demand that the "woman's voice" be heard also invites some further directions in the exploration of women's lives and discourages or excludes others. For reasons mentioned above, systematic, sustained reflection on being a woman—the kind of contemplation that "doing theory" requires—is most likely to be done by women who vis-a-vis other women enjoy a certain amount of political, social and economic privilege because of their skin color, class membership, ethnic identity. There is a relationship between the content of our contemplation and the fact that we have the time to engage in it at some length—otherwise we shall have to say that it is a mere accident of history that white middle-class women in the United States have in the main developed "feminist theory" (as opposed to "Black feminist theory," "Chicana feminist theory," etc.) and that so much of the theory has failed to be relevant to the lives of women who are not white or middle class. Feminist theory—of all kinds—is to be based on, or anyway touch base with, the variety of real life stories women provide about themselves. But in fact, because, among other things, of the structural political and social and economic inequalities among women, the tail has been wagging the dog: feminist theory has not for the most part arisen out of a medley of women's voices; instead, the theory has arisen out of the voices, the experiences, of a fairly small handful of women, and if other women's voices do not sing in harmony with the theory, they aren't counted as women's voices—rather, they are the voices of the woman as Hispana, Black, Jew, etc. There is another sense in which the tail is wagging the dog, too: it is presumed to be the case that those who do the theory know more about those who are theorized than vice versa; hence it ought to be the case that if it is white/Anglo women who write for and about all other women, the white/Anglo women must know more about all other women than other women know about them. But in fact just in order to survive, brown and Black women have to know a lot more about white/Anglo women—not through the sustained contemplation theory requires, but through the sharp observation stark exigency demands.

(*In an Hispana voice*) I think it necessary to explain why in so many cases when women of color appear in front of white/Anglo women to talk about feminism and women of color, we mainly raise a complaint: the complaint of exclusion, of silencing, of being included in a universe we have not chosen. We usually raise the complaint with a certain amount of disguised or undisguised anger. I can only attempt to explain this phenomenon from a Hispanic viewpoint and a fairly narrow one at that: the viewpoint of an Argentinian woman who has lived in the US for 16 years, who has attempted to come to terms with the devaluation of things Hispanic and Hispanic people in "America" and who is most familiar with Hispano life in the Southwest of the US. I am quite unfamiliar with daily Hispano life in the urban centers, though not with some of the themes and some of the salient experiences of urban Hispano life.

When I say "we,"[2] I am referring to Hispanas. I am accustomed to use the "we" in this way. I am also pained by the tenuousness of this "we" given that I am not a native of the United States. Through the years I have come to be recognized and I have come to recognize myself more and more firmly as part of this "we." I also have a profound yearning for this firmness since I am a displaced person and I am conscious of not being of and I am unwilling to make myself of—even if this were possible—the white/Anglo community.

When I say "you" I mean not the non-Hispanic but the white/Anglo women that I address. "We" and "you" do not capture my relation to other non-white women. The complexity of that relation is not addressed here, but it is vivid to me as I write down my thoughts on the subject at hand.

I see two related reasons for our complaint-full discourse with white/Anglo women. Both of these reasons plague our world, they contaminate it through and through. It takes some hardening of oneself, some self-acceptance of our own anger to face them, for to face them is to decide that maybe we can change our situation in self-constructive ways and we know fully well that the possibilities are minimal. We know that we cannot rest from facing these reasons, that the tenderness towards others in us undermines our possibilities, that we have to fight our own niceness because it clouds our minds and hearts. Yet we know that a thoroughgoing hardening would dehumanize us. So, we have to walk through our days in a peculiarly fragile psychic state, one that we have to struggle to maintain, one that we do not often succeed in maintaining.

We and you do not talk the same language. When we talk to you we use your language: the language of your experience and of your theories. We try to use it to communicate our world of experience. But since your language and your theories are inadequate in expressing our experiences, we only succeed in communicating our experience of exclusion. We cannot talk to you in our language because you do not understand it. So the brute facts that we understand your language and that the place where most theorizing about women is taking place is your place, both combine to require that we either use your language and distort our experience not just in the speaking about it, but in the living of it, or that we remain silent. Complaining about exclusion is a way of remaining silent.

You are ill at ease in our world. You are ill at ease in our world in a very different way than we are ill at ease in yours. You are not of our world and again, you are not of our world in a very different way than we are not of yours. In the intimacy of a personal relationship we appear to you many times to be wholly there, to have broken through or to have dissipated the barriers that separate us because you are Anglo and we are raza. When we let go of the psychic state that I referred to above in the direction of sympathy, we appear to ourselves equally whole in your presence but our intimacy is thoroughly incomplete. When we are in your world many times you remake us in your own image, although sometimes you clearly and explicitly acknowledge that we are not wholly there in our being with you. When we are in your world we ourselves feel the discomfort of having our own being Hispanas disfigured or not understood. And yet, we have had to be in your world and learn its ways. We have to participate in it, make a living in it, live in it, be mistreated in it, be ignored in it, and rarely, be appreciated in it. In learning to do these things or in learning to suffer them or in learning to enjoy what is to be enjoyed or in learning to understand your conception of us, we have had to learn your culture and thus your language and self-conceptions. But there is nothing that necessitates that you understand our world: understand, that is, not as an observer understands things, but as a participant, as someone who has a stake in them understands them. So your being ill at ease in our world lacks the features of our being ill at ease in yours precisely because you can leave and you can always tell yourselves that you will be soon out of there and because the wholeness of your selves is never touched by us, we have no tendency to remake you in our image.

But you theorize about women and we are women, so you understand yourselves to be theorizing about us, and we understand you to be theorizing about us. Yet none of the feminist theories developed so far seems to me to help Hispanas in the articulation of our experience. We have a sense that in using them we are distorting our experiences. Most Hispanas cannot even understand the language used in these theories—and only in some cases the reason is that the Hispana cannot understand English. We do not recognize ourselves in these theories. They create in us a schizophrenic split between our concern for ourselves as women and ourselves as Hispanas, one that we do not feel otherwise. Thus they seem to us to force us to assimilate to some version of Anglo culture, however revised that version may be. They seem to ask that we leave our communities or that we become alienated so completely in them that we feel hollow. When we see that you feel alienated in your own communities, this confuses us because we think that maybe every feminist has to suffer this alienation. But we see that recognition of your alienation leads many of you to be empowered into the remaking of your culture, while we are paralyzed into a state of displacement with no place to go.

So I think that we need to think carefully about the relation between the articulation of our own experience, the interpretation of our own experience, and theory making by us and other non-Hispanic women about themselves and other "women."

The only motive that makes sense to me for your joining us in this investigation is the motive of friendship, out of friendship. A non-imperialist feminism requires that you make a real space for our articulating, interpreting, theorizing and reflecting about the connections among them—a real space must be a non-coerced space—and/or that you follow us into our world out of friendship. I see the "out of friendship" as the only sensical motivation for this following because the task at hand for you is one of extraordinary difficulty. It requires that you be willing to devote a great part of your life to it and that you be willing to suffer alienation and self-disruption. Self-interest has been proposed as a possible motive for entering this task. But self-interest does not seem to me to be a realistic motive, since whatever the benefits you may accrue from such a journey, they cannot be concrete enough for you at this time and they may not be worth your while. I do not think that you have any obligation to understand us. You do have an obligation to abandon your imperialism, your universal claims, your reduction of us to your selves simply because they seriously harm us.

I think that the fact that we are so ill at ease with your theorizing in the ways indicated above does indicate that there is something wrong with these theories. But what is it that is wrong? Is it simply that the theories are flawed if meant to be universal but accurate so long as they are confined to your particular group(s)? Is it that the theories are not really flawed but need to be translated? Can they be translated? Is it something about the process of theorizing that is flawed? How do the two reasons for our complaint-full discourse affect the validity of your theories? Where do *we* begin? To what extent are our experience and its articulation affected by our being a colonized people, and thus by your culture, theories and conceptions? Should we theorize in community and thus as part of community life and outside the academy and other intellectual circles? What is the point of making theory? Is theory making a good thing for us to do at this time? When are we making theory and when are we just articulating and/or interpreting our experiences?

Some Questionable Assumptions About Feminist Theorizing

(*Unproblematically in Vicky's and Maria's voice*) Feminist theories aren't just about what happens to the female population in any given society or across all societies; they are about the meaning of those experiences in the lives of women. They are about beings who give their own accounts of what is happening to them or of what they are doing, who have culturally constructed ways of reflecting on their lives. But how can the theorizer get at the meaning of those experiences? What should the relation be between a woman's own account of her experiences and the theorizer's account of it?

Let us describe two different ways of arriving at an account of another woman's experience. It is one thing for both me and you to observe you and come up with our different accounts of what you are doing; it is quite another for me to observe myself and others much like me culturally and in other ways and to develop an account of myself and then use that account to give an account of you. In the first case you are the "insider" and I am the "outsider." When the outsider makes clear that she is an outsider and that this is an outsider's account of your behavior, there is a touch of honesty about what she is doing. Most of the time the "interpretation by an outsider" is left understood and most of the time the distance of outsidedness is understood to mark objectivity in the interpretation. But why is the outsider as an outsider interpreting your behavior? Is she doing it so that you can understand how she sees you? Is she doing it so that other outsiders will understand how you *are*? Is she doing it so that *you* will understand how you are? It would seem that if the outsider wants you to understand how she sees you and you have given your account of how you see yourself to her, there is a possibility of genuine dialogue between the two. It also seems that the lack of reciprocity could bar genuine dialogue. For why should you engage in such a one-sided dialogue? As soon as we ask this question, a host of other conditions for the possibility of a genuine dialogue between us arise: conditions having to do with your position relative to me in the various social, political and economic structures in which we might come across each other or in which you may run face to face with my account of you and my use of your account of yourself. Is this kind of dialogue necessary for me to get at the meaning of your experiences? That is, is this kind of dialogue necessary for feminist theorizing that is not seriously flawed?

Obviously the most dangerous of the understanding of what I—an outsider—am doing in giving an account of your experience is the one that describes what I'm doing as giving an account of who and how you are whether it be given to you or to other outsiders. Why should you or anyone else believe me; that is, why should you or anyone else believe that you are as I say you are? Could I be right? What conditions would have to obtain for my being right? That many women are put in the position of not knowing whether or not to believe outsiders' accounts of their experiences is clear. The pressures to believe these accounts are enormous even when the woman in question does not see herself in the account. She is thus led to doubt her own judgment and to doubt all interpretation of her experience. This leads her to experience her life differently. Since the consequences of outsiders' accounts can be so significant, it is crucial that we reflect on whether or not this type of account can ever be right and if so, under what conditions.

The last point leads us to the second way of arriving at an account of another woman's experience, viz., the case in which I observe myself and others like me culturally and in other ways and use that account to give an account of you. In doing this, I remake you in my own image. Feminist theorizing approaches this remaking insofar as it depends on the concept of women as women. For it has not arrived at this concept as a consequence of dialogue with many women who are culturally different, or by any other kind of investigation of cultural differences which may include different conceptions of what it is to be a woman; it has simply presupposed this concept.

Our suggestion in this paper, and at this time it is no more than a suggestion, is that only when genuine and reciprocal dialogue takes place between "outsiders" and "insiders" can we trust the outsider's account. At first sight it may appear that the insider/outsider distinction disappears in the dialogue, but it is important to notice that all that happens is that we are now both outsider and insider with respect to each other. The dialogue puts us both in position to give a better account of each other's and our own experience. Here we should again note that white/Anglo women are much less prepared for this dialogue with women of color than women of color are for dialogue with them in that women of color have had to learn white/Anglo ways, self-conceptions, and conceptions of them.

But both the possibility and the desirability of this dialogue are very much in question. We need to think about the possible motivations for engaging in this dialogue, whether doing theory jointly would be a good thing, in what ways and for whom, and whether doing theory is in itself a good thing at this time for women of color or white/Anglo women. In motivating the last question let us remember the hierarchical distinctions between theorizers and those theorized about and between theorizers and doers. These distinctions are endorsed by the same views and institutions which endorse and support hierarchical distinctions between men/women, master race/inferior race, intellectuals/manual workers. Of what use is the activity of theorizing to those of us who are women of color engaged day in and day out in the task of empowering women and men of color face to face with them? Should we be articulating and interpreting their experience for them with the aid of theories? Whose theories?

Ways of Talking or Being Talked About That Are Helpful, Illuminating, Empowering, Respectful

(*Unproblematically in Maria's and Vicky's voice*) Feminists have been quite diligent about pointing out ways in which empirical, philosophical and moral theories have been androcentric. They have thought it crucial to ask, with respect to such theories: who makes them? for whom do they make them? about what or whom are the theories? why? how are theories tested? what are the criteria for such tests and where did the criteria come from? Without posing such questions and trying to answer them, we'd never have been able to begin to mount evidence for our claims that particular theories are androcentric, sexist, biased, paternalistic, etc. Certain philosophers have become fond of—indeed, have made their careers on—pointing out that characterizing a statement as true or false is only one of many ways possible of characterizing it; it might also be, oh, rude, funny, disarming, etc.; it may be intended to soothe or to hurt; or it may have the effect, intended or not, of soothing or hurting. Similarly, theories appear to be the kinds of things that are true or false; but they also are the kinds of things that can be, e.g., useless, arrogant, disrespectful, ignorant, ethnocentric, imperialistic. The immediate point is that feminist theory is no less immune to such characterizations than, say, Plato's political theory, or Freud's theory of female psychosexual development. Of course this is not to say that if feminist theory manages to be respectful or helpful it will follow that it must be true. But if, say, an empirical theory is purported to be about "women" and in fact is only about certain women, it is certainly false, probably ethnocentric, and of dubious usefulness except to those whose position in the world it strengthens (and theories, as we know, don't have to be true in order to be used to strengthen people's positions in the world).

Many reasons can be and have been given for the production of accounts of people's lives that plainly have nothing to do with illuminating those lives for the benefit of those living them. It is likely that both the method of investigation and the content of many accounts would be different if illuminating the lives of the people the accounts are about were the aim of the studies. Though we cannot say ahead of time how feminist theory making would be different if all (or many more) of those people it is meant to be about were more intimately part of the theory-making process, we do suggest some specific ways being talked about can be helpful:

1. The theory or account can be helpful if it enables one to see how parts of one's life fit together, for example, to see connections among parts of one's life one hasn't seen before. No account can do this if it doesn't get the parts right to begin with, and this cannot happen if the concepts used to describe a life are utterly foreign.

2. A useful theory will help one locate oneself concretely in the world, rather than add to the mystification of the world and one's location in it. New concepts may be of significance here, but they will not be useful if there is no way they can be translated into already existing concepts. Suppose a theory locates you in the home, because you are a woman, but you know full well that is not where you spend most of your time? Or suppose you can't locate yourself easily in any particular class as defined by some version of Marxist theory?

3. A theory or account not only ought to accurately locate one in the world but also enable one to think about the extent to which one is responsible or not for being in that location. Otherwise, for those whose location is as oppressed peoples, it usually occurs that the oppressed have no way to see themselves as in any way self-determining, as having any sense of being worthwhile or having grounds for pride, and paradoxically at the same time feeling at fault for the position they are in. A useful theory will help people work out just what is and is not due to themselves and their own activities as opposed to those who have power over them.

It may seem odd to make these criteria of a useful theory, if the usefulness is not to be at odds with the issue of the truth of the theory; for the focus on feeling worthwhile or having pride seems to rule out the possibility that the truth might just be that such-and-such a group of people has been under the control of others for centuries and that the only explanation of that is that they are worthless and weak people, and will never be able to change that. Feminist theorizing seems implicitly if not explicitly committed to the moral view that women *are* worthwhile beings, and the metaphysical theory that we are beings capable of bringing about a change in our situations. Does this mean feminist theory is "biased"? Not any more than any other theory, e.g., psychoanalytic theory. What is odd here is not the feminist presupposition that women are worthwhile but rather that feminist theory (and other theory) often has the effect of empowering one group and demoralizing another.

Aspects of feminist theory are as unabashedly value-laden as other political and moral theories. It is not just an examination of women's positions, for it includes, indeed begins with, moral and political judgments about the injustice (or, where relevant, justice) of them. This means that there are implicit or explicit judgments also about what kind of changes constitute a better or worse situation for women.

4. In this connection a theory that is useful will provide criteria for change and make suggestions for modes of resistance that don't merely reflect the situation and values of the theorizer. A theory that is respectful of those about whom it is a theory will not assume that changes that are perceived as making life better for some women are changes that will make, and will be perceived as making, life better for other women. This is *not* to say that if some women do not find a situation oppressive, other women ought never to suggest to the contrary that there might be very good reasons to think that the situation nevertheless *is* oppressive. But it is to say that, e.g., the prescription that life for women will be better when we're in the workforce rather than at home, when we are completely free of religious beliefs with patriarchal origins, when we live in complete separation from men, etc., are seen as slaps in the face to women whose life would be better if they could spend more time at home, whose identity is inseparable from their religious beliefs and cultural practices (which is not to say those beliefs and practices are to remain completely uncriticized and unchanged), who have ties to men—whether erotic or not—such that to have them severed in the name of some vision of what is "better" is, at that time and for those women, absurd. Our visions of what is better are always informed by our perception of what is bad about our present situation. Surely we've learned enough from the history of clumsy missionaries, and the white suffragists of the 19th century (who couldn't imagine why Black women "couldn't see" how crucial getting the vote for "women" was) to know that we can clobber people to destruction with our visions, our versions, of what is better. *But*: this does not mean women are not to offer supportive and tentative criticism of one another. But there is a very important difference between (a) developing ideas together, in a "pre-theoretical" stage, engaged as equals in joint enquiry, and (b) one group developing, on the basis of their own experience, a set of criteria for good change for women—and then reluctantly making revisions in the criteria at the insistence of women to whom such criteria seem ethnocentric and arrogant. The deck is stacked when one group takes it upon itself to develop the theory and then have others criticize it. Categories are quick to congeal, and the experiences of women whose lives do not fit the categories will appear as anomalous when in fact the theory should have grown out of them as much as others from the beginning. This, of course, is why any organization or conference having to do with "women"—with no qualification—that seriously does not want to be "solipsistic" will from the beginning be multi-cultural or state the appropriate qualifications. How we think and what we think about does depend in large part on who is there—not to mention who is expected or encouraged to speak. (Recall the boys in the *Symposium* sending the flute girls out.) Conversations and criticism take place in particular circumstances. Turf matters. So does the fact of who if anyone already has set up the terms of the conversations.

5. Theory cannot be useful to anyone interested in resistance and change unless there is reason to believe that knowing what a theory means and believing it to be true have some connection to resistance and change. As we make theory and offer it up to others, what do we assume is the connection between theory and consciousness? Do we expect others to read theory, understand it, believe it, and have their consciousnesses and lives thereby transformed?

If we really want theory to make a difference to people's lives, how ought we to present it? Do we think people come to consciousness by reading? only by reading? Speaking to people through theory (orally or in writing) is a *very* specific context-dependent activity. That is, theory makers and their methods and concepts constitute a community of people and of shared meanings. Their language can be just as opaque and foreign to those not in the community as a foreign tongue or dialect.[3] Why do we engage in *this* activity and what effect do we think it ought to have? As Helen Longino has asked: "Is 'doing theory' just a bonding ritual for academic or educationally privileged feminist women?" Again, whom does our theory making serve?

Some Suggestions About How to Do Theory That Is Not Imperialistic, Ethnocentric, Disrespectful

(*Problematically in the voice of a woman of color*) What are the things we need to know about others, and about ourselves, in order to speak intelligently, intelligibly, sensitively, and help-fully about their lives? We can show respect, or lack of it, in writing theoretically about others no less than in talking directly with them. This is not to say that here we have a well-worked out concept of respect, but only to suggest that together all of us consider what it would mean to theorize in a respectful way.

When we speak, write, and publish our theories, to whom do we think we are ac-countable? Are the concerns we have in being accountable to "the profession" at odds with the concerns we have in being accountable to those about whom we theorize? Do commit-ments to "the profession," method, getting something published, getting tenure, lead us to talk and act in ways at odds with what we ourselves (let alone others) would regard as ordinary, decent behavior? To what extent do we presuppose that really understanding another person or culture requires our behaving in ways that are disrespectful, even violent? That is, to what extent do we presuppose that getting and/or publishing the requisite information requires or may require disregarding the wishes of others, lying to them, wresting informa-tion from them against their wills? Why and how do we think theorizing about others pro-vides *understanding* of them? Is there any sense in which theorizing about others is a short-cut to understanding them?

Finally, if we think doing theory is an important activity, and we think that some condi-tions lead to better theorizing than others, what are we going to do about creating those conditions? If we think it not just desirable but necessary for women of different racial and ethnic identities to create feminist theory jointly, how shall that be arranged for? It may be the case that at this particular point we ought not even try to do that—that feminist theory by and for Hispanas needs to be done separately from feminist theory by and for Black women, white women, etc. But it must be recognized that white/Anglo women have more power and privilege than Hispanas, Black women, etc., and at the very least they can use such ad-vantage to provide space and time for other women to speak (with the above caveats about implicit restrictions on what counts as "the woman's voice"). And once again it is important to remember that the power of white/Anglo women vis-a-vis Hispanas and Black women is in inverse proportion to their working knowledge of each other.

This asymmetry is a crucial fact about the background of possible relationships between white women and women of color, whether as political co-workers, professional colleagues, or friends.

If white/Anglo women and women of color are to do theory jointly, in helpful, respect-ful, illuminating and empowering ways, the task ahead of white/Anglo women because of this asymmetry, is a very hard task. The task is a very complex one. In part, to make an analogy, the task can be compared to learning a text without the aid of teachers. We all know the lack of contact felt when we want to discuss a particular issue that requires knowledge of a text with someone who does not know the text at all. Or the discomfort and impatience that arise in us when we are discussing an issue that presupposes a text and someone walks into the conversation who does not know the text. That person is either left out or will impose herself on us and either try to engage in the discussion or try to change the subject. Women of color are put in these situations by white/Anglo women and men constantly. Now imagine yourself simply left out but wanting to do theory with us. The first thing to recognize and accept is that you disturb our own dialogues by putting yourself in the left-out position and not leaving us in some meaningful sense to ourselves.

You must also recognize and accept that you must learn the text. But the text is an extraordinarily complex one: viz., our many different cultures. You are asking us to make ourselves more vulnerable to you than we already are before we have any reason to trust that you will not take advantage of this vulnerability. So you need to learn to become unintrusive, unimportant, patient to the point of tears, while at the same time open to learning any possible lessons. You will also have to come to terms with the sense of alienation, of not belonging, of having your world thoroughly disrupted, having it criticized and scrutinized from the point of view of those who have been harmed by it, having important concepts central to it dismissed, being viewed with mistrust, being seen as of no consequence except as an object of mistrust.

Why would any white/Anglo woman engage in this task? Out of self-interest? What in engaging in this task would be, not just in her interest, but perceived as such by her before the task is completed or well underway? Why should we want you to come into our world out of self-interest? Two points need to be made here. The task as described could be entered into with the intention of finding out as much as possible about us so as to better dominate us. The person engaged in this task would act as a spy. The motivation is not unfamiliar to us. We have heard it said that now that Third World countries are more powerful as a bloc, westerners need to learn more about them, that it is in their self-interest to do so. Obviously there is no reason why people of color should welcome white/Anglo women into their world for the carrying out of this intention. It is also obvious that white/Anglo feminists should not engage in this task under this description since the task under this description would not lead to joint theorizing of the desired sort: respectful, illuminating, helpful and empowering. It would be helpful and empowering only in a one-sided way.

Self-interest is also mentioned as a possible motive in another way. White/Anglo women sometimes say that the task of understanding women of color would entail self-growth or self-expansion. If the task is conceived as described here, then one should doubt that growth or expansion will be the result. The severe self-disruption that the task entails should place a doubt in anyone who takes the task seriously about her possibilities of coming out of the task whole, with a self that is not as fragile as the selves of those who have been the victims of racism. But also, why should women of color embrace white/Anglo women's self-betterment without reciprocity? At this time women of color cannot afford this generous affirmation of white/Anglo women.

Another possible motive for engaging in this task is the motive of duty, "out of obligation," because white/Anglos have done people of color wrong. Here again two considerations: coming into Hispano, Black, Native American worlds out of obligation puts white/Anglos in a morally self-righteous position that is inappropriate. You are active, we are passive. We become the vehicles of your own redemption. Secondly, we couldn't want you to come into our worlds "out of obligation." That is like wanting someone to make love to you out of obligation. So, whether or not you have an obligation to do this (and we would deny that you do), or whether this task could even be done out of obligation, this is an inappropriate motive.

Out of obligation you should stay out of our way, respect us and our distance, and forego the use of whatever power you have over us—for example, the power to use your language in our meetings, the power to overwhelm us with your education, the power to intrude in our communities in order to research us and to record the supposed dying of our cultures, the power to engrain in us a sense that we are members of dying cultures and are doomed to assimilate, the power to keep us in a defensive posture with respect to our own cultures.

So the motive of friendship remains as both the only appropriate and understandable motive for white/Anglo feminists engaging in the task as described above. If you enter the task out of friendship with us, then you will be moved to attain the appropriate reciprocity of care for your and our well-being as whole beings, you will have a stake in us and in our world, you will be moved to satisfy the need for reciprocity of understanding that will enable you to follow us in our experiences as we are able to follow you in yours.

We are not suggesting that if the learning of the text is to be done out of friendship, you must enter into a friendship with a whole community and for the purpose of making theory. In order to understand what it is that we are suggesting, it is important to remember that during the description of her experience of exclusion, the Hispana voice said that Hispanas experience the intimacy of friendship with white/Anglo women friends as thoroughly incomplete. It is not until this fact is acknowledged by our white/Anglo women friends and felt as a profound lack in our experience of each other that white/Anglo women can begin to see us. Seeing us in our communities will make clear and concrete to you how incomplete we really are in our relationships with you. It is this beginning that forms the proper background for the yearning to understand the text of our cultures that can lead to joint theory making.

Thus, the suggestion made here is that if white/Anglo women are to understand our voices, they must understand our communities and us in them. Again, this is not to suggest that you set out to make friends with our communities, though you may become friends with some of the members, nor is it to suggest that you should try to befriend us for the purpose of making theory with us. The latter would be a perversion of friendship. Rather, from within friendship you may be moved by friendship to undergo the very difficult task of understanding the text of our cultures by understanding our lives in our communities. This learning calls for circumspection, for questioning of yourselves and your roles in your own culture. It necessitates a striving to understand while in the comfortable position of not having an official calling card (as "scientific" observers of our communities have); it demands recognition that you do not have the authority of knowledge; it requires coming to the task without ready-made theories to frame our lives. This learning is then extremely hard because it requires openness (including openness to severe criticism of the white/Anglo world), sensitivity, concentration, self-questioning, circumspection. It should be clear that it does not consist in a passive immersion in our cultures, but in a striving to understand what it is that our voices are saying. Only then can we engage in a mutual dialogue that does not reduce each one of us to instances of the abstraction called "woman."

Notes

1. For a recent example, see MacKinnon, Catharine. 1982. Feminism, Marxism, method and the state: An agenda for theory. *Signs* 7 (3): 515–544.
2. I must note that when I think this "we," I think it in Spanish—and in Spanish this "we" is gendered, "nosotras." I also use "nosotros" lovingly and with ease and in it I include all members of "La raza cosmica" (Spanish-speaking people of the Americas, la gente de colores: people of many colors). In the US, I use "we" contextually with varying degrees of discomfort: "we" in the house, "we" in the department, "we " in the classroom, "we" in the meeting. The discomfort springs from the sense

of community in the "we" and the varying degrees of lack of community in the context in which the "we" is used.

3. See Bernstein, Basil. 1972. Social class, language, and socialization. In Giglioli, Pier Paolo, ed., *Language and Social Context*, pp. 157–178. Penguin, Harmondsworth, Middlesex. Bernstein would probably, and we think wrongly, insist that theoretical terms and statements have meanings *not* "tied to a local relationship and to a local social structure," unlike the vocabulary of, e.g., working-class children.

Study Questions

1. Why does Spelman (the white/Anglo woman) feel that women should speak out? Does she think that there is *one* woman's voice? Explain your answer.

2. How does Lugones (the Hispana) explain the fact that when women of color appear in front of white women they mainly raise the complaint that they are being excluded? Does she feel that Anglo feminist theory captures her experiences as a Hispana?

3. What are two different ways of arriving at an account of another woman's experience of theorizing?

4. What are some characteristics of a truly helpful feminist theory? Try to find an example of a feminist theory (from your other readings) that would not be "helpful" from the point of view of Lugones and Spelman.

5. What problems does Lugones see with the suggestion that women of different backgrounds "do theory together"? What does she think Anglo women need to do before such joint theorizing can take place? What motives should the Anglo woman not bring to the task of constructing a theory with women of color?

2

Women's Nature and Women's Values

Moral philosophy, traditionally, distinguishes "ought" from "is," that is, it distinguishes prescriptive questions about worth and value from descriptive questions about the nature of things or matters of fact. But "ought" and "is" are intimately related in a number of ways. For one thing, "ought" implies "can." In other words, any judgment about what a person ought to do presupposes judgments about what that person is capable of doing. Thus, questions of moral philosophy cannot be separated from questions about what constitutes human nature.

How has women's nature been traditionally viewed; that is, how has it been viewed from the male perspective? Women's nature has been held to be not only different from men's but also lesser, especially in regard to rationality. Men's nature is taken to be the standard for human nature, and women, presumably, fall short of that standard. Women have been described as emotional rather than rational, intuitive rather than logical, passive rather than active, and so on. This view, in turn, justified the confinement of women to the private/domestic sphere. And because women were held to be unfit for the public (political) sphere, where rationality is supposedly required, they were denied literacy and education and were kept from participating in political, legal, economic, and religious institutions.

Feminist thinkers now challenge the very notion of human nature, and especially women's nature, as androcentrically biased. They argue that what has been called "natural" in regard to sex/gender is, in reality, socially or culturally constructed. They are also critical of the deliberate equation of male nature and human nature, because it serves to exclude women from public life and to justify their subordination as "the second sex."

As a result, feminists are engaged in reconceiving the basic question of "woman's nature." Is it true that women have a distinct nature? If so, are the differences the outcome of social learning and cultural conditioning? Should feminists seek to eliminate these differences, and if so, what would constitute the ideal form of human nature? Or should feminists celebrate any, or all, differences and explore the notion of women's nature as the basis for a system of women's values?

In her survey of classical and contemporary (psychoanalytic) theories of women's nature, Caroline Whitbeck shows how "male-stream" theories devalue women's nature and serve as rationales for the subordination of women. She considers three basic motifs in men's philosophy of women; woman as partial man; the masculine/feminine division as better/worse; and woman as defined by man's needs. Since these motifs fit men's fantasies, she says, women must create their own images.

According to Nancy Holmstrom, theories of women's nature have been used to justify women's exclusion from the public sphere, so women are rightly suspicious of them. Feminist investigators hold that past scientific research has been sexist in its assumptions. Holmstrom calls for a feminist revision of sex-difference theory that would show how women's nature is culturally produced and maintained to serve patriarchal and capitalist ends. In this way, she says, the focus of the discussion of women's nature would be dynamic rather than static. Holmstrom asserts that new social conditions will redefine women's nature.

"Woman is to nature as man is to culture" is the equation Sherry Ortner has formulated to explain the universal devaluation of women. Following de Beauvoir, Ortner sees women as tied to the natural or biological processes (primarily childbearing and childrearing). According to Ortner, man is seen as the creator of culture, which is the distinctively human project that controls nature. Women (nature) are relegated to the private sphere, while men (culture) assume the public sphere unchallenged. The feminist project, she says, is to question and challenge this oppressive dichotomy.

Theories of Sex Difference

Caroline Whitbeck

A survey of the theories which identify and explain differences between women and men in Western philosophy and science reveals three general themes or motifs which recur over a period of twenty-five hundred years, and still have a lively currency. In the space of this paper I shall discuss several ancient and modern theories structured by these motifs, and offer a critique of those which are currently held. In the course of the critique of Freud's and Jung's theories I shall identify factors which may explain the vitality of these motifs. These factors may be seen to contribute to, rather than be a product of, male domination. I end with some conclusions about the implications that the recognition of these motifs have for the task we

From *The Philosophical Forum*, Vol. V, Nos. 1–2 (Fall/Winter 1973–74), pp. 54–80. Reprinted by permission of The Philosophical Forum. (Notes deleted.)

women presently face, the task of articulating our experience and recovering our own consciousness.

The first of these three motifs, and one which is particularly important in structuring scientific theories on this subject, is that of woman as partial man. In theories structured by this motif the principal difference or differences among the sexes is seen as deriving from the supposed fact that women either completely lack, or have less of, some important ingredient in men's makeup. The second major motif entails an identification of two principles in nature and/or human nature. The first of these principles embodies whatever characteristics are seen as accruing to the conscious self and is taken to be male or masculine. The second principle is defined by contrast to the first and so embodies whatever characteristics are seen accruing to the nonself or other.[1] It is taken to be female or feminine.[2] (Frequently, the content ascribed to these two principles associates the masculine with the rational and the feminine with the nonrational or even irrational, but this varies with the view of the conscious self.) The second motif occurs most often in metaphysical and psychological theories. The third and final motif holds that the essence of womanhood is defined in terms of men's needs. This motif figures most prominently in religious and mythological literature and in works which explicitly set down norms. As such the "theories" involved are more prescriptive than descriptive and are part of a social mythology and are not theories proper. However this third motif will be briefly discussed because it is also frequently found in combination with the two previous motifs in theories which do claim to describe and explain the way things are.

(i) Aristotle: Woman as Partial Man

Although we find reference to the putative fact that women are weaker than (in the sense of generally inferior to) men in Plato[3] and the Presocratics, it is Aristotle who provides the first extensive enumeration and explanation of differences between the sexes by the *woman-as-partial-man* motif.[4] Indeed, according to Aristotle, woman is defined by both a quantitative and a qualitative deficiency, though the two are related. It will be seen that his account is in many respects isomorphic to later theories, e.g., Freud's views and at least some accounts of recent findings in endocrinology. . . .

According to Aristotle, women, and likewise the females of other species, have less intrinsic, vital, or soul heat than men, or the males of the species. Thus a woman is unable to concoct, or cook, her menstrual blood to the final stage of refinement, i.e., semen. Therefore Aristotle holds, women do not contribute semen in conception, but only menstrual blood. The latter supplies the matter of the embryo but does not contribute to its form or distinctive character. This view I shall call "the flower pot theory of pregnancy." Woman supplies the container and the earth which nourishes the seed but the seed is solely the man's. The analogy fails only in that actual seeds have a material component[5] and Aristotle envisions semen as being pure movement, which gives form to the embryo but is not itself a body.[6]

It might be objected that since a woman supplies something which the man does not, *viz.*, the material, the analog of the earth-filled flower pot, it is a mistake to say that Aristotle conceives of a woman as a partial man. This objection might be maintained even in the face of the low regard Aristotle has for the material factor in human generation. (He assimilates menstrual fluid to other products of incomplete concoction such as diarrhea.) However he explicitly says that a female is to be viewed as an infertile male and goes on to say

> the female in fact is female on account of an inability of a sort, *viz.*, it lacks the
> power to concoct semen out of the final state of nourishment (this is either blood
> or its counterpart in bloodless animals) because of the coldness of their nature.[7]

Again later in the work he says

> we should look upon the female state as being as it were a deformity though one which occurs in the ordinary course of nature.[8]

As it turns out Aristotle views women as being a bit worse off than females of other species with regard to the possession of innate heat, notwithstanding his view that females of even bloodless species are female on account of their lack of heat. He takes one result of woman's special deficiency in this regard to be the large volume of her menstrual secretions as compared with other mammals. In the human species

> the perfecting of female embryos is inferior to that of male ones since their uterus is inferior in condition. In other animals however the perfecting of female embryos is not inferior to that of male ones.[9]

The view that there is more difference between women and men than between females and males of other species would of course undercut Plato's argument from analogy with other animals for opening all societal activities to women as well as men.

The lack of semen in women has the consequence that the mother does not impart any sentient soul to the fetus but only nutritive soul. Nutritive soul is shared by all species of life including plants. Sentient soul is peculiar to animals. What about rational soul, that which in the Aristotelian scheme differentiates humans from other animals? In the *Politics* Aristotle tells us that it is proper for free adult males to rule over slaves, children and women because in slaves the deliberative faculty is entirely lacking, in children (presumably free and male) it is immature, and in women it is defective or to use the usual translation, a woman has the faculty but it is "without authority."

As we have seen, Aristotle repeatedly expresses the view that what is essential to being female is a lack of certain attributes of the male. Aristotle was one of the first to build a detailed biological theory upon this idea although this idea, and in particular the flower pot theory of pregnancy is to be found in fragments from certain of the Pre-Socratics (*viz.*, Anaxagoras and Diogenes of Apollonia[10]), and Aeschylus in the *Eumenides* has Apollo assert it explicitly and deny that the mother is a parent to the child. . . .

In spite of the fact that Aristotle's account of sex differences is the exemplar of theories structured around the woman-as-partial-man motif, nonetheless Aristotle's thinking does reflect the second principle motif. This motif is revealed in his discussion of the male and female principles of generation. The male principle is, or contributes, form or movement and the female principle is, or contributes, matter. Thus Aristotle frequently speaks as though there were two distinct and perhaps opposing factors. He even says at one point that male and female differ in respect to their *logos*. A succinct expression of the two-principle theme is found in the following sentence:

> Now of course the female, *qua* female, is passive, and the male, *qua* male is active.[11]

We have already seen that Aristotle does not weaken his claim that women are partial or defective men, notwithstanding this talk of two principles. Is there any source from which Aristotle might have inherited this conception of male and female principles? Clearly from Pythagoras or at least the Pythagoreans.

(ii) Pythagoras: The Feminine as the Second of Two Opposing Principles

In the Pythagoreans' account of the Monad and the Dyad we have one of the earliest Western accounts which embodies the second motif. According to the Pythagoreans, the Monad, the Principle of Oneness or unit was the original number. They envisaged it as an indivisible point, the most elementary form which can be imposed on space. Space or the Unlimited was understood as making multiplicity possible and hence the Dyad or Principle of Twoness, was derived from the Monad and Space, jointly. Subsequently, Space or the Unlimited generally was identified with the Dyad so that the Unlimited was identified with the number two, and with the even while Limit or the Limited was associated with the number one and with the odd in general. Indeed Aristotle tells us that the Pythagoreans accounted for the perceptible world in terms of ten oppositions. The first members of each pair were grouped together and identified with the Monad, whereas the second members of each pair were identified with the Dyad.

Limit-Unlimited ⟶ *not individuals*
Odd-Even
One-Many ⟶
Right-Left
Male-Female ⟶ *involuntary*
Rest-Motion ⟶
Straight-Curved
Light-Darkness
Good-Bad
Square-Oblong

You will notice that the Dyad is at once, female, unlimited, bad, and plural, and associated with darkness, and motion. On the face of it this association of motion with the female seems to contradict Aristotle's definition of the male as active and the female as passive. However in the case of motion associated with the Dyad the sense is of change, inconstancy, whereas the motion which Aristotle associates with the male, is goal-directed action of a purposive cause. The above interpretation of the Pythagorean idea is borne out by attention to the last of the opposites identified with the Dyad, oblong. Odd numbers were thought of as square because a square arrangement of any number of units may be seen as the sum of successive odd numbers 1, 3, 5, 7 . . . or displayed in two dimensions
5 5 5
3 3 5 . . . whereas even numbers were thought of as oblong because
1 3 5   6 6 6 6
successive even numbers produce an oblong array 4 4 4 6 . . . the oblong
                                    2 2 4 6
produced has a changeable character in that the ratio of the length of its sides changes as successive even numbers are added. Thus the motion characteristic of the Dyad is not the motion of an efficient cause proceeding rationally to accomplish some end, but recalcitrant unpredictability which Plato, and later Aristotle came to think of as characteristic of matter. For the Pythagoreans number is constitutive of reality and the rational form supplied by number is static, whereas Aristotle has a biologist's concern for the natural course of development, and thus for a dynamic rationality. In both cases however the female principle embodies that which opposes rationality and order.

As it happens the Pythagoreans did deem at least some women worthy of instruction, for Iamblichus (fourth century A.D.) lists all Pythagoreans known by name, and seventeen women are included in this list of two hundred and thirty-five. This fact illustrates the point that there need not be any *simple* relationship between the political and social freedom of women within a group and the theories about sex differences explicitly propounded by that group. It also warns us that what is held to distinguish the feminine principle need not be claimed to be either true of all women or a norm for women, provided that individual variation in this regard is not seen as unnatural, unseemly, or otherwise untoward.

If and when it is claimed that women need not be especially feminine nor men especially masculine, what are we to make of the fact that the terms "masculine" and "feminine" are used? This question will be dealt with below in discussion of the masculine and feminine principles in the work of C. G. Jung. However some light is shed on this question by considering the feminine symbols of astrology. Venus and the Moon are feminine "planets." The glyph for Cancer is thought to represent the breasts, and that for Virgo, the female genitals, and the fourth house represents the home and womb. Finally, the odd signs are regarded as positive, or masculine whereas the even signs are negative or feminine. Masculine here means self-expressive whereas feminine means receptive, or "self-repressive." Thus some elements of a person's destiny and psychological makeup were considered female and symbols for these elements *all* appeared somewhere in each subject's chart. What are these forces? Love and passion, beauty and the emotions in the planet Venus; flux and change, the unconscious, and maternal influences in the moon; the home and domesticity in Cancer and the fourth house; for harmony and close relationship and communication in Libra and the seventh house. In cultures which more or less confine women to the home it is clear why female symbols would be naturally associated with maternal influences, the home and domesticity. What about passion, beauty, close relation, harmony, aesthetics and emotional life in general? These areas of life have a close association with what may be broadly termed sexual feelings and hence are naturally associated with members of the opposite sex. In view of the fact that, with the exception of royalty, horoscopes were originally cast *only for men,* the opposite sex was female. Now that it has become common practice to cast the horoscopes of women, there has been some disagreement over whether in the case of a female subject the sun's positions and aspects ought to represent her own nature, as it does in the case of a man, or whether it should be understood to represent the men in her life. The difficulty arises from the fact that the symbol for the conscious self is a masculine symbol, so that the female is seen as essentially in contrast with that self. Since rationality is the hallmark of the conscious self, the ego, rationality is seen as masculine as opposed to feminine. I will return to this subject in section (iv) below.

(iii) Women as Defined in Terms of Man's Needs

What, finally should be said about the third motif, that of woman as defined in terms of man's needs? This theme exists in a relatively pure form only in mythic religious literature and utopian social writings rather than in philosophical and scientific theories. The "theories" which embody this third motif function prescriptively, drawing morals about how the sexes ought to behave or function rather than how they do, though this is not always explicitly done. Thus this motif is more to be found in social mythology than in theories which purport to have a truth value and identify and explain existing sex differences. However it often structures subsidiary arguments and explanations offered in theories which are primarily structured by one of the two previously discussed motifs and so influences the course of some explanations, proper. Therefore it will be briefly discussed here in some of its purer instances. It is to be found in the second account of creation, the one found in Genesis 2:4b f. We are told that the point of creating woman was to provide man with a helper and companion.

Indeed this was the point of making the animals too, but they did not succeed very well. For that matter woman herself was not a great success, as we shall see. The first chapter of Genesis contains a different account of creation, according to it God created man and woman together. When the narratives were put together scholars had to account for this supposed double creation. Most of the Midrashic commentators held that the first woman, Lilith, was uppity and insisted on full equality with Adam. She found Adam intolerable, and, by pronouncing the Ineffable Name, was able to fly away from Adam. A second woman was then created for Adam. The Midrashic account is as follows:

> The woman destined to become the true companion of man was taken from Adam's body, for "only when like is joined unto like the union is indissoluble." The creation of woman from man was possible because Adam originally had two faces, which were separated at the birth of Eve.
>
> When God was on the point of making Eve, He said: "I will not make her from the head of man, lest she carry her head high in arrogant pride; not from the eye, lest she be wanton-eyed; not from the ear, lest she be an eavesdropper; not from the neck, lest she be insolent; not from the mouth, lest she be a tattler; not from the heart, lest she be inclined to envy; not from the hand, lest she be a meddler; not from the foot, lest she be a gadabout. I will form her from a chaste portion of the body," and to every limb and organ as He formed it, God said, "Be chaste! Be chaste!" Nevertheless, in spite of the great caution used, woman has all the faults God tried to obviate.[12]

Not a great success as a helper. Some of the Midrashic commentators consider the fact that as bearer of children women ought to be much more complicated than men, and thus they contradict the partial man views of woman.

The definition of woman in terms of man's needs admits of variations. In particular it varies depending on whether it is the adult male or the male child's perspective that is regarded as primary. In the first case it is the role of assistant/wife that is considered as definitive for femininity and for "fulfillment" as a woman, in the second case it is the role of mother that is definitive for femininity and womanhood. In our culture the assistant/wife role is seen in terms of such traits and abilities as the following, not necessarily in this order: attractive appearance; a responsiveness to her man which makes him feel attractive; a willingness to take over routine tasks and accomplish them to perfection; the ability to produce a home/office/children which are a credit to him; a personal style which is supportive to her man which enables her to work around and modulate his moods, quirks and neuroses, disguising them even from herself; a loyalty to her man above all else; and the ability to amuse herself when not needed. Maternal worth is seen in terms of such traits and abilities as the following: physical strength, stamina, a disposition which is placid enough to nurse with ease, but versatile enough to change with each new stage of the child's development so that, for example, she is enthralled with physical functions of the infant and can stimulate the intellectual interest of a twelve-year-old. (In short she is able to produce a highly achieving but non-neurotic son.) Furthermore she is devoted to her children above all else, and able to induce their father into taking an interest in them, never sees herself as martyr, and is able to sustain herself as her children outgrow her. I submit that characteristics for the mother role are not only different from but conflict with those of the assistant/wife role. As with all roles there is a negative as well as positive aspect implicit in each, so that a woman *qua woman* is in jeopardy of becoming a *bad* assistant/wife, epitomized in a witch who steals men's potency or even literally steals his penis and the evil mother, epitomized in the witch who kills and even eats children. Success as an assistant/wife runs the danger of making a woman a bad mother, and the perfect mother is at risk for being a bad assistant/wife. What both variants of this theme have *in common* is their emphasis upon the special competence required of a good woman—though not the competence of the conquering hero or intellectual competence which might put her in competition with her man/son. This idea of special competence is foreign to both the woman-as-partial-man motif, and the theme of the feminine or the second (often explicitly non-rational or irrational) principle.

The explanations which fit under the defined-in-terms-of-man's-needs motif appear in the works of those, like the Jungians and Freudians, whose theories about sex differences are primarily structured by one of the other motifs. For example the idea of the "anima woman" whom as we shall see, the Jungians regard as expressing instinctive femininity in her life style, structured by one of the other motifs. For example the Jungians regard what they term an "anima woman" as the type of woman who "expresses instinctive femininity." An anima woman is characterized by the tendency to invite the projection of certain unconscious elements in a man's psyche, and to actively accommodate to them in the manner characteristic of a good assistant/wife. More familiar is the way in which Freudians augment their postulation that the wish to have a baby (to symbolize the missing penis) is the characteristic feminine desire, with the supposition that normal women wish to engage in *caring for* the baby and child. The first is the wish of a partial man. The second is the wish of a natural mother.

(iv) Jung: The Feminine as Non-Ego Traits in the Human Psyche

Next I will consider Jungian views of the structure and content of the masculine and feminine principles. It will be seen that there are numerous difficulties and inconsistencies in the Jungian account of the way in which the feminine principle relates to a woman's psyche. I am led to conclude that many of these difficulties arise because it is only from *the point of view of a man* is it natural to consider the content of the so-called "feminine principle" as feminine, and to associate it with women.

In the Jungian scheme the feminine is conceived of as one pole of a masculine-feminine polarity, in keeping with the rather Heraclitean view, that all psychic energy or libido is organized in polarities. Jungians claim that the feminine is an important element in men's as well as women's psyches. Certain qualities of personality, ways of understanding and foci of concern are viewed as feminine. According to the Jungians the feminine or, as they also term it, the eros principle, encompasses relatedness and value reached through feeling, and is contrasted with the masculine, or logos principle, which encompasses discrimination and interest in objective truth. In this respect, Jung's view is reminiscent of the now familiar supposition, found in Hegel and others, that abstract or analytic thinking and objective judgment are masculine, and that apprehension of the related concrete whole and interest in the personal and emotional side of things are feminine.

There is an empirical basis for the characterization of the eros principle as "feminine," in that Jungian analysts have amassed a body of clinical evidence showing that there is a tendency to personify these qualities in dreams, fantasies and artistic representations by female figures. On the basis of this evidence, Jung postulates the existence of an "inner woman" in the unconscious of each man. This "inner woman" personifies the manifestations of the eros principle in his psyche. Jung calls this structure "the anima." Since "she" embodies relatedness, the anima may function to relate the man's ego to the rest of his psyche (including the so-called collective unconscious or objective psyche with its repository of archetypal and religious images). Evidence in support of Jung's view is not limited to clinical observation. Indeed, a trip through an art museum lends a good deal of credence to it. One sees muses emerging from the artist's head, represented as linking him with his creative energies, the Virgin Mary relating the human and divine, and a host of other female figures represented as relating the artist to some other realm; of course, the artist is a man.

What about women? In order to discuss the relation of women to the feminine or eros principle, we would need an initial distinction between what is held to be true of women and what is held to be true of the feminine, but this is what the Jungians do not supply.

Jung's failure to maintain a distinction between the feminine and women is exemplified in the following passage:

> Too much soul is reserved for God, too little for man. But God himself cannot flourish if man's soul is starved. The *feminine psyche* responds to this hunger, for it is the function of *Eros* to unite what Logos has sundered. The *woman* of today is faced with a tremendous cultural task—perhaps it will be the dawn of a new era.[13] (My emphasis.)

The confusion is related too in this passage from another Jungian, Gerhard Adler.[14]

> (Man) has been obliged to acknowledge the existence of an autonomous and independent psyche. His old established belief in the "superiority" of "logos" has been decisively challenged by an equally important, but diligently overlooked power of the "*eros*." Where this challenge is accepted and answered in a constructive sense, a new and creative relationship between *man* and *woman* as equal partners can be established.[14] (My emphasis.)

The failure on the part of Jungians to maintain the distinction between woman and the feminine may be traced to another tendency, the tendency to adopt the point of view of a man, or at least, a man's ego. Thus, in the passage quoted from Jung, we find that he sees women as performing a task of reintegration for the whole culture, a task which is entirely analogous to the one that the anima, a man's unconscious "feminine" side, performs for the individual man's psyche.

Similarly, if we look into Esther Harding's *The Way of All Women*,[15] we find that Harding's first chapter entitled, "All Things to All Men," is an extended account of what she calls "a man's woman" or an "anima-woman." Harding says of her, "She figures in myths and legends, but she is always shown from the man's point of view." In playing the anima role, such a woman is viewed as being in touch with her "instinctive femininity." In contrast, the other type of woman, not-a-man's woman, is viewed as, to some extent, identified with her animus, her masculine side. It is instructive to see how odd Harding's account would appear turned around: if men were discussed as falling into two basic types depending on whether they did or did not invite animus projection on the part of women, so that a man would be understood to be fully masculine only if he were a woman's man (a lady's man?), and all other men would be viewed as identified to some extent with their unconscious feminine side.

Reading the works of Jungians, one is liable to get the impression that the conscious ego is always masculine. For example, Erich Neumann says, "every archetypal opposition easily assumes a masculine-feminine character and the opposition of the conscious and unconscious is also experienced through this symbolism, the masculine being identified with consciousness and the feminine with the unconscious. This . . . stems from the primary fact . . . that masculine consciousness is born from maternal unconscious (*sic*). . . . Similarly, we find Harding suggesting that the ego of an anima-woman can be largely unconscious. Harding says:

The world of work, however, is essentially a world of competition which forces the ego into consciousness. In the case of the anima-woman, the ego often hides almost entirely in the unconscious. . . .

We may make sense of Harding's statement by supposing her to mean not that a woman's ego is largely unconscious, but that women, or at least "feminine" women, live unreflectively and are thus largely unaware of their own personalities. However, her choice of words is symptomatic of the tendency to associate women with the unconscious in defiance of the fact that conscious ego functioning is as requisite for "women's work" as for other tasks.

Another Jungian, Ann Ulanov in the book *The Feminine*, likewise says that a woman's ego is "less consciously defined than the male's and often less firm. . . . However, she does try to give a better account of women by emphasizing what she calls the "feminine mode consciousness." Thus, she maintains that

In contrast to the frequent identification of the feminine with the unconscious, with non-spiritual and natural processes, the symbolic (i.e., Jungian) approach describes the feminine kind of ego consciousness and its relation to the unconscious. . . .

However, Ulanov is only partially successful in her endeavor, since it turns out that feminine ego consciousness is more primitive according to the usual criteria. She says of it:

Historically, feminine consciousness characterizes the early eras of humanity, and in individual lives, is manifest in childhood, in moments of psychological crisis, and in the creative processes. . . .

In spite of her efforts to present a more favorable account of feminine ego functioning, which Ulanov asserts to be the predominant but not exclusive type of ego functioning available to women, she, like many other female analysts, has fallen into a standpoint which I call "displaced consciousness." She has adopted man's point of view. This displaced consciousness is reflected not only in her ascription to women of a primitive form of ego functioning, and in her general failure to distinguish what is true of women from what is true of the anima, the embodiment of eros in a man's psyche, it is reflected even in her choice of pronouns. In referring to women, Ulanov invariably speaks of "them," "they," and "their experience." However, we find her saying:

When we talk about the feminine, we talk about our concepts of the human person and of relationships between persons. We touch the most intimate aspects of our lives—our relation to sexuality, to *our wives*, our daughters, our mothers, to feminine elements in the male personality, and to the unconscious. . . . (My emphasis.)

If there is anything to the notion that eros characteristics are in some way more directly expressed in the conscious personalities of women, and logos characteristics are in some sense largely unconscious in women, then for women it would be logos or the masculine which would touch "the most intimate aspects of our (women's) lives"—our relation to sexuality, etc. However, logos does not lend itself much to intimacy. The essence of the logos principle is discrimination, differentiation, and relation to impersonal truth. Such a principle is hardly embodied in a warm, passionate and tender lover. Nonetheless, guided by his equal-but-complementary principle, Jung fashioned an account of women's psyches according to which a woman's sexuality is the province of her animus, her "inner man" who embodies the logos principle.

In spite of their expressed concern to give an account of the human psyche in which the eros, or feminine principle is given equal weight with the logos, or masculine principle, the Jungians, like the Freudians, have devoted their principal efforts to constructing a model of a man's psyche, a model which is adequate to a man's experience. They have then derived from the model of a man's psyche their model of a woman's psyche. So it is that in spite of Ulanov's statement that in her book she means to be discussing the feminine as it appears in women, we find that in her section on psychological development, sex unspecified, what she gives is in fact an account of the development of a male! This is revealed in the following passages which are quoted from it:

> The third stage, which Neumann calls patriarchal, corresponds to the prepuberty years and to the onset of puberty itself. Transition to this phase is represented in initiation rituals where the boy leaves the world of women, undergoes challenges, tests, and fulfills rules laid down by the men and then joins their ranks as one of their own. . . .
>
> The fourth stage is called integrative. In this phase, the ego reclaims the elements of the non-rational feminine as woman, as the unconscious, and as anima—characteristics that were all rejected and repressed in the patriarchal. . . .

No mention is made of a girl. It is only somewhat later in the book, following a chapter explicitly devoted to the development of a man, that we finally find a chapter on the development of a woman. In that chapter Ulanov, herself, comes close to recognizing that for *both sexes*, logos characteristics are associated with the conscious ego, while eros characteristics are associated with the attractive other, with the unconscious, and with reunification of the total psyche. She says that for both sexes, it is the masculine, the logos principle, which initiates the final phase of development . . . , and later in the book, she says that in marriage it is important that both partners develop the feminine qualities within themselves and with each other. . . .

In spite of the general inadequacy of the Jungian account of a woman's psyche, the Jungian scheme *does* provide an explanation of the way in which the feminine principle has come to have much of the content that it does in our culture. Thus Ann Ulanov gives an account of the process by which a male child may come to associate eros traits and his own unconscious with women, and also to regard the sexual polarity as central. She first quotes the following passage from Erich Neumann:

> Every archetypal opposition easily assumes a masculine-feminine character and the opposition of conscious and unconscious is also experienced through this symbolism, the masculine being identified with consciousness and the feminine with unconscious. This . . . stems from the primary fact . . . that masculine consciousness is born from the maternal unconscious.

She then goes on to say that in the case of a boy

> The experience of the opposing sexual elements occurs sooner than it does with girls, and it has immediate decisive effects upon him. He experiences his original identity with his mother as a relation of like to unlike, as a relation to a non-self, to an "other," an opposite, symbolized by all the obvious sexual differences. In order to be himself and to have himself to himself he must stand against his early

identity with the non-self; he must free his ego and go his own way. He identifies his ego with consciousness because his self-discovery coincides with his freeing
himself from his mother and from the pre-ego containment in the unconscious
that she symbolizes. . . .

The Jungians have drawn attention to facts about the experiences of most male infants
which make it natural to form the traditional notion of the feminine. Notice that since female
infants are not regularly given primary care by an adult male the complementary identification will not naturally arise in the thinking of girls and women. Indeed the masculine-feminine
polarity is not likely to be a central symbol for girls and women at all.

Because of the impact of the idea of the feminine, Jung may nonetheless be right in
some of what he says about women. It may well be true that in our culture at least, women
are more likely than men to have developed skills for relating, and for integrating unconscious
materials. If this is the case, then Jung may also be right in thinking that women are in a
position to restore the balance in our value system which he claims to have been skewed in
the direction of logos traits.

(v) Freud: Woman as Partial Man

In Freud's theory about sex differences we find many parallels to Aristotle. Like Aristotle
Freud sees women as partial men, and in each case in the equipment "missing" in women
(*vis.*, semen according to Aristotle, and a penis according to Freud) has a sexual character.
Like Aristotle, Freud also equates masculine with active (aims) and feminine with passive (aims).
Freud's view of the primary deficiency is somewhat different from Aristotle's. Freud's suggestion that women have less libido, psychic energy, parallels Aristotle's suggestion that women
have less of that quantity, innate heat, which is the vehicle of the soul, however according
to Freud this quantitative "lack" is not related to the qualitative lack, the lack of a penis,
being "castrated," which is the focal point of his account.

I take it that Freud's views are rather well known in philosophical and feminist circles
and so shall not take space to summarize them further but instead give detailed attention
to specific passages in Freud's account of feminine psychology which reveal two significant
areas of incoherence. These will, I think, shed some light on the phenomenon of the recurrence of the partial man motif.

The first area of incoherence lies in Freud's account of a little girl's fantasies about the
difference between male and female genitals. The term that he uses most often is "castrated."
For example in "Female Sexuality" he says

> She (the female child) acknowledges the *fact of her castration*, and with it too, the
> superiority of the male.
>
> In women the Oedipus complex . . . is not destroyed but *created by the influence
> of castration*.
>
> The point of time when the *discovery of castration* is made varies. (My emphasis).

Now castration implies that the little girl had a penis and it was cut off. This, Freud
tells us, is precisely a little boy's fantasy about why girls and women do not possess penises.
It leads the boy to fear that his penis will be cut off by his father. Who, according to Freud,
does the little girl fantasize cut off her penis? No one. Even Freud's own clinical observations
do not support the view that little girls fantasize that they had a penis and someone cut it
off. As Freud sometimes recognized, a little girl is familiar with her own genitals.

What one would expect then is that she might *at most* regard her equipment as inferior. This, and not a fantasy of castration, is in fact what Freud has observed among his female analysands.

He reports this in the following passages:

> It was a surprise to learn that girls hold their mother responsible for their lack of a penis and do not forgive her for their being thus put at a disadvantage.[16]
>
> At the end of this first phase of attachment to the mother, there emerges, as the girl's strongest motive for turning away from her, the reproach that her mother did not give her a proper penis.[17]

Freud also reports the (presumably rare) analysand who did fantasize she was castrated. But in this case it is the *father* who in fantasy castrated her (as punishment for masturbation). This after all is what one would expect if as Freud supposed, the father is the figure who has the power and authority in the child's eyes. On Freud's account if somebody did any castrating then it should be the father, but as we have seen it is the mother whom his analysands blame for their "inferior" equipment.

For the moment at least I am not concerned with whether all or most girls have this or that fantasy, but only with whether Freud's account of a girl's fantasies is coherent. My first conclusion is that if other facts of psychic life are as Freud claims, little girls would generally not fantasize they are castrated. What Freud has done is to employ a term, "castrated" which derives from the fantasy of boys (and therefore of men) and treat it both as *fact* and as something which *little girls fantasize*. His Freudian slip leads us to ask how much of the rest of his view is a carry-over from the fantasy of little boys.

Another instance of this projection is to be found in his description of what genitals a little girl believes others to possess. We find Freud saying

> To begin with the girl regards her castration as an individual misfortune, and only gradually extends it to other females and finally to her mother as well. Her love was directed to her *phallic* mother; with the *discovery that her mother is castrated* it becomes possible to drop her as object.
>
> As a result of the discovery of a woman's lack of a penis they are debased in value for girls just *as they are for boys and later perhaps for men*.[18] (Second and third emphasis, mine.)

At the least Freud's account assumes that generally little girls learn that (some) males have penises, before they learn that (some) other females do not. A very implausible assumption, at best. However, to get to the heart of the issue I think we must attend to the term "phallic." A phallus as distinct from a penis is, the Freudians claim, a uniquely appropriate symbol for power. Freud consistently speaks of a little boy's regard for his *penis*. Perhaps the little boy connects the idea of this penis with that of a phallus through his experience of his own erections, but the prevalent power symbol is the phallus and the image associated with this symbol is that of an erect (adult) phallus. Now where is the little girl supposed to familiarize herself with an erect phallus? The sight of an infant brother's penis, even in a state of erection, is hardly likely to convey the symbol of the phallus. Well, let us assume that after all children do like to crawl into their parents' bed in the morning, and that little girls may commonly encounter early morning erections of their fathers. But how is the rest of the fantasy to get off the ground? How is the little girl supposed to attribute a phallus to her mother? Is she supposed to be *less* familiar with her mother's than her father's body? A possible but hardly likely situation. Or are little girls supposed to have an innate tendency in this specific instance to deny what they experience of their mother's body when they begin to acquaint themselves with their father's body? Such a specific psychic mechanism, if postulated, would itself require explanation. It should be noted too that empirical studies do not support Freud's description of the so-called Oedipal stage in girls.

Of course matters may be different for a little boy who may well initially assume that all persons have penises, and, having experienced as well as observed his own erections, and having connected these with his own sexual impulses, forms at least a rudimentary notion of a phallus and hence a phallic mother.

We need not impune existence of the clinical evidence supporting Freud's interpretation. Perhaps some of his women patients, having learned the symbolic meaning of the phallus, *read this symbol back* into their recollection of disappointment in their mothers when they realized their mother's subservience or weakness or passivity. (Analysts and psychiatrists are quite accustomed to interpreting hostile and resentful reactions of little boys toward fathers whom they see as subservient, weak or passive.) Such *retrospective* fantasies about the childhood experience even if common in a ''normal'' woman do not give us any insight into ''normal'' female development.

The second area of incoherence lies in Freud's account of psychological masculinity and femininity. Although for many years Freud wrestled with the problem of finding a psychological meaning for ''masculine'' and ''feminine'' the equation of masculinity with active sexual aims and of femininity with passive sexual aims appears without further explanation in his 1931 essay ''Female Sexuality.'' However, a year later in the lecture ''Femininity'' he warns his hearers of what appear to be his own errors in the following tortuous passage:

> We are accustomed to employ ''masculine'' and ''feminine'' as mental qualities as well, and have in the same way transferred the notion of bisexuality to mental life. Thus we speak of a person, whether male or female, as behaving in a masculine way in one connection and in a feminine way in another. But you will soon perceive that this is only giving way to anatomy or to convention. You cannot give the concepts of ''masculine'' and ''feminine'' *any* new connotation. The distinction is not a psychological one; when you say ''feminine'' you usually mean ''passive.'' Now it is true that a relation of the kind exists. The male sex-cell is actively mobile and searches out the female one, and the latter, the ovum, is immobile and waits passively. This behaviour of the elementary sexual organisms is indeed a model for the conduct of sexual individuals during intercourse. The male pursues the female for the purpose of sexual union, seizes hold of her and penetrates into her. But by this you have precisely reduced the characteristic of masculinity to the factor of aggressiveness so far as psychology is concerned. You may well doubt whether you have gained any real advantage from this when you reflect that in some classes of animals the females are the stronger and more aggressive and the male is active only in the single act of sexual union. This is so, for instance, with the spiders. Even the functions of rearing and caring for the young, which strike us as feminine *par excellence*, are not invariably attached to the female sex in animals. In quite high species we find that the sexes share the task of caring for the young between them or even that the male alone devotes himself to it. Even in the sphere of human sexual life you soon see how inadequate it is to make masculine behavior coincide with activity and feminine with passivity. A mother is active in every sense towards her child; the act of lactation itself may equally be described as the mother suckling the baby or as her being suckled by it . . . Women can display great activity in various directions, men

are not able to live in company with their own kind unless they develop a large amount of passive adaptability. If you now tell me that these facts go to prove precisely that both men and women are bisexual in the psychological sense, I shall conclude that you have decided in your own minds to make "active" coincide with "masculine" and "passive" with "feminine." But I advise you against it. It seems to me to serve no useful purpose and adds nothing to our knowledge.

One might consider characterizing femininity psychologically as giving preference to passive aims. This is not, of course, the same thing as passivity; to achieve a passive aim may call for a large amount of activity. It is perhaps the case that in a woman, on the basis of her share in the sexual function, a preference for passive behavior and passive aims is carried over into her life to a greater or lesser extent, in proportion to the limits, restricted or far-reaching, within which her sexual life thus serves as a model. But we must beware in this of underestimating the influence of social customs, which similarly force women into passive situations. All this is still far from being cleared up.[19]

And later Freud says [of the girl in her pre-Oedipal phase]

These wishes represent active as well as passive impulses; if we relate them to the differentiation of the sexes which is to appear later—though we should avoid doing so far as possible—we may call them masculine and feminine.[20]

What remains especially unclear is what is supposed to be the remaining link between what is feminine in the usual sense (i.e., being characteristic of, although not necessarily restricted to, "normal" women and girls), and what is passive in the usual sense.

What are "passive aims" and how are they at once passive and characteristic of girls and women? Freud tells us that in her phallic phase a little girl has active sexual aims and that her mother is the object of her desire but what even these active aims are, Freud admits he is at a loss to discover. All he can say is that in the cases in which a sibling is born, "the little girl wants to believe that she has given her mother the new baby just as the boy wants to.[21] At the next phase of her development, at least according to Freud, the little girl will want a baby "from" her father. As we have seen above. Freud in his *New Introductory Lectures* comes to admit that "a mother is active in every sense towards her child" so what does it come to, to say that for the girl, wanting to have a child is a passive aim? Perhaps we are to assume that the little girl sees the baby as a gift pure and simple, like a doll, or an organ transplant. *Qua* recipient the girl is passive but in this case it is not at all clear how the father could be seen as the object, or how the *sexual* aim could be passive. The aim could be sexual in some sense if the baby symbolizes a penis, as Freud claims, but if what the girl wants is a penis then *that* is what she wants and growing it or making it would be as gratifying as receiving it. If we take the baby on face value, as a baby, sexual gratification could be expected from contact with the baby, but if the aim is for just this contact and the mother is in every sense active towards her child, it is hard to see how predominantly passive aims are served. The more likely possibility is that Freud intends us to understand the giving of a child itself to be much more than giving pure and simple. Most straightforwardly what the little girl might wish to do is make a baby with her father. If that is her sexual aim the talk of *receiving* a baby is misleading. What the little girl wants to do is to make a baby with her father, and the *making* of a baby is the sexual aim. If this is what Freud means then to call this aim "passive" seems quite peculiar. Perhaps he was too impressed by the form of his own words in describing the girl as wanting a child *from* her father.

The phrase is anyhow inappropriate as a description of conception unless one holds something like a flower pot theory of pregnancy, i.e., one which assumes the very equation of masculine with active form and feminine with passive matter whose origin we are trying to discover.

(It might be the case that the girl wishes to be the recipient of solicitous attention, if any, which the mother receives on account of having the baby or being pregnant, but in the case of this straight-forwardly passive aim, having the baby is only a means to this end and not the aim itself.)

The matter is further complicated by the fact that along with the wish to ''get the mother with child'' *the wish to "bear her a child"* is one which Freud attributes to little girls in their active phallic period.

One is left with the conclusion that to make a baby is not in itself an especially passive aim even in Freud's view, but perhaps some particular *way* of making a baby is. In the long passage quoted above we saw that in spite of his caveats with respect to extending the model too far. Freud does offer us the image of the male being the active partner, pursuing and penetrating. Of course this is active *behavior*, and active behavior Freud tells us may be engaged in to achieve a passive aim. However having ruled out the making (giving, getting, bearing) of a child as a relevant passive sexual aim for the girl, we must assume that Freud sees the woman's and girl's desire for coitus with a man as a passive aim. Why passive? It is hard to find any reason other than that she is thought to be passive in the act, but passivity is not *generally* true of women who desire coitus. It is hard then to make much of Freud's thesis that the sexual aims which are feminine are passive.

As far as intercourse goes, *to the male* the female is the object of desire. *Qua* object of the male's active aims, the female is passive, even though in fact the female does not act in a particularly passive way nor does she primarily fantasize herself as mere recipient.

Freud's account of female fantasy makes it concur with male fantasy. However some correlation could also be expected if male fantasy secondarily influences female fantasy. Coincident with the punitive shift from active to passive aims in ''normal'' feminine development is a putative change of object on the part of the little girl. Her mother is replaced by her father as her primary object. Insofar as her father reciprocates (and we may assume that the little girl will be very sensitive to any reciprocation) he will convey his own (male) fantasies about intercourse and sex differences. If you recall the above discussion of ''castration'' and Freud's attribution of male fantasies to a little girl, you have an indication of what fantasies about sex differences will be conveyed. Furthermore if, for example, the male does fear activity on the part of the female, say through fear of castration, this may of course induce in her conscious or unconscious guilt, or fear of rejection which might make her more passive in her behavior and subsequent fantasies.

I would like to approach this issue of secondary influence in another way. Freud tells us that the psychic representation of the mother-substitute or foster mother regularly fuses with that of the mother in the child's consciousness. When, as is becoming more common even in our society, the mother-substitute is the father, and both parents give the infant a full range of care, the infant nonetheless usually grows into a ''normal'' woman or man. (Indeed Margaret Mead in her book *Sex and Temperament* states that the clearest departure from ''normality,'' i.e., inversion [homosexuality, transvestism, etc.] occurs *only* in those cultures with sex stereotypes of temperament.) This ''normal'' outcome of development cannot occur in the manner which Freud describes. We need not follow Horney in postulating the existence of an innate, perhaps biologically based, heterosexual attraction in order to explain this outcome. It is sufficient to suppose that the heterosexual orientation of the parent or parents determines whether it is through identification or through complementing the parents' behavior in some way that the child's libidinal attachment finds most reward. (This may sound like too behavioral a description for some, but I am as willing to describe this in terms of transmission of the parents' conscious and unconscious fantasies.) Such a heterosexual object preference would be likely, although not necessary, in biological parents. We may question whether the mechanisms, whatever their precise character, which act in the above situation do not *also* operate in the more traditional family situation. If they do, then as I have suggested above the father's male fantasies may be expected to commonly influence the way little girls learn their sexual role.

The general conclusion to which the above examination of Freud's theories leads is that if he is right about male development, then his account of female development is more an expression of male fantasies than it is true of the way in which a girl grows into even a "normal" woman.

(vi) Conclusion

We have seen that Freud and the Jungians have supplied us with more than just further examples of two of the basic motifs in explanation of sex differences. In each case we have also been given an account of how a little boy would be expected to arrive at a fantasy or symbolization embodying the motif in question. Freudians and Jungians may have given us a fairly accurate account of the origin of these motifs in the conscious and unconscious mind of boys. If so, we have found not only the source of these motifs, and an explanation of their recurrence throughout history of male-dominated Western history, but we may have located a factor which has been a contributing cause of that male domination, *viz.*, the existence of a small number of fantasies about sex differences which are common to (most) males, and which will determine what theories they will find plausible; and the absence of a similar small number of fantasies about sex differences common to most females, which might compete with the male fantasies. Thus if a little boy's narcissistic investment in his penis is as great as it is thought to be, it may be common for males to see sex differences as primarily consisting in the fact that a penis is "missing" in females. (The case is more plausible if the little boy is more familiar with the anatomy of little girls than with that of a pregnant or lactating woman.) Similarly in situations in which the mother's care of the child far exceeds that given by the father, a circumstance which is probable where breast feeding is necessary, the male child may well hit upon the contrast between the sexes to symbolize the contrast of self with other. In the latter case it is evident that the female child will not be led to either the same or the contrary symbolization by her own experience. What content does accrue to the sexual contrast is likely to vary with the infant girl's subsequent experience with males. Variety may be the rule rather than the exception with regard to a girl's fantasies about anatomical differences too, although this case is less clear.

An awareness of the entrenched motifs which have structured theories about sex differences in Western thought should have several effects. First it should make us more sensitive to those recalcitrant facts which are obscured by the fitting of data to these motifs, and thus enable us to improve the scientific researches conducted into these matters. Second, and perhaps more importantly, if we women are able to recognize the fantasies and symbolizations that arise in the male mind we will be better able to bring to consciousness our own fantasies and to understand the symbolic meaning that our own experience has for us. These reflections then may assist in a more formal way a process which has been underway for some time in rap groups. I take it that these groups are one of the principal products of the collective genius of the women's movement, that they are admirably suited to deal with certain forms of oppression peculiar to women's experience, because they enable us to discover and recover our own various fantasies and to articulate the symbolic meaning of our own experience; to know our own minds in the deepest sense.

Notes

1. Simone de Beauvoir has discussed the idea of *Woman* (though not the feminine principle) as Other in the *Second Sex* but does not discriminate between this and other motifs which I am putting forward.
2. It is common to reserve the terms "female" and "male" to mark biological diamorphism and use the terms "feminine" and "masculine" for psychological traits. Thus some depth psychologists would speak of a "feminine" principle but not a "female" one. However this distinction was not drawn historically, and in early philosophy and science no sharp distinction is drawn between the biological and the psychological contrasts.
3. E.g., Plato, *The Republic*, 455c.
4. Prior to Aristotle we have medical theories of hysteria (in the Hippocratic writings and in ancient Egyptian papyri dating from 1900 B.C.) which view this disease as arising when the uterus wanders about the body. Commentators have been puzzled by the way this conception of the uterus as an autonomous being, or "animal" could have achieved and maintained such currency in the thinking of otherwise astute medical thinkers. (See Ilza Veith *Hysteria: the History of a Disease,* Chicago, 1965.) I maintain that the view of the uterus as a separate being is natural *if one assumes that a woman is a partial man*. Her "extra" equipment which does not fit the model is then be explained away as separate individual.
5. Aristotle recognizes that seeds and eggs have a nutritive component. *Generation of Animals*, 731 a–b 3 and 732 a 29–33.
6. Because western biology and medicine followed Aristotle (and Anaxagoras) rather than Hippocrates, Empedocles, Democritus, Alcmaeon and even Galen, in denying the existence of gametes supplied by the female parent, "semen" came to mean sperm exclusively, so that when the existence of gametes from the female was accepted in the nineteenth century, a different word, "ova," had come into use. Similarly what had been called "testes" in the female came to be called "ovaries."
7. Aristotle, *The Generation of Animals,* translated by A. L. Peck, Cambridge: Harvard University Press, p. 103 (728 a 18). This view is expressed again at 766 b 20.
8. *Ibid.*, 775 a 15. A similar statement is also found 767 b 9.
9. *Ibid.*
10. A useful companion to Diels, *Fragmente der Vorsokratiker* which includes the views of pre-Socratics on sex differences is Kathleen Freeman's *The Pre-Socratic Philosophers*, Oxford: Basil Blackwell, 1959.
11. *Ibid.*, 729 b 14–16, p. 113.
12. Louis Ginsberg, *Legends of the Jews*, Vol. I, Philadelphia: the Jewish Publication Society of America, 1909, p. 66.
13. Carl Jung, "Woman in Europe," *Contributions to Analytical Psychology*, trans. H. G. and Gary F. Baynes (London: Routledge & Kegan Paul, 1928), pp. 132–133.
14. Gerhard Adler, *Studies in Analytical Psychology* (New York: C. G. Jung Foundation, 1966), pp. 242–243.
15. London: Longmans, Green & Co., 1936.
16. Freud "Femininity" lecture 33 of New Introductory Lectures on Psycho-Analysis in Volume 22 of the Standard Edition, edited by James Strachey, p. 127.
17. Freud, Female Sexuality in Volume 21 Standard Edition, p. 234.
18. Freud, "Femininity," p. 126.
19. Freud, "Femininity," pp. 114–116.
20. *Ibid.*, p. 120.
21. Freud, "Female Sexuality," p. 239.

Study Questions

1. What three general motifs, or views of women, does Whitbeck discuss?
2. What, according to Whitbeck, is Aristotle's view of women?
3. What is the Pythagorean view of women? What does Whitbeck think that the fact that there were women Pythagoreans illustrates?
4. What is the third motif Whitbeck delineates? Where can this motif in its present form be found? (Discuss with examples.) What is the definition of woman from the adult male perspective? The male child perspective?

5. What is the Jungian view of woman? To which of the three motifs described earlier is it closest? What contradiction lurks in the Jungian view, as evidenced in the quote from Adler? The Jungian view seems to promote equality, but does it in fact do so?
6. What is Freud's view of women? To which of the three motifs is it related? What are two areas of incoherence in Freud's view of women?

Do Women Have a Distinct Nature?

Nancy Holmstrom

Feminists have good reason to be suspicious of any talk of a distinct women's nature. The very phrase contains a sexist bias in that men are implicitly taken as the norm and women as ''the other,'' to use de Beauvoir's term. Despite some pious talk of complementarity the different characteristics attributed to men and women have always been evaluated differently, and for thousands of years theories of a distinct women's nature have been used to justify the subordination of women to men. The theories are taken to imply that these natures cannot change and also that one ought not even try to change them. Most theories of *human* nature have served a similar function. Either women have been explicitly taken to lack the traits designated by the theories as essentially human, e.g., rationality, or else traits historically more true of men than women, such as participating in politics, have been designated as essentially human. Most of these theories have been exposed by feminists as pseudo-scientific rationalizations of cultural prejudices. Not only has a distinct women's nature not been established, feminists argue, but even if it had no normative implications would follow automatically.[1]

The question can, however, be posed in unbiased terms: are there sex-differentiated natures? In this sense if women have a distinct nature then it is equally true that men have a distinct nature. This question refuses to be disposed of—in part because of the tremendous social importance the answer is presumed to have and also because of the enormous variety and complexity of the issues involved. First of all there are conceptual, methodological and ontological issues: what exactly is a nature or essence? When are similarities between things sufficient to constitute a common nature and when do differences constitute different natures? To help elucidate a methodology, I will turn to biology, which has the most developed and precise system of classifications of things in nature. I will argue that a nature or essence should be understood as an underlying structure that generates laws and that natures in this sense often play a crucial explanatory role. There are also, of course, empirical questions to be answered regarding differences between men and women that might determine their respective social roles. Examining the research on psychological sex differences, I conclude that there probably

From *The Philosophical Forum*, Vol. XIV, No. 1 (Fall 1982), pp. 25–42. Reprinted by permission of The Philosophical Forum. (Notes deleted.)

are significant differences between the sexes. However I also conclude that the most important determinants of these differences are social. The usual inference would be that men and women do not have different natures, and in the traditional sense of "natures," this is correct. However, the traditional conception depends upon a contrast between nature and society that, I argue, is mistaken, particularly in the case of human beings. Natures can also be socially constituted. Whether men and women have different natures depends, I contend, on certain theoretical considerations. As an illustration of what I mean by this claim, I discuss Marx's theory of human nature. In conclusion I discuss what would follow if men and women do have distinct natures in this sense.

Although biology has the most precise system of classifications in nature and involves few, if any, social and political factors, nevertheless, even in biology there is considerable disagreement as to the criteria for differentiating species, behind which lie different philosophies of science.[2] The essentialist, or typological approach, coming from Aristotle, holds that species are differentiated by sets of individually necessary and jointly sufficient characteristics which constitute the nature or essence of that species. Since these essences were supposed to be unchanging, this approach became less dominant after the discovery of evolution. Another contemporary school of taxonomists (called pheneticists) rejects essences and argues that the only proper scientific basis for classification is the overall similarity of things. Taxonomists who emphasize evolution correctly reply that there is no such thing as overall similarity. Every individual is similar to and different from every other individual in a variety of ways. Hence there are always many possible orderings. However, this does not make all classifications arbitrary and all generalizations accidental. What similarities and differences are most important can only be decided in terms of theoretical considerations. Classifications and generalizations backed up by a theory are neither accidental nor arbitrary. Evolutionary and gene theory do not define species in terms of similarity. There can be greater variations of certain kinds within a species, e.g., between a Chihuahua and a St. Bernard, among dogs, than between two species, e.g., dogs and wolves. This is because some differences are more important than others for biological theory. Taxonomists who emphasize evolution conceive of a species as, roughly speaking, a class of individual organisms which (either do or could) consistently interbreed with fertile offspring. The actual distribution of properties among organisms is such that, contrary to the Aristotelian view, most taxa names can only be defined disjunctively. Any of the disjuncts is sufficient and the few properties that are necessary are far from sufficient. Thus most concepts of so-called natural kinds are cluster concepts. These classes of organisms change over time to such an extent that individuals in the later generations are no longer classified as belonging to the same species as those of earlier generations.

Although it is superior to the alternatives discussed, I would agree with those philosophers called realists who argue that the evolutionary approach is still not adequate. Suppose we ask why things that fit that sort of disjunctive definition should figure in evolutionary theory? Why should such a group have the requisite stability? Why is it that they can interbreed? Realists argue that it is necessary to posit some underlying structure common to the things so defined which generates this set of properties and causes the variations in different individuals. In the case of a species, this underlying structure would be the gene pool. The disjunctive definition is sufficient to define the species, if it is, only because it is reflective of the underlying structure. The theories, which back up some generalizations and not others, should provide some account of the mechanisms generative of the regularities. In traditional terminology, the set of properties which justifies the use of the common term is called the nominal essence; the internal constitution which generates these manifest properties in accordance with laws is called the real essence. I am arguing, then, that the notion of a nature or essence—stripped of the metaphysical assumptions found in Plato and Aristotle's use of the concept—often plays an important explanatory function. Whether it is applicable to men and women depends on the facts about the sexes and the theories which explain the facts. However, it should be clear that the concept as I have explained it carries no evaluative implications. If a group has a distinct nature, nothing follows automatically about how its members ought or ought not to behave.

Since the concept of distinct male and female natures has been used to explain and justify distinct social roles for the sexes, the sexual differences we are concerned with are those which would be explanatory of those social roles. Some of the physical differences between the sexes are true by definition—which makes tautological talk of sex-differentiated natures based on these differences. To explain sexual/social roles from distinct natures in this sense would be an empty exercise. Therefore we are only concerned with physical differences between men and women if it can be shown that they determine or dispose men and women to their respective social roles. Now why should biological differences *per se* have such systematic social implications? The linkage is usually made through psychology. Those who emphasize the biological differences between the sexes as critical to their social roles and their natures usually maintain (or simply assume) that the biological differences cause psychological differences and these in turn determine their respective social roles.[3] So what we need to find out, first of all, is whether there are psychological differences between men and women, in terms of cognitive abilities and styles and other personality characteristics, that suit them to their respective social roles, for example, that women are more nurturant than men, and therefore are the primary caretakers of their own and other peoples' children. The second question would be the source of such differences.

As we have seen, the properties that constitute the nature of a group need not be unique or common to all its members. What we should look for as a beginning, then, are statistically significant differences between the sexes. Social scientists approach the question in this way but unfortunately they rarely go further. One problem with *only* looking for statistically significant differences is that even minute differences are statistically significant given a large enough sample.[4] Furthermore it is a measure that is very manipulable. We also need to consider the magnitude of the differences between the sexes and the degree to which they overlap. Even more crucial, as we saw, is that the differences must be of a kind that is theoretically important. We need therefore to look for a theoretical framework in which to evaluate the data. As our discussion of taxonomy revealed, it is often impossible to tell what differences are important without a theory. A new theory can even change our minds about what needs to be explained. Newtonian theory, for example, showed that certain kinds of unaccelerated motion, such as a passenger in a car continuing to move when the car stops suddenly, do not need an explanation, as had previously been supposed. This is one of the reasons that after determining what if any psychological differences there are between the sexes, we then need to determine their source.

The literature in the field of psychological sex differences is actually quite confusing because the experts disagree. However, if we examine the literature we can arrive at conclusions that are fairly reliable. One of the most recent and authoritative books in the field, often cited by feminists, is *The Psychology of Sex Differences* by Eleanor Maccoby and Carol Jacklin,[5] which attempts an exhaustive analysis of the research in the field, with an emphasis on the developmental literature. According to their results, there are fewer psychological differences between men and women than commonly believed (and fewer still that appear to be biologically based). Among the beliefs about sex differences[6] that they conclude to be unfounded are: that girls are more "social" and more "suggestible" than boys, that girls have lower self-esteem and lack achievement motivation, that girls are better at rote learning while boys are more analytic and better at tasks requiring higher cognitive processing. The areas of alleged psychological sex differences that they judge to be, at present, open questions, either because of insufficient evidence or unclear results, are the following: (1) tactile sensitivity, (2) fear, timidity, anxiety, (3) activity level, (4) competitiveness, (5) dominance, (6) compliance, (7) nurturance and "maternal" behavior.[7] The alleged sex differences that they find to be fairly well established are that girls have greater verbal ability while boys have greater visual/spatial and also mathematical ability (though this did not show up until age 12–13) and that males are more "prepared for" aggression. Except for this greater "preparedness" for aggression in boys, their findings simply show that with respect to a few traits more men than women have the trait to a higher degree than most people do (or vice versa). This allows that some women have as much or more of it than any man, and even that a majority of the group may lack the trait found more frequently among their group.[8]

Feminists might feel vindicated by these results, but they should be somewhat surprised too. It would be naive and idealistic to think that the differences in opportunities, expectations, socialization, and, in general, the social environment in which boys and girls and men and women live and function would have so little effect. And in fact there seem to be very good reasons for being skeptical about Maccoby and Jacklin's conclusions. Another expert in the field, Jeanne Block, points out that their conclusions conflict with other surveys of the research in the field and raises very serious questions about their methodology and the evidential support for their conclusions.[9]

One of the most interesting problems that Block points out is that Maccoby and Jacklin concentrate on sex differences in the performance of various tasks and ignore the interrelationships between intellectual performance and personality characteristics. These interrelationships are critical in understanding motivation, and there is much evidence that the differences in how the traits are linked together in the sexes are more important than the differences in average scores on various tests.[10] Achievement motivation in girls brings out the importance of this point. Females appear to have greater needs to be close to people than males. Conflict between these needs and achievement needs cuts into achievement, and since this conflict will occur more frequently in girls, this will reduce their achievement. Girls would rather "lose the game than lose the man." However, level of achievement is not the only factor to consider, because even when, at younger ages, achievement is the same or higher in girls, "it appears that female achievement behavior . . . is motivated by a desire for love rather than mastery."[11]

Most crucial for the concerns of this paper is the criticism that Maccoby and Jacklin's results are based predominantly on pre-adolescent children. Breaking down their results into different age groups, one finds that the percentage of studies in which there are clear and significant sex differences increases significantly with older age groups, especially beginning with adolescence, and this accords with other studies that show personality differences between the sexes increasing with age. All in all, then, it seems that there probably are greater personality differences between the sexes than Maccoby and Jacklin conclude, particularly among the age groups most relevant to our examination of the social roles of men and women.

The next question to consider is the source of the psychological differences between men and women. Hoffman's research suggests that many have their origins in differences in childrearing practices.[12] However, she and others who want to argue that the psychological differences between men and women are due to differences in their socialization and in the social contexts in which they find themselves have insufficient research to appeal to. This neglect of social context is not only an obstacle to discovering the etiology of psychological sex differences but may also lead to incorrect assessment of the facts. Studies of males and females in artificial contexts (like most of Maccoby and Jacklin's data), may yield results that are not predictive of their feelings and behavior in ordinary life, where they find themselves in very different social contexts. Studies of men and women in actual social contexts would likely show greater differences between the sexes. (One reason why there are so many inconsistent findings in this area might be the different contexts in which the studies were done.)

Actually it is not only the social approach to etiology which suffers from inadequate research. As indicated earlier, there is a prevailing hostility within academic research psychology to any theoretical explanatory framework. Research psychologists do not try to determine cause and effect; they only look for statistical relationships. Longitudinal studies, more relevant to establishing cause and effect, are also more costly and more speculative. This empiricist bias obviously makes it very difficult to determine an explanation for relationships they discover.

Given this state of the research, any position on the etiology of psychological sex differences is necessarily somewhat speculative. Although serious questions have been raised as to the likelihood that any specific and variable human behavioral traits are under genetic control, I will ignore this general question about sociobiology. With respect to psychological sex differences in particular, there are a number of findings and arguments which strongly suggest that social factors are far more important determinants than biological ones: (1) Black males and white females, different biologically but with similar social handicaps, are similar in: patterns of achievement scores, fear of success, and conformity and perceptual judgment; (2) Protestant, Jewish and Catholic women (who do not differ biologically) nevertheless experience significant differences in menstrual discomfort. (3) The same physiological state can yield very different emotional states and behavior depending on the social situation. Adrenalin produces a physiological state very much like that present in extreme fear, yet subjects injected with it became euphoric when around another person who acted euphoric and very angry when around another person who acted very angry. Thus even if sex hormonal differences between men and women affect brain functioning, as some psychologists contend, it would not follow that there necessarily would be consistent emotional and behavioral differences between men and women. (4) Different behavioral propensities, thought by many to be biologically based, disappear given certain social conditions. In one study, both sexes were rewarded for aggressive behavior, and the sex differences disappeared.[13] (5) Studies of hermaphrodites show that the crucial variable determining their gender identity is neither chromosomal sex nor hormones administered pre- or postnatally but "the consistency of the experiences of being reared as feminine, especially in the early years."[14] (6) The studies of psychological sex differences are based overwhelmingly on white middle-class Americans living in college towns. The generalizability of these findings cannot be assumed, as evidenced by the differences between whites and blacks discussed above. Moreover, anthropology reveals significant differences in sex roles in different cultures. Although rigorous cross-cultural psychological research has not been done, it appears that the personality differences between the sexes also show some cross-cultural differences.[15] If there is any connection between sex roles and psychological traits (whatever the direction of the causation), then one would expect further research to reveal that psychological sex differences vary cross-culturally. In the absence of a biological explanation, a variation according to culture strongly suggests that there is a social explanation.

The above points seem to offer dramatic evidence in favor of environmental factors as the *primary* determinants of psychological differences. There certainly does not seem to be any direct link between biological and psychological factors. In addition, there is a general methodological argument in favor of taking environmental factors as decisive. It can be summed up as follows: "Although future research may uncover important biological factors, the present data give more than sufficient evidence that environmental shaping of sex-differentiated behavior does exist. At this time it seems evident that the environment in which all American children mature clearly projects sex role stereotypes. These stereotypic expectations and the differential responses they elicit are sufficiently clear and unambiguous to account for the cognitive and personality differences in children that ultimately lead to the different roles that they fulfill."[16] Much the same argument, using the principle of methodological simplicity, is made by J. S. Mill in *The Subjection of Women*, where he argues that there is no basis for talking about the nature of men and women so long as they have only been in the present relations to each other. I would concur with this opinion[17] and thus conclude that the most reasonable position at present is that psychological differences between the sexes are most probably over-whelmingly social in origin.

By "social" I simply mean "not biological." Such factors could include family struc-ture, organization of the economy, and innumerable more specific factors. It is important to note that if psychological differences between the sexes do owe much to family structure, that is, to the fact that women are the primary child rearers,[18] it does not follow that the biological (reproductive) differences between the sexes are the real cause of the psychological differences. Women's ability to bear children does not automatically determine that they are the primary rearers of children. The reproductive differences between the sexes, just because they are universal, cannot explain the social and historical variations in the personalities and roles of men and women. The *significance* of the biological differences depends on social, his-torical facts, and, moreover, is maintained in every society by complicated social practices.

Consider this analogous example. Suppose that the division of slaves into house and field workers was based entirely on the slaves' size and strength, bigger and stronger slaves becoming field workers, smaller and weaker ones becoming house workers. It is well known that there were differences in attitudes and, to some extent, personality between house and field slaves (so-called "house niggers" and "field niggers"). What was the cause of these differences? Most writers point to the differences in work, working conditions and social relations of house and field slaves. If different social conditions would have produced different psychological results, then it would be mistaken to point to the physical differences as the cause—even though they were the basis of their being in their respective social conditions.

It seems then that there probably are not differences in male and female natures—so long as natures are understood as biologically based and immutable. However, this inference depends on certain equations and contrasts that are usually presupposed in this discussion.[19] The natural is contrasted with the social and the former is taken to be biological in origin. What's biological/natural is taken to be inevitable and what's social in origin is taken to be alterable. These assumptions are found in both popular and academic discussions of the issue, e.g., in traditional philosophical theories of essence which exclude socially variant properties as essential.

These assumptions cannot go unquestioned. Our discussion of taxonomy shows how mistaken is the assumption that the biological is unchangeable. In rejecting static essentialism and trying to fit classifications into evolutionary theory, taxonomists have rejected the equa-tion of the natural with the unchangeable. That things change is built into nature, although, of course, until recently the big changes have been quite slow. Not only do biological facts undergo slow change on their own, but they can be changed or their results affected by social conditions and by deliberate human action. For example: the disadvantages of people with Pku deficiency can be removed by human action. We have just discussed other examples of this. So even if the differences between men and women were based more in biology than they seem to be, it would not make those differences inevitable. They could still be outweighed by deliberate human action and by social conditions, e.g., by altering childrearing practices. Therefore whether the differences between men and women are primarily biological or social in origin need not have the momentous importance it is usually assumed to have by people on both sides of the question.

If there is not in fact such a sharp contrast between what is biologically based and what is socially based then there is less reason to maintain a sharp conceptual contrast between what is natural and what is social in origin. Nor should it be assumed that what is natural is inevitable and immutable. This is not true of biological facts, as we have just seen, and if species can be understood as evolving sorts of things, there seems no reason to assume that natures must be unchanging. More precisely, if the classes of organisms classified as a particular species can change to the point where they should be classified as belonging to another species, then why should it be understood as having a different nature? If the underlying genetic basis of the classification into species can change, why can't natures themselves change? In other words, even if natures are taken to be biological in origin there seems little basis for the assumption that natures are unchanging.

Moreover there seems no reason to assume that natures must be exclusively biological. I argued earlier that natures should be understood as underlying structures that explain a range of behavior. What kinds of structures these are depends on the behavior and the organism we are seeking to explain. While human beings are undeniably biological beings they are also social beings with a history. Their biological characteristics have evolved somewhat but their social and cultural characteristics have evolved more rapidly and to a much greater extent. If we are concerned with human beings as distinct from other biological beings, then their natures are biological. But if we are concerned with humans as social beings, then their natures, i.e., the underlying structures that explain their behavior—must be understood as socially constituted and historically evolving. Hence social changes could cause changes in natures even if they had no biological effect. This brings out the point that there are many levels of generating structures, many levels of explanation appropriate to human beings. If one accepts the view that freedom and determinism are not necessarily incompatible, then this account does not deny human freedom; it simply makes clear the constraints within which human agency functions. To what extent people are free depends on the extent to which they can be said to be self-determining. And this depends on the kinds of explanations, the kinds of determining structures of their behavior.

A similar distinction to that just made for human beings can be made for men and women. The distinction between males and females is a biological one. Hence the nature of a woman, *qua* female, is biological. However, the categories ''men'' and ''women'' are also social categories—what is called gender. Hence men and women, *qua* social beings, might have distinct natures which would be explanatory of the sex-related differences in behavior. As we saw, natures in the biological sense cannot by themselves explain sexual/social roles. If the sex differences in personality and cognitive traits discussed earlier are primarily social in origin the natures which generate and explain them would be primarily social in origin. However, this is all hypothetical. As we saw earlier, in the absence of a theoretical framework it is impossible to determine whether the psychological differences between men and women are sufficiently important to constitute differences in natures.

To clarify how a theoretical framework could be applied to help resolve this question I will discuss the example of the Marxist theory of historical materialism, which accords fairly well with the methodology set out earlier in the paper.[20] Marx argued vehemently against theories of a fixed, transhistorical human nature, offering instead a social and historical account. There are few transhistorical features of human beings, he maintained, and those there are—basic needs and capacities—are transformed throughout history and hence are in part socially constituted. ''Hunger is hunger but the hunger gratified by cooked meat eaten with a knife and fork is a different hunger from that which bolts down raw meat with the aid of hand, nail and tooth.''[21] These human needs are expressed, shaped, and even created through the activity of satisfying needs, that is, through labor. Because the labor of society is institutionalized into sets of social practices and social relations, Marx says that by their labor people are thereby producing their whole life. Although biological structures make possible the forms of human labor, they do not determine a particular form as the biology of other animals does. Given that in Marx's theory labor is the key to an explanation of social life and social change—which was his concern—he emphasized the characteristic form of labor rather than the biology.

The differing forms of human labor (and the resultant social practices and institutions) change the mental and physical capacities of human beings. Although there will be some transhistorical features of human beings, there will also then be certain characteristic differences in the psycho-physical structures of people who do very different sorts of labor in different modes of production. These structures would generate and explain a wide range of human behavior within that mode of production which the transhistorical features would not do. These psychophysical structures would constitute the nature of humans *qua* social beings. Although there would be certain common features, these structures as a whole vary from one mode of production to another. Hence there is no transhistorical human nature. However there would be historically specific forms of human nature, that is, human nature specific to feudalism, to capitalism, to socialism, and so on.

This approach can be applied to particular social groups, such as women, as well as to human beings. If particular social groups do labor that is sufficiently different as to generate distinct social relations, practices, and institutions associated with that labor, then they probably have distinct natures as well. There will probably be generalizations subsumable under a theory that would explain much of the group's behavior. Women appear to fit this condition. There are several levels of generalizations (sociological psychological . . .) distinctive of women which are relevant—both as cause and as effect—to their distinct social roles. Using a Marxist theoretical framework in which to evaluate the sexual differences, we would look to see whether they are connected to the different sorts of labor women do in society and the different social relations this puts them in. Although much more investigation needs to be done, particularly cross-cultural research, there is a lot of evidence that this is so. Despite the variations, there is and has always been a sexual division of labor in which women have primary responsibility for childcare and most of the everyday household work, whatever else they do as well. In a society with a significantly different sexual division of labor, this theory implies that other differing generalizations would be true of men and women and where there was no sexual division of labor, there would likely be few or no non-accidental generalizations true of women and not men—other than biological ones, of course, and fewer perhaps of these. The generalizations true of women and not men describe behavioral dispositions reflective of specific cognitive/affective structures found more often among women which generate the different sets of traits found under different conditions. These structures would constitute the distinctive natures of women as social beings.

Much more work is necessary before we can determine whether men and women have distinct social natures. We would need to establish the validity of a particular theoretical framework and do the research dictated by that framework. In the Marxist case we would need to establish both that the sexual differences are due to the sexual division of labor and that this theoretical framework is a valid one. The point of the excursion into Marxist theory was simply to illustrate how a theoretical framework could lead to the conclusion that there are sex-differentiated natures which are social in origin. This question should be pursued with other theories as well.

Suppose men and women do have distinct natures in this social sense—whatever the theoretical grounding. What follows? Well, first of all it is important to see that many of the implications usually thought to follow do not follow when natures are understood in the sense I have explained. This nature is not fixed and inevitable; natures can change. The crucial determinants are social, not biological. That there is a distinct women's nature in this sense would not entail that every woman has this nature. If we recall that most species' names only admit of disjunctive definitions we see that there need not be any one trait that is universally more common to women than to men. There could be a common core of psychological traits found more among women than men around the world, but women of different cultures or subcultures have different subsets of this common core of traits. This would make the concept of women's (social) nature a cluster concept, as are most "natural kinds" concepts. Although probably very few women would have none of the traits generated by the distinctive cognitive/affective structures, some might have them to only a minimal degree. Individual men could have more of this women's nature than do some women. Thus someone might be biologically female but not share the gender of other females. This is because one is a biological category, the other a social category. Even women who have this nature fully do not necessarily have more in common with other such women than with any man. This women's nature is only one aspect of her individual human nature and is not necessarily more determinant than all the other factors, individually much less collectively. Furthermore, and perhaps most important, the statement that women have a distinct nature in this sense has no evaluative implications. Nothing follows about how they ought or ought not to live or how society ought to be structured. This does not logically follow from the traditional view of natures either, but it is a more plausible conclusion to draw, given that if natures are immutable, they certainly set severe constraints on possible social arrangements. Moreover, if women live and become a different way, they will not be violating their nature; their nature will simply have changed. In fact we could predict that new social conditions would redefine women's nature. Less oppressive conditions would develop potentialities presently unrealized. It is quite likely that under some social conditions there would be no sex-differentiated natures.

Given all these disclaimers, given all the ways in which my sense of a women's nature differs from the usual meaning, a reasonable objection might be that I should not call this a nature; in fact, given the sexist associations of most such talk, it is positively dangerous to do so. I agree that the term could be misleading and even dangerous in certain contexts, but "nature" is also a technical, theory-laden term that is useful in summing up certain relationships. To summarize the conditions under which I think it would be useful to employ the term about women (and men): (1) there is a cluster of traits that women tend to have more than men which are systematically related to one another and which are important in explaining a wide range of their behavior (thus not every factor explanatory of women's behavior would be part of a women's nature); (2) it seems probable that there are certain psychic structures distinctive of the sexes which generate these traits; and (3) these sexual differences can in turn be explained within a broader theoretical framework which can also explain where women differ from one another as well as where they are similar. If these conditions are met, then talk of women's (and men's) natures is a way of bringing out the importance that a person's sex, thus far in history, has tended to have for their personality and behavior. Although the term itself is not important, this fact is important and is given its due prominence if the term is used. If "nature" is understood as a theory-laden term, then talk of women's nature carries the implications of that theory. I would argue that if the theory were adequate, the concept of a woman's nature would refer to something dynamic rather than static, primarily social/historical in origin rather than innate, and so on. If understood correctly, then, the concept does have a function and need not be misleading or dangerous.

Notes

1. Joyce Trebilcot, in "Sex Roles: The Argument from Nature," argues that even if there are natural psychological differences between the sexes, it does not follow that there ought to be distinct social/sexual roles. Christine Pierce, "Natural Law Language and Women," is particularly good on the many different and even conflicting senses of the word "natural." Both articles are in *Sex Equality*, ed. Jane English (Englewood Cliffs, NJ: Prentice Hall, 1977), pp. 121–29, 130–42.
2. Radical critics of science (see, e.g., *Radical Science Journal*) would argue that social/political factors come into biological classifications as well.

3. An academic example of this point of view is Judith Bardwick, *Psychology of Women* (New York: Harper and Row, 1971); a more popular example is Steven Goldberg, "The Inevitability of Patriarchy," in *Sex Equality*, pp. 196–204.

4. Such minute differences can prove very significant in some contexts. E.g., it has been proved that a feature that gives only a minute reproductive advantage will completely replace its alternatives in 1–2000 years (pointed out to me by Rohr). However, merely being statistically significant does not make something important or anything more than minute, as is often assumed once it is called "statistically significant."

5. Eleanor Maccoby and Carol Jacklin, *The Psychology of Sex Differences* (Stanford: Stanford University Press, 1974).

6. I am speaking here about statistically significant differences, whatever the cause.

7. Their findings indicate that there may be some sex differences in these areas but that there are not general overall differences in these areas. E.g., there may be different circumstances in which males and females are compliant but no overall difference in compliance.

8. Hence the inadequacy of statistical significance as the sole criterion.

9. Block argues that their data base, their conceptual classifications, and other aspects of their methodology can all be questioned in various ways, and they shape their conclusions against differences between the sexes. For example, the studies vary considerably in statistical power, and Block says "to the extent that sex differences are assessed with respect to scores that are undependable, differences that may exist in fact will go undetected." Studies having to do with other issues are often required to report any sex differences, although there would be no reason whatsoever to expect differences (in fact, there is good reason to expect that there would not be differences since researchers not concerned with sex differences would try to control for that). As a result, "the empirical literature is replete with null findings of inconsequential import." With respect to conceptual rubrics, Block cites several questionable examples. These include: (1) a very broad definition of parental pressures for achievement; equally reasonable narrower definitions would probably reveal greater differences between the sexes; (2) a narrow definition of "impulsivity" only having to do with cognitive qualities; a broader definition including temperament (which Maccoby used in an earlier work) would show greater differences between the sexes. Certain omissions in their bibliography also influence their conclusions in the same direction. Block argues that even using their data, sex differences on several of the traits that claim to be open questions, e.g., dominance, have as much support as others that they conclude are well established. "Issues, Problems and Pitfalls in Assessing Sex Differences: A Critical Review of *The Psychology of Sex Differences*," *Merrill-Palmer Quarterly*, 22, No. 4 (1976), 283–308.

10. *Ibid.*, p. 297.

11. Hoffman, "Early Childhood Experiences and Women's Achievement Motives," *Journal of Social Issues*, 28, No. 1 (1972), 129–55. Related to this objection is the possibility that although boys and girls differ in their propensity to aggressive behavior, they may not differ in their "preparedness for aggression" but rather in the likelihood that they will express it and not inhibit it and in the way they express it, e.g., verbally or physically.

12. She suggests this explanation for the differences in achievement motives: "Since girls as compared to boys have less encouragement for independence, more parental protectiveness, less pressure for establishing an identity separate from the mother, and less mother-child conflict which highlights this separation, they engage in less independent exploration of their environment. As a result they develop neither adequate skills nor confidence but continue to be dependent upon others" (p. 129). Although there is not adequate evidence to definitely establish this at this time, it is consistent with findings that girls are more anxious and less confident in their abilities and their judgment. The same pattern appears to be reinforced by later socialization practices (p. 144).

13. Mischel in Maccoby, pp. 56–81. Maccoby also reports that the greater propensity for aggression in boys disappears when they are given substantial childcare responsibilities. One might argue that the propensity is simply inhibited. I think this is less plausible for various reasons, but in any case it does not affect my point. This is another instance where social conditions prove more important in determining behavior than an (allegedly) biological propensity.

14. Money and Ehrhardt, *Man and Woman, Boy and Girl*, quoted in Beverly Birns' "The Emergence and Socialization of Sex Differences in the Earliest Years," *Merrill Palmer Quarterly*, 22, No. 3 (1976), 250–51.

15. Margaret Mead in *Sex and Temperament* (New York: Morrow, 1963), reports societies where the men have personalities designated as female in our culture (emotionally dependent, spoiled, etc.) and women have "masculine" personalities (independent, dominant). Carol Hoffer, in "Mende and Sherbro Women in High Office," *Canadian Journal of African Studies* (1971), 151–64, reports cultures in which women hold high political office which is enhanced by motherhood.

16. Birns, p. 251.

17. Under two conditions: (1) that natures are taken to be primarily biological and (2) that there are no strong theoretical considerations to support the claim that there are biologically based sex natures.

18. Two recent books, Nancy Chodorow's *The Reproduction of Mothering* (Berkeley: University of California Press, 1978), and Dorothy Dinerstein's *The Mermaid and the Minotaur* (New York: Harper and Row, 1977), offer similar interesting hypotheses. Both authors argue that the near-universal fact that women "mother" (in a psychological as well as the many physical ways) is the key to adult male and female personality structures. Although different from "social learning" approaches (they are both more psychoanalytic), these theories both offer a social explanation in the sense I am using "social" and could easily be combined with other social explanations.
19. E.g., "a crucial issue is whether there is any basis to the claim that there are biologically derived (and therefore inescapable) psychological or personality characteristics that universally differentiate men and women." Nancy Chodorow, "Being and Doing," in *Sisterhood is Powerful*, p. 173.
20. The following is controversial. One of the most controversial areas of Marxist scholarship is whether Marx had a theory of human nature in his later works and, if so, whether it is significantly different from his earlier views. I believe the following to be consistent with both his early and his late work whether or not there are also differences between his early and later ideas.
21. *Grundrisse* (Hammondsworth, England: Penguin Books, 1973), p. 92.

Study Questions

1. According to Holmstrom, why do women have a right to be suspicious of talk about "women's nature"?
2. What view of "species" does Holmstrom accept?
3. Holmstrom discusses a number of issues surrounding empirical psychological research on sex differences. What are some candidates for true sex differences (mentioned in the Maccoby/Jacklin study)?
4. What does Holmstrom think is the likely cause of any such sex differences? On what basis does she reach her conclusion about the likely cause of those differences?
5. What is the Marxist view of human nature? How does Holmstrom think it might apply to "women's nature"?
6. What are a few claims that do *not* follow from the assertion that women have a distinct nature? Discuss in detail why they don't follow.

Is Female to Male as Nature Is to Culture?

Sherry B. Ortner

Much of the creativity of anthropology derives from the tension between two sets of demands: that we explain human universals, and that we explain cultural particulars. By this canon, woman provides us with one of the more challenging problems to be dealt with. The secondary status of woman in society is one of the true universals, a pan-cultural fact. Yet within that universal fact, the specific cultural conceptions and symbolizations of woman are extraordinarily diverse and even mutually contradictory. Further, the actual treatment of women and their relative power and contribution vary enormously from culture to culture, and over different periods in the history of particular cultural traditions. Both of these points—the universal fact and the cultural variation—constitute problems to be explained.

My interest in the problem is of course more than academic: I wish to see genuine change come about, the emergence of a social and cultural order in which as much of the range of human potential is open to women as is open to men. The universality of female subordination, the fact that it exists within every type of social and economic arrangement and in societies of every degree of complexity, indicates to me that we are up against something very profound, very stubborn, something we cannot rout out simply by rearranging a few tasks and roles in the social system, or even by reordering the whole economic structure. In this paper I try to expose the underlying logic of cultural thinking that assumes the inferiority of women; I try to show the highly persuasive nature of the logic, for if it were not so persuasive, people would not keep subscribing to it. But I also try to show the social and cultural sources of that logic, to indicate wherein lies the potential for change.

It is important to sort out the levels of the problem. The confusion can be staggering. For example, depending on which aspect of Chinese culture we look at, we might extrapolate any of several entirely different guesses concerning the status of women in China. In the ideology of Taoism, *yin*, the female principle, and *yang*, the male principle, are given equal weight; "the opposition, alternation, and interaction of these two forces give rise to all phenomena in the universe." . . . Hence we might guess that maleness and femaleness are equally valued in the general ideology of Chinese culture.[1] Looking at the social structure, however, we see the strongly emphasized patrilineal descent principle, the importance of sons, and the absolute authority of the father in the family. Thus we might conclude that China is the archetypal patriarchal society. Next, looking at the actual roles played, power and influence wielded, and material contributions made by women in Chinese society—all of which are, upon observation, quite substantial—we would have to say that women are allotted a great deal of (unspoken) status in the system. Or again, we might focus on the fact that a goddess, Kuan Yin, is the central (most worshipped, most depicted) deity in Chinese Buddhism, and we might be tempted to say, as many have tried to say about goddess-worshipping cultures in prehistoric and early historical societies, that China is actually a sort of matriarchy. In short,

From Michelle Zimbalist Rosaldo and Louise Lamphere, eds., *Woman, Culture, and Society*, pp. 67–87. © 1974 by the Board of Trustees of the Leland Stanford Junior University. Reprinted by permission of the publishers, Stanford University Press. (Notes deleted.)

we must be absolutely clear about *what* we are trying to explain before explaining it.

We may differentiate three levels of the problem:

1. The universal fact of culturally attributed second-class status of woman in every society. Two questions are important here. First, what do we mean by this; what is our evidence that this is a universal fact? And second, how are we to explain this fact, once having established it?

2. Specific ideologies, symbolizations, and sociostructural arrangements pertaining to women that vary widely from culture to culture. The problem at this level is to account for any particular cultural complex in terms of factors specific to that group—the standard level of anthropological analysis.

3. Observable on-the-ground details of women's activities, contributions, powers, influence, etc., often at variance with cultural ideology (although always constrained within the assumption that women may never be officially preeminent in the total system). This is the level of direct observation, often adopted now by feminist-oriented anthropologists.

This paper is primarily concerned with the first of these levels, the problem of the universal devaluation of women. The analysis thus depends not upon specific cultural data but rather upon an analysis of ''culture'' taken generically as a special sort of process in the world. A discussion of the second level, the problem of cross-cultural variation in conceptions and relative valuations of women, will entail a great deal of cross-cultural research and must be postponed to another time. As for the third level, it will be obvious from my approach that I would consider it a misguided endeavor to focus only upon women's actual though culturally unrecognized and unvalued powers in any given society, without first understanding the overarching ideology and deeper assumptions of the culture that render such powers trivial.

The Universality of Female Subordination

What do I mean when I say that everywhere, in every known culture, women are considered in some degree inferior to men? First of all, I must stress that I am talking about *cultural* evaluations; I am saying that each culture, in its own way and on its own terms, makes this evaluation. But what would constitute evidence that a particular culture considers women inferior?

Three types of data would suffice: (1) elements of cultural ideology and informants' statements that *explicitly* devalue women, according them, their roles, their tasks, their products, and their social milieux less prestige than are accorded men and the male correlates; (2) symbolic devices, such as the attribution of defilement, which may be interpreted as *implicitly* making a statement of inferior valuation; and (3) social-structural arrangements that exclude women from participation in or contact with some realm in which the highest powers of the society are felt to reside.[2] These three types of data may all of course be interrelated in any particular system, though they need not necessarily be. Further, any one of them will usually be sufficient to make the point of female inferiority in a given culture. Certainly, female exclusion from the most sacred rite or the highest political council is sufficient evidence. Certainly, explicit cultural ideology devaluing women (and their tasks, roles, products, etc.) is sufficient evidence. Symbolic indicators such as defilement are usually sufficient, although in a few cases in which, say, men and women are equally polluting to one another, a further indicator is required—and is, as far as my investigations have ascertained, always available.

On any or all of these counts, then, I would flatly assert that we find women subordinated to men in every known society. The search for a genuinely egalitarian, let alone matriarchal, culture has proved fruitless. An example from one society that has traditionally been on the credit side of this ledger will suffice. Among the matrilineal Crow, as Lowie (1956) points out, "Women . . . had highly honorific offices in the Sun Dance; they could become directors of the Tobacco Ceremony and played, if anything, a more conspicuous part in it than the men; they sometimes played the hostess in the Cooked Meat Festival; they were not debarred from sweating or doctoring or from seeking a vision." . . . Nonetheless, "Women [during menstruation] formerly rode inferior horses and evidently this loomed as a source of contamination, for they were not allowed to approach either a wounded man or men starting on a war party. A taboo still lingers against their coming near sacred objects at these times." . . . Further, just before enumerating women's rights of participation in the various rituals noted above, Lowie mentions one particular Sun Dance Doll bundle that was not supposed to be unwrapped by a woman. . . . Pursuing this trail we find: "According to all Lodge Grass informants and most others, the doll owned by Wrinkled-face took precedence not only of other dolls but of all other Crow medicines whatsoever. . . . This particular doll was not supposed to be handled by a woman." . . .[3]

In sum, the Crow are probably a fairly typical case. Yes, women have certain powers and rights, in this case some that place them in fairly high positions. Yet ultimately the line is drawn: menstruation is a threat to warfare, one of the most valued institutions of the tribe, one that is central to their self-definition; and the most sacred object of the tribe is taboo to the direct sight and touch of women.

Similar examples could be multiplied ad infinitum, but I think the onus is no longer upon us to demonstrate that female subordination is a cultural universal; it is up to those who would argue against the point to bring forth counterexamples. I shall take the universal secondary status of women as a given, and proceed from there.

Nature and Culture

How are we to explain the universal devaluation of women? We could of course rest the case on biological determinism. There is something genetically inherent in the male of the species, so the biological determinists would argue, that makes them the naturally dominant sex; that "something" is lacking in females, and as a result women are not only naturally subordinate but in general quite satisfied with their position, since it affords them protection and the opportunity to maximize maternal pleasures, which to them are the most satisfying experiences of life. Without going into a detailed refutation of this position, I think it fair to say that it has failed to be established to the satisfaction of almost anyone in academic anthropology. This is to say, not that biological facts are irrelevant, or that men and women are not different, but that these facts and differences only take on significance of superior/inferior within the framework of culturally defined value systems.

If we are unwilling to rest the case on genetic determinism, it seems to me that we have only one way to proceed. We must attempt to interpret female subordination in light of other universals, factors built into the structure of the most generalized situation in which all human beings, in whatever culture, find themselves. For example, every human being has a physical body and a sense of nonphysical mind, is part of a society of other individuals and an inheritor of a cultural tradition, and must engage in some relationship, however mediated, with "nature," or the nonhuman realm, in order to survive. Every human being is born (to a mother) and ultimately dies, all are assumed to have an interest in personal survival, and society/culture has its own interest in (or at least momentum toward) continuity and survival, which transcends the lives and deaths of particular individuals. And so forth. It is in the realm of such universals of the human condition that we must seek an explanation for the universal fact of female devaluation.

I translate the problem, in other words, into the following simple question. What could there be in the generalized structure and conditions of existence, common to every culture, that would lead every culture to place a lower value upon women? Specifically, my thesis is that woman is being identified with—or, if you will, seems to be a symbol of—something that every culture devalues, something that every culture defines as being of a lower order of existence than itself. Now it seems that there is only one thing that would fit that description, and that is "nature" in the most generalized sense. Every culture, or, generically, "culture," is engaged in the process of generating and sustaining systems of meaningful forms (symbols, artifacts, etc.) by means of which humanity transcends the givens of natural existence, bends them to its purposes, controls them in its interest. We may thus broadly equate culture with the notion of human consciousness, or with the products of human consciousness (i.e., systems of thought and technology), by means of which humanity attempts to assert control over nature.

Now the categories of "nature" and "culture" are of course conceptual categories—one can find no boundary out in the actual world between the two states or realms of being. And there is no question that some cultures articulate a much stronger opposition between the two categories than others—it has even been argued that primitive peoples (some or all) do not see or intuit any distinction between the human cultural state and the state of nature at all. Yet I would maintain that the universality of ritual betokens an assertion in all human cultures of the specifically human ability to act upon and regulate, rather than passively move with and be moved by, the givens of natural existence. In ritual, the purposive manipulation of given forms toward regulating and sustaining order, every culture asserts that proper relations between human existence and natural forces depend upon culture's employing its special powers to regulate the overall processes of the world and life.

One realm of cultural thought in which these points are often articulated is that of concepts of purity and pollution. Virtually every culture has some such beliefs, which seem in large part (though not, of course, entirely) to be concerned with the relationship between culture and nature. . . . A well-known aspect of purity/pollution beliefs cross-culturally is that of the natural "contagion" of pollution; left to its own devices, pollution (for these purposes grossly equated with the unregulated operation of natural energies) spreads and overpowers all that it comes in contact with. Thus a puzzle—if pollution is so strong, how can anything be purified? Why is the purifying agent not itself polluted? The answer, in keeping with the present line of argument, is that purification is effected in a ritual context; purification ritual, as a purposive activity that pits self-conscious (symbolic) action against natural energies, is more powerful than those energies.

In any case, my point is simply that every culture implicitly recognizes and asserts a distinction between the operation of nature and the operation of culture (human consciousness and its products); and further, that the distinctiveness of culture rests precisely on the fact that it can under most circumstances transcend natural conditions and turn them to its purposes. Thus culture (i.e., every culture) at some level of awareness asserts itself to be not only distinct from but superior to nature, and that sense of distinctiveness and superiority rests precisely on the ability to transform—to "socialize" and "culturalize"—nature.

Returning now to the issue of women, their pan-cultural second-class status could be accounted for, quite simply, by postulating that women are being identified or symbolically associated with nature, as opposed to men, who are identified with culture. Since it is always culture's project to subsume and transcend nature, if women were considered part of nature, then culture would find it "natural" to subordinate, not to say oppress, them. Yet although this argument can be shown to have considerable force, it seems to oversimplify the case. The formulation I would like to defend and elaborate on in the following section, then, is that women are seen "merely" as being *closer* to nature than men. That is, culture (still equated relatively unambiguously with men) recognizes that women are active participants in its special processes, but at the same time sees them as being more rooted in, or having more direct affinity with, nature.

The revision may seem minor or even trivial, but I think it is a more accurate rendering of cultural assumptions. Further, the argument cast in these terms has several analytic advantages over the simpler formulation; I shall discuss these later. It might simply be stressed here that the revised argument would still account for the pan-cultural devaluation of women, for even if women are not equated with nature, they are nonetheless seen as representing a lower order of being, as being less transcendental of nature than men are. The next task of the paper, then, is to consider why they might be viewed in that way.

Why Is Woman Seen as Closer to Nature?

It all begins of course with the body and the natural procreative functions specific to women alone. We can sort out for discussion three levels at which this absolute physiological fact has significance: (1) woman's *body and its functions*, more involved more of the time with "species life," seem to place her closer to nature, in contrast to man's physiology, which frees him more completely to take up the projects of culture; (2) woman's body and its functions place her in *social roles* that in turn are considered to be at a lower order of the cultural process than man's; and (3) woman's traditional social roles, imposed because of her body and its functions, in turn give her a different *psychic structure*, which, like her physiological nature and her social roles, is seen as being closer to nature. I shall discuss each of these points in turn, showing first how in each instance certain factors strongly tend to align woman with nature, then indicating other factors that demonstrate her full alignment with culture, the combined factors thus placing her in a problematic intermediate position. It will become clear in the course of the discussion why men seem by contrast less intermediate, more purely "cultural" than women. And I reiterate that I am dealing only at the level of cultural and human universals. These arguments are intended to apply to generalized humanity; they grow out of the human condition, as humanity has experienced and confronted it up to the present day.

   1. *Woman's physiology seen as closer to nature.* This part of my argument has been anticipated, with subtlety, cogency, and a great deal of hard data, by de Beauvoir. . . . De Beauvoir reviews the physiological structure, development, and functions of the human female and concludes that "the female, to a greater extent than the male, is the prey of the species." . . . She points out that many major areas and processes of the woman's body serve no apparent function for the health and stability of the individual; on the contrary, as they perform their specific organic functions, they are often sources of discomfort, pain, and danger. The breasts are irrelevant to personal health; they may be excised at any time of a woman's life. "Many of the ovarian secretions function for the benefit of the egg, promoting its maturation and adapting the uterus to its requirements; in respect to the organism as a whole, they make for disequilibrium rather than for regulation—the woman is adapted to the needs of the egg rather than to her own requirements." . . . Menstruation is often uncomfortable, sometimes painful; it frequently has negative emotional correlates and in any case involves bothersome tasks of cleansing and waste disposal; and—a point that de Beauvoir does not mention—in many cultures it interrupts a woman's routine, putting her in a stigmatized state involving various restrictions on her activities and social contacts. In pregnancy many of the woman's vitamin and mineral resources are channeled into nourishing the fetus, depleting her own strength and energies. And finally, childbirth itself is painful and dangerous. . . . In sum, de Beauvoir concludes that the female "is more enslaved to the species than the male, her animality is more manifest." . . .

   While de Beauvoir's book is ideological, her survey of woman's physiological situation seems fair and accurate. It is simply a fact that proportionately more of woman's body space, for a greater percentage of her lifetime, and at some—sometimes great—cost to her personal health, strength, and general stability, is taken up with the natural processes surrounding the reproduction of the species.

De Beauvoir goes on to discuss the negative implications of woman's "enslavement to the species" in relation to the projects in which humans engage, projects through which culture is generated and defined. She arrives thus at the crux of her argument . . . :

> Here we have the key to the whole mystery. On the biological level a species is maintained only by creating itself anew; but this creation results only in repeating the same Life in more individuals. But man assures the repetition of Life while transcending Life through Existence [e.g., goal-oriented, meaningful action]; by this transcendence he creates values that deprive pure repetition of all value. In the animal, the freedom and variety of male activities are vain because no project is involved. Except for his services to the species, what he does is immaterial. Whereas in serving the species, the human male also remodels the face of the earth, he creates new instruments, he invents, he shapes the future.

In other words, woman's body seems to doom her to mere reproduction of life; the male, in contrast, lacking natural creative functions, must (or has the opportunity to) assert his creativity externally, "artificially," through the medium of technology and symbols. In so doing, he creates relatively lasting, eternal, transcendent objects, while the woman creates only perishables—human beings.

This formulation opens up a number of important insights. It speaks, for example, to the great puzzle of why male activities involving the destruction of life (hunting and warfare) are often given more prestige than the female's ability to give birth, to create life. Within de Beauvoir's framework, we realize it is not the killing that is the relevant and valued aspect of hunting and warfare; rather, it is the transcendental (social, cultural) nature of these activities, as opposed to the naturalness of the process of birth: "For it is not in giving life but in risking life that man is raised above the animal; that is why superiority has been accorded in humanity not to the sex that brings forth but to that which kills." . . .

Thus if male is, as I am suggesting, everywhere (unconsciously) associated with culture and female seems closer to nature, the rationale for these associations is not very difficult to grasp, merely from considering the implications of the physiological contrast between male and female. At the same time, however, woman cannot be consigned fully to the category of nature, for it is perfectly obvious that she is a full-fledged human being endowed with human consciousness just as a man is; she is half of the human race, without whose cooperation the whole enterprise would collapse. She may seem more in the possession of nature than man, but having consciousness, she thinks and speaks; she generates, communicates, and manipulates symbols, categories, and values. She participates in human dialogues not only with other women but also with men. As Lévi-Strauss says, "Woman could never become just a sign and nothing more, since even in a man's world she is still a person, and since insofar as she is defined as a sign she must [still] be recognized as a generator of signs." . . .

Indeed, the fact of woman's full human consciousness, her full involvement in and commitment to culture's project of transcendence over nature, may ironically explain another of the great puzzles of "the woman problem"—woman's nearly universal unquestioning acceptance of her own devaluation. For it would seem that, as a conscious human and member of culture, she has followed out the logic of culture's arguments and has reached culture's conclusions along with the men. As de Beauvoir puts it . . . :

> For she, too, is an existent, she feels the urge to surpass, and her project is not mere repetition but transcendence towards a different future—in her heart of hearts she finds confirmation of the masculine pretensions. She joins the men in the festivals that celebrate the successes and victories of the males. Her misfortune is to have been biologically destined for the repetition of Life, when even in her

own view Life does not carry within itself its reasons for being, reasons that are more important than life itself.

In other words, woman's consciousness—her membership, as it were, in culture—is evidenced in part by the very fact that she accepts her own devaluation and takes culture's point of view.

I have tried here to show one part of the logic of that view, the part that grows directly from the physiological differences between men and women. Because of woman's greater bodily involvement with the natural functions surrounding reproduction, she is seen as more a part of nature than man is. Yet in part because of her consciousness and participation in human social dialogue, she is recognized as a participant in culture. Thus she appears as something intermediate between culture and nature, lower on the scale of transcendence than man.

2. *Woman's social role seen as closer to nature.* Woman's physiological functions, I have just argued, may tend in themselves to motivate[4] a view of woman as closer to nature, a view she herself, as an observer of herself and the world, would tend to agree with. Woman creates naturally from within her own being, whereas man is free to, or forced to, create artificially, that is, through cultural means, and in such a way as to sustain culture. In addition, I now wish to show how woman's physiological functions have tended universally to limit her social movement, and to confine her universally to certain social contexts which *in turn* are seen as closer to nature. That is, not only her bodily processes but the social situation in which her bodily processes locate her may carry this significance. And insofar as she is permanently associated (in the eyes of culture) with these social milieux, they add weight (perhaps the decisive part of the burden) to the view of woman as closer to nature. I refer here of course to woman's confinement to the domestic family context, a confinement motivated, no doubt, by her lactation processes.

Woman's body, like that of all female mammals, generates milk during and after pregnancy for the feeding of the newborn baby. The baby cannot survive without breast milk or some similar formula at this stage of life. Since the mother's body goes through its lactation processes in direct relation to a pregnancy with a particular child, the relationship of nursing between mother and child is seen as a natural bond, other feeding arrangements being seen in most cases as unnatural and makeshift. Mothers and their children, according to cultural reasoning, belong together. Further, children beyond infancy are not strong enough to engage in major work, yet are mobile and unruly and not capable of understanding various dangers; they thus require supervision and constant care. Mother is the obvious person for this task, as an extension of her natural nursing bond with the children, or because she has a new infant and is already involved with child-oriented activities. Her own activities are thus circumscribed by the limitations and low levels of her children's strengths and skills:[5] she is confined to the domestic family group; "woman's place is in the home."

Woman's association with the domestic circle would contribute to the view of her as closer to nature in several ways. In the first place, the sheer fact of constant association with children plays a role in the issue; one can easily see how infants and children might themselves be considered part of nature. Infants are barely human and utterly unsocialized; like animals they are unable to walk upright, they excrete without control, they do not speak. Even slightly older children are clearly not yet fully under the sway of culture. They do not yet understand social duties, responsibilities, and morals; their vocabulary and their range of learned skills are small. One finds implicit recognition of an association between children and nature in many cultural practices. For example, most cultures have initiation rites for adolescents (primarily for boys; I shall return to this point below), the point of which is to move the child ritually from a less than fully human state into full participation in society and culture; many cultures do not hold funeral rites for children who die at early ages, explicitly because they are not yet fully social beings. Thus children are likely to be categorized with nature, and woman's close association with children may compound her potential for being seen as closer to nature herself. It is ironic that the rationale for boys' initiation rites in many cultures is that the boys must be purged of the defilement accrued from being around mother and other women so much of the time, when in fact much of the woman's defilement may derive from her being around children so much of the time.

The second major problematic implication of women's close association with the domestic context derives from certain structural conflicts between the family and society at large in any social system. The implications of the "domestic/public opposition" in relation to the position of women have been cogently developed by Rosaldo . . . , and I simply wish to show its relevance to the present argument. The notion that the domestic unit—the biological family charged with reproducing and socializing new members of the society—is opposed to the public entity—the superimposed network of alliances and relationships that *is* the society—is also the basis of Lévi-Strauss's argument in the *Elementary Structures of Kinship.* . . . Lévi-Strauss argues not only that this opposition is present in every social system, but further that it has the significance of the opposition between nature and culture. The universal incest prohibition[6] and its ally, the rule of exogamy (marriage outside the group), ensure that "the risk of seeing a biological family become established as a closed system is definitely eliminated; the biological group can no longer stand apart, and the bond of alliance with another family ensures the dominance of the social over the biological, and of the cultural over the natural." . . . And although not every culture articulates a radical opposition between the domestic and the public as such, it is hardly contestable that the domestic is always subsumed by the public; domestic units are allied with one another through the enactment of rules that are logically at a higher level than the units themselves; this creates an emergent unit—society—that is logically at a higher level than the domestic units of which it is composed.

Now, since women are associated with, and indeed are more or less confined to, the domestic context, they are identified with this lower order of social/cultural organization. What are the implications of this for the way they are viewed? First, if the specifically biological (reproductive) function of the family is stressed, as in Lévi-Strauss's formulation, then the family (and hence woman) is identified with nature pure and simple, as opposed to culture. But this is obviously too simple; the point seems more adequately formulated as follows: the family (and hence woman) represents lower-level, socially fragmenting, particularistic sort of concerns, as opposed to interfamilial relations representing higher-level, integrative, universalistic sorts of concerns. Since men lack a "natural" basis (nursing, generalized to child care) for a familial orientation, their sphere of activity is defined at the level of interfamilial relations. And hence, so the cultural reasoning seems to go, men are the "natural" proprietors of religion, ritual, politics, and other realms of cultural thought and action in which universalistic statements of spiritual and social synthesis are made. Thus men are identified not only with culture, in the sense of all human creativity, as opposed to nature; they are identified in particular with culture in the old-fashioned sense of the finer and higher aspects of human thought—art, religion, law, etc.

Here again, the logic of cultural reasoning aligning woman with a lower order of culture than man is clear and, on the surface, quite compelling. At the same time, woman cannot be fully consigned to nature, for there are aspects of her situation, even within the domestic context, that undeniably demonstrate her participation in the cultural process. It goes without saying, of course, that except for nursing newborn infants (and artificial nursing devices can cut even this biological tie), there is no reason why it has to be mother—as opposed to father, or anyone else—who remains identified with child care. But even assuming that other practical and emotional reasons conspire to keep woman in this sphere, it is possible to show that her activities in the domestic context could as logically put her squarely in the category of culture.

In the first place, one must point out that woman not only feeds and cleans up after children in a simple caretaker operation; she in fact is the primary agent of their early socialization. It is she who transforms newborn infants from mere organisms into cultured humans, teaching them manners and the proper ways to behave in order to become full-fledged members of the culture. On the basis of her socializing functions alone, she could not be more a representative of culture. Yet in virtually every society there is a point at which the socialization of boys is transferred to the hands of men. The boys are considered, in one set of terms or another, not yet "really" socialized; their entrée into the realm of fully human (social, cultural) status can be accomplished only by men. We still see this in our own schools, where there is a gradual inversion in the proportion of female to male teachers up through the grades: most kindergarten teachers are female; most university professors are male.[7]

Or again, take cooking. In the overwhelming majority of societies cooking is the woman's work. No doubt this stems from practical considerations—since the woman has to stay home with the baby, it is convenient for her to perform the chores centered in the home. But if it is true, as Lévi-Strauss has argued . . . , that transforming the raw into the cooked may represent, in many systems of thought, the transition from nature to culture, then here we have woman aligned with this important culturalizing process, which could easily place her in the category of culture, triumphing over nature. Yet it is also interesting to note that when a culture (e.g., France or China) develops a tradition of *haute cuisine*—"real" cooking, as opposed to trivial ordinary domestic cooking—the high chefs are almost always men. Thus the pattern replicates that in the area of socialization—women perform lower-level conversions from nature to culture, but when the culture distinguishes a higher level of the same functions, the higher level is restricted to men.

In short, we see once again some sources of woman's appearing more intermediate than man with respect to the nature/culture dichotomy. Her "natural" association with the domestic context (motivated by her natural lactation functions) tends to compound her potential for being viewed as closer to nature, because of the animal-like nature of children, and because of the infrasocial connotation of the domestic group as against the rest of society. Yet at the same time her socializing and cooking functions within the domestic context show her to be a powerful agent of the cultural process, constantly transforming raw natural resources into cultural products. Belonging to culture, yet appearing to have stronger and more direct connections with nature, she is once again seen as situated between the two realms.

3. *Woman's psyche seen as closer to nature.* The suggestion that woman has not only a different body and a different social locus from man but also a different psychic structure is most controversial. I will argue that she probably *does* have a different psychic structure, but I will draw heavily on Chodorow's paper . . . to establish first that her psychic structure need not be assumed to be innate; it can be accounted for, as Chodorow convincingly shows, by the facts of the probably universal female socialization experience. Nonetheless, if we grant the empirical near universality of a "feminine psyche" with certain specific characteristics, these characteristics would add weight to the cultural view of woman as closer to nature.

It is important to specify what we see as the dominant and universal aspects of the feminine psyche. If we postulate emotionality or irrationality, we are confronted with those traditions in various parts of the world in which women functionally are, and are seen as, more practical, pragmatic, and this-worldly than men. One relevant dimension that does seem pan-culturally applicable is that of relative concreteness vs. relative abstractness: the feminine personality tends to be involved with concrete feelings, things, and people, rather than with abstract entities; it tends toward personalism and particularism. A second, closely related, dimension seems to be that of relative subjectivity vs. relative objectivity: Chodorow cites Carlson's study (1971), which concludes that "males represent experiences of self, others, space, and time in individualistic, objective, and distant ways, while females represent experiences in relatively interpersonal, subjective, immediate ways." . . . Although this and other studies were done in Western societies, Chodorow sees their findings on the differences between male and female personality—roughly, that men are more objective and inclined to relate in terms of relatively abstract categories, women more subjective and inclined to relate in terms of relatively concrete phenomena—as "general and nearly universal differences." . . .

But the thrust of Chodorow's elegantly argued paper is that these differences are not innate or genetically programmed; they arise from nearly universal features of family structure, namely that "women, universally, are largely responsible for early child care and for (at least) later female socialization" . . . and that "the structural situation of child rearing, reinforced by female and male role training, produces these differences, which are replicated and reproduced in the sexual sociology of adult life." . . . Chodorow argues that, because mother is the early socializer of both boys and girls, both develop "personal identification" with her, i.e., diffuse identification with her general personality, behavior traits, values, and attitudes. . . . A son, however, must ultimately shift to a masculine role identity, which involves building an identification with the father. Since father is almost always more remote than mother (he is rarely involved in child care, and perhaps works away from home much of the day), building an identification with father involves a "positional identification," i.e., identification with father's male role as a collection of abstract elements rather than a personal identification with father as a real individual. . . . Further, as the boy enters the larger social world, he finds it in fact organized around more abstract and universalistic criteria . . . , as I have indicated in the previous section; thus his earlier socialization prepares him for, and is reinforced by, the type of adult social experience he will have.

For a young girl, in contrast, the personal identification with mother, which was created in early infancy, can persist into the process of learning female role identity. Because mother is immediate and present when the daughter is learning role identity, learning to be a woman involves the continuity and development of a girl's relationship to her mother, and sustains the identification with her as an individual; it does not involve the learning of externally defined role characteristics. . . . This pattern prepares the girl for, and is fully reinforced by, her social situation in later life; she will become involved in the world of women, which is characterized by few formal role differences . . . , and which involves again, in motherhood, "personal identification" with *her* children. And so the cycle begins anew.

Chodorow demonstrates to my satisfaction at least that the feminine personality, characterized by personalism and particularism, can be explained as having been generated by social-structural arrangements rather than by innate biological factors. The point need not be belabored further. But insofar as the "feminine personality" has been a nearly universal fact, it can be argued that its characteristics may have contributed further to the view of women as being somehow less cultural than men. That is, women would tend to enter into relationships with the world that culture might see as being more "like nature"—immanent and embedded in things as given—than "like culture"—transcending and transforming things through the superimposition of abstract categories and transpersonal values. Woman's relationships tend to be, like nature, relatively unmediated, more direct, whereas man not only tends to relate in a more mediated way, but in fact ultimately often relates more consistently and strongly to the mediating categories and forms than to the persons or objects themselves.

It is thus not difficult to see how the feminine personality would lend weight to a view of women as being "closer to nature." Yet at the same time, the modes of relating characteristic of women undeniably play a powerful and important role in the cultural process. For just as relatively unmediated relating is in some sense at the lower end of the spectrum of human spiritual functions, embedded and particularizing rather than transcending and synthesizing, yet that mode of relating also stands at the upper end of that spectrum. Consider the mother-child relationship. Mothers tend to be committed to their children as individuals, regardless of sex, age, beauty, clan affiliation, or other categories in which the child might participate. Now any relationship with this quality—not just mother and child but any sort of highly personal, relatively unmediated commitment—may be seen as a challenge to culture and society "from below," insofar as it represents the fragmentary potential of individual loyalties vis-à-vis the solidarity of the group. But it may also be seen as embodying the synthesizing agent for culture and society "from above," in that it represents generalized human values above and beyond loyalties to particular social categories. Every society must have social categories that transcend personal loyalties, but every society must also generate a sense of ultimate moral unity for all its members above and beyond those social categories. Thus that psychic mode seemingly typical of women, which tends to disregard categories and to seek "communion" . . . directly and personally with others, although it may appear infracultural from one point of view, is at the same time associated with the highest levels of the cultural process.

The Implications of Intermediacy

My primary purpose in this paper has been to attempt to explain the universal secondary status of women. Intellectually and personally, I felt strongly challenged by this problem; I felt compelled to deal with it before undertaking an analysis of woman's position in any particular society. Local variables of economy, ecology, history, political and social structure, values, and world view—these could explain variations within this universal, but they could not explain the universal itself. And if we were not to accept the ideology of biological determinism, then explanation, it seemed to me, could only proceed by reference to other universals of the human cultural situation. Thus the general outlines of the approach—although not of course the particular solution offered—were determined by the problem itself, and not by any predilection on my part for global abstract structural analysis.

I argued that the universal devaluation of women could be explained by postulating that women are seen as closer to nature than men, men being seen as more unequivocally occupying the high ground of culture. The culture/nature distinction is itself a product of culture, culture being minimally defined as the transcendence, by means of systems of thought and technology, of the natural givens of existence. This of course is an analytic definition, but I argued that at some level every culture incorporates this notion in one form or other, if only through the performance of ritual as an assertion of the human ability to manipulate those givens. In any case, the core of the paper was concerned with showing why women might tend to be assumed, over and over, in the most diverse sorts of world views and in cultures of every degree of complexity, to be closer to nature than men. Woman's physiology, more involved more of the time with "species of life"; woman's association with the structurally subordinate domestic context, charged with the crucial function of transforming animal-like infants into cultured beings; "woman's psyche," appropriately molded to mothering functions by her own socialization and tending toward greater personalism and less mediated modes of relating—all these factors make woman appear to be rooted more directly and deeply in nature. At the same time, however, her "membership" and fully necessary participation in culture are recognized by culture and cannot be denied. Thus she is seen to occupy an intermediate position between culture and nature.

This intermediacy has several implications for analysis, depending upon how it is interpreted. First, of course, it answers my primary question of why woman is everywhere seen as lower than man, for even if she is not seen as nature pure and simple, she is still seen as achieving less transcendence of nature than man. Here intermediate simply means "middle status" on a hierarchy of being from culture to nature.

Second, intermediate may have the significance of "mediating," i.e., performing some sort of synthesizing or converting function between nature and culture, here seen (by culture) not as two ends of a continuum but as two radically different sorts of processes in the world. The domestic unit—and hence woman, who in virtually every case appears as its primary representative—is one of culture's crucial agencies for the conversion of nature into culture, especially with reference to the socialization of children. Any culture's continued viability depends upon properly socialized individuals who will see the world in that culture's terms and adhere more or less unquestioningly to its moral precepts. The functions of the domestic unit must be closely controlled in order to ensure this outcome; the stability of the domestic unit as an institution must be placed as far as possible beyond question. (We see some aspects of the protection of the integrity and stability of the domestic group in the powerful taboos against incest, matricide, patricide, and fratricide.[8]) Insofar as woman is universally the primary agent of early socialization and is seen as virtually the embodiment of the functions of the domestic group, she will tend to come under the heavier restrictions and circumscriptions surrounding that unit. Her (culturally defined) intermediate position between nature and culture, here having the significance of her *mediation* (i.e., performing conversion functions) between nature and culture, would thus account not only for her lower status but for the greater restrictions placed upon her activities. In virtually every culture her permissible sexual activities are more closely circumscribed than man's, she is offered a much smaller range of role choices, and she is afforded direct access to a far more limited range of its social institutions. Further, she is almost universally socialized to have a narrower and generally more conservative set of attitudes and views than man, and the limited social contexts of her adult life reinforce this situation. This socially engendered conservatism and traditionalism of woman's thinking is another—perhaps the worst, certainly the most insidious—mode of social restriction, and would clearly be related to her traditional function of producing well-socialized members of the group.

Finally, woman's intermediate position may have the implication of greater symbolic ambiguity. . . . Shifting our image of the culture/nature relationship once again, we may envision culture in this case as a small clearing within the forest of the larger natural system. From this point of view, that which is intermediate between culture and nature is located on the continuous periphery of culture's clearing; and though it may thus appear to stand both above and below (and beside) culture, it is simply outside and around it. We can begin to understand then how a single system of cultural thought can often assign to woman completely polarized and apparently contradictory meanings, since extremes, as we say, meet. That she often represents both life and death is only the simplest example one could mention.

For another perspective on the same point, it will be recalled that the psychic mode associated with women seems to stand at both the bottom and the top of the scale of human modes of relating. The tendency in that mode is to get involved more directly with people as individuals and not as representatives of one social category or another; this mode can be seen as either "ignoring" (and thus subverting) or "transcending" (and thus achieving a higher synthesis of) those social categories, depending upon the cultural view for any given purpose. Thus we can account easily for both the subversive symbols (witches, evil eye, menstrual pollution, castrating mothers) and the feminine symbols of transcendence (mother goddesses, merciful dispensers of salvation, female symbols of justice, and the strong presence of feminine symbolism in the realms of art, religion, ritual, and law). Feminine symbolism, far more often than masculine symbolism, manifests this propensity toward polarized ambiguity—sometimes utterly exalted, sometimes utterly debased, rarely within the normal range of human possibilities.

If woman's (culturally viewed) intermediacy between culture and nature has this implication of generalized ambiguity of meaning characteristic of marginal phenomena, then we are also in a better position to account for those cultural and historical "inversions" in which women are in some way or other symbolically aligned with culture and men with nature. A number of cases come to mind: the Sirionó of Brazil, among whom, according to Ingham . . . , "nature, the raw, and maleness" are opposed to "culture, the cooked, and femaleness";[9] Nazi Germany, in which women were said to be the guardians of culture and morals; European courtly love, in which man considered himself the beast and woman the pristine exalted object—a pattern of thinking that persists, for example, among modern Spanish peasants. . . . And there are no doubt other cases of this sort, including some aspects of our own culture's view of women. Each such instance of an alignment of women with culture rather than nature requires detailed analysis of specific historical and ethnographic data. But in indicating how nature in general, and the feminine mode of interpersonal relations in particular, can appear from certain points of view to stand both under and over (but really simply outside of) the sphere of culture's hegemony, we have at least laid the groundwork for such analyses.

In short, the postulate that woman is viewed as closer to nature than man has several implications for further analysis, and can be interpreted in several different ways. If it is viewed simply as a *middle* position on a scale from culture down to nature, then it is still seen as lower than culture and thus accounts for the pan-cultural assumption that woman is lower than man in the order of things. If it is read as a *mediating* element in the culture-nature relationship, then it may account in part for the cultural tendency not merely to devalue woman but to circumscribe and restrict her functions, since culture must maintain control over its (pragmatic and symbolic) mechanisms for the conversion of nature into culture. And if it is read as an *ambiguous* status between culture and nature, it may help account for the fact that, in specific cultural ideologies and symbolizations, woman can occasionally be aligned with culture, and in any event is often assigned polarized and contradictory meanings within a single symbolic system. Middle status, mediating functions, ambiguous meaning—all are different readings, for different contextual purposes, of woman's being seen as intermediate between nature and culture.

Conclusions

Ultimately, it must be stressed gain that the whole scheme is a construct of culture rather than a fact of nature. Woman is not "in reality" any closer to (or further from) nature than man—both have consciousness, both are mortal. But there are certainly reasons why she appears that way, which is what I have tried to show in this paper. The result is a (sadly) efficient feedback system: various aspects of woman's situation (physical, social, psychological) contribute to her being seen as closer to nature, while the view of her as closer to nature is in turn embodied in institutional forms that reproduce her situation. The implications for social change are similarly circular: a different cultural view can only grow out of a different social actuality; a different social actuality can only grow out of a different cultural view.

It is clear, then, that the situation must be attacked from both sides. Efforts directed solely at changing the social institutions—through setting quotas on hiring, for example, or through passing equal-pay-for-equal-work laws—cannot have far-reaching effects if cultural language and imagery continue to purvey a relatively devalued view of women. But at the same time efforts directed solely at changing cultural assumptions—through male and female consciousness-raising groups, for example, or through revision of educational materials and mass-media imagery—cannot be successful unless the institutional base of the society is changed to support and reinforce the changed cultural view. Ultimately, both men and women can and must be equally involved in projects of creativity and transcendence. Only then will women be seen as aligned with culture, in culture's ongoing dialectic with nature.

Notes

1. It is true of course that *yin*, the female principle, has a negative valence. Nonetheless, there is an absolute complementarity of *yin* and *yang* in Taoism, a recognition that the world requires the equal operation and interaction of both principles for its survival.

2. Some anthropologists might consider this type of evidence (socialstructural arrangements that exclude women, explicitly or de facto, from certain groups, roles, or statuses) to be a subtype of the second type of evidence (symbolic formulations of inferiority). I would not disagree with this view, although most social anthropologists would probably separate the two types.

3. While we are on the subject of injustices of various kinds, we might note that Lowie secretly bought this doll, the most sacred object in the tribal repertoire, from its custodian, the widow of Wrinkled-face. She asked $400 for it, but this price was "far beyond [Lowie's] means," and he finally got it for $80. . . .

4. Semantic theory uses the concept of motivation of meaning, which encompasses various ways in which a meaning may be assigned to a symbol because of certain objective properties of that symbol, rather than by arbitrary association. In a sense, this entire paper is an inquiry into the motivation of the meaning of woman as a symbol, asking why woman may be unconsciously assigned the significance of being closer to nature. . . .

5. A situation that often serves to make her more childlike herself.

6. David M. Schneider (personal communication) is prepared to argue that the incest taboo is not universal, on the basis of material from Oceania. Let us say at this point, then, that it is virtually universal.

7. I remember having my first male teacher in the fifth grade, and I remember being excited about that—it was somehow more grown-up.

8. Nobody seems to care much about sororicide—a point that ought to be investigated.

9. Ingham's discussion is rather ambiguous itself, since women are also associated with animals: "The contrasts man/animal and man/woman are evidently similar . . . hunting is the means of acquiring women as well as animals." . . . A careful reading of the data suggests that both women and animals are mediators between nature and culture in this tradition.

Study Questions

1. What levels of the problem of the subordination of women does Ortner distinguish? Which does Ortner focus on?

2. What sorts of evidence does Ortner think would prove that a given culture thinks women are inferior? Does Ortner prove her claim that in every human culture, women are considered inferior?

3. How is biological determinism used to explain the universal devaluation of women? On what basis does Ortner reject that explanation?

4. What does Ortner mean by "nature" and "culture"? What leads Ortner to believe that even primitive cultures distinguish nature from culture? How is that distinction relevant to the issue of the devaluation of women?

5. Discuss in detail the reasons women are seen as closer to nature.

6. Discuss the various ways men are identified with culture.

7. Why does Ortner believe that it would be inaccurate to claim that women are considered a part of nature? What implications does women's intermediate status (between nature and culture) have?

3

Social Philosophy

Social philosophy is that area of value theory that deals with questions about the nature of society and social institutions. Social theory has characteristically inquired into the relationship between the self and society. But, according to de Beauvoir, man is constituted as self and woman as other. So, feminists ask: What of woman and society?

Self is the subject, which freely chooses projects. But man has enslaved woman and made her into other, or object. Woman, therefore, has not been subject but object; she has, literally, been sex object. Feminist theorists show how women have been sexually objectified. In every society, women are defined by their sexuality. Catharine MacKinnon writes:

> Implicit in feminist theory is (the) argument: the molding, direction, and expression of sexuality organizes society into two sexes—women and men— which division underlies the totality of social relations.

Feminists demonstrate how society assigns and maintains women's sexuality in determinate social (sex) roles such as daughter, wife, mother, prostitute, lesbian, and the like.

In this section, feminist theorists address these sex roles and the social construction of "the second sex" around them. How do social institutions serve to ensure the subordination of women and the domination of men?

Sarah Hoagland discusses the notion of "femininity," which has been central to feminist theory. She argues that it is not an empirical concept but a political one. As de Beauvoir says, "a woman is made, not born," and a woman is made into the feminine, or that which is desirable to men. Lucy Gilbert and Paula Webster call this process "a formula for surrender." Hoagland describes the means by which women learn to accept their inequality and the cultural definition of woman as inferior, submissive, and vulnerable. In her analysis, Hoagland discusses forms of "resistance" and "sabotage" that women have employed to counter "the forced march to femininity."

In *The Dialectic of Sex*, Shulamith Firestone argues that whereas in the past the procreative function (as wife/mother) was the source of women's subordination, now the pivot of women's oppression is the social institution of romantic love. As she says, "Romanticism develops in proportion to the liberation of women from their biology." Romantic love, she demonstrates, is the means by which women are indoctrinated to accept their inferior status in the sex-class system. Firestone identifies the basic components of romanticism as eroticism, sex-privatization ("the process by which women are blinded to their generality as a class"), and the beauty ideal.

Jeffner Allen investigates the radical feminist formulation that the institution of motherhood maintains women's subordination. Citing de Beauvoir and Firestone, she makes motherhood the focus of her critical analysis. Her "philosophy of evacuation," that women as a class not be synonymous with the class of mother, calls for "women's collective removal of ourselves from all forms of motherhood." She asserts the demand for a world which is open and free of the oppressive constructs of patriarchy.

Another radical feminist critique of motherhood, to which Allen's may interestingly be compared, is Adrienne Rich's *Of Woman Born*. Rich's thesis is that motherhood as an *institution* is to be distinguished from motherhood as *experience*. The institution of motherhood in patriarchy is oppressive. However, Rich says, motherhood as the relationship of women and children may be nonoppressive if experienced, personally and collectively, outside the control of men, in the community of women.

By contrast, a socialist feminist approach to the nature of motherhood is explored by Dorothy Dinnerstein in *The Mermaid and the Minotaur*. In her essay, Ann Snitow summarizes the argument of this text. Utilizing psychoanalytic concepts, Dinnerstein connects the fear and denigration of women to the infantile experience of what seemed an all-powerful mother. As not only the giver but the withholder of gratification, mother inevitably frustrates us. At the same time, the infant fears being "swallowed up" by the mother's totality. So, Dinnerstein says, we seek asylum in the seemingly bounded and rational world of the fathers. The outcome is the devaluation of women, since women are mothers. According to Dinnerstein, amelioration of "the human malaise created by the present sexual arrangements" is to be sought in a fundamental shift so that men as well as women are primary caretakers of infants and children.

Finally, feminist social theory sees prostitution as paradigmatic of woman as sexually objectified. According to Andrea Dworkins, men see women as objectified in the roles of wife/mother *or* prostitute. Alison Jaggar proposes a philosophical investigation into the nature of prostitution. She applies what she has called the "feminist frameworks" of radical feminism, liberal feminism, and socialist feminism to the analysis. These approaches have in common the rejection of the patriarchal ideology that makes woman synonymous with her sexuality and thus objectifies her. However, they differ in their responses to the issues around prostitution. Jaggar believes that prostitution is to be viewed as part of a wider account of social arrangements and of "what is the proper role of sexuality and work in human life."

"Femininity," Resistance, and Sabotage

Sarah Lucia Hoagland

Scientists and other male elite named wimmin "feminine," the most pervasive label infecting our lives. Yet "femininity" is not an empirical concept. It did not arise as a result of, nor is it susceptible to, empirical investigation. It is not based on fact. Instead it is akin to a metaphysical category, and those in power use it to determine perception of fact, to define the social perception of wimmin. Using the feminine stereotype, scientists[1] and conservatives who are not scientists[2] portray female behavior as submissive, and in the process legitimate male domination. I will argue that behaviors typically labeled feminine indicate not submission, but rather *resistance*, to male domination; we will see that the concept "femininity" has been used to obscure and bury female resistance, as well as female autonomy and female bonding.

I have argued elsewhere that "femininity" is not an empirical concept.[3] In the first place particular character traits alleged to fall under the feminine or masculine categories are valued differently depending on whether they apply to wimmin or men. Aggression is regarded as a flaw in wimmin and an asset in men while dependence is regarded as an asset in wimmin but not men. Such valuation indicates at the very least that use of the label "feminine" is prescriptive, not descriptive: when aggression is found among wimmin it is punished. Society attempts to control and limit aggression through social sanctions against those labeled feminine in a way not attempted among those labeled masculine.

More importantly, such traits are not only valued differently, they are *perceived* differently, an indication of the metaphysical nature of femininity. An aggressive man is seen as normal, and a middle-class aggressive man is seen as healthy, confident, and ambitious. An aggressive womon, on the other hand, is seen as frustrated if not neurotic, and heterosexual coercion is embedded in the stereotype because such a womon is seen as in need of a "good" (i.e., more aggressive) man.

The metaphysical nature of the feminine stereotype is apparent in the "humorous" characterization of the differences between businessmen and business wimmin who behave in identical ways:[4]

A businessman is aggressive.
A business woman is pushy.
A well-dressed businessman is fashionable.
A well-dressed business woman is a clothes horse.
He's careful about detail.
She's picky.
He loses his temper because he's involved in his job.
She's bitchy.
He gets depressed from work pressures.

From Mary Vetterling-Braggin, ed., *Femininity, Masculinity, and Androgyny,* (Totowa, NJ: Littlefield, Adams, 1982). Reprinted by permission of Sarah Lucia Hoagland.

She has menstrual tension.
He's a man of the world.
She's been around.
He's confident.
She's conceited.
He's enthusiastic.
She's emotional.
He isn't afraid to say what he thinks.
She's opinionated.
He's a stern task maker.
She's difficult to work for.
He follows through.
She doesn't know when to quit.
He's firm.
She's stubborn.
He's an authority.
She's a tyrant.

Yet another example is Dory Previn's song, "When a Man Wants a Woman":

When a man wants a woman
He says it's a compliment
He says he's only trying to capture her
To claim her; to tame her
When he wants ev'rything ev'rything of her
Her soul, her love, her life forever and more.
He says he's persuading her
He says he's pursuing her
But when a woman wants a man
He says she's threatening him
He says she's only trying to trap him
To train him, to chain him
When she wants anything anything of him
A look, a touch, a moment of his time
He says she's demanding
He swears she's destroying him
Why is it
When a man wants a woman
He's called a hunter
But when a woman wants a man
She's called a predator

These two examples indicate that identical behavior is perceived to be different depending on whether it is attributed to wimmin or men. In both cases when a womon steps outside the limits of the feminine stereotype she is subject to derision, attack, and denial. To suggest the behavior is qualitatively different begs the question; it presupposes that wimmin and men have different natures prior to investigating the hypothesis. More significantly, such a suggestion fails to consider the context of these perceptions—a society based on the rule of the fathers. Femininity exists to limit wimmin; in these cases we are unable to *perceive* certain behavior outside the feminine stereotype.

In other cases, the behavior is detectable as challenging femininity, but it is denied to be either normal or female. If femininity were an empirical concept then female behavior would provide endless counterexamples to the feminine labeling of wimmin's characters.[5] Empirical concepts are subject to challenge and their applications to refutation. Yet wimmin who act in ways which do not fit the feminine model are not treated by scientists as counterexamples to scientific hypotheses (prejudices, prejudgments) about wimmin and wimmin's characters. Instead, scientists and others label wimmin whose behavior is clearly not limited by the feminine model "abnormal." Recently an even more insidious move is underfoot in science. Wimmin who will not remain confined to the feminine stereotype are denied our womonhood. For example, pursuing his hypothesis that hormones pass on specific behavioral traits in conformity with sex-role stereotypes, John Money is developing an ideology that masculine minds appear in female bodies. Such a move whitens out, obliterates the concept of a strong, autonomous womon; she is now a male trapped in a female body.[6] In this view, a strong, autonomous womon must really be a man.

In general, scientists and other men in power discredit and attempt to render invisible counterexamples to the feminine stereotype, using "femininity" as a standard of womonhood, femaleness, even though they may differ on a few of the minor particulars as to what exactly constitutes femininity. Measures or standards determine fact; no amount of research into wimmin's "true natures," no appeal to fact, will either confirm or challenge the concept, the label, "femininity." The importance of realizing the coerciveness of "femininity" lies not in the tired male question of whether we can ever "discover" wimmin's "true nature." The importance lies in realizing how "femininity" determines the social perception of wimmin, and how it is used to enforce male domination and heterosexuality.

Characterizations which ordinarily pass under the label "feminine" include: passive, emotional, irrational or even nonrational, unassuming, cooperative (with whom?), unthreatening (to whom?), behind the scenes (whose scenes?), weak, gullible (when?), childlike, infantile. These characterizations present a significant picture of male fantasy. In 1946 Viola Klein documented the fanciful and contradictory nature of the scientific collection of feminine characteristics. For example, she points to a general paradox while discussing Otto Weininger's work: How can one talk about positive male and female characteristics such that each person has a few from both categories while at the same time depicting one set of those characteristics in negative terms, as voids?[7]

More than being contradictory or simply negative, however, the feminine stereotype as applied to wimmin maintains existing lines of power and promotes heterosexual bias by defining wimmin in relation to men and characterizing as normal the womon who remains totally accessible to male authority. A "normal" womon, under the male-identification of wimmin, does not bond with wimmin and she does not remain autonomous. Caroline Whitbeck has isolated three prevailing theories composing the foundation of the feminine characteristics, all of which define wimmin in relation to men: womon as partial man, womon as opposite man, and womon as helpmate to man.[8]

Following this, one of the most pervasive effects of the male naming of wimmin feminine is the obliteration of any conceptual hint of female resistance to male domination, resistance to attempts to limit or control a womon's integrity. One searches in vain for portraits and historical depictions of female autonomy, female resistance, female bonding. Patrihistorians claim that wimmin have remained content with our lot and have accepted male domination throughout time with the exception of a few suffragists and now a few "aberrant" feminists. Yet upon examination it becomes clear that within the confines of the feminine stereotype, no behavior, no set of actions *count* as resistance. Any behavior that cannot be squeezed into the confines of the feminine, passive stereotype has been discounted as an aberration or it has been buried.[9]

If nothing one can point to or even imagine counts as proof against the claim that all (normal) wimmin are feminine and accept male domination, then the claim is not empirical, it is not based on examination of fact. And we are attempting to work with a closed, coercive conceptual system. We have been unable to recognize resistance to male domination among wimmin because under the male-identified feminine stereotype, resistance is considered abnormal, an indication of insanity, or incredibly, proof of submission.

For example, acts which the namers use to support the feminine stereotype of white middle-class wimmin, the current paradigm of all womonhood, indicate resistance. Alix Kates Shulman in *Memoirs of an Ex-Prom Queen*, portrays a "fluffyheaded" housewife who regularly burns the dinner when her husband brings his boss home unexpectedly.[10] And she periodically packs raw eggs in his lunchbox. Such acts are used as "proof" of wimmin's "lesser rational ability" by those in power, but in fact they indicate resistance—sabotage. Such acts may or may not be openly called sabotage by the saboteurs. But wimmin engage in them as an affirmation of existence in a society which denies us recognition independently of a man. When we are isolated, one from another, through heterosexual coercion, these are rational alternatives to untenable situations, to traps, within a patriarchal context.

Donna Deitch's documentary, "Woman to Woman," offers a classic example of sabotage.[11] Four wimmin, two housewives, a daughter, and the interviewer, sit around a kitchen table. One housewife protests that she is not a housewife, that she is not married to the house. The interviewer asks her to say what she does all day. The womon relates that she starts by getting up, feeding her husband, feeding her children, driving them to the school bus, driving her husband to work, returning to do the dishes, make the beds, going out to do the shopping, returning to do a wash. She continues relating her activities for a normal Monday and half of a Tuesday before she stops, shocked, and says: "Wait a minute, I AM married to the house." She complains of difficulty in getting her husband to give her money for the household, of frustration because he nevertheless holds her responsible for running the house, and of degradation because she must go to him, apologetically, at the end of each week to ask for extra money when he could have provided her with sufficient funds at the beginning of each week. Suddenly she gets a gleam in her eye, lowers her voice and leans forward, saying: "Have you ever bought something you didn't need?" Excitement brews and they all lean closer as she states: "You have to know you're alive, you have to make sure you exist." She has separated herself from her husband's perceptions of her; she is not simply an extension of his purposes, of his will, she is reclaiming (some) agency—sabotage.[12] Yet under the feminine stereotype, we are barred from claiming her as a sister re-sister.

Significantly, femininity is used to characterize any group men in power wish to justify dominating. [In 1971] Kate Millett pointed out that femininity characterizes traits that those in power cherish in subordinates.[13] [In 1968] Naomi Weisstein noted that feminine characteristics add up to typical minority group characteristics.[14] An investigation of the literature shows that Nazis characterized Jews as feminine and used the ideology in the justification of their massacre. Men accused at the Salem witch trials were characterized as feminine.[15] And an investigation of white British anthropological writing reveals that Black South Africans were labeled feminine. The model for oppression in Anglo-European thinking is the male conception of femininity. A feminine being is one who is by nature relatively passive and dependent. It follows that those to whom the label is applied must be seeking protection (domination) by nature and should be subjected to authority "for their own good." "Femininity" portrays those not in power as wanting and needing control. It is a matter of logic, then, that those who refuse control are abnormal.

Consider the fact that white history depicts Black slaves (though not white indentured servants) as lazy, docile, and clumsy on such grounds as that slaves frequently broke tools. Yet a rational woman under slavery, comprehending that her situation is less than human, that she functions as an extension of the will of her master, will not run to pick up tools. She acts instead to differentiate herself from the will of her master, she breaks tools, carries on subversive activities—sabotage. Her master, in turn, perceiving her as subhuman and sub-rational, names her clumsy, childlike, foolish, perhaps, but not a saboteur.

If officially slaves were subhuman and content with their lot and masters were only acting in slaves' best interest, then any resistance to the system would be depicted by those in power as an abnormality or an indication of madness. Indeed, in recollecting the stories of her grandmother's slave days, Annie Mae Hunt tells us that "If you run off, you was considered sick."[16] That is to say, slaves existed in a Weltanschauung where running away from slavery was perceived as an indication not of (healthy) resistance but of mental imbalance. Such was the extent of control the masters exercised through the power of naming—*nothing* one did could be perceived as resistance. In fact the behaviors of slaves out of which the masters constructed and fed the slave stereotypes provide evidence of resistance and sabotage.[17]

During the Holocaust and, more significantly, after it, in the telling of the stories, Nazis as well as liberal historians have depicted Jews under Hitler's reign of terror as cooperative and willing victims. This stereotype, as is true of the slave stereotype, is still alive today. Yet again, one must ask, what would *count* as resistance? For example, Jews at Auschwitz committing suicide by hurling themselves against an electric fence would be depicted as "willing victims," and such behavior has been used to portray Jews as failing to resist Nazi aggression. If fact, Jews in concentration camps committing suicide were not willing victims. In determining the time of their own deaths they were resisting, interfering with the plans of the masters, exercising choice, and so establishing a self, differentiating themselves from the will of the masters. Holocaust literature is full of indications of Jewish resistance, of sabotage, yet the stereotype of the willing (i.e., feminine) Jewish victim persists today.[18] Again, "femininity" is used to obscure resistance.

Consider one paradigm of femininity, the white, upper-class Victorian lady. In *The Yellow Wallpaper*, Charlotte Perkins Gilman portrayed conditions faced by such wimmin in the 1880s.[19] These conditions included a prescription of total female passivity by mind gynecologists such as S. Weir Mitchell, prescriptions arising as a result of male scientists' sudden interest in wimmin as the first wave of feminism attracted their attention, prescriptions enforced by those in control. The heroine is taken by her husband to a summer home for rest. He locks her in a nursery with bars on the windows, a bed bolted to the floor, and hideous wallpaper, shredded in spots. He rebuts her despair with the rhetoric of protection, refusing to indulge her "whims" when she protests the room's atrocity. He also stifles all other attempts at creativity, flying into a rage when he discovers her writing in her diary. In the end, she manages to crawl behind the wallpaper and escape into "madness." Charlotte Perkins Gilman shows us a womon with every avenue of creativity, of integrity, patronizingly and paternalistically cut off for "her own good," to "protect" her, and we watch her slowly construct her resistance. Not surprisingly, male scientists and doctors of the day saw nothing more in the story than a testament to "feminine" insanity.[20]

Resistance, in other words, may even take the form of insanity when one is isolated within the confines of male domination and all means of maintaining integrity have been systematically cut off. Under such conditions insanity becomes a more viable alternative than submission. Mary's long descent into oblivion on morphine in *A Long Day's Journey Into Night* is another example of resistance to domination. But the coerciveness of "femininity" dictates that such behavior be perceived as part of the "mysterious" and "intricate" nature of womon rather than recognized as resistance.

Significantly, one and the same word governs insanity and anger: madness. As Phyllis Chesler has documented, mind gynecologists call wimmin mad whose behavior they can no longer understand as functioning in relation to men.[21] On the other hand, the *Oxford English Dictionary* defines "mad" as it relates to anger as "ungovernable rage or fury." One must ask, "ungovernable" by whom? Madness in anger and madness in "insanity" indicate that men have lost control.[22] When wimmin are labeled mad, it is often because we have become useless to men or a threat to male supremacy.

Thus, to maintain the feminine stereotype men will characterize more obvious forms of resistance as insanity when wimmin engage in them. Thus insanity becomes a part of the "feminine" nature and resistance is rendered institutionally invisible. Just as slaves who ran off were perceived as insane, so are wimmin who fight back against battering husbands. Wimmin who kill long-term battering husbands are, for the most part, forced to use the plea of insanity rather than that of self-defense. The most famous case is that of Francine Hughes who killed her husband after fourteen years of beatings and psychological abuse.[23]

However, institutionally characterizing wimmin who fight back as insane was still not enough. Perceiving the plea of insanity as a license to kill even though it means incarceration for an unspecified amount of time, media men began a campaign against battered wimmin who fight back, depicting them as getting away with murder.[24] Funds for battered wives shelters are now being withdrawn on the grounds that the shelters break up the family. And agencies working on "domestic violence" focus on preserving the family intact, burying the slave conditions of wimmin within the nuclear family by obliterating the distinction between aggressor and victim.[25] Once again, the conceptual framework that renders female resistance invisible comes full circle. The concept of femininity not only blocks any social perception of female resistance, it lays the groundwork for denying the problem of male domination when female resistance threatens to break through the stereotype and become visible.

I have stressed the fact that feminine behaviors indicate resistance to point to the phenomenal reversals those in power have perpetuated. To dominate a people one must first use force, but eventually one must find other means.[26] One effective means of maintaining power is to rob the oppressed of any positive self-concept and so prevent us from identifying with each other. Then one can portray us as accepting, indeed desiring our lot, and each individual sees herself as alone and abnormal when she resists. The feminine stereotype is the most effective tool that exists for this purpose, and scientists who "investigate" femininity under the guise of establishing social fact perpetuate and legislate patriarchal value, both male domination and compulsory heterosexuality.[27]

This is true to such an extent that scientists *condemn* female competence and autonomy as threatening to males and subversive to the patriarchal family, hence as socially undesirable. Thus Daniel P. Moynihan popularized the theory of the Black matriarch who castrates Black men, and implied that for Black men to claim their manhood, Black wimmin must step behind them and become submissive.[28]

Female bonding is so threatening that it is altogether erased. For example, one will find the term "maiden aunt" employed in sociobiology in a lesbian context, burying the idea of a female rejecting a male and promoting the idea that a female is unable to attract one. The latter feeds an unsupported theory of male dominance while the former does not.[29] Among humans, Lesbians are either depicted as men or are rendered invisible.

As a final note, I wish to merely indicate an additional consequence of the heterosexual coerciveness of "femininity." The feminine stereotype provides a basis for the ideology of special protection for wimmin, thus enforcing heterosexuality. For men to maintain the conceptual framework in which they can see themselves as protectors, they must establish and maintain an atmosphere in which wimmin are in danger; they must create our victim (feminine) status. To maintain the ideology of special protection of wimmin, men have portrayed us as helpless, defenseless, innocent—victims, and thereby, targets to be attacked. If we act in self-defense and thus step out of the feminine role, becoming on their terms active and "guilty," men step up overt physical violence against us to reaffirm our victim status. When they cannot control us through protection, the safety valve they fall back on is overt violence, predation (pornography, rape, "domestic violence" [wifebeating], "incest" [daughter rape]). In short, the ideology of special protection of wimmin emerging from femininity sets us up as targets which in turn compels us to turn to men for protection and enforces heterosexuality.[30]

The patriarchal naming of wimmin feminine goes even further. The separate valuation of aggression in men and wimmin affects what is tolerated in society in terms of violence. Male violence against wimmin is an integral part of society, it is expected that men will rape, batter, maim, torture, mutilate, and murder wimmin. Rape, wifebeating and "incest" are at best ignored. But, as noted above, wimmin who fight back face the full brutality of the system.

"Femininity," I have argued, is a label whereby one group of people are defined in relation to another in such a way that domination and submission are portrayed as part of the biological essence of those involved. Under the feminine stereotype, a portrait of naive contentment with being controlled is painted such that resistance is rendered invisible or perceived as abnormal, mad, or of no consequence. Men of minority groups such as Blacks and Jews are slowly and painfully emerging from under the domination of femininity.[31] Unfortunately they often do so by laying claim to "masculinity" which does not challenge the dualism that justifies oppression. Heterosexist ideology and the failure to examine the coercive conceptual framework of "femininity" keeps wimmin locked in an ideology of male domination. Be we Black, Jewish, WASP, Iranian, Hispanic, Native American, Asian American, or a member of any of the many other cultures in which wimmin survive, be we working class, middle class, or upper class,[32] within our various situations we remain saddled with the label "femininity." Female resistance, female autonomy and Lesbian bonding do not exist within patriarchal ontology. Instead scientists and other male elite have limited the boundaries of female behavior and set us up for attack, control, and domination.

Notes

1. See, for example, E. O. Wilson, *Sociobiology: The New Synthesis* (Cambridge, Mass.: Harvard University Press, 1975).
2. See, for example, Marabel Morgan, *The Total Woman,* and *Total Joy* (Old Tappan, N.J.: Flemming H. Revell Co., 1972 and 1976).
3. Sarah L. Hoagland, "On the Status of the Concepts of Masculinity and Femininity," *Transactions of the Nebraska Academy of Sciences* 4 (August 1977): 169–72. The argument that follows is an extension of the arguments I developed in this paper.
4. Loosely adapted from "The Executive Woman," *Family Circle,* May 1976.
5. See footnote 4.
6. See the discussion of Money's thesis in Janice G. Raymond, *The Transsexual Empire: The Making of the She-Male* (Boston: Beacon Press, 1979), Chapter II.
7. Viola Klein, *The Feminine Character* (Chicago: University of Illinois Press, 1971), p. 60.
8. Caroline Whitbeck, "Theories of Sex Difference," in *Women and Philosophy: Toward a Theory of Liberation,* ed. Carol C. Gould and Marx W. Wartofsky (New York: G. P. Putnam's Sons, 1976), pp. 54–81.
9. For example, the Amazons are repeatedly depicted as mythical creatures (with attendant male fantasies such as the alleged removing of one breast) even though there is proof of their existence both in Africa and Asia. For example, in the Fall of 1979, Soviet archeologists uncovered the remains of a tribe of Amazons that lived 1200 years ago in Balabany in the Soviet Republic of Moldavia (*Chicago Sun-Times,* September 9, 1979). I have yet to see further information on this anywhere.
10. Alix Kates Shulman, *Memoirs of an Ex-Prom Queen* (New York: Bantam, 1973).
11. Copies of the film can be obtained from Donna Deitch, 3644 Carnation Avenue, Los Angeles, CA 90026.
12. This material is taken from a paper I presented at the AAAS, January 1979, in which I argue that there is patriarchal deception in science at all three levels: naming, describing, and explaining. I also argue

the problem emanates not simply from observer bias but lies at the heart of scientific methodology. That paper, "Naming, Describing, Explaining: Deception and Science," is available through the Eric Clearing House (Information Analysis Center for Science, Mathematics, and Environmental Education, The Ohio State University, 1700 Chambers Road, 3rd floor, Columbus, Ohio, 43212).

13. Kate Millett, *Sexual Politics* (New York: Avon, 1971), p. 47.
14. Naomi Weisstein, "Psychology Constructs the Female, or: The Fantasy Life of the Male Psychologist," reprint (Boston: New England Free Press, 1968).
15. Research of Betty Carpenter, personal communication, Spring 1978, Lincoln, Nebraska.
16. Ruth Winegarten, "I Am Annie Mae: The Personal Story of a Black Texas Woman," *Chrysalis* 10 (Spring 1980): 15.
17. Since formulating the thesis, I have come across documented evidence of it. See, *Puttin' on Ole Massa,* ed. Gilbert Osofsky (New York: Harper and Row, 1969); *Great Slave Narratives,* ed. Arna Bontemps (Boston: Beacon Press, 1969); and *A Documentary History of Slavery in North America,* ed. Willie Lee Rose (New York: Oxford University Press, 1976).
18. See Simone Wallace, Ellen Ledley, Paula Tobin, letter to *Off Our Backs* (December 1979): 28.
19. Charlotte Perkins Gilman, *The Yellow Wallpaper* (New York: The Feminist Press, 1973).
20. Elaine R. Hedges, "Afterword," Charlotte Perkins Gilman, op. cit.
21. Phyllis Chesler, *Women and Madness* (Garden City, N.Y.: Doubleday and Co., 1972).
22. When reading between the lines, when claiming wimmin from the past, we must examine alternatives available and in that context understand the behavior. Thus insanity itself can be a form of resistance. In addition, other behavior is depicted as insanity. As a result, there is a fine line that fades between insanity and behavior of the resister who is able to maintain the confidence of her perceptions. If everyone around you perceives your behavior in a light other than your intention, your perceptions struggle in a very different world.
23. Ann Jones, *Women Who Kill* (New York: Holt, Rinehart and Winston, 1980), pp. 285–91.
24. Ibid., p. 291.
25. Kathleen Barry, *Female Sexual Slavery* (Englewood Cliffs, N.J.: Prentice-Hall, 1979), p. 142.
26. Pat Robinson (et al.), "A Historical and Critical Essay for Black Women in the Cities," *The Black Woman,* ed. Toni Cade (New York: New American Library, 1970), pp. 198–210.
27. See Adrienne Rich, "Compulsory Heterosexuality and Lesbian Existence," *Signs* 5 (Summer 1980): 631–60. Of interest also is Marilyn Frye, "Assignment: NWSA-Bloomington-1980, Speak on 'Lesbian Perspectives on Women's Studies,'" *Sinister Wisdom* 14 (Summer 1980): 3–7.
28. See Jean Carey Bond and Pat Peery, "Is the Black Male Castrated?" *The Black Woman,* ed. Toni Cade (New York: New American Library, 1970), pp. 113–19.
29. See Sarah Lucia Hoagland, "Androcentric Rhetoric in Sociobiology," *Women's Studies International Quarterly* 3, nos. 2/3 (1980): 285–93.
30. See Sarah Lucia Hoagland, "Violence, Victimization, Violation," *Sinister Wisdom* 15.
31. This is not to say, of course, that the *experience* of Black men or Jewish men has been identical to that of white wimmin or Black wimmin or Jewish wimmin. It is not to say, for example, that Black male slaves and white wimmin who were wives of Southern plantation owners had the same experiences. Black slaves were perceived as beasts. If wives of Southern plantation owners were perceived as animals (pets), still there were significant differences. Even poor white Southern wimmin and upper-class Southern white wimmin did not have the same experiences. My point here is simply that the concept of femininity was used in the justification of the Weltanschauung of dominance and submission in such a way that resistance, in all its various forms, becomes invisible.
32. See Kathleen Barry, *Female Sexual Slavery* (Englewood Cliffs, N.J.: Prentice-Hall, 1979), Chapter 7.

Study Questions

1. What does Hoagland mean when she says that femininity is not an "empirical" concept? What reasons does she offer for her view?
2. What are some standard characterizations of femininity? In what sense are these characterizations negative, and how do they serve to reinforce the existing power relationships?
3. In what ways might seemingly typical feminine behavior (from the male point of view) instead be "resistance" or "sabotage," according to Hoagland?

4. In what way has the male conception of femininity formed the model for oppression in Anglo-European thought?
5. How can resistance sometimes take the form of insanity?
6. How does the concept of femininity promote violence against women? Explain your answer.

═══════════════════════════════

The Culture of Romance

Shulamith Firestone

So far we have not distinguished ''romance'' from love. For there are no two kinds of love, one healthy (dull) and one not (painful) (''My dear, what you need is a mature love relationship. Get over this romantic nonsense.''), but only less-than-love or daily agony. When love takes place in a power context, everyone's ''love life'' must be affected. Because power and love don't make it together.

So when we talk about romantic love we mean love corrupted by its power context—the sex class system—into a diseased form of love that then in turn reinforces this sex class system. We have seen that the psychological dependence of women upon men is created by continuing real economic and social oppression. However, in the modern world the economic and social bases of the oppression are no longer *alone* enough to maintain it. So the apparatus of romanticism is hauled in. (Looks like we'll have to help her out, Boys!)

Romanticism develops in proportion to the liberation of women from their biology. As civilization advances and the biological bases of sex class crumble, male supremacy must shore itself up with artificial institutions, or exaggerations of previous institutions, e.g., where previously the family had a loose, permeable form, it now tightens and rigidifies into the patriarchal nuclear family. Or, where formerly women had been held openly in contempt, now they are elevated to states of mock worship.[1] Romanticism is a cultural tool of male power to keep women from knowing their condition. It is especially needed—and therefore strongest—in Western countries with the highest rate of industrialization. Today, with technology enabling women to break out of their roles for good—it was a near miss in the early twentieth century—romanticism is at an all-time high.

How does romanticism work as a cultural tool to reinforce sex class? Let us examine its components, refined over centuries, and the modern methods of its diffusion—cultural techniques so sophisticated and penetrating that even men are damaged by them.

1. *Eroticism.* A prime component of romanticism is eroticism. All animal needs (the affection of a kitten that has never seen heat) for love and warmth are channeled into genital sex: people must never touch others of the same sex, and may touch those of the opposite sex only when preparing for a genital sexual encounter (''a pass''). Isolation from others makes people starved for physical affection; and if the only kind they can get is genital sex, that's

soon all they crave. In this state of hypersensitivity the least sensual stimulus produces an exaggerated effect, enough to inspire everything from schools of master painting to rock and roll. Thus *eroticism is the concentration of sexuality—often into highly-charged objects ("Chantilly Lace")—signifying the displacement of other social/affection needs onto sex.* To be plain old needy-for-affection makes one a "drip," to need a kiss is embarrassing, unless it is an erotic kiss; only "sex" is O.K., in fact it proves one's mettle. Virility and sexual performance become confused with social worth.[2]

Constant erotic stimulation of male sexuality coupled with its forbidden release through most normal channels are designed to encourage men to look at women as only things whose resistance to entrance must be overcome. For notice that this eroticism operates in only one direction. Women are the only "love" objects in our society, so much so that women regard *themselves* as erotic.[3] This functions to preserve direct sex pleasure for the male, reinforcing female dependence: women can be fulfilled sexually only by vicarious identification with the man who enjoys them. Thus eroticism preserves the sex class system.

The only exception to this concentration of all emotional needs into erotic relationships is the (sometimes) affection within the family. But here, too, unless they are *his* children, a man can no more express affection for children than he can for women. Thus his affection for the young is also a trap to saddle him into the marriage structure, reinforcing the patriarchal system.

2. *The Sex Privatization of Women.* Eroticism is only the topmost layer of the romanticism that reinforces female inferiority. As with any lower class, group awareness must be deadened to keep them from rebelling. In this case, because the distinguishing characteristic of women's exploitation as a class is sexual, a special means must be found to make them unaware that they are considered all alike sexually ("cunts"). Perhaps when a man marries he chooses from this undistinguishable lot with care, for as we have seen, he holds a special high place in his mental reserve for "The One," by virtue of her close association with himself; but in general he can't tell the difference between chicks (Blondes, Brunettes, Redheads).[4] And he likes it that way. ("A wiggle in your walk, a giggle in your talk, THAT'S WHAT I LIKE!") When a man believes all women are alike, but wants to keep women from guessing, what does he do? He keeps his beliefs to himself, and pretends, to allay her suspicions, that what she has in common with other women is precisely what makes her different. Thus her sexuality eventually becomes synonymous with her individuality. *The sex privatization of women is the process whereby women are blinded to their generality as a class which renders them invisible as individuals to the male eye.* Is not that strange Mrs. Lady next to the President in his entourage reminiscent of the discreet black servant at White House functions?

The process is insidious: When a man exclaims, "I love Blondes!" all the secretaries in the vicinity sit up; they take it personally because they have been sex-privatized. The blonde one feels personally complimented because she has come to measure her worth through the physical attributes that differentiate her from other women. She no longer recalls that any physical attribute you could name is shared by many others, that these are accidental attributes not of her own creation, that her sexuality is shared by half of humanity. But in an authentic recognition of her individuality, her blondeness would be loved, but in a different way: She would be loved first as an irreplaceable totality, and then her blondeness would be loved as one of the characteristics of that totality.

The apparatus of sex privatization is so sophisticated that it may take years to detect—if detectable at all. It explains many puzzling traits of female psychology that take such form as:

Women who are personally complimented by compliments to their sex, i.e., "Hats off to the Little Woman!"

Women who are not insulted when addressed regularly and impersonally as Dear, Honey, Sweetie, Sugar, Kitten, Darling, Angel, Queen, Princess, Doll, Woman.

Women who are secretly flattered to have their asses pinched in Rome. (Much wiser to count the number of times other girls' asses are pinched!)

The joys of "prickteasing" (generalized male horniness taken as a sign of personal value and desirability).

The "clotheshorse" phenomenon. (Women, denied legitimate outlets for expression of their individuality, "express" themselves physically, as in "I want to see something 'different.' ")

These are only some of the reactions to the sex privatization process, the confusion of one's sexuality with one's individuality. The process is so effective that most women have come to believe seriously that the world needs their particular sexual contributions to go on. ("She thinks her pussy is made of gold.") But the love songs would still be written without them.

Women may be duped, but men are quite conscious of this as a valuable manipulative technique. That is why they go to great pains to avoid talking about women in front of them ("not in front of a lady")—it would give their game away. To overhear a bull session is traumatic to a woman: So all this time she has been considered only "ass," "meat," "twat," or "stuff," to be gotten a "piece of," "that bitch," or "this broad" to be tricked out of money or sex or love! To understand finally that she is no better than other women but completely indistinguishable comes not just as a blow but as a total annihilation. But perhaps the time that women more often have to confront their own sex privatization is in a lover's quarrel, when the truth spills out: then a man might get careless and admit that the only thing he ever *really* liked her for was her bust ("Built like a brick shithouse") or legs anyway ("Hey, Legs!"), and he can find that somewhere else if he has to.

Thus sex privatization stereotypes women: it encourages men to see women as "dolls" differentiated only by superficial attributes—not of the same species as themselves—and it blinds women to their sexploitation as a class, keeping them from uniting against it, thus effectively segregating the two classes. A side-effect is the converse: if women are differentiated only by superficial physical attributes, men appear more individual and irreplaceable than they really are.

Women, because social recognition is granted only for a *false* individuality, are kept from developing the tough individuality that would enable breaking through such a ruse. If one's existence in its generality is the only thing acknowledged, why go to the trouble to develop real character? It is much less hassle to "light up the room with a smile"— until that day when the "chick" graduates to "old bag," to find that her smile is no longer "inimitable."

3. *The Beauty Ideal.* Every society has promoted a certain ideal of beauty over all others. What that ideal is is unimportant, for any ideal leaves the majority out; ideals, by definition, are modeled on *rare* qualities. For example, in America, the present fashion vogue of French models, or the erotic ideal Voluptuous Blonde are modeled on qualities rare indeed: few Americans are of French birth, most don't look French and never will (and besides they eat too much); voluptuous brunettes can bleach their hair (as did Marilyn Monroe, the sex queen herself), but blondes can't develop curves at will—and most of them, being Anglo-Saxon, simply aren't built like that. If and when, by artificial methods, the majority can squeeze into the ideal, the ideal changes. If it were attainable, what good would it be?

For the exclusivity of the beauty ideal serves a clear political function. Someone—most women—will be left out. And left scrambling, because as we have seen, women have been allowed to achieve individuality only through their appearance—looks being defined as "good" not out of love for the bearer, but because of her more or less successful approximation to an external standard. This image, defined by men (and currently by homosexual men, often misogynists of the worst order), becomes the ideal. What happens? Women everywhere rush to squeeze into the glass slipper, forcing and mutilating their bodies with diets and beauty programs, clothes and makeup, anything to become the punk prince's dream girl. But they have no choice. If they don't the penalties are enormous: their social legitimacy is at stake.

Thus women become more and more look-alike. But at the same time they are expected to express their individuality through their physical appearance. Thus they are kept coming and going, at one and the same time trying to express their similarity and their uniqueness. The demands of Sex Privatization contradict the demands of the Beauty Ideal, causing the severe feminine neurosis about personal appearance.

But this conflict itself has an important political function. When women begin to look more and more alike, distinguished only by the degree to which they differ from a paper ideal, they can be more easily stereotyped as a class: They look alike, they think alike, and even worse, they are so stupid they believe they are not alike.

*   *   *

These are some of the major components of the cultural apparatus, romanticism, which, with the weakening of "natural" limitations on women, keep sex oppression going strong. The political uses of romanticism over the centuries became increasingly complex. Operating subtly or blatantly, on every cultural level, romanticism is now— in this time of greatest threat to the male power role— amplified by new techniques of communication so all-pervasive that men get entangled in their own line. How does this amplification work?

With the cultural portrayal of the smallest details of existence (e.g., deodorizing one's underarms), the distance between one's experience and one's perceptions of it becomes enlarged by a vast interpretive network; If our direct experience contradicts its interpretation by this ubiquitous cultural network, the experience must be denied. This process, of course, does not apply only to women. The pervasion of image has so deeply altered our very relationships to ourselves that even men have become objects—if never *erotic* objects. Images become extensions of oneself; it gets hard to distinguish the real person from his latest image, if indeed, the Person Underneath hasn't evaporated altogether. Arnie, the kid who sat in back of you in the sixth grade, picking his nose and cracking jokes, the one who had a crook in his left shoulder, is lost under successive layers of adopted images: the High School Comedian, the Campus Rebel, James Bond, the Salem Springtime Lover, and so on, each image hitting new highs of sophistication until the person himself doesn't know who he is. Moreover, he deals with others through this image-extension (Boy-Image meets Girl-Image and consummates Image-Romance). Even if a woman could get beneath this intricate image facade—and it would take months, even years, of a painful, almost therapeutic relationship—she would be met not with gratitude that she had (painfully) loved the man for his real self, but with shocked repulsion and terror that she had found him out. What he wants instead is The Pepsi-Cola Girl, to smile pleasantly to his Johnny Walker Red in front of a ski-lodge fire.

But, while this reification affects both men and women alike, in the case of women it is profoundly complicated by the forms of sexploitation I have described. Woman is not only an Image, she is the Image of Sex Appeal. The stereotyping of women expands: now there is no longer the excuse of ignorance. Every woman is constantly and explicitly informed on how to "improve" what nature gave her, where to buy the products to do it with, and how to count the calories she should never have eaten—indeed, the "ugly" woman is now so nearly extinct even she is fast becoming "exotic." The competition becomes frantic, because everyone is now plugged into the same circuit. The current beauty ideal becomes all-pervasive ("Blondes have more fun . . . ").

And eroticism becomes erotomania. Stimulated to the limit, it has reached an epidemic level unequalled in history. From every magazine cover, film screen, TV tube, subway sign, jump breasts, legs, shoulders, thighs. Men walk about in a state of constant sexual excitement. Even with the best of intentions, it is difficult to focus on anything else. This bombardment of the senses, in turn, escalates sexual provocation still further: ordinary means of arousal have lost all effect. Clothing becomes more provocative: hemlines climb, bras are shed. See-through materials become ordinary. But in all this barrage of erotic stimuli, men themselves are seldom portrayed as erotic objects. Women's eroticism, as well as men's, becomes increasingly directed toward women.

One of the internal contradictions of this highly effective propaganda system is to expose to men as well as women the stereotyping process women undergo. Though the idea was to better acquaint women with their feminine role, men who turn on the TV are also treated to the latest in tummy-control, false eyelashes, and floor waxes (Does she . . . or doesn't she?). Such a crosscurrent of sexual tease and exposé would be enough to make any man hate women, if he didn't already.

Thus the extension of romanticism through modern media enormously magnified its effects. If before culture maintained male supremacy through Eroticism, Sex Privatization, and the Beauty Ideal, these cultural processes are now almost too effectively carried out: the media are guilty of "overkill." The regeneration of the women's movement at this moment in history may be due to a backfiring, an internal contradiction of our modern cultural indoctrination system. For in its amplification of sex indoctrination, the media have unconsciously exposed the degradation of "femininity."

In conclusion, I want to add a note about the special difficulties of attacking the sex class system through its means of cultural indoctrination. Sex objects *are* beautiful. An attack on them can be confused with an attack on beauty itself. Feminists need not get so pious in their efforts that they feel they must flatly deny the beauty of the face on the cover of *Vogue*. For this is not the point. The real question is: is the face beautiful in a *human* way— does it allow for growth and flux and decay, does it express negative as well as positive emotions, does it fall apart without artificial props—or does it falsely imitate the very different beauty of an *inanimate* object, like wood trying to be metal?

To attack eroticism creates similar problems. Eroticism is *exciting*. No one wants to get rid of it. Life would be a drab and routine affair without at least that spark. That's just the point. Why has all joy and excitement been concentrated, driven into one narrow, difficult-to-find alley of human experience, and all the rest laid waste? When we demand the elimination of eroticism, we mean not the elimination of sexual joy and excitement but its rediffusion over—there's plenty to go around, it increases with use—the spectrum of our lives.

Notes

1. Gallantry has been commonly defined as "excessive attention to women without serious purpose," but the purpose is very serious: through a false flattery, to keep women from awareness of their lower-class condition.
2. But as every woman has discovered, a man who seems to be pressuring for sex is often greatly relieved to be excused from the literal performance: His ego has been made dependent on his continuously proving himself through sexual conquest; but all he may have really wanted was the excuse to indulge in affection without the loss of manly self-respect. That men are more restrained than are women about exhibiting emotion is because, in addition to the results of the Oedipus Complex, to express tenderness to a woman is to acknowledge her equality. Unless, of course, one tempers one's tenderness—takes it back—with some evidence of domination.

3. Homosexuals are so ridiculed because in viewing the male as sex object they go doubly against the norm: even women don't read Pretty Boy magazines.
4. "As for his other sports," says a recent blurb about football hero Joe Namath, "he prefers Blondes."

Study Questions

1. What does Firestone mean by "romantic love"? What caused it to develop?
2. How does eroticism (one component of romanticism) act to reinforce the sex class system?
3. What is the "sex privatization of women" (another component of romanticism), and how does it act to reinforce the sex class system?
4. What is the Beauty Ideal, and how does it act to reinforce the sex class system?
5. How has romanticism been amplified in modern American culture?

Motherhood: The Annihilation of Women

Jeffner Allen

I would like to affirm the rejection of motherhood on the grounds that motherhood is dangerous to women. If woman, in patriarchy, is she who exists as the womb and wife of man, every woman is by definition a mother: she who produces for the sake of men. A mother is she whose body is used as a resource to reproduce men and the world of men, understood both as the biological children of patriarchy and as the ideas and material goods of patriarchal culture. Motherhood is dangerous to women because it continues the structure within which females must be women and mothers and, conversely, because it denies to females the creation of a subjectivity and world that is open and free.

An active rejection of motherhood entails the development and enactment of a *philosophy of evacuation*.[1] Identification and analysis of the multiple aspects of motherhood not only show what is wrong with motherhood, but also point to a way out. A philosophy of evacuation proposes women's collective removal of ourselves from all forms of motherhood. Freedom is never achieved by the mere inversion of an oppressive construct, that is, by seeing motherhood in a "new" light. Freedom is achieved when an oppressive construct, motherhood, is vacated by its members and thereby rendered null and void.

A small and articulate group of radical feminist and radical lesbian feminist authors agree that motherhood is oppressive to women. Simone de Beauvoir's position in *The Second Sex*, that woman's "misfortune is to have been biologically destined for the repetition of life,"[2] is reaffirmed in her recent interviews: "I think a woman must not fall into the trap of children and marriage. Even if a woman wants to have children, she must think very hard about the

From Joyce Trebilcot, ed., *Mothering,* (Totowa, NJ: Roman & Allanheld, 1984), pp. 315–328. Reprinted by permission of Roman & Allanheld. (Notes deleted.)

conditions in which she will have to bring them up, because child-bearing, at the moment, is real slavery."[3] Shulamith Firestone, following de Beauvoir, finds that, "the heart of woman's oppression is her childbearing and childrearing roles."[4] That woman's "reproductive function . . . is the critical distinction upon which all inequities toward women are grounded" is also asserted by Ti-Grace Atkinson at the beginning of the second wave of the women's liberation movement.[5] Monique Wittig writes that a female becomes a woman and a mother when she is defined first, and above all else, in terms of "the capacity to give birth (biology)."[6]

The claim that a direct connection exists between woman's oppression and her role as breeder within patriarchy also entails the recognition that men impose a type of sexuality on women through the institution of motherhood. De Beauvoir agrees that "frigidity seems . . . , in the present state of malaise created by the power relationship between men and women, a reaction at least more prudent and more reasonable [than woman's being trapped in sexuality] because it reflects this malaise and makes women less dependent on men."[7] Atkinson answers affirmatively the more specific question "Do you still feel that sexual instincts would disappear if 'sexual intercourse' no longer served the function of reproduction?"[8] Wittig holds that, "Sexuality is for us (lesbian feminists) an inevitable battleground insofar as we want to get outside of genitality and of the sexual economy imposed on us by the dominant heterosexuality."[9] Andrea Dworkin states clearly and without equivocation, "There is a continuum of phallic control. In the male system, reproductive and nonreproductive sex are both phallic sex."[10] I engage in a philosophy of evacuation as a radical lesbian feminist who questions, analyzes, and describes how motherhood is dangerous to women.

Speaking of motherhood as the annihilation of women does not disclaim either women's past or present as mothers. Women as mothers make the best of motherhood. Women are mothers because within patriarchy women have no choice except motherhood. Without the institution of motherhood women could and would live otherwise. Just as no single woman, or particular mother, is free in patriarchy, no group of token women, mothers in general, are free in patriarchy. Until patriarchy no longer exists, all females, as historical beings, must resist, rebel against, and avoid producing for the sake of men. Motherhood is not a matter of woman's psychological or moral character. As an ideology by which men mark females as women, motherhood has nothing to do with a woman's selfishness or sacrifice, nurturance or nonviolence. Motherhood has everything to do with a history in which women remain powerless by reproducing the world of men and with a present in which women are expected to do the same. The central publication of the Soviet Women's Committee, for instance, writes, "Considering motherhood to be a woman's most important social function . . ."[11]

I am endangered by motherhood. In evacuation from motherhood, I claim my life, body, world, as an end in itself.

Where Do Children Come From?

The question "Where do babies come from?" is frequently dismissed with a laugh, or cut short by recourse to scientific authority. In present-day discourse, both God's prescience and the stork are generally thought to be inadequate responses. A satisfactory and "progressive" explanation is found in a scientific account of the union of egg and sperm. The appeal to science is misleading, however, for it ignores and conceals the social intercourse which first brings men and women together either indirectly, through the use of medical technology, or directly, by means of physical copulation. The question "Where do babies come from?" might be approached more appropriately through the social and historical circumstances in which conception takes place. *Children come from patriarchal (male) sexuality's use of woman's body as a resource to reproduce men and the world of men.* Similarly, *motherhood* is men's appropriation of women's bodies as a resource to reproduce patriarchy.

The scientific explanation of where children come from avoids placing conception within the continuum of social power relationships that constitute motherhood: heterosexual intercourse, pregnancy, and childraising. Compulsion marks every aspect of the motherhood continuum: the mandatory heterosexuality imposed on women by men is thought ''natural''; pregnancy is viewed as a biological fact; obligatory childraising by women is so ''normal'' that in the United States 39 percent of black families and 12 percent of white families are headed by women.

Seduction and pregnancy, for instance, are remarkably similar: both eroticize women's subordination by acting out and deepening women's lack of power.

> Male instinct can't help ITself; women need IT either because of their sexiness or their maternal instinct. IT, the penis, is big; IT, the child, is large. Woman's body is made for IT. Women's bodies have the right fit, or proportions. Women ask for IT, want IT. IT's a maturing experience in her becoming a woman. She takes IT. No real harm is done.

In seduction and pregnancy the power imbalance between men and women assumes the appearance of sexual difference, regardless of whether such activities are ''affectionate'' or ''brutal.''

> If women didn't want IT, IT wouldn't happen. Therefore, women must choose IT. Since many choose IT, IT must be part of their nature.[12]

I am defenseless within the motherhood continuum.

IT, ''male instinct,'' passes through heterosexual intercourse to become the IT of motherhood. In motherhood, IT, male sexuality as a man-made social power construct, marks females with ITself. IT compels women to ITself: to male sexuality and its consequences, namely, birthing and raising men and the world of men. Children come from IT, from male-defined, male-dominated social intercourse. It names ITself as ''virility'': belonging to, characteristic of a man; the power of procreation, especially for sexual intercourse; the masculine member, the generative organs; force, energy, drive considered typically masculine; to pursue, to hunt.[13] Virility comes from vir, which in Latin means ''man.'' Women's ''misfortune is to have been biologically destined for the repetition of life''[14] precisely because ITs power, force, energy, drive appropriates women's biological possibility in order to produce ITself. IT pursues ITs own continuation, silencing my questions: is IT needed? Is IT desired? IT pursues ITs own evolution, constituting motherhood as a given, as compulsory for women, a danger to women.

The Representation

The question remains: ''Where do children come from?'' Or, more precisely, if children are produced by IT, by male sexuality as a man-made social power construct, how does male sexuality appropriate women's biological possibility in order to reproduce ITself? How do men constitute the motherhood continuum of heterosexual intercourse, pregnancy, and childraising as compulsory for women?

Analysis from a radical lesbian feminist perspective suggests that motherhood is constituted by male sexuality's use of woman's body to represent ITself to ITself. As such, motherhood is a paradigmatic instance of men's creation of representational thinking and of men's appropriation of the ''world'' by means of representational thought.

Representational thinking does not mean the production of a picture, copy, or imitation *of* the world. Representational thinking means, rather, to conceive and grasp the world *as* picture. In representational thinking, man manipulates, pursues, and entraps the world in order to secure it as picture. Man brings into play his unlimited power for the calculating, planning, and molding of all things; by conceiving and grasping the world as picture, he gives the measure and draws up the guidelines for everything that is. As such, he creates and determines what is real, and what is not. Not only is the man who has made the picture already in the picture, he is that which he pictures to himself. Yet, to acknowledge himself as the picture would be to destroy himself as he who conceives and grasps the world as picture. Only by maintaining a privileged stand outside the picture can he claim to be the creator, and not the object, of the activity of representation. Withdrawn from representation as the representer, however, he enters into the picture as "the incalculable," "the gigantic."

The object of representational thought, in turn, is allowed to be only insofar as it can be overpowered—manipulated, pursued, entrapped—by representational thought. Once conceived and grasped as picture, the object is said to call forth, to provoke, the particular way in which it is pictured and the activity of picturing as such. The object can, indeed, must repeat itself exactly as it has been thought. It must even claim to establish, maintain, and justify its objectification. Its sole "activity" is reproductive: the reiteration and reinforcement of itself as picture.

Reproductive thinking thereby generates, unavoidably and of necessity, an ideology that is reproductive: motherhood. Athena is born from the head of Zeus alone; children are born from the head of man alone. Athena springs fully armed from the head of Zeus; a child springs from the head of its father, fully adorned with the markings of patriarchy. Zeus sees his world in his full-grown offspring; man pictures his world in his children who soon will be adults. Even if the child is female, man incorporates the female into his world as picture. The man with the child in his head, with the child as image in his head, represents himself to himself in the child that he has made. In contrast, Athena's mother, Metis, cannot be manipulated, pursued, trapped. She cannot be bound, secured, by man's representational thought. Athena's mother, children's mothers, are not.

In representational thought, woman is made pregnable (from *prehendere,* Latin for "to take"), understood in its literal sense as vulnerable to capture, taken. She is compelled to have man's child, to reproduce throughout her world of experience men's thoughts, words, actions. She must reproduce the life of the species, that is, man and his immortality. Captured by representational thinking, woman can never be genuinely pregnant (*pregnas,* akin to *gignere,* to produce): she cannot provide her own life and world. Woman as what-in-men's-eyes-she-seems-to-be is invisible, except insofar as her body is used by man to reproduce himself and his world. Woman as what-I-am-in-my-own-eyes is not. Motherhood passes through the mind of a man, of a man who does not see woman's body as her body. The man with the child in his head does not see the woman with the child in her body. Throughout the motherhood continuum of heterosexual intercourse, pregnancy, and compulsory childraising, motherhood exists as a dialogue between men about an invisible woman.

Key to the specific mode of representation that defines motherhood, including the articulation of women's sexuality within the confines of motherhood, is male sexuality's setting of the bounds within which life and death are to be recognized. Man, the representer, assumes a greater-than-human power over life and death. Man, the representer, fixates on life and death as the central defining moments of one's life and as the two parts, or pieces, which comprise one's life. Within the framework of man's representation of life and death, woman's body is reduced to a lifeless instrument, even when her body is a carrier of life and death. The very manner in which man represents to himself his own life and death precludes, moreover, an experience of what is always already given: the continuity and discontinuity of an individual life, the strength and power of its ongoing action in the world, the authentic subjectivity of the woman who is *as* she is.

While man is giving birth to himself, woman dies. I, bound to the representation of woman as mother, leave that representation behind: evacuation to another way of thinking, to a productive empowering of the female who has been both woman and mother.

The Mark

The question ''Where do children come from?'' may be answered by a radical lesbian feminist phenomenology of consciousness, in terms of the representation. The representation is that form of consciousness by which patriarchal (male) sexuality constitutes a world in which woman's body is used as a resource to reproduce men and the world of men. ''Where do children come from?'' may also be answered by a similarly radical phenomenology of existence, through reference to the mark. The mark is the form of specific difference imposed on women's bodies when appropriated by men as a resource to reproduce patriarchy. An idealist interpretation of the representation and a materialist analysis of the mark converge so as to portray, when taken together, the social intercourse that is motherhood. A philosophy of evacuation from motherhood proposes, accordingly, that from which women must collectively remove ourselves: patriarchal thinking, the representation, and patriarchal existence, the mark.

One may object that even within patriarchy some types of motherhood are free of the representation and the mark, that some individual women do not occupy woman's traditional position as she who is marked. Such women, when truly exceptional, successfully assume man's traditional position as the representer of motherhood. A distinction must be made, however, between the hope that it expressed by such an objection, i.e., that women might live more freely, and the fact that is ignored by the objection, i.e., how women actually live. Such an objection involves a non-appropriation of the female body, as if motherhood could miraculously pass through woman's mind and not through her body. In fact, a female cannot escape being a mother unless she no longer produces for men, unless she is no longer compelled to reproduce the biological children, material goods, and ideas of patriarchy. Identification with the patterns traced on woman's body by the representation and the mark of motherhood is a necessity for the survival of all women. Indeed, identification with any single aspect of the motherhood continuum is an identification with every aspect of the motherhood continuum, for no single aspect exists as separable from the whole of its context. Women's identification with all women as mothers is a positive endeavor which points to what can be done, to actionary possibilities for the creation of a subjectivity that is genuinely free and open. I am no longer within patriarchy when I and all females have rendered null and void the ideology and institution of motherhood.

A radical lesbian feminist perspective suggests that the mark imposed by patriarchy on the bodies of all women compels all women to exist as mothers. The mark of motherhood inscribes the domination of men into woman's body, making motherhood appear as a natural phenomenon. Yet, motherhood is not a natural phenomenon, and mothers do not exist as a natural group. On the contrary, female biological possibilities are first ''naturalized'' by men as women's specific difference and then claimed as the reason for the existence of motherhood. Through this ''naturalization,'' or marking, the female's biological possibility to give birth is made to appear as the intrinsic cause of women's place in motherhood and as the origin of women's social, economic, and political place in the world. The female's biological possibility to bear a child thereby becomes the defining characteristic of all women.

The closer a mark is to the body, the more indelibly it is associated with the body and the more the individual as a whole is pursued, hunted, trapped. In the case of woman, the mark has absolute permanence, for woman's entire body, and the body of her world, is marked: MOTHER. The permanence of the mark is the sign of the permanence of the male domination that marks all women as mothers.

Marking operates by focusing on isolated fragments of the female body. Such fragments, vagina, breasts, etc., are marked with a significance that is presumed to be intrinsic, eternal, and to characterize the whole of the female body. Forms of activity and character traits termed "natural" to women are then deduced from the marking imposed on the body fragments.

The institution of motherhood is unique among those created by marking in that there is no other institution in which so many persons can be destroyed by the mark, and yet, a sufficient supply of persons to be marked remains. In all other forms of war, attrition eventually threatens the supply of persons who can be marked and thereby usually limits the activity of marking, at least for a time. The mark of motherhood is distinctive in that one of its by-products is the regeneration of more females to be marked as women and mothers.

The object marked, woman as mother, experiences the mark as pain. The inscription of the mark of motherhood on women's bodies is never without pain—the pain of not "owning" our bodies, the pain of physical injury, the pain of being compelled to never produce a life or world of our own. Pain (from Greek *poiné*, punishment, penalty, payment) is the punishment, the penalty we must pay, for being marked by men as woman and mother. Pain has nothing to do with what we do, that is, our success or failure at being good, well-informed, or willing mothers. Pain is a sign that we, as women, are put in danger by men who mark us. *If and when* the pain of the mark is not successfully "naturalized" by men, that is, is not or does not remain imprinted on females as belonging to our nature either physiologically or psychologically, we attempt to evade pain. Our pain breaks through the force of the mark. We do not endure the pain. We do not put up with the mark. We avoid, resist, the mark. We neither need nor desire the mark. We will get out of the mark. The immense amount of pain that marking entails is both an experience that always accompanies the mark of motherhood and an experience that can lead to the end of the mark of motherhood.

Outside the social power relationship within which marking occurs, the mark does not exist. Outside patriarchy, the mark of motherhood cannot even be imagined.

Stamped, firmly imprinted on women's bodies, is the emblem that our bodies have been opened to the world of men: the shape of the pregnant woman's stomach. From conception to abortion, acts which are biologically different and yet symbolically the same, our stomachs are marked: MOTHER.

In present-day patriarchal society, the marking impressed on woman's stomach is man's proof of his virility, that he can reproduce himself. When the mark remains on women's stomachs from conception to the birth of an infant, male virility not only can, but does, reproduce itself. In contrast, when the mark remains imprinted on our stomachs from conception to the abortion of a fetus, male virility can, but does not—yet—reproduce itself. Either the time is judged as not right—yet, or the right time has passed by—already. When abortion is permitted, either officially or unofficially, there need not be an immediate and direct link between conception and the birth of an infant. There must, however, be an indirect link between male virility which can reproduce itself and male virility which does reproduce itself. The right time must eventually be found such that man both can and does reproduce himself, either by means of biological children or through the material goods and ideas of patriarchy. Indeed, within patriarchy the fact that abortion may sometimes be permitted does not make abortion a genuinely free choice, for women have no alternative but abortion if we are already impregnated and do not want to reproduce. Nor does the right to abortion make motherhood voluntary, for a woman in patriarchy cannot abort, or do away with, the mark of motherhood itself. The right to abortion in patriarchy cannot, in principle, recognize that women may choose abortion because we will not reproduce men and the world of men, because we will not be mothers.

The woman who does not remove the mark from her stomach, who does not have an abortion, may be killed: on the West Bank one such Arab woman a week is found "poisoned or burned to death and the murder is made to look accidental."[15] Women who survive an initial decision to not remove the mark from our stomachs, to not have an abortion, in defiance of the traditions of male virility, may be persecuted as non-virgins and unmarried mothers. Yet, the women who do remove the mark from our stomachs, who abort, may also die. Five thousand women a year are estimated to die in Spain and Portugal alone as a result of complications arising from illegal abortions. In Latin America, abortion causes 20 percent to 50 percent of all maternal deaths. Complications from illegal abortions account for 4 percent to 70 percent of maternal deaths in the hospitals of developing countries. "A woman undergoing a properly performed abortion has six times less risk of death from complications than a woman having a child."[16] In childbirth our bodies as a whole are stamped with the mark of pain, terror, and possible death.

To speak of birth without violence is to ignore the violence of childbirth. The most frequent cause of death of women is childbirth:[17]

> In a number of developing countries . . . maternal mortality rates in excess of 500 per 100,000 live births are by no means exceptions. Rates of over 1000 per 100,000 have been reported in parts of Africa.
>
> In the areas with the highest maternal mortality, i.e., most of Africa, West, South, and East Asia, about half a million women die from maternal causes every year.
>
> Age-specific death rates for women rise sharply at ages 20–30 in many countries, where women often have less chance than men of surviving from 15 to 45 years of age.[18]

Already, as female children, women as a whole are marked—"undesirable." College students in the United States, for instance, favor what amounts to a decrease in female births, with the overall ratio of girls to boys desired being 100:116. Also, "from 66 to 92 percent of men have been found to want an only child to be a boy . . . , and from 62 to 80 percent prefer a first child to be a boy,"[19] a chilling thought as the United States, like Western Europe, moves toward zero growth.

As female fetuses, women as a whole are stamped "to be aborted." A recent Chinese report, for example, shows that when sex determination tests were performed on 100 fetuses with the sole purpose being the determination of the fetus's gender, there were 30 planned abortions. Of those 30 aborted fetuses, 29 were female.[20]

As female infants, women as a whole are marked "dead." Men, rather than regulate men and men's use of women, claim that because there is not enough food, resources, etc., "female fertility" must be controlled by the elimination of women. From the Athens of antiquity to the present, infanticide has been, largely and for the most part, femicide.

Women as mothers are marked: Dead. Man the marker continues with himself, his sons, his mark.

The Society of Mothers

Man remains with his representation and his mark. Women need not remain. The representation and the mark, and not existing females *per se,* are integral to motherhood. Indeed, if and when the representation and the mark of motherhood can be affixed to something other than the female body, women may not be at all.

The society of mothers, comprised of all women within motherhood, is dangerous to all its members. The society of mothers continues, by definition, the ideology and institution of motherhood as oppressive to women. The motherhood lived out by the society of mothers is also the annihilation of women. When motherhood involves men's reproduction and marking of females as women and mothers, (a) motherhood may entail our physical death and our non-existence as mothers and as female infants, and (b) motherhood always entails the death of a world in which women are free. In the contemporary ideology and institution of motherhood, women's annihilation is also involved in that (a) men's representation and marking of females as women and mothers may continue and, at the same time, (b) men may represent and mark objects (from the domain of the sciences and technology of reproduction) and persons other than females (from among those men held to be "lesser" in power and merit) to reproduce men and the world of men, such that (c) the class, women as mothers, has no further use function, and thus need no longer be reproduced. Both forms of annihilation are dangerous to women. The specifically contemporary manifestation of motherhood, however, shows clearly that women are not necessary to motherhood. Patriarchal men must represent and mark something as MOTHER, but that which is so designated need not be women.

The society of mothers exhibits, in multiple forms, the dangerous situation of woman, the womb and wife of man, and mother, she who produces for men. In modern times, the collectivity of females who are compelled to live within motherhood is composed of those who must reproduce the biological children of patriarchy and those who must reproduce the material goods and ideas of patriarchal culture. Women who reproduce the biological children of patriarchy do so in widely differing manners. All such women, however, are represented and marked by motherhood. In fact, so determinate is men's regulation of women's reproduction of children that the world population growth is projected as coming to a halt in 130 years, at which time, "nearly nine-tenths of this projected 10.5 billion people will be living in developing countries. The poorest regions of the world—Africa and South Asia—will account for more than 60 percent of the world's people . . . the industrialized world's share of the world population will see a drop of today's 24 percent to about 13 percent.[21]

Members of the society of mothers who reproduce the material goods and ideas of patriarchal culture may manifest the ideology and institution of motherhood in differing ways. Despite such differences, the women remain mothers. The limitation of the society of mothers to those who reproduce only the biological children of men is to ignore that men use women's bodies in a multitude of ways to reproduce patriarchal life. Women who do not give birth to biological children are still involved in the "regeneration" of men, in virtue of our work, unpaid and paid, to continue the products, both ideal and material, of motherhood. Even when men can produce biological children by use of the sciences and technology of reproduction, women may be kept in existence as those who perform various services for men, or women may be bred out of existence. Within a patriarchal context, even the production of females by parthenogenesis need not alter the social and historical circumstances of the society of mothers into which they are born. Men may or may not continue to impose patriarchal (male) sexuality on women. Men may or may not relate in explicitly sexual modes to women, and women may still be kept in our service function as the society of mothers.

The representation and mark of motherhood claim not just the surface, but the whole of women, such that the society of mothers not only reproduces, but often defends, the patriarchal world of men: "Confined to their cities the mothers were no longer separate, free, complete individuals and they fused into an anonymous collective consciousness."[22]

In the production of the son for the father, in the production of goods for the father, for the benefit of the son, we are not our bodies, we are not ourselves. A means to men's ends, never an end in ourselves, we are selfless, worldless, annihilated. The experience of our servitude takes seriously our danger and holds, firmly and strongly, to the conviction that together we must get out of motherhood.

Priorities and Alternatives

To show how motherhood, in its many forms, is dangerous to women is also to suggest how women may get out of motherhood. Further questions such as ''Why do men impose motherhood on women by means of the representation and the mark?'' and ''Why do women form a society of mothers?'' can lead to idle speculation, unless the questioner's focus centers on how motherhood exists in actuality and how women's actions may form a horizon of possibility in light of which all women may succeed in breaking free of the ideology and institution of motherhood.

Central to a philosophy of evacuation from motherhood is the primacy of women's daily lives and the power of our possible, and sometimes actual, collective action. In breaking free from motherhood, I no longer focus on birth and death as the two most important moments of my life. I give priority, rather, to that which is always already given, my life and my world in their actual presence to me. The moment of birth and the moment of death have, in themselves, no special value. They need not determine who I am or who I may become. I—my activities, body, sexuality—am articulated by my actions and choices, which, apart from patriarchy, may be made in the openness of freedom. Similarly, I no longer give a primacy to that which I have reproduced. I claim as primary my life and world as I create and experience them. New modes of thinking and existing emerge as the evacuation from motherhood empowers the female who has been both woman and mother. In that evacuation I, as an individual female, and we, as the community of all females, lay claim, with firmness and strength, to the presence of our own freely chosen subjectivities, to the priorities and alternatives we produce as our own.

Because the evacuation from motherhood does not simply seek to alter motherhood as it exists currently, its focus is not specifically on the development of alternative means of intercourse, pregnancy, or childraising. Women who use artificial insemination and whose children have no known father, as well as women who live as lesbian mothers, clearly challenge, but need not break with, the ideology and institution of motherhood. Each of these alternatives is significant for women's survival within patriarchy, but none is sufficient for women's effective survival, that is, for the creation of a female's self-chosen, nonpatriarchal, existence.

A precondition for women's effective survival may be established, instead, by the female's power to not have children. A decision not to have children may be made, not because a female's biological possibility causes the ideology of motherhood, but because,

1. To not have children opens a time-space for the priority of claiming my life and world as my own and for the creative development of radically new alternatives.
2. The biology from which a child is born does not determine or control the course of that child's life. Females and males, younger and older, create the shapes of our lives through our individual choices.
3. Women who wish to be with younger females or males can do so collectively, with others of similar interests, or individually, through adoption.
4. Currently, there is no question of women's absolute biological extinction.

At present, and for several thousands of years past, women have conceived, borne, and raised multitudes of children without any change in the conditions of our lives as women. In the case that all females were to decide not to have children for the next twenty years, the possibilities for developing new modes of thought and existence would be almost unimaginable.

The necessary condition for women's evacuation from motherhood is, even more significantly, the claiming of our bodies as a source. Our bodies are not resources to be used by men to reproduce men and the world of men while, at the same time, giving death to ourselves. If necessary, women must bear arms, but not children, to protect our bodies from invasion by men. For our effective survival, women's repetitive reproduction of patriarchy must be replaced by the genuine, creative, production of ourselves. In particular, the areas of food, literacy, and energy sources and supplies for women must be reexamined as crucial to the claiming of our bodies as a source.

Women's hunger is one of the specific conditions affecting the possibility for men's continuing success in representing and marking women as mothers. Within the current patriarchal economy, women do not have access to sufficient crops to feed ourselves:

> In many countries where malnutrition is prevalent, up to half the cultivated acreage is growing crops for export to those who can afford them, rather than food stuffs for those who need them. . . . The cash crops are generally cultivated by men while food crops are grown by women. Practically all the agricultural land in developing countries is owned by men. Men always eat first and most of the food: Women and children go hungry and are the vast majority of malnourished everywhere, especially in Asia and Africa.[23]

Nor do women have access to the money necessary to purchase food: in 1979, women living in poverty constituted 12 percent of the total, worldwide, female population and 75 percent of all people living in poverty.

Women's literacy is the second specific condition that enhances the possibility for men's continuing success in maintaining the ideology and institution of women as mothers. Women have insufficient access to the basics of literacy, that is, reading, writing, and simple arithmetic. In fact, from a global perspective, women are two-thirds of the illiterates of the world. In almost all countries, "girls already begin school in fewer numbers than boys; on the average, the difference even at the start of school is 10–20 percent. By the time higher education is reached, the ratio between boys and girls is at least 2:1, but in many cases more."[24] In many African countries, less than 10 percent of the women read and write. The education gap between men and women is growing all over the developing world. Yet, even in industrialized societies, women have no access to determining what constitutes an education, which areas of research are the most pressing, and what comprises the development of more liberating forms of thinking and speaking.

Energy sources and supplies for women are a third area which undermines women's endeavors to break free of motherhood. In African villages, women work about three hours per day more than men because it is the women who must gather the food, water, and fuel necessary for survival. Generally speaking, technological information on alternative means of energy is not made available to such women, any more than it is to most women in industrialized countries. In all societies, women's non-control of energy sources and supplies necessary to our survival keeps us in subordination to men.

Women's non-access to food, education, and energy sources greatly facilitates men's representation and marking of women as mothers and, as such, forms one of the central foundations of the ideology and institution of motherhood. Women's sexual and material oppression by men go hand in hand, as is evidenced by the multiple forms of violence by which men rigidly enforce women's non-access to ourselves. To claim our bodies as a source, to get out of the reproduction of motherhood, females of all ages must work together to establish female-defined alternatives that express and fulfill our current needs and desires for food, education, and energy. The goal of such an endeavor is neither to save the world nor to become "healthy" mothers who reproduce "healthy" children. Female-defined access to food, education, and energy forms a necessary condition for women's collective evacuation from motherhood in that such access claims as a source the whole of our bodies and world. As females who engage in evacuation from motherhood, we shape the whole of ourselves and our world in the present of our own lifetimes.

Notes

1. I am indebted to Julie Murphy for suggesting the phrase "a philosophy of evacuation."
2. Simone de Beauvoir, *The Second Sex,* translated by H. M. Parshley (New York: Vintage Books, 1974), p. 72.
3. De Beauvoir, "Talking to de Beauvoir," *Spare Rib* (March 1977): 2.
4. Shulamith Firestone, *The Dialectic of Sex* (New York: Bantam Books, 1971), p. 72.
5. Ti-Grace Atkinson, *Amazon Odyssey* (New York: Links Books, 1974), p. 1.
6. Monique Wittig and Sande Zeig, *Brouillon pour un dictionnaire des amantes* (Paris: Grasset, 1976), p. 94; and Wittig, "One Is Not Born a Woman," *Feminist Issues* 1, no. 2 (Winter 1981): 1.
7. De Beauvoir, "Talking to de Beauvoir," p. 2.
8. Atkinson, "Interview with Ti-Grace Atkinson," *Off Our Backs* 9, no. 11 (December 1973): 3.
9. Wittig, "Paradigm," in *Homosexualities and French Literature,* edited by George Stambolian and Elaine Marks (Ithaca: Cornell University Press, 1979), pp. 118–19.
10. Andrea Dworkin, *Pornography: Men Possessing Women* (New York: Perigree, 1981), p. 222.
11. *WIN News* 7, no. 4 (1981): 68. Citation from the "Soviet Women's Committee" booklet.
12. Iona Wieder, "Accouche!" *Questions Féministes* 5 (February 1979): 53–72.
13. *The Oxford English Dictionary.*
14. De Beauvoir, *The Second Sex,* p. 72.
15. *WIN News,* vol. 7, no. 2 (1981): 52. From *Journal Americain* (3 January 1981).
16. *WIN News,* vol. 7, no. 3 (1981): 22.
17. *WIN News,* vol. 7, no. 4 (1981): 24. From The Population Institute, *International Dateline.*
18. *WIN News,* vol. 7, no. 3 (1981): 16. From World Health Organization, "Sixth Report on the World Health Situation."
19. Jalna Hanmer, "Sex Predetermination, Artificial Insemination and the Maintenance of Male-Dominated Culture," in *Women, Health and Reproduction,* edited by Helen Roberts (London: Routledge & Kegan Paul, 1981), pp. 167, 168.
20. Ibid., p. 176.
21. *WIN News,* vol. 7, no. 4 (1981): 23. From the Population Institute, *International Dateline.*
22. Wittig and Zeig, *Lesbian Peoples,* p. 76.
23. *WIN News,* vol. 7, no. 4 (1981): 23, 24.
24. *WIN News,* vol. 7, no. 1 (1981): 21. From World Bank Headquarters, "Education: A World Bank Sector Policy Paper."

Study Questions

1. What does Allen mean by posing a "philosophy of evacuation" regarding motherhood?
2. What does Allen mean when she asks, "Where do children come from?"
3. What is "representational thinking"? How have men used this mode of thought to create "motherhood"?
4. What is the "mark of motherhood," according to Allen?
5. In what ways does Allen think the "mark of motherhood" is physically dangerous for women?
6. What is the "society of mothers" for her?
7. What does Allen see as central to her "philosophy of evacuation"? What does that entail about the female's power to not have children? Other powers?

Thinking about
The Mermaid and the Minotaur

Ann Snitow

Summary of the Argument

"Woman" will always be regarded as dangerous and debased as long as it is she, and she alone, who first introduces us as infants to the mixed blessing of being human. This is the core argument of The Mermaid and the Minotaur, *in which Dorothy Dinnerstein describes the asymmetry between men and women which we experience at the heart of all our social and sexual life.*[1] *To Dinnerstein, this asymmetry in sexual roles is being crucially reinforced by the way we continue (though with less and less biological necessity) to maintain infancy as a kingdom ruled only by mother.*

From this core idea proliferates a great number of observations about our partial, tenuous and deformed humanity. Men and women have divided up human traits between them and they have struck a bargain of interdependence.

Men agree to build the world while women agree both to support them in this struggle and to give vent, like harmless jesters, to the knowledge both sexes have that "there is something trivial and empty, ugly and sad, in what he does." A proverb records this bargain: Men must work and women must weep.

Traditionally, both sexes have felt fairly comfortable with this arrangement because both have been mother-reared. That is to say, both began life seeing "Woman" as an all powerful provider. As a result of this first memory of "Woman," she has always been defined as a quasi-person, as a sort of infinitely exploitable natural resource, which, like nature, has the power to turn nasty but which is bounteous when controlled. She bears the guilt for our discovery as infants that we cannot command the world, that we are flesh. Our mother's separate subjectivity, which is invisible to us as infants, later becomes an insult to our childish belief that she is there to serve us. We continue to feel that she is not, or should not be, a complete person in herself.

Males compensate for their original powerlessness by controlling women in the adult world. Female infants have the same ambivalent feelings of passionate love and rapacity toward their mothers, but since they must ultimately become female figures themselves, they split these feelings off from each other. They join with men in distrusting female power and share with men a preference for male leadership in adult life, a leadership they, too, see as cleaner, more finite than the overwhelming first power of "Mother." Women often sacrifice sexual impulsivity and many kinds of spontaneous and natural world-building activity to their fear of overwhelming men. They recognize the quality and source of male fear of woman and know that to call this fear forth is to break the tenuous balance which is the only promise of sexual partnership.

Dinnerstein argues that we are now at a moment in human history when the elaborate symbiosis between the sexes contributes to the undermining of our chances for survival as a species. The male project has gotten out of hand; it's gotten more and more abstracted and farther and farther away from

From *Feminist Studies,* Vol. 4, No. 2 (Summer 1978), pp. 190–98. Reprinted by permission of the publisher, Feminist Studies, Inc., c/o Women's Studies Program, University of Maryland, College Park, M.D. 20742. (Notes deleted.)

the original energies that were progressive in it. And the female absence from the male world-building project excludes traditions of nurturance from the public sphere that are now necessary for human survival.

In this crisis, Dinnerstein worries about the mothers. How will they manage during this period of painful transition? The percentage of time childbearing and childrearing must play in the lifespan of women is reduced; the old sexual divisions of labor are no longer technically necessary and must change if we are to adapt as a species to our shrinking resources. How will this enormous pressure toward change be enacted in our daily life? Right now women are left with their old tasks as mothers; they are asked to do new ones, to participate more directly than before in social change, while men, also aware that the old system is breaking down, are giving women less and less support for either their old tasks or their new.

Yet The Mermaid and the Minotaur *has its own species of qualified optimism. When a system breaks down, as our old sociosexual symbiosis is breaking down, there is a human drive to reconstruct. Dinnerstein offers her book as a suggestive map for this reconstruction. She puts up sign posts: Here, she says, are the reasons why women find it hard to work together in groups. (They fear the powerful mother in each other.) Here are women's strengths for allying with each other. (They have the deep first love of a woman—their mothers—to draw on as a source of intimacy and real sharing.) Here are the reasons why men are increasingly unable to protect and love us. (The world-building project traditionally theirs is in crisis. They must change their relation to that other first parent, mother nature, whom they once believed limitless in bounty or they—and we all—will die.)*

The political implication of Dinnerstein's argument is that men and women have to raise children together. Both men and women must guide children through their first encounter with life, through the pain of being helpless, of not knowing what the world is, of having to be channeled and controlled. Dinnerstein writes:

> *When men start participating as deeply as women in the initiation of infants into the human estate, when both male and female parents come to carry for all of us the special meanings of early childhood, the trouble we have reconciling these meanings with person-ness will finally be faced. The consequence, of course, will be a fuller and more realistic, and kinder and at the same time more demanding, definition of person-ness.*

And there would be other consequences. As long as we can use women as scapegoats for our discontents, we need not face the real tyrants. Dinnerstein insists that "the stone walls that activism runs into have buried foundations." She suspects that as long as we have conquered "Mother," the first tyrant we know, we are often content to suffer under other, less primitively frightening tyrants. Our rebellions are marred by our incomplete grasp of our shared human condition in which each one of us must both work and weep, both enterprise and criticize the products of our enterprise. The old sexual divisions have infantilized us, have bestialized us. To rebel, we must be more fully human.

*   *   *

The problem with summarizing Dinnerstein's argument in The Mermaid and the Minotaur *as I have tried to do here is that in both construction and meaning the book is complex and experimental. Dinnerstein refuses to simplify. Without ever calling the female monopoly of child care the cause of misogyny, oppression, tyranny, or the rape of nature by men, Dinnerstein makes it clear that there is an organic, dialectical connection among these things, that each one helps keep the others in place.*

Dinnerstein's male mentors such as Freud and Norman O. Brown have seen the primacy of "Mother" but they have assumed her symbolic meaning to infants as a biological constant. Dinnerstein's feminism has reordered their material, suddenly bringing female power over children into history and recognizing it as a condition that is always evolving and that now must be more radically and consciously altered if we are to develop in ways that we wish—and that we must—to survive as a species.

Few men have dared to write as circuitously and tentatively as Dinnerstein. Yet what man has said so much about "the division of responsibility, opportunity, and privilege that prevails between male and female humans, and the patterns of psychological interdependence that are implicit in this division," has stitched so many bits and pieces together, without succumbing to the temptation to snip off all the loose ends and neatly present a theory? When I say that Dinnerstein's writing is circular and inver- tebrate I mean that as the beginning of the highest praise. She is so aware that some things cannot be proved, that oversimplification will get us nowhere, and that recriminations are in vain, that she has removed herself from the usual categories of scholarship, science, and political writing. She is, very simply, one of the great humanists we have writing now. With this caveat to anyone who hopes that this summary can be any substitute for the original, rich and complex argument, let me move on to talk about Dinnerstein in quite another way.

A Conversation with Dinnerstein

> We are mermaids or minotaurs,
> only half human. We sense a
> monstrosity about ourselves.
> *Dorothy Dinnerstein*

About the maladaptive relations between man and woman which Dorothy Dinnerstein describes, I, and we all, have much too much experience.

Take the following scenes:

A male friend I've known well for years turns out to have a daughter. This fact comes out because I happen to tell him about *The Mermaid and the Minotaur*; other- wise I might never have known of it.

"How old is your daughter?"

My friend casts his head back and makes counting gestures with his fingers. Then he says, with some surprise, "She must be about six now!"

My friend doesn't think of his daughter as a secret; a perfect repression ob- viates the need for secrets. After making one hospital visit shortly after she was born, he has never seen his daughter again.

To me this fact is so stunning that I would like to take Dinnerstein's ideas about the loss we all sustain through the absence of our fathers during our first introduction to life and carve them with a cleaver on my friend's smooth and empty heart.

Another, pre-Dinnerstein memory:

A man I used to love once confided in me that he didn't think I would be a whole person, ever, if I didn't have a child. In my journal I wrote the following fantasy:

I am pregnant. (My lover dislikes birth control; it offends his potency, which my pregnancy proves.) I give him a choice: an abortion or he keeps the baby, not hiring some other woman to nurse it but taking care of it himself. Hating abortion far worse than birth control, he takes the second alternative. A daughter is born. When my lover brings my daughter to visit me, the baby cries and he is forced to interrupt himself to go and pick her up. The baby's schedule keeps him from taking trips or making money. I have a good job so I give him child support and I say, "A few more years like this, having the experiences of women,

and you'll be the wisest man in America." For the first time he begins to understand me. I stay away and don't mind that my daughter cries on the rare occasions I see her; after all, it's a wise child that knows its blood mother if that
mother has the freedom to go away and lacks the usual guilt to make her stay.
Meanwhile, my lover is bringing up my daughter. This experience is the only
one that could make him into a fit companion.

At the time I made this journal entry, I knew only that my lover had said something
unforgivable, and, worse, something against which I was powerless to defend myself. Now,
reading Dinnerstein has clarified these emotions: I had half thought I was a whole human
being; my friend reminded me that to him I was not. But, as Dinnerstein argues, this idea
is in itself cruelly inhuman. My friend was afraid of me as an autonomous creature, his mother
disturbingly off the leash and on the rampage in the world, or, to use Dinnerstein's metaphor,
his mother arisen from the dark, magical sea to walk on land. My lover told me I would
not be a complete human being without the experience of motherhood. I wrote my journal
entry to contradict him, to claim that it is he who needs this experience in order to be completely human.

These angry fantasies come naturally during our era of breakdown in what Dorothy
Dinnerstein calls our "asymmetrical sexual arrangements." The female desire to carve a political tract on the unresponsive male heart, the self-defeating fantasy of giving a child away—
these extremities are the products of desperation, dizzy efforts to correct an increasingly pathological imbalance in the roles of the sexes.

Motherhood is a condition in crisis. Whichever fantasy each one of us has, either dreaming
of leaving the baby with father forever or dreaming of taking the baby back from father (from
patriarchal control) and never letting him come near it again, either way we must eventually
find whatever is irreducible in motherhood, and whatever is malleable in it, and make a radical
change.

The two stories I have told are Dinnersteinian fables. In the first we see a man who
forgot the existence of his daughter. Her needs can have no modifying influence on what
he does in the world. He is Dinnerstein's minotaur, "mindless, greedy." He has escaped from
mother, and from the mother in himself.

The women in this first story are almost invisible: one is the mother who has been
left alone with her child; the other is the writer who wants to carve the truth of the mother's
oppression and the child's abandonment on the cold father's heart. But neither really knows
how to beard the minotaur in his far-off den. They are Dinnerstein's mermaids, able to love
the child but too socially powerless to do more than impotently rage at its father.

In my second story, the mother is now so angry that she refuses to become Dinnerstein's
"treacherous mermaid, seductive and impenetrable representative of the dark and magic underwater world from which our life comes." She tries to become like the man in the first
story; she leaves her child, ignores it when it cries. The woman in this story is the revolutionary, running fast because she knows the old world is just behind her. But to enter the male
world which is "free from the chagrins of the nursery," she must sacrifice other human parts
of herself. She outruns her own strengths; she exhausts herself. She needs to be nurtured by
the love and support of the man and of the child she has left behind, just as for generations
they both have flourished by being nurtured by her. If the father has been humanized by mothering, has become at last "a fit companion," then she can enjoy being fully human herself.
If he cannot be made a true parent, she is endlessly drawn toward one of two extremes—
either total immersion in motherhood or total renunciation of it—in a seesawing effort to
create a human balance.

In the world Dinnerstein describes and in the world of my stories there is not as yet a well-established middle ground where the humanness of the minotaur's world-building project and the humanness of the nurturant mother can meet. In her interest in the extremes, mermaid and minotaur, Dinnerstein is not saying there is no such middle ground in our actual social life, between these mythic, half-human roles. (In fact, she always insists that actual men and women do not, and luckily *cannot*, fit comfortably or neatly into these sexual roles.) Rather she is using the myths as metaphors to illustrate the barriers we put between ourselves and change: Dinnerstein is showing us the boxes so we can see how much time we actually spend outside them. *Both* sexes live inside the roles and outside them, but it is of course women who now feel this contradiction most sharply. When women struggle to create a human, middle position, to combine work, mothering and loving mother-reared men, we are in a condition of terrible stress. (It will surprise no one that Dorothy Dinnerstein once wrote an essay about Hans Christian Andersen's Little Mermaid who, to gain the love of the prince, gives up her tail and gets legs, a sign of wanting to grow up, love man, and be fully human. Andersen's Little Mermaid ends tragically; her prince is not human *enough*, not yet a fit companion; he doesn't recognize her for who she is and on his wedding day to another, she dies.)

I offer these two anecdotes from my journal almost at random. For me, Dinnerstein throws light everywhere. Speaking primarily about one class in one country, middle-class America, she nevertheless diagnoses social symptoms which I suspect further scholarship will confirm are present, and have been present, in very different classes and cultures. Many women have complained about *The Mermaid and the Minotaur* that they have heard this diagnosis before: Once again it is all the mother's fault; the powerful matriarch must be overthrown in order for civilization to progress. We have already heard more than enough about the fear of woman and very little about how to extricate ourselves from this labyrinth of feeling.

Dinnerstein's unique contribution is that she has given this tradition of the powerful mother its full and crushing weight in our history without finally being overwhelmed by it. She has an explanation for the fear and rejection of mother that makes sense. Without making light of the myth of the terrible mother she nevertheless demythologizes it. Without claiming that mother-centered childcare is the *cause* of inequalities between men and women, she nevertheless sees how it confirms us in these inequalities, makes us comfortable with them.

It's easy to misread Dinnerstein at this point, to think that hers is a reductionist's argument: but she offers no primary cause for female oppression, no simple panacea. Instead her discussion is a web of connections and descriptions proliferating from what is, in fact, a rather humble core. Dinnerstein has one thing to say and she tries to say it keeping all its connections with other matters intact. Instead of a linear argument, her book is really a grid whose lines trail off the page where she cannot always follow them, though one often feels how much she would like to. For this very reason it is easy to be frustrated by *The Mermaid and the Minotaur.* It raises more questions than it can answer. And to make its positive point, it must again emphasize the negative side of mother in a world which we feel has done that enough already.

In fact, in many respects this book is a mother it's easy to reject. There are so many things it cannot do for us. It fails to incorporate theoretically the enormous ego strength of women, and their very real contribution to world-building so far. It fails to offer any material suggestions for how new childrearing structures could enter our society. It fails to identify clearly (though it often mentions) the cracks in our present situation which might be the points at which changes could most easily be made. What about working-class families where the mother is forced to be absent from the home and is a worker in the world? What about large families where children rear each other? What about families where the father is such a tyrant he can never represent for his children an easier alternative to the first, loved parent? Don't other cultures offer evidence of politically suggestive variations in childcare arrangements?

Can countercultural experiments really change the mainstream as Dinnerstein hopes and, if so, by what mechanism? What is to prevent the experimenters from becoming the same sort of useless jesters that Dinnerstein says women have always been? How can we more scientifically assess the metaphoric power of Mother in the first two years of life? For example, in a more sexually balanced social environment could the five-year-old's discoveries of the social similarities between Mommy and Daddy eventually change the overall metaphoric meaning of conscious and subconscious memories? How much can we change the biological primacy of the mother-child tie in the first year of life and how much *should* we change it?

These are legitimate questions about Dinnerstein's work. (In fact, if one reads closely, *The Mermaid and the Minotaur* raises each one of these questions somewhere or other in a box or a note or a parenthesis) but Dinnerstein cannot answer them. At an interview when I asked her these questions she asked them back at me. They are, very simply, our biggest human questions.[2]

Some women have told me they think that Dinnerstein is too accepting of our patriarchal past. (Certainly my two stories are more unfriendly to men than anything in her book.) Indeed she grants the past its charms. As she said to Jane Lazarre, "The way things go between men and women are so deeply tied up with what we need in a positive way, that we have good reasons for being reluctant to let go of them. If it were not for the fact that now our sexual arrangements are part and parcel of what's killing us, I doubt that we would be tampering with them." This is Dinnerstein's profundity as a social thinker, her wisdom as a psychologist. She is friendly toward our peculiar double nature: We have been and still are mermaids and minotaurs, but this asymmetry in our lives has always frustrated us, has always propelled us out of ourselves toward new forms of social life:

> Our prevailing male-female arrangement is rooted in our biological history; it is part of what we have always been. Yet the feelings that make us restless with it—an intolerance of constriction, a resentment of bondage, an urge to grow— are also part of what we have always been.

Dinnerstein admires the human spirit, our capacity for self-transformation. A revolutionary thinker, a historical materialist, she shows us to be always in the process of revolutionizing the conditions of our social life.

She is also a feminist, one who believes that it is women who must make the next step in our species' self-creation. Without calling men villains, Dinnerstein nevertheless believes them to have too many vested interests in the present system to find the strength to change it. Women, she says, will be the ones to change it, if it is to be changed at all.

Notes

1. Dorothy Dinnerstein, author of *The Mermaid and the Minotaur: Sexual Arrangements and Human Malaise* (New York: Harper & Row, 1976) is a professor of psychology at the Institute for Cognitive Studies, Rutgers-Newark.

   Dorothy Dinnerstein is presently working on another piece of the vast project of which *The Mermaid and the Minotaur* is a part, the project of understanding how our species' traditional social arrangements are now threatening our species' very life. As Dinnerstein describes this next project: "What the book will survey—drawing both upon experimental data and upon descriptive analysis of my own and the reader's life experience—is a number of weaknesses (soft spots or cracks, so to speak) in the human sense of reality, weaknesses which have not been grave enough to menace our survival in the past, but which do menace it in the face of the situation we have by this time gotten ourselves into, and which we may be able to outgrow."

2. My long interview with Dr. Dinnerstein (Spring 1977) deals with the implications of her book for women living alone with children, for feminists, etc.

Study Questions

1. In writing about Dorothy Dinnerstein's text *The Mermaid and the Minotaur,* what does Ann Snitow see as Dinnerstein's central argument?
2. What crisis does Dinnerstein say we now face? Why does Snitow say Dinnerstein is in a way an optimist about resolving that crisis?
3. What fundamental shift in male/female relations does Dinnerstein advocate?
4. Snitow recounts a story in which she induces her lover to raise their daughter. What is the point of her parable?
5. How does Snitow address the question: If Dinnerstein is a feminist, why does she seem to place the blame for women's oppression on mothers?

Prostitution

Alison M. Jaggar

Prostitution has long been referred to as "the social evil."[1] "Whore" or "tart" has long been the ultimate epithet to be hurled against women. Social reformers, feminists and government agencies have long sought, in their various ways, to put an end to the sale of sexual services. But there are signs that this centuries-old taboo is about to be reversed. Prostitutes themselves have organized unions calling for the decriminalization of prostitution. A recent survey showed that 59% of Republican voters favored its legalization in the United States. And her supposedly autobiographical series detailing the life of "the happy hooker" have made Xaviera Hollander a best-selling author.

Is there any reason to oppose the decriminalization of prostitution or even the western European innovation of publicly raising capital to finance prostitution hostels? The conditions of modern society appear to have undermined many traditional arguments against prostitution. Venereal disease can be detected quickly and treated effectively. Illegitimacy can be prevented by modern contraceptive techniques; indeed, prostitutes now have a lower fertility rate than other women. And changing sexual mores mean that sexual activity outside the marriage bed is increasingly taken for granted. To decide how to respond to these developments, we need a philosophical theory of prostitution. Such a theory should state exactly what prostitution is, should tell us what, if anything, is wrong with it and should help us determine what, if anything, should be done about it. In this paper, unfortunately, I am not able to offer a full-fledged theory of prostitution. Instead, I compare the relative merits of three attempts to provide such a theory and identify the philosophical basis on which a comprehensive theory of prostitution must rest. Thus I view my paper as a prolegomenon to a theory of prostitution.

From Alan G. Soble, ed., *Philosophy of Sex* (Totowa, NJ: Littlefield, Adams, 1980). © 1980 by Alison Jaggar. Reprinted by permission of Alison Jaggar. (Notes deleted.)

The three approaches to prostitution that I shall discuss are the liberal, the classical Marxist, and the radical feminist approaches. Obviously, these do not comprise all possible views on prostitution. I choose them in part because they are all current views and in part because I find them all, to some extent, plausible. In addition, they provide interesting contrasts not only in moral and political theory but in their accounts of just what they take prostitution to be. Each begins from the paradigm case of the prostitute as a woman selling her sexual services, but each picks out very different features as essential to that situation. Thus, a comparison of these theories of prostitution illustrates an important general point about the appropriate philosophical methodology for approaching not only the issue of prostitution but also a number of other normative social issues.

Liberalism

The standard liberal position on prostitution is that it should be decriminalized. This was the conclusion of the 1963 British *Wolfenden Report of the Committee on Homosexual Offences and Prostitution* and it is the view of the American Civil Liberties Union. The Wolfenden Committee argued that "private immorality should not be the concern of the criminal law."[2] They believed that the function of the law was not "to punish prostitution *per se*," but rather to regulate "those activities which offend against public order and decency or expose the ordinary citizen to what is offensive or injurious."[3] Hence, they argued that prostitutes might be arrested for "importuning" but neither they nor their customers should be subject to any penalties for actually engaging in prostitution.

The American Civil Liberties Union argues that laws prohibiting prostitution are unconstitutional on several grounds. For one thing, they deny equal protection of the law to women. In some states, prostitution statutes apply only to females. Indeed, according to traditional case law, a prostitute is by definition female; thus by legal definition a man cannot be a prostitute. The male customer of a female prostitute, moreover, is rarely subject to legal penalty while the female prostitute invariably is. In these and other ways, prostitution laws discriminate against women. Another argument for the unconstitutionality of prostitution laws is that they often treat the mere status of being a prostitute as an offense, thereby inflicting "cruel and unusual punishment." And the use of loitering as a criterion for prostitution is said to violate a woman's right to due process. Finally, the ACLU argues that prohibitions on prostitution are an invasion of the individual's right to control his or her body without unreasonable interference from the state. This last argument is the most important, for it entails that prohibition laws cannot simply be "tidied up" by such reforms as writing them in gender neutral language or by insisting on strict standards of evidence before convicting someone of prostitution. Instead, it argues that there should be no law prohibiting prostitution.

> The private sexual act involved in prostitution is no less a personal right for being commercial. Therefore, the government should not be able to prohibit it unless the state can meet the very heavy burden of proof that banning it is beneficial to society.[4]

This author even goes beyond the Wolfenden Report by arguing that solicitation for prostitution should be decriminalized. She doubts that it is genuinely offensive to men and claims that "to legalize prostitution while prohibiting solicitation makes as much sense as encouraging free elections but prohibiting campaigning."[5]

Their agreement on the decriminalization of prostitution does not mean that liberals share a common view about its moral status. Liberal feminists have always seen prostitution as degrading to women and conclude that it should receive no encouragement even though it should be decriminalized. This attitude is implicit in the report of the NOW Task Force on prostitution which supports

> full prosecution of any acts of coercion to any person, public agency or group to influence women to become prostitutes.[6]

Others, however, claim to see nothing wrong with prostitution. Some prostitutes view themselves as entrepreneurs, choosing to go into business for themselves rather than to work for someone else. One prostitute remarked that the work was really not tiring, that it was often less humiliating than dating. The prostitute may see herself as the boss because she can say "No" to the deal; as someone, therefore, who is less exploited than exploiting. Thus it may be argued that decriminalization will finally allow "the oldest profession" to take its place among the other professions so that prostitutes will be respected as offering a skilled service.

These liberal reflections on the moral status of prostitution, however, are generally taken as mere side comments. The central liberal line of argument is to stress the need for decriminalization by appeal to classical liberal ideals. Thus, liberal arguments emphasize the importance of equality before the law and of individual rights. They attempt to minimize government interference in the lives of individuals and they assume that there is a "private" sphere of human existence

> comprehending all that portion of a person's life and conduct which affects only himself (*sic*) or if it affects others, only with their free, voluntary and undeceived consent and participation.[7]

Prostitution, they believe, falls obviously within that sphere.

The usual liberal recommendation on prostitution, then, is that it should be treated as an ordinary business transaction, the sale of a service; in this case, of a sexual service. Because the prostitute engages in it out of economic motivation, liberals view prostitution as quite different from a sexual act committed by physical force or under threat of force; they view prostitution as quite different, for instance, from rape. Instead, they see it as a contract like other contracts, entered into by each individual for her or his own benefit, each striking the best bargain that she or he is able. The state has exactly the same interest in the prostitution contract as in all other contracts and may therefore regulate certain aspects by law. For instance, the law may concern itself with such matters as hygiene, control of disease, minimum standards of service and of working conditions, misleading advertising, payment of taxes and social security, etc. It should also ensure equal opportunity by redrawing the legal definition of prostitution so that an individual of either sex may be a prostitute. In these sorts of ways, the state would fulfill its traditional liberal function of ensuring fair trading practices. It should assure consumers of "a clean lay at a fair price."[8]

At first sight, the liberal approach to prostitution seems refreshingly straightforward and uncomplicated. As so often happens, however, this appearance is deceptive. One problem concerns the normative assumption that prostitution is a contract whose legitimacy is equal to that of other business contracts. Although liberals view the paradigmatic social relation as contractual, they do not believe that all contracts are legitimate. Mill, for instance, denied the legitimacy of contracts by which individuals permanently abdicated or alienated their freedom to decide on future courses of action, and on this ground he argued that the state should not enforce either lifelong marriage contracts or contracts where an individual sold her- or himself into slavery. Similarly, Joel Feinberg offers a number of different arguments which suggest why voluntary slavery contracts may be illegitimate. For instance, he suggests that it is inherently immoral to own another person and that such immorality ought to be forbidden by law; and he also suggests, on what he calls Kantian grounds, that we may not dispose of our "humanity" and that attempts to do so should not be recognized by law.[9] Without examining all the liberal arguments in detail, it is clear that the early liberal conviction that the primary purpose of the state was to uphold the sanctity of contracts has been weakened in contemporary times and liberals now also expect the state

> to provide against those contracts being made which, from the helplessness of one of the parties to them, instead of being a security for freedom, become an instrument of disguised oppression.[10]

These restrictions on legitimate contracts might be strong enough to exclude prostitution. It may well be that prostitution constitutes the sort of selling of oneself that a liberal would refuse to countenance. And it is surely not implausible to consider many prostitution contracts as instruments of not very well disguised oppression. Those liberals, therefore, are being too hasty who simply assume the legitimacy of prostitution contracts. In order to establish that prostitution is simply an ordinary business contract, they need a clear theory of what kinds of contracts are legitimate. (Robert Nozick, for instance, believes that the law should recognize and enforce people's right to sell themselves even into slavery.)[11] And they need a clear analysis of prostitution together with a normative theory of sexuality.

Liberal writers have not devoted much attention to the latter question at least. Since they ordinarily assume that sexual relations fall within the "private" realm and hence are outside the sphere of legal regulation, the development of a normative theory of sexuality has not seemed important for their political philosophy. Their main contribution to the analysis of prostitution has been to insist that a prostitute may be either male or female. Thus, liberals would rewrite laws regarding prostitution in gender-neutral language and would also, presumably, wish to revise the first part of the definition of "prostitution" in *Webster's New Twentieth Century Dictionary* which currently reads:

> *prostitute, n.* 1, a woman who engages in promiscuous sexual intercourse for pay; whore; harlot.

Here, liberals would presumably substitute "person" for "woman" and would construe "sexual intercourse" broadly enough to cover sexual encounters between individuals of either sex. Such an interpretation would also allow so-called massage parlors within the definition of "prostitution." This liberal revision of the concept of prostitution may seem at first sight to be in line with common usage, with common sense and with common justice. As we shall see, however, there are other accounts of prostitution which draw the boundaries quite differently.

A final problem with the liberal position on prostitution concerns its assumption that the prostitute enters into the transaction voluntarily. It has often been pointed out in other contexts that the liberal concept of coercion is very weak. It may well turn out that the sorts of economic considerations that impel some persons into prostitution do indeed constitute a sort of coercion and that the prostitution contract may therefore be invalidated on those grounds. This is one of the objections made by the Marxist theory of prostitution, to which I now turn.

Marxism

The Marxist approach to prostitution is considerably wider-ranging than the liberal approach, both because it attempts to understand prostitution in its social context and because it construes prostitution much more broadly. For instance, Marxists view prostitution as including not only the sale of an individual's sexual services; they see it also as the exchange of all those tangible and intangible services that a married woman provides to her husband in return for economic support. Sometimes they believe that prostitution may cover even the exchange of the services that a man provides when he marries a rich woman.

Whether or not marriage is a form of prostitution is determined, for the Marxist, by the economic class of the marriage partners. It is only where property is involved that marriage degenerates into prostitution; where no property is involved, for instance among the proletariat, marriage is based solely on mutual inclination. Thus Engels writes that, within the bourgeoisie,

> the marriage is conditioned by the class position of the parties and is to that extent always a marriage of convenience. . . . this marriage of convenience turns often enough into the crassest prostitution—sometimes of both partners, but far more commonly of the woman, who only differs from the ordinary courtesan in that she does not let out her body on piecework as a wageworker, but sells it once and for all into slavery. And of all marriages of convenience Fourier's words hold true: "As in grammar two negatives make an affirmative, so in matrimonial morality two prostitutions pass for a virtue."[12]

In describing bourgeois marriage as a form of prostitution, Marx and Engels assume not only that men as well as women may prostitute themselves; they assume also that what is sold may not be restricted to sexual services. From this, it is but a short step to describing the sale of a number of other services as types of prostitution. Indeed, in the *Economic and Philosophical Manuscripts*, Marx asserts that all wage labor is a form of prostitution. He writes, "Prostitution (in the ordinary sense) is only a *specific* expression of the *general* prostitution of the *labourer.*"[13]

Someone might object that this usage of Marx's is merely metaphorical, that he is simply utilizing the pejorative connotations of "prostitution" in order to condemn wage labor. But the following entry in *Webster's New Twentieth Century Dictionary* supports the claim that Marx's broader usage is not metaphorical:

> *prostitute, n.* 2. a person, as a writer, artist, etc., who sells his services for low or unworthy purposes.

If *Webster's* too is mistaken, and if there is indeed a philosophically significant distinction to be made between the woman who sells sexual services and the individual who sells services of any kind, then that distinction must be given a philosophical rationale.

Does the Marxist corpus contain such a rationale or does it, on the other hand, provide a reason for assimilating wage labor to prostitution? I think that it contains traces of both but that the tendency to assimilate prostitution to wage labor is probably stronger. Some of Engel's objections to prostitution in the narrower sense seem to depend on two specific normative beliefs about sexuality, that sex should be linked with love and that "sexual love is by its nature exclusive."[14] It is because of the latter belief that he worries, since he views both monogamy and prostitution as results of the same state of affairs (namely, male ownership of the means of production), whether "prostitution [can] disappear without dragging monogamy with it into the abyss?"[15] He is anxious to make monogamy, or at any rate sexual fidelity, "a reality—also for men."[16] Similarly, he wants to make the "paper"[17] description of bourgeois marriage into a reality by turning an economic transaction into a free agreement based on mutual sex-love. He writes:

> Full freedom of marriage can therefore only be generally established when the abolition of capitalist production and of the property relations created by it has

> removed all the accompanying economic considerations which still exert such a powerful influence on the choice of a marriage partner. For then there is no other motive left except mutual inclination.[18]

Unfortunately, the theory of sexuality on which these objections to prostitution are based is left undeveloped. We are given no reason to believe that Engels's notion of "modern individual sex-love," which he describes as "the greatest moral advance we owe to [monogamy],"[19] is in fact anything more than a romantic Victorian prejudice.

Even if our intuitions about sexual relations do not agree with Engels's, however, I do not think that we are necessarily thrown back to the liberal view about prostitution. Instead I believe that it is possible to draw from the Marxist corpus another, more searching, more plausible, and more specifically Marxist critique of prostitution. This critique, however, is very similar to the critique of wage labor and thus leads us in the direction of assimilating female prostitution to the wage labor of either sex.

There are a number of different ways of explaining Marx's critique of the system of wage labor. In his earlier works, Marx stresses the concept of alienation, the estrangement of wage laborers from the process and the product of their work, from their co-workers and from their humanity itself. In his later works, Marx drops the terminology of alienation; there is considerable controversy over whether he retained the central ideas or whether there is an "epistemological break" between his earlier and his later work. Certainly in his later work Marx seems concerned to detail in a more concrete way the devastating consequences to the worker of the capitalist system. He shows how the bodies of wage laborers are distorted by industrial diseases and how their minds are damaged by the boredom of repetitive tasks. Under capitalism, he argues, workers become mere appendages to their machines, no longer human beings but merely factors in the capitalist production process. Their human capacity to work becomes reduced to the commodity of labor power and the value of this is measured not in terms of its ability to provide useful products but merely in terms of its price on the labor market. In both his earlier and his later work, Marx stresses the lack of genuine freedom that exists under capitalism. In particular, he argues that so-called free wage labor is free only in the sense that it is no longer limited by the medieval laws restricting entry into the labor market. But although individuals are free to decide for which capitalist enterprise they want to work, they are not free to refuse wage labor entirely. In order to survive, they are forced to become wage laborers. The Marxist analysis of the position of women under capitalism is notoriously sketchy; in fact, the classic analysis was left to Engels after Marx's death. Engels's explanation of the special oppression faced by women under capitalism appeals to women's exclusion from wage labor and argues that women's liberation requires that they should be drawn into "public production." Nevertheless, in spite of the importance that they place on the distinction between those who are engaged in capitalist production and those who are not, there are a number of places where Marx and Engels seem to draw parallels between the situation of women under capitalism and the situation of wage-laborers. For instance, in *The Communist Manifesto* Marx and Engels claim that the bourgeois fear that the communists will introduce "community of women" stems from the fact that

> the bourgeois sees in his wife a mere instrument of production. He hears that the instruments of production are to be exploited in common, and, naturally, can come to no other conclusions than that the lot of being common to all will likewise fall to women.[20]

Both the bourgeois wife and the wage laborer, therefore, can be seen as "instruments of production," the latter of commodities, the former of babies. Prostitutes in the narrower, more conventional sense cannot be viewed in this way, of course. They perform a service rather than create a product. Nevertheless, Marx presents prostitution as a paradigm case of the sort of alienated relationships that are created by capitalism, where money substitutes for concrete human characteristics. He writes that, under capitalism,

> What I am and can do is, therefore, not at all determined by my individuality. I am ugly, but I can buy the most beautiful woman for myself. Consequently, I am not ugly, for the effect of ugliness, its power to repel, is annulled by money.[21]

Just as the capacity to labor becomes a commodity under capitalism, so does sexuality, especially the sexuality of women. Thus prostitutes, like wage laborers, have an essential human capacity alienated. Like wage laborers, they become dehumanized and their value as persons is measured by their market price. And like wage laborers, they are compelled to work by economic pressure; prostitution, if not marriage, may well be the best option available to them.

On the Marxist view, prostitution and wage labor (in so far as they are still separable) degrade not only the prostitute and the wage laborer. They dehumanize also the prostitute's client and the laborer's employer. Marx writes:

> in the approach to *woman* as the spoil and handmaid of communal lust is expressed the infinite degradation in which man exists for himself.[22]

Engels goes further. He writes that prostitution

> demoralizes men far more than women. Among women, prostitution degrades only the unfortunate ones who become its victims, and even these by means to the extent commonly believed. But it degrades the whole male world.[23]

(The last sentence provides an interesting comment on the extent of prostitution in Victorian England.) Marx describes the capitalist in a similar way:

> Prostitution is only a *specific* expression of the *general* prostitution of the *labourer*, and since it is a relationship in which falls not the prostitute alone, but also the one who prostitutes—and the latter's abomination is still greater—the capitalist, etc., also comes under this head.[24]

Given this critique, it is hardly surprising to find in *The Communist Manifesto* the explicit statement that it is necessary to abolish "prostitution both public and private."[25] But Marx and Engels certainly do not suggest that this end may be achieved by legal prohibition. Since all forms of prostitution result from inequality of wealth, such inequality must be eliminated. And in our time this means that capitalism must be abolished. For it is capitalism that gives men control over the means of production, thus forcing women to sell their bodies and allowing men to maintain a sexual double standard in marriage. And of course it is capitalism, by definition, that maintains the wage system and so forces the majority of the population to prostitute themselves by selling whatever capacities to labor that they may possess. Thus Marxists believe that the elimination of prostitution demands a full communist revolution. Until then, in one way or another, "capital screws us all."

The Marxist discussion of prostitution is illuminating in many respects. It brings out the real economic coercion underlying the apparently free market contract and the parallels between prostitution and wage labor must still raise questions for some people, as no doubt they did for a Victorian audience, about the moral status of the system of wage labor. (It is perhaps a measure of how far contemporary populations have internalized bourgeois values that it is possible for liberals nowadays to use the comparison not to discredit wage labor but rather to rehabilitate prostitution.) Certainly, the philosophical assimilation of prostitution to wage labor is supported by the two entries in *Webster's Dictionary*. But this assimilation may not only be illuminating. It may also obscure certain important differences between prostitution and wage labor. It may not be a matter of indifference whether the prostitute is male or female or whether it is an individual's sexuality that is sold rather than her or his capacity to labor. Radical feminism argues that an adequate account of prostitution requires an emphasis on the feminine gender of the prostitute and the sexual nature of her service.

Radical Feminism

For contemporary radical feminists, prostitution is the archetypal relationship of women to men. Karen Lindsey sums it up this way:

> We have long held that all women sell themselves: that the only available roles of a woman—wife, secretary, girlfriend— all demand the selling of herself to one or more men.[26]

Even a century ago, some feminists saw marriage as a form of prostitution and as long ago as 1909 Cicely Hamilton wrote that, although a woman cannot predict before marriage which of an infinite variety of possible tasks her husband may expect her to perform,

> the only thing she can be fairly certain of is that he will require her to fulfill his idea of personal attractiveness. As a matter of business, then, and not purely from vanity, she specialises in personal attractiveness.[27]

Contemporary radical feminists have extended this insight and now perceive most social interaction between women and men as some form of prostitution. Thus, they believe that almost every man/woman encounter has sexual overtones and typically is designed to reinforce the sexual dominance of men. Correspondingly, men reward this sexual service in a variety of ways: the payment may range from a very tangible dinner to the intangible but nonetheless essential provision of male approval and patronage. Paradoxically, radical feminists argue, some women are even forced to prostitute themselves by selling their celibacy. They may retain their alimony or their social security payments only by remaining ''chaste.''[28]

This radical feminist view contrasts both with liberalism and with Marxism in its insistence that prostitutes must be defined as women. It differs from liberalism in its broad construal of what constitutes sexual services and from Marxism in its refusal to assimilate prostitution to other types of wage labor. It sees the social function of prostitution primarily as a means neither for sexual enjoyment nor for profit. Instead, radical feminists see prostitution as an institution to assert the dominance and power of men over women.

With respect to prostitution in the narrow conventional sense, radical feminists admit that it may indeed satisfy the physical desires of men, but they see this as being only a subsidiary function. Primarily, they believe,

> Prostitution exists to meet the desire of men to degrade women. Studies made by men reveal that very few even pretend they frequent prostitutes primarily for sexual gratification. Young boys admit they go to achieve a sense of male camaraderie and freedom. They usually go in groups and gossip about it at length afterward in a way that is good for their egos. Other men have expressed the prime motive as the desire to reaffirm the basic ''filth'' of all women; or to clearly separate

"good" from "bad" women in their minds, or for the opportunity to treat another person completely according to personal whim.[29]

In addition, conventional prostitution is seen as a way of controlling other women who are not culturally defined as prostitutes.

> The existence of a category of women defined by this function of sex object, plus the fact that every woman must guard against "slipping" into this category or being assigned to it (and the absence of a comparable group of men), is suffi-cient to understanding prostitution as oppressive to all women. By the ubiqui-tous "threat" of being treated like a "common prostitute" we are kept in our places and our freedom is further contracted.[30]

Thus,

> The [prostitution] laws are fundamental to the male protection racket—to main-taining most women as private rather than public property.[31]

From this account of prostitution, it is clear that the radical feminist does not regard it as a morally neutral institution, either in the narrow or in the broad form. The radical feminist denies the liberal contention that conventional prostitution is a victimless crime. The victims are all women, but particularly the prostitutes themselves, outcast, degraded and ex-ploited by all the men who, directly or indirectly, enjoy the benefits of prostitution. Prostitu-tion in its broad form is, of course, no more acceptable to the radical feminist. But,

> Unlike religious reforms of the past, feminists do not base opposition to pros-titution on anti-sex values. Just as with marriage, our opposition is to the economics of the situation. Sex is a fine thing when it is the free choice of the individuals involved—free of economic coercion. No one should be dependant on selling herself for support; all love should be free love.[32]

So it is the economic coercion underlying prostitution, which requires that a woman's sex-uality can be expressed only in a manner pleasing to men, that provides the basic feminist objection to prostitution. This economic coercion means that ultimately the moral status of prostitution is identical with that of rape. Like rape, prostitution perpetuates the oppression of women by encouraging the view that women are mere sexual objects, hence reinforcing male dominance and female inferiority.

Needless to say, radical feminists want to eliminate prostitution in all its forms. For this, they see two preconditions. One is that the male demand for prostitutes should be eliminated. This requires a total transformation of men's attitudes toward women and it also requires the abandonment of such conventional myths about male sexuality as that men have a much stronger biological appetite for sex than women. When masculinity is no longer so inseparably tied to heterosexual performance, feminists hypothesize that men will no longer demand prostitutes.

Recognition that the demand for prostitutes is not a biological inevitability is a com-paratively recent insight in our culture. But feminists have always recognized that the *supply* of prostitutes is a function of women's inferior social status. Over fifty years ago Emma Goldman remarked:

> Nowhere is woman treated according to the merit of her work but rather as a sex. It is therefore almost inevitable that she should pay for her right to exist,

to keep a position in whatever line, with sex favors. Thus it is merely a question of degree whether she sells herself to one man, in or out of marriage, or to many men. Whether our reformers admit it or not, the economic and social inferiority of woman is responsible for prostitution.[33]

Radical feminists believe, therefore, that the eradication of prostitution requires the abolition of the male monopoly of economic power together with an abandonment of the view that women are primarily sexual objects. So long as these two interdependent conditions exist, almost any significant transaction between a woman and a man must be a form of prostitution. Susan Brownmiller sums it up:

> Prostitution will not end in this country until men see women as equals. And men will never see women as equals until there's an end to prostitution. So it seems that we will have to work for the full equality of women and the end to prostitution side by side.[34]

These two tasks are indistinguishable. And, until they are achieved, radical feminists believe that, contrary to what conventional morality may indicate, women are confronted by a choice which is morally indistinguishable: it is the choice between "sucking cock and kissing ass."[35]

To many people and especially to many men, the radical feminist account of prostitution seems startling and offensive. A number of objections to it spring immediately to mind. In order to try to make the radical feminist account more plausible, I shall outline some of these objections and probable radical feminist answers to them.

One common objection to the radical feminist view of prostitution argues that it is preposterous to suppose that, when a man brings gifts to a woman he loves or takes her out to dinner, he is treating her as a prostitute. Such gestures are intended and should be received simply as tokens of affection. The radical feminist answer to this objection is that individuals' intentions do not necessarily indicate the true nature of what is going on. Both man and woman might be outraged at the description of their candlelit dinner as prostitution, but the radical feminist argues this outrage is due simply to the participants' failure or refusal to perceive the social context in which their dinner date occurs. This context is deeply sexist: the chances are that the man has more economic power than the woman; and it is certain that much of woman's social status depends on her attractiveness as defined by men. For women in our society are defined culturally as sexual objects so that "every day in a woman's life is a walking Miss America contest."[36] In these circumstances, it is almost inevitable that the man is buying "his idea of personal attractiveness."

But "almost inevitable" is not inevitable. It may be true that many more dinner dates are forms of prostitution than would appear at first sight. But surely it is not logically necessary that a man is prostituting a woman when he takes her out to dinner. What about the occasions when she pays for herself? Or even when she pays for him? Surely it is logically possible for a woman to treat a man as a prostitute? Some men even define themselves as prostitutes.

Here again the radical feminists point to the social context. They point out that the customers of so-called male prostitutes are invariably men and they argue that much of the indignity of being a so-called prostitute, for a man, is that he is being forced to assume what is paradigmatically a woman's role, that he is being feminized. Radical feminists argue that there is an asymmetry in social attitudes towards man's and women's sexuality. The portly, grey-haired man with the young blonde woman on his arm is viewed with nudges, envy and even admiration. But the portly, grey-haired woman, if she were ever able to induce a young blonde man to lend her his arm, would be viewed with scorn, ridicule or pity. She is viewed as being "used" by her young gigolo in a way that even a "golddigging" young woman is not able to use her older lover. For, given the different social status of women and men in our society, it is always true that, in sexual encounters between women and men, a man "has" and a woman "is had." And when a man "has" another man, he is depriving him of his masculine status. Young dependent males in prison are even referred to as "women."

In arguing that prostitution is paradigmatically a relation of women to men, radical feminists are remembering the sexism that has structured our history and that continues to pervade every aspect of contemporary life. They are remembering that women appear to have been defined always as "sexual objects" and that the "traffic in women" appears to have been the earliest form of exchange.[37] They are remembering that people's personal identity is grounded on their gender-identity so firmly that, while they may "pass" for black or white or be upwardly or downwardly mobile from their class, any attempt to change their gender is met inevitably with extreme anxiety, confusion and even hostility. They are remembering that a defining feature of gender is the way in which sexuality is expressed so that homosexuals, for instance, are commonly viewed as failing to be appropriately masculine or feminine. And finally, radical feminists are remembering that not only is gender in general tied up inextricably with sexuality but also that femininity in particular is defined in large part by the ability to be attractive sexually to men. Most women have internalized the need to be "attractive" in this way and even those who have not done so usually cannot afford to be indifferent to men's opinions. Whether housewife or wage-earner, therefore, and whether or not she allows genital contact, a woman must sell her sexuality. And since, unlike a man, she is defined largely in sexual terms, when she sells her sexuality she sells herself.

Toward a Philosophical Theory of Prostitution

Although these arguments may not establish conclusively the correctness of the radical feminist approach to prostitution, they do make it much more plausible. And the questions raised by radical feminism help to determine what is required for a philosophical account of prostitution that is adequate.

First of all, an adequate account of prostitution requires a philosophical theory of sexuality. Such a theory must be in part conceptual, in part normative. It must help us to draw the conceptual boundaries of sexual activity, enabling us to answer both how nongenital activity can still be sexual and even how genital activity may not be sexual. Given our ordinary ways of thinking, this latter suggestion may sound paradoxical but it is becoming a commonplace for feminists to define rape as a form of physical assault rather than as a form of sexual expression. Similarly, some feminists are now insisting that prostitution raises no issues of *sexual* privacy: "Prostitution is a professional or economic option, unrelated to sexual/emotional needs."[38] And we have seen other feminists deny that the main purpose of prostitution is sexual, even for men. Not only must the needed philosophical theory of sexuality help us to identify just what sexual activity is; it must also help us to make the conceptual connections and distinctions between forms of sexual expression on the one hand and gender and personal identity on the other hand. It must clarify the relationship, if any, between sexual expression and love. And it must compare the human capacity for sexual activity to the human capacity to labor. Thus it must tell us, for instance, whether there is anything especially degrading about the sale of sexual services.

An adequate account of prostitution also rests, obviously, on a philosophical account of coercion. In particular, we need to know whether economic inducements are coercive and, if so, in what circumstances. Only from this philosophical basis can we work out the conceptual relationships between prostitution, rape and "free enterprise."

In addition to these conceptual and normative presuppositions, a useful account of prostitution also requires an investigation of the way in which the institution functions in contemporary society. We need to know why women engage in prostitution and why men do so. We need to understand the relationship between "the traffic in women" and other forms of exchange in our society; in other words, we need to understand the political economy of prostitution. Without such knowledge, our account of prostitution will remain at a very high level of abstraction; we will not be able to understand the specific phenomenon of prostitution in contemporary society, we shall not be able to determine what, if anything, is wrong with it and what, if anything, ought to be done about it.

But how can we ever arrive at these decisions when the various theorists, liberal, Marxist and radical feminist, all hold such widely different concepts of prostitution? Not only do the theorists disagree on what is wrong with prostitution and on what ought to be done about it; they even disagree on what it is. They each accept the paradigm case of a woman selling sexual services, but each presents a very different analysis of that paradigm case. For example, the radical feminist argues that the gender of the seller is essential to determining whether a situation is a case of prostitution, the liberal insists that it is the sale of a sexual service that is the central feature, while the Marxist focuses on the sale of an important human capacity by an individual of either sex.

How is this disagreement to be resolved? Is there a single correct analysis of prostitution on which we must agree before we can construct a normative moral and political theory about it? And is such a correct analysis to be found by looking up dictionary definitions or paying closer attention to ordinary usage?

I do not think so. I think that the issue of prostitution presents a clear example of the futility of that conventional wisdom which recommends that we begin by defining our terms. For the divergence in the competing definitions of prostitution does not result from failing to consult the dictionary or from paying insufficient attention to ordinary usage. It results from normative disagreements on what constitutes freedom, on the moral status of certain activities and, ultimately, on a certain view of what it means to be human. Thus, the disagreement on what constitutes prostitution is merely a surface manifestation of a disagreement over the fundamental categories to be used in describing social activities and over what are the important features of social life which need to be picked out. The inability of moral theorists to agree on what constitutes prostitution is an instance of the interdependence of principles and intuitions, of theory and data, even of fact and value.

The only conclusion that I draw from all this is perhaps the obvious one that prostitution is far from being a self-contained moral or political issue. What prostitution is, what is wrong with it and what should be done about it can be determined only within the context of a comprehensive social philosophy. This philosophy must explain what it is to be human, what it is to be a man or a woman, what kind of relationships should exist between individuals of the same and different sexes, what kind of social relationships will permit the institution of such relationships and what is the proper role of sexuality and work in human life. Reflections on the issues raised by prostitution shows the need for such a philosophy, but prostitution will be only one of the areas where it helps us determine what is to be done.

Notes

1. Leo Kanowitz, *Woman and the Law: The Unfinished Revolution* (Albuquerque: University of New Mexico Press, 1969), p. 15.
2. *The Wolfenden Report: Report of the Committee on Homosexual Offences and Prostitution,* Authorized American edition (New York: Stein and Day, 1963), p. 132. Another argument commonly given for the decriminalization of prostitution is that it would lessen the opportunities for blackmail, police pay-offs and protection rackets and hence break the current connection between prostitution and such crimes as blackmail, theft, rape, assault, drunkenness, drug abuse and bribery. Some prostitutes are in favor of this in the hope that it will legitimize their work.
3. *Ibid.,* p. 163.
4. Marilyn G. Haft, "Hustling for Rights," *The Civil Liberties Review* 1, Issue 2 (Winter/Spring 1974), p. 16.

5. *Ibid.,* p. 20.
6. NOW Resolution 141, passed at the sixth national conference of the National Organization for Women in Washington, D.C., in February, 1973.
7. John Stuart Mill, *On Liberty,* reprinted in *The Utilitarians* (New York: Anchor Books, 1973), p. 486.
8. Susan Brownmiller, "Speaking Out on Prostitution," in Anne Koedt and Shulamith Firestone, eds., *Notes From the Third Year* (New York: Notes From the Second Year, Inc., 1971), p. 38.
9. Joel Feinberg, "Legal Paternalism," *Canadian Journal of Philosophy,* No. 1 (1971), pp. 105–124.
10. T. H. Green, *Liberal Legislation and Freedom of Contract* III, p. 388, quoted in D. J. Manning, *Liberalism* (New York: St. Martin's Press, 1976), p. 20.
11. Robert Nozick, *Anarchy, State and Utopia* (New York: Basic Books, 1974), p. 331.
12. Frederick Engels, *The Origin of the Family, Private and the State* (New York: International Publishers, 1942), p. 63.
13. Karl Marx, *The Economic and Philosophical Manuscripts of 1844,* edited with an introduction by Dirk J. Struik (New York: International Publishers, 1964), p. 133, footnote.
14. Engels, *op. cit.,* p. 42. I do not know how far Marx shared this belief, but it is certainly echoed in Lenin's rejection of "the glass-of-water" theory of sex in communist society. "To be sure, thirst has to be quenched. But would a normal person normally lie down in the gutter and drink from a puddle? Or even from a glass whose edge has been greased by many lips?" V. I. Lenin, *The Emancipation of Women* (New York: International Publishers, 1934), p. 106.
15. Engels, *op. cit.,* p. 67.
16. *Ibid.*
17. *Ibid.,* p. 72.
18. *Ibid.*
19. *Ibid.,* p. 61.
20. Karl Marx and Frederick Engels, "Manifesto of the Communist Party," reprinted in *Selected Works of Marx and Engels* (Moscow and New York: New World Paperbacks, 1968), p. 50.
21. Marx, *op. cit.,* p. 167.
22. *Ibid.,* p. 134.
23. Engels, *op. cit.,* p. 66.
24. Marx, *op. cit.,* p. 133, footnote.
25. Marx and Engels, *op. cit.,* p. 51.
26. Karen Lindsey, "Prostitution and the Law," *The Second Wave* 1, No. 4 (1972), p. 6.
27. Cicely Hamilton, *Marriage as a Trade* (London: Chapman & Hall, Ltd., 1909); selections reprinted in Nancy Reeves, *Womankind* (Chicago: Aldine-Atherton, 1971), p. 209. Some authors go so far as to charge that, contrary to public belief, marriage is less of an "honorable estate" than prostitution. "The wife who married for money, compared with the prostitute," says Havelock Ellis, "is the true scab. She is paid less, gives much more in return in labor and care, and is absolutely bound to her master. The prostitute never signs away the right over her own person, she retains her freedom and personal rights, nor is she always compelled to submit to man's embrace." Quoted by Emma Goldman, *The Traffic in Women* (New York: Times Change Press, 1970), p. 26. Contemporary radical feminists voice a similar point of view. "Wifehood is slavery with a measure of status and security; prostitution is a bit of freedom coupled with the stigma of outcast." Barbara Mehrhof and Pamela Kearon, "Prostitution," *Notes from the Third Year, op. cit.,* p. 72.
28. Mary Lathan, "Selling Celibacy," *Women: A Journal of Liberation* 3, No. 1 (1972), pp. 24–25.
29. Mehrhof and Kearon, *op. cit.,* p. 72. A similar claim is made by one of the prostitutes interviewed by Kate Millett: "There's a special indignity in prostitution, as if sex were dirty and men can only enjoy it with someone low. It involves a type of contempt, a kind of disdain, and a kind of triumph over another human being." Kate Millett, *op. cit.,* p. 54.
30. Mehrhof and Kearon, *op. cit.,* p. 74.
31. Jackie MacMillan, "Prostitution as Sexual Politics," *Quest: A Feminist Quarterly* IV, No. 1 (Summer, 1977), p. 43.
32. Linda Thurston, "Prostitution and the Law," *op. cit.,* p. 8.
33. Emma Goldman, *op. cit.,* p. 20.
34. Susan Brownmiller, *op cit.,* p. 39.
35. Cathy Nossa, "Prostitution: Who's Hustling Whom?" *Women: A Journal of Liberation* 3, No. 1 (1972), p. 29.
36. Carol Hanisch, "A Critique of the Miss American Protest" in Shulamith Firestone and Anne Koedt, eds. *Notes from the Second Year: Women's Liberation* (New York: Radical Feminism, 1970), p. 88.
37. Gayle Rubin, "The Traffic in Women," in Ranya Reiter, ed., *Towards an Anthropology of Women* (New York: Monthly Review Press, 1975), pp. 157–210.
38. Jackie MacMillan, *op. cit.,* p. 47.

Study Questions

1. What is the liberal position regarding prostitution?
2. What is the radical feminist position regarding prostitution?
3. What is the Marxist position regarding prostitution, according to Jaggar?
4. Why does Jaggar deny that the difference between these views is primarily "semantical"? In what sense does she think the issue of prostitution is answerable?

4

Political Philosophy

Traditionally, political philosophy has focused on the concepts of power and authority and their relation to the state. Political philosophy has asked: What governmental system is the best, what rights do individuals possess, what limitations to state power should exist, and so on. From the feminist point of view, traditional political theory has dealt exclusively with the public realm, from which women have been systematically excluded, and has ignored the private realm, to which women have universally been consigned. Feminists have accordingly sought to reshape political theory.

The feminist imperative is to move women, personally and collectively, from power-lessness to power and in so doing to redefine the nature and function of power. Catharine MacKinnon holds that "Feminism has no theory of the state. It has a theory of power: . . . The man/woman difference and the dominance/submission dynamic define each other." In the past, women were empowered by such means as enfranchisement; the present feminist project is for women to empower themselves by a range of possible practices. The following essays present some of these.

Ti-Grace Atkinson delineates the radical feminist position, which she calls a *causal class analysis* of the oppressor class (men) and the oppressed class (women). Women, as the oppressed, she holds, were the first political class and were defined as such by their sexual/procreative function. Atkinson shows how the sexual politics of dominance and submission have been generated and maintained by men out of their own needs for potency. She calls for a programmatic analysis to ground women's tactics and strategies for feminist revolution.

Charlotte Bunch outlines the case for lesbian-feminism as a political philosophy. The basic tenet of lesbian-feminist theory is that the institution of heterosexuality is the corner-stone of male supremacy. The political ideology of heterosexism assumes that women wish to be "bonded to men—that each woman exists for a man." According to Bunch, "les-bianism is a threat to the ideological and political basis of male supremacy," because it challenges male domination in behalf of all women and, as she says, "is not for lesbians only." She calls on lesbians, however, to form their own political movement.

Separatism has been a significant political strategy for feminists. Exploring the feminist notion of female separatism as a counter to male supremacy, Marilyn Frye describes its basic modes. She discusses the notion of separatism as a conscious and systematic strategy for women, personally and politically. Frye analyzes separatism as women's denial of (men's) access to themselves. She holds that separatist practices may be instrumental in defining and empowering women.

Barbara Omolade voices the point of view of women of color, who want to speak for themselves instead of being spoken for by others (either white women or black men). Race as well as class divide women and prevent their being heard. Omolade insists that black women point out their material differences from white women and develop their own feminist politics, independent of the frameworks—radical, socialist, liberal, separatist— that have been developed by others.

As Barbara Smith writes: "The fact that we [black feminists] face oppression specific to our combined racial, sexual, and class status means that we will also develop specific theory and practice to fight our oppression."

Radical Feminism: Declaration of War

Ti-Grace Atkinson

Almanina Barbour, a black militant woman in Philadelphia, once pointed out to me: "The Women's Movement is the first in history with a war on and no enemy." I winced. It was an obvious criticism. I fumbled about in my mind for an answer. Surely the enemy must have been defined at some time. Otherwise, what had we been shooting at for the last couple of years? into the air?

Only two responses came to me, although in looking for those two I realized that it was a question carefully avoided. The first and by far the most frequent answer was "society." The second, infrequently and always furtively, was "men."

If "society" is the enemy, what could that mean? If women are being oppressed, there's only one group left over to be doing the oppressing: men. Then why call them "society"? Could "society" mean the "institutions" that oppress women? But institutions must be maintained, and the same question arises: by whom? The answer to "who is the enemy?" is so obvious that the interesting issue quickly becomes "why has it been avoided?"

The master might tolerate many reforms in slavery but none that would threaten his essential role as master. Women have known this, and since "men" and "society" are in

---

From Ti-Grace Atkinson, *Amazon Odyssey* (1974), pp. 46–55. Reprinted by permission of Hyperion Press. (Notes deleted.)

effect synonymous, they have feared confronting him. Without this confrontation and a detailed understanding of what *his* battle strategy has been that has kept us so successfully pinned down, the "Women's Movement" is worse than useless. It invites backlash from men, and no progress for women.

There has never been a feminist analysis. While discontent among women and the attempt to resolve this discontent have often implied that women form a class, no political or *causal* class analysis has followed. To rephrase my last point, the persecution of women has never been taken as the starting point for a political analysis of society.

Considering that the last massing of discontent among women continued some 70 years (1850–1920) and spread the world and the recent accumulation of grievances began some three years ago here in America, the lack of a structural understanding of the problem is at first sight incomprehensible. It is the understanding of the *reasons* for this devastating omission and of the *implications* of the problem that forces one to "radical feminism."

Women who have tried to solve their problems as a class have proposed not solutions but dilemmas. The traditional feminists want equal rights for women with men. But on what grounds? If women serve a different *function* from men in society, wouldn't this necessarily affect women's "rights"? For example, do *all* women have the "right" not to bear children? Traditional feminism is caught in the dilemma of demanding equal treatment for unequal functions, because it is unwilling to challenge political (functional) classification by sex.

Radical women, on the other hand, grasp that women as a group somehow fit into a political analysis of society, but err in refusing to explore the significance of the fact that women form a class, the uniqueness of this class, and the implications of this description to the system of political classes. Both traditional feminists and radical women have evaded questioning any part of their *raison d'être*: women are a class, and the terms that make up this initial assumption must be examined.

The feminist dilemma is that it is as women—or "females"—that women are persecuted, just as it was as slaves—or "blacks"—that slaves were persecuted in America. In order to improve their condition, those individuals who are today defined as women must eradicate their own definition. Women must, in a sense, commit suicide, and the journey from womanhood to a society of individuals is hazardous. The feminist dilemma is that we have the most to do, and the least to do it with. We must create, as no other group in history has been forced to do, from the very beginning.

The "battle of the sexes" is a commonplace, both over time and distance. But it is an inaccurate description of what has been happening. A "battle" implies some balance of powers, whereas when one side suffers all the losses, such as in some kinds of raids (often referred to as the "rape" of an area), that is called a *massacre*. Women have been massacred as human beings over history, and this destiny is entailed by their definition. As women begin massing together, they take the first step from *being* massacred to *engaging in* battle (resistance). Hopefully, this will eventually lead to negotiations—in the *very* far future—and peace.

When any person or group of persons is being mistreated or, to continue our metaphor, is being attacked, there is a succession of responses or investigations:

1. Depending on the severity of the attack (short of an attack on life), the victim determines how much damage was done and what it was done with.
2. Where is the attack coming from? from whom? located where?
3. How can you win the immediate battle? defensive measures? holding actions?
4. Why did he attack you?
5. How can you win (end) the war? offensive measures. moving within his boundaries.

These first five questions are necessary but should be considered diplomatic maneuvers. They have never been answered by the so-called "Women's Movement," and for this reason I think one cannot properly call that Movement "political." It could not have had any direction relevant to women as a class.

If diplomacy fails, that is, if your enemy refuses to stop attacking you, you must force him to stop. This requires a strategy, and this strategy requires a map of the relevant landscape, including such basic information as

1. Who is the enemy?
2. Where is he located?
3. Is he getting outside support? material? manpower? from whom?
4. Where are his forces massed?
5. What's the best ammunition to knock them out?
6. What weapons is he using?
7. How can you counteract them?
8. What is your plan of attack on him to force diplomatic negotiations? program of action (including priorities). techniques.

I am using some military terminology, and this may seem incongruous. But why should it? We accept the phrase "battle of the sexes." It is the proposal that *women* fight *back* that seems incongruous. It has been necessary to program women's psychic structure to nonresistance on their own behalf—for obvious reasons—they make up over half the population of the world.

Without a programmatic analysis, the "Women's Movement" has been as if running blindly in the general direction of where they *guess* the last missile that just hit them was based. For the first two years of the last organizing, I was very active in this running-blind approach. It's true that we were attacking evils, but why *those* particular evils? Were they the central issues in the persecution of women? There was no map so I couldn't be sure, but I could see no reason to believe that we knew what the key issues were, much less that we were hitting them.

It became increasingly clear to me that we were incorporating many of our external problems (e.g., power hierarchies) into our own movement, and in understanding this and beginning to ask myself some of the obvious questions I've listed above, I cam to the conclusion that at this time the most radical *action* that any woman or group of women could take was a feminist analysis. The implications of such an analysis is a greater threat to the opposition to human rights for women than all the actions and threatened actions put together up until this time by women.

With this introduction to the significance of a feminist analysis, I will outline what we have so far.

As I mentioned before, the *raison d'être* of all groups formed around the problem of women is that women are a class. What is meant by that? What is meant by "women" and what is meant by "class"?

Does "women" include all women? Some groups have been driven back from the position of *all* women to some proposed "special" class such as "poor" women and eventually concentrated more on economic class than sexual class. But if we're interested in women and how women *qua* women are oppressed, this class must include *all* women.

What separates out a particular individual from other individuals as a "woman"? We recognize it's a sexual separation and that this separation has two aspects, "sociological" and "biological." The term for the sociological function is "woman" (wifman); the term for the biological function is "female" (to suckle). Both terms are descriptive of functions in the interests of someone other than the possessor.

And what is meant by "class"? We've already briefly covered the meaning as the characteristic by which certain individuals are grouped together. In the "Women's Movement" or "feminism," individuals group together to *act* on behalf of women as a class in opposition to the *class* enemies of women. It is the interaction between classes that defines political action. For this reason I call the feminist analysis a *causal class analysis*.

We have established that women are a political class characterized by a sexual function. It is clear that women, at the present time at any rate, have the *capacity* to bear children. But the question arises: "how did this biological classification become a political classification?" How or why did this elaborate superstructure of coercion develop on top of a capacity (which normally implies choice)?

It is generally agreed that women were the first political class. (Children do not properly constitute a political class since the relevant characteristic of its members [namely, age] is unstable for any given member by definition.) "Political" classes are usually defined as classes treated by other classes in some special manner distinct from the way other classes are treated. What is frequently omitted is that "political" classes are *artificial*; they define persons with certain capacities *by* those capacities, changing the contingent to the necessary, thereby appropriating the *capacities* of an individual as a *function* of society. (Definition of "political class" = individuals grouped together by other individuals as a function of the grouping individuals, depriving the grouped individuals of their human status.) A "function" of society cannot be a free individual: exercising the minimal human rights of physical integrity and freedom of movement.

If women were the first political class, and political classes must be defined by individuals outside that class, who defined them, and why, and how? It is reasonable to assume that at some period in history the population was politically undifferentiated; let's call that mass "Mankind" (generic).

The first dichotomous division of this mass is said to have been on the grounds of sex: male and female. But the genitals *per se* would be no more grounds for the human race to be divided in two than skin color or height or hair color. The genitals, in connection with a particular activity, have the *capacity* for the initiation of the reproductive process. But, I submit, it was because one half the human race bears the *burden* of the reproductive *process* and because man, the "rational" animal, had the wit to take advantage of that that the childbearers, or the "beasts of burden," were corralled into a political class. The biologically contingent burden of childbearing was equivocated into a political (or necessary) penalty, thereby modifying those individuals' definition thereby defined from the human to the functional—or animal.

There is no justification for using any individual as a function of others. Didn't *all* members of society have the right to decide if they even *wanted* to reproduce? Because one half of humanity was and still is forced to bear the burden of reproduction at the will of the other half, the first political class is defined not by its sex—sexuality was only relevant originally as a means to reproduction—but by the function of being the *container* of the reproductive process.

Because women have been taught to believe that men have protective feelings toward women (men have protective feelings toward their functions [property], not other human beings!), we women are shocked by these discoveries and ask ourselves *why* men took and continue to take advantage of us.

Some people say that men are naturally, or biologically, aggressive. But this leaves us at an impasse. If the values of society are power-oriented, there is no chance that men would agree to be medicated into a humane state.

The other alternative that has been suggested is to eliminate men as biologically incapable of humane relationships and therefore a menace to society. I can sympathize with the frustration and rage that leads to this suggestion.

But the proposal to eliminate men, as I understand it, assumes that men constitute a kind of social disease, and that by "men" is meant those individuals with certain typical genital characteristics. These genital characteristics are held to determine the organism in every biochemical respect thus determining the psychic structure as well. It may be that as in other mental derangements, and I do believe that men behave in a mentally deranged manner toward women, there is a biochemical correspondence, but this would be ultimately behaviorally determined, not genetically.

I believe that the sex roles—both male and female—must be destroyed, not the individuals who happen to possess either a penis or a vagina, or both, or neither. But many men I have spoken with see little to choose from between the two positions and feel that without the role they'd just as soon die.

Certainly it is the master who resists the abolition of slavery, especially when he is offered no recompense in power. I think that the *need* men have for the role of Oppressor is the source and foundation of all human oppression. Men suffer from a disease peculiar to Mankind which I call "metaphysical cannibalism." Men must, at the very least, cooperate in curing themselves.

Study Questions

1. What sort of feminist analysis does Atkinson propose? Why is it necessary?
2. What does Atkinson mean by "women as a class"? As "the first political class"?
3. How were women made into the first political class?
4. How does Atkinson feel men can be dealt with?

Lesbians in Revolt

Charlotte Bunch

The development of Lesbian-Feminist politics as the basis for the liberation of women is our top priority: this article outlines our present ideas. In our society, which defines all people and institutions for the benefit of the rich, white male, the Lesbian is in revolt. In revolt because she defines herself in terms of women and rejects the male definitions of how she should feel, act, look, and live. To be a Lesbian is to love oneself, woman, in a culture that denegrates and despises women. The Lesbian rejects male sexual/political domination; she defies his world, his social organization, his ideology, and his definition of her as inferior. Lesbianism puts women first while the society declares the male supreme. Lesbianism threatens male supremacy at its core. When politically conscious and organized, it is central to destroying our sexist, racist, capitalist, imperialist system.

Male society defines Lesbianism as a sexual act, which reflects men's limited view of women: they think of us only in terms of sex. They also say Lesbians are not real women,

---

From *Lesbianism and the Women's Movement* (Diana Press, 1975). Copyright © 1975 by Charlotte Bunch. *Editor's note:* This essay should be read in the context of the Women's Movement of the early 1970s and of the kind of anger out of which these ideas arose. Lesbian feminist theory was being formulated at that time.

so a real woman is one who gets fucked by men. We say that a Lesbian is a woman whose sense of self and energies, including sexual energies, center around women—she is woman identified. The woman-identified-woman commits herself to other women for political, emotional, physical, and economic support. Women are important to her. She is important to herself. Our society demands that commitment from women be reserved for men.

The Lesbian, woman-identified-woman, commits herself to women not only as an alternative to oppressive male/female relationships but primarily because she *loves* women. Whether consciously or not, by her actions, the Lesbian has recognized that giving support and love to men over women perpetuates the system that oppresses her. If women do not make a commitment to each other, which includes sexual love, we deny ourselves the love and value traditionally given to men. We accept our second-class status. When women do give primary energies to other women, then it is possible to concentrate fully on building a movement for our liberation.

Woman-identified Lesbianism is, then, more than a sexual preference, it is a political choice. It is political because relationships between men and women are essentially political, they involve power and dominance. Since the Lesbian actively rejects that relationship and chooses women, she defies the established political system.

Of course, not all Lesbians are consciously woman-identified, nor are all committed to finding common solutions to the oppression they suffer as women and Lesbians. Being a Lesbian is part of challenging male supremacy, but not the end. For the Lesbian or heterosexual woman, there is no individual solution to oppression.

The Lesbian may think that she is free since she escapes the personal oppression of the individual male/female relationship. But to the society she is still a woman, or worse, a visible Lesbian. On the street, at the job, in the schools, she is treated as an inferior and is at the mercy of men's power and whims. (I've never heard of a rapist who stopped because his victim was a Lesbian.) This society hates women who love women, and so, the Lesbian, who escapes male dominance in her private home, receives it doubly at the hands of male society; she is harassed, outcast, and shuttled to the bottom. Lesbians must become feminists and fight against woman oppression, just as feminists must become Lesbians if they hope to end male supremacy.

U.S. society encourages individual solutions, apolitical attitudes, and reformism to keep us from political revolt and out of power. Men who rule, and male leftists who seek to rule, try to depoliticize sex and the relations between men and women in order to prevent us from acting to end our oppression and challenging their power. As the question of homosexuality has become public, reformists define it as a private question of who you sleep with in order to sidetrack our understanding of the politics of sex. For the Lesbian-Feminist, it is not private; it is a political matter of oppression, domination, and power. Reformists offer solutions which make no basic changes in the system that oppresses us, solutions which keep power in the hands of the oppressor. The only way oppressed people end their oppression is by seizing power: People whose rule depends on the subordination of others do not voluntarily stop oppressing others. Our subordination is the basis of male power.

Sexism Is the Root of All Oppression

The first division of labor, in pre-history, was based on sex: men hunted, women built the villages, took care of children, and farmed. Women collectively controlled the land, language, culture, and the communities. Men were able to conquer women with the weapons that they developed for hunting when it became clear that women were leading a more stable, peaceful, and desirable existence. We do not know exactly how this conquest took place, but it is clear that the original imperialism was male over female: the male claiming the female body and her service as his territory (or property).

Having secured the domination of women, men continued this pattern of suppressing people, now on the basis of tribe, race, and class. Although there have been numerous battles over class, race, and nation during the past 3000 years, none has brought the liberation of women. While these other forms of oppression must be ended, there is no reason to believe that our liberation will come with the smashing of capitalism, racism, or imperialism today. Women will be free only when we concentrate on fighting male supremacy.

Our war against male supremacy does, however, involve attacking the latter-day dominations based on class, race, and nation. As Lesbians who are outcasts from every group, it would be suicidal to perpetuate these man-made divisions among ourselves. We have no heterosexual privileges, and when we publicly assert our Lesbianism, those of us who had them lose many of our class and race privileges. Most of our privileges as women are granted to us by our relationships to men (fathers, husbands, boyfriends) whom we now reject. This does not mean that there is no racism or class chauvinism within us, but we must destroy these divisive remnants of privileged behavior among ourselves as the first step toward their destruction in the society. Race, class, and national oppressions come from men, serve ruling class white men's interests, and have no place in a woman-identified revolution.

Lesbianism Is the Basic Threat to Male Supremacy

Lesbianism is a threat to the ideological, political, and economic basis of male supremacy. The Lesbian threatens the ideology of male supremacy by destroying the lie about female inferiority, weakness, passivity, and by denying women's "innate" need for men. Lesbians literally do not need men (even for procreation if the science of cloning is developed).

The Lesbian's independence and refusal to support one man undermines the personal power that men exercise over women. Our rejection of heterosexual sex challenges male domination in its most individual and common form. We offer all women something better than submission to personal oppression. We offer the beginning of the end of collective and individual male supremacy. Since men of all races and classes depend on female support and submission for practical tasks and feeling superior, our refusal to submit will force some to examine their sexist behavior, to break down their own destructive privileges over other humans, and to fight against those privileges in other men. They will have to build new selves that do not depend on oppressing women and learn to live in social structures that do not give them power over anyone.

Heterosexuality separates women from each other; it makes women define themselves through men; it forces women to compete against each other for men and the privilege which comes through men and their social standing. Heterosexual society offers women a few privileges as compensation if they give up their freedom: for example, mothers are respected and "honored," wives or lovers are socially accepted and given some economic and emotional security, a woman gets physical protection on the street when she stays with her man, etc. The privileges give heterosexual women a personal and political stake in maintaining the status quo.

The Lesbian receives none of these heterosexual privileges or compensations since she does not accept the male demands on her. She has little vested interest in maintaining the present political system since all of its institutions—church, state, media, health, schools—work to keep her down. If she understands her oppression, she has nothing to gain by supporting white rich male America and much to gain from fighting to change it. She is less prone to accept reformist solutions to women's oppression.

Economics is a crucial part of woman oppression, but our analysis of the relationship between capitalism and sexism is not complete. We know that Marxist economic theory does not sufficiently consider the role of women or Lesbians, and we are presently working on this area.

However, as a beginning, some of the ways that Lesbians threaten the economic system are clear: In this country, women work for men in order to survive, on the job and in the home. The Lesbian rejects this division of labor at its roots; she refuses to be a man's property, to submit to the unpaid labor system of housework and childcare. She rejects the nuclear family as the basic unit of production and consumption in capitalist society.

The Lesbian is also a threat on the job because she is not the passive/part-time woman worker that capitalism counts on to do boring work and be part of a surplus labor pool. Her identity and economic support do not come through men, so her job is crucial and she cares about job conditions, wages, promotion, and status. Capitalism cannot absorb large numbers of women demanding stable employment, decent salaries, and refusing to accept their traditional job exploitation. We do not understand yet the total effect that this increased job dissatisfaction will have. It is, however, clear that as women become more intent upon taking control of their lives, they will seek more control over their jobs, thus increasing the strains on capitalism and enhancing the power of women to change the economic system.

Lesbians Must Form Our Own Movement to Fight Male Supremacy

Feminist-Lesbianism, as the most basic threat to male supremacy, picks up part of the Women's Liberation analysis of sexism and gives it force and direction. Women's Liberation lacks direction now because it has failed to understand the importance of heterosexuality in maintaining male supremacy and because it has failed to face class and race as real differences in women's behavior and political needs. As long as straight women see Lesbianism as a bedroom issue, they hold back the development of politics and strategies which would put an end to male supremacy and they give men an excuse for not dealing with their sexism.

Being a Lesbian means ending identification with, allegiance to, dependence on, and support of heterosexuality. It means ending your personal stake in the male world so that you join women, individually and collectively, in the struggle to end your oppression. Lesbianism is the key to liberation and only women who cut their ties to male privilege can be trusted to remain serious in the struggle against male dominance. Those who remain tied to men, individually or in political theory, cannot always put women first. It is not that heterosexual women are evil or do not care about women. It is because the very essence, definition, and nature of heterosexuality is men first. Every woman has experienced that desolation when her sister puts her man first in the final crunch: heterosexuality demands that she do so. As long as women still benefit from heterosexuality, receive its privileges and security, they will at some point have to betray their sisters, especially Lesbian sisters who do not receive those benefits.

Women in women's liberation have understood the importance of having meetings and other events for women only. It has been clear that dealing with men divides us and saps our energies and that it is not the job of the oppressed to explain our oppression to the oppressor. Women also have seen that collectively, men will not deal with their sexism until they are forced to do so. Yet, many of these same women continue to have primary relationships with men individually and do not understand why Lesbians find this oppressive. Lesbians cannot grow politically or personally in a situation which denies the basis of our politics: that Lesbianism is political, that heterosexuality is crucial to maintaining male supremacy.

Lesbians must form our own political movement in order to grow. Changes which will have more than token effects on our lives will be led by woman-identified Lesbians who understand the nature of our oppression and are therefore in a position to end it.

Study Questions

1. What does Bunch set out to show in her paper?
2. What is lesbian feminism, and how has it evolved over the last decade?

3. In what way is "woman-identified-woman" a common identification around which lesbians and feminists should unite?
4. What is the ideology of heterosexism, and how does it help to oppress women?
5. In what ways does lesbianism threaten patriarchal society?
6. Why does Bunch hold that lesbians should form their own political movement?

Some Reflections On Separatism and Power

Marilyn Frye

I have been trying to write something about separatism almost since my first dawning of feminist consciousness, but it has always been for me somehow a mercurial topic which, when I tried to grasp it, would softly shatter into many other topics like sexuality, man-hating, so-called reverse discrimination, apocalyptic utopianism, and so on. What I have to share with you today is my latest attempt to get to the heart of the matter.

In my life, and within feminism as I understand it, separatism is not a theory or a doctrine, nor a demand for certain specific behaviors on the part of feminists, though it is undeniably connected with lesbianism. Feminism seems to me to be kaleidoscopic—something whose shapes, structures and patterns alter with every turn of feminist creativity; and one element which is present through all the changes is an element of separation. This element has different roles and relations in different turns of the glass—it assumes different meanings, is variously conspicuous, variously determined or determining, depending on how the pieces fall and who is the beholder. The theme of separation, in its multitude variations, is there in everything from divorce to exclusive lesbian separatist communities, from shelters for battered women to witch covens, from women's studies programs to women's bars, from expansion of daycare to abortion on demand. The presence of this theme is vigorously obscured, trivialized, mystified and outright denied by many feminist apologists, who seem to find it embarrassing, while it is embraced, explored, expanded and ramified by most of the more inspiring theorists and activists. The theme of separation is noticeably absent or heavily qualified in most of the things I take to be personal solutions and band-aid projects, like legalization of prostitution, liberal marriage contracts, improvement of the treatment of rape victims and affirmative action. It is clear to me, in my own case at least, that the contrariety of assimilation and separation is one of the main things that guides or determines assessments of various theories, actions and practices as reformist or radical, as going to the root of the thing or being relatively superficial. So my topical question comes to this: What is it about separation, in any or all of its many forms and degrees, that makes it so basic and so sinister, so exciting and so repellent?

From *The Politics of Reality: Essays in Feminist Theory* (Trumansburg, New York: The Crossing Press, 1983). Reprinted by permission of the publisher. (Notes deleted.)

Feminist separation is, of course, separation of various sorts or modes from men and from institutions, relationships, roles and activities which are male-defined, male-dominated and operating for the benefit of males and the maintenance of male privilege—this separation being initiated or maintained, at will, *by women*. (Masculist separatism is the partial segregation of women from men and male domains *at the will of men*. This difference is crucial.) The feminist separation can take many forms. Breaking up or avoiding close relationships or working relationships; forbidding someone to enter your house; excluding someone from your company, or from your meeting; withdrawal from participation in some activity or institution, or avoidance of participation; avoidance of communications and influence from certain quarters (not listening to music with sexist lyrics, not watching tv); withholding commitment or support; rejection of or rudeness toward obnoxious individuals.[1] Some separations are subtle realignments of identification, priorities and commitments, or working with agendas which only incidentally coincide with the agendas of the institution one works in. Ceasing to be loyal to something or someone is a separation; and ceasing to love. The feminist's separations are rarely if ever sought or maintained directly as ultimate personal or political ends. The closest we come to that, I think, is the separation which is the instinctive and self-preserving recoil from the systematic misogyny that surrounds us.[2] Generally, the separations are brought about and maintained for the sake of something else like independence, liberty, growth, invention, sisterhood, safety, health, or the practice of novel or heretical customs.[3] Often the separations in question evolve, unpremeditated, as one goes one's way and finds various persons, institutions or relationships useless, obstructive or noisome and leaves them aside or behind. Sometimes the separations are consciously planned and cultivated as necessary prerequisites or conditions for getting on with one's business. Sometimes the separations are accomplished or maintained easily, or with a sense of relief, or even joy; sometimes they are accomplished or maintained with difficulty, by dint of constant vigilance, or with anxiety, pain or grief.

Most feminists, probably all, practice some separation from males and male-dominated institutions. A separatist practices separation consciously, systematically, and probably more generally than the others, and advocates thorough and "broad-spectrum" separation as part of the conscious strategy of liberation. And, contrary to the image of the separatist as a cowardly escapist, hers is the life and program which inspires the greatest hostility, disparagement, insult and confrontation and generally she is the one against whom economic sanctions operate most conclusively. The penalty for refusing to work with or for men is usually starvation (or, at the very least, doing without medical insurance); and if one's policy of noncooperation is more subtle, one's livelihood is still constantly on the line, since one is not a loyal partisan, a proper member of the team, or what have you. The penalties for being a lesbian are ostracism, harassment and job insecurity or joblessness. The penalty for rejecting men's sexual advances is often rape and, perhaps even more often, forfeit of such things as professional or job opportunities. And the separatist lives with the added burden of being assumed by many to be a morally depraved man-hating bigot. But there is a clue here: if you are doing something that is so strictly forbidden by the patriarchs, you must be doing something right.

There is an idea floating around in both feminist and antifeminist literature to the effect that females and males generally live in a relation of parasitism,[4] a parasitism of the male on the female . . . that it is, generally speaking, the strength, energy, inspiration and nurturance of women that keeps men going, and not the strength, aggression, spirituality and hunting of men that keeps women going.

It is sometimes said that the parasitism goes the other way around, that the female is the parasite. But one can conjure the appearance of the female as parasite only if one takes a very narrow view of human living—historically parochial, narrow with respect to class and race, and limited in conception of what are the necessary goods. Generally, the female's contribution to her material support is and always has been substantial; in many times and places it has been independently sufficient. One can and should distinguish between a partial and contingent material dependence created by a certain sort of money economy and class structure, and the nearly ubiquitous spiritual, emotional and material dependence of males on females. Males presently provide, off and on, a portion of the material support of women, within circumstances apparently designed to make it difficult for women to provide them for themselves. But females provide and generally have provided for males the energy and spirit for living; the males are nurtured by the females. And this the males apparently cannot do for themselves, even partially.

The parasitism of males on females is, as I see it, demonstrated by the panic, rage and hysteria generated in so many of them by the thought of being abandoned by women. But it is demonstrated in a way that is perhaps more generally persuasive by both literary and sociological evidence. Evidence cited in Jesse Bernard's work in *The Future of Marriage* and in George Gilder's *Sexual Suicide* and *Men Alone* convincingly shows that males tend in shockingly significant numbers and in alarming degree to fall into mental illness, petty crime, alcoholism, physical infirmity, chronic unemployment, drug addiction and neurosis when deprived of the care and companionship of a female mate, or keeper. (While on the other hand, women without male mates are significantly healthier and happier than women with male mates.) And masculist literature is abundant with indications of male cannibalism, of males deriving essential sustenance from females. Cannibalistic imagery, visual and verbal, is common in pornography: images likening women to food, and sex to eating. And, as documented in Millett's *Sexual Politics* and many other feminist analyses of masculist literature, the theme of men getting high off beating, raping or killing women (or merely bullying them) is common. These interactions with women, or rather, these actions upon women, make men feel good, walk tall, feel refreshed, invigorated. Men are drained and depleted by their living by themselves and with and among other men, and are revived and refreshed, re-created, by going home and being served dinner, changing to clean clothes, having sex with the wife; or by dropping by the apartment of a woman friend to be served coffee or a drink and stroked in one way or another; or by picking up a prostitute for a quicky or for a dip in favorite sexual escape fantasies; or by raping refugees from their wars (foreign and domestic). The ministrations of women, be they willing or unwilling, free or paid for, are what restore in men the strength, will and confidence to go on with what they call living.

If it is true that a fundamental aspect of the relations between the sexes is male parasitism, it might help to explain why certain issues are particularly exciting to patriarchal loyalists. For instance, in view of the obvious advantages of easy abortion to population control, to control of welfare rolls, and to ensuring sexual availability of women to men, it is a little surprising that the loyalists are so adamant and riled up in their objection to it. But look . . .

The fetus lives parasitically. It is a distinct animal surviving off the life (the blood) of another animal creature. It is incapable of surviving on its own resources, of independent nutrition; incapable even of symbiosis. If it is true that males live parasitically upon females, it seems reasonable to suppose that many of them and those loyal to them are in some way sensitive to the parallelism between their situation and that of the fetus. They could easily identify with the fetus. The woman who is free to see the fetus as a parasite[5] might be free to see the man as a parasite. The woman's willingness to cut off the life line to one parasite suggests a willingness to cut off the life line to another parasite. The woman who is capable (legally, psychologically, physically) of decisively, self-interestedly, independently rejecting the one parasite, is capable of rejecting, with the same decisiveness and independence, the like burden of the other parasite. In the eyes of the other parasite, the image of the wholly self-determined abortion, involving not even a ritual submission to male veto power, is the mirror image of death.

Another clue here is that one line of argument against free and easy abortion is the slippery slope argument that if fetuses are to be freely dispensed with, old people will be next. Old people? Why are old people next? And why the great concern for them? Most old people are women, indeed, and patriarchal loyalists are not generally so solicitous of the welfare of any women. Why old people? Because, I think, in the modern patriarchal divisions of labor, old people too are parasites on women. The antiabortionist folks seem not to worry about wife beating and wife murder—there is no broad or emotional popular support for stopping these violences. They do not worry about murder and involuntary sterilization in prisons, nor murder in war, nor murder by pollution and industrial accidents. Either these are not real to them or they cannot identify with the victims; but anyway, killing in general is not what they oppose. They worry about the rejection *by women, at women's discretion*, of something which lives parasitically on women. I suspect that they fret not because old people are next, but because men are next.

There are other reasons, of course, why patriarchal loyalists should be disturbed about abortion on demand; a major one being that it would be a significant form of female control of reproduction, and at least from certain angles it looks like the progress of patriarchy *is* the progress toward male control of reproduction, starting with possession of wives and continuing through the invention of obstetrics and the technology of extrauterine gestation. Giving up that control would be giving up patriarchy. But such an objection to abortion is too abstract, and requires too historical a vision, to generate the hysteria there is now in the reaction against abortion. The hysteria is, I think, to be accounted for more in terms of a much more immediate and personal presentiment of ejection by the woman-womb.

I discuss abortion here because it seems to me to be the most publicly emotional and most physically dramatic ground on which the theme of separation and male parasitism is presently being played out. But there are other locales for this play. For instance, women with newly raised consciousnesses tend to leave marriages and families, either completely through divorce, or partially, through unavailability of their cooking, housekeeping and sexual services. And women academics tend to become alienated from their colleagues and male mentors and no longer serve as sounding board, ego booster, editor, mistress or proofreader. Many awakening women become celibate or lesbian, and the others become a very great deal more choosy about when, where and in what relationships they will have sex with men. And the men affected by these separations generally react with defensive hostility, anxiety and guilt-tripping, not to mention descents into illogical argument which match and exceed their own most fanciful images of female irrationality. My claim is that they are very afraid because they depend very heavily upon the goods they receive from women, and these separations cut them off from those goods.

Male parasitism means that males *must have access* to women; it is the Patriarchal Imperative. But feminist no-saying is more than a substantial removal (redirection, reallocation) of goods and services because Access is one of the faces of Power. Female denial of male access to females substantially cuts off a flow of benefits, but it has also the form and full portent of assumption of power.

Differences of power are always manifested in asymmetrical access. The President of the United States has access to almost everybody for almost anything he might want of them, and almost nobody has access to him. The super-rich have access to almost everybody; almost nobody has access to them. The resources of the employee are available to the boss as the resources of the boss are not to the employee. The parent has unconditional access to the child's room; the child does not have similar access to the parent's room. Students adjust to professors' office hours; professors do not adjust to students' conference hours. The child is required not to lie; the parent is free to close out the child with lies at her discretion. The slave is unconditionally accessible to the master. Total power is unconditional access; total powerlessness is being unconditionally accessible. The creation and manipulation of power is constituted of the manipulation and control of access.

All-woman groups, meetings, projects seem to be great things for causing controversy and confrontation. Many women are offended by them; many are afraid to be the one to announce the exclusion of men; it is seen as a device whose use needs much elaborate justification. I think this is because conscious and deliberate exclusion of men by women, from anything, is blatant insubordination, and generates in women fear of punishment and reprisal (fear which is often well-justified). Our own timidity and desire to avoid confrontations generally keep us from doing very much in the way of all-woman groups and meetings. But when we do, we invariably run into the male champion who challenges our right to do it. Only a small minority of men go crazy when an event is advertised to be for women only—just one man tried to crash our women-only Rape Speak-Out, and only a few hid under the auditorium seats to try to spy on a women-only meeting at a NOW convention in Philadelphia. But these few are onto something their less rabid com-patriots are missing. The woman-only meeting is a fundamental challenge to the structure of power. It is always the privilege of the master to enter the slave's hut. The slave who decides to exclude the master from her hut is declaring herself not a slave. The exclusion of men from the meeting not only deprives them of certain benefits (which they might survive without); it is a controlling of access, hence an assumption of power. It is not only mean, it is arrogant.

It becomes clearer now why there is always an off-putting aura of negativity about separatism—one which offends the feminine pollyanna in us and smacks of the purely defensive to the political theorist in us. It is this: First: When those who control access have made you totally accessible, your first act of taking control must be denying access, or must have denial of access as one of its aspects. This is not because you are charged up with (unfeminine or politically incorrect) negativity; it is because of the logic of the situation. When we start from a position of total accessibility there *must* be an aspect of no-saying (which is the beginning of control) in *every effective* act and strategy, the effective ones being precisely those which *shift power*, i.e., ones which involve manipulation and control of access. Second: Whether or not one says "no," or withholds or closes out or rejects, on this occasion or that, the capacity and ability to say "no" (with effect) is logically necessary to control. When we are in control of access to ourselves there will be some no-saying, and when we are more accustomed to it, when it is more common, an ordinary part of living, it will not seem so prominent, obvious, or strained . . . . we will not strike ourselves or others as being particularly negative. In this aspect of ourselves and our lives, we will strike ourselves pleasingly as active beings with momentum of our own, with sufficient shape and structure—with sufficient integrity—to generate friction. Our experience of our no-saying will be an aspect of our experience of our definition.

When our feminist acts or practices have an aspect of separation, we are assuming power by controlling access and simultaneously by undertaking definition. The slave who excludes the master from her hut thereby declares herself *not a slave*. And *definition* is another face of power.

The powerful normally determine what is said and sayable. When the powerful label something or dub it or baptize it, the thing becomes what they call it. When the Secretary of Defense calls something a peace negotiation, for instance, then whatever it is that he called a peace negotiation is an instance of negotiating peace. If the activity in question is the working out of terms of a trade-off of nuclear reactors and territorial redistributions, complete with arrangements for the resulting refugees, that is peacemaking. People laud it, and the negotiators get Noble Piece Prizes for it. On the other hand, when I call a certain speech act a rape, my "calling" it does not make it so. At best, I have to explain and justify and make clear exactly what it is about this speech act which is assaultive in just what way, and then the others acquiesce in saying the act was *like* rape or could figuratively be called a rape. My counterassault will not be counted a simple case of self-defense. And what I called rejection of parasitism, they call the loss of the womanly virtues of compassion and "caring." And generally, when renegade women call something one thing and patriarchal loyalists call it another, the loyalists get their way.*

Women generally are not the people who do the defining, and we cannot from our isolation and powerlessness simply commence saying different things than others say and make it stick. There is a humpty-dumpty problem in that. But we are able to arrogate definition to ourselves when we repattern access. Assuming control of access, we draw new boundaries and create new roles and relationships. This, though it causes some strain, puzzlement and hostility, is to a fair extent within the scope of individuals and small gangs, as outright verbal redefinition is not, at least in the first instance.

One may see access as coming in two sorts, "natural" and humanly arranged. A grizzly bear has what you might call natural access to the picnic basket of the unarmed human. The access of the boss to the personal services of the secretary is humanly arranged access; the boss exercises institutional power. It looks to me, looking from a certain angle, like institutions are humanly designed patterns of access—access to persons and their services. But institutions are artifacts of definition. In the case of intentionally and formally designed institutions, this is very clear, for the relevant definitions are explicitly set forth in by-laws and constitutions, regulations and rules. When one defines the term "president," one defines presidents in terms of what they can do and what is owed them by other offices, and "what they can do" is a matter of their access to the services of others. Similarly, definitions of *dean, student, judge,* and *cop* set forth patterns of access, and definitions of *writer, child, owner,* and of course, *husband, wife,* and *man* and *girl.* When one changes the pattern of access, one forces new uses of words on those affected. The term "man" has to shift in meaning when rape is no longer possible. When we take control of sexual access to us, of access to our nurturance and to our reproductive function, access to mothering and sistering, we redefine the word "woman." The shift of usage is pressed on others by a change in social reality; it does not await their recognition of our definitional authority.

When women separate (withdraw, break out, regroup, transcend, shove aside, step outside, migrate, say *no*), we are simultaneously controlling access and defining. We are doubly insubordinate, since neither of these is permitted. And access and definition are fundamental ingredients in the alchemy of power, so we are doubly, and radically, insubordinate.

---

* This paragraph and the succeeding one are the passage which has provoked the most substantial questions from women who read the paper. One thing that causes trouble here is that I am talking from a stance or position that is ambiguous—it is located in two different and noncommunicating systems of thought-action. *Re* the patriarchy and the English language, there is general usage over which I/we do not have the control that elite males have (with the cooperation of all the ordinary patriarchal loyalists). *Re* the new being and meaning which are being created now by lesbian-feminists, we *do* have semantic authority, and, collectively, can and do define with effect. I think it is only by maintaining our boundaries through controlling concrete access to us that we can enforce on those who are not-us our definitions of ourselves, hence force on them *the fact of our existence* and thence open up the *possibility* of our having semantic authority with them. (I wrote some stuff that's relevant to this in the last section of my paper "Male Chauvinism—A Conceptual Analysis.")⁶ Our unintelligibility to patriarchal loyalists is a source of pride and delight, in some contexts; but if we don't have an effect on their usage while we continue, willy nilly, to be subject to theirs, being totally unintelligible to them could be fatal. (A friend of mine had a dream where the women were meeting in a cabin at the edge of town, and they had a sort of inspiration through the vision of one of them that they should put a sign on the door which would connect with the patriarchs' meaning-system, for otherwise the men would be too curious/frightened about them and would break the door down to get in. They put a picture of a fish on the door.) Of course, you might say that *being* intelligible to them might be fatal. Well, perhaps it's best to be in a position to make tactical decisions about when and how to be intelligible and unintelligible.

If these, then, are some of the ways in which separation is at the heart of our struggle, it helps to explain why separation is such a hot topic. If there is one thing women are queasy about it is *actually taking power*. As long as one stops just short of that, the patriarchs will for the most part take an indulgent attitude. We are afraid of what will happen to us when we really frighten them. This is not an irrational fear. It is our experience in the movement generally that the defensiveness, nastiness, violence, hostility and irrationality of the reaction to feminism tends to correlate with the blatancy of the element of separation in the strategy or project which triggers the reaction. The separations involved in women leaving homes, marriages and boyfriends, separations from fetuses, and the separation of lesbianism are all pretty dramatic. That is, they are dramatic and blatant when perceived from within the framework provided by the patriarchal world view and male parasitism. Matters pertaining to marriage and divorce, lesbianism and abortion touch individual men (and their sympathizers) because they can feel the relevance of these to themselves—they can feel the threat that they might be the next. Hence, heterosexuality, marriage and motherhood, which are the institutions which most obviously and individually maintain female accessibility to males, form the core triad of antifeminist ideology; and all-woman spaces, all-woman organizations, all-woman meetings, all-woman classes, are outlawed, suppressed, harassed, ridiculed and punished—in the name of that other fine and enduring patriarchal institution, Sex Equality.

To some of us these issues can seem almost foreign . . . strange ones to be occupying center stage. We are busily engaged in what seem to *us* our blatant insubordinations: living our own lives, taking care of ourselves and one another, doing our work, and in particular, telling it as we see it. Still, the original sin is the separation which these presuppose, and it is that, not our art or philosophy, not our speechmaking, nor our "sexual acts" (or abstinences), for which we will be persecuted, when worse comes to worst.

Notes

1. Adrienne Rich: " . . . makes me question the whole idea of 'courtesy' or 'rudeness'—surely *their* constructs, since women become 'rude' when we ignore or reject male obnoxiousness, while male 'rudeness' is usually punctuated with the 'Haven't you a sense of humor' tactic." Yes; me too. I embrace rudeness; our compulsive/compulsory politeness so often is what coerces us into their "fellowship."
2. Ti-Grace Atkinson: "Should give more attention here to our vulnerability to assault and degradation, and to separation as *protection*." Okay, but then we have to re-emphasize that it has to be separation at *our* behest— we've had enough of their imposed separation for our "protection." (There's no denying that in my real-life life, protection and maintenance of places for healing are major motives for separation.)
3. See "Separatism and Sexual Relationships," in *A Philosophical Approach to Women's Liberation*, eds. S. Hill and M. Weinzweig (Wadsworth, Belmont, California, 1978).
4. I first noticed this when reading *Beyond God the Father*, by Mary Daly (Beacon Press, Boston, 1973). See also *Women's Evolution*, by Evelyn Reed (Pathfinder Press, New York, 1975) for rich hints about male cannibalism and male dependence.
5. Caroline Whitbeck: "Cross-cultural evidence suggests it's not the fetus that gets rejected in cultures where abortion is common, it is the role of motherhood, the burden, in particular, of 'illegitimacy'; where the institution of illegitimacy does not exist, abortion rates are pretty low." This suggests to me that the woman's rejection of the fetus is even more directly a rejection of the male and his world than I had thought.
6. In (improbably enough) *Philosophy and Sex*, edited by Robert Baker and Frederick Elliston (Prometheus Books, Buffalo, New York, 1976).

Study Questions

1. In what ways is the theme of separation present in radical feminism and absent in liberal feminism?

2. What does the systematic separatist experience? What can she conclude from what she experiences?
3. What leads Frye to think that men parasitize women, and not vice versa? How does she think that male parasitism helps explain opposition to abortion?
4. In what way does female separatism upset the power relationship between men and women?
5. How is definition another aspect of the power relations between men and women?

Black Women and Feminism

Barbara Omolade

The question of black women's relationship to feminism has been raised primarily to discover why black women have not joined the women's movement in large numbers and have been generally hostile to feminism. In other words, it has been raised as a strategic and organizational issue by white feminists in order to develop better ways to recruit black women into their movement. The question rarely gets raised as a political or theoretical issue seeking greater clarity and understanding of black women and white women: their differences and similarities, their separate histories and possible common interests. In discussing this issue, there is a need to put aside the narrow and limited confines of feminism as defined and dominated by mainly middle- and upper-class white women to reach a broader analysis that could include the experiences of all women under white male domination. By confining their theories to their own particular history and culture, white feminists have denied the history and culture of women of color and have objectively excluded them from equal participation in the women's movement.

White feminists claim that sexism and women's oppression cut beyond all racial and cultural boundaries and reach back to the fundamental purpose and function of the patriarchal family, which limited women to being childbearers and homemakers. But this view cannot be merely rhetorically spouted to get black women to march for the Equal Rights Amendment. For black women to begin to consider political alliances with white women, the rhetoric has to be either documented and proven or abandoned.

Even the most cursory examination of the cultures and history of black women, for example, would force feminists to raise questions about the universal oppression of women under patriarchy. The experiences of black women in West Africa before the colonial period, prior to 1490, and the experiences of white women in Western Europe during the same period (the Middle Ages) were quite different. Women in Western Europe were nonpeople, citizens without basic civil rights,[1] while black women enjoyed high status, and the civil and human

From Hester Eisenstein and Alice Jardine, eds., *The Future of Difference* (Boston: G. K. Hall, 1980), pp. 247–257. Reprinted by permission of Barbara Omolade. (Notes deleted.)

rights accorded all tribal members.[2] A thorough study of the role of women in traditional cultures has to be undertaken by African feminists; here we merely pose the theoretical framework and directions of that research. We assert simply that black women are not white women with color but are women whose color has obscured their historical and cultural experiences as Africans, as chattel slaves and as more than half the population of the black community. Their color has also obscured *their* assessment and understanding of their own experiences. Therefore, any attempt at dialogue between black women and white feminists must begin with a knowledge of the history of black women as *they* understand it, and the limitation of feminist theory as developed thus far.

Black women came to this country as captured chattel slaves from tribal communities that dotted the West African coast. Like their male counterparts they came against their will and under the force of European men possessing superior military technology. The 500 years of domination by white Europeans over the world's peoples of color wreaked havoc with the underpinnings and interworkings of the societies it exploited. Propped up by racism and male chauvinism, European cultural imperialism distorted, dismissed, and mocked the thoughts and actions of black women in traditional African societies. Black women and men in traditional African societies were conscious human beings who designed and constructed their own societies to meet their defined human needs. This seemingly self-evident statement is often overlooked by historical studies that depict black people beginning as slaves with no thoughts and ideas about the world.

African women in traditional culture were human, were citizens, and were valuable members of society. There is no concept in Africa that designates people as sub- or nonhuman, existing apart from the range of tribal law or human consideration. In contrast to European society, which continued the Greek tradition of granting the father the absolute right to sell, kill, or abandon his children,[3] African societies never condoned the mistreatment and abandonment of children regardless of their sex. There was sex-role differentiation: men and women had clearly designated roles and tasks. But this did not undermine the rights of women to participate in the tribal decision-making process, i.e., tribal and family councils; to have redress against mistreatment even by their husbands; and to have the right to own property and accumulate personal wealth and goods from their labor. As Chancellor Williams points out in *Destruction of African Civilization*, Africans were operating under a continent-wide constitution which outlined the rights of each member of the community, including women.[4]

African women were valued as childbearers, a sign to many feminists of oppression and restriction. But Africans viewed motherhood as an honor necessary for the tribe's continuance. Motherhood had a more critical place in the society than fatherhood; "the mother is sacred, her authority is so to speak unlimited."[5] In addition, African women did not belong to the husband's family, but continued to belong to their own family after marriage and were only temporarily separated from it. Feminists might legitimately raise the question of paternal rule over the women's family, since the African woman was still not free from patriarchal domination and protection. The crucial aspect here is not an assertion that African women were liberated in the context of industrialized twentieth-century societies, but whether they were citizens with political rights and economic freedoms that differed from European women living at the same time.

Preindustrialized traditional societies were characteristically overwhelmed by the struggle for physical survival. "In those primitive ages," Diop asserts, "when the security of the group was the primary concern, the respect enjoyed by either of the sexes was connected with its contribution to this collective security."[6] It is in this context that African tribal unity and egalitarianism must be understood.

When comparing black women in traditional African society and women in Europe, a qualitative difference in world view emerges. In Europe between 1500 and 1700 millions of women were burned at the stake as witches, ostensibly for communicating with God or practicing medicine outside the male-dominated church. But the witch hunts were a systematic attempt to eradicate any "heretical" thinking as well as independent activity of women. In contrast, female organizations in Western African tribes flourished and were responsible for educating women about sexuality, obstetrics, and gynecology. Men were forbidden by tribal law to interfere: even clitoridectomy was originally part of the practices of these female societies. There was no religiously reinforced system justifying male domination or a male priesthood controlling knowledge and excluding women in Africa. African men never pondered, as medieval church fathers did, whether women "had immortal souls" or were bestial in nature.[7] The religious systems in Africa included powerful female gods that often designated men and women as their god-children, requiring both to emulate and be obedient to her.

There was no economic system in Africa where women were either appendages, household ornaments, or worthless drudges. African women were workers encouraged to work and participate in the survival of the tribe and clan. Wealthy men were proud of their wives for working and managing market stalls which traded goods and crafts. Their activities enhanced the family's status and wealth.

Thus African women captured as slaves were brutally wrested from a society where they participated as human beings with firmly entrenched rights and status. It is not surprising, therefore, that from the beginning African women as well as men independently and collectively resisted enslavement. They did not want to leave Africa and clearly understood that their human rights were left on its shore.

There was no chattel slavery in Africa. The slaves of traditional African society were captured in wars, and had rights to manumission, to a family, and even entry into certain tribes as equal members. The trickling African slave trade began with the trade of African slaves to the Europeans. As more and more wealth began to accumulate in the hands of unscrupulous kings and tribal chieftains vying for power, unrestrained by more egalitarian tribal law, tribal members were taken and sold as slaves for minor offenses or without cause. This process was accelerated by Europeans attempting to foster the tribal divisions in Africa so they could reap profit and power for themselves.

African women captives were given no special privileges because of their sex. Men and women were force-marched, carrying heavy loads, to the coast to meet the Europeans and their ships. In addition, African women were systematically raped by slave catchers and slave holders. (This slavery-initiated practice has continued until fairly recently; because of their racial and class status, black women have been the source of available sex for white men.)

Irrespective of whether the father was rapist, slave-holder, or lover, slave women were expected to reproduce slaves, to assure even greater profits for the slaveholder. However, the prime reason black women and men were brought here as slaves was to work, to develop and extend the plantation system. The skills and strength of African women and men in large-tract agriculture, practiced communally in Western Africa, made them the most profitable source of labor for the white ruling class. Tremendous profits were realized in spite of the two-month slaveship journey, the loss of life due to disease and torture, and the "seasoning" process which turned captive Africans into productive slaves.

As workers, as mothers, and as forced sex partners, slave women were basic to the success of the slave system. On their sheer physical strength to work twelve hours in the field, bear and raise babies, and have sex on demand rested the fortunes of the slave owners. The brutal oppression suffered by black women gave rise to their militant resistance to the slave system. In this resistance the black woman was not alone, but was supported by the equally brutalized black man. For he, too, had been stripped of his birthright of liberty and the cultural right to define his own manhood. In fact, the use of men and women as chattel slaves gave rise to a unity and equality in resistance probably unknown before in the history of male/female relationships. Patriarchal protection of women ended when black women were enslaved, irrespective of their sex-defined roles in tribal law. They were on their own in facing the oppression, and thus worked hard with the black man in developing strategies and tactics for resisting slavery. Petitioning, escape, noncooperation, and armed struggle were the means they used.

This resistance took place within the context of a developing black society. The forging of a black society with cultural integrity and independence as its binding force and human and civil rights as its goal has long been neglected in studying the history of black people in this country. The black society has been able to build religious and educational institutions and develop social and community programs. The most important function of the black society, with black communities as its geographic base, has been the protection and sustenance of black people against the ravages of a racist and often fascist system.

In ignoring the existence and importance of a black society, historians have emphasized the roles of so-called exceptional and exemplary black people in Afro-American and American history. The individual contributions of Frederick Douglass, Harriet Tubman, and Sojourner Truth, though they were great, are discussed as if their achievements were miracles for black people to attain. Given the theoretical basis of unity in the black community and the practical need for a collective response to oppression, Harriet Tubman could not have emerged by herself. She was not merely affected by the brutality of her individual slave experiences, but represented the collective aspirations of all slaves for freedoms. Her revolutionary consciousness was shaped by those collective aspirations, which enabled her to "see" herself as an instrument to free her people. More concretely, Harriet Tubman could not have helped free slaves without the support of the slave community which lied and covered for runaway slaves, giving them an edge on pursuing masters, which stole food and protected runaways and isolated spies and betrayers. She could not have helped free slaves without the "free" black community being there to receive slaves when they escaped and to defend them against slave catchers.

By denying our collective aspirations for freedom and emphasizing certain individuals, feminists and feminist historians dismiss the question of political ideology and the conscious organizational response of black women and men to slavery. For example, they begin accounts of the abolitionist movement in the white community with William Lloyd Garrison, the Grimke sisters, and others. Their mention of blacks is cursory and matter-of-fact. They ignore the fact that it was black people who first called in an organized way for the abolition of slavery.

The call emerged as part of a growing movement by black people from pre-Revolutionary days which linked the struggle for an end to racism in the North with the struggle to resist slavery in the South.

> Under the impact of this revolutionary spirit, Negroes themselves, led by Absalom Jones, Prince Hall, and William Cuffee, became involved in the struggles; they protested the payment of taxes to a government denying them the rights of citizens; and they demanded freedom as a reward for fighting in defense of their country. Negroes also organized resistance to the slave trade and, in New England, even petitioned state legislatures for emancipation. . . . These early protests against American slavery yielded rich rewards. By 1808 the African slave trade was abolished, slaves were freed in Vermont, New Hampshire, Massachusetts, and Ohio, and gradual emancipation was provided for in Rhode Island, Pennsylvania, New Jersey, New York, and Connecticut. Although slave labor in these states had already decreased in importance as an economic factor and was being replaced by free labor, these early anti-slavery activities hastened the day of freedom.[8]

Thus, at least fifty years before 1832, when local and national abolition societies met in Philadelphia to form the American Anti-Slavery Society, black people had begun to organize resistance to slavery. The American Anti-Slavery Society apparently grew from the second annual meeting of the Convention of Colored Men, who had organized the year before to oppose emigration of black people to Africa as a solution to slavery and to press the demand for ''life, liberty, and the pursuit of happiness'' for black people. In 1831 the Convention invited Garrison, Lundy, the Tappan brothers, and other white abolitionist leaders to attend also. The next year the American Anti-Slavery Society launched its work with black people to end slavery.

The abolition movement brought together white women and the black community in a united front organized against white male power around the question of the abolition of slavery. White women correctly linked the oppression of slaves with their own oppression as women while the black community understood that alliances with white women would benefit their struggle against chattel slavery. However, the united front did not assure the equal inclusion of black women into feminist circles. There was outright racist exclusion such as the dissolution of the Massachusetts Female Anti-Slave Society at Fall River in 1838 when black women began attending meetings. And there was subtle racist exclusion such as failing to link their early concerns about women's rights with black women organized in antislave societies and the underground railroad. Both kinds weakened the unity between black and white women in fighting both racism and male chauvinism. It was not surprising therefore that white women viewed black abolitionist support, including that of early black feminist/abolitionist Frances Harper, for the Fifteenth Amendment, giving former slaves (male) citizenship and voting rights, as a betrayal of their own struggle for suffrage. Though Frederick Douglass and Frances Harper attempted to explain the difference between white women getting the vote and black people, former chattel slaves, getting the vote as legal recognition of their citizenship, white women nonetheless went ahead and formed the National Women's Suffrage Association. Thus white women formally broke the organized united front between those opposing racism and slavery and those opposing male chauvinism.

White women continued to organize as women, excluding black women, either explicitly or de facto. White women organized for entry as equals in the white-male-dominated economic and political system, while black women and the black community continued their struggles against racist and economic exploitation. This division continues to exist today, with white women organizing in opposition to white men, while black women have united with black men to struggle for national liberation from white male rule. These separate paths, though shaped by racist and class exploitation, come directly from the histories of black and white women before they came to this country. White women have had to fight for identity within a culture which has denied them a place as human or equal, while black women have had to fight for the survival of a culture which had defined them as equal and human but whose values and practices were undermined by European imperialism.

Furthermore, black women have joined white women's organizations and helped to develop feminist ideas and strategies, especially around suffrage, and have helped to lobby for white women to support black community struggles against racism. White women, on the other hand, have largely ignored the work of black women within their own community. Thus the tradition of black women organizers for social change has been neglected, especially by many feminist organizers.

One of these black women organizers, Ella Baker, bears closer examination because of her impact on the recent civil rights movement and her influence in shaping and defining the role of black women political activists in the last thirty years. She began organizing consumer cooperatives in New York City during the Depression but by the end of the 1930s was a field organizer for the National Association for the Advancement of Colored People, recruiting members primarily in the South. She traveled, often alone, throughout the South organizing people to join the NAACP as a way of fighting the racism in the rural South.

She tried to awaken the black people in their communities to a feeling of common need and that in numbers there is strength. She started with where people were at, helping them to identify the organization with the people they knew and who had helped them.[9] She believed "very firmly in the right of people who are under the heel to be the ones to decide the action they are going to take."[10]

These views, enabling people in the community to decide the direction and form of political action, were critical to building the mass movement in the black South against segregation and racism. The Montgomery Bus Boycott was initiated by Rosa Park, a black woman whose personal refusal to accept segregated seating on a bus precipitated the boycott and the later Freedom Rides. One year after four students sat in in protest against not being served food at a lunch counter, 70,000 students sat in throughout the South. Both these mass movements demonstrated the influence and soundness of Ms. Baker's theory of organizing community people. Ms. Baker worked for the Southern Christian Leadership Conference, which grew out of the Montgomery Bus Boycott at the time of the sit-ins.

> She called a conference of the students who were from the sit-ins to better coordinate their activities. The SCLC felt that they could influence how things went. They were interested in having the students become an arm of SCLC. "They were confident that this would be their baby because I was their functionary and had called the meeting." She refused to participate in persuading the students to join SCLC and subsequently resigned.[11]

She went to work for the Student Non-violent Coordinating Committee, the independent student group that became one of the most powerful black grass-roots organizations during the 1960s.

Though essential to the administrative development of three major civil rights organizations and critical to their reaching black community people throughout the South, Ms. Baker has insisted upon a supportive and back-seat role. She states,

> I knew from the beginning that as a woman, an older woman in a group of ministers who are accustomed to having women largely as supporters, there was no place for me to have come into a leadership role. The competition wasn't worth it![12]

Neither was the feminist theory and practice available which could have supported Ms. Baker in taking that leadership. There was no organized women's movement. The revolutionary examples of women in Vietnam, China, Cuba, and Angola were either not known or were yet to happen. There was no theory of revolutionary feminism to help her "come into a leadership role." She did not have a feminist perspective, though she acknowledges the significant role of black church women in the civil rights movement. Nor does she advocate anyone following her pattern, though most black women who participated in the civil rights movement did.

Following the legacy of Ella Baker, activist black women organizers have defined their role as supporting black male leadership, rather than "splitting" the unity of the movement for black liberation. Many have chosen to ignore or condemn the call of feminists to join them in fighting sexist oppression, as a ploy to sidetrack them from the larger issue of racism. Unfortunately, black men and their black women supporters lacked the understanding, though they experienced it, of the link between racism and sexism. The very biology of black women embodies that link. The separation and prioritizing has prevented the black community from correctly understanding the insidious and vicious nature of capitalism, which is propped up by racism and male chauvinism simultaneously. In fact, many black male leaders have restricted, rather than developed, the political participation of black women in their liberation struggle.

White feminists who could have educated and helped black women understand the nature of male chauvinism were blinded and confused by their own racism. They failed to develop a feminist view of racism which sees the interrelationship between racism and sexism, expressing itself in a militant and activist stand against racism. Instead, white feminists have frequently defined women's liberation in terms of employment opportunities and changing sex roles. They successfully ignore the history of black women as workers in Africa and this country, which have proven that economic independence from men is not liberation. Even more striking, most of black women's work has been under the direct supervision of white women as domestics or office workers. Even in hospitals, where many black women are employed, they are frequently supervised by white females. These women have been as domineering, arbitrary, and racist as white men. How can they ask black women to join them if they haven't even acknowledged white skin privilege?

The racism of white feminists has prevented unified and effective actions around issues that concern all women, such as rape. The definition of the issue of rape as posed by white women has excluded black women. White women speak out only about brutal rape and sneak attacks in the night, and rarely mention the business rape that women of color face from white men who own the factories and head the households where they work as servants. White women have also turned to the criminal justice system to prosecute rapists as a solution. But many black women are raped by black men, and reporting them to white cops, aside from raising questions about loyalty to black people in the face of common enemies, places them in positions of being ignored, mocked, or even threatened with rape by the policemen themselves.

In conclusion, to enable black women to pursue a dialogue with white feminists, a feminist theory needs to be developed and expanded to include our priorities and experiences. We have to begin to speak of a feminism that is black in its essence and historical roots and that is not isolated from the black community. We must speak of a feminism that seeks the root cause of our oppression under capitalism and links our struggles with the liberation struggles of other peoples of color in the world. Our feminism must expand the theories of revolutionary nationalism. It must aim at destroying male chauvinism in our brothers, while understanding that they have been the staunchest ally of black women in our fight for freedom. But this feminism cannot be defined or demanded on our behalf by white women or black men. No other group can demand liberation for us, because in doing so they take away our own capacity to organize and speak for ourselves.

The racism of white women will not allow them to give us the right to speak on our own behalf, and the male chauvinism of black men will not allow them to give us the right to speak on our own behalf. *We must take the right to speak from them.* The feminism of white women does not define us, nor can it lead us. When black women begin to organize in large numbers and become a political force, white women will have to say either that they only speak for themselves or that they stand with us against racist and sexist oppression.

Notes

1. Eleanor Flexner, *Century of Struggle* (Cambridge: Belknap Press, 1959, rev. 1979), p. 7.
2. Chancellor Williams, *Destruction of Black Civilizations* (Chicago: Third World Press, 1974), pp. 180–85.
3. Robert Flacelliere, "Daily Life in Greece at the Time of Pericles," in Michael Cherniavsky and Arthur Slavin, *Social Textures of Western Civilization: The Lower Depths* (Lexington, Mass.: Xerox College Publication, 1972), p. 129.
4. Williams, *Black Civilization*, pp. 180–85.
5. Cheikh Anta Diop, *Cultural Unity of Black Africa* (Chicago: Third World Press, 1959), p. 37.
6. Ibid., p. 34.
7. Sheila Rowbotham, *Women, Resistance and Revolution* (New York: Vintage Books, 1974), p. 20.

8. Philip Foner, ed., *Life and Writings of Frederick Douglass* (New York: International Publishers, 1975), Vol. I, p. 29.
9. Ellen Canterow and Susan O'Malley, "Ella Baker: Organizing for Civil Rights," in *Moving the Mountain: Women Working for Social Change* (New York: Feminist Press, 1980), pp. 9–13.
10. Ibid., p. 18.
11. Ibid.
12. Gerda Lerner, *Black Women in White America: A Documentary History* (New York: Vintage Books, 1973), p. 351.

Study Questions

1. In what way does Omolade think that white feminists have too narrowly defined feminism?
2. How does the history of black women differ from that of white women? How does this run against the grain of white feminist theory?
3. Specifically, how did black women's experience in slavery develop black male/female cooperation? How does that difference complicate feminist theory? How have white feminist historians "rewritten" this period of black history?
4. "The Abolition movement brought white and black women together." Does Omolade think this statement is absolutely true?
5. What division between black and white women exists at the present time?
6. What role have present-day black activist women defined for themselves?

5

Philosophy of Law

Laws—and the sanctions by which they are enforced—represent the authority of political institutions. Accordingly, philosophers have devoted considerable attention to substantive issues surrounding legal systems: What is a just law? Should an unjust law be obeyed? What is the relationship between law and morality?

Feminist philosophers have seen the centrality of legal issues for women. And women have looked to laws and the courts for redress for the inequities and crimes that impinge upon women privately and publicly. How well do legal institutions serve women? Is there gender-balance in the courts?

In response to such questions, feminists have explored areas of law that are of special concern to women: rape, sexual slavery, pornography, incest, sexual harassment in the workplace, sex discrimination, and the like. As Rosemarie Tong writes, feminists hope "to probe the nature and limits of the law—insofar as women and their sexuality are concerned."

According to feminists, sexual harassment is sex discrimination because it endangers a woman's job and threatens her economic livelihood. Rosemarie Tong wants to show the connection between women's social inequality and the sexual harassment of women in the marketplace. As Catharine MacKinnon writes, "Sexual harassment at work connects the jobs most women do—in which a major part of their work is to be there for men—with the structure of sexual relations—in which their role is also to be there for men." Tong holds that the legal system has not fully recognized this configuration. To demonstrate the claim that sexual harassment is sex discrimination, Tong shows its connection to women's social inequality.

Many, though by no means all, feminists have viewed pornography, in the words of Robin Morgan, as "the theory of which rape is the practice." Consequently, they have organized to campaign for antipornography laws. Helen Longino argues for the antipornography position on the grounds that pornography, unlike erotica, is women-degrading.

That is, it portrays women as sexually objectified, and it depicts disrespect for women as sexual beings. Thus, Longino defends the use of censorship. She contends that pornography itself is a form of violence against women since it supports the devaluation of women as a sex class.

Susan Griffin's analysis connects the criminal act of rape with the expression of culturally held norms about women's sexuality and availability in regard to men. Rape, she argues, is not an isolated or aberrant phenomenon but is, as Andrea Dworkin says, "in fact an exaggerated expression of accepted sexual relations between men and women." Griffin contends that rape is a threat to all women in that it reinforces men's dominance.

In their essay, Marilyn Frye and Carolyn Shafer examine what rape means to women and how it acts to keep women "in their place." Is rape primarily a violent act, a sexual act, or both? Finding out calls for a re-examination of what women have considered "normal" in heterosexual intercourse. Frye and Shafer believe that existing legislation on rape reflects the view of women as property, and they call for the concept of "woman as person."

In these and other issues, feminist principles are put into practice, challenging a perceived gender bias in the legal system, that is, the manner in which sexual inequalities are enforced by the laws themselves.

Sexual Harassment

Rosemarie Tong

A March 1980 article in *Newsweek* begins:

> It may be as subtle as a leer and a series of off-color jokes, or as direct as grabbing a woman's breast. It can be found in typing pools and factories, Army barracks and legislature suites, city rooms and college lecture halls. It is fundamentally a man's problem, an exercise of power almost analogous to rape, for which women pay with their jobs, and sometimes their health. It's as traditional as underpaying women—and now appears to be just as illegal. Sexual harassment, the boss's dirty little fringe benefit, has been dragged out of the closet.[1]

Indeed, sexual harassment has been brought out into the open and, unlike pornography and prostitution, which have been perceived as feminist issues, sexual harassment has been labeled a woman's issue: an issue that can directly affect any women in this country. It is surely odd to distinguish between feminist and women's issues, as if the two were mutually exclusive.

But this is the way the public tends to think. Nonetheless, had it not been for feminists, the problem of sexual harassment would never have been named, let alone confronted.

From Rosemarie Tong, *Women, Sex and the Law* (Totowa, NJ: Rowman and Littlefield, 1983). By permission of the author. (Notes deleted.)

Before the 1970s women largely accepted as an unpleasant fact of life what some of them called the "little rapes." With the emergence of consciousness-raising groups, many women (especially working women and students) began to feel that they need not and should not have to submit to these nagging violations of their persons. Speaking to women, Andrea Medea and Kathleen Thompson observed:

> If you are subjected . . . to this kind of violation every day, a gradual erosion begins—an erosion of your self-respect and privacy. You lose a little when you are shaken out of your daydreams by the whistles and comments of the construction workers you have to pass. You lose a little when a junior executive looks down your blouse or gives you a familiar pat at work. You lose a little to the obnoxious drunk at the next table, to that man on the subway, to the guys in the drive-in.[2]

As a result of people realizing that such abuses are common, the problem of sexual harassment was named in 1975. No sooner was the problem named than its seriousness as well as pervasiveness became apparent. For example, a 1976 issue of *Redbook* (by no means a feminist publication) reported that out of a sample of 9,000 readers, 88 percent had experienced some form of sexual harassment, and 92 percent considered the problem of sexual harassment serious.[3] Most women find that their job or academic performance degenerates as they are forced to take time and energy away from work or school to deal with sexual harassers. Indeed, fending off offensive sexual advances, especially if they are sustained over several weeks, months, or years, causes women tension, anxiety, frustration, and above all anger. Unfortunately, many women turn this anger not against their harassers, but against themselves. Gradually, they transform their initial feelings of righteous indignation into feelings of shame or guilt. Shame is experienced when a woman feels that she has not lived up to a self-imposed ideal image of herself as a person who can control men's reactions to her body. In contrast, guilt is experienced when a woman feels that she has not lived up to society's standards for female behavior, one of which instructs women to meet men's sexual wants and needs with grace, generosity, and good humor. Plagued by intense feelings of shame (failure) or guilt (transgression), an increasing number of women workers and students suffer from what has been termed "sexual harassment syndrome." Victims of this syndrome can experience psychological depression, if not also physical ailments, such as "stomachaches, headaches, nausea, involuntary muscular spasms, insomnia, hypertension, and other medical illnesses."[4]

Unfortunately, victims of sexual harassment syndrome are sometimes scoffed at. When five women students and a male assistant professor filed a class-action suit at Yale, contending that male faculty members had engaged in sexually offensive behavior, resulting in a multitude of harms, university officials responded in a defensive manner. As one spokesman for Yale said, "It's not a new thing, but it is also not a major problem." Another university official added, "There is a stronger argument that if women students aren't smart enough to outwit some obnoxious professor, they shouldn't be here in the first place. Like every other institution, Yale has its share of twisted souls."[5]

Given such varied reactions to sexual harassment and its deleterious consequences, it poses problems of definition analogous to those posed by pornography and prostitution. This article will discuss recent attempts to define sexual harassment and to distinguish it clearly from sexual attraction. Standard as well as preferred feminist legal responses to sexual harassment will be evaluated, noting that the former tend to invoke versions of both the offense principle and the harm principle, whereas the latter tend to invoke only the harm principle. Finally, the discussion will focus on when the appropriate response to an incident of sexual harassment is a legal remedy and when it is an extralegal remedy, arguing that the law is best invoked when the price one must pay for her sexual integrity is an education or occupational opportunity/position.

The Ubiquitous Phenomenon

Although definitions of sexual harassment are by no means uniform, many feminist antiharassers agree that sexual harassment involves four conditions: (1) an annoying or unwelcome sexual advance or imposition; (2) a negative response to this sexual advance/imposition; (3) the presence of intimidation or coercion when the sexual harasser holds more power than the person sexually harassed and, frequently, (4) the suggestion that institutionally inappropriate rewards or penalties will result from compliance or refusal to comply.

This preliminary definition, critics point out, leaves much to be desired. First, it fails to illuminate the connection between the sexual advance/imposition, the negative response, and the institutional consequences. For instance, how forceful must the response be? How serious must the consequences be? Second, the definition fails to make clear who this society's power-holders are. Must one be an employer or a professor in order to have power over a woman employee or a woman student? Or does the mere fact that a person is male give him an automatic power over a female's fate? Third, it fails to distinguish between the kind of coercion that consists of a threatened penalty and the kind that consists of a promised reward. Properly speaking, is not the latter form of coercion more aptly described as a pressure tactic or an incentive technique? Fourth, and most important, the definition fails to indicate which of the four conditions are necessary for sexual harassment and which are sufficient.

In response to these criticisms, but especially the last one, feminists have refined their definition of sexual harassment. As they see it, there are two types of sexual harassment: coercive and noncoercive. Coercive sexual harassment includes (1) sexual misconduct that offers a benefit or reward to the person to whom it is directed, as well as (2) sexual misconduct that threatens some harm to the person to whom it is directed. An example of the first instance would be offering someone a promotion only if she provides a sexual favor. An example of the second instance would be stating that one will assign a student a failing grade unless she performs a sexual favor. In contrast, noncoercive sexual harassment denotes sexual misconduct that merely annoys or offends the person to whom it is directed. Examples of noncoercive sexual misconduct are repeatedly using a lewd nickname (''Boobs'') to refer to an attractive co-worker, or prowling around the women's dormitory after midnight. What coercive and noncoercive modes of sexual harassment have in common, of course, is that they are unsolicited, unwelcome, and generally unwanted by the women to whom they are directed.[6]

Coercive Sexual Harassment

According to feminists, a coercive act is ''one where the person coerced is made to feel compelled to do something he or she would not normally do.''[7] This compulsion is accomplished by the coercer's ''adversely changing the options available for the victim's choosing.''[8] The paradigm case of coercion is, of course, the use of physical or psychological restraint, but *threats* of physical or psychological restraint/reprisal are also coercive to a lesser degree. Although it is difficult to determine whether a sexual harasser has in fact narrowed for the worse the options available for a woman's choosing, John Hughes and Larry May provide two tests to facilitate such determinations: would the woman have ''freely chosen'' to change her situation before the alleged threat was made for her situation after the broaching of the alleged threat; and, would the woman be made ''worse off'' than she otherwise would be by not complying with the offer?[9]

Relying on Hughes and May's twofold test, feminists maintain that sexual advances/impositions that threaten some harm to the person to whom they are directed are clearly coercive. "If you don't go to bed with me, Suzy, I'll fail you in this course." Assuming that Suzy has not been secretly longing to sleep with her professor or to flunk her course, she would not freely choose to change her situation to one in which the only way she can attain a passing grade is by sleeping with him. Therefore, because Suzy's professor has adversely altered her options, he has coerced her into a very tight corner; and since a coercive sexual advance is by definition an instance of sexual harassment, Suzy's professor is guilty of sexual harassment.

In contrast to sexual advances backed by threats, feminists admit that sexual advances backed by offers do not constitute clear cases of sexual harassment. Nonetheless, like sexual threats, sexual offers are coercive. It is just that the bitter pill of coercion is coated with a sugary promise: "If you go to bed with me, Suzy, I'll give you an 'A' in this course." According to critics, however, feminists confuse seduction with sexual harassment when they conflate sexual offers with sexual threats—when they insist that every time a man pressures a woman for a sexual favor by promising her a reward he coerces her into saying an unwilling yes to his request. In this connection, Michael Bayles asks feminists to ponder the following hypothetical case:

> Assume there is a mediocre woman graduate student who would not receive an assistantship. Suppose the department chairman offers her one if she goes to bed with him, and she does so. In what sense has the graduate student acted against her will? She apparently preferred having the assistantship and sleeping with the chairman to not sleeping with the chairman and not having the assistantship . . . the fact that choice has undesirable consequences does not make it against one's will. One may prefer having clean teeth without having to brush them; nonetheless, one is not acting against one's will when one brushes them.[10]

As Bayles sees it, the department chairman has not coerced the graduate student to sleep with him. Rather he has seduced her to sleep with him. Consequently, whatever the chairman is guilty of, it is not sexual harassment. Bayles's reasons for insisting that the graduate student has not been coerced are two. First, she would have freely chosen to move from the preoffer stage (no chance of an assistantship) to the postoffer stage (a chance of an assistantship). Second, her options after the sexual offer are not worse than before. If she refuses the sexual offer, she will not lose a chance for an assistantship because she was never in the running; and if she accepts the sexual offer, she will have not only a chance for an assistantship, but an assistantship. Despite the superficial plausibility of Bayle's analysis, feminists (once again following Hughes and May) insist that a deeper reading of the graduate student's dilemma indicates that she has in fact been coerced by her department chairman. In the first place, assuming the graduate student has not been dying to go to bed with her chairman, and that she is not a calculating mercenary who has been hoping for a sexual offer to bail her out of a dead-end career trajectory, it is not clear that she would have freely chosen to move from the preoffer stage to the postoffer stage. The best reason for her not wishing to move to the postoffer stage is that it places her in a "damned if you do, damned if you don't" predicament.

On the one hand, if the graduate student refuses to sleep with her chairman, she will of course *not* receive an undeserved assistantship. In addition, she will place herself at considerable risk. Perhaps the chairman is talking sweetly today only because he thinks the graduate student will be in his bed tomorrow. Should she disappoint him, he may turn against her. This is a real possibility, given the unpredictable character of sexual feelings and the history of reprisals against women who turn down sexual offers. On the other hand, if the graduate student agrees to sleep with the chairman—either because she wants an assistantship or because she fears angering him (a possibility that Bayles overlooks)—she increases her vulnerability to other professors as well as to the chairman. Other professors might imitate their chairman's behavior—after all, he got away with it—adding a degree of instability and potential for arbitrary treatment not only to this particular student's future, but to all female graduate students' futures. Once such considerations are factored in, feminists observe that the chairman has in fact boxed his graduate student into a corner from which she cannot emerge unscathed. Consequently, whatever else the chairman is guilty of (such as depriving a worthy candidate of an assistantship), he is also guilty of sexual harassment.

Noncoercive Sexual Harassment

Clear cases of coercive sexual harassment affect a woman's options so adversely that she gives in to her harasser's threats or offers simply because her other options seem so much worse. Unlike the sexual seducer who showers a woman with gifts so that she will at long last *willingly* leap into his arms, the coercive sexual harasser waves his stick or carrot in front of a woman, not caring how *unwilling* she is when she jumps into his bed. Significantly, what distinguishes the noncoercive sexual harasser from both the sexual seducer and the coercive sexual harasser is that his primary aim is not to get a woman to perform sexually for him, but simply to annoy or offend her.

Although it is possible to argue that the ogler's, pincher's, or squeezer's sexual misconduct is coercive, it is difficult. Many women fear calling attention not only to the sexual misconduct of their employers and professors, who can cost them their jobs or academic standing, but also to the sexual misconduct of strangers—strangers who have no long-term economic or intellectual power over them, but who nonetheless have the short-term power of physical strength over them. For example, in a recent *New York Times* article, Victoria Balfour reported that although women are frequently sexually harassed at movie theaters, they very rarely complain to theater managers. One highly educated woman who had been afraid to report an incident of sexual harassment to the theater manager commented: "He might think that somehow I had done something that made the man want to bother me, that I had provoked him. To me, harassment has its implications, like rape."[11] Two other women silently endured a harasser for the duration of another film. Although their harasser's behavior was extremely offensive, they did not report the incident: "He was staring heavily, breathing heavily and making strange noises. We didn't move because we were afraid if we got somebody to deal with him, he'd be waiting outside afterward with a knife."[12] All three of these women kept silent because they feared provoking their harassers to some heinous deed.

To claim that these theatergoers were *coerced* into silence is, according to feminists, to accomplish some good at the risk of effecting considerable harm. On the one hand, the public ought to realize that, for women, being bothered at the movies, in the subways, and on the streets by youthful girl-watchers, middle-aged creeps, and dirty old men is a routine occurrence. On the other hand, women ought not to think of themselves as helpless victims who dare not confront their harassers for fear of retaliatory violence. Therefore, on balance, feminists are of the opinion that it is best to reserve the term *coercive* for cases of sexual harassment that involve specific threats or offers, especially if these threats or offers are made in the context of the workplace or academy. This is not to suggest, however, that feminists think that cases of noncoercive sexual harassment are always less serious than cases of coercive sexual harassment. No woman wants to be coerced into a man's bed; but neither does a woman want to be hounded by a man who takes delight in insulting, belittling, or demeaning her, and who may even find satisfaction in driving her to distraction. This being the case, feminists insist that the law attend to cases of unwanted *noncoercive* as well as unwanted coercive sexual harassment. But this is no light request to make of a law that, like some Freudians, is still wondering what women really want.

Standard Legal Responses

Although the law is better suited to deal with cases of coercive sexual harassment than with cases of noncoercive sexual harassment, it has attempted to provide remedies for both types of misconduct. Traditionally, the two major legal avenues open to victims of sexual harassment have been criminal proceedings and civil suits, which invoke tort law. The rationale behind the criminal-proceedings approach depends straightforwardly on the harm principle, whereas the rationale behind civil suits relies on a mixture of the harm and offense principles. The fact that these two rationales differ is not without consequence. The civil law (= tort law) tends to take sexual harassment even less seriously than the criminal law does.

Criminal Proceedings: Invoking the Harm Principle

Criminal proceedings are now, as in the past, less frequently employed than civil suits. This is not surprising given that the criminal sanction is appropriate only if the sexually harassed woman is a victim of rape, indecent assault, common assault, assault causing bodily harm, threats, intimidation, or solicitation. That is, unless a woman is *seriously* harmed by her harasser, a prosecutor is not likely to press criminal charges, and if she is seriously harmed, the prosecutor is not likely to charge her harasser with sexual harassment but with rape, indecent assault, and so on.

   The prosecutor's course of action is prima facie rational. If a woman's "harasser" is in no way connected with her place of education or employment, it is confusing and trivializing to describe his rape of her as an extreme incident of sexual harassment. But if a woman is coerced to submit to sexual intercourse as a condition of successful employment or education, then her rape is technically best described as aggravated sexual harassment. If the prosecutor wishes to be precise about the whole affair, then he should work toward an aggravated sexual harassment conviction rather than a rape conviction. But be this as it may, a victim of sexual harassment who seeks the aegis of the criminal law is not likely to get very far. Should an adult working woman or an adult student complain of indecent assault, the police are not likely either to lay charges for her or to pursue her case absent of witnesses, other than herself, to the episode. Says one police officer:

> If a girl came to us and told us her boss had called her into the office, put his arm around her, and grabbed her breast, we would first investigate to see if there was some additional evidence. No judge would convict without further evidence. Out practice is that we will not deal with complaints of this kind without some corroborating evidence. It's just too easy for her employer, an upstanding man in the community, to testify that she had asked him for a raise, that he had turned her down, and that this false cry of assault was her ploy to get even.[13]

   If a victim of sexual harassment encounters such a police officer, she may, in absence of his support, lay criminal charges herself. Should she pursue this course of action, however, the district attorney would probably not argue her case. She would be forced to hire a private prosecutor to do her arguing and "it is common knowledge that the judges who hear private prosecutors treat them with much less concern than they do police-laid charges."[14] Realizing this, victims of sexual harassment have tended to bypass the criminal sanction unless they are able to find other women who have been similarly harassed by the particular man involved. The sole victim of *even* extreme forms of sexual harassment is unlikely to be taken seriously. Oftentimes police officers and prosecutors are unable to recognize the special coercion, the extra harm, inherent in extreme forms of sexual harassment that occur in the workplace or the academy. They are apt to think that such cases are episodes of mutually agreeable sexual relations gone awry: "A guy and a gal are together—she's prepared to go along for a few months—after that she wants to cut it off and he doesn't."[15] In short, male members of the criminal justice system are quite reluctant to invoke the harm principle against sexual harassers because they remain unconvinced, on some level, that sexual harassment can indeed constitute a serious harm to a woman's physical or psychological integrity.

Civil Torts: Invoking the Harm and Offense Principles

Given the criminal law's limitations, victims of sexual harassment have turned instead to the civil law, which seems better suited to succor the individual woman who has been sexually harassed. Whereas criminal liability exists to exact a penalty from a wrongdoer in order to protect society as a whole, tort liability exists primarily to compensate the injured person by requiring the wrongdoer to pay for the damage he or she has done. Like criminal law, tort law designates that liability is progressively greater as the defendant's actions range from mere inadvertence, to negligence of likely consequences, to intentional invasion of another's rights under the mistaken notion that no harm is being committed, to instances where the motive is a "malevolent desire to do harm."[16] Because tort law is oriented to victim compensation in a way that the criminal law is not, and because guilty tort-feasors are punished less severely than guilty criminal offenders, in many more instances than the criminal law, tort law will take a strict liability approach, often requiring even the person who merely acted inadvertently or negligently to compensate the individual(s) harmed by his or her thoughtless or careless action(s). Likewise, tort law will, in many more instances than the criminal law, address what I have termed "offenses" (behavior that embarrasses, shames, disgusts, or annoys someone), sometimes requiring the merely offensive person to compensate his or her victim.

1. *Types of Torts:* While new torts are emerging all the time, there are several existing torts that may be particularly applicable to cases of sexual harassment: battery, assault, and the intentional infliction of mental or emotional disturbance.

a. *The Battery Tort:* Battery is defined as "an intentional and unpermitted contact, other than that permitted by social usage."[17] While contact must be intentional, intent to cause all the damages that resulted from the contact is not necessary to establish liability. In other words, a harasser may be guilty of battery simply because he intended to touch a woman without her consent, even though he meant her no harm or offense. So, for example, battery includes instances in which a compliment is intended. Absent her consent, it is tortious, for example, to kiss an "unappreciative woman" under the mistletoe. Because the battery tort considers contact with the body or anything already in contact with the body (such as clothing), it is a useful tort for victims to use against harassers who go beyond verbal abuse. Usually physical contact is not tortious unless it represents socially unacceptable behavior ("breast squeezing" or "fanny-pinching"). Nonetheless, in some cases, socially acceptable behavior ("cheek kissing" or "hand pressing") may be tortious if it is known by the harassers that the receiver of such contacts objects to and does not permit them. In either event, the victim of battery may win her suit, especially since she need not prove—as the victim of rape has had to prove until recently—her lack of consent through some show of resistance.

b. *The Assault Tort:* Where physical contact has not occurred, the tort of assault may be actionable. Assault is "an intentional act, short of contact, which produces *apprehension* of a battery."[18] As Catharine MacKinnon notes, the tort of assault applies to the person placed in fear of an immediately harmful and minimally offensive "touching of the mind, if not the body." Since the invasion is mental, the defendant must have intended at least to arouse psychic apprehension in his victim. Although the fear-producing event must consist of "more than words alone," without words the intentions of the harasser may remain equivocal.[19]

Because the lines between psychic and physical battery are easily crossed, battery and assault doctrines are frequently combined in practice. Catharine MacKinnon provides several examples of successful torts brought under this combined doctrine in the early 1900s. In an age of heightened sexual sensibilities, it was not unusual for cases to be brought forward such as the one in which "a railroad was found responsible for the embarrassment and humiliation of a woman passenger caused when a drunken man, of whose boisterous conduct and inebriated condition the railroad was aware, fell down on top of her and kissed her on the cheek."[20] In another case, "a woman recovered damages for assault and battery against a man who squeezed her breast and laid his hand on her face."[21]

The Intentional Infliction of Mental or Emotional Disturbance Tort

Contemporary sexual mores make it difficult to take altogether seriously the cases MacKinnon describes in today's courts. Unlike her early twentieth-century counterpart, today's woman does not take umbrage at every peck on the cheek or laying on of hands. This does not mean, however, that today's woman either *does* or *should* take in stride every obnoxious ogle, every offensive touch, and every suggestive gesture. As in the past, unwanted or annoying sexual advances/impositions can affect a woman adversely. For this reason, the tort of intentional infliction, in words or acts, of mental or emotional disturbance is gaining currency. Although this tort may be the most difficult to use against sexual harassers, because it includes only those offenses that cause "purely emotional disturbance,"[22] it is also the most promising in that it probably covers those forms of sexual harassment calculated to wear down a woman's resistance.

Consider, for example, the specific tort of intentional infliction of nervous shock. In order for this tort to apply, the sexual harasser must have either purposely, knowingly, or recklessly desired to cause alarm or fright in his victim. Moreover, his conduct must have been serious enough to cause nervous shock in a normal person (unless he was aware of his victim's peculiar susceptibility to emotional shock), and the victim's nervous shock must have physical or psychopathological consequences. Given that sexual harassers often badger their victims systematically over a long period of time, some women do suffer from nervous shock, or sexual harassment syndrome. An example may clarify matters. Over an eight-month period, David Eccles had "persistently telephoned" Marcia Samms at all hours of the night or day, begging her to have sexual intercourse with him. Although Mrs. Samms repeatedly told Eccles to stop bothering her, he kept on soliciting her. Eventually, Mrs. Samms became so emotionally distressed that she brought suit against Eccles for three thousand dollars in damages. The Supreme Court of Utah in *Samms* v. *Eccles* (1961) found that Mrs. Samms had grounds for suit (cause of action).[23] The court decision reads:

> We quite agree with the idea that under usual circumstances, the solicitation to sexual intercourse would not be actionable even though it may be offensive to the offeree. It seems to be a custom of longstanding and one which in all likelihood will continue. The assumption is usually indulged that most solicitations occur under such conditions as to fall within the well known phrase of Chief Judge Magruder that "there is no harm in asking." The Supreme Court of Kentucky has observed that an action will not lie in favor of a woman against a man who,

without trespass or assault, makes such a request; and that the reverse is also true: that a man would have no right of action against a woman for such a solicitation. But the situation just described, where tolerance for the conduct referred to is indulged, is clearly distinguishable from the aggravated circumstances the plaintiff claims existed here.[24]

1. *Problems with the Tort Approach:* This case is important in that it offers recourse to women who are subjected to both aggravated and severely disturbing sexual harassment. Nonetheless, for at least three reasons the tort approach is problematic not only in this form, but in its battery and assault forms.

a. *The Issue of Consent:* At least in battery cases, the harasser may claim that the woman consented to his sexual advances. This objection is significant because the harasser is not liable for his actions if the woman agreed to submit to them. Unfortunately, it is no easy matter to determine if a woman consented to a sexual advance. For this reason, in cases of sexual harassment, as in cases of rape and woman-battering, the law has straddled between two approaches: One focuses on whether the sexual misconduct was clearly consented to; the other focuses on the consequences of the sexual misconduct without emphasizing issues of consent. Where the law has favored the consent strategy, it has adopted methods similar to those it uses in rape cases. That is, it has sought to establish consent (a mental state) by looking to the victim's resistance or lack thereof (a behavioral manifestation).

In some sense the victim who fails to resist the man who paws her does consent to his pawing. But given that women are still socialized to be "nice" to men, it will take a strong woman to say a loud "No, thank you" to a man who has more arms than an octopus has tentacles. Andrea Medea and Kathleen Thompson report that one woman went so far as to follow her eventual rapist into a dark alley because she feared "offending" him by implying that he might rape her. Rather than berating the woman for her naivete, Medea and Thompson ask their female readers to recall all those times and places in which they paid attention to a man for fear of hurting his feelings.

Realizing that many women are currently unable to express forcefully their nonconsent to an unwanted sexual advance/imposition, the law has recently experimented with the so-called consequences approach. This approach assumes that it is easier to measure the effect that unwanted sexual propositions have on female victims than it is to determine whether a female victim's lack of overt resistance to them is a sign of her tacit consent to them. If Jane experiences depression, anxiety, frustration, and even nausea or vomiting as a result of being repeatedly manhandled by Dick, she has been sexually harassed whether or not she was able to communicate her nonconsent to Dick by telling him to "shove off" or by splashing a glass of ice water on his face.

The consequences approach is an *effective* way to handle sexual harrassment cases. But critics wonder whether it is a *fair* way to handle such cases, since Dick, for example, may have sincerely believed that Jane was enjoying his pawings and pattings. Under such circumstances, it does not seem unambiguously just to penalize Dick, since much of Anglo-American law teaches that unless a man knowingly or recklessly harms someone, he is not to be sanctioned for the harm he effects, unless, of course, a standard of negligence is employed. This being the case, even when the consequences approach is employed and the harassed woman does not have to prove her lack of consent, her case is strengthened where she has made her dissent quite clear through words and actions.

b. *The Issue of Hypersensitivity:* Where consent is not an issue, the harasser may claim that he had no reason to believe that the woman he touched or threatened to touch would be offended or frightened. That is, he had no reason to believe that his target was a hypersensitive individual. In such cases, the harasser will be liable only if his conduct would have been offensive to a person of ordinary sensibilities. So, for example, Dick is liable for the battery of Jane, whom he patted on the posterior, if, but only if, a person of ordinary sensibilities would have been offended by such physical contact. But since this person of ordinary sensibilities is generally termed "the ordinary *man*," problems could arise for the female victim of sexual harassment. As Catharine MacKinnon notes:

> Ordinary women probably find offensive sexual contact and proposals that ordinary men find trivial or sexually stimulating coming from women. Sex is peculiarly an area where a presumption of gender sameness, or judgments by men of women, are not illuminating as standards for equal treatment, since to remind a man of his sexuality is to build his sense of potency, while for a man to remind a woman of hers is often experienced as intrusive, denigrating, and depotentiating.[25]

To summarize, although a typical man in this culture may like it when a strange woman squeezes muscles, a typical woman will probably not like it when a strange man squeezes her breasts or buttocks. And there will be times when a man will not be able to understand, say, why a woman does not always (or usually) appreciate wolf whistles. Of course, these differences of perspective could be remedied by a supplemental ordinary *woman* test, but this would require the law to confront squarely its male-biases—a major review for which it may not be ready.

2. *The Issue of Harm:* Where neither consent nor hypersensitivity is an issue, the harasser may argue that his victim did not suffer the harm she claims to have suffered. Such a defense is likely to set off a battle between *his* medical experts and *her* medical experts, the former arguing that Jane is of sound body and mind, the latter insisting that Jane is the shell of her former self. Unless such battles can be avoided, it may not be worth the victim's time, energy, and reputation to sue her harasser.

Feminist Legal Responses: Antidiscrimination Law

Even if it can be shown that a woman has not consented to her harasser's sexual advances, that she is not a hypersensitive individual, and that she has indeed suffered harm as a result of her harasser's sexual misconduct, it is not clear that the tort approach best serves sexually harassed women's interests. Catharine MacKinnon notes that the "aura of the pedestal," more properly viewed as a "cage," distorts cases such as the one in which a judge preached, "every woman has the right to assume that a passenger car is not a brothel and that when she travels in it, she will meet nothing, see nothing, hear nothing, to wound her delicacy or insult her womanhood."[26] But to construe resistance to sexual harassment as a return to prudery is, according to feminists, to miss the point: Sexual harassment is not so much an issue of offensive behavior as an issue of abusive power.

But if sexual harassment is more an issue of power than an issue of offense, the tort approach, which emphasizes unseemly sexual conduct, must, in the estimation of feminists, be supplemented by a legal approach stressing that women often submit to unwanted sexual advances simply because their position in society is inferior relative to men. Not only are most men physically more powerful than most women, but it is men and not women who hold the balance of power in the political, economic, and social institutions that govern us all. Because antidiscrimination law is sensitive to these power dynamics, it can accomplish more for sexually harassed women than tort law. Whereas tort law views sexual harassment as an outrage to an individual woman's sensibilities and to a society's purported values, antidiscrimination law casts the same act either as one of *economic* coercion, in which the material survival of women in general is threatened, or as one of *intellectual* coercion, in which the spiritual survival of women in general is similarly jeopardized. If a woman wishes to argue that she has been sexually harassed not because she is vulnerable Sally Jones, but because she is a woman, a member of a gender that suffers from institutionalized inferiority and relative powerlessness, then the antidiscrimination approach obviously suits her purposes best.

Discriminatory Sexual Harassment: A Historical Survey

Despite the cogency of this line of reasoning, feminists were *initially* unable to convince the courts that sexual harassment could in fact constitute sex-based discrimination in the workplace and in the academy. The workplace decisions, resting on Title VII, which prohibits sex-based discrimination in employment, represent an upward struggle from the first case brought under it, *Corne v. Bausch and Lomb, Inc.*,[27] through several subsequent cases (*Miller v. Bank of America*[28] and *Tomkins v. Public Service Electric and Gas Co.*,[29] to the landmark case *Barnes v. Costle*).[30] To a greater or lesser extent all these cases reveal two attitudes the courts had to overcome on the way to recognizing discriminatory sexual harassment: (1) sexual attraction between a man and a woman is a personal matter in which the courts should not intervene; and (2) the practice of sexual harassment is so prevalent that if courts became involved they would be flooded with complaints, many of which might be false or trivial.

In *Corne v. Bausch and Lomb, Inc.*, two female clerical workers sued for a violation of their civil rights based on sex discrimination. As a result of the offensive and unwelcome sexual liberties their male supervisor had taken with them, these two women were forced to resign their positions. In dismissing their complaint, the court gave several reasons, the chief of which was that sexual harassment is a "personal proclivity, peculiarity, or mannerism," which employers can not be expected to extirpate in their employees.[31] Said the court, "The only sure way an employer could avoid such charges would be to have employees who were asexual."[32] Incidentally, the trial judge found unimaginable precisely what Margaret Mead has encouraged; namely, that society establish a sexual taboo in the workplace (and by parity of reasoning, in the academy). Flatly stated, Mead's incest taboo asserts that "You don't make passes at or sleep with the people you work with."[33]

Although many feminists think Mead's asexual approach is too drastic, it gains strength in view of *Miller v. Bank of America*. In this case the court dismissed the complaint of a female bank worker who was fired when she refused to be "sexually cooperative" with her male supervisor. The court concluded that "The attraction of males to females and females to males is a natural sex phenomenon and it is probable that this attraction plays at least a subtle part in most personnel decisions. Such being the case, it would seem wise for the courts to refrain from delving into these matters."[34] This decision is particularly distressing not only because it conflates sexual attraction (a desirable social phenomenon) with sexual harassment (an undesirable social phenomenon), but because it suggests that unwanted manhandling is something that "big girls" must accept unless the company that employs their harassers *explicitly* endorses such hanky panky as a matter of policy (or some sort of fringe benefit for male employees).

That the courts have had trouble taking sexual harassment seriously as well as distinguishing between sexual attraction and sexual harassment is even more apparent in a case that followed *Miller*. In *Tomkins v. Public Service Electric and Gas Co.*, the court dismissed Tomkins's complaint, commenting that a sexually motivated assault that takes place in a "corporate corridor" is no more the concern of Title VII than a sexually motivated assault that takes place in a "back alley."[35] Title VII does not address the labyrinthine issue of sexual desires, and were the courts to encourage women to sue male co-workers and employees whose sexual attentions they had tired of, "an invitation to dinner could become an invitation to a federal lawsuit, if some harmonious relationship turned sour at a later time.''[36] This court decision supposes that vindictive women would sue their male subordinates on trumped-up charges; similarly, hysterical or hypersensitive women would sue their male superordinates for the most trivial of reasons.

Fortunately, not all courts are as benighted as those that ruled in *Corne, Miller,* and *Tomkins.* In *Barnes* v. *Train (Costle),* the Washington, D.C., District Court originally found against the plaintiff, a woman who was first denied promotion and then fired for having refused the sexual advances of her supervisor. Ironically, the woman's supervisor was none other than the director of the Environmental Protection Agency's Equal Employment Opportunities Division. The suit was initially rejected on the grounds that sexual harassment does not constitute sex discrimination. The court contended that the woman plaintiff had been denied promotion not because of her sex, but because of her refusal to accede to the director's sexual demands. Conceding that the supervisor's behavior may have been inexcusable, the court nonetheless insisted that the behavior did not constitute an ''arbitrary barrier to continued employment based on plaintiff's sex.''[37] On appeal, the D.C. circuit court reversed, declaring that discrimination *was* involved, since the declined invitation had been issued only because the plaintiff was a woman. Said Judge Robinson for the court:

> But for her womanhood, from aught that appears, her participation in sexual activity would never have been solicited. To say, then, that she was victimized in her employment simply because she declined the invitation is to ignore the asserted fact that she was invited only because she was a woman subordinate to the inviter in the hierarchy of agency personnel. Put another way, she became the target of her superior's sexual desires because she was a woman, and was asked to bow to his demands as the price for holding her job.[38]

As a result of this decision, the courts now seem prepared to find sex-based discrimination in the workplace.

In the same way that Title VII is an available remedy for sexually harassed working women, Title IX (1972 Education Amendments) is an available remedy for sexually harassed students. With the exception of the still-pending *Alexander* v. *Yale* case, in which five women students and a male assistant professor filed a class-action suit, contending that male faculty members had engaged in sexually offensive conversations and behavior resulting in a multitude of harms, the courts have not, as yet, handled Title IX cases.[39] However, should such cases be generated and processed, they will probably follow Title VII precedents. Such litigations explicitly promise to reveal the limits of antidiscrimination law as it has developed so far. In handling the grievances of working women and also of female students (who are sexually harassed more frequently by their fellow students than by their male professors), the courts will have to confront squarely the problem of peer-on-peer sexual harassment, a type of harassment that they have already encountered in *Continental Can Co.* v. *Minnesota.*[40] In this case, the Minnesota Supreme Court extended employer liability beyond the actions of supervisory personnel to those of co-workers. To the degree that *Continental Can Co.* sets a precedent for other jurisdictions, it requires the courts to rethink the three major conditions for discriminatory sexual harassment outlined in *Barnes.* There the court ruled that sex-based discrimination may be found only (1) when the victims of sexual harassment are of only one sex; (2) when the harasser is in a position to affect the terms or conditions of the victim's employment; and (3) when the harassment has a verifiably adverse impact on the victim (that is, it is not trivial).

Discriminatory Sexual Harassment: A Doctrinal Analysis

The first major condition for discriminatory sexual harassment is that it does not exist unless *only women* or *only men* are being harassed by a particular supervisor or professor. Arguably, neither Title VII nor Title IX prohibits a bisexual male supervisor/professor from sexually harassing his employees/students—provided that he harasses men as well as women.

1. *The Disparate Treatment Approach:* Regarding Title VII, sexual harassment is discriminatory when a male supervisor, for example, sexually pursues a woman simply because she is a woman, pawing and patting her when there is nothing except her sexuality to separate her from similarly situated male employees. Likewise, it is discriminatory when a female supervisor sexually pursues a man simply because he is a man, coming on to him when there is nothing except his sexuality to separate him from similarly situated female employees. Much the same could be said about male homosexual or lesbian supervisors with the necessary adjustments.

The problem with the "disparate-treatment" approach is that only a fraction of women/men present in an employment situation is likely to be victimized by any particular incident of sexual harassment. As a result, there will be a tendency to detach the incident from the group referent necessary to establish a case under Title VII. This is precisely what happened in the cases preceding *Barnes* v. *Costle*. In these cases the courts suggested that the female employees had been singled out for sexual attention not so much because they were members of the gender group women, but either because of their unique personal characteristics, such as red hair, or because of their sex-specific characteristics, such as large breasts. (A sex-specific characteristic is one that is not shared by both genders and which is possessed by only a subset of the gender class in question.) Since there is no sex discrimination unless a plaintiff can show that her personal injury contains a sufficient gender referent, a red-headed, large-breasted, sexually harassed woman employee must be able to explain why her employer has not harassed similarly situated blond, flat-chested women, if all he was interested in was *a woman* and not a specific kind of woman with red hair and large breasts. Supposedly, if she cannot explain this, she does not have cause to invoke title VII, although she may have grounds for an assault or battery tort action.

But all this seems rather ludicrous. The sexually harassed red-haired or large-breasted woman does have an explanation for her employer's conduct: He would not be sexually harassing her were she a man or were she her employer's boss. In other words, when a woman invokes Title VII rather than slapping her harasser with an assault or battery suit, she wants to stress that had she not been a female employee in a subordinate position she would not have been sexually harassed.

Implicit in this argument is the suggestion that harassment is not an expression of sexual lust, but a show of power. Contrary to the *Tomkins* court, there is a difference, at least of degree, between an incident of sexual harassment that occurs in a "corporate corridor" and one that occurs in a "back alley." An employer has control over one's life in a way that a stranger does not. And when a company tolerates the sexual harassment of one female employee, it makes an implicit statement to all female employees, telling them that their merits are to be measured not in terms of their skills or job performance, but in terms of their sexual attractiveness and compliance. In short, when a heterosexual male employer harasses only one female employee, he not only treats her disparately but also affects her reference group disparately.

2. *The Disparate-Impact Approach:* According to the "disparate-impact" approach to discriminatory sexual harassment, the motivating impetus for harassment is indeed sexuality (whether male or female), which results in discrimination "only when conjoined with social traditions of male heterosexual predominance in academic and employment hierarchies."[41] Therefore, this approach suggests that when an individual male employee is sexually harassed by

a female employer, the discrimination he experiences is of the disparate-treatment rather than the disparate-impact variety. Given the way society is still structured, men are less likely than women to become fearful as a group when one of their number is sexually harassed by an employer of the opposite sex.

3. *Comparing the Disparate-Treatment and Disparate-Impact Approaches:* Regarding women, the disparate-impact approach to discriminatory sexual harassment seems more serviceable and promising than the disparate-treatment approach. Because the disparate-impact approach focuses on structural considerations (women's general position in society), it reminds the courts that women have yet to achieve parity with men either in the workplace or in the academy. In the past, the courts were either not served this reminder or they chose to ignore it. More recently, the courts have taken off their blinders. Increasingly, they are realizing that sexual harassment is a serious problem for many working and learning women. For example, the female worker may find herself at the mercy of her male supervisor, who, in an attempt to avoid liability and follow the letter of his company's official antiharassment policy, may not discharge or demote her, but may instead make working conditions so intolerable for her that she will "voluntarily" resign. Fortunately, the courts have come to see these "voluntary" resignations for what they are: "constructive discharges."

As a result of such realizations, the courts are taking a stronger line with respect to those institutions that fail to protect their employees from even the more subtle forms of adverse consequences attendant upon discriminatory sexual harassment: the assignment of undesirable work, close surveillance of performance, failure to enlist co-worker cooperation where necessary, unwillingness to provide adequate training, and failure to release recommendations for promotion. Despite a history of vacillation, the courts now seem prepared to hold employers liable for all acts of sexual harassment perpetrated by their employees, "regardless of whether the employer knew or should have known of their occurrence" except sexual harassment by co-workers.[42] In other words, if Tilly is sexually harassed by her foreman, then the foreman's employer is liable for his actions. It matters not that the employer did not know, or should not have been expected to know, what his foreman was doing. The employer is strictly liable. In contrast, if Tilly is harassed by her co-worker Joe, then the employer must have *actual* or constructive knowledge of Joe's misbehavior in order to be liable for it.

This last point is worth developing because most sexual harassment occurs between peers. There is no reason to view such sexual harassment as discriminatory, however offensive it may be, unless an employer (such as a corporation or a university) is understood to tolerate, endorse, or condone it. By failing to sanction the sexually-harassing conduct of its nonmanagerial and nonsupervisory employees, the employer lets them poison the work atmosphere. If the men on the assembly line are making passes at Rosy the Riveter and Betty the Bolter, and the employer, Cast Iron Works, does nothing to stop them, even though its managers and supervisors either know or should know what is going on, then Cast Iron Works is liable for their misbehavior where the other tests of liability under Title VII are met. Similarly, if the fraternity boys are sexually harassing members of the Feminist Alliance and the university does nothing to stop them, even though its deans and professors either know or should know what is going on, then the university is liable for their misbehavior when the other tests of liability under Title IX are met.

Extralegal Remedies

The current trend of the courts is to hold employers (corporations or universities) responsible for what goes on in the workplace or in the academy. In fact, Title IX already requires universities to adopt and publish grievance procedures providing for prompt and equitable resolution of student complaints of sexual harassment. Because sexual harassment has been kept in the closets of colleges and universities for many years, most grievance procedures are not capable of providing prompt and equitable resolution of student complaints. In the past, students have complained about members of the faculty or school who have harassed them, and some of this harassment has been explicitly sexual; however, quite a bit of it has been so-called gender harassment.

Gender harassment is related to sexual harassment as genus is to species: Sexual harassment is a form of gender harassment. Catharine MacKinnon comments "Gender *is* a power division and sexuality is one sphere of its expression. One thing wrong with sexual harassment . . . is that it eroticizes women's subordination. It acts out and deepens the powerlessness of women as a gender, *as women.*"[43] Whereas gender harassment is a relatively abstract way to remind women that their gender role is one of subordination, sexual harassment is an extremely concrete way to remind women that their subordination as a gender is intimately tied to their sexuality, in particular to their reproductive capacities and in general to their bodily contours.

Examples of verbal sexual harassment include those comments (in this case, written comments) to which female coal miners were subjected at the Shoemaker Mine in the late 1970s. Because women had never worked in the mine before, they were, from the moment they appeared on the scene, scrutinized by male eyes. Although the tension between the female and male coal miners was considerable, it was bearable until a rash of graffiti appeared on the mine walls. The graffiti focused on the women's physical characteristics. For example, one woman who had small breasts was called "inverted nipples," and another woman who supposedly had protruding lower vaginal lips was called the "low-lip express."[44] Subjected to such offensive social commentary on this and other occasions, the female miners found it increasingly difficult to maintain their sense of self-respect, and their personal and professional lives began to deteriorate.

In contrast to these examples of verbal sexual harassment stand more sanitized but not necessarily less devastating examples of verbal gender harassment. Unlike instances of verbal sexual harassment that focus on women's bodies, these latter comments, illustrations, and jokes call attention to women's gender traits and roles. It is interesting that a gender harasser may describe female gender traits and roles either in negative terms (women are irrational, hysterical, defective) or in seemingly positive terms (women are nurturing, self-sacrificing, closer to nature). In both cases, however, the gender harasser will add credence to the *"kinder, kirche, kuche"* theory of womanhood, according to which women's biology and psychology naturally suit them for bearing and raising children, praying in church, and cooking.

Although women are routinely subjected to gender harassment, society as a whole remains unconvinced that female students, for example, should take umbrage when their professors gender harass them. Nonetheless, given the educational mission of academic institutions, and the fact that women students may be more vulnerable to their professors' sexist remarks ("Women can't do math") than their professors' sexual innuendos ("It's a joy having your body—oops! your *person*—in this class, Miss Jones"), Title IX should, and probably does, cover cases of gender harassment.

In this connection, it is important to note that Title VII has already covered several gender-harassment cases. Recently, for example, a woman named Ms. Bay, who was employed by EFCS (Executive Financial Counselling Service) in Philadelphia, won a successful sex-discrimination suit against her boss, Gordon Campbell. Although Mr. Campbell never sexually harassed Ms. Bay by calling attention to or touching her body in any way, he did gender-harass her. On one occasion Mr. Campbell asked Ms. Bay whether her husband would "suffer for food and clean clothes while she was away on business trips." On other occasions he contacted clients, on his own initiative, to inquire whether they objected to dealing with a woman and to see what they thought of Ms. Bay, "although such evaluations had never been requested for a male member of the EFCS staff." On still another occasion he arranged a seminar training program for a male employee while providing no such training program for Ms. Bay, despite her requests and despite Mr. Campbell's private comments to his superiors that her seminar performance was weak and in need of improvement. After listening to the recounting of these and other incidents, the judge ruled that, although Ms. Bay quit, she was really fired because "any reasonable person would have reacted to the situation at EFCS much as she did."[45]

Realizing that liability for sexual harassment and gender harassment belong to them as well as to authorities in the workplace, academic deans and other college personnel have tried to handle student harassment complaints informally. Their attempts have not always been successful. Not wanting to make mountains out of molehills, and arguing that young women frequently "imagine" things, some college officials have downplayed student reports of gender and sexual harassment. Even where they have taken such reports seriously and acted upon them, they have tended to keep them quiet in the name of discretion, preferring to let things "cool off" or "work themselves out." As a result of the students' rights movement, students have pressed their respective colleges and universities to handle such matters in a more formal and public manner. Students have also become much more concerned about student-on-student sexual harassment, which is a very pervasive fact of campus life. Understandably, deans and professors, who have by and large abandoned their *in loco parentis* roles, fear to invade their students' privacy. Realizing that students who come from diverse backgrounds will, as a matter of course, experience some difficulty in adjusting to one another's sexual mores, they fear making an issue out of what may be nothing more than normal social adjustment. And even when college officials discern a problem on campus, they resist setting up quasi-legal procedures to handle it. Predictably, deans and professors tend to argue that the way to handle sensitive problems such as sexual harassment is through educational forums rather than litigation.

Indeed, education is needed. Despite the breakdown of many sexual stereotypes, the macho ideal of the strong man lives on, as does the ideal of the vulnerable female. In large measure, this fact explains the growing incidence of "date-rape" on campuses. Crossed signals and mixed messages characterize many student sexual relations. Says one man:

> I get told "no," . . . and I keep going. I guess if someone said, "Look, sorry, I thought I wanted to, but I changed my mind, no way!" I'd listen, but if we're lying on the bed and she puts her little hands up in front of her chest and says, "Oh, please, no, I'm not sure about this," I ignore it. Nobody complains afterward."[46]

Women have to learn to say no, and men have to learn to take a *no* at face value. Moreover, women have to stop blaming themselves when men sexually harass them. This may be particularly difficult for a young woman to do. She may not have met enough different types of men to realize that it's not always something about her or her body that turns a man on, but something about his need to assert himself. Arguably, the more secure a man is about his masculinity, the less need he will have to harass women sexually or otherwise. Failing to understand this, a young woman may berate herself for her harasser's conduct. She may punish herself for being sexed by starving or neglecting her body. The epidemic of anorexia on many campuses is not unrelated to young women's fear of their own sexuality; and the unkempt appearance of some young women is often evidence of their attempt to kill the "temptress" in themselves.

Not surprisingly, educators want to help students escape these destructive prisons. But, as always, education is a long-term process. In the interim, college officials must set up and enforce internal grievance procedures to handle both faculty-on-student and student-on-student sexual harassment. Such quasi-legal remedies are not in opposition to a college's educational mission. On the contrary, they serve to remind the college community that it is susceptible to the same human foibles and power plays that characterize society in general.

Internal grievance procedures have been set up in many workplaces as well as at many academic institutions even though Title VII does not require employers to *maintain* grievance procedures. Since agreement has arisen in Title VII sexual harassment cases that there is no cause for judicial action *if* the employer takes prompt and remedial action upon acquiring knowledge of an incident, prudent employers have decided to set up mechanisms that can facilitate quick and corrective action. Unfortunately, these internal grievance procedures can be subverted. Company officials can convince all but the most determined of women that it is in her best interest to keep things quiet. One government official, who was interviewed by Constance Backhouse and Leah Cohen, opined that women should avoid both internal grievance procedures and complaints made directly to a personnel manager or management:

> The personnel director will most likely go to the sexual harasser and have a quiet little chat and a good laugh and express any number of the following statements:
>
> > She brought it on herself.
> >
> > She can take care of herself.
> >
> > She was obviously willing.
> >
> > She is vindictive, as a result of a love affair gone sour.
> >
> > In fact, this is an isolated incident, not a serious problem.
> >
> > She is a troublemaker.[47]

This official went on to add that, if at all possible, the sexually harassed woman should either start looking for another job—''A woman is in real jeopardy if she can't get along in government. Who will hire you in private industry, if you are fired by the government?''—or if this is not a viable option, she should start looking for a ''tough feminist lawyer'' who will take the case as a ''personal challenge.''[48]

Conclusion

Sexual harassment is a phenomenon deeply rooted in the sexist assumptions that women can turn men ''on'' or ''off'' at will, and that sexual harassment is nothing more serious than old-fashioned flirtation. As such, it clearly must be approached on social and cultural as well as legal levels. However, because of its intangible or blurry-edged nature, sexual harassment often seems to be a problem with which the law, in its insistence on clear definitions and consistent guidelines, does not seem best suited to deal. The broad concept of institutional liability, which encourages the development of internal grievance procedures and internal education programs, may thus be the ideal way of confronting and remedying cases of sexual harassment. But the ideal is not always realized, and women—especially women workers and students—find themselves without effective remedies, short of quitting their jobs or leaving school. As Catharine MacKinnon has noted, the sexual subordination of women interacts with other forms of social power that men have over women. To be precise: ''Economic power is to sexual harassment as physical force is to rape.''[49] And regarding Title IX, intellectual power is to gender harassment on the campus as economic power is to gender or sexual harassment in the workplace as physical force is to rape anywhere. Rape and harassment are abuses of power as well as expressions of male sexuality. The power that makes rape or harassment effective derives from the superior position that the rapist or harasser holds by virtue of his social position.

As in the past, men remain powerful today. Their power is currently derived not so much from their brawn or their brains as from the fact that the major institutions of society—law, education, medicine, government, business, and science—are still largely controlled by them. Only when these institutions, for whatever reasons, begin to evolve in ways that allow women full access to them will the balance of power between men and women equalize. Fortunately, this institutional evolution is already in process.

In particular, the law is being tailored to fit women's as well as men's needs. Avenues of legal action against sexual harassers are both a powerful educational tool and an important means for women to assert and protect their rights to personal respect and self-determination, especially in the workplace and in the academy, while they wait for those rights to be accepted into the canon of cultural assumptions.

Faced with the possibility of legal consequences, men may be forced to reconsider their assumptions about women, employers may be forced to recognize their workers as workers rather than sexually exploitable conveniences, and institutes of higher education may be forced to extend their promise of an environment supportive rather than inhibitive of intellectual growth to female students. Once this happens, the incidences of gender harassment, especially its sexual forms, are likely to decrease. Where neither men nor women have superior power as a group, there is no need to use "sexuality" as a cruel weapon, reminding the powerless just how limited their options are.

Notes

1. A. Press et al., "Abusing Sex at the Office," *Newsweek*, March 10, 1980, p. 81.
2. Andrea Medea and Kathleen Thompson, *Against Rape* (New York: Farrar, Straus and Giroux, 1974), p. 50.
3. Constance Backhouse and Leah Cohen, *Sexual Harassment on the Job* (Englewood Cliffs, N.J.: Prentice-Hall, 1982), p. 34.
4. Ibid., pp. 38–39.
5. Ibid., pp. 39–40.
6. John C. Hughes and Larry May, "Sexual Harassment," *Social Theory and Practice* 6 (Fall 1980): 251.
7. Ibid., p. 252.
8. Ibid.
9. Ibid.
10. Ibid., p. 249; cf. Michael Bayles, "Coercive Offers and Public Benefits," *The Personalist* 55 (Spring 1974): 142–43.
11. Victoria Balfour, "Harassment at Movies: Complaints Rare," *New York Times*, November 17, 1982, p. C24.
12. Ibid.
13. Backhouse and Cohen, *Sexual Harassment on the Job*, p. 101.
14. Ibid.
15. Ibid., p. 103.
16. Frank J. Till, *Sexual Harassment: A Report on the Sexual Harassment of Students* (Washington, D.C.: National Advisory Council on Women's Educational Programs, 1980), pt. II, p. 13.
17. Ibid.
18. Ibid.
19. Catharine MacKinnon, *Sexual Harassment of Working Women* (New Haven, Conn.: Yale University Press, 1979), pp. 165–66.
20. Ibid., p. 166.
21. Ibid.
22. Ibid., p. 167.
23. *Samms* v. *Eccles* (1961), in Wright I. Linden, *Canadian Tort Law*, 6th ed. (Toronto: Butterworths, 1975), pp. 52–54.
24. Ibid.
25. MacKinnon, *Sexual Harassment of Working Women*, p. 171.
26. Ibid., p. 172.
27. 390 F. Supp. 161 (1975), U.S. Dist. Ct., D. Arizona.
28. 418 F. Supp. 233 (1976), U.S. Dist. Ct., N.D. California.

29. 422 F. Supp. 553 (1976), U.S. Dist. Ct., New Jersey.
30. 561 F. 2nd. 983 (1977), U.S. Ct. of Appeals, D.C. Circuit.
31. Backhouse and Cohen, *Sexual Harassment on the Job*, p. 119.
32. Ibid.
33. Margaret Mead, "A Proposal: We Need Taboos on Sex at Work," *Redbook*, April 1978, p. 31.
34. *Miller v. Bank of America*, 418 F. Supp. 233 (1976), U.S. Dist. Ct., N.D. California.
35. Backhouse and Cohen, *Sexual Harassment on the Job*, p. 121.
36. Ibid., p. 122.
37. *Barnes v. Train* (Costle), 13 FEP Cases 123, 124 (D.D.C. 1974).
38. *Barnes v. Costle*, 561 F. 2d at 992, n. 68 (D.C. Cir. 1977).
39. *Alexander et al. v. Yale University*, 459 F. Supp. 1 (D. Conn. 1977).
40. *Continental Can Co. v. Minnesota* (Minn. S.C. 1980).
41. Ibid., pp. 260–61.
42. Till, *Sexual Harassment*, pt. II, p. 9.
43. MacKinnon, *Sexual Harassment of Working Women*, pp. 220–21.
44. Raymond M. Lane, "A Man's World: An Update on Sexual Harassment," *The Village Voice*, December 16, 1981, p. 20.
45. *Philadelphia Inquirer*, September 9, 1982, p. 1A.
46. Karen Barrett, "Sex on a Saturday Night," *Ms.*, September 1982, p. 50.
47. Backhouse and Cohen, *Sexual Harassment on the Job*, p. 72.
48. Ibid.
49. MacKinnon, *Sexual Harassment of Working Women*, pp. 217–18.

Study Questions

1. Why might one call sexual harassment a *women's* issue as opposed to a *feminist* issue? Does Tong agree with that characterization?
2. Why and how do feminists distinguish between coercive and noncoercive sexual harassment? What tests can be applied to tell whether coercion has taken place?
3. Consider the case of the "mediocre woman graduate student." How does Bayles argue that such a case is *not* sexual harassment? How does Tong reply? Do you agree with her reply?
4. Why are criminal proceedings rarely employed in sexual harassment cases?
5. What is tort law? How does it differ from criminal law? Why is tort law possibly a more adequate avenue of attack against sexual harassment? In what way is the tort approach problematic?
6. Why do feminists think that the tort approach needs to be supplemented by an antidiscrimination approach? What obstacles did the view initially face in the courts? What case proved a turning point? Why?

Pornography, Oppression, and Freedom: A Closer Look

Helen E. Longino

A question which is often asked at the beginning of any discussion on pornography is "How do you define it?" The answer is difficult. A good clear definition of pornography has eluded everyone. Twenty years ago, the United States Supreme Court was defining pornography as material which "taken as a whole appeals to prurient interest." Ten years later, Justice Potter Stewart said, "I can't define it, but I know it when I see it." Today federal law states that the definition of pornography is to be left up to the individual communities to decide. This, of course, has totally confused the country. What seems to be acceptable in San Francisco may be appalling in a small town, and communities themselves are having trouble deciding what they think is "patently offensive" and without "serious literary, artistic, political or scientific value." Feminists have a further objection to this definition: If pornography does not offend local community standards, we say, then something is wrong because it should!

In this paper, . . . feminist philosopher Helen Longino puts forth a serious definition of pornography which we believe withstands a rigorous and critical examination and which may prove helpful to teachers, doctors, laypeople, and jurists—anyone, in fact, who is interested in a good working definition of the term. She goes on to apply this definition to the question of pornography and the First Amendment.

Introduction

The much-touted sexual revolution of the 1960's and 1970's not only freed various modes of sexual behavior from the constraints of social disapproval, but also made possible a flood of pornographic material. According to figures provided by WAVPM (Women Against Violence in Pornography and Media), the number of pornographic magazines available at newsstands has grown from zero in 1953 to forty in 1977, while sales of pornographic films in Los Angeles alone have grown from $15 million in 1969 to $85 million in 1976.

Traditionally, pornography was condemned as immoral because it presented sexually explicit material in a manner designed to appeal to "prurient interests" or a "morbid" interest in nudity and sexuality, material which furthermore lacked any redeeming social value and which exceeded "customary limits of candor." While these phrases, taken from a definition of "obscenity" proposed in the 1954 American Law Institute's *Model Penal Code*, require some criteria of application to eliminate vagueness, it seems that what is objectionable is the explicit description or representation of bodily parts or sexual behavior for the purpose of inducing sexual stimulation or pleasure on the part of the reader or viewer. This kind of objection is part of a sexual ethic that subordinates sex to procreation and condemns all sexual interactions outside of legitimized marriage. It is this code which was the primary target of

From Laura Lederer, ed., *Take Back the Night* (New York: Morrow, 1980), pp. 26–39. Reprinted by permission of Helen E. Longino. (Notes deleted.)

the sexual revolutionaries in the 1960's, and which has given way in many areas to more open standards of sexual behavior.

One of the beneficial results of the sexual revolution has been a growing acceptance of the distinction between questions of sexual mores and questions of morality. This distinction underlies the old slogan, "Make love, not war," and takes harm to others as the defining characteristic of immorality. What is immoral is behavior which causes injury to or violation of another person or people. Such injury may be physical or it may be psychological. To cause pain to another, to lie to another, to hinder another in the exercise of her or his rights, to exploit another, to degrade another, to misrepresent and slander another are instances of immoral behavior. Masturbation or engaging voluntarily in sexual intercourse with another consenting adult of the same or the other sex, as long as neither injury nor violation of either individual or another is involved, are not immoral. Some sexual behavior is morally objectionable, but not because of its sexual character. Thus, adultery is immoral not because it involves sexual intercourse with someone to whom one is not legally married, but because it involves breaking a promise (of sexual and emotional fidelity to one's spouse). Sadistic, abusive, or forced sex is immoral because it injures and violates another.

The detachment of sexual chastity from moral virtue implies that we cannot condemn forms of sexual behavior merely because they strike us as distasteful or subversive of the Protestant work ethic, or because they depart from standards of behavior we have individually adopted. It has thus seemed to imply that no matter how offensive we might find pornography, we must tolerate it in the name of freedom from illegitimate repression. I wish to argue that this is not so, that pornography is immoral because it is harmful to people.

What Is Pornography

I define pornography as *verbal or pictorial explicit representations of sexual behavior that*, in the words of the Commission on Obscenity and Pornography, *have as a distinguishing characteristic "the degrading and demeaning portrayal of the role and status of the human female . . . as a mere sexual object to be exploited and manipulated sexually."* In pornographic books, magazines, and films, women are represented as passive and as slavishly dependent upon men. The role of female characters is limited to the provision of sexual services to men. To the extent that women's sexual pleasure is represented at all, it is subordinated to that of men and is never an end in itself as is the sexual pleasure of men. What pleases women is the use of their bodies to satisfy male desires. While the sexual objectification of women is common to all pornography, women are the recipients of even worse treatment in violent pornography, in which women characters are killed, tortured, gang-raped, mutilated, bound, and otherwise abused, as a means of providing sexual stimulation or pleasure to the male characters. It is this development which has attracted the attention of feminists and been the stimulus to an analysis of pornography in general.

Not all sexually explicit material is pornography, nor is all material which contains representations of sexual abuse and degradation pornography.

A representation of a sexual encounter between adult persons which is characterized by mutual respect is, once we have disentangled sexuality and morality, not morally objectionable. Such a representation would be one in which the desires and experiences of each participant were regarded by the other participants as having a validity and a subjective importance equal to those of the individual's own desires and experiences. In such an encounter, each participant acknowledges the other participant's basic human dignity and personhood. Similarly, a representation of a nude human body (in whole or in part) in such a manner that the person shown maintains self-respect—e.g., is not portrayed in a degrading position—

would not be morally objectionable. The educational films of the National Sex Forum, as well as a certain amount of erotic literature and art, fall into this category. While some erotic materials are beyond the standards of modesty held by some individuals, they are not for this reason immoral.

A representation of a sexual encounter which is not characterized by mutual respect, in which at least one of the parties is treated in a manner beneath her or his dignity as a human being, is no longer simple erotica. That a representation is of degrading behavior does not in itself, however, make it pornographic. Whether or not it is pornographic is a function of contextual features. Books and films may contain descriptions or representations of a rape in order to explore the consequences of such an assault upon its victim. What is being shown is abusive or degrading behavior which attempts to deny the humanity and dignity of the person assaulted, yet the context surrounding the representation, through its exploration of the consequences of the act, acknowledges and reaffirms her dignity. Such books and films, far from being pornographic, are (or can be) highly moral, and fall into the category of moral realism.

What makes a work a work of pornography, then, is not simply its representation of degrading and abusive sexual encounters, but its implicit, if not explicit, approval and recommendation of sexual behavior that is immoral, i.e., that physically or psychologically violates the personhood of one of the participants. Pornography, then, is verbal or pictorial material which represents or describes sexual behavior that is degrading or abusive to one or more of the participants *in such a way as to endorse the degradation*. The participants so treated in virtually all heterosexual pornography are women or children, so heterosexual pornography is, as a matter of fact, material which endorses sexual behavior that is degrading and/or abusive to women and children. As I use the term "sexual behavior," this includes sexual encounters between persons, behavior which produces sexual stimulation or pleasure for one of the participants, and behavior which is preparatory to or invites sexual activity. Behavior that is degrading or abusive includes physical harm or abuse, and physical or psychological coercion. In addition, behavior which ignores or devalues the real interests, desires, and experiences of one or more participants in any way is degrading. Finally, that a person has chosen or consented to be harmed, abused, or subjected to coercion does not alter the degrading character of such behavior.

Pornography communicates its endorsement of the behavior it represents by various features of the pornographic context: the degradation of the female characters it represented as providing pleasure to the participant males and, even worse, to the participant females, and there is no suggestion that this sort of treatment of others is inappropriate to their status as human beings. These two features are together sufficient to constitute endorsement of the represented behavior. The contextual features which make material pornographic are intrinsic to the material. In addition to these, extrinsic features, such as the purpose for which the material is presented—i.e., the sexual arousal/pleasure/satisfaction of its (mostly) male consumers —or an accompanying text, may reinforce or make explicit the endorsement. Representations which in and of themselves do not show or endorse degrading behavior may be put into a pornographic context by juxtaposition with others that are degrading, or by a text which invites or recommends degrading behavior toward the subject represented. In such a case the whole complex—the series of representations or representations with text—is pornographic.

The distinction I have sketched is one that applies most clearly to sequential material— a verbal or pictorial (filmed) story—which represents an action and provides a temporal context for it. In showing the before and after, a narrator or film-maker has plenty of opportunity to acknowledge the dignity of the person violated or clearly to refuse to do so. It is somewhat more difficult to apply the distinction to single still representations. The contextual features cited above, however, are clearly present in still photographs or pictures that glamorize degradation and sexual violence. Phonograph album covers and advertisements offer some prime examples of such glamorization. Their representations of women in chains (the Ohio Players), or bound by ropes and black and blue (the Rolling Stones) are considered high-quality commercial "art" and glossily prettify the violence they represent. Since the standard function of prettification and glamorization is the communication of desirability, these albums and ads are communicating the desirability of violence against women. Representations of women bound or chained, particularly those of women bound in such a way as to make their breasts, or genital or anal areas vulnerable to any passerby, endorse the scene they represent by the absence of any indication that this treatment of women is in any way inappropriate.

To summarize: Pornography is not just the explicit representation or description of sexual behavior, nor even the explicit representation or description of sexual behavior which is degrading and/or abusive to women. Rather, it is material that explicitly represents or describes degrading and abusive sexual behavior so as to endorse and/or recommend the behavior as described. The contextual features, moreover, which communicate such endorsement are intrinsic to the material; that is, they are features whose removal or alteration would change the representation or description.

This account of pornography is underlined by the etymology and original meaning of the word "pornography." *The Oxford English Dictionary* defines pornography as "Description of the life, manners, etc., of prostitutes and their patrons [from πόρνη (porne) meaning "harlot" and γράφειν (graphein) meaning "to write"]; hence the expression or suggestion of obscene or unchaste subjects in literature or art."

Let us consider the first part of the definition for a moment. In the transactions between prostitutes and their clients, prostitutes are paid, directly or indirectly, for the use of their bodies by the client for sexual pleasure.[1] Traditionally males have obtained from female prostitutes what they could not or did not wish to get from their wives or women friends, who, because of the character of their relation the the male, must be accorded some measure of human respect. While there are limits to what treatment is seen as appropriate toward women as wives or women friends, the prostitute as prostitute exists to provide sexual pleasure to males. The female characters of contemporary pornography also exist to provide pleasure to males, but in the pornographic context no pretense is made to regard them as parties to a contractual arrangement. Rather, the anonymity of these characters makes each one Everywoman, thus suggesting not only that all women are appropriate subjects for the enactment of the most bizarre and demeaning male sexual fantasies, but also that this is their primary purpose. The recent escalation of violence in pornography—the presentation of scenes of bondage, rape, and torture of women for the sexual stimulation of the male characters or male viewers—while shocking in itself, is from this point of view merely a more vicious extension of a genre whose success depends on treating women in a manner beneath their dignity as human beings.

Pornography: Lies and Violence Against Women

What is wrong with pornography, then, is its degrading and dehumanizing portrayal of women (and *not* its sexual content). Pornography, by its very nature, requires that women be subordinate to men and mere instruments for the fulfillment of male fantasies. To accomplish this, pornography must lie. Pornography lies when it says that our sexual life is or ought to be subordinate to the service of men, that our pleasure consists in pleasing men and not ourselves, that we are depraved, that we are fit subjects for rape, bondage, torture, and murder. Pornography lies explicitly about women's sexuality, and through such lies fosters more lies about our humanity, our dignity, and our personhood.

Moreover, since nothing is alleged to justify the treatment of the female characters of pornography save their womanhood, pornography depicts all women as fit objects of violence by virtue of their sex alone. Because it is simply being female that, in the pornographic vision, justifies being violated, the lies of pornography are lies about all women. Each work of pornography is on its own libelous and defamatory, yet gains power through being reinforced by every other pornographic work. The sheer number of pornographic productions expands the moral issue to include not only assessing the morality or immorality of individual works, but also the meaning and force of the mass production of pornography.

The pornographic view of women is thoroughly entrenched in a booming portion of the publishing, film, and recording industries, reaching and affecting not only all who look to such sources for sexual stimulation, but also those of us who are forced into an awareness of it as we peruse magazines at newsstands and record albums in record stores, as we check the entertainment sections of city newspapers, or even as we approach a counter to pay for groceries. It is not necessary to spend a great deal of time reading or viewing pornographic material to absorb its male-centered definition of women. No longer confined within plain brown wrappers, it jumps out from billboards that proclaim "Live X-rated Girls!" or "Angels in Pain" or "Hot and Wild," and from magazine covers displaying a woman's genital area being spread open to the viewer by her own fingers.[2] Thus, even men who do not frequent pornography shops and movie houses are supported in the sexist objectification of women by their environment. Women, too, are crippled by internalizing as self-images those that are presented to us by pornographers. Isolated from one another and with no source of support for an alternative view of female sexuality, we may not always find the strength to resist a message that dominates the common cultural media.

The entrenchment of pornography in our culture also gives it a significance quite beyond its explicit sexual messages. To suggest, as pornography does, that the primary purpose of women is to provide sexual pleasure to men is to deny that women are independently human or have a status equal to that of men. It is, moreover, to deny our equality at one of the most intimate levels of human experience. This denial is especially powerful in a hierarchical, class society such as ours, in which individuals feel good about themselves by feeling superior to others. Men in our society have a vested interest in maintaining their belief in the inferiority of the female sex, so that no matter how oppressed and exploited by the society in which they live and work, they can feel that they are at least superior to someone or some category of individuals—a woman or women. Pornography, by presenting women as wanton, depraved, and made for the sexual use of men, caters directly to that interest.[3] The very intimate nature of sexuality which makes pornography so corrosive also protects it from explicit public discussion. The consequent lack of any explicit social disavowal of the pornographic image of women enables this image to continue fostering sexist attitudes even as the society publicly proclaims its (as yet timid) commitment to sexual equality.

In addition to finding a connection between the pornographic view of women and the denial to us of our full human rights, women are beginning to connect the consumption of pornography and committing rape and other acts of sexual violence against women. Contrary to the findings of the Commission on Obscenity and Pornography, a growing body of research is documenting (1) a correlation between exposure to representations of violence and the committing of violent acts generally, and (2) a correlation between exposure to pornographic materials and the committing of sexually abusive or violent acts against women. While more study is needed to establish precisely what the causal relations are, clearly so-called hard-core pornography is not innocent.

From "snuff" films and miserable magazines in pornographic stores to *Hustler*, to phonograph album covers and advertisements, to *Vogue*, pornography has come to occupy its own niche in the communications and entertainment media and to acquire a quasi-institutional character (signaled by the use of diminutives such as "porn" or "porno" to refer to pornographic material, as though such familiar naming could take the hurt out). Its acceptance by the mass media, whatever the motivation, means a cultural endorsement of its message. As much as the materials themselves, the social tolerance of these degrading and distorted images of women in such quantities is harmful to us, since it indicates a general willingness to see women in ways incompatible with our fundamental human dignity and thus to justify treating us in those ways.[4] The tolerance of pornographic representations of the rape, bondage, and torture of women helps to create and maintain a climate more tolerant of the actual physical abuse of women.[5] The tendency on the part of the legal system to view the victim of a rape as responsible for the crime against her is but one manifestation of this.

In sum, pornography is injurious to women in at least three distinct ways:

1. Pornography, especially violent pornography, is implicated in the committing of crimes of violence against women.
2. Pornography is the vehicle for the dissemination of a deep and vicious lie about women. It is defamatory and libelous.
3. The diffusion of such a distorted view of women's nature in our society as it exists today supports sexist (i.e., male-centered) attitudes, and thus reinforces the oppression and exploitation of women.

Society's tolerance of pornography, especially pornography on the contemporary massive scale, reinforces each of these modes of injury. By not disavowing the lie, it supports the male-centered myth that women are inferior and subordinate creatures. Thus, it contributes to the maintenance of a climate tolerant of both psychological and physical violence against women.

Pornography and the Law

Congress shall make no law respecting the establishment of religion, or prohibiting the free exercise thereof; or abridging the freedom of speech, or of the press; or the right of the people peaceably to assemble, and to petition the Government for a redress of grievances.

—First Amendment, Bill of Rights
of the United States Constitution

Pornography is clearly a threat to women. Each of the modes of injury cited above offers sufficient reason at least to consider proposals for the social and legal control of pornography. The almost universal response from progressives to such proposals is that constitutional guarantees of freedom of speech and privacy preclude recourse to law. While I am concerned about the erosion of constitutional rights and also think for many reasons that great caution must be exercised before undertaking a legal campaign against pornography, I find objections to such a campaign that are based on appeals to the First Amendment or to a right to privacy ultimately unconvincing.

Much of the defense of the pornographer's right to publish seems to assume that, while pornography may be tasteless and vulgar, it is basically an entertainment that harms no one but its consumers, who may at worst suffer from the debasement of their taste; and that therefore those who argue for its control are demanding an unjustifiable abridgment of the rights to freedom of speech of those who make and distribute pornographic materials and of the rights to privacy of their customers. The account of pornography given above shows that the assumptions of this position are false. Nevertheless, even some who acknowledge its harmful character feel that it is granted immunity from social control by the First Amendment, or that the harm that would ensue from its control outweighs the harm prevented by its control.

There are three ways of arguing that control of pornography is incompatible with adherence to constitutional rights. The first argument claims that regulating pornography involves an unjustifiable interference in the private lives of individuals. The second argument takes the First Amendment as a basic principle constitutive of our form of government, and claims that the production and distribution of pornographic material, as a form of speech, is an activity protected by that amendment. The third argument claims not that the pornographer's rights are violated, but that others' rights will be if controls against pornography are instituted.

The privacy argument is the easiest to dispose of. Since the open commerce in pornographic materials is an activity carried out in the public sphere, the publication and distribution of such materials, unlike their use by individuals, is not protected by rights to privacy. The distinction between the private consumption of pornographic material and the production and distribution of, or open commerce in, it is sometimes blurred by defenders of pornography. But I may entertain, in the privacy of my mind, defamatory opinions about another person, even though I may not broadcast them. So one might create without restraint—as long as no one were harmed in the course of preparing them—pornographic materials for one's personal use, but be restrained from reproducing and distributing them. In both cases what one is doing—in the privacy of one's mind or basement—may indeed be deplorable, but immune from legal proscription. Once the activity becomes public, however—i.e., once it involves others—it is no longer protected by the same rights that protect activities in the private sphere.[6]

In considering the second argument (that control of pornography, private or public, is wrong in principle), it seems important to determine whether we consider the right to freedom of speech to be absolute and unqualified. If it is, then obviously all speech, including pornography, is entitled to protection. But the right is, in the first place, not an unqualified right: There are several kinds of speech not protected by the First Amendment, including the incitement to violence in volatile circumstances, the solicitation of crimes, perjury and misrepresentation, slander, libel, and false advertising.[7] That there are forms of proscribed speech shows that we accept limitations on the right to freedom of speech if such speech, as do the forms listed, impinges on other rights. The manufacture and distribution of material which defames and threatens all members of a class by its recommendation of abusive and degrading behavior toward some members of that class simply in virtue of their membership in it seems a clear candidate for inclusion on the list. The right is therefore not an unqualified one.

Nor is it an absolute or fundamental right, underived from any other right: If it were there would not be exceptions or limitations. The first ten amendments were added to the Constitution as a way of guaranteeing the "blessings of liberty" mentioned in its preamble, to protect citizens against the unreasonable usurpation of power by the state. The specific rights mentioned in the First Amendment—those of religion, speech, assembly, press, petition—reflect the recent experiences of the makers of the Constitution under colonial government as well as a sense of what was and is required generally to secure liberty.

It may be objected that the right to freedom of speech is fundamental in that it is part of what we mean by liberty and not a right that is derivative from a right to liberty. In order to meet this objection, it is useful to consider a distinction explained by Ronald Dworkin in his book *Taking Rights Seriously*. As Dworkin points out, the word "liberty" is used in two distinct, if related, senses: as "license," i.e., the freedom from legal constraints to do as one pleases, in some contexts; and as "independence," i.e., "the status of a person as independent and equal rather than subservient," in others. Failure to distinguish between these senses in discussions of rights and freedoms is fatal to clarity and understanding.

If the right to free speech is understood as a partial explanation of what is meant by liberty, then liberty is perceived as license: The right to do as one pleases includes a right to speak as one pleases. But license is surely not a condition the First Amendment is designed to protect. We not only tolerate but require legal constraints on liberty as license when we enact laws against rape, murder, assault, theft, etc. If everyone did exactly as she or he pleased at any given time, we would have chaos if not lives, as Hobbes put it, that are "nasty, brutish, and short." We accept government to escape, not to protect, this condition.

If, on the other hand, by liberty is meant independence, then freedom of speech is not necessarily a part of liberty; rather, it is a means to it. The right to freedom of speech is not a fundamental, absolute right, but one derivative from, possessed in virtue of, the more basic right to independence. Taking this view of liberty requires providing arguments showing that the more specific rights we claim are necessary to guarantee our status as persons "independent and equal rather than subservient." In the context of government, we understand independence to be the freedom of each individual to participate as an equal among equals in the determination of how she or he is to be governed. Freedom of speech in this context means that an individual may not only entertain beliefs concerning government privately, but may express them publicly. We express our opinions about taxes, disarmament, wars, social-welfare programs, the function of the police, civil rights, and so on. Our right to freedom of speech includes the right to criticize the government and to protest against various forms of injustice and the abuse of power. What we wish to protect is the free expression of ideas even when they are unpopular. What we do not always remember is that speech has functions other than the expression of ideas.

Regarding the relationship between a right to freedom of speech and the publication and distribution of pornographic materials, there are two points to be made. In the first place, the latter activity is hardly an exercise of the right to the free expression of ideas as understood above. In the second place, to the degree that the tolerance of material degrading to women supports and reinforces the attitude that women are not fit to participate as equals among equals in the political life of their communities, and that the prevalence of such an attitude effectively prevents women from so participating, the absolute and fundamental right of women to liberty (political independence) is violated.

This second argument against the suppression of pornographic material, then, rests on a premise that must be rejected, namely, that the right to freedom of speech is a right to utter anything one wants. It thus fails to show that the production and distribution of such material is an activity protected by the First Amendment. Furthermore, an examination of the issues involved leads to the conclusion that tolerance of this activity violates the rights of women to political independence.

The third argument (which expresses concern that curbs on pornography are the first step toward political censorship) runs into the same ambiguity that besets the arguments based on principle. These arguments generally have as an underlying assumption that the maximization of freedom is a worthy social goal. Control of pornography diminishes freedom—directly the freedom of pornographers, indirectly that of all of us. But again, what is meant by "freedom"? It cannot be that what is to be maximized is license—as the goal of a social group whose members probably have at least some incompatible interests, such a goal would be internally inconsistent. If, on the other hand, the maximization of political independence is the goal, then that is in no way enhanced by, and may be endangered by, the tolerance of pornography. To argue that the control of pornography would create a precedent for suppressing political speech is thus to confuse license with political independence. In addition, it ignores a crucial basis for the control of pornography, i.e., its character as libelous speech. The prohibition of such speech is justified by the need for protection from the injury (psychological as well as physical or economic) that results from libel. A very different kind of argument would be required to justify curtailing the right to speak our minds about the institutions which govern us. As long as such distinctions are insisted upon, there is little danger of the government's using the control of pornography as precedent for curtailing political speech.

In summary, neither as a matter of principle nor in the interests of maximizing liberty can it be supposed that there is an intrinsic right to manufacture and distribute pornographic material.

The only other conceivable source of protection for pornography would be a general right to do what we please as long as the rights of others are respected. Since the production and distribution of pornography violates the rights of women—to respect and to freedom from defamation, among others—this protection is not available.

Conclusion

I have defined pornography in such a way as to distinguish it from erotica and from moral realism, and have argued that it is defamatory and libelous toward women, that it condones crimes against women, and that it invites tolerance of the social, economic, and cultural oppression of women. The production and distribution of pornographic material is thus a social and moral wrong. Contrasting both the current volume of pornographic production and its growing infiltration of the communications media with the status of women in this culture makes clear the necessity for its control. Since the goal of controlling pornography does not conflict with constitutional rights, a common obstacle to action is removed.

Appeals for action against pornography are sometimes brushed aside with the claim that such action is a diversion from the primary task of feminists—the elimination of sexism and of sexual inequality. This approach focuses on the enjoyment rather than the manufacture of pornography, and sees it as merely a product of sexism which will disappear when the latter has been overcome and the sexes are socially and economically equal. Pornography cannot be separated from sexism in this way: Sexism is not just a set of attitudes regarding the inferiority of women but the behaviors and social and economic rules that manifest such attitudes. Both the manufacture and distribution of pornography and the enjoyment of it are instances of sexist behavior. The enjoyment of pornography on the part of individuals will presumably decline as such individuals begin to accord women their status as fully human. A cultural climate which tolerates the degrading representation of women is not a climate which facilitates the development of respect for women. Furthermore, the demand for pornography is stimulated not just by the sexism of individuals but by the pornography industry itself. Thus, both as a social phenomenon and in its effect on individuals, pornography, far from being a mere product, nourishes sexism. The campaign against it is an essential component of women's struggle for legal, economic, and social equality, one which requires the support of all feminists.[8]

Notes

1. In talking of prostitution here, I refer to the concept of, rather than the reality of, prostitution. The same is true of my remarks about relationships between women and their husbands or men friends.
2. This was a full-color magazine cover seen in a rack at the check-out counter of a corner delicatessen.
3. Pornography thus becomes another tool of capitalism. One feature of some contemporary pornography—the use of Black and Asian women in both still photographs and films—exploits the racism as well as the sexism of its white consumers. For a discussion of the interplay between racism and sexism under capitalism as it relates to violent crimes against women, see Angela Y. Davis, "Rape, Racism, and the Capitalist Setting," *The Black Scholar*, Vol. 9, No. 7, April 1978.
4. This tolerance has a linguistic parallel in the growing acceptance and use of nonhuman nouns such as "chick," "bird," "filly," "fox," "doll," "babe," "skirt," etc., to refer to women, and of verbs of harm

such as "fuck," "screw," "bang" to refer to sexual intercourse. See Robert Baker and Federick Elliston, " 'Pricks' and 'Chicks': A Plea for Persons." *Philosophy and Sex* (Buffalo, N.Y.: Prometheus Books, 1975).

5. This is supported by the fact that in Denmark the number of rapes committed has increased while the number of rapes reported to the authorities has decreased over the past twelve years. See *WAVPM Newspage*, Vol. II, No. 5, June, 1978, quoting M. Harry, "Denmark Today—The Causes and Effects of Sexual Liberty" (paper presented to The Responsible Society, London, England, 1976). See also Eysenck and Nias, *Sex, Violence and the Media* (New York: St. Martin's Press, 1978), pp. 120–124.

6. Thus, the right to use such materials in the privacy of one's home, which has been upheld by the United States Supreme Court (*Stanley* v. *Georgia*, 394 U.S. 557), does not include the right to purchase them or to have them available in the commercial market. See also *Paris Adult Theater I* v. *Slaton*, 431 U.S. 49.

7. The Supreme Court has also traditionally included obscenity in this category. As not everyone agrees it should be included, since as defined by statutes, it is a highly vague concept, and since the grounds accepted by the Court for including it miss the point, I prefer to omit it from this list.

8. Many women helped me to develop and crystallize the ideas presented in this paper. I would especially like to thank Michele Farrell, Laura Lederer, Pamela Miller, and Dianne Romain for their comments in conversation and on the first written draft. Portions of this material were presented orally to members of the Society for Women in Philosophy and to participants in the workshops on "What Is Pornography?" at the Conference on Feminist Perspectives on Pornography, San Francisco, November 17, 18, and 19, 1978. Their discussion was invaluable in helping me to see problems and to clarify the ideas presented here.

Study Questions

1. According to Longino, what is one of the benefits of the sexual revolution? What does she think constitutes immorality?

2. How does Longino define "pornography"? How does her definition differ from the earlier traditional one?

3. According to Longino, how are women and children portrayed in pornography?

4. What does Longino mean when she says that "pornography communicates its endorsement of the behavior it represents by various features of the pornographic context?"

5. How does pornography lie? How, according to the author, do these lies serve men's purposes?

6. Longino considers three arguments that attempt to show that control of pornography is incompatible with adherence to constitutional rights. What are these arguments, and how does she respond to them?

Rape: The All-American Crime

Susan Griffin

I have never been free of the fear of rape. From a very early age I, like most women, have thought of rape as part of my natural environment—something to be feared and prayed against like fire or lightning. I never asked why men raped; I simply thought it one of the many mysteries of human nature.

From *Ramparts*, September 1971, pp. 26–35. Reprinted by permission of Susan Griffin.

I was, however, curious enough about the violent side of humanity to read every crime magazine I was able to ferret away from my grandfather. Each issue featured at least one "sex crime," with pictures of a victim, usually in a pearl necklace, and of the ditch or the orchard where her body was found. I was never certain why the victims were always women, nor what the motives of the murderer were, but I did guess that the world was not a safe place for women. I observed that my grandmother was meticulous about locks, and quick to draw the shades before anyone removed so much as a shoe. I sensed that danger lurked outside.

At the age of eight, my suspicions were confirmed. My grandmother took me to the back of the house where the men wouldn't hear, and told me that strange men wanted to do harm to little girls. I learned not to walk on dark streets, not to talk to strangers, or get into strange cars, to lock doors, and to be modest. She never explained why a man would want to harm a little girl, and I never asked.

If I thought for a while that my grandmother's fears were imaginary, the illusion was brief. That year, on the way home from school, a schoolmate a few years older than I tried to rape me. Later, in an obscure aisle of the local library (while I was reading *Freddy the Pig*) I turned to discover a man exposing himself. Then, the friendly man around the corner was arrested for child molesting.

My initiation to sexuality was typical. Every woman has similar stories to tell—the first man who attacked her may have been a neighbor, a family friend, an uncle, her doctor, or perhaps her own father. And women who grow up in New York City always have tales about the subway.

But though rape and the fear of rape are a daily part of every woman's consciousness, the subject is so rarely discussed by that unofficial staff of male intellectuals (who write the books which study seemingly every other form of male activity) that one begins to suspect a conspiracy of silence. And indeed, the obscurity of rape in print exists in marked contrast to the frequency of rape in reality, for *forcible rape is the most frequently committed violent crime in America today*. The Federal Bureau of Investigation classes three crimes as violent: murder, aggravated assault and forcible rape. In 1968, 31,600 rapes were *reported*. According to the FBI and independent criminologists, however, to approach accuracy this figure must be multiplied by at least a factor of ten to compensate for the fact that most rapes are not reported; when these compensatory mathematics are used, there are more rapes committed than aggravated assaults and homicides.

When I asked Berkeley, California's Police Inspector in charge of rape investigation if he knew why men rape women, he replied that he had not spoken with "these people and delved into what really makes them tick, because that really isn't my job. . . ." However, when I asked him how a woman might prevent being raped, he was not so reticent, "I wouldn't advise any female to go walking around alone at night . . . and she should lock her car at all times." The Inspector illustrated his warning with a grisly story about a man who lay in wait for women in the back seats of their cars, while they were shopping in a local super-market. This man eventually murdered one of his rape victims. "Always lock your car," the Inspector repeated, and then added, without a hint of irony, "Of course, you don't have to be paranoid about this type of thing."

The Inspector wondered why I wanted to write about rape. Like most men he did not understand the urgency of the topic, for, after all, men are not raped. But like most women I had spent considerable time speculating on the true nature of the rapist. When I was very young, my image of the "sexual offender" was a nightmarish amalgamation of the bogey man and Captain Hook: he wore a black cape, and he cackled. As I matured, so did my image of the rapist. Born into the psychoanalytical age, I tried to "understand" the rapist. Rape, I came to believe, was only one of many unfortunate evils produced by sexual repression. Reasoning by tautology, I concluded that any man who would rape a woman must be out of his mind.

Yet, though the theory that rapists are insane is a popular one, this belief has no basis in fact. According to Professor Menachem Amir's study of 646 rape cases in Philadelphia, *Patterns in Forcible Rape*, men who rape are not abnormal. Amir writes, "Studies indicate that sex offenders do not constitute a unique or psychopathological type; nor are they as a group invariably more disturbed than the control groups to which they are compared." Alan Taylor, a parole officer who has worked with rapists in the prison facilities at San Luis Obispo, California, stated the question in plainer language, "Those men were the most normal men there. They had a lot of hang-ups, but they were the same hang-ups as men walking out on the street."

Another canon in the apologetics of rape is that, if it were not for learned social controls, all men would rape. Rape is held to be natural behavior, and not to rape must be learned. But in truth rape is not universal to the human species. Moreover, studies of rape in our culture reveal that, far from being impulsive behavior, most rape is planned. Professor Amir's study reveals that in cases of group rape (the "gangbang" of masculine slang) 90 percent of the rapes were planned; in pair rapes, 83 percent of the rapes were planned; and in single rapes, 58 percent were planned. These figures should significantly discredit the image of the rapist as a man who is suddenly overcome by sexual needs society does not allow him to fulfill.

Far from the social control of rape being learned, comparisons with other cultures lead one to suspect that, in our society, it is rape itself that is learned. (The fact that rape is against the law should not be considered proof that rape is not in fact encouraged as part of our culture.)

This culture's concept of rape as an illegal, but still understandable, form of behavior is not a universal one. In her study *Sex and Temperament*, Margaret Mead describes a society that does not share our views. The Arapesh do not ". . . have any conception of the male nature that might make rape understandable to them." Indeed our interpretation of rape is a product of our conception of the nature of male sexuality. A common retort to the question, why don't women rape men, is the myth that men have greater sexual needs, that their sexuality is more urgent than women's. And it is the nature of human beings to want to live up to what is expected of them.

And this same culture which expects aggression from the male expects passivity from the female. Conveniently, the companion myth about the nature of female sexuality is that all women secretly want to be raped. Lurking beneath her modest female exterior is a subconscious desire to be ravished. The following description of a stag movie, written by Brenda Starr in Los Angeles' underground paper, *Everywoman*, typifies this male fantasy. The movie "showed a women in her underclothes reading on her bed. She is interrupted by a rapist with a knife. He immediately wins her over with his charm and they get busy sucking and fucking." An advertisement in the *Berkeley Barb* reads, "Now as all women know from their daydreams, rape has a lot of advantages. Best of all it's so simple. No preparation necessary, no planning ahead of time, no wondering if you should or shouldn't; just whang! bang!" Thanks to Masters and Johnson even the scientific canon recognizes that for the female, "whang! bang!" can scarcely be described as pleasurable.

Still, the male psyche persists in believing that, protestations and struggles to the contrary, deep inside her mysterious feminine soul, the female victim has wished for her own fate. A young woman who was raped by the husband of a friend said that days after the incident the man returned to her home, pounded on the door and screamed to her, "Jane, Jane. You loved it. You know you loved it."

The theory that women like being raped extends itself by deduction into the proposition that most or much of rape is provoked by the victim. But this too is only myth. Though provocation, considered a mitigating factor in a court of law, may consist of only "a gesture," according to the Federal Commission on Crimes of Violence, only 4 percent of reported rapes involved any precipitative behavior by the woman.

The notion that rape is enjoyed by the victim is also convenient for the man who, though he would not commit forcible rape, enjoys the idea of its existence, as if rape confirms that enormous sexual potency which he secretly knows to be his own. It is for the pleasure of the armchair rapist that detailed accounts of violent rapes exist in the media. Indeed, many men appear to take sexual pleasure from nearly all forms of violence. Whatever the motivation, male sexuality and violence in our culture seem to be inseparable. James Bond alternately whips out his revolver and his cock, and though there is no known connection between the skills of gun-fighting and love-making, pacifism seems suspiciously effeminate.

In a recent fictional treatment of the Manson case, Frank Conroy writes of his vicarious titillation when describing the murders to his wife:

> "Every single person there was killed." She didn't move.
> "It sounds like there was torture," I said. As the words left my mouth I knew there was no need to say them to frighten her into believing that she needed me for protection.

The pleasure he feels as his wife's protector is inextricably mixed with pleasure in the violence itself. Conroy writes, "I was excited by the killings, as one is excited by catastrophe on a grand scale, as one is alert to pre-echoes of unknown changes, hints of unrevealed secrets, rumblings of chaos. . . ."

The attraction of the male in our culture to violence and death is a tradition Manson and his admirers are carrying on with tireless avidity (even presuming Manson's innocence, he dreams of the purification of fire and destruction). It was Malraux in his *Anti-Memoirs* who said that, for the male, facing death was *the* illuminating experience analogous to childbirth for the female. Certainly our culture does glorify war and shroud the agonies of the gun-fighter in veils of mystery.

And in the spectrum of male behavior, rape, the perfect combination of sex and violence, is the penultimate act. Erotic pleasure cannot be separated from culture, and in our culture male eroticism is wedded to power. Not only should a man be taller and stronger than a female in the perfect love-match, but he must also demonstrate his superior strength in gestures of dominance which are perceived as amorous. Though the law attempts to make a clear division between rape and sexual intercourse, in fact the courts find it difficult to distinguish between a case where the decision to copulate was mutual and one where a man forced himself upon his partner.

The scenario is even further complicated by the expectation that, not only does a woman mean "yes" when she says "no," but that a really decent woman ought to begin by saying "no," and then be led down the primrose path to acquiescence. Ovid, the author of Western Civilization's most celebrated sex-manual, makes this expectation perfectly clear:

> . . . and when I beg you to say "yes," say "no." Then let me lie outside your bolted door. . . . So love grows strong. . . .

That the basic elements of rape are involved in all heterosexual relationships may explain why men often identify with the offender in this crime. But to regard the rapist as the victim, a man driven by his inherent sexual needs to take what will not be given him, reveals a basic ignorance of sexual politics. For in our culture heterosexual love finds an erotic expression through male dominance and female submission. A man who derives pleasure from raping a woman clearly must enjoy force and dominance as much or more than the simple pleasures of the flesh. Coitus cannot be experienced in isolation. The weather, the state of the nation, the level of sugar in the blood—all will affect a man's ability to achieve orgasm. If a man can achieve sexual pleasure after terrorizing and humiliating the object of his passion, and in fact while inflicting pain upon her, one must assume he derives pleasure directly from terrorizing, humiliating and harming a woman. According to Amir's study of forcible rape, on a statistical average the man who has been convicted of rape was found to have a normal sexual personality, tending to be different from the normal, well-adjusted male only in having a greater tendency to express violence and rage.

And if the professional rapist is to be separated from the average dominant heterosexual, it may be mainly a quantitative difference. For the existence of rape as an index to masculinity is not entirely metaphorical. Though this measure of masculinity seems to be more publicly exhibited among "bad boys" or aging bikers who practice sexual initiation through group rape, in fact, "good boys" engage in the same rites to prove their manhood. In Stockton, a small town in California which epitomizes silent-majority America, a bachelor party was given last summer for a young man about to be married. A woman was hired to dance "topless" for the amusement of the guests. At the high point of the evening the bride-groom-to-be dragged the woman into a bedroom. No move was made by any of his companions to stop what was clearly going to be an attempted rape. Far from it. As the woman described, "I tried to keep him away—told him of my Herpes Genitalis, et cetera, but he couldn't face the guys if he didn't screw me." After the bridegroom had finished raping the woman and returned with her to the party, far from chastizing him, his friends heckled the woman and covered her with wine.

It was fortunate for the dancer that the bridegroom's friends did not follow him into the bedroom for, though one might suppose that in group rape, since the victim is outnumbered, less force would be inflicted on her, in fact, Amir's studies indicate, "the most excessive degrees of violence occurred in group rape." Far from discouraging violence, the presence of other men may in fact encourage sadism, and even cause the behavior. In an unpublished study of group rape by Gilbert Geis and Duncan Chappell, the authors refer to a study by W. H. Blanchard which relates, "The leader of the male group . . . apparently precipitated and maintained the activity, despite misgivings, because of a need to fulfill the role that the other two men had assigned to him. 'I was scared when it began to happen,' he says. 'I wanted to leave but I didn't want to say it to the other guys—you know—that I was scared.' "

Thus it becomes clear that not only does our culture teach men the rudiments of rape, but society, or more specifically other men, encourage the practice of it.

Every man I meet wants to protect me. Can't figure out what from.

Mae West

If a male society rewards aggressive, domineering sexual behavior, it contains within itself a sexual schizophrenia. For the masculine man is also expected to prove his mettle as a protector of women. To the naive eye, this dichotomy implies that men fall into one of two categories: those who rape and those who protect. In fact, life does not prove so simple. In a study euphemistically entitled "Sex Aggression by College Men," it was discovered that men who believe in a double standard of morality for men and women, who in fact believe most fervently in the ultimate value of virginity, are more liable to commit "this aggressive variety of sexual exploitation."

(At this point in our narrative it should come as no surprise that Sir Thomas Malory, creator of that classic tale of chivalry, *The Knights of the Round Table*, was himself arrested and found guilty for repeated incidents of rape.)

In the system of chivalry, men protect women against men. This is not unlike the protection relationship which the mafia established with small businesses in the early part of this century. Indeed, chivalry is an age-old protection racket which depends for its existence on rape.

According to the male mythology which defines and perpetuates rape, it is an animal instinct inherent in the male. The story goes that sometime in our pre-historical past, the male, more hirsute and burly than today's counterparts, roamed about an uncivilized landscape until he found a desirable female. (Oddly enough, this female is *not* pictured as more muscular than the modern woman.) Her mate does not bother with courtship. He simply grabs her by the hair and drags her to the closest cave. Presumably, one of the major advantages of modern civilization for the female has been the civilizing of the male. We call it chivalry.

But women do not get chivalry for free. According to the logic of sexual politics, we too have to civilize our behavior. (Enter chastity. Enter virginity. Enter monogamy.) For the female, civilized behavior means chastity before marriage and faithfulness within it. Chivalrous behavior in the male is supposed to protect that chastity from involuntary defilement. The fly in the ointment of this otherwise peaceful system is the fallen woman. She does not behave. And therefore she does not deserve protection. Or, to use another argument, a major tenet of the same value system: what has once been defiled cannot again be violated. One begins to suspect that it is the behavior of the fallen woman, and not that of the male, that civilization aims to control.

The assumption that a woman who does not respect the double standard deserves whatever she gets (or at the very least "asks for it") operates in the courts today. While in some states a man's previous rape convictions are not considered admissible evidence, the sexual reputation of the rape victim is considered a crucial element of the facts upon which the court must decide innocence or guilt.

The court's respect for the double standard manifested itself particularly clearly in the case of the People v. Jerry Plotkin. Mr. Plotkin, a 36-year-old jeweler, was tried for rape last spring in a San Francisco Superior Court. According to the woman who brought the charges, Plotkin, along with three other men, forced her at gunpoint to enter a car one night in October 1970. She was taken to Mr. Plotkin's fashionable apartment where he and the three other men first raped her and then, in the delicate language of the *S.F. Chronicle*, "subjected her to perverted sex acts." She was, she said, set free in the morning with the warning that she would be killed if she spoke to anyone about the event. She did report the incident to the police who then searched Plotkin's apartment and discovered a long list of names of women. Her name was on the list and had been crossed out.

In addition to the woman's account of her abduction and rape, the prosecution submitted four of Plotkin's address books containing the names of hundreds of women. Plotkin claimed he did not know all of the women since some of the names had been given to him by friends and he had not yet called on them. Several women, however, did testify in court that Plotkin had, to cite the *Chronicle*, "lured them up to his apartment under one pretext or another, and forced his sexual attentions on them."

Plotkin's defense rested on two premises. First, through his own testimony Plotkin established a reputation for himself as a sexual libertine who frequently picked up girls in bars and took them to his house where sexual relations often took place. He was the Playboy. He claimed that the accusation of rape, therefore, was false—this incident had simply been one of many casual sexual relationships, the victim one of many playmates. The second premise of the defense was that his accuser was also a sexual libertine. However, the picture created of the young woman (fully 13 years younger than Plotkin) was not akin to the light-hearted, gay-bachelor image projected by the defendant. On the contrary, the day after the defense cross-examined the woman, the *Chronicle* printed a story headlined, "Grueling Day for Rape

Case Victim." (A leaflet passed out by women in front of the courtroom was more succinct, "rape was committed by four men in a private apartment in October; on Thursday, it was done by a judge and a lawyer in a public courtroom.")

Through skillful questioning fraught with innuendo, Plotkin's defense attorney James Martin MacInnis portrayed the young woman as a licentious opportunist and unfit mother. MacInnis began by asking the young woman (then employed as a secretary) whether or not it was true that she was "familiar with liquor" and had worked as a "cocktail waitress." The young woman replied (the *Chronicle* wrote "admitted") that she had worked once or twice as a cocktail waitress. The attorney then asked if she had worked as a secretary in the financial district but had "left that employment after it was discovered that you had sexual intercourse on a couch in the office." The woman replied, "That is a lie. I left because I didn't like working in a one-girl office. It was too lonely." Then the defense asked if, while working as an attendant at a health club, "you were accused of having a sexual affair with a man?" Again the woman denied the story, "I was never accused of that."

Plotkin's attorney then sought to establish that his client's accuser was living with a married man. She responded that the man was separated from his wife. Finally he told the court that she had "spent the night" with another man who lived in the same building.

At this point in the testimony the woman asked Plotkin's defense attorney, "Am I on trial? . . . It is embarrassing and personal to admit these things to all these people. . . . I did not commit a crime. I am a human being." The lawyer, true to the chivalry of his class, apologized and immediately resumed questioning her, turning his attention to her children. (She is divorced, and the children at the time of the trial were in a foster home.) "Isn't it true that your two children have a sex game in which one gets on top of another and they—" "That is a lie!" the young woman interrupted him. She ended her testimony by explaining "They are wonderful children. They are not perverted."

The jury, divided in favor of acquittal ten to two, asked the court stenographer to read the woman's testimony back to them. After this reading, the Superior Court acquitted the defendant of both the charges of rape and kidnapping.

According to the double standard a woman who has had sexual intercourse out of wedlock cannot be raped. Rape is not only a crime of aggression against the body; it is a transgression against chastity as defined by men. When a woman is forced into a sexual relationship, she has, according to the male ethos, been violated. But she is also defiled if she does not behave according to the double standard, by maintaining her chastity, or confining her sexual activities to a monogamous relationship.

One should not assume, however, that a woman can avoid the possibility of rape simply by behaving. Though myth would have it that mainly "bad girls" are raped, this theory has no basis in fact. Available statistics would lead one to believe that a safer course is promiscuity. In a study of rape done in the District of Columbia, it was found that 82 percent of the rape victims had a "good reputation." Even the Police Inspector's advice to stay off the streets is rather useless, for almost half of reported rapes occur in the home of the victim and are committed by a man she has never before seen. Like indiscriminate terrorism, rape can happen to any woman, and few women are ever without this knowledge.

But the courts and the police, both dominated by white males, continue to suspect the rape victim, *sui generis*, of provoking or asking for her own assault. According to Amir's study, the police tend to believe that a woman without a good reputation cannot be raped. The rape victim is usually submitted to countless questions about her own sexual mores and behavior by the police investigator. This preoccupation is partially justified by the legal requirements for prosecution in a rape case. The rape victim must have been penetrated, and she must have made it clear to her assailant that she did not want penetration (unless of course she is unconscious). A refusal to accompany a man to some isolated place to allow him to touch her does not, in the eyes of the court, constitute rape. She must have said "no" at the crucial genital moment. And the rape victim, to qualify as such, must also have put up a physical struggle—unless she can prove that to do so would have been to endanger her life.

But the zealous interest the police frequently exhibit in the physical details of a rape case is only partially explained by the requirements of the court. A woman who was raped in Berkeley was asked to tell the story of her rape four different times "right out in the street," while her assailant was escaping. She was then required to submit to a pelvic examination to prove that penetration had taken place. Later, she was taken to the police station where she was asked the same questions again: "Were you forced?" "Did he penetrate?" "Are you sure your life was in danger and you had no other choice?" This woman had been pulled off the street by a man who held a 10-inch knife at her throat and forcibly raped her. She was raped at midnight and was not able to return to her home until five in the morning. Police contacted her twice again in the next week, once by telephone at two in the morning and once at four in the morning. In her words, "The rape was probably the least traumatic incident of the whole evening. If I'm ever raped again, . . . I wouldn't report it to the police because of all the degradation. . . ."

If white women are subjected to unnecessary and often hostile questioning after having been raped, third-world women are often not believed at all. According to the white male ethos (which is not only sexist but racist), third-world women are defined from birth as "impure." Thus the white male is provided with a pool of women who are fair game for sexual imperialism. Third-world women frequently do not report rape and for good reason. When blues singer Billie Holliday was 10 years old, she was taken off to a local house by a neighbor and raped. Her mother brought the police to rescue her, and she was taken to the local police station crying and bleeding:

> When we got there, instead of treating me and Mom like somebody who called the cops for help, they treated me like I'd killed somebody. . . . I guess they had me figured for having enticed this old goat into the whorehouse. . . . All I know for sure is they threw me into a cell . . . a fat white matron . . . saw I was still bleeding, she felt sorry for me and gave me a couple glasses of milk. But nobody else did anything for me except give me filthy looks and snicker to themselves.
>
> After a couple of days in a cell they dragged me into a court. Mr. Dick got sentenced to five years. They sentenced me to a Catholic institution.

Clearly the white man's chivalry is aimed only to protect the chastity of "his" women.

As a final irony, that same system of sexual values from which chivalry is derived has also provided womankind with an unwritten code of behavior, called femininity, which makes a feminine woman the perfect victim of sexual aggression. If being chaste does not ward off the possibility of assault, being feminine certainly increases the chances that it will succeed. To be submissive is to defer to masculine strength; is to lack muscular development or any interest in defending oneself; is to let doors be opened, to have one's arm held when crossing the street. To be feminine is to wear shoes which make it difficult to run; skirts which inhibit one's stride; underclothes which inhibit the circulation. Is it not an intriguing observation that those very clothes which are thought to be flattering to the female and attractive to the male are those which make it impossible for a woman to defend herself against aggression?

Each girl as she grows into womanhood is taught fear. Fear is the form in which the female internalizes both chivalry and the double standard. Since, biologically speaking, women in fact have the same if not greater potential for sexual expression as do men, the woman who is taught that she must behave differently from a man must also learn to distrust her own carnality. She must deny her own feelings and learn not to act from them. She fears herself. This is the essence of passivity, and of course, a woman's passivity is not simply sexual but functions to cripple her from self-expression in every area of her life.

Passivity itself prevents a woman from ever considering her own potential for self-defense and forces her to look to men for protection. The woman is taught fear, but this time fear of the other; and yet her only relief from this fear is to seek out the other. Moreover, the passive woman is taught to regard herself as impotent, unable to act, unable even to perceive, in no way self-sufficient, and, finally, as the object and not the subject of human behavior. It is in this sense that a woman is deprived of the status of a human being. She is not free to be.

Since Ibsen's Nora slammed the door on her patriarchical husband, woman's attempt to be free has been more or less fashionable. In this 19th-century portrait of a woman leaving her marriage, Nora tells her husband, "Our home has been nothing but a playroom. I have been your doll-wife just as at home I was papa's doll-child." And, at least on the stage, "The Doll's House" crumbled, leaving audiences with hope for the fate of the modern woman. And today, as in the past, womankind has not lacked examples of liberated women to emulate: Emma Goldman, Greta Garbo and Isadora Duncan all denounced marriage and the double standard, and believed their right to freedom included sexual independence; but still their example has not affected the lives of millions of women who continue to marry, divorce and remarry, living out their lives dependent on the status and economic power of men. Patriarchy still holds the average woman prisoner not because she lacks the courage of an Isadora Duncan, but because the material conditions of her life prevent her from being anything but an object.

In the *Elementary Structures of Kinship*, Claude Levi-Strauss gives to marriage this universal description, "It is always a system of exchange that we find at the origin of the rules of marriage." In this system of exchange, a woman is the "most precious possession." Levi-Strauss continues that the custom of including women as booty in the marketplace is still so general that "a whole volume would not be sufficient to enumerate instances of it." Levi-Strauss makes it clear that he does not exclude Western Civilization from his definition of "universal" and cites examples from modern wedding ceremonies. (The marriage ceremony is still one in which the husband and wife become one, and "that one is the husband.")

The legal proscription against rape reflects this possessory view of women. An article in the 1952-53 *Yale Law Journal* describes the legal rationale behind laws against rape: "In our society sexual taboos, often enacted into law, buttress a system of monogamy based upon the law of 'free bargaining' of the potential spouses. Within this process the woman's power to withhold or grant sexual access is an important bargaining weapon." Presumably then, laws against rape are intended to protect the right of a woman, not for physical self-determination, but for physical "bargaining." The article goes on to explain explicitly why the preservation of the bodies of women is important to men:

> The consent standard in our society does more than protect a significant item of social currency for women; it fosters, and is in turn bolstered by, a masculine pride in the exclusive possession of a sexual object. The consent of a woman to sexual intercourse awards the man a privilege of bodily access, a personal "prize" whose value is enhanced by sole ownership. An additional reason for the man's condemnation of rape may be found in the threat to his status from a decrease in the "value" of his sexual possession which would result from forcible violation.

The passage concludes by making clear whose interest the law is designed to protect. "The man responds to this undercutting of his status as *possessor* of the girl with hostility toward the rapist; no other restitution device is available. The law of rape provides an orderly outlet for his vengeance." Presumably the female victim in any case will have been sufficiently socialized so as not to consciously feel any strong need for vengeance. If she does feel this need, society does not speak to it.

The laws against rape exist to protect rights of the male as possessor of the female body, and not the right of the female over her own body. Even without this enlightening passage from the *Yale Law Review*, the laws themselves are clear: In no state can a man be accused of raping his wife. How can any man steal what already belongs to him? It is in the sense of rape as theft of another man's property that Kate Millett writes, "Traditionally rape has been viewed as an offense one male commits against another—a matter of abusing his woman." In raping another man's woman, a man may aggrandize his own manhood and concurrently reduce that of another man. Thus a man's honor is not subject directly to rape, but only indirectly, through "his" woman.

If the basic social unit is the family, in which the woman is a possession of her husband, the superstructure of society is a male hierarchy, in which men dominate other men (or patriarchal families dominate other patriarchal families). And it is no small irony that, while the very social fabric of our male-dominated culture denies women equal access to political, economic and legal power, the literature, myth and humor of our culture depicts women not only as the power behind the throne, but the real source of the oppression of men. The religious version of this fairy tale blames Eve for both carnality and eating of the tree of knowledge, at the same time making her gullible to the obvious devices of a serpent. Adam, of course, is merely the trusting victim of love. Certainly this is a biased story. But no more biased than the one television audiences receive today from the latest slick comedians. Through a media which is owned by men, censored by a State dominated by men, all the evils of this social system which make a man's life unpleasant are blamed upon "the wife." The theory is: were it not for the female who waits and plots to "trap" the male into marriage, modern man would be able to achieve Olympian freedom. She is made the scapegoat for a system which is in fact run by men.

Nowhere is this more clear than in the white racist use of the concept of white womanhood. The white male's open rape of black women, coupled with his overweening concern for the chastity and protection of his wife and daughters, represents an extreme of sexist and racist hypocrisy. While on the one hand she was held up as the standard for purity and virtue, on the other the Southern white woman was never asked if she wanted to be on a pedestal, and in fact any deviance from the male-defined standards for white womanhood was treated severely. (It is a powerful commentary on American racism that the historical role of Blacks as slaves, and thus possessions without power, has robbed black women of legal and economic protection through marriage. Thus black women in Southern society and in the ghettoes of the North have long been easy game for white rapists.) The fear that black men would rape white women was, and is, classic paranoia. Quoting from Ann Breen's unpublished study of racism and sexism in the South "*The New South: White Man's Country*," Frederick Douglass legitimately points out that, had the black man wished to rape white women, he had ample opportunity to do so during the civil war, when white women, the wives, sisters, daughters and mothers of the rebels, were left in the care of Blacks. But yet not a single act of rape was committed during this time. The Ku Klux Klan, who tarred and feathered black men and lynched them in the honor of the purity of white womanhood, also applied tar and feathers to a Southern white woman accused of bigamy, which leads one to suspect that Southern white men were not so much outraged at the violation of the woman as a person, in the few instances where rape was actually committed by black men, but at the violation of his property rights." In the situation where a black man was found to be having sexual relations with a white woman, the white woman could exercise skin-privilege, and claim that she had been raped, in which case the black man was lynched. But if she did not claim rape, she herself was subject to lynching.

In constructing the myth of white womanhood so as to justify the lynching and oppression of black men and women, the white male has created a convenient symbol of his own power which has resulted in black hostility toward the white "bitch," accompanied by an unreasonable fear on the part of many white women of the black rapist. Moreover, it is not surprising that after being told for two centuries that he wants to rape white women, occasionally a black man does actually commit that act. But it is crucial to note that the frequency of this practice is outrageously exaggerated in the white mythos. Ninety percent of reported rape is intra- not inter-racial.

In *Soul on Ice*, Eldridge Cleaver has described the mixing of a rage against white power with the internalized sexism of a black man raping a white woman. "Somehow I arrived at the conclusion that, as a matter of principle, it was of paramount importance for me to have an antagonistic, ruthless attitude toward white women. . . . Rape was an insurrectionary act. It delighted me that I was defying and trampling upon the white man's law, upon his system of values and that I was defiling his women—and this point, I believe, was the most satisfying to me because I was very resentful over the historical fact of how the white man has used the black woman." Thus a black man uses white women to take out his rage against white men. But in fact, whenever a rape of a white woman by a black man does take place, it is again the white man who benefits. First, the act itself terrorizes the white woman and makes her more dependent on the white male for protection. Then, if the woman prosecutes her attacker, the white man is afforded legal opportunity to exercise overt racism. Of course, the knowledge of the rape helps to perpetuate two myths which are beneficial to white male rule—the bestiality of the black and the desirability of white women. Finally, the white man surely benefits because he himself is not the object of attack—he has been allowed to stay in power.

Indeed, the existence of rape in any form is beneficial to the ruling class of white males. For rape is a kind of terrorism which severly limits the freedom of women and makes women dependent on men. Moreover, in the act of rape, the rage that one man may harbor toward another higher in the male hierarchy can be deflected toward a female scapegoat. For every man there is always someone lower on the social scale on whom he can take out his aggressions. And this is any woman alive.

This oppressive attitude towards women finds its institutionalization in the traditional family. For it is assumed that a man "wears the pants" in his family—he exercises the option of rule whenever he so chooses. Not that he makes all the decisions—clearly women make most of the important day-to-day decisions in a family. But when a conflict of interest arises, it is the man's interest which will prevail. His word, in itself, is more powerful. He lords it over his wife in the same way his boss lords it over him, so that the very process of exercising his power becomes as important an act as obtaining whatever it is his power can get for him. This notion of power is key to the male ego in this culture, for the two acceptable measures of masculinity are a man's power over women and his power over other men. A man may boast to his friends that "I have 20 men working for me." It is also aggrandizement of his ego if he has the financial power to clothe his wife in furs and jewels. And, if a man lacks the wherewithal to acquire such power, he can always express his rage through equally masculine activities—rape and theft. Since male society defines the female as a possession, it is not surprising that the felony most often committed together with rape is theft. As the following classic tale of rape points out the elements of theft, violence and forced sexual relations merge into an indistinguishable whole.

The woman who told this story was acquainted with the man who tried to rape her. When the man learned that she was going to be staying alone for the weekend, he began early in the day a polite campaign to get her to go out with him. When she continued to refuse his request, his chivalrous mask dropped away:

I had locked all the doors because I was afraid, and I don't know how he got in; it was probably through the screen door. When I woke up, he was shaking my leg. His eyes were red, and I knew he had been drinking or smoking. I thought I would try to talk my way out of it. He started by saying that he wanted to sleep with me, and then he got angrier and angrier, until he started to say, "I want pussy," "I want pussy." Then, I got scared and tried to push him away. That's when he started to force himself on me. It was awful. It was the most humiliating, terrible feeling. He was forcing my legs apart and ripping my clothes off. And it was painful. I did fight him—he was slightly drunk and I was able to keep him away. I had taken judo a few years back, but I was afraid to throw a chop for fear that he'd kill me. I could see he was getting more and more violent. I was thinking wildly of some way to get out of this alive, and then I said to him, "Do you want money. I'll give you money." We had money but I was also thinking that if I got to the back room I could telephone the police—as if the police would have even helped. It was a stupid thing to think of because obviously he would follow me. And he did. When he saw me pick up the phone, he tried to tie the cord around my neck. I screamed at him that I did have the money in another room, that I was going to call the police because I was scared, but that I would never tell anybody what happened. It would be an absolute secret. He said, okay, and I went to get the money. But when he got it, all of a sudden he got this crazy look in his eye and he said to me, "Now I'm going to kill you." Then I started saying my prayers. I knew there was nothing I could do. He started to hit me—I still wasn't sure if he wanted to rape me at this point—or just to kill me. He was hurting me, but hadn't yet gotten me into a strangle-hold because he was still drunk and off balance. Somehow we pushed into the kitchen where I kept looking at this big knife. But I didn't pick it up. Somehow, no matter how much I hated him at that moment, I still couldn't imagine putting the knife in his flesh, and then I was afraid he would grab it and stick it into me. Then he was hitting me again and somehow we pushed through the back door of the kitchen and onto the porch steps. We fell down the steps and that's when he started to strangle me. He was on top of me. He just went on and on until finally I lost consciousness. I did scream, though my screams sounded like whispers to me. But what happened was that a cab driver happened by and frightened him away. The cab driver revived me—I was out only a minute at the most. And then I ran across the street and I grabbed the woman who was our neighbor and screamed at her, "Am I alive? Am I still alive?"

Rape is an act of aggression in which the victim is denied her self-determination. It is an act of violence which, if not actually followed by beatings or murder, nevertheless always carries with it the threat of death. And finally, rape is a form of mass terrorism, for the victims of rape are chosen indiscriminately, but the propagandists for male supremacy broadcast that it is women who cause rape by being unchaste or in the wrong place at the wrong time—in essence, by behaving as though they were free.

The threat of rape is used to deny women employment. (In California, the Berkeley Public Library, until pushed by the Federal Employment Practices Commission, refused to hire female shelvers because of perverted men in the stacks.) The fear of rape keeps women off the streets at night. Keeps women at home. Keeps women passive and modest for fear that they be thought provocative.

It is part of human dignity to be able to defend oneself, and women are learning. Some women have learned karate; some to shoot guns. And yet we will not be free until the threat of rape and the atmosphere of violence is ended, and to end that the nature of male behavior must change.

But rape is not an isolated act that can be rooted out from patriarchy without ending patriarchy itself. The same men and power structure who victimize women are engaged in the act of raping Vietnam, raping Black people and the very earth we live upon. Rape is a classic act of domination where, in the words of Kate Millett, "the emotions of hatred, contempt, and the desire to break or violate personality," takes place. This breaking of the personality characterizes modern life itself. No simple reforms can eliminate rape. As the symbolic expression of the white male hierarchy, rape is the quintessential act of our civilization, one which, Valerie Solanis warns, is in danger of "humping itself to death."

Study Questions

1. How does Griffin think all women get initiated to sexuality?
2. Does Griffin believe that rapists are insane? Explain your answer.
3. Does Griffin believe that if it weren't for social control all men would rape? Explain.
4. What two myths about sexuality, according to Griffin, are prevalent in our culture?
5. "In our culture male eroticism is wedded to power." What does Griffin mean by this, and how does it tie in with the existence of rape? Does it mean that the difference between a "normal" man and the rapist is merely a matter of degree?
6. Does Griffin believe that the system of chivalry is incompatible with the existence of rape? Explain your answer.
7. In what way is the rape victim often "put on trial"?
8. Griffin says "femininity" makes sexual aggression against women easier. Explain what she means by this.
9. What view of women is implicit in the institution of monogamy? How does it account for the existence of laws against rape?
10. How does rape in any form benefit males as a class? How does the threat of rape serve to oppress women, according to Griffin?

Rape and Respect

Carolyn M. Shafer
Marilyn Frye

It is part of public piety to hold rape in low regard. Rape is, in fact, generally counted among the crimes of great moral moment. At the same time, there is a certain warm solicitude for the accused rapist, more than for the accused murderer, for instance. This seems to be due to the prevalence of a belief that a hugely disproportionate number of accused rapists are falsely

From Mary Vetterling-Braggin, Frederick A. Elliston, and Jane English, eds., *Feminism and Philosophy* (Totowa, NJ: Rowman and Littlefield, 1977), pp. 336–346. Reprinted by permission of Rowman and Allenheld.

accused, innocent, and in need of unusual legal and moral protection, and that real rape—real, culpable criminal rape—is in fact very rare. It might have been supposed that such an attitude was justified because the very heinousness of the crime deflated the enthusiasm of all but the most hardened aspiring rapists. Quite recently, however, this belief has been discredited by the public discovery of the actual and frequent occurrence of rape. This discovery was a significant moral advance, one for which we are indebted to the feminists.

The present state of affairs presents at least two significant problems. First, what exactly is so bad about rape? Traditional mutterings about loss of purity, chastity, and honor, and about the diminution of the woman's value as the property of her father, husband, or other male keeper will hardly account for the rage and horror feminists express about the matter. Nor, to be fair, do they seem to capture fully the professed public sentiments about rape. Second, the existence of a general public stance of unqualified moral condemnation of rape, in tandem with a general public pretense that rape almost never happens and an attitude of skepticism and reproach toward purported victims of rape, intimates the presence of some ulterior motivation in the public psyche. This raises the question: what unsavory social purposes could this piece of hypocrisy be serving? We will offer answers to both these questions.

What we shall here refer to as ''rape'' is sexual intercourse performed without the consent of the woman involved. As conservatives on the matter tirelessly remind us, rape is not done only by males or suffered only by females. So long as one is speaking strictly in terms of the anatomical characteristics of the participants, we certainly have no quarrel with this. But using the terms ''man'' and ''woman'' and invoking their associations with social and political roles rather than their associations with anatomical characteristics, one may nonetheless sensibly claim that rape is a man's act, whether it is a male or a female man and whether it is a man relatively permanently or relatively temporarily; and being raped is a woman's experience, whether it is a female or a male woman and whether it is a woman relatively permanently or relatively temporarily. We will speak of women and men as though all women were female and all men male, bearing in mind that what we say must be capable of extension to instances where this is not the case and also to instances where the sexual acts in question would not comfortably fit under the rubric ''sexual intercourse.'' With these caveats, we shall proceed to presume that rape is sexual intercourse performed without the consent of the woman. Since we share the public view that rape is morally wrong and gravely so, and since we would not want to say that there is anything morally wrong with sexual intercourse per se, we conclude that the wrongness of rape rests with the matter of the woman's consent.[1]

Giving consent is a conventional, institutional speech act and shares the general characteristics of such acts. There is an explicit verbal formula, ''I (hereby) consent,'' by which it may be performed, though other phrases or gestures may be employed more frequently and colloquially and though consent is often tacitly given. The act of consenting is a formal one and is sharply to be distinguished from the emotional states which ideally accompany it and which it is often presumed to express, most notably a feeling of willingness.

To consent is to reverse a prima facie presumption about what may and may not be done. For example, there is a prima facie presumption that one person should not use another's books; after the owner gives consent, however, it is prima facie all right for the person to whom it is given to use those books on a particular occasion or occasions. In the case where a person grants general consent, a general prima facie presumption is reversed. Without general consent, one may not use a person's library unless she says one may; with general consent, one may use her books unless she says one may not. The person who gives a general consent does not yield up the right to alter, qualify, or revoke that consent. If one day the owner of the library tells you to leave a particular book on the shelf and you spirit it away even so, you have taken it without her consent, and this is theft—regardless of the fact that you had and still have general consent to use the library. At any time and without explanation she may revoke her consent, and this act will constitute the immediate reversal once again of the presumption about your use of her library: you may no longer remove a book unless she says you may.

(It becomes clear, now, that a married woman cannot correctly be said to have granted general consent to intercourse with her husband, since she does not retain the right to revoke or modify this so-called consent at will.)

As in the case of other speech acts, there are preconditions for a felicitous act of consenting. There is the usual requirement that performance of the act not be secured by coercion or fraud, but there are conditions more peculiar to consent as well. In the first place, one can have power of consent only over something that could in principle be effected or affected by human agency. One cannot consent to the occurrence of a thunderstorm or to the laws of physics. Within the range where one might have power of consent there are further limitations. Because of the conventional nature of the act of consent, one can effectively consent or withhold consent only where others are prone to consider one's wishes—that is, where one's act of giving consent can secure uptake. In another dimension, one can properly consent or withhold consent only where one has a right to exercise control. Obviously, the range of one's actual, effective power of consent may or may not coincide with the range within which, morally, one ought to have power of consent, for one's effective power of consent depends upon the acknowledgment of others.

The proper scope of one's power of consent depends on one's *domain*, and the notion of domain is inextricably linked with that of personhood, for it is as a person that one has a domain. The concept of personhood is a peculiarly behavioral one: a certain respect is accorded to a creature because it has certain traits and capabilities which normally result in, and are exercised in, certain behaviors. What is held in high regard is not the behaviors but the properties and capacities assumed to reside inside the black box. (This is confirmed by expressed moral intuitions about the personhood of fetuses, small children, once competent paralyzed adults, robots and so on.) But the only way we know a creature has those traits and capacities is that they are manifest in its behavior. It is recognized that temporary or explicable absence of the characteristic behavior does not necessarily indicate the absence of the privileged properties, especially if impediments to the behavior are readily discernible; but complete absence of the behaviors (as with someone in a lengthy coma) or constitutional inability to manifest recognizable behaviors of the appropriate sort (as with porpoises or machines) tend to disqualify a creature as a person.

The list of traits and capacities regarded as characteristic of persons is much debated, and the question of the number of these properties a creature must possess, and in what degree, in order to satisfy personhood criteria is usually answered by consulting the intestines rather than the brain. Nevertheless, it seems fairly safe to list among the more popular traits intelligence, self-awareness, linguistic ability, emotional sensibility, moral sense, and the ability to choose and make decisions. Perhaps another way to put this point is to say that to qualify as a person, a candidate must be the sort of creature that is capable of identifying its own interests, choosing a fairly wide range of more or less complex goals for itself, and engaging in communication about and pursuit of those interests and goals. And the behavior by which it manifests these abilities is the evident exercise of them.

(There are numerous indications that personhood can come in degrees—as our perception of small children, idiots , and the senile will testify. But in order to reveal the fundamental moral situation, we shall carry on here as though all persons were paradigm cases of full personhood.)

Now we can say quite simply what a domain is. A domain is where this sort of creature, a person, lives. The very center of the domain is the highly touted person-properties themselves and their physical locus, the body. In this context, theories on whether or how the properties and the body are related are irrelevant. In dealing with persons, one is dealing with behaving bodies, and it is these that have domains. It is to be noted that the body is not the property of a person who possesses it along with the rest of the domain. Rather, the behaving body *is* a person, the sort of thing which acts and owns and consents, and cannot be owned or consented over, even by itself.[2] The disposition of the body, because in one aspect it directly affects and in another it is that body's behavior, is also central to the person's domain. Since biological life and health are prerequisites for the pursuit of any other interests and goals whatever, everything necessary for their maintenance and sustenance evidently will fall very close to the center of the domain. Anything which exerts an influence on the person-properties themselves—which, for example, bends a person's will or dulls its intelligence or affects its own sense of its identity—also comes very near the center of the domain. Whatever has a relatively permanent effect on the person, whatever affects its relatively constant surroundings, whatever causes it discomfort or distress—in short, whatever a person has to live with—is likely to fall squarely within its domain. A person's domain includes the activities, the tools and materials, and the physical spaces used in the pursuit of that person's goals and the carrying out of its projects; its domain includes the resources of its work, play, recreation, exercise, solace, and amusement. This domain becomes attenuated as the items in question are removed from physical, temporal, or emotional proximity to the person—that is, from the center of the domain.

What makes a person's domain the delimiter of the morally proper scope of that person's power of consent is that intruding into a person's domain comes dangerously (sometimes indistinguishably) close to treading upon the person itself. It seems obvious that a person, which is a person precisely in virtue of traits that give it among other things a capacity for and a tendency toward self-determination, ought to have power of consent over anything that seriously affects it, and that violation of a person's domain can be justified only by reference to some higher principle. Upon examination, most if not all higher principles commonly suggested seem reducible to rules for settling conflicts among domains. This does introduce a problem. A lone person in the world would seem to have a right to power of consent over any and every thing it could (and cared to) control—except that it makes no sense to talk of consent in the absence of other persons. The fact is that there are a multitude of persons in the world, and their domains can and frequently do overlap; this is just what makes the convention of consent necessary. It also necessitates some principle for resolving conflicts between scopes of powers of consent resulting from the overlap of domains. Each person qua person has as much right to power of consent within its own domain as any other has within its domain. When domains overlap, it seems only reasonable to concede the power of consent in a conflict over a given item to the person to whose domain it is more central—that is, to the one more profoundly affected by it. If an item is of equal centrality to the domains of the opponents, they should negotiate the matter. If and only if that fails, direct confrontation and struggle may be permissible, so long as each recognizes the prima facie equal right of the other. *Possibly* if an item is equally central to several persons the decision of the majority should carry, though those outnumbered should not be expected to relinquish their claims. *Possibly* a lesser effect on a great many persons can outweigh a greater effect on just one. And so on. The conceivable configurations are endless and endlessly complex, but the appropriate general principle and attitude seem clear enough. A person's domain is the physical, emotional, psychological, and intellectual space it lives in. The space, diminished only by overlap with the domains of others, defines the rightful scope of the person's power of consent. It should be noticed that one person, being itself the center of a domain and a sort of thing which cannot be *in* a domain, can never properly fall under another's power of consent.

The morally appropriate attitude upon encountering another person is one of respect: recognition of its domain, and deference to its rightful power of consent. Ideally, the range of a person's effective power of consent should coincide with that of its rightful power of consent, but the conventionality of consent allows for considerable slippage. It is quite possible honestly to misperceive or misjudge the extent of a person's domain and consequently to accord it a greater or lesser effective power of consent than that to which it is entitled. Such an error is probably not morally reprehensible, so long as one has taken seriously the moral requirement of deferring to the other within the range of its rightful power of consent. This, of course, involves taking seriously the business of discerning the boundaries of the other's domain. It is also quite possible disingenuously and self-deceptively to misperceive or misjudge the extent of another's domain, usually because there appears to be some advantage to (or survival value in) doing so. This also can result in the concession to another of a greater or lesser effective power of consent than is proper; such attitudes we label obsequious or overbearing. A common example of such attitudes flourishing in symbiosis can be observed in the relationship of many an enterprising junior executive with his boss. It is furthermore quite possible for a person to have a clear and accurate perception of the domain of another and to disregard it deliberately nonetheless. While it is possible thus to aggrandize the domain of another, it seems likely that the rightful scope of a person's power of consent is more often blatantly flouted by diminishing than by expanding its effective power of consent.

Because of the conventional, linguistic nature of the act of consent, the corresponding uptake has a communicative function as well. Whatever the moral status of the processes from which it results, the concession of a particular range of effective power of consent to a person constitutes a statement about the domain of that person and, in the light of the intimate connection between a person and its domain, about the person itself. It is prima facie far more culpable to refuse to grant a person its rights than to grant it unwarranted privileges; and on the other hand, the expansion of one person's effective power of consent is almost inevitably correlated with the diminution of someone else's. Therefore we shall concentrate here on the significance of conceding to someone an effective power of consent narrower than its rightful one. Failure to defer to someone's expressed wishes is in effect either a formal denial that the person is within its domain or a formal assertion that the item in question is more central to your domain than it is to the other person's. Now, on our view, the extent of a person's domain is determined by the person-qualities themselves, while the shape (or, so to speak, the intensity) of the domain is determined by the person's personal identity (its ordering of things according to their centrality to itself). So to fail to defer to a person's rightful power of consent is to deny either the actual extent of its personhood or its actual personal identity. Either is flagrantly disrespectful, and thus grievously wrong. The closer the item is to the center of the domain of the person whose rightful power of consent over it is not recognized, the more violent is the attack upon the creature's personhood itself. To presume to wield an effective power of consent over the personal properties and/or the body of that creature, the center of its domain, is ipso facto to deny that there is a person there at all. The ultimate in disrespect is to exercise the power of consent over those properties and the body in action (that is, over the creature's behavior), for it is precisely as a behaving body that the creature is a person and is the person that it is. The ultimate disrespect is, then, the exercise of the power of consent over another *person*. And this is exactly what rape is.

As we mentioned at the beginning, there is a standing public pretense that rape is rare. And it would be rare if women were in general creatures viewed with respect. When among people whose acts are motivated, guided, and restricted by respect, no one has to attend with any great vigilance to threats of assault, either physical or emotional. When one is among friends, one need not worry that someone is going suddenly to get a notion to pursue steadfastly an end which requires as a means one's murder or one's humiliation. But a woman, in the world we live in, is not among friends. A woman does not have this sort of security. There are people around her who will suddenly take it into their heads to rape her—to coerce her submission to sexual intercourse. This naturally raises the question, why would anyone take it into his head to do this?

One answer given by conventional wisdom is that men do this out of sexual need or desire. That a man would rape with such motivation reveals his unwillingness to exercise a certain kind and degree of control where he should be deferring to the wishes of another. In fact, it is a rather extreme case. He is controlling not just the disposition of things which are within the range of the woman's rightful power of consent, but the woman herself, through the manipulation of her body. He is not merely diverting her resources or using her property to further ends other than hers, he is using *her* in furtherance of ends other than hers. Moreover, the ends for which he is using her body are ends which are *contrary* to hers, given that her ends include the maintenance of her bodily integrity and health. The use of a person in the advancement of interests contrary to its own is a limiting case of disrespect. It reveals the perception of the person simply as an object which can serve some purpose, a tool or a bit of material, and one which furthermore is dispensable or replaceable and thus of little value even as an object with a function.

But the phenomena of rape present us with a maze of humiliations more complex yet than this. The victim of this sort of rape is not, of course, an insensate object, and this event is not without meaning to her. It conveys to her that she is seen as an object with a sexual function. The person raping her sees her through a perceptual schema which presents her and anything she does as something associated or connected with sexual intercourse—with his penetration and ejaculation. The rape represents to her his sexual perception of her; it gives her a picture of herself as a being within someone's domain and not as a being which has domain. The rape means that she is not seen as a person; and she is the observer *to whom* it means this.

The plot thickens when we shift from rape as a sort of simple, selfish act of appropriation and look at rape in the boudoir, between friends, lovers, or spouses. When a person with whom a woman has a friendly or personal or intimate relationship rapes her, it is typically with some intension more complicated than merely the satisfaction of his sexual desires. The act of rape itself has the same meaning in such cases, perhaps, but it is done with the intention that it have this meaning. The boudoir rapist acts with the intention of informing, reminding, or telling the woman of his sexual perception of her. This intention is involved in or subserves other more specific communication intentions which vary with the sort of situation the pair are in and the sorts of things he may have to say to her.

Many of the relationships women and men enter into within our society are more or less analogues of those in which the two people implicitly strike a sort of bargain. Facing the world alone, the woman discovers or rediscovers that she is chronically liable to exploitation and victimization so long as she is without male support and protection. The man, facing the world alone, discovers or senses that his happiness and peace of mind are precarious at best if he does not have a wife or mistress. The woman and the man form an alliance: he provides her with male sponsorship and she provides him with sexual and other services. In such a situation, if she shows unwillingness or lack of inclination to engage with him in sexual intercourse, he may wish to remind her of the nature of the bargain they struck. The act of rape may serve conveniently as a communicative vehicle for reminding her of the situation from which she negotiated this arrangement, in such a way as to threaten to return her to that situation if she withholds sexual services. The situation from which she started was that of a being without respect; and treating her as such in the act of rape, he may communicate his message with considerable clarity and directness.

Rape is an act which belies respect, and it is often an act actually intended to communicate the fact of disrespect. Whether it is the rapist's intention or not, being raped conveys for the woman the message that she is a being without respect, that she is not a person. And it is in part because of this that the institution of rape can play the role it does in the structure of intersexual relations in general.

Women in this society live generally under the threat of rape. The threat of sexual assault limits the movements of women about their communities, restricts their access to various services and amusements, restricts their pursuit both of comfort and of self-expression in their clothes and personal styles, portends penalty and punishment for various assertions of their interests and claims to domain, and greatly restricts the range of possible exploration of sexual experience and expression. Even if the threat were simple and direct and open, it would have these effects to a considerable degree. But it is not generally posed as an open threat.

The public denial that rape is common, or even that it happens at all, is effectively also a public denial that there is any significant threat of rape. This denial is at best an insult to women's common sense; at worst it is the sort of public denial of the veracity of a person's perceptions that, if sustained, can simply drive a person mad. The woman is subjected not only to the controlling influence of the threat, but at the same time to the maddening influence of the denial that the threat exists.

Although the threat of physical assault of any sort could no doubt be fairly effective as a means of social control of a large population, one would expect such a threat to have to be made plausible through considerable open advertisement and vivid examples. But the threat of rape is very effective even though its existence is publicly denied, and no great amount of resource is expended in publicity and enforcement. This remarkable efficiency is attained by there being another twist in the mechanism.

What is threatened when rape is threatened is not just physical assault, but the vigorous revelation of the simple fact that rape happens. Rape is the exposure of the public lie that women are respected persons. It reveals to the woman that she is viewed in such a way that men do not have prohibitive moral compunctions about using her as an object whose function is their sexual gratification and expression—as an object, like a sheep in the field, with regard to which no question of its consent or the lack of it arises. The threat of rape operates like a form of blackmail. It is the threat of exposure of the woman as a being without respect, or, as some women experience it, exposure of the woman as a being unworthy of respect.

A woman knows her status in this society—her status as a being generally not respected. It is taught her from the crib. But it is an ugly and painful fact, and she is likely to be all too willing to be persuaded that it isn't really so. It is also of value in a society such as ours that populations being controlled and used should in general be self-deceived about it, for then they will be less prone to railing and rebellion. There is here a perfect role for the gentleman and the pedestal.

Many women in many aspects of their lives are treated relatively gently and with a fair amount of generosity by the males around them. They live in the house of some male, like a child living under a broad blanket of general consents in its parents' home. Generous and open-minded parents grant their children the privilege of acting to a fair extent as though they had domains of their own, like frequent and welcome visitors enjoying a broad hospitality. And women often enjoy such privileges as well—often as comfortably as their menfolk can financially manage. It is easy to mistake the privilege of freedom of movement and choice within another's domain for the right of power of consent within one's own domain. And the kindly granting of the privilege can be mistaken for the recognition of the right; the condescending deference to a cherished object in a man's domain mistaken for the deference given a person in its own domain.[3]

Taking kindness and humane treatment for respect, the woman can convince herself, or be convinced, that she is a respected being, while living in a society where in general she is not and where she constantly receives hints and reminders of this fact. While rueing the fact of her willingness to be deceived or to deceive herself, we may see that this may be absolutely necessary to her survival. The clear-eyed perception that one is not in general respected (when others say one is) is, other things being equal, a challenging threat to one's maintenance of self-respect. To maintain one's sense of being a person and respectable, it is surely in some situations essential to avoid the influence of the public perception to the contrary. The position a woman has by birth in this sexist society makes it valuable, in some cases essential, for her to exercise some self-deception and to cooperate in some trickery in order to view herself as a creature viewed with respect. This can coerce her into collaboration with her oppressors in their disrespectful behavior. And once again we see the woman herself being used in furtherance of ends inimical to her own well-being.

The woman's (coerced) collusion in the myth of her respectability would make her doubly susceptible to the blackmail involved in the threat of rape. The thing threatened (in addition to mere assault) is the disclosure of the evil fact of her real status, a fact in whose cover-up the woman herself is implicated by her willingness to collaborate in the deception. Welcoming neither the disclosure of the fact of her status nor the disclosure of her betrayal of herself, she will go to great lengths to accommodate the blackmailer.[4]

Looked at microscopically, an individual rape on the street, as it were, done by a stranger simply in pursuit of sexual gratification (if there are such cases—the motivation is usually more complex) is bad in the way assault in general is, but its wickedness is compounded by the fact that it is a use of a person, not just the injury of a person, and a use of a person in pursuit of ends not its own and/or contrary to its own. That is profoundly disrespectful and a clear case of failing to treat a person *as* a person. It is also a use of a person which involves tampering with parts of its self which are for most people centrally rather than peripherally involved in their personal identity.

Looked at macroscopically, rape is the point of application of a monstrous device of social control in which insult and injury are heaped upon one another in such complex abundance that one can scarcely keep the accounts, much less stomach the contemplation of it.

The public discovery of rape and women's boldly facing the terrible fact of their status in society can disarm the machine. One who knows and acknowledges the grim fact cannot be tricked into the treachery of self-deception or frightened by the threat or the actuality of the fact's disclosure. One has then to deal merely with the widespread threat of intentional violation of one's domain, and the out-and-out disregard of one's power of consent by persons who see one as an object with a purely sexual function—persons who are therefore unlikely to be moved to desist by the mere withholding of one's consent to sexual intercourse.

Notes

1. Some of Pamela Foa's observations move in a different direction from ours at this point. She notes that though an enlightened view may reveal that sexual intercourse per se is morally neutral, there is in our culture a strong tradition of classifying it as taboo, forbidden, or sinful, and this whether misguided or not, complicates the politics of rape. . . . Our account is intended to explore the intuition that rape has peculiar moral features even *apart* from the odd moral sentiments about sex which pervade this culture. Sexual intercourse, even if not felt to be sinful or taboo in itself, has a peculiar role in the moral and political intercourse between the sexes in a sexist culture.
2. In much of the debate about abortion, the conflicting positions seem to share the presupposition that a human body is a piece of property; once the rhetorical smokescreens dissipate, the disputants seem to be disagreeing merely about who owns which body—that is, who has property rights over what.
3. Conversations I have had with women who are either not middle class or not white, or not either, suggest that not only are they less accustomed to being treated so gently and granted such privileges, they are also less intimidated by the fear of rape than are those who are white and middle class. M.F.

4. The assault on the woman's personhood is exacerbated by the fact that in this culture the act by which it is accomplished is taboo. According to some of the prevailing mores, she is defiled and made into a transgressor, and to the extent that she is susceptible to their influence, she feels herself to be such. The "assertion" that she is not a person is made in such a way as to be self-verifying, for the act through which it is asserted itself *casts* her outside the taboo-defined community of persons.

Study Questions

1. According to the authors, what hypocrisy about rape is prevalent among the public?
2. According to Frye and Shafer, in what sense is rape "a man's act."
3. Why is the notion of "consent" important to the discussion of rape? How is consent normally indicated? What are some preconditions of consenting?
4. Explain in some detail what a "domain" is.
5. How is the notion of a person's domain tied to the notion of consent?
6. According to the authors, what are the reason(s) or intention(s) underlying rape.
7. Is rape rare (in Frye and Shafer's opinion)? Why or why not? How is the threat of rape like blackmail?
8. What do the authors mean when they say that the respectability of women is a myth?

6

Philosophy of Religion

Religious institutions profoundly affect our public lives as well as our private lives. Religion affects our public lives in that religious values permeate political, social, legal, and educational structures. Religion also affects our private lives in that religious attitudes inform our domestic and sexual relationships. Thus philosophers have been concerned with the nature and function of those religious values.

Philosophers, historically, have raised such questions as: What is the function of religion? What is the nature of religious concepts? Does God exist, and if so, what is God's nature? How can religious statements be established, and for whom are they valid?

Some feminist thinkers have a strong interest in these matters. From the woman's point of view, the most important questions about religion have not yet been addressed. So feminists are raising such issues as: Is religion by its very nature patriarchal and oppressive? Should women involve themselves with religious institutions to make them more responsive to us? What would it mean to have women-centered religion, which would express matriarchal values or feminist spirituality?

Mary Daly calls for women to reject world religions and their "processions," since they all legitimate patriarchy and are not salvageable. She proposes that women exorcize their minds of patriarchal religious myths by means of "ludic cerebration." Daly speaks of "the qualitative leap" by which women will move "beyond God the Father" and live their own transcendence, in their own time/space. She calls this process "the journey of *becoming.*"

Theology may be distinguished from the philosophy of religion as that area that deals with the concept of deity. Carol Christ proposes "thealogy" or the study of the Goddess concept. In positing a male God, she believes that patriarchal religion has supported the devaluation of women. Christ argues that a Goddess symbol would empower women by affirming female strength, by reclaiming the female body, and by valuing female energy.

Women's spirituality is not synonymous with the Goddess symbol but may take several forms. Sally Gearhart defends diverse feminist spiritual practices, from the charge that they divert women from political action. She believes that women's religion is one of several strategies women may employ in their struggle against capitalist patriarchy. She sees the others as reform, revolution, and alternate structures (separatism). Women's spirituality, Gearhart asserts, may alternate with political modes and serve as a "re-sourcement" of women's energy and women's culture.

The Qualitative Leap Beyond Patriarchal Religion

Mary Daly

The writing of this article presents a minor dilemma. I do not wish simply to rewrite ideas which I have presented elsewhere. Yet there is a background, or frame of reference, or context, out of which the present article is written. To resolve this I am setting forth in very skeletal form, in the form of twenty-three statements, a context discussed at length in a number of articles and in two books.[1]

Prolegomena

1. There exists a planetary sexual caste system, essentially the same in Saudi Arabia and in New York, differing only in degree.
2. This system is masked by sex role segregation, by the dual identity of women, by ideologies and myths.
3. Among the primary loci of sexist conditioning is grammar.
4. The "methods" of the various "fields" are not adequate to express feminist thought. Methodolatry requires that women perform Methodicide, an act of intellectual bravery.
5. All of the major world religions function to legitimate patriarchy. This is true also of the popular cults such as the Krishna movement and the Jesus Freaks.
6. The myths and symbols of Christianity are essentially sexist. Since "God" is male, the male is God. God the Father legitimates all earthly Godfathers, including Vito Corleone, Pope Paul, President Gerald Ford, the Godfathers of medicine (e.g., the American Medical Association), of science (e.g., NASA), of the media, of psychiatry, of education, and of all the -ologies.
7. The myth of feminine evil, expressed in the story of the Fall, is reinforced by the myth of salvation/redemption by a single human being of the male

From *Quest*, Vol. 1, No. 4 (Spring 1975), pp. 20–40. Reprinted by permission of Mary Daly.

sex. The idea of a unique divine incarnation in a male, the God-man of the "hypostatic union," is inherently sexist and oppressive. Christolatry is idolatry.

8. A significant and growing cognitive minority of women, radical feminists, are breaking out from under the sacred shelter of patriarchal religious myths.

9. This breaking out, facing anomy when the meaning structures of patriarchy are seen through and rejected, is a communal, political event. It is a revelatory event, a creative, political ontophany.

10. The bonding of the growing cognitive minority of women who are radical feminists, commonly called *sisterhood,* involves a process of new naming, in which words are wrenched out of their old semantic context and heard in a new semantic context. For example, the "sisterhoods" of patriarchy, such as religious congregations of women, were really mini-brotherhoods. *Sisterhood* heard with new ears is bonding for women's own liberation.

11. There is an inherent dynamic in the women's revolution in Judeo-Christian society which is Antichurch, whether or not feminists specifically concern ourselves with churches. This is so because the Judeo-Christian tradition legitimates patriarchy—the prevailing power structure and prevailing world view—which the women's revolution leaves behind.

12. The women's revolution is not only Antichurch. It is a postchristian spiritual revolution.

13. The ethos of Judeo-Christian culture is dominated by The Most Unholy Trinity: Rape, Genocide, and War. It is rapism which spawns racism. It is gynocide which spawns genocide, for sexism (rapism) is fundamental socialization to objectify "the other."

14. The women's revolution is concerned with transvaluation of values, beyond the ethics dominated by The Most Unholy Trinity.

15. The women's revolution is not merely about equality within a patriarchal society (a contradiction in terms). It is about *power* and redefining power.

16. Since Christian myths are inherently sexist, and since the women's revolution is not about "equality" but about power, there is an intrinsic dynamic in the feminist movement which goes beyond efforts to reform Christian churches. Such efforts eventually come to be recognized as comparable to a Black person's trying to reform the Ku Klux Klan.

17. Within patriarchy, power is generally understood as power *over* people, the environment, things. In the rising consciousness of women, power is experienced as *power of presence* to ourselves and to each other, as we affirm our own being against and beyond the alienated identity (non-being) bestowed upon us within patriarchy. This is experienced as *power of absence* by those who would objectify women as "the other," as magnifying mirrors.

18. The presence of women to ourselves which is *absence* to the oppressor is the essential dynamic opening up the women's revolution to human liberation. It is an invitation to men to confront non-being and hence affirm their be-ing.

19. It is unlikely that many men will accept this invitation willingly, or even be able to hear it, since they have profound vested (though self-destructive) interest in the present social arrangements.

20. The women's movement is a new mode of relating to the self, to each other, to men, to the environment—in a word—to the cosmos. It is self-affirming, refusing objectification of the self and of the other.

21. Entrance into new feminist time/space, which is moving time/space located on the boundaries of patriarchal institutions, is active participation in ultimate

reality, which is de-reified, recognized as Verb, as intransitive Verb with no object to block its dynamism.

22. Entrance into radical feminist consciousness involves recognition that all male-dominated "revolutions," which do not reject the universally oppressive reality which is patriarchy, are in reality only reforms. They are "revolutions" only in the sense that they are spinnings of the wheels of the same senescent system.

23. Entrance into radical feminist consciousness implies an awareness that the women's revolution is the "final cause" (pun intended) in the radical sense that it is the cause which can move the other causes. It is the catalyst which can bring about real change, since it is the rising up of the universally and primordially objectified "Other," discrediting the myths which legitimate rapism. Rapism is by extension the objectification and destruction of all "others" and inherently tends to the destruction of the human species and of all life on this planet.

Radical feminism, the becoming of women, is very much an Otherworld Journey. It is both discovery and creation of a world other than patriarchy. Some observation reveals that patriarchy is "everywhere." Even outer space and the future have been colonized. As a rule, even the more imaginative science fiction writers (seemingly the most foretelling futurists) cannot/will not create a space and time in which women get far beyond the role of space stewardess. Nor does this situation exist simply "outside" women's minds, securely fastened into institutions which we can physically leave behind. Rather, it is also internalized, festering inside women's heads, even feminist heads.

The journey of women *becoming*, then, involves exorcism of the internalized Godfather, in his various manifestations (His name is legion). It involves dangerous encounters with these demons. Within the Christian tradition, particularly in medieval times, evil spirits have some-times been associated with the Seven Deadly Sins, both as personifications and as causes.[2] A "standard" and prevalent listing of the Sins is, of course, the following: pride, avarice, anger, lust, gluttony, envy, and sloth.[3] I am contending that these have all been radically misnamed, that is, inadequately and even perversely "understood" within Christianity. These concepts have been used to victimize the oppressed, particularly women. They are particularized ex-pressions of the overall use of "evil" to victimize women. The feminist journey involves con-frontations with the demonic distortions of evil.

Why has it seemed "appropriate" in this culture that a popular book and film (*The Exorcist*) center around a Jesuit who "exorcises" a girl-child who is "possessed"? Why is there no book or film about a woman who exorcises a Jesuit?[4] Within a culture possessed by the myth of feminine evil, the naming, describing, and theorizing about good and evil has constituted a web of deception, a Maya. The journey of women becoming is breaking through this web—a Fall into free space. It is reassuming the role of subject, as opposed to object, and naming good and evil on the basis of our own intuitive intellection.

Breaking through the web of the Male Maya is both exorcism and ecstasy. These are two aspects of the same journey. Since women have been prohibited from real journeying, that is, from encountering the strange, the unknown, the women's movement is movement into uncharted territory. The process involves removal of the veils which prevent confronta-tion with the unknown. Let it be noted that "journey" is a multidimensional word and that the various meanings and images conjured up by the word are not sharply distinguishable. One thinks of mystical journeys, quests, adventurous travel, advancement in skills, in sports, in intellectual probing, in psychological integration and transformation. So also the "veils," the insulations against the unknown imposed upon women by male mediators, are multi-dimensional and intertwined. The veils are woven of religious myths (for example, the myth of the "good woman," the Virgin Mother who has only a Son, not a Daughter), legal restrictions, social customs, medical and psychoanalytic ideologies and practices, academic restrictions (withholding of access to "higher" education, to certain professions), grammatical conditioning ("he" supposedly includes "she"), economic limitations. The very process of exorcism, of casting off the blinding veils, is movement outside the patriarchally imposed sense of reality and identity. This demystification process, standing/moving outside The Lie, *is* ecstasy.

The process of encountering the unknown, of overcoming the "protection" racket, also involves a continual conversion of the previously unknown into the familiar.[5] This requires the use of tools and instruments now in the possession of women's captors. Amazon expeditions into the male-controlled "fields" such as law, medicine, psychology, philosophy, theology, literature, history, sociology, biology, and physics are necessary in order to leave the Fathers' cave and live in the sun. A crucial problem has been to learn how to plunder righteously while avoiding being caught too long in the cave. In universities, and in virtually all of the professions, there are poisonous gases which are almost invisible and odorless, and which gradually stifle women's minds and spirits. Those who carry out the necessary expeditions run the risk of shrinking into the mold of the mystified Athena, the twice-born who forgets and denies her Mother and Sisters. "Reborn" from the Father, she becomes Daddy's Girl, the mutant who serves the master's purposes. The token woman, who in reality is enchained, possessed, "knows" that she is free. She is a useful tool of the patriarchs, particularly against her sister Artemis, who knows better, respects her womanself, bonds with her sisters, and refuses to sell her freedom, her original birthright, for a mess of respectability.

Exorcism, Processions, and Remythologization

What clues can we find concerning the "nature" and direction of the Other-world journey of radically feminist (i.e., conscious) women? Some important hints can be discovered in *Three Guineas,* an astonishing book published in the 1930s by a prophetic foremother. In that book Virginia Woolf links processions (e.g., academic, churchly, military, judicial) with professions and processions. She asks: What are these ceremonies and why should we take part in them? What are these professions and why should we make money out of them? Where, in short, is it leading us, the procession of the sons of educated men?[6]

Clearly, they are leading us to destruction of the human species and of the planet. The rigid, stylized, hierarchical, gynocidal and genocidal processions of male-controlled professions—of church, state, university, army—are all intimately interconnected. These processions capture and reify process. They are deadly. It is important to understand them in order to understand what feminist process/journeying is *not*.

Patriarchal processions both generate and reflect the archetypal image of "procession" from and return to God the Father. In Christian myth, this is a cyclic pattern: separation and return. Christians participate in the procession—they join the parade—through Baptism, which explicitly contains a rite of exorcism. This mythic symbolic procession toward "God," then, begins with belief in possession by evil forces ("possession" technically in a broad sense, of course), release from which requires captivity by the church. What is ultimately sought is reconciliation with the Father.

Clearly, the ultimate symbol of "procession" is the All Male Trinity itself. In various abstruse ways theologians have elaborated upon the "mystery," or as some would say, the "symbol," of the Trinity. What is of great significance here is the fact that this is a myth of Father and Son (no Mother or Daughter involved) in total unity, so total that this "love" is expressed by the Third Person, the Holy Spirit. This is the epitome of male bonding beyond the wildest dreams of Lionel Tiger. It is (almost?) erotic male homosexual mythos, the perfect All Male Marriage, the All Male Divine Family. It is asymmetric patriarchy carried to the sublime absurdity of contradiction, christened "mystery." To the timid objections sometimes voiced by Christian women, the classic answer has been: "You're included. The Holy Spirit is feminine." The conclusion of this absurd logic arrives quickly if one asks: How then, did "he" impregnate the Virgin Mary?

Mere human males, of course, cannot fully identify with the divine Son. Perfect consubstantiality with the Father, therefore, cannot be achieved. The earthly processions of the sons of men have as their basic paradigm an attempted identification with the Father. (God the Father, the Godfather, the Oedipal Father). The junior statesman dreams of becoming The President. The academic junior scholar (disciple) dreams of becoming The Professor (Master). The acolyte dreams of becoming The Priest. And, as Woolf recognized, the death-oriented military processions reveal the real direction of the whole scenario, which is a funeral procession of the human species. God the Father requires human sacrifice.

Women becoming must indeed recognize the fact of having been possessed by the structures of evil. However, the solution is not "rebirth" or Baptism by the Father's surrogates, for it is this socialized "rebirth" which is the captivity from which we are trying to escape. Radical feminism is *not* reconciliation with the Father. It begins with saying "No" to the Father, who attempts to eradicate our Mother and to transform us into mutants by forcing "rebirth" (whether from the head of Zeus or from the rib of Adam or from baptismal "grace"). More than this: radical feminism means saying "Yes" to our original birth, the original movement-surge toward life. This is both a remembering and a rediscovering. Athena remembers and rediscovers her Mother. That which is generated between us is Sisterhood. We are then no longer confined by our identities as "Mother" or "Daughter." The Daughter is *not* obedient to the Mother "unto death." The Mother does not send her forth to be crucified for the sins of women or of men. Rather, they go forth as Sisters. Radical feminism releases the inherent dynamic in the Mother-Daughter relationship toward Sisterhood, which is thwarted within the Male-mastered system. The Mother does *not* demand self-sacrifice of the Daughter. Rather, both demand of each other affirmation of the self and of each other in an ongoing personal/political process which is mythic in its depths—which is both exorcising and remythologizing process. The "sacrifice" that is required is not mutilation at the hands of men, but rather the discipline needed for action together, for self-defense and self-actualization on a planet dominated by the Reign of Terror which is the Reign of the Godfathers. It is important that we consider the actual conditions of this terrain through which we must make our journey.

The Land of the Fathers

As Phyllis Chesler has pointed out, the story of the Virgin Mary, impregnated by God to bring forth his only Son, is classic patriarchal rape-incest myth. The Madonna has no Divine Daughter. Moreover, as the same author perceptively says, she foregoes sexual pleasure, physical prowess, and economic and intellectual power in order to become a "mother" for her "divine" son.[7] And this is the primary role-model for women in our culture. This is the life that women are condemned to live out—an alienation which is personal, social, mythic—and which is all the deeper because unrecognized, unacknowledged.

In a society in which women are in fact *robbed* of physical prowess, of economic and intellectual power, we live in a State of Siege.[8] As Jeanne Lafferty and Evelyn Clark wrote:

> Every female person knows the humiliation of being constantly harassed and solicited by males. Having her person talked at, whistled at, yelled at, grunted at, hooted and howled at, visually dismembered or stared and winked at by males everywhere—on the street, at work, at school, at home—everywhere.[9]

This is the very real condition of women in a rapist society. Moreover, the dismemberment is not always only visual. Male fetishism concerning women's bodies, the cutting into objectified parts which is the prime material of advertising and pornography, has as its logical outcome the brutal rape murders and actual physical dismemberments which take place in such a society. In a world ruled by God the Father this is not considered a serious problem. A feminist author wrote:

> "Rape is too personal and too terrible a crime to be left to the punishment of indifferent male law."[10]

In a society possessed by the sexual caste system, that is, in a rapist society, there is a deep struggle on the part of those designated "victims" to cast out the deception that warps the soul. The deception inflicted upon women is a kind of mindbinding comparable to the footbinding procedure which mutilated millions of Chinese women for a thousand years.[11] Just as footbinding destroyed the capacity for physical movement—walking, running, dancing—mindbinding damages the capacity for autonomous creativity, action, thinking, imagining, willing. Stripping away the mindbindings of lies that reduce women to the status of physical, mental, and spiritual rapes is the basic loving act in such a society.

The Qualitative Leap

Creative, living, political hope for movement beyond the gynocidal reign of the Fathers will be fulfilled only if women continue to make qualitative leaps in living our transcendence. A short-circuited hope of transcendence has caused many to remain inside churches, and patriarchal religion sometimes has seemed to satisfy the hunger for transcendence. The problem has been that both the hunger and the satisfaction generated within such religions have to a great extent alienated women from our deepest aspirations. Spinning in vicious circles of false needs and false consciousness, women caught on the patriarchal wheel have not been able to experience women's own experience.

I suggest that what is required is *ludic cerebration,* the free play of intuition in our own space, giving rise to thinking that is vigorous, informed, multidimensional, independent, creative, tough. *Ludic cerebration* is thinking out of experience. I do not mean the experience of dredging out All That Was Wrong with Mother, or of instant intimacy in group encounters, or of waiting at the doctoral dispensary, or of self-lobotomization in order to publish, perish, and then be promoted. I mean the experience of being. *Be-ing* is the verb that says the dimensions of depth in all verbs, such as intuiting, reasoning, loving, imaging, making, acting, as well as the couraging, hoping, and playing that are always there when one is really living.

It may be that some new things happen within patriarchy, but one thing essentially stays the same: women are always marginal beings. From this vantage point of the margin it is possible to look at what is between the margins with the lucidity of The Compleat Outsider. To change metaphors: the systems within the System do not appear so radically different from each other to those excluded by all. Hope for a qualitative leap lies in *us* by reason of that deviance from the "norm" which was first imposed but which can also be *chosen* on our own terms. This means that there has to be a shift from "acceptable" female deviance (characterized by triviality, diffuseness, dependence upon others for self-definition, low self-esteem, powerlessness) to deviance which may be unacceptable to others but which is acceptable to the self and *is* self-acceptance.

For women concerned with philosophical/theological questions, it seems to me, this implies the necessity of some sort of choice. One either tries to avoid "acceptable" deviance ("normal" female idiocy) by becoming accepted as a male-identified professional, or else one tries to make the qualitative leap toward self-acceptable deviance as ludic cerebrator, questioner of everything, madwoman, and witch.

I do mean witch. The heretic who rejects the idols of patriarchy is the blasphemous creatrix of her own thoughts. She is finding her life and intends not to lose it. The witch that smolders within every woman who cared and dared enough to become a philosophically/spiritually questing feminist in the first place seems to be crying out these days: "Light my fire!" The qualitative leap, the light of those flames of spiritual imagination and cerebral fantasy can be a new dawn.

On "Androgyny"

Feminists have searched for a word to express the concept/reality of psychic wholeness, of integration, which we are just beginning to glimpse intuitively, experientially, as realizable. In this search for the right word we have experienced the poverty of the language bequeathed to us, and we have recognized the manner in which it constricts and even distorts our thought. In my book *Beyond God the Father*, I frequently use the word "androgyny" to express this intuition and incipient experience of wholeness which transcends sex-role stereotyping—the societally imposed "eternal feminine" and "eternal masculine." Feminist ethicist Janice Raymond has written perceptively of an "intuition of androgyny" as identical with the intuition of being.[12] Two young theologians, graduates of Harvard Divinity School, used the term to convey a feminist understanding of wholeness in a much discussed jointly published article.[13] Feminist poet Adrienne Rich used the word in her poem *The Stranger*, which concludes with the following lines:

> I am the androgyne
> I am the living mind you fail to
> describe
> in your dead language
> the lost noun, the verb surviving
> only in the infinitive
> the letters of my name are written
> under the lids
> of the newborn child.[14]

All of these authors now experience some hesitancy about using the word "androgyny" to express our vision(s). This hesitancy is at least in part due to an increasing understanding of the political use and abuse of language. This increased sophistication has resulted from some distressing misinterpretations of the word.

In speaking to audiences, I have sometimes had the impression that people hearing this term vaguely envisage two distorted halves of a human being stuck together—something like John Wayne and Brigitte Bardot scotchtaped together—as if two distorted "halves" could make a whole. That is, there is a kind of reification of wholeness, instead of recognition that what is being described is continual process. This non-understanding of "androgyny," which feminists have used when attempting to describe the *process* of integration, is also reflected in the assumption on the part of some women (and men) that a woman who is successful in a career on male terms (for example, a successful business executive) and at the same time a model housewife has achieved "androgyny." In fact, this career housewife as described fails to criticize radically either the "masculine" or the "feminine" roles/worlds. She simply compartmentalizes her personality in order to function within both, instead of recognizing/rejecting/transcending the inherent oppressiveness of such institutions as big business and the nuclear family.

When one becomes conscious of the political usages of language, she recognizes also that the term "androgyny" is adaptable to such mystifying usage as the expression "human liberation" has been subjected to. That is, it can easily be used to deflect attention from the fact that women and men at this point in history cannot simply "get together and work it out," ignoring the profound differences in socialization and situation within the sexual caste system. Both "androgyny" and "human liberation" function frequently to encourage false transcendence, masking—even though unintentionally—the specific content of the oppression of women, and suggesting that wholeness depends upon identification with men. Some of us do still use the term "androgyny," of course, but less frequently, more circumspectly, and with some apprehension that we will be misunderstood.

Some feminists began to feel somewhat less comfortable with the word "androgyny" when the implications of a small terse fact surfaced to consciousness. That fact is etymological: the first part of the word obviously is derived from the Greek *aner, andros* (man), while the second part is from *gyne* (woman). This, of course, carries its own message. A first reaction was to employ the word "gynandry," which, from the perspective of women's becoming, is more appropriate. But it soon became evident that the priority problem in the etymology of the word was really symptomatic of deeper problems.

In fact, the term "androgyny" comes to us heavily fraught with traditional associations, that is, associations of male-centered tradition(s). The image conveyed by the word is that of a "feminized" male. This fact has been brought home to me in public discussions with male Christian theologians who, confronted with the problem of the inherent oppressiveness of Christolatry, have responded earnestly that there really is no problem since "Jesus was androgynous." Whatever this may mean, it has little relevance to the problem of women's becoming *now*, and in fact it distracts from the real issues confronting us. Dressing up old symbols just will not work for women who are conscious of sexist religiosity.

"Gynandry" helps to shift images away from the traditional biases, but only to a limited degree. Placing the female part of the word first does not dissolve the inherent dependency of the word itself upon stereotypes in order that there be any meaningful content at all. To put it another way, in an "androgynous" or "gynandrous" society it would be senseless to speak of "androgyny" or "gynandry," since people would have no idea of the sex-stereotyped characteristics and/or roles referred to by the components of the terms. Use of these terms at this point in history is dysfunctional to the extent that it encourages on some level a perpetuation of stereotypes (as is the case with Jungian ideology of the "anima" and "animus"). "Gynandry" or "androgyny" *can* function in a liberating way if they are seen as "transitional" words, or, more precisely, as self-liquidating words. They should be understood as having a built-in planned obsolescence.[15]

Wanted: "God" or "The Goddess"?

Feminist consciousness is experienced by a significant number of women as ontological becoming, that is, being. This process requires existential courage, courage to be and to *see*, which is both revolutionary and revelatory, revealing our participation in ultimate reality as Verb, as intransitive Verb.

The question obviously arises of the need for anthropomorphic symbols for this reality. There is no inherent contradiction between speaking of ultimate reality as Verb and speaking of this as personal. The Verb is more personal than a mere static noun. However, if we choose to *image* the Verb in anthropomorphic symbols, we can run into a problematic phenomenon which sociologist Henri Desroche calls "crossing." "Crossing" refers to a notable tendency among oppressed groups to attempt to change or adapt the ideological tools of the oppressor, so that they can be used *against* him and *for* the oppressed. The problem here is the fact that the functioning of "crossing" does not generally move far enough outside the ideological framework it seeks to undermine. In the "Black theology" of James Cone, for example, we find a Black God and a Black Messiah, but this pigmentation operation does not significantly alter the behavior of Jahweh & Son. Cone's Black God is as revengeful and sexist as his White prototype. For feminist eyes it is clear that this God is at least as oppressive as the old (for black women as well as for white women). The message in the alteration of symbol is simply about *which* male-ruled racial group will be on top and which will be on the bottom. The basic presupposition of *hierarchy* remains unaltered: that is, the presupposition that there must be an "us" or a "them" on top, and a corresponding "them" or "us" on the bottom.

Some women religious leaders within Western culture in modern times have performed something like a "crossing" operation, notably such figures as Mary Baker Eddy and Ann Lee, in stressing the "maternal" aspect of the divinity. The result has been mixed. Eddy's "Father-Mother God" is, after all, the Christian God. Nor does Ann Lee really move completely outside the Christian framework. It is interesting that their writings lack the thirst for vengeance that characterizes Cone's all too Christian Black theology, which is certainly in their favor. But it is also necessary to note that their theologies lack explicit relevance to the concrete problems of the oppression of women. Intellection and spirituality remain cut off from creative political movement. In earlier periods also there were women within the Christian tradition who tried to "cross" the Christian all-male God and Christ to some degree. An outstanding example was Juliana of Norwich, an English recluse and mystic who lived in the last half of the fourteenth century. Juliana's "God" and "Jesus" were—if language conveys anything—hermaphroditic constructs, with the primary identity clearly male. While there are many levels on which I could analyze Juliana's words about "our beloved Mother, Jesus, (who) feeds us with himself,"[16] suffice it to say here that this hermaphroditic image is somewhat less than attractive. The "androgynous" God and Jesus present problems analogous to and related to those problems which occur in connection with the use of the term "androgyny" to describe the direction of women's becoming. There is something like a "liberation of the woman within" the (primarily male) God and Jesus.

Indeed, it is harder to perform a transsexual operation on the Judeo-Christian divinity than a mere pigmentation operation. This is one reason, no doubt, why Cone is able to achieve a purely Black God and Black Messiah rather than a Mulatto, whereas the Christian women mentioned brought forth hermaphrodites, with emphasis upon maleness. Indeed, they did something on the symbolic level which is analogous to "liberating the woman within the man." Since they went only this far, they accomplished little or nothing, in social or mythic terms, toward the genuine liberation of women.

One fact that stands out here is that these were women whose imaginations were still partially controlled by Christian myth. My contention is that they were caught in a contradiction (which is not the case in the work of Black *male* theologians). I am saying that there is a profound contradiction between the inherent logic of radical feminism and the inherent logic of the Christian symbol system. I would not have said this ten years ago, at the time of writing the original edition of *The Church and the Second Sex*, which expressed hope for reform of Christianity in general and Roman Catholicism in particular. Nor would some women today say this—women who still perceive their identity as both Christian and feminist.

Both the reformers and those who leave Judaism and Christianity behind are contributing and will contribute in different ways to the process of the becoming of women. The point here is not to place value judgments upon individual persons and their efforts—and there are heroic efforts at all points of the feminist spectrum. Rather, it is to disclose an inherent logic in feminism. The courage which some women have in affirming this logic comes in part from having been on the feminist journey for quite awhile. Encouragement comes also from knowing increasing numbers of women who have chosen the route of the logical conclusion. Some of these women have "graduated" from Christianity or religious Judaism, and some have never even been associated closely with church or synagogue, but have discovered spiritual and mythic depths in the women's movement itself. What we share is a sense of becoming in cosmic process, which I prefer to call the Verb, Be-ing, and which some would still call "God."

For some feminists concerned with the spiritual depth of the movement, the word "God" is becoming increasingly problematic, however. This by no means indicates a movement in the direction of "atheism" or "agnosticism" or "secularism," as these terms are usually understood. Rather, the problem arises precisely because of the spiritual and mythic quality perceived in feminist process itself. Some use expressions such as "power of being." Some reluctantly still use the word "God" while earnestly trying to divest the term of its patriarchal associations, attempting to think perhaps of the "God of the philosophers" rather than the overtly masculist and oppressive "God of the theologians." But the problem becomes increasingly troublesome, the more the "God" of the various Western philosophers is subjected to feminist analysis. "He'—'Jahweh'—still often hovers behind the abstractions, stunting our own thought, giving us a sense of contrived double-think. The word "God" just may be inherently oppressive.

Indeed, the word "Goddess" has also been problematic, but for different reasons. Some have been worried about the problem of "crossing." However, that difficulty appears more and more as a pseudo-difficulty when it is recognized that "crossing" is likely to occur only when one is trying to work *within* a sexist tradition. For example, Christian women who in their "feminist liturgies" experiment with referring to "God" as "she" and to the Trinity as "The Mother, the Daughter, and the Holy Spirit," are still working within all the boundaries of the same symbolic framework and the same power structure. Significantly, their services are at the same place and time as "the usual," and are regarded by most of the constituency of the churches as occasional variations of "business as usual."

As women who are outside the Christian church inform ourselves of evidence supporting the existence of ancient matriarchy and of evidence indicating that the Gods of patriarchy are indeed contrived, pale derivatives and reversals of the Great Goddess of an earlier period, the fear of mere "crossing" appears less appropriate and perhaps even absurd. There is also less credibility allowable to the notion that "Goddess" would function like "God" in reverse, that is, to legitimate an oppressive "female-dominated" society, if one is inclined to look seriously at evidence that matriarchal society was not structured like patriarchy, that it was non-hierarchical.[17]

Would "Goddess" be likely to function oppressively, like "God"? Given the present situation of women, the danger is not imminent. "Would it function that way in the future?" My inclination is to think not, but it is not my intention to attempt to "prove" this point at this time. The question has a quality of "abstraction" and remoteness from the present social realities and it is, it seems to me, diversionary. When it is raised, and it is usually raised by men, one senses an "atmosphere" about the question, an aroma of masculine hysteria, a fear of invading hordes of "matriarchs" (read; female patriarchs) taking over The Man's world.

There are, however, two points concerning the symbol "Goddess" which I think *are* relevant to the existing situation. First, it can at the very least be pointed out that whenever the pendulum has swung extremely in one direction (and it *has*—for millennia), it is psychologically/socially/ethically important to emphasize "the other side." The hermaphroditic image hardly seems satisfactory for anyone. For an increasing minority of women—and even for some men[18]—"Goddess" is becoming more functional, meaningful, and loaded with healing associations. As this minority grows, Western society will be shaken by the presence of gynarchic symbolism in a new and potent way. It should be noted that women are inclined to speak and write of "The Goddess," whereas one seldom says "The God." In our culture it has been assumed that "goddesses" are many and trivial, whereas the "real" divinity *is*

"God," who does not even require the definite article. The use of the expression, "The Goddess," is a way of confronting this trivialization, of exorcising the male "God," and of affirming a different myth/reality.

A second, and related, point has to do with the fact that the "self-transcending immanence," the sense of giving birth to ourselves, the sense of power of being within, which is being affirmed by many women, does not seem to be denoted, imaged, adequately pointed to, or perhaps even associated with the term "God." With her permission, I will relate a story told to me by a theologian for whose insights I have the greatest respect. This woman told me that in the past when riding in planes (and feeling fearful about the situation) she often conjured up images remembered from childhood of "God" as "having the whole world in his hands." Later, this image/prayer? became meaningless. When she was on a plane recently, the ride suddenly became extremely "bumpy" and rough. It occurred to her to "try on" the name/image "Goddess." The result, as she described it, was immediate, electrifying, consoling. She sensed a presence and had/heard? the thought: "Just let go. Just sit on the seat and sit on the air waves and ride." The ride, though as rough as before, became a joyful experience.[19]

Clearly, it would be inappropriate and arrogant to try to "explain" or "interpret" this experience of another person. I can only comment that many women I know are finding power of being within the self, rather than in "internalized" father images. As a philosopher, my preference has been for abstractions. Indeed I have always been annoyed and rather embarrassed by "anthropomorphic" symbols, preferring terms such as "ground and power of being" (Tillich), "beyond subjectivity and objectivity" (James), "the Encompassing" (Jaspers), or the commonly used "Ultimate Reality," or "cosmic process." More recently I have used the expression "Intransitive Verb." Despite this philosophical inclination, and also because of it, I find it impossible to ignore the realm of symbols, or to fail to recognize that many women are experiencing and participating in a remythologizing process, which is a new dawn.

It is necessary to add a few remarks about the functioning of the confusing and complex "Mary" symbol within Christianity. Through it, the power of the Great Goddess symbol is enchained, captured, used, cannibalized, tokenized, domesticated, tranquillized. In spite of this, I think that many women and at least some men, when they have heard of or imaged the "Mother of God," have, by something like a selective perception process, screened out the standardized, lobotomized, dull, derivative and dwarfed Christian reflections of a more ancient symbol; they have perceived something that might more accurately be described as the Great Goddess, and which, in human terms, can be translated into "the strong woman who can relate because she can stand alone." A woman of Jewish background commented that "Mother of God" had always seemed strange and contradictory to her. Not having been programmed to "know" about the distinctions between the "divine" and the "human" nature of "Christ," or to "know" that the "Mother of God" is less than God, this woman had been able to hear the expression with the ears of an extraenvironmental listener. It sounded, she said, something like "infinite plus one."[20] When this symbolic nonsense is recognized, it is more plausible simply to *think* "infinite," and to *image* something like "Great Mother," or "Goddess."

It may appear that the suffix "-ess" presents a problem, when one considers other usages of that suffix, for example, in "poetess," or in "authoress." In these cases, there is a tone of depreciation, a suggestion that women poets and authors are in a separate and "inferior" category to be judged by different standards than their male counterparts. However, the suffix does not always function in this "diminishing" way. For example, there appear to be no "diminuitive" overtones suggested by the word "actress." So also it seems that the term "Goddess"—or "The Goddess"—*is not only non-diminuitive*, but very strong. Indeed, it calls before the mind images of a powerful and ancient tradition before, behind, and beyond Christianity. These are multi-dimensional images of women's present and future becoming/be-ing.

"Priests" or "Priestesses"?

I would suggest that "priestess" has diminuitive connotations if it is applied within the framework of Christianity (Episcopalian priestesses?), since of course within the limitations of that framework the role "acted out" by women has to be seen as derivative. It is only when one considers the possibility that the Christian tradition is itself derivative from a far more ancient and woman-centered tradition, that one's perception of priesthood changes. For women to be priestesses then is no longer perceived simply as a derivative phenomenon, but as primary and authentic. But then neither is it a Christian phenomenon. The priesthood of women need not seek legitimation within Christian churches. Nor need it be seen as a title or office conferred upon certain officially designated women to the exclusion of others.

Moreover, there are impossible contradictions in the idea of woman-identified Christian priests. While it may be possible for a twice-born Athena to "say Mass," or to commit baptism "in the name of the Father and of the Son and of the Holy Ghost," this sort of behavior presents incredible problems, that is, problems of credibility. Moreover, as I have said, it is inconsistent simply to try to fit a "feminine" symbolism into these sclerotic vessels. The "form" would still be the message, with some alterations in "content."

Is it true, as Malcolm Boyd has recently argued, that "when the (Christian) priest is a woman, even God is no longer a male"?[21] At one time, some years ago, I might have agreed with this. However, it is important to look at Protestant churches which have been ordaining women for years. Clearly, their God (and Gods) are still male. Large patriarchal institutions are still male. Large patriarchal institutions are still quite capable of absorbing a few tokens and in fact of profiting from this, appearing "liberal" while at the same time attracting women who are doubly devoted to the task of serving male Gods. I say "doubly devoted" because, as the cliché goes, a woman has to be twice as "good" as a man to get half as much recognition.

It is instructive to read the list of 110 Catholic signers who have called for the ordination of women "to the priesthood of the universal church."[22] Having read some writings of some of them, I question (1) whether they can possibly understand what the logic of feminism is all about (i.e., leaving behind and thus leaving to die the inherently oppressive structures of patriarchal religions); (2) whether they *do* "understand" what the logic of feminism is about and see "containment" as an important tactic for holding women in bondage as long as possible.

The women's movement *is* about refusal to be merely contained as well as refusal to be mere containers. It is about saying "Yes" to ourselves, which is the deepest way of saying "Yes" to others. At some point in her history a woman may sincerely see ordination to the Christian priesthood as her way of saying this "Yes." It is my hope that such women will *continue* their journey. Ambition to "ordination" perhaps reaches a respectable altitude for the jet age, but it does not reach very far, I think, into feminist space/time. It is my hope that these sisters will raise their ambitions and their self-respect higher, immeasurably higher, that they will one day outgrow their books of common prayer and dream less common dreams.

Notes

1. *Beyond God the Father: Toward a Philosophy of Women's Liberation* (Boston: Beacon Press, 1973); *The Church and the Second Sex*, With a New Feminist Postchristian Introduction by the Author (New York: Harper Colophon, 1975).
2. An elaborate historical study of the Sins is to be found in Morton W. Bloomfield, *The Seven Deadly Sins* (Michigan State University Press, 1952, 1967).
3. Bloomfield gives a variety of "listings" of Deadly Sins in different periods and cultures, with useful contextual information
4. See Dolores Bargowski's review of the film in *Quest: A Feminist Quarterly* I, No. 1 (Summer, 1974), pp. 53–57.

5. This idea is developed in a remarkable article. See Peggy Allegro, "The Strange and the Familiar," *Amazon Quarterly*, I, 1, pp. 29–41.
6. Virginia Woolf, *Three Guineas* (New York: Harcourt, Brace, and World, Inc., 1938, 1966), p. 63.
7. Phyllis Chesler, *Women and Madness*, (New York: Doubleday, 1972), pp. 24–26.
8. This expression was used by Emily Culpepper in an unpublished paper titled "Reflections on Ethics and Self Defense: Establishing a Firm Stance."
9. "Self Defense and the Preservation of Females," in *The Female State: A Journal of Female Liberation*, Issue 4 (April 1970), p. 96.
10. Elizabeth Gould Davis, author of *The First Sex* (New York: G. P. Putnam's Sons, 1971), wrote this in an article about her own devastating rape in *Prime Time*, June, 1974, p. 3.
11. The horrors of footbinding are recounted by Andrea Dworkin, *Woman Hating* (New York: Dutton, 1974), pp. 95–117. These "tiny feet" were malodorous, mutilated humps. Women fell from one to the other. These stumps were described in fantastically deceptive euphemistic language and were the objects of sadistic male fetishism.
12. "Beyond Male Morality," in *Women and Religion*, Revised Edition, edited by Judith Plaskow and Joan Romero (Missoula, Montana: American Academy of Religion and The Scholars' Press, 1974), pp. 115–125.
13. Linda L. Barufaldi and Emily E. Culpepper, "Androgyny and the Myth of Masculine/Feminine," *Christianity and Crisis*, April 16, 1973, pp. 69–71.
14. Adrienne Rich, *Diving into the Wreck Poems*, 1971–72 (New York: W. W. Norton, 1973).
15. In a speech delivered at the Modern Languages Association Forum, December, 1973, Cynthia Secor noted that there is no "Androgyne Quarterly"—most probably because there are no androgynes around to publish it.
16. Juliana of Norwich, *Revelations of Divine Love*, edited by Clifton Walters (Baltimore, Maryland: 1966), Ch. 61.
17. See Robert Briffault, *The Mothers* (New York: Macmillan, 1927), Vol. I. See also J. J. Bachofen, *Myth, Religion and Mother-Right*, trans. by Ralph Manheim (Princeton: Princeton University Press, 1967).
18. Kenneth Pitchford chooses Goddess imagery, which occurs frequently in his more recent poems.
19. The story was told by Professor Nelle Morton of Drew Theological Seminary, and paraphrased by myself.
20. Comment of Linda Franklin, Boston College student.
21. *Ms.*, December, 1974.
22. Reported in *National Catholic Reporter*, November 8, 1974, p. 5.

Study Questions

1. What does Daly mean when she says that women must exorcise the internalized Godfather?
2. What does Daly think of "Amazon expeditions into the male-controlled" fields?
3. What does Daly think of the male-controlled professions?
4. How does Daly view the notion of the Trinity? Of the story of the Virgin Mary?
5. What does it mean to say our society is "rapist"?
6. What is "ludic cerebration," and why does Daly recommend it for women as a "qualitative leap"?
7. How does Daly view the desirability of androgyny?
8. What does Daly think of attempts to perform a "crossing" operation on the concept of the Christian God?
9. Does Daly think that Christian women should try to become ordained ministers or priests in their churches?
10. Does Daly think that feminists should substitute the concept of "Goddess" for that of "God"?

Why Women Need the Goddess: Phenomenological, Psychological, and Political Reflections

Carol P. Christ

At the close of Ntosake Shange's stupendously successful Broadway play "For Colored Girls Who Have Considered Suicide When the Rainbow Is Enuf," a tall beautiful black woman rises from despair to cry out, "I found God in myself and I loved her fiercely."[1] Her discovery is echoed by women around the country who meet spontaneously in small groups on full moons, solstices, and equinoxes to celebrate the Goddess as symbol of life and death powers and waxing and waning energies in the universe and in themselves.[2]

> It is the night of the full moon. Nine women stand in a circle, on a rocky hill above the city. The western sky is rosy with the setting sun; in the east the moon's face begins to peer above the horizon. . . . The woman pours out a cup of wine onto the earth, refills it and raises it high. "Hail, Tana, Mother of mothers!" she cries. "Awaken from your long sleep, and return to your children again!"[3]

What are the political and psychological effects of this fierce new love of the divine in themselves for women whose spiritual experience has been focused by the male God of Judaism and Christianity? Is the spiritual dimension of feminism a passing diversion, an escape from difficult but necessary political work? Or does the emergence of the symbol of Goddess among women have significant political and psychological ramifications for the feminist movement?

To answer this question, we must first understand the importance of religious symbols and rituals in human life and consider the effect of male symbolism of God on women. According to anthropologist Clifford Geertz, religious symbols shape a cultural ethos, defining the deepest values of a society and the persons in it. "Religion," Geertz writes, "is a system of symbols which act to produce powerful, pervasive, and long-lasting moods and motivations"[4] in the people of a given culture. A "mood" for Geertz is a psychological attitude such as awe, trust, and respect, while a "motivation" is the *social* and *political* trajectory created by a mood that transforms mythos into ethos, symbol system into social and political reality. Symbols have both psychological and political effects, because they create the inner conditions (deep-seated attitudes and feelings) that lead people to feel comfortable with or to accept social and political arrangements that correspond to the symbol system.

Because religion has such a compelling hold on the deep psyches of so many people, feminists cannot afford to leave it in the hands of the fathers. Even people who no longer "believe in God" or participate in the institutional structure of patriarchal religion still may not be free of the power of the symbolism of God the Father. A symbol's effect does not depend on rational assent, for a symbol also functions on levels of the psyche other than the

---

From *Heresies* (Spring 1978), in C. P. Christ and J. Plaskow, eds., *Womanspirit Rising* (New York: Harper & Row, 1979), Chapter IV. Reprinted by permission of Carol P. Christ. (Notes deleted.)

rational. Religion fulfills deep psychic needs by providing symbols and rituals that enable people to cope with limit situations in human life (death, evil, suffering) and to pass through life's important transitions (birth, sexuality, death). Even people who consider themselves completely secularized will often find themselves sitting in a church or synagogue when a friend or relative gets married, or when a parent or friend has died. The symbols associated with these important rituals cannot fail to affect the deep or unconscious structures of the mind of even a person who has rejected these symbolisms on a conscious level—especially if the person is under stress. The reason for the continuing effect of religious symbols is that the mind abhors a vacuum. Symbol systems cannot simply be rejected, they must be replaced. Where there is not any replacement, the mind will revert to familiar structures at times of crisis, bafflement, or defeat.

Religions centered on the worship of a male God create "moods" and "motivations" that keep women in a state of psychological dependence on men and male authority, while at the same legitimating the *political* and *social* authority of fathers and sons in the institutions of society.

Religious symbol systems focused around exclusively male images of divinity create the impression that female power can never be fully legitimate or wholly beneficent. This message need never be explicitly stated (as, for example, it is in the story of Eve) for its effect to be felt. A woman completely ignorant of the myths of female evil in biblical religion nonetheless acknowledges the anomaly of female power when she prays exclusively to a male God. She may see herself as like God (created in the image of God) only by denying her own sexual identity and affirming God's transcendence of sexual identity. But she can never have the experience that is freely available to every man and boy in her culture, of having her full sexual identity affirmed as being in the image and likeness of God. In Geertz' terms, her "mood" is one of trust in male power as salvific and distrust of female power in herself and other women as inferior or dangerous. Such a powerful, pervasive, and longlasting "mood" cannot fail to become a "motivation" that translates into social and political reality.

In *Beyond God the Father*, feminist theologian Mary Daly detailed the psychological and political ramifications of father religion for women. "If God in 'his' heaven is a father ruling his people," she wrote, "then it is the 'nature' of things and according to divine plan and the order of the universe that society be male dominated. Within this context, a *mystification of roles* takes place: The husband dominating his wife represents God 'himself.' The images and values of a given society have been projected into the realm of dogmas and 'Articles of Faith,' and these in turn justify the social structures which have given rise to them and which sustain their plausibility."[5]

Philosopher Simone de Beauvoir was well aware of the function of patriarchal religion as legitimater of male power. As she wrote, "Man enjoys the great advantage of having a god endorse the code he writes; and since man exercises a sovereign authority over women it is especially fortunate that this authority has been vested in him by the Supreme Being. For the Jew, Mohammedans, and Christians, among others, man is Master by divine right; the fear of God will therefore repress any impulse to revolt in the downtrodden female."[6]

This brief discussion of the psychological and political effects of God religion puts us in an excellent position to begin to understand the significance of the symbol of Goddess for women. In discussing the meaning of the Goddess, my method will first be phenomenological. I will isolate a meaning of the symbol of the Goddess as it has emerged in the lives of contemporary women. I will then discuss its psychological and political significance by contrasting the "moods" and "motivations" engendered by Goddess symbols with those engendered by Christian symbolism. I will also correlate Goddess symbolism with themes that have emerged in the women's movement, in order to show how Goddess symbolism undergirds and legitimates the concerns of the women's movement, much as God symbolism in

Christianity undergirded the interests of men in patriarchy. I will discuss four aspects of Goddess symbolism here: the Goddess as affirmation of female power, the female body, the female will, and women's bonds and heritage. There are, of course, many other meanings of the Goddess that I will not discuss here.

The sources for the symbol of the Goddess in contemporary spirituality are traditions of Goddess worship and modern women's experience. The ancient Mediterranean, pre-Christian European, native American, Mesoamerican, Hindu, African, and other traditions are rich sources for Goddess symbolism. But these traditions are filtered through modern women's experiences. Traditions of Goddesses, subordination to Gods, for example, are ignored. Ancient traditions are tapped selectively and eclectically, but they are not considered authoritative for modern consciousness. The Goddess symbol has emerged spontaneously in the dreams, fantasies, and thoughts of many women around the country in the past several years. Kirsten Grimstad and Susan Rennie reported that they were surprised to discover widespread interest in spirituality, including the Goddess, among feminists around the country in the summer of 1974.[7] *WomanSpirit* magazine, which published its first issue in 1974 and has contributors from across the United States, has expressed the grass roots nature of the women's spirituality movement. In 1976, a journal, *Lady Unique*, devoted to the Goddess emerged. In 1975, the first women's spirituality conference was held in Boston and attended by 1,800 women. In 1978, a University of Santa Cruz course on the Goddess drew over 500 people. Sources for this essay are these manifestations of the Goddess in modern women's experiences as reported in *WomenSpirit*, *Lady Unique*, and elsewhere, and as expressed in conversations I have had with women who have been thinking about the Goddess and women's spirituality.

The simplest and most basic meaning of the symbol of Goddess is the acknowledgment of the legitimacy of female power as a beneficent and independent power. A woman who echoes Ntosake Shange's dramatic statement, "I found God in myself and I loved her fiercely," is saying "Female power is strong and creative." She is saying that the divine principle, the saving and sustaining power, is in herself, that she will no longer look to men or male figures as saviors. The strength and independence of female power can be intuited by contemplating ancient and modern images of the Goddess. This meaning of the symbol of Goddess is simple and obvious, and yet it is difficult for many to comprehend. It stands in sharp contrast to the paradigms of female dependence on males that have been predominant in Western religion and culture. The internationally acclaimed novelist Monique Wittig captured the novelty and flavor of the affirmation of female power when she wrote, in her mythic work *Les Guerilleres*,

> There was a time when you were not a slave, remember that. You walked alone, full of laughter, you bathed bare-bellied. You say you have lost all recollection of it, remember . . . you say there are no words to describe it, you say it does not exist. But remember. Make an effort to remember. Or, failing that, invent.[8]

While Wittig does not speak directly of the Goddess here, she captures the "mood" of joyous celebration of female freedom and independence that is created in women who define their identities through the symbol of Goddess. Artist Mary Beth Edelson expressed the political "motivations" inspired by the Goddess when she wrote,

> The ascending archetypal symbols of the feminine unfold today in the psyche of modern Every woman. They encompass the multiple forms of the Great Goddess. Reaching across the centuries we take the hands of our Ancient Sisters. The Great Goddess alive and well is rising to announce to the patriarchs that their 5,000 years are up—Hallelujah! Here we come.[9]

The affirmation of female power contained in the Goddess symbol has both psychological and political consequences. Psychologically, it means the defeat of the view engendered by patriarchy that women's power is inferior and dangerous. This new "mood" of affirmation of female power also leads to new "motivations"; it supports and undergirds women's trust in their own power and the power of other women in family and society.

If the simplest meaning of the Goddess symbol is an affirmation of the legitimacy and beneficence of female power, then a question immediately arises, "Is the Goddess simply female power writ large, and if so, why bother with the symbol of Goddess at all? Or does the symbol refer to a Goddess 'out there' who is not reducible to a human potential?" The many women who have rediscovered the power of Goddess would give three answers to this question: (1) The Goddess is divine female, a personification who can be invoked in prayer and ritual; (2) the Goddess is symbol of the life, death, and rebirth energy in nature and culture, in personal and communal life and (3) the Goddess is symbol of the affirmation of the legitimacy and beauty of female power (made possible by the new becoming of women in the women's liberation movement). If one were to ask these women which answer is the "correct" one, different responses would be given. Some would assert that the Goddess definitely is *not* "out there," that the symbol of a divinity "out there" is part of the legacy of patriarchal oppression, which brings with it the authoritarianism, hierarchicalism, and dogmatic rigidity associated with biblical monotheistic religions. They might assert that the Goddess symbol reflects the sacred power within women and nature, suggesting the connectedness between women's cycles of menstruation, birth, and menopause, and the life and death cycles of the universe. Others seem quite comfortable with the notion of Goddess as a divine female protector and creator and would find their experience of Goddess limited by the assertion that she is not *also* out there as well as within themselves and in all natural processes. When asked what the symbol of Goddess means, feminist priestess Starhawk replied, "It all depends on how I feel. When I feel weak, she is someone who can help and protect me. When I feel strong, she is the symbol of my own power. At other times I feel her as the natural energy in my body and the world." How are we to evaluate such a statement? Theologians might call these the words of a sloppy thinker. But my deepest intuition tells me they contain a wisdom that Western theological thought has lost.

To theologians, these differing views of the "meaning" of the symbol of Goddess might seem to threaten a replay of the trinitarian controversies. Is there, perhaps, a way of doing theology, which would not lead immediately into dogmatic controversy, which would not require theologians to say definitively that one understanding is true and the others are false? Could people's relation to a common symbol be made primary and varying interpretations be acknowledged? The diversity of explications of the meaning of the Goddess symbol suggests that symbols have a richer significance than any explications of their meaning can express, a point literary critics have long insisted on. This phenomenological fact suggests that theologians may need to give more than lip service to a theory of symbol in which the symbol is viewed as the primary fact and the meanings are viewed as secondary. It also suggests that a *thea*logy of the Goddess would be very different from the *theo*logy we have known in the West. But to spell out this notion of the primacy of *symbol* in thealogy in contrast to the primacy of the *explanation* in theology would be the topic of another paper. Let me simply state that women, who have been deprived of a female religious symbol system for centuries, are therefore in an excellent position to recognize the power and primacy of symbols. I believe women must develop a theory of symbol and thealogy congruent with their experience at the same time as they "remember and invent" new symbol systems.

A second important implication of the Goddess symbol for women is the affirmation of the female body and the life cycle expressed in it. Because of women's unique position as menstruants, birthgivers, and those who have traditionally cared for the young and the dying, women's connection to the body, nature, and this world has been obvious. Women were denigrated because they seemed more carnal, fleshy, and earthy than the culture-creating males. The misogynist anti*body* tradition in Western thought is symbolized in the myth of Eve who is traditionally viewed as a sexual temptress, the epitome of women's carnal nature. This tradition reaches its nadir in the *Malleus Maleficarum (The Hammer of Evil-Doing Women)*, which states, "All witchcraft stems from carnal lust, which in women is insatiable."[10] The Virgin Mary, the positive female image in Christianity does not contradict Christian denigration of the female body and its powers. The Virgin Mary is revered because she, in her perpetual virginity, transcends the carnal sexuality attributed to most women.

The denigration of the female body is expressed in cultural and religious taboos surrounding menstruation, childbirth, and menopause in women. While menstruation taboos may have originated in a perception of the awesome powers of the female body, they degenerated into a simple perception that there is something "wrong" with female bodily functions. Menstruating women were forbidden to enter the sanctuary in ancient Hebrew and premodern Christian communities. Although only Orthodox Jews still enforce religious taboos against menstruant women, few women in our culture grow up affirming their menstruation as a connection to sacred power. Most women learn that menstruation is a curse and grow up believing that the bloody facts of menstruation are best hidden away. Feminists challenge this attitude to the female body. Judy Chicago's art piece "Menstruation Bathroom" broke these menstrual taboos. In a sterile white bathroom, she exhibited boxes of Tampax and Kotex on an open shelf, and the wastepaper basket was overflowing with bloody tampons and sanitary napkins.[11] Many women who viewed the piece felt relieved to have their "dirty secret" out in the open.

The denigration of the female body and its powers is further expressed in Western culture's attitudes toward childbirth. Religious iconography does not celebrate the birthgiver, and there is no theology or ritual that enables a woman to celebrate the process of birth as a spiritual experience. Indeed, Jewish and Christian traditions also had blood taboos concerning the woman who had recently given birth. While these religious taboos are rarely enforced today (again, only by Orthodox Jews), they have secular equivalents. Giving birth is treated as a disease requiring hospitalization, and the woman is viewed as a passive object, anesthetized to ensure her acquiescence to the will of the doctor. The women's liberation movement has challenged these cultural attitudes, and many feminists have joined with advocates of natural childbirth and home birth in emphasizing the need for women to control and take pride in their bodies, including the birth process.

Western culture also gives little dignity to the postmenopausal or aging woman. It is no secret that our culture is based on a denial of aging and death, and that women suffer more severely from this denial than men. Women are placed on a pedestal and considered powerful when they are young and beautiful, but they are said to lose this power as they age. As feminists have pointed out, the "power" of the young woman is illusory, since beauty standards are defined by men, and since few women are considered (or consider themselves) beautiful for more than a few years of their lives. Some men are viewed as wise and authoritative in age, but old women are pitied and shunned. Religious iconography supports this cultural attitude toward aging women. The purity and virginity of Mary and the female saints is often expressed in the iconographic convention of perpetual youth. Moreover, religious mythology associates aging women with evil in the symbol of the wicked old witch. Feminists have challenged cultural myths of aging women and have urged women to reject patriarchal beauty standards and to celebrate the distinctive beauty of women of all ages.

The symbol of Goddess aids the process of naming and reclaiming the female body and its cycles and processes. In the ancient world and among modern women, the Goddess symbol represents the birth, death and rebirth processes of the natural and human worlds.

The female body is viewed as the direct incarnation of waxing and waning, life and death, cycles in the universe. This is sometimes expressed through the symbolic connection between the twenty-eight-day cycles of menstruation and the twenty-eight-day cycles of the moon. Moreover, the Goddess is celebrated in the triple aspect of youth, maturity, and age, or maiden, mother, and crone. The potentiality of the young girl is celebrated in the nymph or maiden aspect of the Goddess. The Goddess as mother is sometimes depicted giving birth, and giving birth is viewed as a symbol for all the creative, life-giving powers of the universe. The life-giving powers of the Goddess in her creative aspect are not limited to physical birth, for the Goddess is also seen as the creator of all the arts of civilization, including healing, writing, and the giving of just law. Women in the middle of life who are not physical mothers may give birth to poems, songs, and books, or nurture other women, men, and children. They too are incarnations of the Goddess in her creative, life-giving aspect. At the end of life, women incarnate the crone aspect of the Goddess. The wise old woman, the woman who knows from experience what life is about, the woman whose closeness to her own death gives her a distance and perspective on the problems of life, is celebrated as the third aspect of the Goddess. Thus, women learn to value youth, creativity, and wisdom in themselves and other women.

The possibilities of reclaiming the female body and its cycles have been expressed in a number of Goddess-centered rituals. Hallie Mountainwing and Barbry MyOwn created a summer solstice ritual to celebrate menstruation and birth. The women simulated a birth canal and birthed each other into their circle. They raised power by placing their hands on each other's bellies and chanting together. Finally they marked each other's faces with rich, dark menstrual blood saying, "This is the blood that promises renewal. This is the blood that promises sustenance. This is the blood that promises life."[12] From hidden dirty secret to symbol of the life power of the Goddess, women's blood has come full circle. Other women have created rituals that celebrate the crone aspect of the Goddess. Z. Budapest believes that the crone aspect of the Goddess is predominant in the fall, especially at Halloween, an ancient holiday. On this day, the wisdom of the old woman is celebrated, and it is also recognized that the old must die so that the new can be born.

The "mood" created by the symbol of the Goddess in triple aspect is one of positive, joyful affirmation of the female body and its cycles and acceptance of aging and death as well as life. The "motivations" are to overcome menstrual taboos, to return the birth process to the hands of women, and to change cultural attitudes about age and death. Changing cultural attitudes toward the female body could go a long way toward overcoming the spirit-flesh, mind-body dualisms of Western culture, since, as Ruether has pointed out, the denigration of the female body is at the heart of these dualisms. The Goddess as symbol of the revaluation of the body and nature thus also undergirds the human potential and ecology movements. The "mood" is one of affirmation, awe, and respect for the body and nature, and the "motivation" is to respect the teachings of the body and the rights of all living beings.

A third important implication of the Goddess symbol for women is the positive valuation of will in a Goddess-centered ritual, especially in Goddess-centered ritual magic and spellcasting in womanspirit and feminist witchcraft circles. The basic notion behind ritual magic and spellcasting is energy as power. Here the Goddess is a center or focus of power and energy; she is the personification of the energy that flows between beings in the natural and human worlds. In Goddess circles, energy is raised by chanting or dancing. According to Starhawk, "Witches conceive of psychic energy as having form and substance that can be perceived and directed by those with a trained awareness. The power generated within the circle is built into a cone form, and at its peak is released—to the Goddess, to reenergize the members of the coven, or to do a specific work such as healing."[13] In ritual magic, the energy raised is directed by willpower. Women who celebrate in Goddess circles believe they can achieve their wills in the world.

The emphasis on the will is important for women, because women traditionally have been taught to devalue their wills, to believe that they cannot achieve their will through their own power, and even to suspect that the assertion of will is evil. Faith Wildung's poem "Waiting," from which I will quote only a short segment, sums up women's sense that their lives are defined not by their own will, but by waiting for others to take the initiative.

> Waiting for my breasts to develop
> Waiting to wear a bra
> Waiting to menstruate
>
> . . .
>
> Waiting for life to begin, Waiting—
> Waiting to be somebody
>
> . . .
>
> Waiting to get married
> Waiting for my wedding day
> Waiting for my wedding night
>
> . . .
>
> Waiting for the end of the day
> Waiting for sleep. Waiting . . . [14]

Patriarchal religion has enforced the view that female initiative and will are evil through the juxtaposition of Eve and Mary. Eve caused the fall by asserting her will against the command of God, while Mary began the new age with her response to God's initiative, "Let it be done to me according to thy word" (Luke 1:38). Even for men, patriarchal religion values the passive will subordinate to divine initiative. The classical doctrines of sin and grace view sin as the prideful assertion of will and grace as the obedient subordination of the human will to the divine initiative or order. While this view of will might be questioned from a human perspective, Valerie Saiving has argued that it has particularly deleterious consequences for women in Western culture. According to Saiving, Western culture encourages males in the assertion of will, and thus it may make some sense to view the male form of sin as an excess of will. But since culture discourages females in the assertion of will, the traditional doctrines of sin and grace encourage women to remain in their form of sin, which is self-negation or insufficient assertion of will.[15] One possible reason the will is denigrated in a patriarchal religious framework is that both human and divine will are often pictured as arbitrary, self-initiated, and exercised without regard for other wills.

In a Goddess-centered context, in contrast, the will is valued. *A woman is encouraged to know her will, to believe that her will is valid, and to believe that her will can be achieved in the world,* three powers traditionally denied to her in patriarchy. In a Goddess-centered framework, a woman's will is not subordinated to the Lord God as king and ruler, nor to men as his representatives. Thus a woman is not reduced to waiting and acquiescing in the wills of others as she is in patriarchy. But neither does she adopt the egocentric form of will that pursues self-interest without regard for the interests of others.

The Goddess-centered context provides a different understanding of the will than that available in the traditional patriarchal religious framework. In the Goddess framework, will can be achieved only when it is exercised in harmony with the energies and wills of other beings. Wise women, for example, raise a cone of healing energy at the full moon or solstice when the lunar or solar energies are at their high points with respect to the earth. This discipline encourages them to recognize that not all times are propitious for the achieving of every will. Similarly, they know that spring is a time for new beginnings in work and love, summer a time for producing external manifestations of inner potentialities, and fall or winter times for stripping down to the inner core and extending roots. Such awareness of waxing and waning processes in the universe discourages arbitrary ego-centered assertion of will, while at the same time encouraging the assertion of individual will in cooperation with natural energies and the energies created by the wills of others. Wise women also have a tradition that whatever is sent out will be returned and this reminds them to assert their wills in cooperative and healing rather than egocentric and destructive ways. This view of will allows women to begin to recognize, claim, and assert their wills without adopting the worst characteristics of the patriarchal understanding and use of will. In the Goddess-centered framework, the "mood" is one of positive affirmation of personal will in the context of the energies of other wills or beings. The "motivation" is for women to know and assert their wills in cooperation with other wills and energies. This of course does not mean that women always assert their wills in positive and life-affirming ways. Women's capacity for evil is, of course, as great as men's. My purpose is simply to contrast the differing attitudes toward the exercise of will *per se*, and the female will in particular, in Goddess-centered religion and in the Christian God-centered religion.

The fourth and final aspect of Goddess symbolism that I will discuss here is the significance of the Goddess for a revaluation of woman's bonds and heritage. As Virginia Woolf has said, "Chloe liked Olivia," a statement about a woman's relation to another woman, is a sentence that rarely occurs in fiction. Men have written the stories, and they have written about women almost exclusively in their relations to men.[16] The celebrations of women's bonds to each other, as mothers and daughters, as colleagues and coworkers, as sisters, friends, and lovers, is beginning to occur in the new literature and culture created by women in the women's movement. While I believe that the revaluing of each of these bonds is important, I will focus on the mother-daughter bond, in part because I believe it may be the key to the others.

Adrienne Rich has pointed out that the mother-daughter bond, perhaps the most important of woman's bonds, "resonant with charges . . . the flow of energy between two biologically alike bodies, one of which has lain in amniotic bliss inside the other, one of which has labored to give birth to the other,"[17] is rarely celebrated in patriarchal religion and culture. Christianity celebrates the father's relation to the son and the mother's relation to the son, but the story of mother and daughter is missing. So, too, in patriarchal literature and psychology the mothers and the daughters rarely exist. Volumes have been written about the oedipal complex, but little has been written about the girl's relation to her mother. Moreover, as de Beauvoir has noted, the mother-daughter relation is distorted in patriarchy because the mother must give her daughter over to men in a male-defined culture in which women are viewed as inferior. The mother must socialize her daughter to become subordinate to men, and if her daughter challenges patriarchal norms, the mother is likely to defend the patriarchal structures against her own daughter.[18]

These patterns are changing in the new culture created by women in which the bonds of women to women are beginning to be celebrated. Holly Near has written several songs that celebrate women's bonds and women's heritage. In one of her finest songs she writes of an "old-time woman" who is "waiting to die." A young woman feels for the life that has passed the old woman by and begins to cry, but the old woman looks her in the eye and says, "If I had not suffered, you wouldn't be wearing those jeans/Being an old-time woman ain't as bad as it seems."[19] This song, which Near has said was inspired by her grandmother, expresses and celebrates a bond and a heritage passed down from one woman to another. In another of Near's songs, she sings of "a hiking-boot mother who's seeing the world/For the first time with her own little girl." In this song, the mother tells the drifter who has been traveling with her to pack up and travel alone if he thinks "traveling three is a drag" because "I've got a little one who loves me as much as you need me/And darling, that's loving enough."[20] This song is significant because the mother places her relationship to her daughter above her relationship to a man, something women rarely do in patriarchy.

Almost the only story of mothers and daughters that has been transmitted in Western culture is the myth of Demeter and Persephone that was the basis of religious rites celebrated by women only, the Thesmophoria, and later formed the basis of the Eleusian mysteries, which were open to all who spoke Greek. In this story, the daughter, Persephone, is raped away from her mother, Demeter, by the God of the underworld. Unwilling to accept this state of affairs, Demeter rages and withholds fertility from the earth until her daughter is returned to her. What is important for women in this story is that a mother fights for her daughter and for her relation to her daughter. This is completely different from the mother's relation to her daughter in patriarchy. The "mood" created by the story of Demeter and Persephone is one of celebration of the mother-daughter bond, and the "motivation" is for mothers and daughters to affirm the heritage passed on from mother to daughter and to reject the patriarchal pattern where the primary loyalties of mother and daughter must be to men.

The symbol of Goddess has much to offer women who are struggling to be rid of the "powerful, pervasive, and long-lasting moods and motivations" of devaluation of female power, denigration of the female body, distrust of female will, and denial of the women's bonds and heritage that have been engendered by patriarchal religion. As women struggle to create a new culture in which women's power, bodies, will, and bonds are celebrated, it seems natural that the Goddess would reemerge as symbol of the newfound beauty, strength, and power of women.

Notes

1. From the original cast album, Buddah Records, 1976.
2. See Susan Rennie and Kristen Grimstad, "Spiritual Explorations Cross-Country," *Quest*, 1975, *I* (4), 1975, 49–51; and *WomanSpirit* magazine.
3. See Starhawk, "Witchcraft and Women's Culture," *WomanSpirit Rising* (New York: Harper & Row, 1979).
4. "Religion as a Cultural System," in William L. Lessa and Evon V. Vogt, eds., *Reader in Comparative Religion*, 2nd ed. (New York: Harper & Row, 1972), p. 206
5. Boston: Beacon Press, 1974, p. 13, italics added.
6. *The Second Sex*, trans. H. M. Parshleys (New York: Alfred A. Knopf, 1953).
7. See Grimstad and Rennie.
8. *Les Guerilleres*, trans. David LeVay (New York: Avon Books, 1971), p. 89. Also quoted in Morgan MacFarland, "Witchcraft: The Art of Remembering," *Quest*, 1975, *I* (4), 41.
9. "Speaking for Myself," *Lady Unique*, 1976, *I*, 56.
10. Heinrich Kramer and Jacob Sprenger (New York: Dover, 1971), p. 47.
11. *Through the Flower* (New York: Doubleday & Company, 1975), plate 4, pp. 106–107.
12. Barbry MyOwn, "Ursa Maior: Menstrual Moon Celebration," in Anne Kent Rush, ed., *Moon, Moon* (Berkeley, Calif., and New York: Moon Books and Random House, 1976), pp. 374–387.
13. Starhawk.
14. In Judy Chicago, pp. 213–217.
15. "The Human Situation: A Feminine View," in *Journal of Religion*, 1960, *40*, 100–112.
16. *A Room of One's Own* (New York: Harcourt Brace Jovanovich, 1928), p. 86.
17. Rich, p. 226.
18. De Beauvoir, pp. 448–449.
19. "Old Time Woman," lyrics by Jeffrey Langley and Holly Near, from *Holly Near: A Live Album*, Redwood Records, 1974.
20. "Started Out Fine," by Holly Near from *Holly Near: A Live Album*.

Study Questions

1. Why does religion have such a compelling hold on people?
2. What "mood" does the traditional religious symbol system create in women, and why?
3. What is the basic meaning of the Goddess symbol? Why is that meaning so difficult for some to comprehend?
4. What controversy surrounds the question "Does the Goddess really exist?" Need a thealogy (as opposed to a theology) take such a question as all-important?

5. What implications does the Goddess symbol have for women's view of their bodies? How does this contrast with male-created theology? How does the Goddess symbol help "reclaim" the female body?
6. How does the Goddess symbol aid the positive valuation of the will? Why is that important for women?
7. How does the Goddess symbol aid the positive valuation of the bonds between women?

Womanpower: Energy Re-Sourcement

Sally Gearhart

In the past two years I have come to a firm point of conviction about what is happening to us as a woman's movement, and I want to share some of my thinking about that. I believe that politically conscious women move toward the transformation of society through one of four distinct approaches. By "politically conscious" I mean women who do not believe in the values or functions of monopoly capitalism, who want to bring that whole economic system to dust.

Strategy #1: Some women move in *revolutionary actions against the system* either through *violence* ("terrorist acts" as the press names them) or through *radical political organizing*.

Strategy #2: Far more women believe in *seizing power within the system through consciously chosen reforms so as to make the system work for us*.

Strategy #3: A number of women put energy into *alternative organizations* or *structures*.

It is clear to me now that in terms of these first three strategies we have already lost. Daily the system anoints and assimilates more reforms into itself and regularly another multinational corporation entrenches itself into the culture of a developing nation; bombings and kidnappings frighten us step-by-paranoid-step into the police state; alternative organizations seem less and less like alternatives or cease to exist altogether. All the while the futility of our struggles becomes clearer and clearer. The dreadful has already happened. In the world of these first three strategies there is no antidote for the pell-mell rush to annihilation because all the rules there are devised and revised constantly by the dominant culture and enough of us can never become skilled enough fast enough to beat that system at its own game. Only something as powerful as that system itself can threaten it.

A fourth strategy, I believe, has the potential to be that threat. I have called the strategy "re-sourcement" because it suggests we must go to a new place for our energy. To re-source

From *Womanspirit*, Vol. 2, No. 7 (Spring 1976), in Charlene Spretnak, ed., *The Politics of Women's Spirituality* (New York: Doubleday, 1982), pp. 194–206. © Sally Miller Gearhart, 1976. Reprinted by permission of Sally Miller Gearhart.

is to find another source, an entirely different and prior one, a source deeper than the patriarchy and one that allows us to stand in the path of continuous and cosmic energy. That new source is discovered only by moving inward to the self, and it is being experienced most widely these days by women who are finding our individual or *intra*personal energy flow. Once we are at home there—as more and more of us are becoming—then we can begin to develop authentic forms of *inter*personal energy or that energy which flows between people. What we have experienced with the patriarchy (the arena of the first three strategies) is *inter*personal energy which has not first been founded on, which has never been connected to, *intra*personal energy, or the internal source.

What I am calling re-sourcement is the activity of women who are reaching out for new ways of understanding and viewing reality, i.e., *they are articulating a new epistemology:* astrology, the Tarot, numerology, the I Ching, the Kabala—all these and others reinterpreted and/or redeemed from their masculist emphases and filtered anew through the channels of womanknowing, womansight; also dreams, visions, dream-and-vision-sharing, womanmusic, womanart, storytelling, rituals, dramas, celebrations, memory, games, fantasy, Witchcraft, an attention to the personal and collective unconscious, an affirmation of the intuitive, a song of praise to the non-logical, a greeting of the right-brained analogical capacity; a rediscovery and a reunderstanding of anthropological data in a reconstruction of reality that will be unequalled in history.

Second, women are re-sourcing and reformulating their attitudes toward the material world, i.e., *they are articulating a new value system, a new ethic:* the human body—discovery of its victimization by allopathic medicine, new healings, the introduction of feminist uses of the martial arts, the meaning of discipline to the female body, learnings about the laying on of hands, about loving and healing, new seeings about health, nutrition, natural cures, connections between physical health and psychological realities, questions about reproduction, midwifery, cloning, parthenogenesis, self-nuturing, and mothering; the Earth Herself and the healing of Her ten-thousand-year-long rape—the tending of the ground, farming, food production, relationship to animals, to plants, to artifacts, careful ecological reflections and commitments, connections to the biosphere, action in the face of the deeper meaning of death and life, a new assessment of the significance and destiny of a species which has ravaged its own home.

I believe that the conscious women who are exploring a new epistemology and a new value system, the women who are working in the fourth approach to social change, are all, in one form or another, attempting a *re-sourcing of energy*. They are addressing themselves to the very fundamental discovery: *that there is a source or kind of power qualitatively different from the one we have been taught to accept and to operate with; further, the understanding, the protection, the development of that source and the allowing of it to reach its full dimensions could mean the redemption of the entire globe from the devastation of the last ten thousand years.*

The more we get into re-sourcement the more we realize that patriarchal or "power-over" energy is of a victor/victim design and that the first step in the manufacture of a victim (or of a victor) is the *alienation* of the individual from her internal energy source. Further, we realize that the search for the internal source requires an absence of the dominant (external or interpersonal) energy patterns, that only in the absence of competitiveness and power-over activity can the subdued and devalued inner source find any expression. In a world where every nook and cranny has been filled with superficialized and competitivized external energy, it is no wonder that any internally sourced power has had trouble being expressed—much less valued. Hence the move on the part of thousands of women to isolate themselves (with other women of like understandings) from those power-ridden dominant energy forms; hence, that is, *the need for separatism: the separation of women from the patriarchal system in quantities great enough to make a qualitative difference in history.*

I believe that the new power (not power-over) that will emerge from re-sourcement will be *womanpower*, and that it will come from women not only because we are uniquely in tune with internal sourcing but further because there is a uniquely female capacity for collective functioning which will make possible more life-giving uses of energy in the future.

Women (probably all women but so as not to beg the question I will assume Western women) are uniquely in touch with the internal source out of at least three necessities.

1. Our historical separation from each other and from the activities of the Man's world has afforded us near constant access to the wells of *intra*personal energy. To be sure, within families and in bourgeoise social circles, women have also been relied upon to be peacemakers and relational agents, but our participation in the competitive or power-over mode has always been limited or at best ''second rate''; women still have had hours-per-day and decades-per-century for visiting with ourselves within our own space.

2. Middle-class women (at least) move now in Western society toward a disavowal of sex-role socialization; many of us understand that movement to be a rejection of the most fundamental of all power-over dynamics and as well a throwing off of the self-hatred/woman-hatred engendered by sex roles. The first milestone in a developing feminist consciousness seems to mark a loving and affirmative embrace of the self as a whole entity and an internal energy flow from that holistically experienced self. We have often testified in the movement to the reality of long-dormant energy and how it can be released and expressed when it is touched by one's own self-loving hand.

3. Finally biology for sure is destiny in this sense, that as women we *are* what the patriarchy has labelled us: vessels, containers, receptacles, carriers, shelters, houses, nurturers, incubators, holders, enfolders, listeners. We are *not only* those things but neither is it accurate to say ''we are also aggressors, penetrators, attackers, etc.,'' for if we can be said to be those last things it is out of a context that is wholly different (and therefore manifests itself in a totally different behavior pattern) from the one that men have operated from in their aggression/penetration/etc. . . .

There is not much penetrating about our bodies and there is lots that enfolds and holds and eases. We are built to receive. Let's say that loud and clear. We are also built to give, but even our giving is in our own mode and that mode is totally different from the mis-sourced *inter*personal energy exercised by most men (and unfortunately by many women). Instead of probing or invading, our natural giving takes the path of wrapping around the givee, of being available to her/him without insisting; our giving is a *presence*, an *offering*, an *opening*, a *surrounding*, a *listening*, a *vulnerability*, a *trust*. At the very most our giving takes the form of a push toward freedom for the givee, as in the act of *giving* birth.

So in the reclaiming of our bodies, let's also affirm some propaganda: We are what our fathers and husbands and sons and lovers have called us, but what they have not known, or what they knew and suppressed because of its potential paralyzing threat, is that in our listening is all meaning, in our vesseling is the home, in our shelter is survival, in our nurturing is all possibility. In our enfolding, in short, is ultimately all power. But in the force and thrust of renegade and exclusive *inter*personal (external and externalized) energy, there can be only havoc and destruction.

Re-sourcement calls for the energy of receptivity, the energy of the listening ear, of the open meadow, of the expansive embrace. It calls for an energy generated from within the individual's own territory and for an affirmation of that energy as the genesis of both individual and societal transformation. Women know that territory; in our centuries of waiting we have baptized it with our blood. Now it remains only for women to reclaim that homeland so that the redemption of the biosphere can begin.

Collectivity,* I think, and women's special capacity for it, needs to be talked about elsewhere and by many of us. My own thoughts on it right now are that we are uniquely capable of it because (1) we are *in touch with* the internal energy source; (2) we are *conscious* of what we are in touch with; and (3) we have the *intentionality to share* that energy. That makes us anarchists of sorts, whose only government is self-government. Then, I'm thinking, we are uniquely capable of collectivity because we are beginning to practice—in very incomplete and frustrating ways—a new use of *inter*personal energy. We have started to look at things non-hierarchically and to take seriously the lessons we have learned on the battlefield of romantic love. As a result we occasionally find ourselves (1) respecting and/or loving one another, (2) trusting one another, and (3) beginning to dialogue with each other.

If men have ever found an internal energy flow, and even if they have been conscious of what a cosmic force they have thus tapped, they have been unable, I believe, to take the next step: intending to share that power. My continuing experience of men is that they feel they need women in order to do these things, that really respecting and loving one another, trusting one another, and dialoguing with one another are functions they cannot or will not reach out for by themselves, as men. Even the struggles of gay men toward non-power brotherhood suggest to me that collectivizing internal power may not be men's gift; they may use that power in some other way—perhaps use it creatively—but sharing it in non-power forms is perhaps at this time and place not a possibility for the male psyche.

I now realize that the power we want as women, the power that we have uniquely within us as women, the power that we are developing in order to redeem ten thousand years of extreme and misdirected relational energy, has very little to do with political parties, with money, or with revolution in the common sense of that term.

The power that is emerging from women working in the fourth strategy for change is *womanpower* itself. It is re-sourced energy that is collectively shared among women.

If our real power lies in this fourth strategy, then how do we assess the radical women's movement, at least in the United States? The fourth strategy is the politics of a rapidly growing *minority* of women, and not all those who believe in it are able to separate entirely from society in order to practice re-sourcement skills or to create a woman's culture; others of the "believers" may only be able to separate occasionally—a weekend or so out of linear time or a few moments each day in the at-homeness of the self. They/we will testify that re-sourcement in the thick of the patriarchy is difficult-to-impossible—but also *crucial*.

The majority of feminists have commitments to one of the other three strategies and for a variety of good reasons. But to be working there is dangerous. We have all watched creative women go wagging off down the well-worn path toward masculist power and glory. In some part of themselves they must know that they will make no fundamental change there, that they are only riding on temporary highs (like blood sugar rushes) and only copying the very patterns that afflict us all in the first place. It hurts to see them flexing their hierarchical muscles as the system grants them power or as they join the march of every revolution in history— revolutions which have invariably failed to address the primary problem: the dominance of male over female. While women march in the service of one of the first three strategies *believing that there we can make fundamental change,* we are victims still of patriarchy and only repeat the errors of the ages.

---

*There is no word yet to carry the full meaning of women-togethering or women-being-present-with-themselves-while-presencing-with-others. "Collective" is inadequate for it calls up notions of a pooling, an aggregate. Further, history has tried collective action only within settings where power-over energy has been dominant. Maybe "syzygy" (sizzagee) is the word we need, meaning "yoked" (forget "paired") or "conjunction of organisms without loss of identity" or "a related group of rational(!) integral functions." "Syzygious" would then be the adjective, and the entity resulting from women being together in this state would be a "syzygium."

The secret lies in that phrase, "believing . . . change." Since the majority of us do work "there," what's important, I believe, is that we understand that that work is not the essential work of the revolution, for that essential work is in re-sourcement.

The function of the first three strategies for change is to draw the enemy's fire, to operate as a kind of holding action, to stave off the knowledge and reaction of the patriarch so that time and room are bought for the essential work of genuine transformation. To be sure, each of the three strategies serves the immediate needs of some women; further, the work that is done in these areas can bring significantly closer the ideal of worldwide economic equality. Yet the *fundamental* changes, the changes that do not repeat the age-old mistakes of a competitive system, cannot come from any one or all of these three sources. If we give woman-power room and time it will work for all of us, but let's not fool ourselves that there is hope in any of these patriarchal forms.

It seems to me that women deep at work in re-sourcement, appreciating the fact that their work could not continue if that buffer state failed, need to acknowledge the protection of women working in the other three strategies. For their part, women in the buffer state—if they believe in it—need to work with the knowledge that they are protecting the re-sourcement; if they don't believe it to be the essential strategy, then they can at least affirm it as a valid part of a vast movement of women; hopefully they will lend *critical* support, openly talking about differences with and listening to women who do consider the movement's deepest task to be re-sourcement.

Criticism of this fourth strategy comes easily and is often scathing. When I allow myself to get into those criticisms, they come out like this:

1. Most obviously, since it is extra-rational in much of its expression, the re-sourcement approach seems kooky, supernatural, all a matter of faith. What these spiritualist women are asking us to believe rings too soundly of old-time religion. We can't sit around and simply contemplate our navels or wallow in self-love any more than we can lay it all on Jesus and let him take care of it. People are dying at the hand of imperialist powers and every off-the-wall fad that privileged women fall into only bolsters up the corrupt system. Not only are such crazy women not working for the revolution; they actually aid the enemy.

2. Further, it's a trap. In turning away from the direct struggles with the system itself, these energy-concerned women seem to believe about themselves as women just what the patriarchy has always wanted us to believe, i.e., that we are incapable of functioning in a male world, that we are the passive, receptive, quiet, non-violent, introverted sex, that it is our sphere to be religious and mystical. By withdrawing to the more occult or esoteric realms we yield up to men the real world, the world of power and excitement and achievement. It's an individual solution, the old "trip to the self," the attention to the personal at the sacrifice of significant social action. Women are right back inside ourselves, in the skin-encapsulated ego, isolated and alone, just as men have trained us to be.

3. Third, it's too slow. And furthermore the women involved in it tell us that things can't be pushed, that urgency contradicts the process of re-sourcement. But the world is burning and in the face of that, this fourth approach comes out as lazy, fun, mellow, the good, unstruggled-for life—as long as you can rip off the system for foodstamps or as long as you have nice white skin and aren't a single mother balancing on a piddling minimum wage between starvation and bare subsistence. But where is the real political commitment? Where is the realization that things have to change immediately, that women have political clout if they'll only use it? There is nothing visible happening within the re-sourcement arena. We have no time to mutter little incantations or to wait for "the flow," or to hope for some supernatural occurrence. Slowly, they say, it comes slowly. By the time "it" gets here the revolution will have passed on by.

It is no wonder that feminists committed to "real" political work doubt the value of the re-sourcement approach. It is no wonder that resentment sometimes runs high. I should use my earning power or my brain or my energy struggling every day against the dehumanizing establishment while some listless unpolitical sisters chant around a solstice fire or space out on their dreams? I should spend my life and consciousness believing that dropped-out sisters will come to Something Bigger Than All of Us, that by burning their menstrual blood in the light of the full moon they will be in touch with the Great Mother and somehow make the patriarchy go "poof"? I should stifle my giggles when they speak so seriously of faith healing and procreation-without-men and obliterated matriarchies? And I should do all this, if you please, because the Tarot speaks and Taurus is at the midheaven and perseverance furthers while a little comfrey, Goddess be praised, heals it all?

The answer I am now making to all that is *yes*. That is exactly what I have to do. Even though my criticism of it is strong and vital to my consciousness, it does not shake my belief. (1) Of course it's kooky and all a matter of faith; of course it jars us. It is a whole new posture that violates every dogma of our upbringing. But not to allow it is in itself fascism. When we hear this criticism from socialist sisters, it's good to remind ourselves that Marx' fundamental view (*Early Philosophical Manuscripts*) was a religious one—beyond proof, beyond empirical demonstration; it was a view of *unalienated* humanity. (2) Of course the re-sourcement attitude affirms qualities that the system wants us to believe we have. But we affirm that we are those things *and* far more. If re-sourcement is an individual solution, then my response is, "It's about time." I suggest that no mass movement will ever be more than mimicry if it is not founded on just such an individual base. (3) Of course it's slow. But if we do not dare to slow down, to alter our own speed to be with the sisters into re-sourcement, then at least we have to remember what we've learned in these past eight years if we've learned anything at all: that, like it or not, there's no forcing any other woman into a full trot or a gallop; she *will* move at her own pace, but at her own pace we can be sure she will *move*. At this point I always remind myself that the patriarchal use of crash programs is antithetical to organic movement; in a crash program the theory goes that if you can get nine women pregnant you can have a baby in one month; it takes women, I suppose, to understand that it doesn't work that way.

On the surface re-sourcement can seem to be just another version of humanism. But I think there are two reasons why it is more than that. First, the re-sourcement is a movement of women, and that means it has *a strong and unashamed lesbian component*. At its base humanism is a socio-psychological attitude initiated by men in speaking about men, for the benefit of men; at its patriarchal roots even humanism, for all its "acceptance," cannot tolerate the love of women for each other if for a single instant that love excludes men. Secondly, re-sourcement is not "just humanism" because it hopefully retains within itself *a high radical consciousness of economic realities*. This does not mean that its proponents have to work in factories—either of necessity or in order to organize with workers—though we may do so; it does not have to mean, though it may, that women believing in the fourth strategy spend a maximum of time fighting racism. What it does mean is that through study, confrontation, and dialogue-like communication women believing in the fourth strategy (whether we ourselves are separatists or not) are aware of the privilege exercised by any who separate even temporarily from the patriarchy in order to work in isolation on a woman's culture. If I can move out of the patriarchy for my re-sourcement, then I do indeed march to a different drummer; but I have to march with the consciousness in my very bones of the cost in blood and pain and death that is somewhere being paid for my personal growth. These two characteristics not only clearly differentiate the re-sourcement strategy from humanism; as well, they distinguish the strategy from any other women's movement in history and from any other political revolution.

I've called re-sourcement a political strategy but when I ask questions usually applicable to a political movement, I find unorthodox answers. Who is the enemy? There may be no "enemy" except a system. How do we deal with "the enemy"? As seldom as possible but when necessary by opening the way for his transformation into not-the-enemy. What weapons do we use? Our healing, our self-protection, our health, our fantasies, our collective care. How do we protect our ranks? By a buffer zone of women working in the patriarchy. How do we train for the battles? By practicing our arational skills.

Most startling was the term that came to me when I asked myself, how do we gain members, i.e., what is our outreach program? The term was "religious conversion." I had to dwell on that one awhile because my memory flew immediately to all that I know of Christian conversion, the extreme of which is "if you won't believe that you're redeemed by my redeemer's blood, then I'll drown you in your own." I recalled my own "conversion" to Christianity, which really never happened. I had put it all together intellectually and then prepared myself—in vain—for the emotional undergirding that they had promised me would come. Picture me, the Bible under one arm and *The Augsburg Confession* under the other, waiting on the plains of Texas with my knees eternally flexed for the leap of faith.

Then I recalled my "conversion" to feminism which took place, I discovered, over a period of five years—actually four separate conversions and each one a revelation, each an agony, each an ecstasy. The first change was *theological:* At 5:00 in the morning someone said "God is dead" and for the first time the words had meaning. My intestines and my heart exchanged places, resettled again properly, and my life was thenceforth changed. The second movement was *personal,* two years later: Five years of celibacy had been far too long. That summer brought a *professional* transformation: One trip to California and another authoritarian teacher bites the dust. Finally, two years beyond that, the *politicization:* Still smarting from just having been royally ripped off by General Motors, I saw the National Guard maliciously beat up some of my hippie friends. Four conversion experiences. The coming of my feminism. All born right out of my self, but surrounding them all a climate that allowed the changes, a climate of intolerable conditions or supportive ones, old patterns becoming unbearable or new, special people suddenly entering my life.

I now better understand the dynamics of those changes—and my further "conversion to" or "believing in" the re-sourcement strategy. Mao has helped me with his analogy of the egg and the stone: how the egg with the internal basis for change will never hatch unless it is placed in the proper external conditions for change—heat and moisture—and how the stone, void of the internal basis, can sit in the proper external conditions forever and never hatch.

First, it is true that with each step *I* changed my life. No one changed it for me, I became no one's disciple, and I wasn't even seriously promised "sisterhood." That's what I didn't know as I waited and hoped on the plains of Texas, that *I* could change my life. (Trapped, still, in the female-as-passive role!) Second, while it is true that *I* changed my life, it is also true that those external conditions were a climate, not a force. They did not constitute a god or a being outside myself that required praise and worship because of the revelation he (or she!) gave to me. It has been conversion, right enough, occurring only when I am internally ready and only in an atmosphere conducive to that change.

Here's the hard part for me when I think of re-sourcement as a political strategy. We know we can't change other women, that they must convert themselves. Our job is to continue in our own growth and thus to create the atmosphere (in this case supportive and exemplary) in which their internal bases for change can break through. But if we get too far into this attitude, we will not be political at all but only "groovy," "far-out" women, each doing her own thing and assuring each other every now and again that by living our mellowed-out lives we are thus doing our bit, creating the atmosphere, *tra-la!,* in which Toots and Amy and the governor's wife and the woman hanging out diapers in Middle America are all some-day going to blossom into feminists—re-sourcement feminists, at that. I suggest that unless we read and think and talk and study and practice with our vision constantly in mind and with our political sensibilities consistently sharpened, unless we somehow conceptualize that vision (knowing it will change) and ritualize the expression of it, we may forget entirely that we are a dynamic force in history.

We might also do well to build into our separatism some healthy examinations of reality and some speculations about the future. For instance, as the world situation grows worse, more people will be turning to what is called the irrational, to religion, to all the freaked and fanatic doctrines that are bound to turn up. From that perspective our job may well be to get our selves so together (both individually and collectively) with our arational skills that we'll be able to cope with the onslaught of chaos. I see, too, an ugly revival of orthodoxy within Christendom which could mean Witch hunts twentieth-century-style, complete with the use of satellite search and Kirlian photography. When I lapse into thinking how easy and mellow it is to be in the re-sourcement mode, I remind myself that when the backlash comes it will be weirdo women who will be chased down first, arrested, and separated from each other. That thought sobers me and keeps me from getting lazy. It makes me think that these days we are in a golden age of spirituality, that we will not always be so safe. I don't like to spend a lot of time in that kind of thinking, but I keep it tucked away in an accessible spot; with it available there, I cease to be worried that we won't have enough women; my concern becomes that we won't have enough women *conscious of the political nature of our re-sourced lives.*

Every now and again I get overwhelmed by the significance of the times I am living in. I have been waiting, it seems, all my life, all my lives, for the movement that is now hap-pening among women, for the birth of the womanpower that is presently on the rise. I believe that it is on the rise *now* because the human species and its planet home are at a critical point in their interrelationship; history needs now the different energy that only conscious women can bring to it.

It was not yet time when they burned Witches one by one or even ten by ten. It was not yet time when some of our self-findings and self-lovings had to be hidden from a world that called such discoveries "perversion" and "sin." It was not yet time for countless women throughout recorded history who could not conform to the demands of their culture.

It is time now. The power is ours. And that power is not on Capitol Hill or Wall Street or in any military might. It is flowing from an authentic source, its only authentic source—from women—and that is the first time in history that it has ever happened that way; it is thus absolutely distinct from the power-over models we have been trained to respect. We will use the power that is rising within us, in the midst of us, to redeem the whole human enterprise. And if we fail in that venture, then our role may be helping our species gracefully to extinguish itself from the cosmos.

It is time.

It is ours.

We move now toward the womanwide recognition of how vast and deep an enterprise we are engaged in.

Study Questions

1. What three strategies for societal transformation does Gearhart examine, and why does she reject them? What strategy does she advocate?
2. What does "re-sourcement" consist of? What lies behind it?

3. What does Gearhart think of the maxim "woman's biology is her destiny"?
4. What objections to her fourth strategy (bringing social change through personal "re-sourcement") does Gearhart explore? How does she reply to them?
5. Is the sort of spiritual approach favored by Gearhart just a form of humanism? Why or why not?

7

Philosophy of Art

Art, like religion, is an aspect of human activity found in all cultures. The field of philosophy that deals with the nature and function of art and the relation of art and society is *esthetics*. Like ethics, esthetics is concerned with value judgments and their validity. (In the case of esthetics, the judgments are about the worth of works of art.)

Feminist theorists are changing the focus of philosophy of art. Feminist philosophers in this field address such questions as: Is there a women's art? How does women's art relate to women's culture and experience? What criteria should feminists apply to assess film, literature, visual arts, music, architecture, and the like?

E. Ann Kaplan's essay offers a critical analysis of art in the patriarchal setting. Specifically, she examines the way in which women are sexually objectified in art, and in turn, how women learn to accept this objectification. In film, this takes the form of "the gaze," which is the cinematic expression of men's objectification of women's bodies and the internalization of this process by women themselves. Kaplan seeks new approaches to film art and esthetics.

Literary criticism, traditionally, has been a male bastion. In response, feminist literary criticism has emerged. The dimensions of this new mode of critical approach are broad, but at its core, feminist literary criticism seeks to consider literary texts in the light of women's experience and women's culture. Thus it examines closely the writings of women as well as the figuration of women in the literary canon. Kate Millett's reading of texts by male authors, in *Sexual Politics*, showed the sexism and misogyny in their portrayal of women.

In her essay, Annette Kolodny explores the development of a women-centered critical canon for literary texts that derives from women's lives. She also discusses the nature and function of feminist textual "readings" and considers how these readings may or may not differ from those of their masculinist counterparts.

In their dialogue, Arlene Raven and Ruth Iskin take up the question of women-centered visual arts and art criticism. Developing the notion of feminist art, they explore women's art for what they call "lesbian sensibility." This sensibility is characterized by the expression of women-identification in its modes and themes. Since art, for Raven and Iskin, cannot be divorced from life, they suggest that the inspiration for lesbian art is rooted in lesbian experience and culture.

Is the Gaze Male?

E. Ann Kaplan

Since the beginning of the recent women's liberation movement, American feminists have been exploring the representation of female sexuality in the arts—literature, painting, film, and television.[1] The first wave of feminist critics adopted a broadly sociological approach, looking at sex roles women were seen to occupy in all kinds of imaginative works, from high art to mass entertainment. Roles were assessed as "positive" or "negative" according to some externally constructed criteria for the fully autonomous, independent woman.

Feminist film critics were the first to object to this prevailing critical approach, largely because of the general developments taking place in film theory at the beginning of the 1970s.[2] They noted the lack of awareness about the way images are constructed through the mechanism of whatever artistic practice is involved; representations, they pointed out, are mediations, embedded through the art form in the dominant ideology. Influenced by the work of Claude Lévi-Strauss, Roland Barthes, Jacques Lacan, Christian Metz, Julia Kristeva, and others, women began to apply the tools of psychoanalysis, semiology, and structuralism in analyzing the representation of women in film.[3] I will not duplicate the history of these theoretical developments here; let it suffice to note, by way of introduction, that increasing attention has been given first, to cinema as a signifying practice, to *how meaning is produced* in film rather than to something that used to be called its "content"; and second, to the links between the processes of psychoanalysis and those of cinema.[4] Feminists have been particularly concerned with how sexual difference is constructed psychoanalytically through the Oedipal process, especially as this is read by Lacan.[5] For Lacan, woman cannot enter the world of the symbolic, of language, because at the very moment of the acquisition of language, she learns that she lacks the phallus, the symbol that sets language going through a recognition of difference; her relation to language is a negative one, a lack. In patriarchal structures, thus, woman is located as other (enigma, mystery), and is thereby viewed as outside of (male) language.

The implications of this for cinema are severe: dominant (Hollywood) cinema is seen as constructed according to the unconscious of patriarchy, which means that film narratives are constituted through a phallocentric language and discourse that parallels the language of the unconscious. Women in film, thus, do not function as signifiers for a signified (a real woman) as sociological critics have assumed, but signifier and signified have been elided into a sign that represents something in the male unconscious.[6]

From Ann Snitow, Christine Stansell, and Sharon Thompson, eds., *Powers of Desire*, (New York: Monthly Review Press, 1983), pp. 309–327. Reprinted by permission of E. Ann Kaplan. (Notes deleted.)

Two basic Freudian concepts—voyeurism and fetishism—have been used to explain what exactly woman represents and the mechanisms that come into play for the male spectator watching a female screen image. (Or, to put it rather differently, voyeurism and fetishism are mechanisms the dominant cinema uses to *construct* the male spectator in accordance with the needs of his unconscious.) The first, voyeurism, is linked to the scopophilic instinct (i.e., the male pleasure in his own sexual organ transferred to pleasure in watching other people having sex). Critics argue that the cinema relies on this instinct, making the spectator essentially a voyeur. The drive that causes little boys to peek through keyholes of parental bedrooms to learn about their sexual activities (or to get sexual gratification by thinking about these activities) comes into play when the male adult watches films, sitting in a dark room. The original eye of the camera, controlling and limiting what can be seen, is reproduced by the projector aperture that lights up one frame at a time; and both processes (camera and projector) duplicate the eye at the keyhole, whose gaze is confined by the keyhole "frame." The spectator is obviously in the voyeur position when there are sex scenes on the screen, but screen images of women are sexualized no matter what the women are doing literally, or what kind of plot may be involved.

According to Laura Mulvey (the British filmmaker and critic whose theories are central to new developments), this eroticization of women on the screen comes about through the way the cinema is structured around three explicitly male looks or gazes: there is the look of the camera in the situation where events are being filmed (called the profilmic event)—while technically neutral, this look, as we have seen, is inherently voyeuristic and usually "male" in the sense of a man doing the filming; there is the look of the men within the narrative, which is structured so as to make women objects of their gaze; and finally there is the look of the male spectator that imitates (or is necessarily in the same position as) the first two looks.[7]

But if women were simply eroticized and objectified, things might not be too bad, since objectification may be an inherent component of both male and female eroticism. (As I will show later on, however, things in this area are not symmetrical.) But two further elements enter in: to begin with, men do not simply look; their gaze carries with it the power of action and of possession that is lacking in the female gaze. Women receive and return a gaze, but cannot act on it. Second, the sexualization and objectification of women is not simply for the purposes of eroticism; from a psychoanalytic point of view, it is designed to annihilate the threat that woman (as castrated, and possessing a sinister genital organ) poses. In her 1932 article "The Dread of Woman," Karen Horney goes to literature to show that "men have never tired of fashioning expressions for the violent force by which man feels himself drawn to the woman, and side by side with his longing, the dread that through her he might die and be undone."[8] Later on, Horney conjectures that even man's glorification of women "has its source not only in his cravings for love, but also in his desire to conceal his dread. A similar relief, however, is also sought and found in the disparagement of women that men often display ostentatiously in their "attitudes."[9] Horney goes on to explore the basis of the dread of women not only in castration (more related to the father), but in fear of the vagina.

But psychoanalysts agree that, for whatever reason—the fear of castration (Freud), or the attempt to deny the existence of the sinister female genital (Horney)—men endeavor to find the penis in women.[10] Feminist film critics have seen this phenomenon (clinically known as fetishism) operating in the cinema; the camera (unconsciously) fetishizes the female form, rendering it phallus-like so as to mitigate woman's threat. Men, that is, turn "the represented figure itself into a fetish so that it becomes reassuring rather than dangerous" (hence overvaluation, the cult of the female star).[11]

The apparently contradictory attitudes of glorification and disparagement pointed out by Horney thus turn out to be a reflection of the same ultimate need to annihilate the dread that woman inspires. In the cinema, the twin mechanisms of fetishism and voyeurism represent two different ways of handling this dread. As Mulvey points out, fetishism "builds up the physical beauty of the object, turning it into something satisfying in itself,'' while voyeurism, linked to disparagement, has a sadistic side, and is involved with pleasure through control or domination, and with punishing the woman (guilty for being castrated).[12] For Claire Johnston, both mechanisms result in woman's not being presented qua *woman* at all. Extending the *Cahiers du Cinéma* analysis of *Morocco*, Johnston argues that Sternberg represses "the idea of woman as a social and sexual being," thus replacing the opposition man/woman with male/nonmale.[13]

With this brief look at feminist film theories as background, we can turn to the question of the gaze: as it stands, current work using psychoanalysis and semiology has demonstrated that the dominant cinematic apparatus is constructed by men for a male spectator. Women as women are absent from the screen *and* from the audience. Several questions now arise: first, is the gaze *necessarily* male (i.e., for reasons inherent in the structure of language, the unconscious, all symbolic systems, and thereby all social structures)? Or would it be possible to structure things so that women own the gaze? Second, would women want to own the gaze, if it were possible? Third, in either case, what does it mean to be a female spectator? Women are in fact present in audiences: what is happening to them as they watch a cinematic apparatus that constructs a male viewer? Does a woman spectator of female images have any choice other than either identifying as female object of desire, or if subject of desire, then appropriating the male position? Can there be such a thing as the female subject of desire? Finally, if a female subject is watching images of lesbians, what can this mean to her? How do such images inform women's actual, physical relations with other women?

It is extremely important for feminist film critics to begin to address these questions. First, behind these questions, posed largely in structural terms, lie the larger questions concerning female desire and female subjectivity: Is it possible for there to be a female voice, a female discourse? What can a feminine specificity mean? Second, those of us working within the psychoanalytic system need to find a way out of an apparently overwhelming theoretical problem that has dramatic consequences for the way we are constituted, and constitute ourselves, not just in representation but also in our daily lives. Is there any escape from the overdetermined, phallocentric sign? The whole focus on the materialization of the signifier has again brought daily experience and art close together. Now critics read daily life as structured according to signifying practices (like art, "constructed," not naively experienced), rather than the earlier oversimplification of seeing art as a mere reflection/imitation of lived experience (mirroring it, or, better, presenting it as through a transparent pane of glass).

Finally, the growing interest in psychoanalytic and semiological approaches has begun to polarize the feminist film community, and I want to begin by addressing some objections to current theoretical work, since they will lead us back to the larger questions of the female gaze and female desire. In a roundtable discussion in 1979, some women voiced their displeasure with theories that were themselves originally devised by men, and with women's preoccupation with how we have been seen/placed/positioned by the dominant male order. Julia LeSage, for instance, argues that the use of Lacanian criticism has been destructive in reifying women "in a childlike position that patriarchy has wanted to see them in"; for LeSage, the Lacanian framework establishes "a discourse which is totally male."[14] And Ruby Rich objects to theories that rest with the apparent elimination of women from both screen and audience. She asks how we can move beyond our placing, rather than just analyzing it.

As if in response to Rich's request, some feminist film critics have begun to take up the challenge of moving beyond the preoccupation with how women have been constructed in patriarchal cinema. In a recent paper on *Gentlemen Prefer Blondes*, Lucie Arbuthnot and Gail Seneca attempt to appropriate for themselves some of the images hitherto defined as repressive. They begin by expressing their dissatisfaction not only with current feminist film theory as outlined above, but also with the new theoretical feminist films, which, they say, "focus more on denying men their cathexis with women as erotic objects than in connecting women with each other." In addition, these films, by "destroying the narrative and the possibility for viewer identification with the characters, destroy both the male viewer's pleasure and our pleasure."[15] Asserting their need for identification with strong female screen images, they argue that Hollywood films offer many examples of pleasurable identification; in a clever analysis, the relationship between Marilyn Monroe and Jane Russell in *Gentlemen Prefer Blondes* is offered as an example of strong women, who care for one another, providing a model we need.

However, looking at the construction of the film as a whole, rather than simply isolating certain shots, it is clear that Monroe and Russell are positioned, and position themselves, as objects for a specifically male gaze. The men's weakness does not mitigate their diegetic power, leaving to the women merely the limited control they can wield through their sexuality. The film constructs them as "to-be-looked-at," and their manipulations end up merely comic, since "capturing" the men involves their "being captured." The images of Monroe show her fetishized placement, aimed at reducing her sexual threat, while Russell's stance is a parody of the male position.[16] The result is that the two women repeat, in exaggerated form, dominant gender stereotypes.

Yet Arbuthnot and Seneca begin from important points: first, the need for films that construct *women* as the spectator and yet do not offer *repressive* identifications (as, for example, Hollywood women's films do); and second, the need for feminist films that satisfy our craving for *pleasure*. In introducing the notion of pleasure, Arbuthnot and Seneca pinpoint a central and little-discussed issue. Mulvey was aware of the way feminist films as counter-cinema would deny pleasure, but she argued that this denial was a necessary prerequisite for freedom, and did not go into the problems involved. Arbuthnot and Seneca locate the paradox in which feminist film critics have been caught without realizing it: namely, that we have been analyzing Hollywood (rather than, say, avant-garde) films, largely because they bring us pleasure; but we have (rightly) been wary of admitting the degree to which the pleasure comes from identifying with our own objectification. Our positioning as "to-be-looked-at," as object of the gaze, has, through our positioning, come to be sexually pleasurable.

However, it will not do to simply enjoy our oppression unproblematically; to appropriate Hollywood images to ourselves, taking them out of the context of the total structure in which they appear, will not get us very far. In order to fully understand *how it is* that women take pleasure in the objectification of women, one has to have recourse to psychoanalysis. Since criticisms like those voiced by LeSage, Rich, and Arbuthnot and Seneca are important, and reflect the deepening rift in the feminist film community, it is worth dwelling for a moment on why psychoanalysis is necessary as a feminist tool at this point in our history.

As Christian Metz, Stephen Heath, and others have shown, the processes of cinema mimic in many ways those of the unconscious. The mechanisms Freud distinguishes in relation to dream and the unconscious have been likened to the mechanisms of film.[17] In this analysis, film narratives, like dreams, symbolize a latent, repressed content, only now the "content" refers not to an individual unconscious but to that of patriarchy in general. If psychoanalysis is a tool that will unlock the meaning of dreams, it should also unlock that of films.

But of course the question still remains as to the ideology of psychoanalysis: is it true, as Talking Lips argues at the start of the film *Sigmund Freud's Dora*, that psychoanalysis is a discourse shot through with bourgeois ideology, functioning "almost as an Ideological State Apparatus," with its focus the individual, "outside of real history and real struggle?"[18] Or is psychoanalysis, although developed at a time when bourgeois capitalism was the dominant form, a theory that applies *across* history rather than being *embedded in* history?

Of these two possibilities, the first seems to me to be true. Psychoanalysis and cinema are inextricably linked both to each other and to capitalism, because both are products of a particular stage of capitalist society. The psychic patterns created by capitalist social and interpersonal structures (especially the nuclear family) required at once a machine for their unconscious release and an analytic tool for understanding and adjusting disturbances caused by the structures confining people. To this extent, both mechanisms support the status quo; but they are not eternal and unchanging, being rather inserted in history and linked to the particular social formation that produced them.

For this very reason, we have to begin by using psychoanalysis if we want to understand how we have been constituted, and the kind of linguistic and cultural universe we live in. Psychoanalysis may indeed have been used to oppress women, in the sense of forcing us to accept a positioning that is inherently antithetical to subjectivity and autonomy; but if that is the case, we need to know exactly *how* this has functioned to repress what we could potentially become. Given our positioning as women raised in a historical period dominated by Oedipal structuring and discourse, we must start by examining the psychoanalytic processes as they have worked to position us as other (enigma, mystery), and as eternal and unchanging, however paradoxical this may appear. For it is only in this way that we can begin to find the gaps and fissures through which we can reinsert woman in history, and begin to change ourselves as a first step toward changing society.

Let us now return to the question of women's pleasure in being objectified and see what we can learn about it through psychoanalysis. We saw earlier that the entry of the father as the third term disrupts the mother/child dyad, causing the child to understand the mother's castration and possession by the father. In the symbolic world the girl now enters she learns not only subject/object position but the sexed pronouns ''he'' and ''she.'' Assigned the place of object (since she lacks the phallus, the symbol of the signifier), she is the recipient of male desire, the passive recipient of his gaze. If she is to have sexual pleasure, it can only be constructed around her objectification; it cannot be a pleasure that comes from desire for the other (a subject position)—that is, her desire is to be desired.

Given the male structuring around sadism that I have already discussed, the girl may adopt a corresponding masochism. In practice, this masochism is rarely reflected in more than a tendency for women to be passive in sexual relations; but in the realm of fantasy, masochism is often quite prominent. In an interesting paper, ''The 'Woman's Film': Possession and Address,'' Mary Ann Doane has shown that in the one film genre that constructs a female spectator, that spectator is made to participate in what is essentially a masochistic fantasy. Doane notes that in the major classical genres, the female body *is* sexuality, providing the erotic object for the male spectator. In the woman's film, the gaze must be de-eroticized (since the spectator is now assumed to be female), but in doing this the films effectively disembody their spectator. The repeated masochistic scenarios are designed to immobilize the female viewer, refuse her the imaginary identification that, in uniting body and identity, gives back to the male spectator his idealized (mirror) self, together with a sense of mastery and control.

Later on in her paper, Doane shows that Freud's ''A Child Is Being Beaten'' is important in distinguishing the way a common masochistic fantasy works out for boys and for girls. In the male fantasy, ''sexuality remains on the surface'' and the man ''retains his own role and his own gratification in the context of the scenario. The 'I' of identity remains.'' But the female fantasy is, first, desexualized, and, second, ''necessitates the woman's assumption of the position of spectator, outside of the event.'' In this way, the girl manages, as Freud says, ''to escape from the demands of the erotic side of her life altogether.''[19]

Perhaps we can phrase this a little differently and say that in locating herself in fantasy in the erotic, the woman places herself as either passive recipient of male desire, or, at one remove, positions herself as *watching* a woman who is passive recipient of male desires and sexual actions. Although the evidence we have to go on is slim, it does seem that women's sexual fantasies would confirm the predominance of these positionings. Nancy Friday's volumes, for instance, provide discourses on the level of dream, and, however questionable as scientific evidence, show narratives in which the woman speaker largely arranges the scenario for her sexual pleasure so that things are done to her, or in which she is the object of men's lascivious gaze.[20] Often, there is pleasure in anonymity, or in a strange man approaching her when she is with her husband. Rarely does the dreamer initiate the sexual activity, and the man's large, erect penis usually is central in the fantasy. Nearly all the fantasies have the dominance-submission pattern, with the woman in the latter place.

It is significant that in the lesbian fantasies that Friday has collected women occupy *both* positions, the dreamer excited either by dominating another woman, forcing her to have sex, or enjoying being so dominated. These fantasies suggest either that the female positioning is not as monolithic as critics often imply, or that women occupy the "male" position when they become dominant. Whichever the case may be, the prevalence of the dominance-submission pattern as a sexual turn-on is clear. At a discussion about pornography organized by Julia LeSage at the Northwestern Conference on Feminist Film Criticism, gay and straight women admitted their pleasure (in both fantasy and actuality) in being "forced" or "forcing" someone else. Some women claimed that this was a result of growing up in Victorian-style households where all sexuality was repressed, but others denied that it had anything to do with patriarchy. Women wanted, rightly, to accept themselves sexually, whatever the turn-on mechanism.[21] But to simply celebrate whatever gives us sexual pleasure seems to me both problematic and too easy: we need to analyze how it is that certain things turn us on, how sexuality has been constructed in patriarchy to produce pleasure in the dominance-submission forms, before we advocate these modes.

It was predictable that many of the male fantasies in Friday's book *Men in Love* would show the speaker constructing events so that he is in control: again, the "I" of identity remains central, as it was not in the female narrations.[22] Many male fantasies focus on the man's excitement arranging for his woman to expose herself (or even give herself) to other men, while he watches. The difference between this male voyeurism and the previous female form is striking: the women do not own the desire, even when they watch; their watching is to place responsibility for sexuality at yet one more remove, to distance themselves from sex; the man, on the other hand, owns the desire and the woman, and gets pleasure from exchanging the woman, as in Lévi-Strauss' kinship system.

Yet some of the fantasies in Friday's book show men's wish to be taken over by an aggressive woman who would force them to become helpless, like the little boy in his mother's hands. The Women Against Pornography guided trip around Times Square corroborated this; after a slide show that focused totally on male sadism and violent sexual exploitation of women, we were taken on a tour that showed literature and film loops expressing as many fantasies of male as of female submission. The situations were the predictable ones, showing young boys (but sometimes men) seduced by women in a form of authority—governesses, nursemaids, nurses, schoolteachers, stepmothers. (Of course, it is significant that the corresponding dominance-submission female fantasies have men in authority positions that carry much more status—professors, doctors, policemen, executives: these men seduce the innocent girls, or young wives, who cross their paths.)

Two interesting things emerge from all this: one is that dominance-submission patterns are apparently a crucial part of both male and female sexuality as constructed in western capitalism. The other is that men have a far wider range of positions available: more readily both dominant and submissive, they vacillate between supreme control and supreme abandonment. Women, meanwhile, are more consistently submissive, but not excessively abandoned. In their own fantasies, women do not position themselves as exchanging men, although a man might find being exchanged an exciting fantasy.

But the important question remains: when women are in the dominant position, are they in the *masculine* position? Can we envisage a female dominant position that would differ qualitatively from the male form of dominance? Or is there merely the possibility for both sex genders to occupy the positions we now know as masculine and feminine?

The experience of recent films of the 1970s and 1980s would support the latter possibility, and explain why many feminists have not been excited by the so-called liberated woman on the screen, or by the fact that some male stars have recently been made to seem the object of the female gaze. Traditionally male stars did not necessarily (or even primarily) derive their glamour from their looks or their sexuality, but from the power they were able to wield within the filmic world in which they functioned (i.e., John Wayne); these men, as Laura Mulvey has shown, became ego ideals for the men in the audience, corresponding to the image in the mirror, who was more in control of motor coordination than the young child looking in. "The male figure," Mulvey notes, "is free to command the stage . . . of spatial illusion in which he articulates the look and creates the action."[23]

Recent films have begun to change this pattern: a star like John Travolta (*Saturday Night Fever, Urban Cowboy, Moment by Moment*) has been rendered the object of women's gaze and in some of the films (i.e., *Moment by Moment*) placed explicitly as a sexual object to a woman who controlled the film's action. Robert Redford likewise has begun to be used as the object of female desire (i.e., in *Electric Horseman*). But it is significant that in all these films, when the man steps out of his traditional role as the one who controls the whole action, and when he is set up as a sex object, the woman then takes on the masculine role as bearer of the gaze and initiator of the action. She nearly always loses her traditionally feminine characteristics in so doing—not those of attractiveness, but rather of kindness, humaneness, motherliness. She is now often cold, driving, ambitious, manipulating, just like the men whose position she has usurped.

Even in a supposedly feminist film like *My Brilliant Career* the same processes are at work. The film is interesting because it places in the foreground the independent-minded heroine's dilemma in a clearly patriarchal culture: in love with a wealthy neighbor, the heroine makes him the object of her gaze, but the problem is that, as female, her desire has no power. Men's desire naturally carries power with it, so when the hero finally concedes his love for her, he comes to get her. However, being able to conceive of "love" only as "submission," an end to autonomy and to her life as a creative writer, the heroine now refuses. The film thus plays with established positions, but is unable to work through them to something else.

What we can conclude from the discussion so far is that our culture is deeply committed to clearly demarcated sex differences, called masculine and feminine, that revolve on, first, a complex gaze-apparatus; and, second, dominance-submission patterns. This positioning of the two sex genders clearly privileges the male through the mechanisms of voyeurism and fetishism, which are male operations, and because his desire carries power/action, where woman's usually does not. But as a result of the recent women's movement, women have been permitted in representation to assume (step into) the position defined as masculine, as long as the man then steps into *her* position, so as to keep the whole structure intact.

It is significant, of course, that while this substitution is made to happen relatively easily in the cinema, in real life any such "swapping" is fraught with the immense psychological difficulties that only psychoanalysis can unravel. In any case, such "exchanges" do not do much for either sex, since nothing has essentially changed: the roles remain locked into their static boundaries. Showing images of mere reversal may in fact provides a safety valve for the social tensions that the women's movement has created by demanding a more dominant role for women.

We have thus arrived at the point where we must question the necessity for the dominance-submission structure. The gaze is not necessarily male (literally), but to own and activate the gaze, given our language and the structure of the unconscious, is to be in the masculine position. It is for this reason that Julia Kristeva and others have said that it is impossible to know what the feminine might be; while we must reserve the category "women" for social demands and publicity. Kristeva says that by "woman" she means "that which is not represented, that which is unspoken, that which is left out of meanings and ideologies."[24]

For similar reasons, Sandy Flitterman and Judith Barry have argued that feminist artists must avoid claiming a specific female power residing in the body of women that represents "an inherent feminine artistic essence which could find expression if allowed to be explored freely." The impulse toward this kind of art is understandable in a culture that denies satisfaction in being a woman, but it results in motherhood's being redefined as the seat of female creativity, while women, "are proposed as the bearers of culture, albeit an alternative one."[25]

Barry and Flitterman argue that this form of feminist art, along with some others that they outline, is dangerous in not taking into account "the social contradictions involved in 'femininity.' " They suggest that "a radical feminist art would include an understanding of how women are constituted through social practices in culture," and argue for "an aesthetics designed to subvert the production of 'woman' as commodity," much as Claire Johnston and Laura Mulvey had earlier stated that to be feminist, a cinema had to be a counter-cinema.[26]

The problem with all these arguments is that they leave women trapped in the position of negativity—subverting rather than positing. Although the feminists asserting this point of view are clearly right in placing in the foreground women's repression in representation and culture (and in seeing this work as a necessary first step), it is hard to see how women can move forward from these awarenesses. If certain feminist groups (i.e., Women Against Pornography) err on the side of eliding reality with fantasy (i.e., in treating an image's violating of women on the same level as a literal act of violation on the street), feminist critics err on the side of seeing a world constructed only of signifiers, of losing contact with the "referred" world of the social formation.

The first error was in positing an unproblematic relationship between art and life in the sense that (1) art was seen as able simply to imitate life, as if through a transparent pane of glass; and (2) that representation was thought to affect social behavior directly; but the second error is to see art and life as both equally "constructed" by the signifying practices that define and limit each sphere. The signifier is here made material, in the sense that it is all there is to know. Discussing semiology in relation to Marxism, Terry Eagleton points out the dangers of this way of seeing for a Marxist view of history. History evaporates in the new scheme, since the signified can never be grasped, we cannot talk about our reality as human subjects. But, as he goes on to show, more than the signified (which in Saussure's scheme obediently followed the signifier, despite its being arbitrary) is at stake: "It is also," he says "a question of the referent, which we all long ago bracketed out of being. In re-materializing the sign, we are in imminent danger of de-materializing its referent; a linguistic materialism gradually reverts itself into a linguistic idealism."[27]

Eagleton no doubt overstates the case when he talks about "sliding away from the referent," since neither Saussure nor Althusser denied that there *was* a referent. But it is true that while semiologists talk about the eruption of "the real" (i.e., accidents, death, revolution), on a daily basis they tend to be preoccupied with life as dominated by the prevailing signifying practices of a culture. It may be true that all lived experience is mediated through signifying practices, but we should not therefore pay exclusive attention to this level of things. In attempting to get rid of an unwelcome dualism, inherent in western thought at least since Plato, and rearticulated by Kant on the brink of the modern period, some semiologists run the danger of collapsing levels of things that need to remain distinct if we are to work effectively in the political arena to bring about change.

Thus while it is essential for feminist film critics to examine signifying processes carefully in order to fully understand the way women have been constructed in language and the nonverbal arts, it is equally important not to lose sight of the need to find strategies for changing discourse, since these changes would, in turn, affect the structuring of the social formation.

Some feminist film critics have begun to face this challenge. The directors of *Sigmund Freud's Dora*, for example, suggest that raising questions is the first step toward establishing a female discourse, or, perhaps, that asking questions is the only discourse available to women as a resistance to patriarchal domination. Since questions lead to more questions, a kind of movement is in fact taking place, although it is in a nontraditional mode. Sally Potter structured her film *Thriller* around this very notion, and allowed her heroine's investigation of herself as heroine to lead to some (tentative) conclusions. And Laura Mulvey has suggested that even if one accepts the psychoanalytic positioning of women, all is not lost, since the Oedipus complex is not completed in women; she notes that "there's some way in which women aren't colonized," having been "so specifically excluded from culture and language."[28]

From this position, psychoanalytic theory allows us to see that there is more possibility for women to change themselves (and perhaps to bring about social change) just because they have not been processed, as have little boys, through a clearly defined, and ultimately simple, set of psychic stages. The girl's relationship to her mother remains forever unresolved, incomplete; in heterosexuality, she is forced to turn away from her primary love object, destined never to return to it, while the boy, through marrying someone like his mother, can regain his original plenitude in another form. The girl must transfer her need for love to the father, who, as Nancy Chodorow has shown, never completely satisfies.[29]

Mulvey thus suggests that patriarchal culture is not monolithic, not cleanly sealed. There are gaps, fissures through which women can begin to ask questions and introduce change. The directors of *Sigmund Freud's Dora* end their film with a series of letters from a daughter (who is sometimes called Dora) read out by her mother, some of which deal with the place of the mother in psychoanalysis. The daughter's comments illuminate the fact that Freud dismisses Dora's mother (in his famous account of the case history), instead of talking about her "as the site of the intersection of many representations" (of which the historical mother is just one). She suggests that Freud's omission was not merely an oversight, but, given his system, a necessity.

Mulvey and Wollen's earlier film, *Riddles of the Sphinx*, confronted the repression of mothering in patriarchal culture directly; the film argued that women "live in a society ruled by the father, in which the place of the mother is repressed. Motherhood, and how to live it or not to live it, lies at the root of the dilemma."[30] In an interview, Mulvey noted the influence of psychoanalysis on her conception of the mother-child exchange ("the identification between the two, and the implications that has for narcissism and recognition of the self in the 'other' "), but she went on to say that this is an area rarely read from the mother's point of view.[31]

Motherhood thus becomes one place from which to begin to reformulate our position as women, just because men have not dealt with it theoretically or in the social realm (i.e., by providing free childcare, free abortions, maternal leave, after-school child programs, etc.). Motherhood has been repressed on all levels except that of hypostatization, romanticization, and idealization. Yet women have been struggling with lives as mothers—silently, quietly, often in agony, often in bliss, but always on the periphery of a society that tries to make us all, men and women, forget our mothers.

But motherhood, and the fact that we were all mothered, will not be repressed; or, if the attempt is made, there will be effects signaling "the return of the repressed." The entire construction of woman in patriarchy as a lack could be viewed as emerging from the need to repress mothering and the painful memory traces it has left in the man. The phallus as signified can be set in motion only given the other with a lack, and this has resulted in the male focus on castration. But is it possible that this focus was designed to mask an even greater threat that mothering poses? And if we look from the position of women, need this lack in reality have the dire implications men would have us believe? The focus on women as (simply) sex object, or (more complexly) as fetishized (narcissistic male desire) that we have been tracing through Hollywood films, may be part of the apparatus that represses mothering.

The insistence on rigidly defined sex roles, and the dominance-submission, voyeurism-fetishism mechanisms may be constructed to this end.

In placing the problem of mothering in the foreground in this way, one is not necessarily falling into the trap of essentialism. First, I am not denying that motherhood has been constructed in patriarchy by its very place as repressed; nor, second, am I saying that women are inherently mothers; nor, third, that the only ideal relationship that can express female specificity is mothering. I am saying, rather, that motherhood is one of the areas that has been left vague, allowing us to reformulate the position as given, rather than discovering a specificity outside the system we are in. It is a place to start rethinking sex-difference, not an end.

Let me review briefly some of the main ways in which motherhood can be thought of within psychoanalysis. First, and most conservatively, motherhood has been analyzed as an essentially narcissistic relationship, and as involved with the problem of castration. In this way, it parallels male fetishism; just as men fetishize women in order to reduce their threat (finding themselves thus in the other), so women fetishize the child, looking in the child for the phallus to "make up" for castration; second, motherhood can be seen as narcissistic, not in the sense of finding the phallus in the child, but of finding *the self* in the child (this parallels male fetishizing of women in another way); women here do not relate to the child as other, but as an extension of their own egos; third, and most radically (but this is also the position that can lead to essentialism), one could argue that since the law represses mothering, a gap is left through which it may be possible to subvert patriarchy.

The problem with this latter (and most hopeful) position, however, is that of how to express motherhood after the period of the imaginary. One could argue that women are faced with an impossible dilemma: to remain in blissful unity with the child in the imaginary (or to try to hold onto this realm as long as possible), or to enter the symbolic in which mothering is repressed, cannot be "spoken," cannot represent a position of power. Here the only resistance is silence.

But is this not one of those places where a rigid adherence to the theoretical formulation of imaginary and symbolic betrays the inadequacy of the theory? Is not mothering, in fact, now being "spoken," even through patriarchal discourse? Both Dorothy Dinnerstein and Nancy Chodorow "speak" a discourse about mothering that, while remaining within psychoanalysis, breaks new ground.[32] And the feminist films about mothering now appearing begin to investigate and move beyond patriarchal representations.[33]

On the social/historical level, in addition, we are living in a period in which mothers are increasingly living alone with their children, offering the possibility for new psychic patterns to emerge; fathers are increasingly becoming involved with childrearing, and also living alone with their children. Freud's own kind of science (which involved studying the people brought up in strict Victorian, bourgeois households) applied rigorously to people today results in very different conclusions. Single mothers are forced to make themselves subject in relation to their children; they are forced to invent new symbolic roles, which combine positions previously assigned to fathers with traditional female ones. The child cannot position the mother as object to the father's law, since in single-parent households *her* desire sets things in motion.

A methodology is often not per se either revolutionary or reactionary, but open to appropriation for a variety of usages. At this point, feminists may have to use psychoanalysis, but in a manner opposite to the traditional one. Other kinds of psychic processes obviously can exist and may stand as models for when we have worked our way through the morass that confronts us as people having grown up in western capitalist culture. Julia Kristeva, for example, suggests that desire functions in a very different manner in China, and urges us to explore Chinese culture, from a very careful psychoanalytic point of view, to see what is possible.[34]

Many of the mechanisms we have found in Hollywood films which echo deeply embedded myths in western capitalist culture are thus not inviolable, eternal, unchanging, or inherently necessary. They rather reflect the unconscious of patriarchy, including a fear of the pre-Oedipal plenitude with the mother. The domination of women by the male gaze is part of men's strategy to contain the threat that the mother embodies, and to control the positive and negative impulses that memory traces of being mothered have left in the male unconscious. Women, in turn, have learned to associate their sexuality with domination by the male gaze, a position involving a degree of masochism in finding their objectification erotic. We have participated in and perpetuated our domination by following the pleasure principle, which leaves us no options, given our positioning.

Everything, thus, revolves around the issue of pleasure, and it is here that patriarchal repression has been most negative. For things have been structured to make us forget the mutual, pleasurable bonding that we all, male and female, enjoyed with our mothers. Some recent experimental (as against psychoanalytic) studies have shown that the gaze is first set in motion in the mother-child relationship. But this is a *mutual* gazing, rather than the subject-object kind that reduces one of the parties to the place of submission. Patriarchy has worked hard to prevent the eruption of a (mythically) feared return of the matriarchy that might take place were the close mother-child bonding returned to dominance, or allowed to stand in place of the law of the father.

This is by no means to argue that a return to matriarchy would be either possible or desirable. What rather has to happen is that we move beyond long-held cultural and linguistic patterns of oppositions: male/female (as these terms currently signify); dominant/submissive; active/passive; nature/civilization; order/chaos; matriarchal/patriarchal. If rigidly defined sex differences have been constructed around fear of the other, we need to think about ways of transcending a polarity that has only brought us all pain.

Notes

1. See works by Kate Millet, Linda Nochlin, Molly Haskell, articles in the few issues of *Women in Film* (1972–1975), and articles in *Screen* and *Screen Education* throughout the 1970s. For a summary of early developments across the arts, see Lucy Arbuthnot's Ph.D. diss., New York University, 1982.
2. See especially work by Christian Metz, Jean-Louis Comolli, Raymond Bellour, Roland Barthes, and essays in *Cahiers du Cinema* in France; in England, the work by Stephen Heath, Colin McCabe, Paul Willémen, and others in *Screen* and elsewhere.
3. See especially the work of Claire Johnston, Pam Cook, and Laura Mulvey from England, and subsequent work by the *Camera Obscura* group.
4. Christine Gledhill, "Recent Developments in Feminist Film Criticism," *Quarterly Review of Film Studies* 3, no. 4 (1978): 458–93; E. Ann Kaplan, "Aspects of British Feminist Film Criticism," *Jump Cut*, nos. 12–13 (December 1976): 52–56; and Kaplan, "Integrating Marxist and Psychoanalytic Concepts in Feminist Film Criticism," *Millenium Film Journal* (April 1980): 8–17.
5. Jacques Lacan, "The Mirror Phase as Formative of the Function of the 'I' " (1949), in *New Left Review* 51 (September/October 1968): 71–77. See also essays on Lacan in Anthony Wilden, *System and Structure: Essays in Communication and Exchange* (London: Tavistock Publications, 1972).
6. For a background to semiological concepts, see work by Roland Barthes, Julia Kristeva, and Umberto Eco among others. Terence Hawkes, *Structuralism and Semiology* (London: Methuen, 1977), and Rosalind Coward and John Ellis, *Language and Materialism* (London: Routledge and Kegan Paul, 1977) provide useful summaries of relevant material.
7. Laura Mulvey, "Visual Pleasure and Narrative Cinema," *Screen* 16, no. 3 (Autumn 1975): 6–18.
8. Karen Horney, "The Dread of Woman" (1932), in *Feminine Psychology* (New York: W. W. Norton, 1967), p. 134.
9. Ibid., p. 136.
10. For a useful discussion of fetishism, see Otto Fenichel, *The Psychoanalytic Theory of Neurosis* (New York: W. W. Norton, 1945), pp. 341–345.
11. Mulvey, "Visual Pleasure," p. 14.
12. Ibid.
13. Claire Johnston, "Woman's Cinema as Counter-Cinema," in *Notes on Women's Cinema*, ed. Claire Johnston (London: Screen Pamphlet, 1973), p. 26.
14. "Women and Film: A Discussion of Feminist Aesthetics," *New German Critique* 13 (Winter 1978): 93.

15. Lucy Arbuthnot and Gail Seneca, "Pre-Text and Text in *Gentlemen Prefer Blondes*," paper delivered at the Conference on Feminist Film Criticism, Northwestern University, November 1980.
16. See Maureen Turim, "Gentlemen Consume Blondes," in *Wideangle* 1, no. 1 (1979): 52–59. Carol Rowe also (if somewhat mockingly) shows Monroe's phallicism in her film *Grand Delusion*.
17. See the essays in *Edinburgh Magazine* 1 (1977) by Coward, Metz, Heath, and Johnston. Also the issue of *Screen* 16, no. 2 (Summer 1975), on "Psychoanalysis and Cinema," especially the piece by Metz.
18. See E. Ann Kaplan, "Feminist Approaches to History, Psychoanalysis, and Cinema in *Sigmund Freud's Dora*," *Millenium Film Journal* 7/8/9 (Fall/Winter 1979): 173–85.
19. Mary-Anne Doane, "The Woman's Film: Possession and Address," paper delivered at the Conference on Cinema History, Asilomar, Monterey, May 1981, pp. 3–8.
20. Nancy Friday, *My Secret Garden: Women's Sexual Fantasies* (New York: Pocket Books, 1981).
21. Unpublished transcript of a discussion, organized by Julia LeSage, at the Conference on Feminist Criticism, Northwestern University, November 1980. See also for discussion of dominance-submission patterns, Pat Califa, "Feminism and Sadomasochism," *Heresies* 12, pp. 32ff.
22. Nancy Friday, *Men in Love* (New York: Dell, 1980).
23. Mulvey, "Visual Pleasure," pp. 12–13.
24. Julia Kristeva, "La femme ce n'est jamais ça," trans. Marilyn A. August, in *New French Feminisms*, ed. E. Marks and I. de Courtivron (Amherst: University of Massachusetts Press, 1980), p. 37.
25. Sandy Flitterman and Judith Barry, "Textual Strategies: The Politics of Art-Making," *Screen* 2, no. 3 (Summer 1980): 37.
26. Ibid., p. 36.
27. Terry Eagleton, "Aesthetics and Politics," *New Left Review* (1978).
28. "Women and Representation: A Discussion with Laura Mulvey" (collective project by Jane Clarke, Sue Clayton, Joanna Clelland, Rosie Elliott, and Mandy Merck), *Wedge* (London) 2 (Spring 1979): 49.
29. Nancy Chodorow, "Psychodynamics of the Family," in *The Reproduction of Mothering* (Berkeley: University of California Press, 1978), pp. 191–209.
30. "*Riddles of the Sphinx*: A Film by Laura Mulvey and Peter Wollen; Script," *Screen* 18, no. 2 (Summer 1977): 62.
31. Jacquelyn Suter and Sandy Flitterman, "Textual Riddles: Woman as Enigma or Site of Social Meanings? An Interview with Laura Mulvey," *Discourse* 1, no. 1 (Fall 1979): 107.
32. Dinnerstein, *The Mermaid and the Minotaur* (New York: Harper and Row, 1976) and Chodorow, *The Reproduction of Mothering*.
33. See, for example, films by Laura Mulvey and Peter Wollen, Michelle Citron, Marjorie Keller, and Helke Sander.
34. Kristeva, "Les Chinoises à 'contre-courant,'" *New French Feminisms*, p. 240.

Study Questions

1. How has feminist film criticism changed as a consequence of the work by Lacan and others?
2. How has the Freudian concept of voyeurism been used to explain what women (in film) represent? In Laura Mulvey's view, how does the voyeurism manifest itself in the types of looks or gazes involved in cinema?
3. In what way has the phenomenon of fetishism operated in the cinema?
4. In what ways have the growing use of psychoanalytic and semiological approaches to cinema polarized feminist film criticism?
5. In what two ways might a feminist critic view *Gentlemen Prefer Blondes*?
6. Kaplan indicates that pleasure (in film viewing) is an important issue, one often over-looked by feminists. Why does she say this? How does she think psychoanalysis can help us understand women's pleasure in being objectified?
7. Why does Kaplan believe that dominance/submission patterns are apparently a crucial part of sexuality in a capitalist system?
8. What does Kaplan think that the films of the present time showing "women as liberated" really tell us about dominance and masculinity? How does "the gaze" figure in respect to those films?
9. In Kaplan's view, how has much feminist art criticism failed in the attempt to create a true female discourse? How have some feminist film critics begun to face the challenge?
10. Why, from the point of view of psychoanalytic theory, is there more possibility for women than men to change themselves? In what ways might women invent new symbolic roles?

Dancing Through the Minefield:
Some Observations on the Theory, Practice,
and Politics of a Feminist Literary Criticism

Annette Kolodny

Had anyone the prescience [in 1968] to pose the question of defining a "feminist" literary criticism, she might have been told, in the wake of Mary Ellmann's *Thinking About Women*,[1] that it involved exposing the sexual stereotyping of women in both our literature and our literary criticism and, as well, demonstrating the inadequacy of established critical schools and methods to deal fairly or sensitively with works written by women. In broad outline, such a prediction would have stood well the test of time, and, in fact, Ellmann's book continues to be widely read and to point us in useful directions. What could not have been anticipated in 1968, however, was the catalyzing force of an ideology that, for many of us, helped to bridge the gap between the world as we found it and the world as we wanted it to be. For those of us who studied literature, a previously unspoken sense of exclusion from authorship, and a painfully personal distress at discovering whores, bitches, muses, and heroines dead in childbirth where we had once hoped to discover ourselves, could—for the first time—begin to be understood as more than "a set of disconnected, unrealized private emotions."[2] With a renewed courage to make public our otherwise private discontents, what had once been "felt individually as personal insecurity" came at last to be "viewed collectively as structural inconsistency"[3] within the very disciplines we studied. Following unflinchingly the full implications of Ellmann's percipient observations, and emboldened by the liberating energy of feminist ideology—in all its various forms and guises—feminist criticism very quickly moved beyond merely "expos[ing] sexism in one work of literature after another,"[4] and promised, instead, that we might at last "begin to record new choices in a new literary history."[5] So powerful was that impulse that we experienced it, along with Adrienne Rich, as much "more than a chapter in cultural history": it became, rather, "an act of survival."[6] What was at stake was not so much literature or criticism as such, but the historical, social, and ethical consequences of women's participation in, or exclusion from, either enterprise.

The pace of inquiry [since the late sixties] has been fast and furious—especially after Kate Millett's 1970 analysis of the sexual politics of literature[7] added a note of urgency to what had earlier been Ellmann's sardonic anger—while the diversity of that inquiry easily outstripped all efforts to define feminist literary criticism as either a coherent system or a unified set of methodologies. Under its wide umbrella, everything has been thrown into question: our established canons, our aesthetic criteria, our interpretative strategies, our reading habits, and, most of all, ourselves as critics and as teachers. To delineate its full scope would require nothing less than a book—a book that would be outdated even as it was being composed. For the sake of brevity, therefore, let me attempt only a summary outline.

Perhaps the most obvious success of this new scholarship has been the return to circulation of previously lost or otherwise ignored works by women writers. Following fast upon the initial success of the Feminist Press in reissuing gems such as Rebecca Harding Davis's

From *Feminist Studies* 6, No. 1 (Spring 1980). Copyright © 1979 by Annette Kolodny. Reprinted by permission of Annette Kolodny.

1861 novella, *Life in the Iron Mills*, and Charlotte Perkins Gilman's 1892 *The Yellow Wallpaper*, published in 1972 and 1973, respectively,[8] commercial trade and reprint houses vied with one another in the reprinting of anthologies of lost texts and, in some cases, in the reprinting of whole series. For those of us in American literature especially, the phenomenon promised a radical reshaping of our concepts of literary history and, at the very least, a new chapter in understanding the development of women's literary traditions. So commercially successful were these reprintings, and so attuned were the reprint houses to the political attitudes of the audiences for which they were offered, that many of us found ourselves wooed to compose critical introductions, which would find in the pages of nineteenth-century domestic and sentimental fictions, some signs of either muted rebellions or overt radicalism, in anticipation of the current wave of "new feminism." In rereading with our students these previously lost works, we inevitably raised perplexing questions as to the reasons for their disappearance from the canons of "major works," and we worried over the aesthetic and critical criteria by which they had been accorded diminished status.

This increased availability of works by women writers led, of course, to an increased interest in what elements, if any, might comprise some sort of unity or connection among them. The possibility that women had developed either a unique, or at least a related tradition of their own, especially intrigued those of us who specialized in one national literature or another, or in historical periods. Nina Baym's *Woman's Fiction: A Guide to Novels by and about Women in America, 1820–1870*[9] demonstrates the Americanists' penchant for examining what were once the "best sellers" of their day, the ranks of the popular fiction writers, among which women took a dominant place throughout the nineteenth century, while the feminist studies of British literature emphasized instead the wealth of women writers who have been regarded as worthy of canonization. Not so much building upon one another's work as clarifying, successively, the parameters of the questions to be posed, Sydney Janet Kaplan, Ellen Moers, Patricia Meyer Spacks, and Elaine Showalter, among many others, concentrated their energies on delineating an internally consistent "body of work" by women that might stand as a female countertradition. For Kaplan, in 1975, this entailed examining women writers' various attempts to portray feminine consciousness and self-consciousness, not as a psychological category, but as a stylistic or rhetorical device.[10] That same year, arguing essentially that literature publicizes the private, Spacks placed her consideration of a "female imagination" within social and historical frames, to conclude that, "for readily discernible historical reasons women have characteristically concerned themselves with matters more or less peripheral to male concerns," and she attributed to this fact an inevitable difference in the literary emphases and subject matters of female and male writers.[11] The next year, Moers's *Literary Women: The Great Writers* focused on the pathways of literary influence that linked the English novel in the hands of women.[12] And, finally, in 1977, Showalter took up the matter of a "female literary tradition in the English novel from the generation of the Brontes to the present day" by arguing that, because women in general constitute a kind of "subculture within the framework of a larger society," the work of women writers, in particular, would thereby demonstrate a unity of "values, conventions, experiences, and behaviors impinging on each individual" as she found her sources of "self-expression relative to a dominant [and, by implication, male] society."[13]

At the same time that women writers were being reconsidered and reread, male writers were similarly subjected to a new feminist scrutiny. The continuing result—to put years of difficult analysis into a single sentence—has been nothing less than an acute attentiveness to the ways in which certain power relations—usually those in which males wield various forms of influence over females—are inscribed in the texts (both literary and critical), that we have inherited, not merely as subject matter, but as the unquestioned, often unacknowledged *given* of the culture. Even more important than the new interpretations of individual texts are the probings into the consequences (for women) of the conventions that inform those texts. For example, in surveying selected nineteenth- and early twentieth-century British novels which employ what she calls "the two suitors convention," Jean E. Kennard sought to understand why and how the structural demands of the convention, even in the hands of women writers, inevitably work to imply "the inferiority and necessary subordination of women." Her 1978 study, *Victims of Convention*, points out that the symbolic nature of the marriage which conventionally concludes such novels "indicates the adjustment of the protagonist to society's values, a condition which is equated with her maturity." Kennard's concern, however, is with the fact that the structural demands of the form too often sacrifice precisely those "virtues of independence and individuality," or, in other words, the very "qualities we have been invited to admire in" the heroines.[14] Kennard appropriately cautions us against drawing from her work any simplistically reductive thesis about the mimetic relations between art and life. Yet her approach nonetheless suggests that what is important about a fiction is not whether it ends in a death or a marriage, but what the symbolic demands of that particular conventional ending imply about the values and beliefs of the world that engendered it.

Her work thus participates in a growing emphasis in feminist literary study on the fact of literature as a social institution, embedded not only within its own literary traditions, but also within the particular physical and mental artifacts of the society from which it comes. Adumbrating Millett's 1970 decision to anchor her "literary reflections" to a preceding analysis of the historical, social, and economic contexts of sexual politics,[15] [subsequent] work—most notably Lillian Robinson's—begins with the premise that the process of artistic creation "consists not of ghostly happenings in the head but of a matching of the states and processes of symbolic models against the states and processes of the wider world."[16] The power relations inscribed in the form of conventions within our literary inheritance, these critics argue, reify the encodings of those same power relations in the culture at large. And the critical examination of rhetorical codes becomes, in their hands, the pursuit of ideological codes, because both embody either value systems or the dialectic of competition between value systems. More often than not, these critics also insist upon examining not only the mirroring of life in art, but also the normative impact of art on life. Addressing herself to the popular art available to working women, for example, Robinson is interested in understanding not only "the forms it uses," but, more importantly, "the myths it creates, the influence it exerts." "The way art helps people to order, interpret, mythologize, or dispose of their own experience," she declares, may be "complex and often ambiguous, but it is not impossible to define."[17]

Whether its focus be upon the material or the imaginative contexts of literary invention; single texts or entire canons; the relations between authors, genres, or historical circumstances; lost authors or well-known names, the variety and diversity of all feminist literary criticism finally coheres in its stance of almost defensive rereading. What Adrienne Rich had earlier called "re-vision," that is, "the act of looking back, of seeing with fresh eyes, of entering an old text from a new critical direction,"[18] took on a more actively self-protective coloration in 1978, when Judith Fetterley called upon the woman reader to learn to "resist" the sexist designs a text might make upon her—asking her to identify against herself, so to speak, by manipulating her sympathies on behalf of male heroes, but against female shrew or bitch characters.[19] Underpinning a great deal of this critical rereading has been the not-unexpected alliance between feminist literary study and feminist studies in linguistics and language-acquisition. Tillie Olsen's common-sense observation of the danger of "perpetuating—by continued usage—entrenched, centuries-old oppressive power realities, early-on incorporated into language,"[20] has been given substantive analysis in the writings of feminists who study "language as a symbolic system closely tied to a patriarchal social structure." Taken together, their work demonstrates "the importance of language in establishing, reflecting, and maintaining an asymmetrical relationship between women and men."[21]

To consider what this implies for the fate of women who essay the craft of language is to ascertain, perhaps for the first time, the real dilemma of the poet who finds her most cherished private experience "hedged by taboos, mined with false-namings."[22] It also [explains] the dilemma of the male reader who, in opening the pages of a woman's book, finds himself entering a strange and unfamiliar world of symbolic significance. For if, as Nelly Furman insists, neither language use nor language acquisition are "gender-neutral," but are, instead, "imbued with our sex-inflected cultural values,"[23] and if, additionally, reading is a process of "sorting out the structures of signification"[24] in any text, then male readers who find themselves outside of and unfamiliar with the symbolic systems that constitute female experience in women's writings, will necessarily dismiss those systems as undecipherable, meaningless, or trivial. And male professors will find no reason to include such works in the canons of "major authors." At the same time, women writers, coming into a tradition of literary language and conventional forms already appropriated, for centuries, to the purposes of male expression, will be forced virtually to "wrestle" with that language in an effort "to remake it as a language adequate to our conceptual processes."[25] To all of this, feminists concerned with the politics of language and style have been acutely attentive. "Language conceals an invincible adversary," observes French critic Helene Cixous, "because it's the language of men and their grammar."[26] But equally insistent, as in the work of Sandra M. Gilbert and Susan Gubar, has been the understanding of the need for *all* readers—male and female alike—to learn to penetrate the otherwise unfamiliar universes of symbolic action that comprise women's writings, past and present.[27]

To have attempted so many difficult questions and to have accomplished so much—even acknowledging the inevitable false starts, overlapping, and repetition—in so short a time, should certainly have secured feminist literary criticism an honored berth on that ongoing intellectual journey which we loosely term in academia, "critical analysis." Instead of being welcomed onto the train, however, we've been forced to negotiate a minefield. The very energy and diversity of our enterprise have rendered us vulnerable to attack on the grounds that we lack both definition and coherence; while our particular attentiveness to the ways in which literature encodes and disseminates cultural value systems calls down upon us imprecations echoing those heaped upon the Marxist critics of an earlier generation. If we are scholars dedicated to rediscovering a lost body of writings by women, then our finds are questioned on aesthetic grounds. And if we are critics, determined to practice revisionist readings, it is claimed that our focus is too narrow, and our results are only distortions or, worse still, polemical misreadings.

The very vehemence of the outcry, coupled with our total dismissal in some quarters, suggests not our deficiencies, however, but the potential magnitude of our challenge. For what we are asking be scrutinized are nothing less than shared cultural assumptions so deeply rooted and so long ingrained that, for the most part, our critical colleagues have ceased to recognize them as such. In other words, what is really being bewailed in the claims that we distort texts or threaten the disappearance of the great Western literary tradition itself is not so much the disappearance of either text or tradition but, instead, the eclipse of that particular *form* of the text, and that particular *shape* of the canon, which previously reified male readers' sense of power and significance in the world. Analogously, by asking whether, as readers, we ought to be "really satisfied by the marriage of Dorothea Brooke to Will Ladislaw? of Shirley Keelder to Louis Moore?" or whether, as Kennard suggests, we must reckon with the ways in which "the qualities we have been invited to admire in these heroines [have] been sacrificed to structural neatness,"[28] is to raise difficult and profoundly perplexing questions about the ethical implications of our otherwise unquestioned aesthetic pleasures. It is, after all, an imposition of high order to ask the viewer to attend to Ophelia's sufferings in a scene where, before, he'd always so comfortably kept his eye fixed firmly on Hamlet. To understand all this, then, as the real nature of the challenge we have offered and, in consequence, as the motivation for the often overt hostility we've aroused, should help us learn to negotiate the minefield, if not with grace, then with at least a clearer comprehension of its underlying patterns.

The ways in which objections to our work are usually posed, of course, serve to obscure their deeper motivations. But this may, in part, be due to our own reticence at taking full responsibility for the truly radicalizing premises that lie at the theoretical core of all we have so far accomplished. It may be time, therefore, to redirect discussion, forcing our adversaries to deal with the substantive issues and pushing ourselves into a clearer articulation of what, in fact, we are about. Up until now, I fear, we have only piecemeal dealt with the difficulties inherent in challenging the authority of established canons and then justifying the excellence of women's traditions, sometimes in accord with standards to which they have no intrinsic relation.

At the very point at which we must perforce enter the discourse—that is, claiming excellence or importance for our "finds"—all discussion has already, we discover, long ago been closed. "If Kate Chopin were *really* worth reading," an Oxford-trained colleague once assured me, "she'd have lasted—like Shakespeare"; and he then proceeded to vote against the English department's crediting a women's studies seminar I was offering in American women writers. The canon, for him, conferred excellence; Chopin's exclusion demonstrated only her lesser worth. As far as he was concerned, I could no more justify giving English department credit for the study of Chopin than I could dare publicly to question Shakespeare's genius. Through hindsight, I've now come to view that discussion as not only having posed fruitless oppositions, but also as having entirely evaded the much more profound problem lurking just beneath the surface of our disagreement. That is, that the fact of canonization puts any work beyond questions of establishing its merit and, instead, invites students to offer only increasingly more ingenious readings and interpretations, the purpose of which is to validate the greatness already imputed by canonization.

Had I only understood it for what it was then, into this circular and self-serving set of assumptions I might have interjected some statement of my right to question why *any* text is revered and my need to know what it tells us about "how we live, how we have been living, how we have been led to imagine ourselves, [and] how our language has trapped as well as liberated us."[29] The very fact of our critical training within the strictures imposed by an established canon of major works and authors, however, repeatedly deflects us from such questions. Instead, we find ourselves endlessly responding to the *riposte* that the overwhelmingly male presence among canonical authors was only an accident of history—and never intentionally sexist—coupled with claims to the "obvious" aesthetic merit of those canonized texts. It is, as I say, a fruitless exchange, serving more to obscure than to expose the territory being protected and dragging us, again and again, through the minefield.

It is my contention that current hostilities might be transformed into a true dialogue with our critics if we at last made explicit what appear, to this observer, to constitute the three crucial propositions to which our special interests inevitably give rise. They are, moreover, propositions which, if handled with care and intelligence, could breathe new life into now moribund areas of our profession: (1) Literary history (and with that, the historicity of literature) is a fiction; (2) insofar as we are taught how to read, what we engage are not texts but paradigms; and, finally, (3) that since the grounds upon which we assign aesthetic value to texts are never infallible, unchangeable, or universal, we must reexamine not only our aesthetics but, as well, the inherent biases and assumptions informing the critical methods which (in part) shape our aesthetic responses. For the sake of brevity, I won't attempt to offer the full arguments for each but, rather, only sufficient elaboration to demonstrate what I see as their intrinsic relation to the potential scope of and present challenge implied by feminist literary study.

1. *Literary history (and, with that, the historicity of literature) is a fiction.* To begin with, an established canon functions as a model by which to chart the continuities and discontinuities, as well as the influences upon and the interconnections between works, genres, and authors.

That model we tend to forget, however, is of our own making. It will take a very different shape, and explain its inclusions and exclusions in very different ways, if the reigning critical ideology believes that new literary forms result from some kind of ongoing internal dialectic within preexisting styles and traditions or if, by contrast, the ideology declares that literary change is dependent upon societal development and thereby determined by upheavals in the social and economic organization of the culture at large. Indeed, whenever in the previous century of English and American literary scholarship one alternative replaced the other, we saw dramatic alterations in canonical "wisdom."

This suggests, then, that our sense of a "literary history" and, by extension, our confidence in a "historical" canon, is rooted not so much in any definitive understanding of the past, as it is in our need to call up and utilize the past on behalf of a better understanding of the present. Thus, to paraphrase David Couzens Hoy, it becomes "necessary to point out that the understanding of art and literature is such an essential aspect of the present's self-understanding that this self-understanding conditions what even gets taken" as comprising that artistic and literary past. To quote Hoy fully, "this continual reinterpretation of the past goes hand in hand with the continual reinterpretation by the present of itself."[30] In our own time, uncertain as to which, if any, model truly accounts for our canonical choices or accurately explains literary history, and pressured further by the feminists' call for some justification of the criteria by which women's writings were largely excluded from both that canon and history, we suffer what Harold Bloom has called "a remarkable dimming" of "our mutual sense of canonical standards."[31]

Into this apparent impasse, feminist literary theorists implicitly introduce the observation that our choices and evaluations of current literature have the effect either of solidifying or of reshaping our sense of the past. The authority of any established canon, after all, is reified by our perception that current work seems to grow, almost inevitably, out of it (even in opposition or rebellion), and is called into question when what we read appears to have little or no relation to what we recognize as coming before. So, were the larger critical community to begin to seriously attend to the recent outpouring of fine literature by women, this would surely be accompanied by a concomitant researching of the past, by literary historians, in order to account for the present phenomenon. In that process, literary history would itself be altered: works by seventeenth-, eighteenth-, or nineteenth-century women, to which we had not previously attended, might be given new importance as "precursors" or as prior influences upon present-day authors; while selected male writers might also be granted new prominence as figures whom the women today, or even yesterday, needed to reject. I am arguing, in other words, that the choices we make in the present inevitably alter our sense of the past that led to them.

Related to this is the feminist challenge to that patently mendacious critical fallacy that we read the "classics" in order to reconstruct the past "the way it really was," and that we read Shakespeare and Milton in order to apprehend the meanings that they intended. Short of time machines or miraculous resurrections, there is simply no way to know, precisely or surely, what "really was," what Homer intended when he sang, or Milton when he dictated. Critics more acute than I have already pointed up the impossibility of grounding a reading in the imputation of authorial intention because the further removed the author is from us, so too must be her or his systems of knowledge and belief, points of view, and structures of vision (artistic and otherwise). (I omit here the difficulty of finally either proving or disproving the imputation of intentionality because, inescapably, the only appropriate authority is unavailable: deceased.) What we have really come to mean when we speak of competence in reading historical texts, therefore, is the ability to recognize literary conventions which have survived through time—so as to remain operational in the mind of the reader—and, where these are lacking, the ability to translate (or perhaps transform?) the text's ciphers into more current and recognizable shapes. But we never really reconstruct the past in its own terms. What we gain when we read the ''classics,'' then, is neither Homer's Greece nor George Eliot's England *as they knew it* but, rather, an approximation of an already fictively imputed past made available, through our interpretive strategies, for present concerns. Only by understanding this can we put to rest that recurrent delusion that the ''continuing relevance'' of the classics serves as ''testimony to perennial features of human experience.''[32] The only ''perennial feature'' to which our ability to read and reread texts written in previous centuries testifies is our inventiveness—in the sense that all of literary history is a fiction which we daily re-create as we reread it. What distinguishes feminists in this regard is their desire to alter and extend what we take as historically relevant from out of that vast storehouse of our literary inheritance and, further, feminists' recognition of the storehouse for what it really is: a resource for remodeling our literary history, past, present, and future.

2. *Insofar as we are taught how to read, what we engage are not texts but paradigms.* To pursue the logical consequences of the first proposition leads, however uncomfortably, to the conclusion that we appropriate meaning from a text according to what we need (or desire) or, in other words, according to the critical assumptions or predispositions (conscious or not) that we bring to it. And we appropriate different meanings, or report different gleanings, at different times—even from the same text—according to our changed assumptions, circumstances, and requirements. This, in essence, constitutes the heart of the second proposition. For insofar as literature is itself a social institution, so, too, reading is a highly socialized—or learned—activity. What makes it so exciting, of course, is that it can be constantly relearned and refined, so as to provide either an individual or an entire reading community, over time, with infinite variations of the same text. It *can* provide that, but, I must add, too often it does not. Frequently our reading habits become fixed, so that each successive reading experience functions, in effect, normatively, with one particular kind of novel stylizing our expectations of those to follow, the stylistic devices of any favorite author (or group of authors) alerting us to the presence or absence of those devices in the works of others, and so on. ''Once one has read his first poem,'' Murray Krieger has observed, ''he turns to his second and to the others that will follow thereafter with an increasing series of preconceptions about the sort of activity in which he is indulging. In matters of literary experience, as in other experiences,'' Krieger concludes, ''one is a virgin but once.''[33]

For most readers, this is a fairly unconscious process, and not unnaturally, what we are taught to read well and with pleasure, when we are young, predisposes us to certain specific kinds of adult reading tastes. For the professional literary critic, the process may be no different, but it is at least more conscious. Graduate schools, at their best, are training grounds for competing interpretive paradigms or reading techniques: affective stylistics, structuralism, and semiotic analysis, to name only a few of the more recent entries. The delight we learn to take in the mastery of these interpretive strategies is then often mistakenly construed as our delight in reading specific texts, especially in the case of works that would otherwise be unavailable or even offensive to us. In my own graduate career, for example, with superb teachers to guide me, I learned to take great pleasure in *Paradise Lost*, even though as both a Jew and a feminist, I can subscribe neither to its theology nor to its hierarchy of sexual valuation. If, within its own terms (as I have been taught to understand them), the text manipulates my sensibilities and moves me to pleasure—as I will affirm it does—then, at least in part, that must be because, in spite of my real-world alienation from many of its basic tenets, I have been able to enter that text through interpretive strategies which allow me to displace less comfortable observations with others to which I have been taught pleasurably to attend. Though some of my teachers may have called this process ''learning to read the text properly,'' I have now come to see it as learning to effectively manipulate the critical strategies which they taught me so well. Knowing, for example, the poem's debt to epic conventions, I am able to discover in it echoes and reworkings of both lines and situations from Virgil and Homer; placing it within the ongoing Christian debate between Good and Evil, I comprehend both the philosophic and the stylistic significance of Satan's ornate rhetoric as compared to God's majestic simplicity in Book III. But, in each case, an interpretative model, already assumed, had guided my discovery of the evidence for it.

When we consider the implications of these observations for the processes of canon formation and for the assignment of aesthetic value, we find ourselves locked in a chicken-and-egg dilemma, unable easily to distinguish as primary the importance of *what* we read as opposed to *how* we have learned to read it. For, simply put, we read well, and with pleasure, what we already know how to read; and what we know how to read is to a large extent dependent upon what we have already read (works from which we've developed our expectations and learned our interpretive strategies). What we then choose to read—and, by extension, teach and thereby "canonize"—usually follows upon our previous reading. Radical breaks are tiring, demanding, uncomfortable, and sometimes wholly beyond our comprehension.

Though the argument is not usually couched in precisely these terms, a considerable segment of the most recent feminist rereadings of women writers allows the conclusion that, where those authors have dropped out of sight, the reason may be due not to any lack of merit in the work but, instead, to an incapacity of predominantly male readers to properly interpret and appreciate women's texts—due, in large part, to a lack of prior acquaintance. The fictions which women compose about the worlds they inhabit may owe a debt to prior, influential works by other women or, simply enough, to the daily experience of the writer herself or, more usually, to some combination of the two. The reader coming upon such fiction, with knowledge of neither its informing literary traditions nor its real-world contexts, will thereby find himself hard-pressed, though he may recognize the words on the page, to competently decipher its intended meanings. And this is what makes the studies by Spacks, Moers, Showalter, Gilbert and Gubar, and others so crucial. For, by attempting to delineate the connections and interrelations that make for a female literary tradition, they provide us invaluable aids for recognizing and understanding the unique literary traditions and sex-related contexts out of which women write.

The (usually male) reader who, both by experience and by reading, has never made acquaintance with those contexts—historically, the lying-in room, the parlor, the nursery, the kitchen, the laundry, and so on—will necessarily lack the capacity to fully interpret the dialogue or action embedded therein; for, as every good novelist knows, the meaning of any character's action or statement is inescapably a function of the specific situation in which it is embedded. Virginia Woolf therefore quite properly anticipated the male reader's disposition to write off what he could not understand, abandoning women's writings as offering "not merely a difference of view, but a view that is weak, or trivial, or sentimental because it differs from his own." In her 1929 essay on "Women and Fiction," Woolf grappled most obviously with the ways in which male writers and male subject matter had already preempted the language of literature. Yet she was also tacitly commenting on the problem of (male) audience and conventional reading expectations when she speculated that the woman writer might well "find that she is perpetually wishing to alter the established values [in literature]—to make serious what appears insignificant to a man, and trivial what is to him important."[34] "The 'competence' necessary for understanding [a] literary message . . . depends upon a great number of codices," after all; as Cesare Segre has pointed out, to be competent, a reader must either share or at least be familiar with, "in addition to the code language . . . the codes of custom, of society, and of conceptions of the world"[35] (what Woolf meant by "values"). Males ignorant of women's "values" or conceptions of the world will necessarily, thereby, be poor readers of works that in any sense recapitulate their codes.

The problem is further exacerbated when the language of the literary text is largely dependent upon figuration. For it can be argued, as Ted Cohen has shown, that while "in general, and with some obvious qualifications . . . all literal use of language is accessible to all whose language it is . . . figurative use can be inaccessible to all but those who share information about one another's knowledge, beliefs, intentions, and attitudes.''[36] There was nothing accidental, for example, in Charlotte Perkins Gilman's decision to situate the progressive mental breakdown and increasing incapacity of the protagonist of *The Yellow Wallpaper* in an upstairs room that had once served as a nursery (with barred windows, no less). But the reader unacquainted with the ways in which women traditionally inhabited a household might not have taken the initial description of the setting as semantically relevant; and the progressive infantilization of the adult protagonist would thereby lose some of its symbolic implications. Analogously, the contemporary poet who declares, along with Adrienne Rich, the need for ''a whole new poetry beginning here''is acknowledging that the materials available for symbolization and figuration from women's contexts will necessarily differ from those that men have traditionally utilized:

> Vision begins to happen in such a life
> as if a woman quietly walked away
> from the argument and jargon in a room
> and sitting down in the kitchen, began turning in her lap
> bits of yarn, calico and velvet scraps, . . .
>
> pulling the tenets of a life together
> with no mere will to mastery,
> only care for the many-lived, unending
> forms in which she finds herself.[37]

What, then, is the fate of the woman writer whose competent reading community is composed only of members of her own sex? And what, then, the response of the male critic who, on first looking into Virginia Woolf or Doris Lessing, finds all of the interpretative strategies at his command inadequate to a full and pleasurable deciphering of their pages? Historically, the result has been the diminished status of women's products and their consequent absence from major canons. Nowadays, however, by pointing out that the act of ''interpreting language is no more sexually neutral than language use or the language system itself,'' feminist students of language, like Nelly Furman, help us better understand the crucial linkage between our gender and our interpretive, or reading, strategies. Insisting upon ''the contribution of the . . . reader [in] the active attribution of significance to formal signifiers,''[38] Furman and others promise to shake us all—female and male alike—out of our canonized and conventional aesthetic assumptions.

    3. *Since the grounds upon which we assign aesthetic value to texts are never infallible, unchangeable, or universal, we must re-examine not only our aesthetics but, as well, the inherent biases and assumptions informing the critical methods which (in part) shape our aesthetic responses.* I am, on the one hand, arguing that men will be better readers, or appreciators, of women's books when they have read more of them (as women have always been taught to become astute readers of men's texts). On the other hand, it will be noted, the emphasis of my remarks shifts the act of critical judgment from assigning aesthetic valuations to texts and directs it, instead, to ascertaining the adequacy of any interpretive paradigm to a full reading of both female and male writing. My third proposition—and, I admit, perhaps the most controversial—thus calls into question that recurrent tendency in criticism to establish norms for the evaluation of literary works when we might better serve the cause of literature by developing standards for evaluating the adequacy of our critical methods. This does not mean that I wish to discard aesthetic valuation. The choice, as I see it, is not between retaining or discarding aesthetic values; rather, the choice is between having some awareness of what constitutes (at least in part) the bases of our aesthetic responses and going without such an awareness. For it is my view that insofar as aesthetic responsiveness continues to be an integral aspect of our human response system—in part spontaneous, in part learned and educated—we will inevitably develop theories to help explain, formalize, or even initiate those responses.

In challenging the adequacy of received critical opinion or the imputed excellence of established canons, feminist literary critics are essentially seeking to discover how aesthetic value is assigned in the first place, where it resides (in the text or in the reader), and, most importantly, what validity may really be claimed by our aesthetic "judgments." What ends do those judgments serve, the feminist asks; and what conceptions of the world or ideological stances do they (even if unwittingly) help to perpetuate? In so doing, she points out, among other things, that any response labeled "aesthetic" may as easily designate some immediately experienced moment or event as it may designate a species of nostalgia, a yearning for the components of a simpler past, when the world seemed known or at least understandable. Thus the value accorded an opera or a Shakespeare play may well reside in the viewer's immediate viewing pleasure, or it may reside in the play's nostalgic evocation of a once-comprehensible and ordered world. At the same time, the feminist confronts, for example, the reader who simply cannot entertain the possibility that women's worlds are symbolically rich, the reader who, like the male characters in Susan Glaspell's 1917 short story, "A Jury of Her Peers," has already assumed the innate "insignificance of kitchen things."[39] Such a reader, she knows, will prove himself unable to assign significance to fictions that attend to "kitchen things" and will, instead, judge such fictions as trivial and as aesthetically wanting. For her to take useful issue with such a reader, she must make clear that what appears to be a dispute about aesthetic merit is, in reality, a dispute about the *contexts of judgment*; and what is at issue, then, is the adequacy of the prior assumptions and reading habits brought to bear on the text. To put it bluntly: we have had enough pronouncements of aesthetic value for a time; it is now our task to evaluate the imputed norms and normative reading patterns that, in part, led to those pronouncements.

By and large, I think I've made my point. Only to clarify it do I add this coda: when feminists turn their attention to the works of male authors which have traditionally been accorded high aesthetic value and, where warranted, follow Olsen's advice that we assert our "right to say: this is surface, this falsifies reality, this degrades,"[40] such statements do not necessarily mean that we will end up with a diminished canon. To question the source of the aesthetic pleasures we've gained from reading Spenser, Shakespeare, Milton, and so on, does not imply that we must deny those pleasures. It means only that aesthetic response is once more invested with epistemological, ethical, and moral concerns. It means, in other words, that readings of *Paradise Lost* which analyze its complex hierarchal structures but fail to note the implications of gender within that hierarchy; or which insist upon the inherent (or even inspired) perfection of Milton's figurative language but fail to note the consequences, for Eve, of her specifically gender-marked weakness, which, like the flowers to which she attends, requires "propping up"; or which concentrate on the poem's thematic reworking of classical notions of martial and epic prowess into Christian (moral) heroism but fail to note that Eve is stylistically edited out of that process—all such readings, however useful, will no longer be deemed wholly adequate. The pleasures we had earlier learned to take in the poem will not be diminished thereby, but they will become part of an altered reading attentiveness.

These three propositions I believe to be at the theoretical core of most current feminist literary criticism, whether acknowledged as such or not. If I am correct in this, then that criticism represents more than a profoundly skeptical stance toward all other preexisting and contemporaneous schools and methods, and more than an impassioned demand that the variety and variability of women's literary expression be taken into full account, rather than written off as caprice and exception, the irregularity in an otherwise regular design. It represents that locus in literary study where, in unceasing effort, female self-consciousness turns in upon itself, attempting to grasp the deepest conditions of its own unique and multiplicitous realities, in the hope, eventually, of altering the very forms through which the culture perceives, expresses, and knows itself. For, if what the larger women's movement looks for in the future is a transformation of the structures of primarily male power which now order our society, then the feminist literary critic demands that we understand the ways in which those structures have been—and continue to be—reified by our literature and by our literary criticism. Thus, along with other "radical" critics and critical schools, though our focus remains the power of the word to both structure and mirror human experience, our overriding commitment is to a radical alteration—an improvement, we hope—in the nature of that experience.

What distinguishes our work from those similarly oriented "social consciousness" critiques, it is said, is its lack of systematic coherence. Pitted against, for example, psychoanalytic or Marxist readings, which owe a decisive share of their persuasiveness to their apparent internal consistency as a system, the aggregate of feminist literary criticism appears woefully deficient in system, and painfully lacking in program. It is, in fact, from all quarters, the most telling defect alleged against us, the most explosive threat in the minefield. And my own earlier observation that, as of 1976, feminist literary criticism appeared "more like a set of interchangeable strategies than any coherent school or shared goal orientation," has been taken by some as an indictment, by others as a statement of impatience. Neither was intended. I felt then, as I do now, that this would "prove both its strength *and* its weakness,"[41] in the sense that the apparent disarray would leave us vulnerable to the kind of objection I've just alluded to; while the fact of our diversity would finally place us securely where, all along, we should have been: camped out, on the far side of the minefield, with the other pluralists and pluralisms.

In our heart of hearts, of course, most critics are really structuralists (whether or not they accept the label) because what we are seeking are patterns (or structures) that can order and explain the otherwise inchoate; thus, we invent, or believe we discover, relational patternings in the texts we read which promise transcendence from difficulty and perplexity to clarity and coherence. But, as I've tried to argue in these pages, to the imputed "truth" or "accuracy" of these findings, the feminist must oppose the painfully obvious truism that what is attended to in a literary work, and hence what is reported about it, is often determined not so much by the work itself as by the critical technique or aesthetic criteria through which it is filtered or, rather, read and decoded. All the feminist is asserting, then, is her own equivalent right to liberate new (and perhaps different) significances from these same texts; and, at the same time, her right to choose which features of a text she takes as relevant because she is, after all, asking new and different questions of it. In the process, she claims neither definitiveness nor structural completeness for her different readings and reading systems, but only their usefulness in recognizing the particular achievements of woman-as-author and their applicability in conscientiously decoding woman-as-sign.

That these alternate foci of critical attentiveness will render alternate readings or interpretations of the same text—even among feminists—should be no cause for alarm. Such developments illustrate only the pluralist contention that, "in approaching a text of any complexity . . . the reader must choose to emphasize certain aspects which seem to him crucial" and that, "in fact, the variety of readings which we have for many works is a function of the selection of crucial aspects made by the variety of readers." Robert Scholes, from whom I've been quoting, goes so far as to assert that "there is no single 'right' reading for any complex literary work," and, following the Russian formalist school, he observes that "we do not speak of readings that are simply true or false, but of readings that are more or less rich, strategies that are more or less appropriate."[42] Because those who share the term "feminist" nonetheless practice a diversity of critical strategies, leading, in some cases, to quite different readings, we must acknowledge among ourselves that sister critics, "having chosen to tell a different story, may in their interpretation identify different aspects of the meanings conveyed by the same passage.''[43]

Adopting a ''pluralist'' label does not mean, however, that we cease to disagree; it means only that we entertain the possibility that different readings, even of the same text, may be differently useful, even illuminating, within different contexts of inquiry. It means, in effect, that we enter a dialectical process of examining, testing, even trying out the contexts—be they prior critical assumptions or explicitly stated ideological stances (or some combination of the two)—that led to the disparate readings. Not all will be equally acceptable to every one of us, of course, and even those prior assumptions or ideologies that are acceptable may call for further refinement and/or clarification. But, at the very least, because we will have grappled with the assumptions that led to it, we will be better able to articulate *why* we find a particular reading or interpretation adequate or inadequate. This kind of dialectical process, moreover, not only makes us more fully aware of what criticism is, and how it functions; it also gives us access to its future possibilities, making us conscious, as R. P. Blackmur put it, ''of what we have done,'' ''of what can be done next, or done again,''[44] or, I would add, of what can be done differently. To put it still another way: just because we will no longer tolerate the specifically sexist omissions and oversights of earlier critical schools and methods does not mean, that, in their stead, we must establish our own ''party line.''

In my view, our purpose is not and should not be the formulation of any single reading method or potentially procrustean set of critical procedures nor, even less, the generation of prescriptive categories for some dreamed-of nonsexist literary canon. Instead, as I see it, our task is to initiate nothing less than a playful pluralism, responsive to the possibilities of multiple critical schools and methods, but captive of none, recognizing that the many tools needed for our analysis will necessarily be largely inherited and only partly of our own making. Only by employing a plurality of methods will we protect ourselves from the temptation of so oversimplifying any text—and especially those particularly offensive to us—that we render ourselves unresponsive to what Scholes has called ''its various systems of meaning and their interaction.''[45] Any text we deem worthy of our critical attention is usually, after all, a locus of many and varied kinds of (personal, thematic, stylistic, structural, rhetorical, etc.) relationships. So, whether we tend to treat a text as a *mimesis*, in which words are taken to be re-creating or representing viable worlds; or whether we prefer to treat a text as a kind of equation of communication, in which decipherable messages are passed from writers to readers; and whether we locate meaning as inherent in the text, the act of reading, or in some collaboration between reader and text—whatever our predilection, let us not generate from it a straitjacket that limits the scope of possible analysis. Rather, let us generate an ongoing dialogue of competing potential possibilities—among feminists and, as well, between feminist and nonfeminist critics.

The difficulty of what I describe does not escape me. The very idea of pluralism seems to threaten a kind of chaos for the future of literary inquiry while, at the same time, it seems to deny the hope of establishing some basic conceptual model which can organize all data— the hope which always begins any analytical exercise. My effort here, however, has been to demonstrate the essential delusions that inform such objections: If literary inquiry has historically escaped chaos by establishing canons, then it has only substituted one mode of arbitrary action for another—and, in this case, at the expense of half the population. And if feminists openly acknowledge ourselves as pluralists, then we do not give up the search for patterns of opposition and connection—probably the basis of thinking itself; what we give up is simply the arrogance of claiming that our work is either exhaustive or definitive. (It is, after all, the identical arrogance we are asking our nonfeminist colleagues to abandon.) If this kind of pluralism appears to threaten both the present coherence of and the inherited aesthetic criteria for a canon of ''greats,'' then, as I have earlier argued, it is precisely that threat which, alone, can free us from the prejudices, the strictures, and the blind spots of the past. In feminist hands, I would add, it is less a threat than a promise.

What unites and repeatedly invigorates feminist literary criticism, then, is neither dogma nor method but, as I have indicated earlier, an acute and impassioned *attentiveness* to the ways in which primarily male structures of power are inscribed (or encoded) within our literary inheritance; the consequences of that encoding for women—as characters, as readers, and as writers; and, with that, a shared analytic *concern* for the implications of that encoding not only for a better understanding of the past, but also for an improved reordering of the present and future as well. If that *concern* identifies feminist literary criticism as one of the many academic arms of the larger women's movement, then that *attentiveness*, within the halls of academe, poses no less a challenge for change, generating, as it does, the three propositions explored here. The critical pluralism that inevitably follows upon those three propositions, however, bears little resemblance to what Robinson has called "the greatest bourgeois theme of all, the myth of pluralism, with its consequent rejection of ideological commitment as 'too simple' to embrace the (necessarily complex) truth.''[46] Only ideological commitment could have gotten us to enter the minefield, putting in jeopardy our careers and our livelihood. Only the power of ideology to transform our conceptual worlds, and the inspiration of that ideology to liberate long-suppressed energies and emotions, can account for our willingness to take on critical tasks that, in an earlier decade, would have been "abandoned in despair or apathy.''[47] The fact of differences among us proves only that, despite our shared commitments, we have nonetheless refused to shy away from complexity, preferring rather to openly disagree than to give up either intellectual honesty or hard-won insights.

Finally, I would argue, pluralism informs feminist literary inquiry not simply as a description of what already exists but, more importantly, as the only critical stance consistent with the current status of the larger women's movement. Segmented and variously focused, the different women's organizations neither espouse any single system of analysis nor, as a result, express any wholly shared, consistently articulated ideology. The ensuing loss in effective organization and political clout is a serious one, but it has not been paralyzing; in spite of our differences, we have united to *act* in areas of clear mutual concern (the push for the Equal Rights Amendment is probably the most obvious example). The trade-off, as I see it, has made possible an ongoing and educative dialectic of analysis and proferred solutions, protecting us thereby from the inviting traps of reductionism and dogma. And so long as this dialogue remains active, both our politics and our criticism will be free of dogma—but never, I hope, of feminist ideology, in all its variety. For, "whatever else ideologies may be—projections of unacknowledged fears, disguises for ulterior motives, phatic expressions of group solidarity" (and the women's movement, to date, has certainly been all of these, and more)—whatever ideologies express, they are, as Geertz astutely observes, "most distinctively, maps of problematic social reality and matrices for the creation of collective conscience." And despite the fact that "ideological advocates . . . tend as much to obscure as to clarify the true nature of the problems involved," as Geertz notes, "they at least call attention to their existence and, by polarizing issues, make continued neglect more difficult. Without Marxist attack, there would have been no labor reform; without Black Nationalists, no deliberate speed.''[48] Without Seneca Falls, I would add, no enfranchisement of women, and without "consciousness raising," no feminist literary criticism nor, even less, women's studies.

Ideology, however, only truly manifests its power by ordering the *sum* of our actions. If feminist criticism calls anything into question, it must be that dog-eared myth of intellectual neutrality. For, what I take to be the underlying spirit, or message, of any consciously ideologically premised criticism—that is, that ideas are important *because* they determine the ways we live, or want to live, in the world—is vitiated by confining those ideas to the study, the classroom, or the pages of our books. To write chapters decrying the sexual stereotyping of women in our literature, while closing our eyes to the sexual harassment of our women students and colleagues; to display Katherine Hepburn and Rosalind Russell in our courses on "The Image of the Independent Career Women in Film," while managing not to notice the paucity of female administrators on our own campus; to study the women who helped make universal enfranchisement a political reality, while keeping silent about our activist colleagues who are denied promotion or tenure; to include segments on "Women in the Labor Movement" in our American studies or women's studies courses, while remaining willfully ignorant of the department secretary fired for her efforts to organize a clerical workers' union; to glory in the delusions of "merit," "privilege," and "status" which accompany campus life in order to insulate ourselves from the millions of women who labor in poverty—all this is not merely hypocritical; it destroys both the spirit and the meaning of what we are about. It puts us, however unwittingly, in the service of those who laid the minefield in the first place. In my view, it is a fine thing for many of us, individually, to have traversed the minefield; but that happy circumstance will only prove of lasting importance if, together, we expose it for what it is (the male fear of sharing power and significance with women) and deactivate its components, so that others, after us, may literally dance through the minefield.

Notes

"Dancing Through the Minefield" was the winner of the 1979 Florence Howe Essay Contest, which is sponsored by the Women's Caucus of the Modern Language Association.

Some sections of this essay were composed during the time made available to me by a grant from the Rockefeller Foundation, for which I am most grateful.

1. Mary Ellmann, *Thinking About Women* (New York: Harcourt Brace Jovanovich, Harvest, 1968).
2. See Clifford Geertz, "Ideology as a Cultural System," in his *The Interpretation of Cultures: Selected Essays* (New York: Basic Books, 1973), p. 232.
3. Ibid., p. 204.
4. Lillian S. Robinson, "Cultural Criticism and the *Horror Vacui*," *College English* 33, no. 1 (1972); reprinted as "The Critical Task" in her *Sex, Class, and Culture* (Bloomington: Indiana University Press, 1978), p. 51.
5. Elaine Showalter, *A Literature of Their Own: British Women Novelists From Bronte to Lessing* (Princeton: Princeton University Press, 1977), p. 36.
6. Adrienne Rich, "When We Dead Awaken: Writing as Re-Vision," *College English* 34, no. 1 (October 1972); reprinted in *Adrienne Rich's Poetry*, ed. Barbara Charlesworth Gelpi and Albert Gelpi (New York: W. W. Norton Co., 1975), p. 90.
7. Kate Millett, *Sexual Politics* (Garden City, N.Y.: Doubleday and Co., 1970).
8. Rebecca Harding Davis, *Life in the Iron Mills*, originally published in *The Atlantic Monthly*, April 1861; reprinted with "A Biographical Interpretation" by Tillie Olsen (New York: Feminist Press, 1972). Charlotte Perkins Gilman, *The Yellow Wallpaper*, originally published in *The New England Magazine*, May 1892; reprinted with an Afterword by Elaine R. Hedges (New York: Feminist Press, 1973).
9. Nina Baym, *Woman's Fiction: A Guide to Novels by and about Women in America, 1820–1870* (Ithaca: Cornell University Press, 1978).
10. In her *Feminine Consciousness in the Modern British Novel* (Urbana: University of Illinois Press, 1975), p. 3, Sydney Janet Kaplan explains that she is using the term "feminine consciousness" "not simply as some general attitude of women toward their own femininity, and not as something synonymous with a particular sensibility among female writers. I am concerned with it as a literary device: a method of characterization of females in fiction."
11. Patricia Meyer Spacks, *The Female Imagination* (New York: Avon Books, 1975), p. 6.
12. Ellen Moers, *Literary Women: The Great Writers* (Garden City, N.Y.: Doubleday and Co., 1976).
13. Showalter, *A Literature of Their Own*, p. 11.
14. Jean E. Kennard, *Victims of Convention* (Hamden, Conn.: Archon Books, 1978), pp. 164, 18, 14.
15. See Millett, *Sexual Politics*, pt. 3, "The Literary Reflection," pp. 235–361.
16. The phrase is Geertz's, "Ideology as a Cultural System," p. 214.
17. Lillian Robinson, "Criticism—and Self-Criticism," *College English* 36, no. 4 (1974) and "Criticism: Who Needs It?" in *The Uses of Criticism*, ed. A. P. Foulkes (Bern and Frankfurt: Lang, 1976); both reprinted in *Sex, Class, and Culture*, pp. 67, 80.

18. Rich, "When We Dead Awaken," p. 90.
19. Judith Fetterley, *The Resisting Reader: A Feminist Approach to American Fiction* (Bloomington: Indiana University Press, 1978).
20. Tillie Olsen, *Silences* (New York: Delacorte Press/Seymour Lawrence, 1978), pp. 239–240.
21. See Cheris Kramer, Barrie Thorne, and Nancy Henley, "Perspectives on Language and Communication," Review Essay in *Signs* 3, no. 3 (Summer 1978): 646.
22. See Adrienne Rich's discussion of the difficulty in finding authentic language for her experience as a mother in her *Of Woman Born* (New York: W. W. Norton and Co., 1976), p. 15.
23. Nelly Furman, "The Study of Women and Language: Comment on Vol. 3, no. 3" in *Signs* 4, no. 1 (Autumn 1978): 184.
24. Again, my phrasing comes from Geertz, "Thick Description: Toward an Interpretive Theory of Culture," p. 9.
25. Julia Penelope Stanley and Susan W. Robbins, "Toward a Feminist Aesthetic," *Chrysalis*, no. 6 (1977): 63.
26. Helene Cixous, "The Laugh of the Medusa," trans. Keith Cohen and Paula Cohen, *Signs* 1, no. 4 (Summer 1976): 887.
27. In *The Madwoman in the Attic: The Woman Writer and the Nineteenth-Century Literary Imagination* (New Haven: Yale University Press, 1979), Sandra M. Gilbert and Susan Gubar suggest that women's writings are in some sense "palimpsestic" in that their "surface designs conceal or obscure deeper, less accessible (and less socially acceptable) levels of meaning" (p. 73). It is, in their view, an art designed "both to express and to camouflage" (p. 81).
28. Kennard, *Victims of Convention*, p. 14.
29. Rich, "When We Dead Awaken," p. 90.
30. David Couzens Hoy, "Hermeneutic Circularity, Indeterminacy, and Incommensurability," *New Literary History* 10, no. 1 (Autumn 1978): 166–67.
31. Harold Bloom, *Map of Misreading* (New York: Oxford University Press, 1975), p. 36.
32. Charles Altieri, "The Hermeneutics of Literary Indeterminacy: A Dissent from the New Orthodoxy," *New Literary History* 10, no. 1 (Autumn 1978): 90.
33. Murray Krieger, *Theory of Criticism: A Tradition and Its System* (Baltimore: The Johns Hopkins University Press, 1976), p. 6.
34. Virginia Woolf, "Women and Fiction," *Granite and Rainbow: Essays* (London: Hogarth, 1958), p. 81.
35. Cesare Segre, "Narrative Structures and Literary History," *Critical Inquiry* 3, no. 2 (Winter 1976): 272–73.
36. Ted Cohen, "Metaphor and the Cultivation of Intimacy," *Critical Inquiry* 5, no. 1 (Autumn 1978): 9.
37. From Adrienne Rich's "Transcendental Etude" in her *The Dream of a Common Language: Poems 1974–1977* (New York: W. W. Norton and Co., 1978), pp. 76–77.
38. Furman, "The Study of Women and Language," p. 184.
39. For a full discussion of the Glaspell short story which takes this problem into account, please see my "A Map for Re-Reading: Or, Gender and the Interpretation of Literary Texts," Special Issue on Narrative, *New Literary History* (1980): 451–467.
40. Olsen, *Silences*, p. 45.
41. Annette Kolodny, "Literary Criticism," Review Essay in *Signs* 2, no. 2 (Winter 1976): 420.
42. Robert Scholes, *Structuralism in Literature* (New Haven: Yale University Press, 1974), p. 144–45. These comments appear within his explication of Tzvetan Todorov's theory of reading.
43. I borrow this concise phrasing of pluralistic modesty from M. H. Abrams's "The Deconstructive Angel," *Critical Inquiry* 3, no. 3 (Spring 1977): 427. Indications of the pluralism that was to mark feminist inquiry were to be found in the diversity of essays collected by Susan Koppelman Cornillon for her early and ground-breaking anthology, *Images of Women in Fiction: Feminist Perspectives* (Bowling Green, Ohio: Bowling Green University Popular Press, 1972).
44. R. P. Blackmur, "A Burden for Critics," *The Hudson Review* 1 (1948): 171. Blackmur, of course, was referring to the way in which criticism makes us conscious of how art functions; I use his wording here because I am arguing that that same awareness must also be focused on the critical act itself. "Consciousness," he avers, "is the way we feel the critic's burden."
45. Scholes, *Structuralism in Literature*, pp. 151–52.
46. Lillian Robinson, "Dwelling in Decencies: Radical Criticism and the Feminist Perspective," *College English* 32, no. 8 (May 1971); reprinted in *Sex, Class, and Culture*, p. 11.
47. "Ideology bridges the emotional gap between things as they are and as one would have them be, thus insuring the performance of roles that might otherwise be abandoned in despair or apathy," comments Geertz in "Ideology as a Cultural System," p. 205.
48. Ibid., p. 220, 205.

Study Questions

1. According to Kolodny, what view of women authors was prevalent in the late fifties and early sixties? How did it change in the late sixties?
2. Of what did early feminist literary criticism consist?
3. What is perhaps the most obvious success of more recent feminist literary scholarship?
4. Put in a single sentence, what has been the focus since the late sixties of feminist literary analysis? Discuss some examples mentioned by Kolodny.
5. Has recent feminist literary criticism been noticed by male literary critics? Why or why not?
6. How can the hostilities between male academic literary critics and feminist literary critics be turned into a true dialogue?
7. In what sense is literary history a fiction?
8. Why does Kolodny speak of reading as engaging paradigms rather than texts?
9. In what sense should we re-examine our esthetics and even our critical method?
10. Will a feminist re-examination of the "canon" of esteemed male authors necessarily preclude a feminist from enjoying or admiring those authors?
11. In what sense does Kolodny think that feminist literary criticism is structuralist? What "obvious truism" should the feminist literary critic emphasize, and how should she employ it?

Through the Peephole: Toward a Lesbian Sensibility in Art

Arlene Raven and Ruth Iskin

The following dialogue on lesbian sensibility is based on the artwork created in the Feminist Studio Workshop at the Woman's Building, Los Angeles, * *and on our experiences in that community. Over the past several years, many women who have participated in our community have created art which manifests a lesbian sensibility. These works have been rich and various—explicit iconography of scenes from everyday lesbian lives, photographic portraits of contemporary lesbians accompanied by short interviews, videotapes exploring female outcast and outlaw roles, performances of a lesbian couple enacting their fantasy of a lesbian family, a book exploring the nature of passion among women, a shrine of the Goddess as lesbian, and a lavish modern dance performance involving 30 dancers exploring nurturance, support, and respectful, loving interactions among women in a grand-scale baroque setting. These artworks are not only about contemporary lesbian experiences; rather, they explore the entire world from a lesbian/feminist point of view, and they create a new and wholly positive imagery, vision, and imagination inspired by a lesbian perspective.*

---

*The Feminist Studio Workshop is a feminist community which conducts an intensive two-year program for women in the arts and humanities.

From *Chrysalis*, No. 4, pp. 20–31. Reprinted by permission of Arlene Raven.

In our participation at the Feminist Studio Workshop, we have observed that lesbian sensibility arises spontaneously in a community in which woman-identification is the structure and content underlying creative activity—that is, a feminist community which supports lesbianism, has as its base shared goals and values of feminism, and is de facto homosexual in the sense that it is exclusively female. In such a community women create their social relations in a new and fundamentally different way— supporting one another's work, collaborating, working collectively, forming important and complete friendships, and generally experiencing the nourishment of an extended women-identified family. For the lesbian this female community is her total environment, providing substantial support for all her activities. This new environment alters the premises under which the feminist creator labors as well as her work— such premises as for whom the work is made and why, or what messages the artist intends to convey.

The experiences women have as a matter of course in a feminist community are in direct opposition to those available to women in the antithetical environment of patriarchy. In contrast, lesbian expressions that are created in isolation often reflect the antipathy of patriarchial culture toward lesbianism. These are no less powerful or articulate statements of the lesbian experience, but the lesbian experience lived and expressed by a lesbian who is isolated in a heterosexist environment differs from that of the lesbian/feminist who is supported by a lesbian/feminist community. The support community creates a new space of freedom of thought, fantasy, and scale which allows for the creation of a lesbian art dealing with lesbianism as everything that is possible—a woman-centered world view—rather than being limited by the constrictions of a lesbian reality dictated by a patriarchal and heterosexual world.

RUTH ISKIN: In discussing lesbian sensibility in art, many questions arise: Does it exist? What is it, or what could it be? Under what conditions does it develop? How much is it related to the artist's sexual practice? What does it say about, and how does it influence, dominant culture?

ARLENE RAVEN: There are also some assertions that we can make in regard to lesbian sensibility:

Lesbianism can symbolize and express feminism. The lesbian is an exemplary symbol— the woman who takes risks, who dares to be a creator in a new territory, who does not follow rules, who declares herself the source of her artistic creation. Lesbians in the women's movement may likewise prefigure what many women would wish to become as feminists— strong, powerfully creative, and effective in the world. It is not surprising that large numbers of feminist women have made this connection and claimed themselves lesbians in the supportive context of lesbian/feminist communities.

"Lesbian sensibility" does not describe an aesthetic quality only. Lesbian sensibility is an active manifestation of the transformation of personal identity, social relations, political analysis, and creative thought which has long been among the aspirations of revolutionary thinkers. Work produced in a feminist/lesbian community has the possibility of acknowledging the radical transformation of self through revolutionary social practice.

I link a feminist world view with lesbian sensibility because I want to challenge the prevailing tendency to narrow down lesbian sensibility or identity as much as possible so that it affects as few people as possible. That narrowing is an expression of the bad feelings the culture has about lesbianism. Opening up the category by making these kinds of connections allows us to express the pride and achievement of the lesbian creator that we discover in the context of lesbian history and culture.

The new lesbian sensibility associated with feminism can develop only in a support community, not in isolation, because it is the expression of a social experience lived in community. But where do we find our communities? In consciousness-raising groups, alternative institutions, communes, and collectives, or in the informal network of female creators nationally and internationally.

RUTH: The transition we see in lesbian artists' environments is not from no context to context, but rather from a private to a public context. The 19th century painter Rosa Bonheur, for example, created a private context for herself: She shared her life with another artist, Natalie

Dara Robinson, *Censored*, mixed media

The censorship of lesbian love. But the photos progressively fly off the frame, out of the conventional framework, and away from those restrictions.—A.R.

Micas, living in the protected privacy of her chateau in the country at By on the border of the Forest of Fontainbleau, surrounded by a wide variety of animals which were the primary subject of her art; in later years the two also spent the winter months in a villa Bonheur built in Nice when Micas' health required a warmer climate.

The private rather than public context has not only been the prevailing tradition of lesbian lifestyle, for obvious reasons, but also the lot of women's culture and a tradition of women's communication in general. Quilting parties are an example of an alternative female context that existed for women's work—these groups were underground female support communities. Today, however, we are in the midst of a developing public context that has the sanction of a political movement in which lesbians are deeply involved on every level—the women's movement.

ARLENE: The important difference between the private and public contexts is that the private context you described would not spawn a lesbian sensibility which could enter the public domain intact. Sanction is also significant, however, because the context for our work is always patriarchy, and our expressions are prey to gross misinterpretation by all but the few who can choose to interpret them through lesbian history and culture. "Deviant" individuals are often crushed by an alien culture: We increase our control and power when we form communities and express our point of view through the institution of the community.

Lesbian sensibility reflects a new process, form, and content because it expresses the transformational process that takes place in a feminist community. Personal relationships—which might form the private context—happen within the community, but the important factor for work is that there is enough immediate support so that one can turn to the interface between the community and the public. Lesbian sensibility is a positive woman-identified sensibility. It communicates publicly that woman-identified lesbian images and social relations transformed in a feminist community provide a world-view free of sexism—a way of life and consciousness in an environment free of patriarchy. It is true that economically privileged women like Rosa Bonheur were also able to live their lives in relative freedom; but unlike Rosa Bonheur—who, though habitually wearing pants, kept a closet full of frilly dresses as a concession to "femininity"—women today don't have to make those kinds of compromises.

RUTH: Despite the fact that as a result of the women's movement the issue of lesbianism is much discussed, and, relatively speaking, there is now a great deal more freedom of expression for lesbians, there are still many problems we encounter when we address the subject of lesbian art or a lesbian sensibility in the visual arts.

ARLENE: There are three major problems—homophobia (fear of homosexuals), misogyny (hatred of women), and paranoia on all sides about seriously considering lesbianism as a legitimate source for creativity. There are unusual scholarly problems, but in fact they are the real issues. Usually when either of us writes about any subject, we first review the literature and find out what the main questions are. But there is almost no existing literature on the subject of lesbian art, and the scholarly problems are complicated and altered by the social implications and the response to lesbianism itself. For instance, most contemporary female artists who are lesbians would probably feel insulted if we were to talk about their work in this particular context. The societal taboos against homosexuality influence interpretations of facts and artists' works. Scholars often circumvent crucial issues in this area by interpreting facts about artists as academic rather than confronting the relevant social issues that these facts suggest. An example is Rosa Bonheur's habit of wearing male clothing, which has only been related to her going to the slaughterhouses to study anatomy and not at all to her rejection of the female role and her assertion of freedom as an artist and a lesbian.

RUTH: For the same societal reasons that art historians have distorted these issues, many women today are also apprehensive about considering a lesbian sensibility—in much the same way that women were apprehensive about being labeled "women artists" at the beginning of the women's art movement in the early 1970's. The source for this apprehension is fear that such women and their art will be devalued. It is still a taboo and in bad taste to mention that a female artist is a lesbian, although (and this is well known in art circles) some of the best artists today are lesbians.

ARLENE: Women who want appreciation and a broad interpretation for their art know that asserting that they are feminists, lesbians, or even women artists will automatically narrow the critical categories for interpretation of their work—not because art is neutral, but because woman is despised and the woman who loves women doubly despised.

RUTH: Another issue we must consider is that the sexual practice of an artist does not necessarily influence her work, although it may. An artist who is a lesbian in her sexual orientation will not necessarily manifest a lesbian or feminist sensibility in her work. On the other hand, we cannot rule out the possibility that an artist who is heterosexual, bisexual, or celibate may act and live as a strong, independent woman, and those "lesbian" feminist ideals may be apparent or dominant in her work. Can or should we say then that her work manifests a lesbian sensibility?

ARLENE: Yes, why not? Not only would we be challenging the fear associated with lesbianism, but we would keep the field of investigation open and broad and provide a large and important space for lesbian sensibility. Besides, the issue of lesbian sensibility is more complicated than the occurrence of a lesbian sexual experience in a woman's life. In beginning to explore lesbian sensibility, I would ask some basic questions:

1. What provides the source for what we see or sense as lesbian sensibility? (As opposed to what forms, colors, content we can pick out and label "lesbian.")
2. How does the lesbian creator perceive and approach her work?
3. How, if at all, are her sources and approach manifested in her work?

The only historical evidence we have for the source of a lesbian sensibility is the last major manifestation of lesbian art in the 1920's—the art of Romaine Brooks and the writing of the women in her circle. Some of the sources for her art were the space and confidence provided by the first wave of feminism, changes in attitudes toward homosexuals, and, most important, Brooks's supportive context of feminist, homosexual, and artistic communities. That she was independently wealthy was, of course, a first requisite for her ability to pursue her career at all. The portraits of lesbian contemporaries—including Natalie Barney, Renata Borgatti, and Una Troubridge—that she painted during the 1920's are unique in the history of Western art because they are the only body of work portraying lesbians as successful, talented, independent women choosing their way of life with conviction. Brooks was not the only female artist creating explicit lesbian images at this time (although she was the only visual artist). A number of her colleagues, such as Virginia Woolf, Rose O'Neill, and Natalie Barney, expressed their devotion to independence and the life of the androgynous creator through

Candace Compton and Nancy Angelo, *Nun and Deviant*, videotape, 1976.

Nancy Fried *Woman Bathing*, dough, watercolor, acrylic

Nancy Fried gives the lesbian experience and everyday scenes in the feminist community a lovely, real setting. The beauty of these works lies in their wholesomeness—a tollhouse cookie!—and in the level of caring in color, design and detail. The accessibility of her style and her material—bread dough—present this radically new content in gentle, agreeable ways. Her highly detailed bread dough reliefs *are* like cookies, or other things we make for our friends. They are creations both in and outside of the art category, because they assert their legitimacy as art and have a real function—of giving and storytelling—in the community.—A.R.

lesbian imagery. Romaine Brooks's art, appreciated by lesbians, has never been understood by art historians because her community has never been acknowledged. She didn't move in Left Bank art circles in Paris like Picasso, but in Right Bank literary circles; for that, she has traditionally been seen as isolated!

RUTH: A crucial relationship to be addressed as an aspect of a feminist lesbian sensibility is that between the artist and her work.

The traditional heterosexual relationship between the artist and his work has been replaced by a homosexual relationship between the artist and her work. We are familiar with portrayals of male artists and their female muses, models, or mistresses, such as *Raphael and La Fornarina* by Ingres, or Picasso's *Suite 347*. These works give clues to a pervasive underlying concept of artistic creation in Western art—the heterosexual love relationship between male artists and the female who inspires or symbolizes his art as the standard metaphor for the relationship of artist to art. In view of that, for a female artist to identify as creator she has to either adopt a "male" role identity or create an alternative concept with which she can identify. Instead of simply reversing the heterosexual model as an alternative, women artists have created an exclusively female relationship between the female creator and her work. For example, when we look at paintings such as Marie Laurencin's *Poet and Her Muse* or Angelica Kauffmann's self-portrait as the personification of Design listening to her muse, Music, we notice that both the artist and her muse are female. Sitting side by side, the two female figures in Kauffmann's painting are represented as equals. The relationship between the artist and her muse or her art is represented as reciprocal—it is mutual inspiration and creation. The question that I want to ask is how does such a female-female relationship—a lesbian relationship—between the artist and her art influence her artistic process and product? It is a difficult

Nancy Fried *To Arlene on Wings of Love*, dough, watercolor, acrylic

question and even trickier when we deal with abstract art. Yet, I believe we can begin to provide some speculative answers.

When we look at contemporary abstract art by women we can find that their abstract forms represent the same ideals of reciprocity, mutuality, and equality between the artists and her inspiration or art, which we clearly see in Angelica Kauffmann's figurative painting. Many contemporary feminist abstract artists express these metaphors in the content, media, and process of their art. Many of these artists have replaced the implicit heterosexual model of male (erotic) domination over women/art/materials (in the case of abstract art) with a reciprocal and harmonious relationship.* This reciprocal, equal, organically growing relationship reconciles a longstanding dichotomy between the active creator and the passive model/artwork, which

---

*For a more elaborate analysis of such an alternative female relationship to art-making, see Ruth Iskin, "Toward a Feminist Imperative: The Art of Joan Snyder," *Chrysalis*, Vol. 1; No. 1 (February 1977), especially pp. 105–107. For an analysis of the erotic heterosexual male model, see Ruth Iskin, "Sexuality and Self-Imagery in Art," *Womanspace Journal*, Vol. 1, No. 3 (Summer 1973), and Carol Duncan, "The Esthetics of Power in Modern Erotic Art," *Heresies*, Vol. 1, No. 1 (February 1977), as well as Carol Duncan, "Male Domination and Virility in 20th Century Art," *Artforum* (December 1973).

is acted upon. The artistic act as *attack* or *thrust* of active artist on canvas, for example, is replaced with an essentially *additive* act of building and integrating. The additive process is predominant in the traditional crafts and arts invented and dominated for a long time by women: pottery, basketry, quilts, lace, weaving, and embroidery. The similarity in the use of the additive process is communicated in the product. The additive process of making art is slow; the whole is created by a repetition of a small and consistent element. In the additive process the act of artistic creation is one of rhythmic repetition of the kind that one finds in rituals, rather than the singular thrust. (If one wants to scrutinize this theory of the additive process, the simplest and most obvious approach is to search for some good examples of male artists who do not subscribe to the Pygmalion and Galathea myth—the model of heterosexual love—in their underlying concept of artistic creation. Not surprisingly, one may find such cases, especially in looking at male homosexual artists. But even if we were to find heterosexual male artists whose artistic art is not at all symbolized or inspired by the Galathea myth, such isolated exceptions would not necessarily change the rule. In fact, we might learn more about the general rule by carefully studying those exceptions: What kind of historical factors, for example, could influence a fundamental change in this basic relationship?)

In the sense that the homosexual relationship replaces the heterosexual relationship as the primary metaphor for the underlying myth of art-making, the lesbian relationship as metaphor stands at the heart of feminist art and has on some level affected every feminist's work. Moreover, we must face the fact that male art traditionally has been created in a male/heterosexual environment based on a male/heterosexual model of interaction. By contrast, women's traditional arts and crafts, as well as some contemporary feminist art, have been created in a different context—one in which women provide the inspiration, assistance, collaboration, and audience for one another. All these factors influence the sensibility visible in women's art; in fact, they constitute the female muse for the female artist. After all, the idea of the muse—inspiration for one's work—is embodied in reality in one's immediate historical circumstances. The muse that inspires one's work is one's *milieu*, one's support community, and for women artists it is the community of women at its broadest, and specifically the community of feminist women in the arts and various work-oriented feminist groups. It would be an interesting line of investigation to explore whether art created by lesbian artists differs from other feminist art in terms of lesbian love used as a metaphor for art-making.

ARLENE: In order to interpret works of art in relation to any sensibility, I agree—one cannot simply look at the art activity leading directly to the product, but rather one must take into account and interpret the entire broad set of activities which are related to the act of making art. The inherent structures of women's lives are reflected in the choice of materials, the process, and the art product.

In regard to context and equality, men have always had an equalized professional peer relationship. But men's art-making comes not only out of this professional context, but also from the support system of their families. Today in the feminist community women support one another in many ways—as colleagues *and* as families and/or lovers. In this case one's lifestyle is pertinent to one's art. A woman who sees her primary association with a nuclear family may not primarily identify herself with a community of women. The sources for her art and her intended audience—the primary sources for a lesbian sensibility—may thus be different from those of women who are members of a women's support community.

ARLENE: And who is the lesbian artist making her art for? Against the background of misogyny, there will be very few female artists who will say that they are making their art for women. We are nervous about that; we want to say that we are making our art for everyone. And perhaps we are making our art for everyone. The fact is that not many men are interested in the female experience, let alone the lesbian experience, much less the revolutionary implications that we might draw from the articulation of these experiences—which may be one reason why we are making our art for one another now.

Sometimes the sources of a woman's art are hidden because the facts of her life do not really reveal the impact that various aspects of her experience had on her. Georgia O'Keeffe said that she spent 30 years in New York, but it passed like a dream. She lived there, and interacted with colleagues who should have been very influential; yet her sensibility was not tied in there but rather in some entirely different place.

RUTH: If an artist seeks support from a male audience, her art is likely to represent values that are digestible to that audience; as we know, this would not include radical feminist values at this point in history. Men and male-identified women are still very threatened by feminist content, not to mention lesbian content, and also generally by a different kind of consciousness and values than those they are accustomed to and feel secure with. An additional aspect of lesbian sensibility could mean the artistic expression of love and sexual feelings for women. Yet the concept of lesbian sensibility is much broader than a sexual relationship.

ARLENE: Yes, and therefore the expression of a lesbian sexual relationship would be an experience within the broad category of a lesbian sensibility. The basic nature of relationships in feminist, lesbian/feminist, or separatist communities (and feminist communities are separatist communities in nature even though the participants may not have separatist points of view) is a lovers' relationship in the sense of each member having the well-being of others in mind and feeling identified with others—including all the notions that we have about love apart from the sterotypes of romantic love. That is the relationship women have with one another—family love, sensuous love, companionship. We can describe a relationship of love among women which is lesbian regardless of whether or not their sexual practice is with women.

RUTH: Given our tradition of feminism, this description could be what we all want sisterhood to be.

ARLENE: That's what we mean by sisterhood, particularly if we imagine a time when being a sister or a friend or collaborator may not necessarily have meant being nonsexual or nonsensual; that was before the Fall. Feminist community is both a before-the-Fall and a post-patriarchy concept. In our feminist community the concept of the lover in its fullest sense has been reclaimed. But here it is love transformed in work, which is what I believe Rita Mae Brown intended in saying, "An army of lovers cannot fail."

Study Questions

1. What does Raven mean by "lesbian sensibility"? How is it related to a feminist world view?
2. What are some problems about or obstacles to the study of lesbian art?
3. Why are some artists apprehensive about being labeled "lesbian artists"?
4. What is the significance of the art of Romaine Brooks for the basic questions about lesbian sensibility?
5. How is lesbian sensibility different from male heterosexual sensibility regarding the relation between the artist and the artist's work?
6. How might the associations (of family, friendship, and love) of the artist's private life affect the style of his or her art? How do lesbian associations affect lesbian art?

8

Feminist Ethics

Ethics is the philosophy of morality and, with esthetics, makes up the centrality of the philosophy called axiology (value theory). Ethics is concerned with questions of right and wrong conduct, the nature of moral obligation, and the notion of the good life. The core question, posed by Aristotle, is "What kind of life shall I best lead?"

Feminist ethics starts, in one sense, with the realization that Aristotle's famous question in "male-stream" philosophy does not—or has not—applied to women. As de Beauvoir says, women have been objects and not subjects. By that she means that women have been denied the right to be full moral agents; they have not been those who "choose a life."

Feminist ethics, therefore, now poses the question: Is it good for women? (This is a recurring question in the feminist manifestoes of the second wave.) In this way, feminist theorists seek the re-visioning of moral philosophy. The feminist imperative is to challenge the hegemony of male ethical theory and to insist on "the woman's voice."

Feminist ethics, then, arises directly out of women's lives and women's issues. (These had been given only passing consideration in patriarchal value theory.) For example, we see much concern with reproductive rights, since these reflect the centrality of women's demand for control over "our bodies, ourselves."

The moral issues concerning abortion have been, accordingly, the subject of significant analysis by feminist philosophers. Paradigmatic of female sexual autonomy, abortion issues affect all women, directly or indirectly. Judith Thomson's argument for abortion was one of the first systematic analyses. Her discussion focuses on the question of what one person owes another and the kind of use one person can make of another's body. This changes the locus of concern from the personhood of the fetus to the notion of rights to one's person.

In response to Thomson's article, Mary Anne Warren contends that personhood is indeed the central issue in the question of abortion, but she returns the discussion to the personhood of the fetus. She introduces the notion of the moral community as the basis for legitimating personhood and for validating judgments of the kind involved in decisions affecting abortion.

Another feminist response to Thomson's argument is offered in the essay by Kathryn Addelson. She compares Thomson's approach to the issue with the approach of a feminist abortion clinic. Addelson believes that this comparison yields a contrast between two ways of organizing morality. The first, the dominant tradition, uses concepts and categories such as ''rights,'' ''property,'' and ''contract,'' while the second, or feminist mode, asks, ''What leads to a meaningful life for women?'' Addelson believes that Thomson's argument is characteristic of the dominant viewpoint rather than of the viewpoint of women, who are socially subordinate. Her discussion leads to an exploration of moral concepts and their significance for a feminist re-visioning.

In the last set of writings, feminist thinking is brought to bear on the central question of feminist ethical theory: Is there a women's morality? And, if so, what are its main features? In other words, what is a feminist ethics? According to Hester Eisenstein, and as the selections show, it is ''a woman-centered analysis which presupposes the centrality, normality, and value of women's experience and women's culture.''

Women's moral development may be different from men's, according to Carol Gilligan, and traditional moral theory does not account for this difference. Gilligan believes that women's morality centers on the notions of caring and responsibility. She contrasts this ethics with the ''standard'' ethics of rights and rules that men have formulated. Like Addelson, Gilligan believes that women's moral development must be recognized and women's morality validated by our ethical theory.

All women, whether as mothers or daughters, are involved in maternal practices, according to Sara Ruddick. She argues for the rational configuration of what she calls ''maternal thinking,'' which arises out of these practices. She also sees maternal thinking as expressive of ethical modes such as the notion of ''attentive love,'' and she proposes that these modes transform morality in general.

Adrienne Rich speaks to the notion of women-bonding and to the kind of morality that will support this goal. She says that in the past women were not expected to have honor: ''they lied and were lied to.'' Rich exhorts women to create a climate of honor among themselves, and she states that it is especially important for women to take truthfulness to each other seriously if they are to have a life together.

In the final essay, Joyce Trebilcot considers women's morality in terms of a re-visioning of certain central concepts such as ''nurturance,'' ''strength,'' and ''lesbian.'' Trebilcot believes that women are redefining themselves, and she shows how a feminist naming of ourselves is called for in order to create ourselves as moral subjects.

A Defense of Abortion

Judith Jarvis Thomson

Most opposition to abortion relies on the premise that the fetus is a human being, a person, from the moment of conception. The premise is argued for, but, as I think, not well. Take, for example, the most common argument. We are asked to notice that the development of a human being from conception through birth into childhood is continuous; then it is said that to draw a line, to choose a point in this development and say "before this point the thing is not a person, after this point it is a person" is to make an arbitrary choice, a choice for which in the nature of things no good reason can be given. It is concluded that the fetus is, or anyway that we had better say it is, a person from the moment of conception. But this conclusion does not follow. Similar things might be said about the development of an acorn into an oak tree, and it does not follow that acorns are oak trees, or that we had better say they are. Arguments of this form are sometimes called "slippery slope arguments"—the phrase is perhaps self-explanatory—and it is dismaying that opponents of abortion rely on them so heavily and uncritically.

I am inclined to agree, however, that the prospects for "drawing a line" in the development of the fetus look dim. I am inclined to think also that we shall probably have to agree that the fetus has already become a human person well before birth. Indeed, it comes as a surprise when one first learns how early in its life it begins to acquire human characteristics. By the tenth week, for example, it already has a face, arms and legs, fingers and toes; it has internal organs, and brain activity is detectable.[1] On the other hand, I think that the premise is false, that the fetus is not a person from the moment of conception. A newly fertilized ovum, a newly implanted clump of cells, is no more a person than an acorn is an oak tree. But I shall not discuss any of this. For it seems to me to be of great interest to ask what happens if, for the sake of argument, we allow the premise. How, precisely, are we supposed to get from there to the conclusion that abortion is morally impermissible? Opponents of abortion commonly spend most of their time establishing that the fetus is a person, and hardly any time explaining the step from there to the impermissibility of abortion. Perhaps they think the step too simple and obvious to require much comment. Or perhaps instead they are simply being economical in argument. Many of those who defend abortion rely on the premise that the fetus is not a person, but only a bit of tissue that will become a person at birth; and why pay out more arguments than you have to? Whatever the explanation, I suggest that the step they take is neither easy nor obvious, that it calls for closer examination than it is commonly given, and that when we do give it this closer examination we shall feel inclined to reject it.

I propose, then, that we grant that the fetus is a person from the moment of conception. How does the argument go from here? Something like this, I take it. Every person has a right to life. So the fetus has a right to life. No doubt the mother has a right to decide what shall happen in and to her body; everyone would grant that. But surely a person's right to life is stronger and more stringent than the mother's right to decide what happens in and

From *Philosophy & Public Affairs,* Vol. 1, No. 1 (Fall 1971), pp. 47–66. Copyright © 1971 by Princeton University Press. Reprinted by permission of Princeton University Press.

to her body, and so outweighs it. So the fetus may not be killed; an abortion may not be performed.

It sounds plausible. But now let me ask you to imagine this. You wake up in the morning and find yourself back to back in bed with an unconscious violinist. A famous unconscious violinist. He has been found to have a fatal kidney ailment and the Society of Music Lovers has canvassed all the available medical records and found that you alone have the right blood type to help. They have therefore kidnapped you, and last night the violinist's circulatory system was plugged into yours, so that your kidneys can be used to extract poisons from his blood as well as your own. The director of the hospital now tells you, "Look, we're sorry the Society of Music Lovers did this to you—we would never have permitted it if we had known. But still, they did it, and the violinist now is plugged into you. To unplug you would be to kill him. But never mind, it's only for nine months. By then he will have recovered from his ailment, and can safely be unplugged from you." Is it morally incumbent on you to accede to this situation? No doubt it would be very nice of you if you did, a great kindness. But do you *have* to accede to it? What if it were not nine months, but nine years? Or longer still? What if the director of the hospital says, "Tough luck, I agree, but you've now got to stay in bed, with the violinist plugged into you, for the rest of your life. Because remember this. All persons have a right to life, and violinists are persons. Granted you have a right to decide what happens in and to your body, but a person's right to life outweighs your right to decide what happens in and to your body. So you cannot ever be unplugged from him." I imagine you would regard this as outrageous, which suggests that something really is wrong with that plausible-sounding argument I mentioned a moment ago.

In this case, of course, you were kidnapped; you didn't volunteer for the operation that plugged the violinist into your kidneys. Can those who oppose abortion on the ground I mentioned make an exception for a pregnancy due to rape? Certainly. They can say that persons have a right to life only if they didn't come into existence because of rape; or they can say that all persons have a right to life, but that some have less of a right to life than others, in particular, that those who came into existence because of rape have less. But these statements have a rather unpleasant sound. Surely the question of whether you have a right to life at all, or how much of it you have, shouldn't turn on the question of whether or not you are the product of a rape. And in fact the people who oppose abortion on the ground I mentioned do not make this distinction, and hence do not make an exception in case of rape.

Nor do they make an exception for a case in which the mother has to spend the nine months of her pregnancy in bed. They would agree that would be a great pity, and hard on the mother; but all the same, all persons have a right to life, the fetus is a person, and so on. I suspect, in fact, that they would not make an exception for a case in which, miraculously enough, the pregnancy went on for nine years, or even the rest of the mother's life.

Some won't even make an exception for a case in which continuation of the pregnancy is likely to shorten the mother's life; they regard abortion as impermissible even to save the mother's life. Such cases are nowadays very rare, and many opponents of abortion do not accept this extreme view. All the same, it is a good place to begin: a number of points of interest come out in respect to it.

1. Let us call the view that abortion is impermissible even to save the mother's life "the extreme view." I want to suggest first that it does not issue from the argument I mentioned earlier without the addition of some fairly powerful premises. Suppose a woman has become pregnant, and now learns that she has a cardiac condition such that she will die if she carries the baby to term. What may be done for her? The fetus, being a person, has a right to life, but as the mother is a person too, so has she a right to life. Presumably they have an equal right to life. How is it supposed to come out that an abortion may not be performed? If mother and child have an equal right to life, shouldn't we perhaps flip a coin?

Or should we add to the mother's right to life her right to decide what happens in and to her body, which everybody seems to be ready to grant—the sum of her rights now outweighing the fetus' right to life?

The most familiar argument here is the following. We are told that performing the abortion would be directly killing[2] the child, whereas doing nothing would not be killing the mother, but only letting her die. Moreover, in killing the child, one would be killing an innocent person, for the child has committed no crime, and is not aiming at his mother's death. And then there are a variety of ways in which this might be continued. (1) But as directly killing an innocent person is always and absolutely impermissible, an abortion may not be performed. Or, (2) as directly killing an innocent person is murder, and murder is always and absolutely impermissible, an abortion may not be performed.[3] Or, (3) as one's duty to refrain from directly killing an innocent person is more stringent than one's duty to keep a person from dying, an abortion may not be performed. Or, (4) if one's only options are directly killing an innocent person or letting a person die, one must prefer letting the person die, and thus an abortion may not be performed.[4]

Some people seem to have thought that these are not further premises which must be added if the conclusion is to be reached, but that they follow from the very fact that an innocent person has a right to life.[5] But this seems to me to be a mistake, and perhaps the simplest way to show this is to bring out that while we must certainly grant that innocent persons have a right to life, the theses in (1) through (4) are all false. Take (2), for example. If directly killing an innocent person is murder, and thus is impermissible, then the mother's directly killing the innocent person inside her is murder, and thus is impermissible. But it cannot seriously be thought to be murder if the mother performs an abortion on herself to save her life. It cannot seriously be said that she *must* refrain, that she *must* sit passively by and wait for her death. Let us look again at the case of you and the violinist. There you are, in bed with the violinist, and the director of the hospital says to you, "It's all most distressing, and I deeply sympathize, but you see this is putting an additional strain on your kidneys, and you'll be dead within the month. But you *have* to stay where you are all the same. Because unplugging you would be directly killing an innocent violinist, and that's murder, and that's impermissible." If anything in the world is true, it is that you do not commit murder, you do not do what is impermissible, if you reach around to your back and unplug yourself from that violinist to save your life.

The main focus of attention in writings on abortion has been on what a third party may or may not do in answer to a request from a woman for an abortion. This is in a way understandable. Things being as they are, there isn't much a woman can safely do to abort herself. So the question asked is what a third party may do, and what the mother may do, if it is mentioned at all, is deduced, almost as an afterthought, from what it is concluded that third parties may do. But it seems to me that to treat the matter in this way is to refuse to grant to the mother that very status of person which is so firmly insisted on for the fetus. For we cannot simply read off what a person may do from what a third party may do. Suppose you find yourself trapped in a tiny house with a growing child. I mean a very tiny house, and a rapidly growing child—you are already up against the wall of the house and in a few minutes you'll be crushed to death. The child on the other hand won't be crushed to death; if nothing is done to stop him from growing he'll be hurt, but in the end he'll simply burst open the house and walk out a free man. Now I could well understand it if a bystander were to say, "There's nothing we can do for you. We cannot choose between your life and his, we cannot be the ones to decide who is to live, we cannot intervene." But it cannot be concluded that you too can do nothing, that you cannot attack it to save your life. However innocent the child may be, you do not have to wait passively while it crushes you to death. Perhaps a pregnant woman is vaguely felt to have the status of house, to which we don't allow the right of self-defense. But if the woman houses the child, it should be remembered that she is a person who houses it.

I should perhaps stop to say explicitly that I am not claiming that people have a right to do anything whatever to save their lives. I think, rather, that there are drastic limits to the right of self-defense. If someone threatens you with death unless you torture someone else to death, I think you have not the right, even to save your life, to do so. But the case under consideration here is very different. In our case there are only two people involved, one whose life is threatened, and one who threatens it. Both are innocent: the one who is threatened is not threatened because of any fault, the one who threatens does not threaten because of any fault. For this reason we may feel that we bystanders cannot intervene. But the person threatened can.

In sum, a woman surely can defend her life against the threat to it posed by the unborn child, even if doing so involves its death. And this shows not merely that the theses in (1) through (4) are false; it shows also that the extreme view of abortion is false, and so we need not canvass any other possible ways of arriving at it from the argument I mentioned at the outset.

2. The extreme view could of course be weakened to say that while abortion is permissible to save the mother's life, it may not be performed by a third party, but only by the mother herself. But this cannot be right either. For what we have to keep in mind is that the mother and the unborn child are not like two tenants in a small house which has, by an unfortunate mistake, been rented to both: the mother *owns* the house. The fact that she does adds to the offensiveness of deducing that the mother can do nothing from the supposition that third parties can do nothing. But it does more than this: it casts a bright light on the supposition that third parties can do nothing. Certainly it lets us see that a third party who says "I cannot choose between you" is fooling himself if he thinks this is impartiality. If Jones has found and fastened on a certain coat, which he needs to keep him from freezing, but which Smith also needs to keep him from freezing, then it is not impartiality that says "I cannot choose between you" when Smith owns the coat. Women have said again and again "This body is *my* body!" and they have reason to feel angry, reason to feel that it has been like shouting into the wind. Smith, after all, is hardly likely to bless us if we say to him, "Of course it's your coat, anybody would grant that it is. But no one may choose between you and Jones who is to have it."

We should really ask what it is that says "no one may choose" in the face of the fact that the body that houses the child is the mother's body. It may be simply a failure to appreciate this fact. But it may be something more interesting, namely the sense that one has a right to refuse to lay hands on people, even where it would be just and fair to do so, even where justice seems to require that somebody do so. Thus justice might call for somebody to get Smith's coat back from Jones, and yet you have a right to refuse to be the one to lay hands on Jones, a right to refuse to do physical violence to him. This, I think, must be granted. But then what should be said is not "no one may choose," but only "*I* cannot choose," and indeed not even this, but "*I* will not *act*," leaving it open that somebody else can or should, and in particular that anyone in a position of authority, with the job of securing people's rights, both can and should. So this is no difficulty. I have not been arguing that any given third party must accede to the mother's request that he perform an abortion to save her life, but only that he may.

I suppose that in some views of human life the mother's body is only on loan to her, the loan not being one which gives her any prior claim to it. One who held this view might well think it impartiality to say "I cannot choose." But I shall simply ignore this possibility. My own view is that if a human being has any just, prior claim to anything at all, he has a just, prior claim to his own body. And perhaps this needn't be argued for here anyway, since, as I mentioned, the arguments against abortion we are looking at do grant that the woman has a right to decide what happens in and to her body.

But although they do grant it, I have tried to show that they do not take seriously what is done in granting it. I suggest the same thing will reappear even more clearly when we turn away from cases in which the mother's life is at stake, and attend, as I propose we now do, to the vastly more common cases in which a woman wants an abortion for some less weighty reason than preserving her own life.

3. Where the mother's life is not at stake, the argument I mentioned at the outset seems to have a much stronger pull. "Everyone has a right to life, so the unborn person has a right to life." And isn't the child's right to life weightier than anything other than the mother's own right to life, which she might put forward as ground for an abortion?

This argument treats the right to life as if it were unproblematic. It is not, and this seems to me to be precisely the source of the mistake.

For we should now, at long last, ask what it comes to, to have a right to life. In some views having a right to life includes having a right to be given at least the bare minimum one needs for continued life. But suppose that what in fact *is* the bare minimum a man needs for continued life is something he has no right at all to be given? If I am sick unto death, and the only thing that will save my life is the touch of Henry Fonda's cool hand on my fevered brow, then all the same, I have no right to be given the touch of Henry Fonda's cool hand on my fevered brow. It would be frightfully nice of him to fly in from the West Coast to provide it. It would be less nice, though no doubt well meant, if my friends flew out to the West Coast and carried Henry Fonda back with them. But I have no right at all against anybody that he should do this for me. Or again, to return to the story I told earlier, the fact that for continued life that violinist needs the continued use of your kidneys does not establish that he has a right to be given the continued use of your kidneys. He certainly has no right against you that *you* should give him continued use of your kidneys. For nobody has any right to use your kidneys unless you give him such a right; and nobody has the right against you that you shall give him this right—if you do allow him to go on using your kidneys, this is a kindness on your part, and not something he can claim from you as his due. Nor has he any right against anybody else that *they* should give him continued use of your kidneys. Certainly he had no right against the Society of Music Lovers that they should plug him into you in the first place. And if you now start to unplug yourself, having learned that you will otherwise have to spend nine years in bed with him, there is nobody in the world who must try to prevent you, in order to see to it that he is given something he has a right to be given.

Some people are rather stricter about the right to life. In their view, it does not include the right to be given anything, but amounts to, and only to, the right not to be killed by anybody. But here a related difficulty arises. If everybody is to refrain from killing that violinist, then everybody must refrain from doing a great many different sorts of things. Everybody must refrain from slitting his throat, everybody must refrain from shooting him—and everybody must refrain from unplugging you from him. But does he have a right against everybody that they shall refrain from unplugging you from him? To refrain from doing this is to allow him to continue to use your kidneys. It could be argued that he has a right against us that *we* should allow him to continue to use your kidneys. That is, while he had no right against us that we should give him the use of your kidneys, it might be argued that he anyway has a right against us that we shall not now intervene and deprive him of the use of your kidneys. I shall come back to third-party interventions later. But certainly the violinist has no right against you that *you* shall allow him to continue to use your kidneys. As I said, if you do allow him to use them, it is a kindness on your part, and not something you owe him.

The difficulty I point to here is not peculiar to the right to life. It reappears in connection with all the other natural rights; and it is something which an adequate account of rights must deal with. For present purposes it is enough just to draw attention to it. But I would stress that I am not arguing that people do not have a right to life—quite to the contrary, it seems to me that the primary control we must place on the acceptability of an account of rights is that it should turn out in that account to be a truth that all persons have a right to life. I am arguing only that having a right to life does not guarantee having either a right to be given the use of or a right to be allowed continued use of another person's body—even if one needs it for life itself. So the right to life will not serve the opponents of abortion in the very simple and clear way in which they seem to have thought it would.

4. There is another way to bring out the difficulty. In the most ordinary sort of case, to deprive someone of what he has a right to is to treat him unjustly. Suppose a boy and his small brother are jointly given a box of chocolates for Christmas. If the older boy takes the box and refuses to give his brother any of the chocolates, he is unjust to him, for the brother has been given a right to half of them. But suppose that, having learned that otherwise it means nine years in bed with that violinist, you unplug yourself from him. You surely are not being unjust to him, for you gave him no right to use your kidneys, and no one else can have given him any such right. But we have to notice that in unplugging yourself, you are killing him; and violinists, like everybody else, have a right to life, and thus in the view we were considering just now, the right not to be killed. So here you do what he supposedly has a right you shall not do, but you do not act unjustly to him in doing it.

The emendation which may be made at this point is this: the right to life consists not in the right not to be killed, but rather in the right not to be killed unjustly. This runs a risk of circularity, but never mind: it would enable us to square the fact that the violinist has a right to life with the fact that you do not act unjustly toward him in unplugging yourself, thereby killing him. For if you do not kill him unjustly, you do not violate his right to life, and so it is no wonder you do him no injustice.

But if this emendation is accepted, the gap in the argument against abortion stares us plainly in the face: it is by no means enough to show that the fetus is a person, and to remind us that all persons have a right to life—we need to be shown also that killing the fetus violates its right to life, i.e., that abortion is unjust killing. And is it?

I suppose we may take it as a datum that in a case of pregnancy due to rape the mother has not given the unborn person a right to the use of her body for food and shelter. Indeed, in what pregnancy could it be supposed that the mother has given the unborn person such a right? It is not as if there were unborn persons drifting about the world, to whom a woman who wants a child says "I invite you in."

But it might be argued that there are other ways one can have acquired a right to the use of another person's body than by having been invited to use it by that person. Suppose a woman voluntarily indulges in intercourse, knowing of the chance it will issue in pregnancy, and then she does become pregnant; is she not in part responsible for the presence, in fact the very existence, of the unborn person inside her? No doubt she did not invite it in. But doesn't her partial responsibility for its being there itself give it a right to the use of her body?[6] If so, then her aborting it would be more like the boy's taking away the chocolates, and less like your unplugging yourself from the violinist—doing so would be depriving it of what it does have a right to, and thus would be doing it an injustice.

And then, too, it might be asked whether or not she can kill it even to save her own life: If she voluntarily called it into existence, how can she now kill it, even in self-defense?

The first thing to be said about this is that it is something new. Opponents of abortion have been so concerned to make out the independence of the fetus, in order to establish that it has a right to life, just as its mother does, that they have tended to overlook the possible support they might gain from making out that the fetus is *dependent* on the mother, in order to establish that she has a special kind of responsibility for it, a responsibility that gives it rights against her which are not possessed by any independent person—such as an ailing violinist who is a stranger to her.

On the other hand, this argument would give the unborn person a right to its mother's body only if her pregnancy resulted from a voluntary act, undertaken in full knowledge of the chance a pregnancy might result from it. It would leave out entirely the unborn person whose existence is due to rape. Pending the availability of some further argument, then, we would be left with the conclusion that unborn persons whose existence is due to rape have no right to the use of their mothers' bodies, and thus that aborting them is not depriving them of anything they have a right to and hence is not unjust killing.

And we should also notice that it is not at all plain that this argument really does go even as far as it purports to. For there are cases and cases, and the details make a difference. If the room is stuffy, and I therefore open a window to air it, and a burglar climbs in, it would be absurd to say, "Ah, now he can stay, she's given him a right to the use of her house—for she is partially responsible for his presence there, having voluntarily done what enabled him to get in, in full knowledge that there are such things as burglars, and that burglars burgle." It would be still more absurd to say this if I had had bars installed outside my windows, precisely to prevent burglars from getting in, and a burglar got in only because of a defect in the bars. It remains equally absurd if we imagine it is not a burglar who climbs in, but an innocent person who blunders or falls in. Again, suppose it were like this: people-seeds drift about in the air like pollen, and if you open your windows, one may drift in and take root in your carpets or upholstery. You don't want children, so you fix up your windows with fine mesh screens, the very best you can buy. As can happen, however, and on very, very rare occasions does happen, one of the screens is defective; and a seed drifts in and takes root. Does the person-plant who now develops have a right to the use of your house? Surely not—despite the fact that you voluntarily opened your windows, you knowingly kept carpets and upholstered furniture, and you knew that screens were sometimes defective. Someone may argue that you are responsible for its rooting, that it does have a right to your house, because after all you *could* have lived out your life with bare floors and furniture, or with sealed windows and doors. But this won't do—for by the same token anyone can avoid a pregnancy due to rape by having a hysterectomy, or anyway by never leaving home without a (reliable!) army.

It seems to me that the argument we are looking at can establish at most that there are *some* cases in which the unborn person has a right to the use of its mother's body, and therefore *some* cases in which abortion is unjust killing. There is room for much discussion and argument as to precisely which, if any. But I think we should sidestep this issue and leave it open, for at any rate the argument certainly does not establish that all abortion is unjust killing.

5. There is room for yet another argument here, however. We surely must all grant that there may be cases in which it would be morally indecent to detach a person from your body at the cost of his life. Suppose you learn that what the violinist needs is not nine years of your life, but only one hour: all you need do to save his life is to spend one hour in that bed with him. Suppose also that letting him use your kidneys for that one hour would not affect your health in the slightest. Admittedly you were kidnapped. Admittedly you did not give anyone permission to plug him into you. Nevertheless it seems to me plain you *ought* to allow him to use your kidneys for that hour—it would be indecent to refuse.

Again, suppose pregnancy lasted only an hour, and constituted no threat to life or health. And suppose that a woman becomes pregnant as a result of rape. Admittedly she did not voluntarily do anything to bring about the existence of a child. Admittedly she did nothing at all which would give the unborn person a right to the use of her body. All the same it might well be said, as in the newly emended violinist story, that she *ought* to allow it to remain for that hour—that it would be indecent of her to refuse.

Now some people are inclined to use the term "right" in such a way that it follows from the fact that you ought to allow a person to use your body for the hour he needs, that he has a right to use your body for the hour he needs, even though he has not been given that right by any person or act. They may say that it follows also that if you refuse, you act unjustly toward him. This use of the term is perhaps so common that it cannot be called wrong; nevertheless it seems to me to be an unfortunate loosening of what we would do better to keep a tight rein on. Suppose that box of chocolates I mentioned earlier has not been given to both boys jointly, but was given only to the older boy. There he sits, stolidly eating his way through the box, his small brother watching enviously. Here we are likely to say "You ought not to be so mean. You ought to give your brother some of those chocolates." My own view is that it just does not follow from the truth of this that the brother has any right to any of the chocolates. If the boy refuses to give his brother any, he is greedy, stingy, callous—but not unjust. I suppose that the people I have in mind will say it does follow that the brother has a right to some of the chocolates, and thus that the boy does act unjustly if he refuses to give his brother any. But the effect of saying this is to obscure what we should keep distinct, namely the difference between the boy's refusal in this case and the boy's refusal in the earlier case, in which the box was given to both boys jointly, and in which the small brother thus had what was from any point of view clear title to half.

A further objection to so using the term "right" that from the fact that A ought to do a thing for B, it follows that B has a right against A that A do it for him, is that it is going to make the question of whether or not a man has a right to a thing turn on how easy it is to provide him with it; and this seems not merely unfortunate, but morally unacceptable. Take the case of Henry Fonda again. I said earlier that I had no right to the touch of his cool hand on my fevered brow, even though I needed it to save my life. I said it would be frightfully nice of him to fly in from the West Coast to provide me with it, but that I had no right against him that he should do so. But suppose he isn't on the West Coast. Suppose he has only to walk across the room, place a hand briefly on my brow—and lo, my life is saved. Then surely he ought to do it, it would be indecent to refuse. Is it to be said "Ah, well, it follows that in this case she has a right to the touch of his hand on her brow, and so it would be an injustice in him to refuse"? So that I have a right to it when it is easy for him to provide it, though no right when it's hard? It's rather a shocking idea that anyone's rights should fade away and disappear as it gets harder and harder to accord them to him.

So my own view is that even though you ought to let the violinist use your kidneys for the one hour he needs, we should not conclude that he has a right to do so—we should say that if you refuse, you are, like the boy who owns all the chocolates and will give none away, self-centered and callous, indecent in fact, but not unjust. And similarly, that even supposing a case in which a woman pregnant due to rape ought to allow the unborn person to use her body for the hour he needs, we should not conclude that he has a right to do so; we should conclude that she is self-centered, callous, indecent, but not unjust, if she refuses. The complaints are no less grave; they are just different. However, there is no need to insist on this point. If anyone does wish to deduce "he has a right" from "you ought," then all the same he must surely grant that there are cases in which it is not morally required of you that you allow that violinist to use your kidneys, and in which he does not have a right to use them, and in which you do not do him an injustice if you refuse. And so also for mother and unborn child. Except in such cases as the unborn person has a right to demand it—and we were leaving open the possibility that there may be such cases—nobody is morally *required* to make large sacrifices, of health, of all other interests and concerns, of all other duties and commitments, for nine years, or even for nine months, in order to keep another person alive.

6. We have in fact to distinguish between two kinds of Samaritan: the Good Samaritan and what we might call the Minimally Decent Samaritan. The story of the Good Samaritan, you will remember, goes like this:

> A certain man went down from Jerusalem to Jericho, and fell among thieves, which stripped him of his raiment, and wounded him, and departed, leaving him half dead.
>
> And by chance there came down a certain priest that way; and when he saw him, he passed by on the other side.
>
> And likewise a Levite, when he was at the place, came and looked on him, and passed by on the other side.
>
> But a certain Samaritan, as he journeyed, came where he was; and when he saw him he had compassion on him.
>
> And went to him, and bound up his wounds, pouring in oil and wine, and set him on his own beast, and brought him to an inn, and took care of him.
>
> And on the morrow, when he departed, he took out two pence, and gave them to the host, and said unto him, "Take care of him; and whatsoever thou spendest more, when I come again, I will repay thee."
>
> *(Luke 10:30–35)*

The Good Samaritan went out of his way, at some cost to himself, to help one in need of it. We are not told what the options were, that is, whether or not the priest and the Levite could have helped by doing less than the Good Samaritan did, but assuming they could have, then the fact they did nothing at all shows they were not even Minimally Decent Samaritans, not because they were not Samaritans, but because they were not even minimally decent.

These things are a matter of degree, of course, but there is a difference, and it comes out perhaps most clearly in the story of Kitty Genovese, who, as you will remember, was murdered while thirty-eight people watched or listened, and did nothing at all to help her. A Good Samaritan would have rushed out to give direct assistance against the murderer. Or perhaps we had better allow that it would have been a Splendid Samaritan who did this, on the ground that it would have involved a risk of death for himself. But the thirty-eight not only did not do this, they did not even trouble to pick up a phone to call the police. Minimally Decent Samaritanism would call for doing at least that, and their not having done it was monstrous.

After telling the story of the Good Samaritan, Jesus said "Go, and do thou likewise." Perhaps he meant that we are morally required to act as the Good Samaritan did. Perhaps he was urging people to do more than is morally required of them. At all events it seems plain that it was not morally required of any of the thirty-eight that he rush out to give direct assistance at the risk of his own life, and that it is not morally required of anyone that he give long stretches of his life—nine years or nine months—to sustaining the life of a person who has no special right (we were leaving open the possibility of this) to demand it.

Indeed, with one rather striking class of exceptions, no one in any country in the world is *legally* required to do anywhere near as much as this for anyone else. The class of exceptions is obvious. My main concern here is not the state of the law in respect to abortion, but it is worth drawing attention to the fact that in no state in this country is any man compelled by law to be even a Minimally Decent Samaritan to any person; there is no law under which charges could be brought against the thirty-eight who stood by while Kitty Genovese died. By contrast, in most states in this country women are compelled by law to be not merely

Minimally Decent Samaritans, but Good Samaritans to unborn persons inside them. This doesn't by itself settle anything one way or the other, because it may well be argued that there should be laws in this country—as there are in many European countries—compelling at least Minimally Decent Samaritanism.[7] But it does show that there is a gross injustice in the existing state of the law. And it shows also that the groups currently working against liberalization of abortion laws, in fact working toward having it declared unconstitutional for a state to permit abortion, had better start working for the adoption of Good Samaritan laws generally, or earn the charge that they are acting in bad faith.

I should think, myself, that Minimally Decent Samaritan laws would be one thing, Good Samaritan laws quite another, and in fact highly improper. But we are not here concerned with the law. What we should ask is not whether anybody should be compelled by law to be a Good Samaritan, but whether we must accede to a situation in which somebody is being compelled—by nature, perhaps—to be a Good Samaritan. We have, in other words, to look now at third-party interventions. I have been arguing that no person is morally required to make large sacrifices to sustain the life of another who has no right to demand them, and this even where the sacrifices do not include life itself; we are not morally required to be Good Samaritans or anyway Very Good Samaritans to one another. But what if a man cannot extricate himself from such a situation? What if he appeals to us to extricate him? It seems to me plain that there are cases in which we can, cases in which a Good Samaritan would extricate him. There you are, you were kidnapped, and nine years in bed with that violinist lie ahead of you. You have your own life to lead. You are sorry, but you simply cannot see giving up so much of your life to the sustaining of his. You cannot extricate yourself, and ask us to do so. I should have thought that—in light of his having no right to the use of your body—it was obvious that we do not have to accede to your being forced to give up so much. We can do what you ask. There is no injustice to the violinist in our doing so.

7. Following the lead of the opponents of abortion, I have throughout been speaking of the fetus merely as a person, and what I have been asking is whether or not the argument we began with, which proceeds only from the fetus' being a person, really does establish its conclusion. I have argued that it does not.

But of course there are arguments and arguments, and it may be said that I have simply fastened on the wrong one. It may be said that what is important is not merely the fact that the fetus is a person, but that it is a person for whom the woman has a special kind of responsibility issuing from the fact that she is its mother. And it might be argued that all my analogies are therefore irrelevant—for you do not have that special kind of responsibility for that violinist, Henry Fonda does not have that special kind of responsibility for me. And our attention might be drawn to the fact that men and women both *are* compelled by law to provide support for their children.

I have in effect dealt (briefly) with this argument in section 4 above; but a (still briefer) recapitulation now may be in order. Surely we do not have any such "special responsibility" for a person unless we have assumed it, explicitly or implicitly. If a set of parents do not try to prevent pregnancy, do not obtain an abortion, and then at the time of birth of the child do not put it out for adoption, but rather take it home with them, then they have assumed responsibility for it, they have given it rights, and they cannot *now* withdraw support from it at the cost of its life because they now find it difficult to go on providing for it. But if they have taken all reasonable precautions against having a child, they do not simply by virtue of their biological relationship to the child who comes into existence have a special responsibility for it. They may wish to assume responsibility for it, or they may not wish to. And I am suggesting that if assuming responsibility for it would require large sacrifices, then they may refuse. A Good Samaritan would not refuse—or anyway, a Splendid Samaritan, if the sacrifices that had to be made were enormous. But then so would a Good Samaritan assume responsibility for that violinist; so would Henry Fonda, if he is a Good Samaritan, fly in from the West Coast and assume responsibility for me.

8. My argument will be found unsatisfactory on two counts by many of those who want to regard abortion as morally permissible. First, while I do argue that abortion is not impermissible, I do not argue that it is always permissible. There may well be cases in which carrying the child to term requires only Minimally Decent Samaritanism of the mother, and this is a standard we must not fall below. I am inclined to think it a merit of my account precisely that it does *not* give a general yes or a general no. It allows for and supports our sense that, for example, a sick and desperately frightened fourteen-year-old schoolgirl, pregnant due to rape, may *of course* choose abortion, and that any law which rules this out is an insane law. And it also allows for and supports our sense that in other cases resort to abortion is even positively indecent. It would be indecent in the woman to request an abortion, and indecent in a doctor to perform it, if she is in her seventh month, and wants the abortion just to avoid the nuisance of postponing a trip abroad. The very fact that the arguments I have been drawing attention to treat all cases of abortion, or even all cases of abortion in which the mother's life is not at stake, as morally on a par ought to have made them suspect at the outset.

Secondly, while I am arguing for the permissibility of abortion in some cases, I am not arguing for the right to secure the death of the unborn child. It is easy to confuse these two things in that up to a certain point in the life of the fetus it is not able to survive outside the mother's body; hence removing it from her body guarantees its death. But they are importantly different. I have argued that you are not morally required to spend nine months in bed, sustaining the life of that violinist; but to say this is by no means to say that if, when you unplug yourself, there is a miracle and he survives, you then have a right to turn round and slit his throat. You may detach yourself even if this costs him his life; you have no right to be guaranteed his death, by some other means, if unplugging yourself does not kill him. There are some people who will feel dissatisfied by this feature of my argument. A woman may be utterly devastated by the thought of a child, a bit of herself, put out for adoption and never seen or heard of again. She may therefore want not merely that the child be detached from her, but more, that it die. Some opponents of abortion are inclined to regard this as beneath contempt—thereby showing insensitivity to what is surely a powerful source of despair. All the same, I agree that the desire for the child's death is not one which anybody may gratify, should it turn out to be possible to detach the child alive.

At this place, however, it should be remembered that we have only been pretending throughout that the fetus is a human being from the moment of conception. A very early abortion is surely not the killing of a person, and so is not dealt with by anything I have said here.

Notes

1. Daniel Callahan, *Abortion: Law, Choice and Morality* (New York, 1970), p. 373. This book gives a fascinating survey of the available information on abortion. The Jewish tradition is surveyed in David M. Feldman, *Birth Control in Jewish Law* (New York, 1968), Part 5; the Catholic tradition in John T. Noonan, Jr., "An Almost Absolute Value in History," in *The Morality of Abortion*, ed. John T. Noonan, Jr. (Cambridge, Mass., 1970).

2. The term "direct" in the arguments I refer to is a technical one. Roughly, what is meant by "direct killing" is either killing as an end in itself, or killing as a means of some end, for example, the end of saving someone else's life. See footnote 5 for an example of its use.

3. Cf. *Encyclical Letter of Pope Pius XI on Christian Marriage*, St. Paul Editions (Boston, n.d.), p. 32: "however much we may pity the mother whose health and even life is gravely imperiled in the performance of the duty allotted to her by nature, nevertheless what could ever be a sufficient reason for excusing in any way the direct murder of the innocent? This is precisely what we are dealing with here." Noonan (*The Morality of Abortion*, p. 43) reads this as follows: "What cause can ever avail to excuse in any way the direct killing of the innocent? For it is a question of that."

4. The thesis in (4) is in an interesting way weaker than those in (1), (2), and (3): they rule out abortion even in cases in which both mother *and* child will die if the abortion is not performed. By contrast, one who held the view expressed in (4) could consistently say that one needn't prefer letting two persons die to killing one.

5. Cf. the following passage from Pius XII, *Address to the Italian Catholic Society of Midwives:* "The baby in the maternal breast has the right to life immediately from God.—Hence there is no man, no human authority, no science, no medical, eugenic, social, economic or moral 'indication' which can establish or grant a valid juridical ground for a direct deliberate disposition of an innocent human life, that is a disposition which looks to its destruction either as an end or as a means to another end perhaps in itself not illicit.—The baby, still not born, is a man in the same degree and for the same reason as the mother" (quoted in Noonan, *The Morality of Abortion,* p. 45).

6. The need for a discussion of this argument was brought home to me by members of the Society for Ethical and Legal Philosophy, to whom this paper was originally presented.

7. For a discussion of the difficulties involved, and a survey of the European experience with such laws, see *The Good Samaritan and the Law,* ed. James M. Ratcliffe (New York, 1966).

Study Questions

1. What premise of the antiabortion argument does Thomson grant for the sake of argument?
2. What specifically is Thomson trying to show by using the example of the violinist?
3. What is the extreme view, according to Thomson, on the impermissibility of abortion? What are the major arguments for this view? How does she reply?
4. How does Thomson respond to the objection that a pregnant woman who voluntarily engaged in sexual intercourse is responsible for the existence of the fetus, and thus it would be unjust for her to deprive the fetus of life?
5. In what way does Thomson think that it might be true that you ought to do something for another person, even though that person has no right to expect that you do?
6. What is Thomson trying to prove by distinguishing between a Good Samaritan and a Minimally Decent Samaritan?
7. Does Thomson think that all abortions are morally acceptable? Why or why not?

On the Moral and Legal Status of Abortion

Mary Anne Warren

We will be concerned with both the moral status of abortion, which for our purposes we may define as the act which a woman performs in voluntarily terminating, or allowing another person to terminate, her pregnancy, and the legal status which is appropriate for this act. I will argue that, while it is not possible to produce a satisfactory defense of a woman's right to obtain an abortion without showing that a fetus is not a human being, in the morally

From *The Monist,* Vol. 57, No. 1 (1973). Reprinted by permission of *The Monist,* La Salle, Illinois 61301.

relevant sense of that term, we ought not to conclude that the difficulties involved in determining whether or not a fetus is human make it impossible to produce any satisfactory solution to the problem of the moral status of abortion. For it is possible to show that, on the basis of intuitions which we may expect even the opponents of abortion to share, a fetus is not a person, and hence not the sort of entity to which it is proper to ascribe full moral rights.

Of course, while some philosophers would deny the possibility of any such proof,[1] others will deny that there is any need for it, since the moral permissibility of abortion appears to them to be too obvious to require proof. But the inadequacy of this attitude should be evident from the fact that both the friends and the foes of abortion consider their position to be morally self-evident. Because proabortionists have never adequately come to grips with the conceptual issues surrounding abortion, most, if not all, of the arguments which they advance in opposition to laws restricting access to abortion fail to refute or even weaken the traditional antiabortion argument, i.e., that a fetus is a human being, and therefore abortion is murder.

These arguments are typically of one of two sorts. Either they point to the terrible side effects of the restrictive laws, e.g., the deaths due to illegal abortions, and the fact that it is poor women who suffer the most as a result of these laws, or else they state that to deny a woman access to abortion is to deprive her of her right to control her own body. Unfortunately, however, the fact that restricting access to abortion has tragic side effects does not, in itself, show that the restrictions are unjustified, since murder is wrong regardless of the consequences of prohibiting it; and the appeal to the right to control one's body, which is generally construed as a property right, is at best a rather feeble argument for the permissibility of abortion. Mere ownership does not give me the right to kill innocent people whom I find on my property, and indeed I am apt to be held responsible if such people injure themselves while on my property. It is equally unclear that I have any moral right to expel an innocent person from my property when I know that doing so will result in his death.

Furthermore, it is probably inappropriate to describe a woman's body as her property, since it seems natural to hold that a person is something distinct from her property, but not from her body. Even those who would object to the identification of a person with his body, or with the conjunction of his body and his mind, must admit that it would be very odd to describe, say, breaking a leg, as damaging one's property, and much more appropriate to describe it as injuring one*self.* Thus it is probably a mistake to argue that the right to obtain an abortion is in any way derived from the right to own and regulate property.

But however we wish to construe the right to abortion, we cannot hope to convince those who consider abortion a form of murder of the existence of any such right unless we are able to produce a clear and convincing refutation of the traditional antiabortion argument, and this has not, to my knowledge, been done. With respect to the two most vital issues which that argument involves, i.e., the humanity of the fetus and its implication for the moral status of abortion, confusion has prevailed on both sides of the dispute.

Thus, both proabortionists and antiabortionists have tended to abstract the question of whether abortion is wrong to that of whether it is wrong to destroy a fetus, just as though the rights of another person were not necessarily involved. This mistaken abstraction has led to the almost universal assumption that if a fetus is a human being, with a right to life, then it follows immediately that abortion is wrong (except perhaps when necessary to save the woman's life), and that it ought to be prohibited. It has also been generally assumed that unless the question about the status of the fetus is answered, the moral status of abortion cannot possibly be determined.

Two recent papers, one by B. A. Brody,[2] and one by Judith Thomson,[3] have attempted to settle the question of whether abortion ought to be prohibited apart from the question of whether or not the fetus is human. Brody examines the possibility that the following two statements are compatible: (1) that abortion is the taking of innocent human life, and therefore wrong; and (2) that nevertheless it ought not to be prohibited by law, at least under the present circumstances.[4] Not surprisingly, Brody finds it impossible to reconcile these two statements, since, as he rightly argues, none of the unfortunate side effects of the prohibition of abortion is bad enough to justify legalizing the *wrongful* taking of human life. He is mistaken, however, in concluding that the incompatibility of (1) and (2), in itself, shows that "the legal problem about abortion cannot be resolved independently of the status of the fetus problem" [p. 369].

What Brody fails to realize is that (1) embodies the questionable assumption that if a fetus is a human being, then of course abortion is morally wrong, and that an attack on *this* assumption is more promising, as a way of reconciling the humanity of the fetus with the claim that laws prohibiting abortion are unjustified, than is an attack on the assumption that if abortion is the wrongful killing of innocent human beings then it ought to be prohibited. He thus overlooks the possibility that a fetus may have a right to life and abortion still be morally permissible, in that the right of a woman to terminate an unwanted pregnancy might override the right of the fetus to be kept alive. The immorality of abortion is no more demonstrated by the humanity of the fetus, in itself, than the immorality of killing in self-defense is demonstrated by the fact that the assailant is a human being. Neither is it demonstrated by the *innocence* of the fetus, since there may be situations in which the killing of innocent human beings is justified.

It is perhaps not surprising that Brody fails to spot this assumption, since it has been accepted with little or no argument by nearly everyone who has written on the morality of abortion. John Noonan is correct in saying that "the fundamental question in the long history of abortion is, How do you determine the humanity of a being?"[5] He summarizes his own antiabortion argument, which is a version of the official position of the Catholic Church, as follows:

> . . . it is wrong to kill humans, however poor, weak, defenseless, and lacking in opportunity to develop their potential they may be. It is therefore morally wrong to kill Biafrans. Similarly, it is morally wrong to kill embryos.[6]

Noonan bases his claim that fetuses are human upon what he calls the theologians' criterion of humanity: that whoever is conceived of human beings is human. But although he argues at length for the appropriateness of this criterion, he never questions the assumption that if a fetus is human then abortion is wrong for exactly the same reason that murder is wrong.

Judith Thomson is, in fact, the only writer I am aware of who has seriously questioned this assumption; she has argued that, even if we grant the antiabortionist his claim that a fetus is a human being, with the same right to life as any other human being, we can still demonstrate that, in at least some and perhaps most cases, a woman is under no moral obligation to complete an unwanted pregnancy.[7] Her argument is worth examining, since if it holds up it may enable us to establish the moral permissibility of abortion without becoming involved in problems about what entitles an entity to be considered human, and accorded full moral rights. To be able to do this would be a great gain in the power and simplicity of the proabortion position, since, although I will argue that these problems can be solved at least as decisively as can any other moral problem, we should certainly be pleased to be able to avoid having to solve them as part of the justification of abortion.

On the other hand, even if Thomson's argument does not hold up, her insight, i.e., that it requires *argument* to show that if fetuses are human then abortion is properly classified as murder, is an extremely valuable one. The assumption she attacks is particularly invidious, for it amounts to the decision that it is appropriate, in deciding the moral status of abortion, to leave the rights of the pregnant woman out of consideration entirely, except possibly when her life is threatened. Obviously, this will not do; determining what moral rights, if any, a fetus possesses is only the first step in determining the moral status of abortion. Step two, which is at least equally essential, is finding a just solution to the conflict between whatever rights the fetus may have, and the rights of the woman who is unwillingly pregnant. While the historical error has been to pay far too little attention to the second step, Ms. Thomson's suggestion is that if we look at the second step first we may find that a woman has a right to obtain an abortion *regardless* of what rights the fetus has.

Our own inquiry will also have two stages. In Section I, we will consider whether or not it is possible to establish that abortion is morally permissible even on the assumption that a fetus is an entity with a full-fledged right to life. I will argue that in fact this cannot be established, at least not with the conclusiveness which is essential to our hopes of convincing those who are skeptical about the morality of abortion, and that we therefore cannot avoid dealing with the question of whether or not a fetus really does have the same right to life as a (more fully developed) human being.

In Section II, I will propose an answer to this question, namely, that a fetus cannot be considered a member of the moral community, the set of beings with full and equal moral rights, for the simple reason that it is not a person, and that it is personhood, and not genetic humanity, i.e., humanity as defined by Noonan, which is the basis for membership in this community. I will argue that a fetus, whatever its stage of development, satisfies none of the basic criteria of personhood, and is not even enough *like* a person to be accorded even some of the same rights on the basis of this resemblance. Nor, as we will see, is a fetus's *potential* personhood a threat to the morality of abortion, since, whatever the rights of potential people may be, they are invariably overridden in any conflict with the moral rights of actual people.

I

We turn now to Professor Thomson's case for the claim that even if a fetus has full moral rights, abortion is still morally permissible, at least sometimes, and for some reasons other than to save the woman's life. Her argument is based upon a clever, but I think faulty, analogy. She asks us to picture ourselves waking up one day, in bed with a famous violinist. Imagine that you have been kidnapped, and your bloodstream hooked up to that of the violinist, who happens to have an ailment which will certainly kill him unless he is permitted to share your kidneys for a period of nine months. No one else can save him, since you alone have the right type of blood. He will be unconscious all that time, and you will have to stay in bed with him, but after the nine months are over he may be unplugged, completely cured, that is provided that you have cooperated.

Now then, she continues, what are your obligations in this situation? The antiabortionist, if he is consistent, will have to say that you are obligated to stay in bed with the violinist: for all people have a right to life, and violinists are people, and therefore it would be murder for you to disconnect yourself from him and let him die [p. 174]. But this is outrageous, and so there must be something wrong with the same argument when it is applied to abortion. It would certainly be commendable of you to agree to save the violinist, but it is absurd to suggest that your refusal to do so would be murder. His right to life does not obligate you to do whatever is required to keep him alive; nor does it justify anyone else in forcing you to do so. A law which required you to stay in bed with the violinist would clearly be an unjust law, since it is no proper function of the law to force unwilling people to make huge sacrifices for the sake of other people toward whom they have no such prior obligation.

Thomson concludes that, if this analogy is an apt one, then we can grant the antiabortionist his claim that a fetus is a human being, and still hold that it is at least sometimes the case that a pregnant woman has the right to refuse to be a Good Samaritan towards the fetus, i.e., to obtain an abortion. For there is a great gap between the claim that x has a right to life, and the claim that y is obligated to do whatever is necessary to keep x alive, let alone that he ought to be forced to do so. It is y's duty to keep x alive only if he has somehow contracted a *special* obligation to do so; and a woman who is unwillingly pregnant, e.g., who was raped, has done nothing which obligates her to make the enormous sacrifice which is necessary to preserve the conceptus.

This argument is initially quite plausible, and in the extreme case of pregnancy due to rape it is probably conclusive. Difficulties arise, however, when we try to specify more exactly the range of cases in which abortion is clearly justifiable even on the assumption that the fetus is human. Professor Thomson considers it a virtue of her argument that it does not enable us to conclude that abortion is *always* permissible. It would, she says, be ''indecent'' for a woman in her seventh month to obtain an abortion just to avoid having to postpone a trip to Europe. On the other hand, her argument enables us to see that ''a sick and desperately frightened schoolgirl pregnant due to rape may *of course* choose abortion, and that any law which rules this out is an insane law'' [p. 187]. So far, so good; but what are we to say about the woman who becomes pregnant not through rape but as a result of her own carelessness, or because of contraceptive failure, or who gets pregnant intentionally and then changes her mind about wanting a child? With respect to such cases, the violinist analogy is of much less use to the defender of the woman's right to obtain an abortion.

Indeed, the choice of a pregnancy due to rape, as an example of a case in which abortion is permissible even if a fetus is considered a human being, is extremely significant; for it is only in the case of pregnancy due to rape that the woman's situation is adequately analogous to the violinist case for our intuitions about the latter to transfer convincingly. The crucial difference between a pregnancy due to rape and the *normal* case of an unwanted pregnancy is that in the normal case we cannot claim that the woman is in no way responsible for her predicament; she could have remained chaste, or taken her pills more faithfully, or abstained on dangerous days, and so on. If, on the other hand, you are kidnapped by strangers, and hooked up to a strange violinist, then you are free of any shred of responsibility for the situation, on the basis of which it could be argued that you are obligated to keep the violinist alive. Only when her pregnancy is due to rape is a woman clearly just as nonresponsible.[8]

Consequently, there is room for the antiabortionist to argue that in the normal case of unwanted pregnancy a woman has, by her own actions, assumed responsibility for the fetus. For if x behaves in a way which he could have avoided, and which he knows involves, let us say, a 1 percent chance of bringing into existence a human being, with a right to life, and does so knowing that if this should happen then that human being will perish unless x does certain things to keep him alive, then it is by no means clear that when it does happen x is free of any obligation to what he knew in advance would be required to keep that human being alive.

The plausibility of such an argument is enough to show that the Thomson analogy can provide a clear and persuasive defense of a woman's right to obtain an abortion only with respect to those cases in which the woman is in no way responsible for her pregnancy, e.g., where it is due to rape. In all other cases, we would almost certainly conclude that it was necessary to look carefully at the particular circumstances in order to determine the extent of the woman's responsibility, and hence the extent of her obligation. This is an extremely unsatisfactory outcome, from the viewpoint of the opponents of restrictive abortion laws, most of whom are convinced that a woman has a right to obtain an abortion regardless of how and why she got pregnant.

Of course a supporter of the violinist analogy might point out that it is absurd to suggest that forgetting her pill one day might be sufficient to obligate a woman to complete an unwanted pregnancy. And indeed it *is* absurd to suggest this. As we will see, the moral right to obtain an abortion is not in the least dependent upon the extent to which the woman is responsible for her pregnancy. But unfortunately, once we allow the assumption that a fetus has full moral rights, we cannot avoid taking this absurd suggestion seriously. Perhaps we can make this point more clear by altering the violinist story just enough to make it more analogous to a normal unwanted pregnancy and less to a pregnancy due to rape, and then seeing whether it is still obvious that you are not obligated to stay in bed with the fellow.

Suppose, then, that violinists are peculiarly prone to the sort of illness the only cure for which is the use of someone else's bloodstream for nine months, and that because of this there has been formed a society of music lovers who agree that whenever a violinist is stricken they will draw lots and the loser will, by some means, be made the one and only person capable of saving him. Now then, would you be obligated to cooperate in curing the violinist if you had voluntarily joined this society, knowing the possible consequences, and then your name had been drawn and you had been kidnapped? Admittedly, you did not promise ahead of time that you would, but you did deliberately place yourself in a position in which it might happen that a human life would be lost if you did not. Surely this is at least a prima facie reason for supposing that you have an obligation to stay in bed with the violinist. Suppose that you had gotten your name drawn deliberately; surely *that* would be quite a strong reason for thinking that you had such an obligation.

It might be suggested that there is one important disanalogy between the modified violinist case and the case of an unwanted pregnancy, which makes the woman's responsibility significantly less, namely, the fact that the fetus *comes into existence* as the result of the woman's actions. This fact might give her a right to refuse to keep it alive, whereas she would not have had this right had it existed previously, independently, and then as a result of her actions become dependent upon her for its survival.

My own intuition, however, is that x has no more right to bring into existence, either deliberately or as a foreseeable result of actions he could have avoided, a being with full moral rights (y), and then refuse to do what he knew beforehand would be required to keep that being alive, than he has to enter into an agreement with an existing person, whereby he may be called upon to save that person's life, and then refuse to do so when so called upon. Thus, x's responsibility for y's existence does not seem to lessen his obligation to keep y alive, if he is also responsible for y's being in a situation in which only he can save him.

Whether or not this intuition is entirely correct, it brings us back once again to the conclusion that once we allow the assumption that a fetus has full moral rights it becomes an extremely complex and difficult question whether and when abortion is justifiable. Thus the Thomson analogy cannot help us produce a clear and persuasive proof of the moral permissibility of abortion. Nor will the opponents of the restrictive laws thank us for anything less; for their conviction (for the most part) is that abortion is obviously *not* a morally serious and extremely unfortunate, even though sometimes justified act, comparable to killing in self-defense or to letting the violinist die, but rather is closer to being a morally neutral act, like cutting one's hair.

The basis of this conviction, I believe, is the realization that a fetus is not a person, and thus does not have a full-fledged right to life. Perhaps the reason why this claim has been so inadequately defended is that it seems self-evident to those who accept it. And so it is, insofar as it follows from what I take to be perfectly obvious claims about the nature of personhood, and about the proper grounds for ascribing moral rights, claims which ought, indeed, to be obvious to both the friends and foes of abortion. Nevertheless, it is worth examining these claims, and showing how they demonstrate the moral innocuousness of abortion, since this apparently has not been adequately done before.

II

The question which we must answer in order to produce a satisfactory solution to the problem of the moral status of abortion is this: How are we to define the moral community, the set of beings with full and equal moral rights, such that we can decide whether a human fetus is a member of this community or not? What sort of entity, exactly, has the inalienable rights to life, liberty, and the pursuit of happiness? Jefferson attributed these rights to all *men*, and it may or may not be fair to suggest that he intended to attribute them *only* to men. Perhaps he ought to have attributed them to all human beings. If so, then we arrive, first, at Noonan's problem of defining what makes a being human, and second, at the equally vital question which Noonan does not consider, namely, What reason is there for identifying the moral community with the set of all human beings, in whatever way we have chosen to define that term?

1. Defining "Human"

One reason why this vital second question is so frequently overlooked in the debate over the moral status of abortion is that the term "human" has two distinct, but not often distinguished, senses. This fact results in a slide of meaning, which serves to conceal the fallaciousness of the traditional argument that since (1) it is wrong to kill innocent human beings, and (2) fetuses are innocent human beings, then (3) it is wrong to kill fetuses. For if "human" is used in the same sense in both (1) and (2) then, whichever of the two senses is meant, one of these premises is question-begging. And if it is used in two different senses then of course the conclusion doesn't follow.

Thus, (1) is a self-evident moral truth,[9] and avoids begging the question about abortion, only if "human being" is used to mean something like "a full-fledged member of the moral community." (It may or may not also be meant to refer exclusively to members of the species *Homo sapiens*.) We may call this the *moral* sense of "human." It is not to be confused with what we will call the *genetic* sense, i.e., the sense in which *any* member of the species is a human being, and no member of any other species could be. If (1) is acceptable only if the moral sense is intended, (2) is non-question-begging only if what is intended is the genetic sense.

In "Deciding Who Is Human," Noonan argues for the classification of fetuses with human beings by pointing to the presence of the full genetic code, and the potential capacity for rational thought (p. 135). It is clear that what he needs to show, for his version of the traditional argument to be valid, is that fetuses are human in the moral sense, the sense in which it is analytically true that all human beings have full moral rights. But, in the absence of any argument showing that whatever is genetically human is also morally human, and he gives none, nothing more than genetic humanity can be demonstrated by the presence of the human genetic code. And, as we will see, the *potential* capacity for rational thought can at most show that an entity has the potential for *becoming* human in the moral sense.

2. Defining the Moral Community

Can it be established that genetic humanity is sufficient for moral humanity? I think that there are very good reasons for not defining the moral community in this way. I would like to suggest an alternative way of defining the moral community, which I will argue for only to the extent of explaining why it consists of all and only *people*, rather than all and only human beings,[10] and probably the best way of demonstrating its self-evidence is by considering the concept of personhood, to see what sorts of entity are and are not persons, and what the decision that a being is or is not a person implies about its moral rights.

What characteristics entitle an entity to be considered a person? This is obviously not the place to attempt a complete analysis of the concept of personhood, but we do not need such a fully adequate analysis just to determine whether and why a fetus is or isn't a person. All we need is a rough and approximate list of the most basic criteria of personhood, and some idea of which, or how many, of these an entity must satisfy in order to properly be considered a person.

In searching for such criteria, it is useful to look beyond the set of people with whom we are acquainted, and ask how we would decide whether a totally alien being was a person or not. (For we have no right to assume that genetic humanity is necessary for personhood.) Imagine a space traveler who lands on an unknown planet and encounters a race of beings utterly unlike any he has ever seen or heard of. If he wants to be sure of behaving morally toward these beings, he has to somehow decide whether they are people, and hence have full moral rights, or whether they are the sort of thing which he need not feel guilty about treating as, for example, a source of food.

How should he go about making this decision? If he has some anthropological background, he might look for such things as religion, art, and the manufacturing of tools, weapons, or shelters, since these factors have been used to distinguish our human from our prehuman ancestors, in what seems to be closer to the moral than the genetic sense of "human." And no doubt he would be right to consider the presence of such factors as good evidence that the alien beings were people, and morally human. It would, however, be overly anthropocentric of him to take the absence of these things as adequate evidence that they were not, since we can imagine people who have progressed beyond, or evolved without ever developing, these cultural characteristics.

I suggest that the traits which are most central to the concept of personhood, or humanity in the moral sense, are, very roughly, the following:

1. Consciousness (of objects and events external and/or internal to the being), and in particular the capacity to feel pain
2. Reasoning (the *developed* capacity to solve new and relatively complex problems)
3. Self-motivated activity (activity which is relatively independent of either genetic or direct external control)
4. The capacity to communicate, by whatever means, messages of an indefinite variety of types, that is, not just with an indefinite number of possible contents, but on indefinitely many possible topics
5. The presence of self-concepts, and self-awareness, either individual or racial, or both.

Admittedly, there are apt to be a great many problems involved in formulating precise definitions of these criteria, let alone in developing universally valid behavioral criteria for deciding when they apply. But I will assume that both we and our explorer know approximately what (1)–(5) mean, and that he is also able to determine whether or not they apply. How, then, should he use his findings to decide whether or not the alien beings are people? We needn't suppose that an entity must have *all* of these attributes to be properly considered a person; (1) and (2) alone may well be sufficient for personhood, and quite probably (1)–(3) are sufficient. Neither do we need to insist that any one of these criteria is *necessary* for personhood, although once again (1) and (2) look like fairly good candidates for necessary conditions, as does (3), if "activity" is construed so as to include the activity of reasoning.

All we need to claim, to demonstrate that a fetus is not a person, is that any being which satisfies *none* of (1)–(5) is certainly not a person. I consider this claim to be so obvious that I think anyone who denied it, and claimed that a being which satisfied none of (1)–(5) was a person all the same, would thereby demonstrate that he had no notion at all of what a person is—perhaps because he had confused the concept of a person with that of genetic humanity. If the opponents of abortion were to deny the appropriateness of these five criteria, I do not know what further arguments would convince them. We would probably have to admit that our conceptual schemes were indeed irreconcilably different, and that our dispute could not be settled objectively.

I do not expect this to happen, however, since I think that the concept of a person is one which is very nearly universal (to people), and that it is common to both proabortionists and antiabortionists, even though neither group has fully realized the relevance of this concept to the resolution of their dispute. Furthermore, I think that on reflection even antiabortionists ought to agree not only that (1)–(5) are central to the concept of personhood, but also that it is a part of this concept that all and only people have full moral rights. The concept of a person is in part a moral concept; once we have admitted that *x* is a person we have recognized, even if we have not agreed to respect, *x*'s right to be treated as a member of the moral community. It is true that the claim that *x* is a *human being* is more commonly voiced as part of an appeal to treat *x* decently than is the claim that *x* is a person, but this is either because "human being" is here used in the sense which implies personhood, or because the genetic and moral senses of "human" have been confused.

Now if (1)–(5) are indeed the primary criteria of personhood, then it is clear that genetic humanity is neither necessary nor sufficient for establishing that an entity is a person. Some human beings are not people, and there may well be people who are not human beings. A man or woman whose consciousness has been permanently obliterated but who remains alive is a human being which is no longer a person; defective human beings, with no appreciable mental capacity, are not and presumably never will be people; and a fetus is a human being which is not yet a person, and which therefore cannot coherently be said to have full moral rights. Citizens of the next century should be prepared to recognize highly advanced, self-aware robots or computers, should such be developed, and intelligent inhabitants of other worlds, should such be found, as people in the fullest sense, and to respect their moral rights. But to ascribe full moral rights to an entity which is not a person is as absurd as to ascribe moral obligations and responsibilities to such an entity.

3. Fetal Development and the Right to Life

Two problems arise in the application of these suggestions for the definition of the moral community to the determination of the precise moral status of a human fetus. Given that the paradigm example of a person is a normal adult human being, then (1) How like this paradigm, in particular how far advanced since conception, does a human being need to be before it begins to have a right to life by virtue, not of being fully a person as of yet, but of being *like* a person? and (2) To what extent, if any, does the fact that a fetus has the *potential* for becoming a person endow it with some of the same rights? Each of these questions requires some comment.

In answering the first question, we need not attempt a detailed consideration of the moral rights of organisms which are not developed enough, aware enough, intelligent enough, etc., to be considered people, but which resemble people in some respects. It does seem reasonable to suggest that the more like a person, in the relevant respects, a being is, the stronger is the case for regarding it as having a right to life, and indeed the stronger its right to life is. Thus we ought to take seriously the suggestion that, insofar as "the human individual develops biologically in a continuous fashion . . . the rights of a human person might develop in the same way."[11] But we must keep in mind that the attributes which are relevant in determining whether or not an entity is enough like a person to be regarded as having some of the same moral rights are no different from those which are relevant to determining whether or not it is fully a person—i.e., are no different from (1)–(5)—and that being genetically human or having recognizably human facial and other physical features, or detectable brain activity, or the capacity to survive outside the uterus, are simply not among these relevant attributes.

Thus it is clear that even though a seven- or eight-month fetus has features which make it apt to arouse in us almost the same powerful protective instinct as is commonly aroused by a small infant, nevertheless it is not significantly more personlike than is a very small embryo. It is *somewhat* more personlike; it can apparently feel and respond to pain, and it may even have a rudimentary form of consciousness, insofar as its brain is quite active. Nevertheless, it seems safe to say that it is not fully conscious, in the way that an infant of a few months is, and that it cannot reason, or communicate messages of indefinitely many sorts, does not engage in self-motivated activity, and has no self-awareness. Thus, in the *relevant* respects, a fetus, even a fully developed one, is considerably less personlike than is the average mature mammal, indeed the average fish. And I think that a rational person must conclude that if the right to life of a fetus is to be based upon its resemblance to a person, then it cannot be said to have any more right to life than, let us say, a newborn guppy (which also seems to be capable of feeling pain), and that a right of that magnitude could never override a woman's right to obtain an abortion, at any stage of her pregnancy.

There may, of course, be other arguments in favor of placing legal limits upon the stage of pregnancy in which an abortion may be performed. Given the relative safety of the new techniques of artificially inducing labor during the third trimester, the danger to the woman's life or health is no longer such an argument. Neither is the fact that people tend to respond to the thought of abortion in the later stages of pregnancy with emotional repulsion, since mere emotional responses cannot take the place of moral reasoning in determining what ought to be permitted. Nor, finally, is the frequently heard argument that legalizing abortion, especially late in the pregnancy, may erode the level of respect for human life, leading, perhaps, to an increase in unjustified euthanasia and other crimes. For this threat, if it is a threat, can be better met by educating people to the kinds of moral distinctions which we are making here than by limiting access to abortion (which limitation may, in its disregard for the rights of women, be just as damaging to the level of respect for human rights).

Thus, since the fact that even a fully developed fetus is not personlike enough to have any significant right to life on the basis of its personlikeness shows that no legal restrictions upon the stage of pregnancy in which an abortion may be performed can be justified on the grounds that we should protect the rights of the older fetus; and since there is no other apparent justification for such restrictions, we may conclude that they are entirely unjustified. Whether or not it would be *indecent* (whatever that means) for a woman in her seventh month to obtain an abortion just to avoid having to postpone a trip to Europe, it would not, in itself, be *immoral,* and therefore it ought to be permitted.

We have seen that a fetus does not resemble a person in any way which can support the claim that it has even some of the same rights. But what about its *potential,* the fact that if nurtured and allowed to develop naturally it will very probably become a person? Doesn't that alone give it at least some right to life? It is hard to deny that the fact that an entity is a potential person is a strong prima facie reason for not destroying it; but we need not conclude from this that a potential person has a right to life, by virtue of that potential. It may be that our feeling that it is better, other things being equal, not to destroy a potential person is better explained by the fact that potential people are still (felt to be) an invaluable resource, not to be lightly squandered. Surely, if every speck of dust were a potential person, we would be much less apt to conclude that every potential person has a right to become actual.

Still, we do not need to insist that a potential person has no right to life whatever. There may well be something immoral, and not just imprudent, about wantonly destroying potential people, when doing so isn't necessary to protect anyone's rights. But even if a potential person does have some prima facie right to life, such a right could not possibly outweigh the right of a woman to obtain an abortion, since the rights of any actual person invariably outweigh those of any potential person, whenever the two conflict. Since this may not be immediately obvious in the case of a human fetus, let us look at another case.

Suppose that our space explorer falls into the hands of an alien culture, whose scientists decide to create a few hundred thousand or more human beings, by breaking his body into its component cells, and using these to create fully developed human beings, with, of course, his genetic code. We may imagine that each of these newly created men will have all of the original man's abilities, skills, knowledge, and so on, and also have an individual self-concept, in short that each of them will be a bona fide (though hardly unique) person. Imagine that the whole project will take only seconds, and that its chances of success are extremely high, and that our explorer knows all of this, and also knows that these people will be treated fairly. I maintain that in such a situation he would have every right to escape if he could, and thus to deprive all of these potential people of their potential lives; for his right to life outweighs all of theirs together, in spite of the fact that they are all genetically human, all innocent, and all have a very high probability of becoming people very soon, if only he refrains from acting.

Indeed, I think he would have a right to escape even if it were not his life which the alien scientists planned to take, but only a year of his freedom, or, indeed, only a day. Nor would he be obligated to stay if he had gotten captured (thus bringing all these people-potentials into existence) because of his own carelessness, or even if he had done so deliberately, knowing the consequences. Regardless of how he got captured, he is not morally obligated to remain in captivity for *any* period of time for the sake of permitting any number of potential people to come into actuality, so great is the margin by which one actual person's right to liberty outweighs whatever right to life even a hundred thousand potential people have. And it seems reasonable to conclude that the rights of a woman will outweigh by a similar margin whatever right to life a fetus may have by virtue of its potential personhood.

Thus, neither a fetus's resemblance to a person, nor its potential for becoming a person provides any basis whatever for the claim that it has any significant right to life. Consequently, a woman's right to protect her health, happiness, freedom, and even her life,[12] by terminating an unwanted pregnancy, will always override whatever right to life it may be appropriate to ascribe to a fetus, even a fully developed one. And thus, in the absence of any overwhelming social need for every possible child, the laws which restrict the right to obtain an abortion, or limit the period of pregnancy during which an abortion may be performed, are a wholly unjustified violation of a woman's most basic moral and constitutional rights.

Postscript on Infanticide

Since the publication of this article, many people have written to point out that my argument appears to justify not only abortion, but infanticide as well. For a newborn infant is not significantly more personlike than an advanced fetus, and consequently it would seem that if the destruction of the latter is permissible so too must be that of the former. Inasmuch as most people, regardless of how they feel about the morality of abortion, consider infanticide a form of murder, this might appear to represent a serious flaw in my argument.

Now, if I am right in holding that it is only people who have a full-fledged right to life, and who can be murdered, and if the criteria of personhood are as I have described them, then it obviously follows that killing a new-born infant isn't murder. It does *not* follow, however, that infanticide is permissible, for two reasons. In the first place, it would be wrong, at least in this country and in this period of history, and other things being equal, to kill a new-born infant, because even if its parents do not want it and would not suffer from its destruction, there are other people who would like to have it, and would, in all probability, be deprived of a great deal of pleasure by its destruction. Thus, infanticide is wrong for reasons analogous to those which make it wrong to wantonly destroy natural resources, or great works of art.

Secondly, most people, at least in this country, value infants and would much prefer that they be preserved, even if foster parents are not immediately available. Most of us would rather be taxed to support orphanages than allow unwanted infants to be destroyed. So long as there are people who want an infant preserved, and who are willing and able to provide the means of caring for it, under reasonably humane conditions, it is *ceteris paribus,* wrong to destroy it.

But, it might be replied, if this argument shows that infanticide is wrong, at least at this time and in this country, doesn't it also show that abortion is wrong? After all, many people value fetuses, are disturbed by their destruction, and would much prefer that they be preserved, even at some cost to themselves. Furthermore, as a potential source of pleasure to some foster family, a fetus is just as valuable as an infant. There is, however, a crucial difference between the two cases: so long as the fetus is unborn, its preservation, contrary to the wishes of the pregnant woman, violates her rights to freedom, happiness, and self-determination. Her rights override the rights of those who would like the fetus preserved, just as if someone's life or limb is threatened by a wild animal, his right to protect himself by destroying the animal overrides the rights of those who would prefer that the animal not be harmed.

The minute the infant is born, however, its preservation no longer violates any of its mother's rights, even if she wants it destroyed, because she is free to put it up for adoption. Consequently, while the moment of birth does not mark any sharp discontinuity in the degree to which an infant possesses the right to life, it does mark the end of its mother's right to determine its fate. Indeed, if abortion could be performed without killing the fetus, she would never possess the right to have the fetus destroyed, for the same reasons that she has no right to have an infant destroyed.

On the other hand, it follows from my argument that when an unwanted or defective infant is born into a society which cannot afford and/or is not willing to care for it, then its destruction is permissible. This conclusion will, no doubt, strike many people as heartless and immoral; but remember that the very existence of people who feel this way, and who are willing and able to provide care for unwanted infants, is reason enough to conclude that they should be preserved.

Notes

1. For example, Roger Wertheimer, who in "Understanding the Abortion Argument," *Philosophy and Public Affairs,* 1, no. 1 (Fall, 1971), [*supra,* pp. 43–57], argues that the problem of the moral status of abortion is insoluble, in that the dispute over the status of the fetus is not a question of fact at all, but only a question of how one responds to the facts.
2. B. A. Brody, "Abortion and the Law," *The Journal of Philosophy,* 68, no. 12 (June 17, 1971), 357–69.
3. Judith Thomsom, "A Defense of Abortion," *Philosophy and Public Affairs,* 1, no. 1 (Fall, 1971), [*infra,* pp. 173–87].
4. I have abbreviated these statements somewhat, but not in a way which affects the argument.
5. John Noonan, "Abortion and the Catholic Church: A Summary History," *Natural Law Forum,* 12 (1967), 125.
6. John Noonan, "Deciding Who Is Human," *Natural Law Forum,* 13 (1968), 134.
7. "A Defense of Abortion."
8. We may safely ignore the fact that she might have avoided getting raped, e.g., by carrying a gun, since by similar means you might likewise have avoided getting kidnapped, and in neither case does the victim's failure to take all possible precautions against a highly unlikely event (as opposed to reasonable precautions against a rather likely event) mean that she is morally responsible for what happens.
9. Of course, the principle that it is (always) wrong to kill innocent human beings is in need of many other modifications, e.g., that it may be permissible to do so to save a greater number of other innocent human beings, but we may safely ignore these complications here.

10. We use "human" to mean genetically human, since the moral sense seems closely connected to, and perhaps derived from, the assumption that genetic humanity is sufficient for membership in the moral community.
11. Thomas L. Hayes, "A Biological View," *Commonweal, 85* (March 17, 1967), 677–78; quoted by Daniel Callahan, in *Abortion, Law, Choice, and Morality* (London: Macmillan & Co., 1970).
12. That is, insofar as the death rate, for the woman, is higher for childbirth than for early abortion.

Study Questions

1. What two common proabortion arguments does Warren reject, and why?
2. What assumption does Warren believe most writers on abortion make without argument?
3. To what analogy offered by Thomson does Warren object? What was Thomson trying to show by that analogy, and what is Warren's objection? How does Warren modify the Thomson analogy to bring out her objection to it?
4. What criteria of personhood does Warren offer? Under these criteria, what types of human beings are not persons? Do you agree with her point?
5. Does Warren believe that a seven- or eight-month fetus is very much like a person in the morally relevant respects? Explain her reasons. Do you agree?
6. What is Warren's reply to the objection that a fetus has a right to life because it is a potential person?
7. Does Warren's defense of abortion commit her to defending infanticide? Why or why not?

Moral Revolution

Kathryn Pyne Addelson

Part I: Introduction

Has a covert bias been introduced into our world view by the near exclusion of women from the domain of intellectual pursuits?

Philosophers and scientists both have argued long and hard that it is a virtue of science that the sex, race, ethnic background, or creed of the investigator is irrelevant to scientific results, provided only that scientific method is practiced correctly. They have taken that to be one consequence of the *objectivity* of science, and some have even felt that the remedy for bias is to become *more* scientific. Although philosophers and scientists generally conclude that there is no bias, the question somehow keeps arising. One reason it cannot be laid to rest is that detecting bias is itself a philosophic or scientific enterprise, and the methods used in the detection may themselves be questioned as to bias. In fact, the major question concerns how to define what bias amounts to.

Revised and condensed from Julia A. Sherman and Evelyn T. Beck, eds., *The Prism of Sex* (Madison, WI: University of Wisconsin Press, 1979). Copyright © 1978 by Kathryn Pyne Parsons. Reprinted by permission of Kathryn Pyne Addelson. (Notes deleted.)

Sometimes bias in intellectual work has been said to be the result of doing "bad science," or "bad philosophy." In principle, the work is biased because of the biases of the investigators using the theory. Let me give an example from Judith Jarvis Thomson's paper, "A Defense of Abortion,"[1] which I'll consider in some detail in Part II below. In this paper, she says that most philosophical discussions of abortion have taken the point of view of a third party (lawgiver, abortionist, interested onlooker) and not the point of view of the pregnant woman. She argues that the moral decision from the point of view of the pregnant woman is quite different and that we can't generalize from the third-party point of view to hers. For example, considerations of self-defense may enter for the pregnant woman when they don't enter for an outsider. This criticism Judith Thomson raises shows bias in the *application* of the philosophical theory she is working with. It doesn't correct the philosophical theory itself. Her criticism shows that other papers on abortion have been biased *in the use of the theory.* The bias would be corrected by reforming the way the theory is applied.

Some criticisms of bias in the use of a theory show that fairly basic assumptions of the theory may need to be corrected to do "good science" with it. Let's take an example from sociology. Arlene Daniels reports on a paper by Joan Acker:

> [Joan Acker] points out that stratification literature—whether written by func-
> tionalists, Marxists, or others—contains assumptions about the social position
> of women that are quite inadequate. The first assumption is that the family is
> the unit in the stratification system. From this view, a number of other assump-
> tions are derived, such as that the social position of a family is determined by
> the male head of household or that the status of females living in families is deter-
> mined by the males to whom they are attached. But these assumptions do not
> accurately reflect the actual state of relationships for large segments of the popula-
> tion. There are many females and female heads of households who are not attached
> to males. Why should such persons be ignored or placed in some residual category
> indicating their irrelevance to any major analysis of the stratification system? No
> male stratification theorists have previously questioned the usefulness of a world
> view that excludes the conditions of so much of the population from considera-
> tion. But it has been convenient to assume that females have no relevant role in
> stratification processes independent of their ties to men.[2]

In this passage, Arlene Daniels isn't suggesting that the functionalist or Marxist theories have to be thrown out because they are sexist. She is saying that they contain inadequate assumptions about the social position of women, and that those assumptions need to be corrected by reforming the theory.

There is a more radical kind of bias that may infect a theory, a kind which can't be corrected by reforming the application of the theory or a few of its assumptions. To reform this kind of bias, we need a scientific revolution in which the old theory is scrapped and a new theory introduced. Let me give another example from sociology. In *Another Voice,* Lyn Lofland reviewed urban sociology. She says:

> . . . women in that portion of the literature of urban sociology here under review
> are mostly and simply, just there. They are part of the locale or neighborhood
> or area—described like other important aspects of the setting such as income,
> ecology, or demography—but largely irrelevant to the analytic *action.* . . . To the
> degree that urban researchers have taken seriously (and of course many have not)
> the Blumerian injunction to "look upon human group life as chiefly a vast inter-
> pretative process in which people, singly and collectively, *guide themselves by defin-
> ing* the objects, events and situations they encounter," they have done so primarily

for the male participants in the human group life. The female participants are "just there."[3]

Lyn Lofland feels a radical change in urban sociology is necessary to correct this bias and that no mere reform will do. She says: ". . . the problems which lead to the portrayal of women as 'only there' are among the central conceptual, focal, and methodological difficulties of urban sociology itself."[4] She suggests that to remedy this bias, completely new models, concepts, and variables would have to be developed out of studies which gave proper investigation to women; the resulting theory, she feels, would very likely differ in a radical way from the one currently used by many urban sociologists. Such a radical change in theory is a *scientific revolution.*

Since the publication of Thomas Kuhn's *Structure of Scientific Revolutions* in 1962, a good deal of research has been done on scientific revolutions.[5] Charles Darwin's evolutionary theory constituted a scientific revolution of very great magnitude, since it brought with it a revolution in patterns of thinking in philosophy of science and many other sciences in addition to biology. Lavoisier's revolution, which transformed alchemy to chemistry, was important but of smaller magnitude. The Copernican revolution in astronomy and the Newtonian in physics were also far-reaching.

The bias which Lyn Lofland found in urban sociology has ancient roots. In this paper, as a philosopher, I shall be investigating a bias of the third sort in contemporary American moral philosophy. A main bias in moral philosophy for two millenia has been the bias which Lyn Lofland points out in urban sociology: the moral-social world has been taken to be the world as men know it. A meaningful life (or a "good life") has been a life seen from the perspective of males and open only to males—and in fact, only to higher-class white adult males, so that the bias is classist and racist and ageist as well as sexist. I believe a moral, social, and philosophical revolution is necessary to change it.

Part II: A Defense of Abortion

In September 1971, the first issue of *Philosophy and Public Affairs* was published. It was a very different kind of journal from the philosophy journals existing then. Its purpose was to highlight the philosophical dimension in issues of public concern and to encourage "philosophically inclined writers from various disciplines . . . [to] bring their distinctive methods to bear on problems that concern everyone." The journal had an effect on the direction of work in philosophy.

In the first issue of *Philosophy and Public Affairs,* there was a paper by Judith Jarvis Thomson titled "A Defense of Abortion." In the paper, Judith Thomson considers whether or not abortion is ever morally justifiable, concluding that it sometimes is. In the years since this paper was published, it has become one of the classic works used when the abortion problem is considered in philosophy courses and in medicine and ethics courses. It is an example of excellent work in its tradition—which I'll call the "Judith Thomson tradition," even though its roots lie in the seventeenth century, and even though some philosophers in the tradition today disagree with some of Judith Thomson's analyses.

Analyzing Arguments

There is a particular pattern of analysis, a particular method, which philosophers in Judith Thomson's tradition use, and there is a particular pattern of thinking which they take to be *moral reasoning. Moral reasoning* constitutes a technical category within this philosophic tradition, but it is really supposed to capture the kind of thinking people would do in moral matters if they were thinking properly. Let me go over the Judith Thomson paper to show the method and to indicate what moral reasoning is supposed to be.

In the introduction to an anthology in which Judith Thomson's abortion paper is reprinted, editor Joel Feinberg says: "Abortion raises subtle problems for private conscience, public policy, and constitutional law. Most of these problems are essentially philosophical, requiring a degree of clarity about basic concepts that is seldom achieved in legislative debates and letters to the newspaper."[6] As the analytic philosopher sees it, matters of private conscience have to do with a *moral agent* doing whatever *moral reasoning* is necessary to decide whether a *moral act* (or kind of moral act) is *morally justifiable.* Moral reasoning may show that an act is morally unjustifiable as well, of course. One way of showing that an act is justifiable is by finding a *moral principle* which covers it. One moral principle that Judith Thomson considers is "Every person has a right to life." Often, though, the matter is much more complicated, and the moral reasoning requires a *moral argument.*

Philosophers in this tradition spend a great deal of time analyzing arguments. It is a main part of their method. In the process of examining arguments, the philosopher clarifies and develops concepts, and often establishes the basis for a new position. Superficially, the widely used tactic of examining arguments makes this philosophy seem destructive and merely critical. But this is misleading. Razing buildings in a city would look merely destructive unless you realized that the buildings were unsafe for people to live in and that, perhaps, the neighborhood people wanted to build a park on the site.

Here is the line of argument Judith Thomson criticizes:

A. The fetus is a *person* from the moment of conception.
B. Every person has a *right to life.*
∴ C. The fetus has a *right to life.*
D. The mother has a *right* to decide what will happen in and to her body.
E. A person's *right to life* is stronger and more stringent than the mother's *right* to decide what happens in and to her own body and so outweighs it.
∴ F. The fetus may not be killed.

Since aborting the birth amounts (in nearly all cases) to killing the fetus, the conclusion of interest is

∴ G. Abortion is impermissible.

Using the word *mother* here reflects a bias—not Judith Thomson's bias, since she is just citing an argument which some "right-to-lifers" give. A pregnant woman is not a mother, nor is a woman giving birth a mother, except in the barest of biological senses. In the context of this argument, using *mother* constitutes an emotional and moral bias, and it begs the question. So I'll use the term *pregnant woman.*

The method of examining arguments is an exact science in philosophy, and there are various questions to ask in doing the examination. For example, a foremost question to ask is whether the argument is *valid.* That amounts to asking whether the conclusion follows by the laws of logic from the premises. In the argument I set out above, which Judith Thomson will be examining, C is a conclusion from premises A and B. Conclusions may also be premises, and C is in fact a premise in the argument which has F as a conclusion. So a question which Judith Thomson raises is whether the argument having A, B, C, D, and E as premises, and F as conclusion is valid.

In fact, that argument is not valid. Like nearly all arguments given in real life, it is *enthymematic*—that is, it has many suppressed premises not set out explicitly in the argument.

If our arguments in real life weren't enthymematic, we would all die of boredom because the premises which have to be made explicit include enormous numbers of trivial premises that everyone would agree to and which everyone realized are presupposed. Sometimes, however, the suppressed premises are not at all obvious, and they may include unacknowledged prejudices and presuppositions which would be rejected if they were brought to light. For example, Judith Thomson's criticism of many arguments about abortion which I mentioned in the introduction to this paper—that they assume that the pregnant woman's moral decision is on a par with the decision of any other moral agent—is a criticism which reveals an unacknowledged prejudice and presupposition. There are other suppressed premises, or "gaps," in the argument from A to E to conclusion F which Judith Thomson reveals in the course of her paper.

Using Hypothetical Cases

One tactic which Judith Thomson used, and one which is a staple in her tradition, is that of introducing hypothetical cases. Philosophers in this tradition suppose moral agents understand the arguments they are using, although that understanding may need clarification; and they suppose moral agents grasp the concepts involved in the arguments. The philosopher (so they say) merely clarifies the thinking and the concepts which the moral agent already grasps. The philosopher adds nothing new. In fact, adding something new would not be doing philosophy, they claim. It would be doing substantive morality, or moral persuasion. Sometimes philosophers talk of this in terms of clarifying the *meaning of the moral terms*. In that phrasing, it may seem even more obvious that the philosopher is merely dealing with what the moral agents already understand, and clarifying it.

Let me give the main hypothetical case which Judith Thomson uses in her paper:

> . . . let me ask you to imagine this. You wake up in the morning and find yourself in bed with an unconscious violinist. A famous violinist. He has been found to have a fatal kidney ailment, and the Society of Music Lovers has canvassed all the available medical records and found that you alone have the right blood type to help. They have therefore kidnapped you, and last night the violinist's circulatory system was plugged into yours, so that your kidneys can be used to extract poisons from his blood as well as your own. The director of the hospital now tells you, "Look, we're sorry the Society of Music Lovers did this to you—we would never have permitted it if we had known." But still, they did it, and the violinist now is plugged into you. To unplug you would be to kill him. But never mind, it's only for nine months. By then he will have recovered from his ailment, and can safely be unplugged from you. (Pp. 48–49)

Judith Thomson takes this hypothetical case to have obvious analogies to the abortion case, analogies she will use in examining the antiabortion argument. I'll trace the outline of her discussion.

The conclusion of the antiabortion argument is

F. Abortion is impermissible.

Does this mean that the abortion is impermissible absolutely, under any and all circumstances? Or does it mean that it is impermissible under normal circumstances, but that there are extraordinary circumstances in which it might be permissible? To work that out, Judith Thomson begins clarifying premise E.

> E. A person's right to life is stronger and more stringent than the mother's right to decide what happens in and to her own body and outweighs it.

But, she asks, what if the pregnant woman will die if the fetus is not aborted? In that case, we have the pregnant woman's right to life balanced against the fetal right to life. Judith Thomson insists that in order for the valid conclusion to be that abortion is absolutely impermissible, two important, suppressed premises have to be made explicit. They are

> E(1) Performing an abortion would be *directly killing* the fetus and doing nothing will merely be *letting* the mother *die.*
> E(2) Directly killing an innocent person is always and absolutely impermissible.

Judith Thomson now tests premise E(2) by bringing in the hypothetical violinist example. Suppose your kidneys will break down under the strain of purifying the violinist's blood and your own? If someone walks in and unplugs the violinist from you, he will be directly killing the violinist, which is impermissible, by E(2). But, she asks, what if you turn around and unplug *yourself* from the violinist. Is that impermissible? A low murmur rises from all the comfortable nooks in which people are reading Judith Thomson's paper. "Surely not," goes the murmur. "Surely unplugging *yourself* is not impermissible." The moral principle embodied in E(2), that directly killing an innocent person is absolutely impermissible, is overridden by a principle of self-defense (or perhaps qualified by a principle of self-defense). We can see this clearly in the violinist example. But the abortion case also falls under E(2). So if it is not impermissible for you to unplug yourself from the violinist in the hypothetical case, then it is not impermissible for the pregnant woman to abort the fetus.

In the course of her discussion of the pregnant woman's decision to abort, Judith Thomson criticized other writings on abortion for having what amounts to a sexist bias (though she doesn't use that term):

> The main focus of attention in writings on abortion has been on what a third party may or may not do in answer to a request from a woman for an abortion. . . . So, the question asked is what a third party may do, and what the mother may do is decided, almost as an afterthought, from what it is concluded that the third party may do. But it seems to me that to treat the matter in this way is to refuse to grant to the mother that very status of person which is so firmly insisted on for the fetus. (P. 52)

This is a prime example of a woman working within the methods of a particular tradition in philosophy and correcting a bias which has its roots in sexism.

Clarifying Concepts

So far, we see that abortion is not *absolutely* impermissible. In some cases, the pregnant woman may abort herself—or at least her decision to do so may be morally justifiable. Now Judith Thomson goes on to argue that the pregnant woman's right to life and the fetus's right to life aren't on a par. She does this by using an analogy. The pregnant woman and the child, she says, aren't simply like "two tenants in a small house which has, by unfortunate mistake, been rented to both. The mother *owns* the house" (p. 53). She goes on to clarify this with another hypothetical example: "If Jones has found and fastened on a certain coat which he needs to keep him from freezing, but which Smith also needs to keep him from freezing, then it is not impartiality that says, 'I cannot choose between you' when Smith owns the coat. Women have said again and again, 'This body is *my* body!' " (p. 53). At this point, some readers may raise their eyebrows and ask what owning a house or coat has to do with the right to life. Many philosophers, including Judith Thomson, would say that property rights are the very model we work with in discussing rights, that our picture of what rights are, and our understanding of what they are, is gained by focusing on property rights.[7] The reader should pay heed also to the fact that Judith Thomson analyzes the pregnant woman's relation to her body by analogy with the legal relation of property ownership (as distinct from the legal relation of tenancy). She then uses this clarification in terms of property relations to help clarify the question of whether abortion is impermissible.

At this point, the murmur rising from the comfortable nooks may show ripples of shock. "Does this mean *I* have an obligation to seize the coat from Jones so that Smith won't freeze to death?" (Or, by analogy, to seize the woman's body back from the fetus by helping her with an abortion?) Judith Thomson saves us from such actions. We *decide* that it is right that Smith have the coat (or that the woman have her body), but we need not ourselves be the agent who does the confiscating. We must grant, she says, that a person has a right to refuse to confiscate that coat: "But then what should be said is . . . 'I will not *act,*' leaving it open that somebody else can or should and, in particular, that anyone in a position of authority with the job of securing people's rights, both can and should" (p. 54).

Judith Thomson's process of clarifying concepts here has been to show their links with other concepts in the broad conceptual scheme which we moral agents allegedly work within. This network includes the concept of *property* and also the concept of the *law,* which is presupposed in the concepts of property and tenancy (those being legalistic concepts). She also links the concept of rights to the concept of a *legitimate authority* who has the *responsibility* for seeing that rights are secured. We shall see later that these linkages are important. But at the moment, the concept of the right to life needs further clarification—a clarification which involves bringing in the additional moral concept of *justice.*

The Right to Life

Investigating the concept of a right to life is part of clarifying premises B and E of the anti-abortion argument:

> B. Every person has a *right to life.*
> E. A person's *right to life* is stronger and more stringent than the mother's *right to decide* what happens in and to her own body and so outweighs it.

Judith Thomson investigates the concept of the right to life in stages. First she asks, "Does having a right to life mean that you have the right to be given the bare minimum you need to continue life?" This is a specific application of the general question of whether having a right to something means that a person has the right to the means to that something, and is one of the very general clarifications of rights which she will make. Looking at the violinist example again, she concludes that although the violinist has a right to life, and he may need to use my kidneys as his means to keep on living, he has no right to their use. What is important here is that Judith Thomson has distinguished between having the right to something and having the right to the means to that something. She claims it is a feature of all rights and something any adequate account of rights must deal with (p. 56).

If the right to life doesn't necessarily involve the right to the means essential to life, what does it involve? Judith Thomson finally concludes that the right to life must simply be the right not to be killed *unjustly*. She then clarifies the concept of justice she is using by a hypothetical example, once again leaning on the concept of property rights (p. 60).

Suppose two brothers are given a single box of chocolates for Christmas, that is, it is their joint possession. Suppose further that the big brother grabs the box, won't let the little brother have any of the chocolates, and instead eats them all himself. We would all surely agree, she says, that the big brother is treating the little one unjustly, because the little brother has been given a right to half of them (p. 56). She goes on with the example. Suppose the older brother had been given the chocolates for his very own and he ate them all himself, refusing to give the little brother even a single one. He wouldn't be treating the little boy unjustly unless he had somehow given him a right to some of the chocolates. The big boy might be greedy, stingy, callous, and mean. But he would not be unjust.[8]

There are many different concepts of justice, and some of them certainly bear a resemblance to this one, which Judith Thomson claims is one we moral agents use. But according to her concept of justice, one may have a right to something by owning it, or by having been given a right to it (by its rightful owner or perhaps by God or by whatever gives natural rights). To act unjustly, then, seems to mean not letting someone have or use something that person has a right to. Having a right to life comes down to not being deprived of life unjustly.

The question of whether abortion is permissible in a given case, then, seems to turn on whether the woman has given the fetus a right to use her body. Once the area of explicit legal contract and long-standing custom is left behind, it becomes very difficult to decide under what conditions someone has given someone else a right to use something. In trying to clarify this in the abortion case, Judith Thomson brings in some of her most memorable hypothetical examples, about people seeds which float in through the living room windows and root themselves in the carpets. But the upshot is that there are cases of pregnancy in which the woman has not given the fetus a right to use her body and in which the fetus may be aborted without killing it unjustly. And so there are cases in which abortion is not impermissible.

Matters of Public Policy

I have discussed work in the Judith Thomson tradition so far as matters of private conscience go. But Joel Feinberg also said that the abortion issue raised questions for public policy and constitutional law, so it would seem that the tradition deals with moral aspects of those things too. I won't take up the question of constitutional law, but it is important to say some things about the way the tradition handles the moral aspects of matters of public policy.[9]

In Judith Thomson's discussion of rights, a person makes his or her decision of private conscience against a background environment that is fixed so far as the distinction of rights goes. Some rights everyone has, like the right to life. Other rights not everyone has, particularly rights to property or rights to some of the means which are necessary to exercise rights which everyone has. The result is that not everyone can exercise even the rights that everyone has. This background distribution may be changed by actions based on individual conscience; for example, the pregnant woman may decide that she ought to give the fetus a right to use her body. In the main, however, the distribution is changed by public policy; for example, the legislature or the courts may decide that public funds must be used to pay for the abortions of indigent women.

Interestingly enough, philosophers in this tradition clarify questions of public policy in the same way as they clarify questions of private conscience. The only difference they see is that in private conscience, individuals without special status are making decisions about their personal lives; and in public policy, individuals who are acting in certain offices (congressmen, circuit court justices, heads of public health divisions) are making policy decisions which will have effects on the public at large. These philosophers suppose that the process of moral reasoning is the same in both cases. In the public case, each individual supposedly clarifies his or her conscience and then votes. In cases of legislation or in board decisions this is exactly what happens. Executive decisions may be construed as decisions of one-member groups. In this view, public policy is made by aggregates of individuals each of whom reasons his or her way through the moral arguments and then votes.

This should serve as enough of a discussion of work in the Judith Thomson tradition to give the reader a feel for the style and to set out enough of the method, categories, and concepts so that I may later argue for bias in the tradition. I'll now turn to an altogether different sort of discussion of abortion.

Part III: Jane

In 1969, most state laws prohibited abortion unless the life of the pregnant woman was threatened.[10] A few states had reformed their abortion laws to allow abortion by doctors in hospitals in cases of threat to the health of the woman, threat of fetal deformity, or rape.[11] In the mid-1960s, the estimated death rate for abortions performed in hospitals was 3 deaths per 100,000 abortions; the rate for illegal abortions was guessed to be over eight times that—30 deaths per 100,00 abortions was a rough estimate and almost certainly conservative.[12] For minority and poorer women, it was certainly very much higher.

The women's liberation movement was in its infancy in 1969. In that year, a group of Chicago women who had been active in radical politics formed an organization called Jane. Over the next year and a half, Jane evolved from an abortion counseling and referral service to a service in which abortions were actually performed by the Jane members themselves. By 1973 when they closed the service, over 12,000 abortions had been performed under Jane's auspices. The medical record equalled that of abortions done under legal, licensed conditions by physicians in hospitals. The service charged on a sliding scale; eventually all abortions were cheaper than the going rate, and some women paid nothing. Jane served many poor women, black women, and very young women who could not have had an abortion otherwise.

My discussion of Jane is based on one newspaper series and an interview with one member. Perhaps not all Jane members will agree with this member's interpretation, but that isn't the point here because I'm not doing a sociological study. I am investigating patterns of moral thinking and acting which the Judith Thomson tradition makes invisible. The fact that one person's thinking and action are concealed is enough to show bias. Pauline B. Bart has done a broader based study.[13]

What Jane Did

This is the way Jane operated, as reported in the June 1973 Hyde Park-Kenwood *Voices* article on the organization: "Jane was the pseudonym we chose to represent the service. A phone was opened in her name and an answering service secured, later replaced by a tape recorder. Jane kept all records and served as control-central." "Jane" was not a particular woman but the code name for whichever counselor was taking calls and coordinating activities on a given day.

> For four years, Jane kept the same phone number. . . . At first she received only eight to ten calls a week. A year later she was receiving well more than 100 calls a week.

All phoned-in messages were returned the same day: "Hello, Marcia. This is Jane from women's liberation returning your call. We can't talk freely over the phone, but I want you to know that we can help you."

Then Jane would refer the name to a counselor, who would meet personally with the woman and talk with her at length about available alternatives.

The counselor would also help the woman arrange finances and, whenever possible, collect a $25 donation for the service loan fund. The counseling session was also a screening process for detecting conflicts and potential legal threats.[14]

Jane worked with several male abortionists. One of these was "Dr. C." Dr. C worked alone with his nurse in motel rooms until the day an abortion was interrupted by a pounding on the door and a man's voice shouting, "Come on out of there, baby killer!" After a wild chase between buildings and down alleys, Dr. C escaped the irate husband. When he caught his breath, he decided that it might be better to quit working in motels.

Jane members then began renting apartments for Dr. C and his nurse to work in. Jane describes the first day they used a rented apartment: "Seven women were done that day, in a setting where they could relax and talk with other women in a similar predicament. And when the first woman walked out of the bedroom, feeling fine and no longer pregnant, the other six were noticeably relieved. They asked her questions and got firsthand answers."[15] Another advantage of the new arrangement was that Jane counselors were with a woman during the abortion, giving her psychological and moral support and explaining what was going on to her. Still another was that the counselors gradually began assisting Dr. C in the abortion itself, and he began training them in the abortion procedures.

After a few months of operation, members of Jane had begun inducing miscarriages for women more than twelve weeks pregnant.[16] During this time, Dr. C was teaching the women of Jane more and more about the process of doing direct abortions. Finally, some counselors were doing the entire direct abortion themselves, under Dr. C's eye. In the midst of all this, they learned that Dr. C was no doctor at all, but just a man who had become an expert in the giving of abortions. Later, they broke off the relationship with Dr. C and began doing all of their own abortions. For good or ill, this meant that they had a sudden abundance of funds, since the abortion fee went to Jane instead of to Dr. C. In the eyes of the law, they became fullfledged abortionists: "We could no longer hide behind the label of 'counselor' or expect 'Dr. C' to act as a buffer, with his know-how and ready cash for dealing with a bust."[17] Jane members were arrested only once, although they were harassed by the police.[18]

The change in the abortion service meant that Jane members had to accept the full consequences of what they were doing—even if it resulted in illness, personal tragedy, or death— and they had to bear this without the protection that the doctor's professionalism gives him.[19] They worked under these conditions until 1 April 1973. Then, two months after the United States Supreme Court passed its opinion on the constitutionality of restrictive abortion laws, Jane officially closed.

What Jane Meant

In describing what Jane did, I selected data to a certain purpose. It was a selection different in many respects from the selection someone in Judith Thomson's tradition would have made. I didn't, however, use any special technical concepts or categories from some philosophical theory. In this section, I shall use Jane as a basis for discussing a moral theory which competes with theories of the Judith Thomson tradition, in order to reveal value implications of bias in that tradition.

Jane was an abortion clinic, and the women of Jane were working out moral and political beliefs and activities, not constructing a theory. I want to try to give a fragment of a theory which is able to capture their thinking and their work. The theory should be taken as *hypothesis* about what Jane meant, subject to correction through further investigation of Jane and groups like Jane, and through seeing what comes of acting on the theory. I believe the theory is based on anarchist, or anarchist-feminist principles, but I won't discuss that. Instead I'll call the tradition out of which the theory arises the Jane tradition, to contrast with the Judith Thomson tradition.

In March 1977, I interviewed one of the founders of Jane. She said that the women who founded the organization had been active in civil rights or anti-war work in the late 1960s. They wanted to begin work in the newly born women's liberation movement. But how should they begin? What should they do? Someone suggested abortion as an issue. It was a difficult decision, and they struggled over it for months. Deciding on an issue required an analysis of a network of larger issues, and of the place of the abortion issue in that network. According to the woman I interviewed, the question was one of a woman's opportunities for life choices: "It was a question of free choice about reproduction, free choice about life style, because the old roles for women weren't viable any more. In frontier times, childbearing was valuable and important. So was housework. But that role is gone. The old ways are gone. We felt nothing *could* come in to replace them unless women could make a choice about childbearing. That seemed necessary for any other choice." These alternatives had to be *created* within our social system. The members of Jane hoped that other groups within the women's movement would work on other alternatives—offering alternative living arrangements, working on ways that women could become economically independent, and so on—while Jane members tried to offer the alternative of choosing not to have the child by aborting. That is, they thought in terms of a division of labor among women working to change the society so that women would have real alternatives for meaningful lives.

As I mentioned in the introduction, the concept of a *meaningful life* (more often called "a good life") has traditionally been a central concept in moral philosophy. The pattern of thinking Jane members use requires a holistic analysis of the society in terms of the resources it actually offers for women to have meaningful lives, plus an analysis of how to change the society so that it can offer such resources. I'll take this up in more detail in Part IV.

In offering the alternative of abortion, Jane was offering a service that was badly needed. The alternative was open to all kinds of women—rich and poor, older and young, white and nonwhite, but it was a service most desperately needed by the poorer, younger, and minority women. One author says:

> In a comparison of blacks and whites, both for premarital and marital conceptions, we find that whites have higher percentages ending in induced abortions at the lower educational levels, while at the higher educational levels there is little or no difference between blacks and whites . . . the data point to the greater reliance upon abortion on the part of whites over blacks and on the part of the more affluent or more educated over the less affluent and less educated.[20]

When they did turn to illegal abortion methods, poorer and nonwhite women came out far worse. Nationally in 1968, the black death rate from abortion was six times that of the white death rate. In New York in the early 1960s, 42 percent of the pregnancy-related deaths resulted from illegal abortions; and of those women who died, half were black and 44 percent were Puerto Rican. Only 6 percent were white.[21]

More affluent women were also able to pay the high fees which all good, illegal abortionists charged.[22] Jane overcame this by calculating fees on a sliding scale according to income. Some women paid nothing.

Jane's purpose, however, was not simply to provide a service for women, however valuable that service might be. The Jane group could not provide abortions to all Chicago women who needed them. More than that, Jane members knew that when abortion was legalized, their service would have to disappear. Jane's purpose was to show women a much broader alternative than simply not having a baby, to show that by acting together, women can change society so that all women can have an opportunity to choose a meaningful life. They tried to show this in different ways. One way was through the sliding scale for fees. Counselors explained to a woman paying $300 that she was helping pay the cost for a woman who could pay only $5.00. She was, in a small way, helping to undercut the unfairness of a society which would allow her an abortion but not the poorer woman.

Jane itself was the most dramatic demonstration of an alternative for women acting together. Jane members were themselves future or past candidates for abortion, and in the present, they were doing something dangerous, exhausting, and illegal for the sake of changing society for all women. Jane showed that women could take change into their own hands. By coming to Jane for their abortions, other women were also acting for this change. They were trusting women to do things which traditionally were done by men in their society, and legally done only by doctors (overwhelmingly male) within the rigid, hierarchically ordered medical profession. This was a leap of trust.

In the structure of their service, Jane members were trying to build an alternative kind of medical structure as well.[23]

> We—the counselors—we learned the medical mystiques are just bullshit. That was a great up for us. Do you know, you're required to have a license as a nurse just to give a shot. Nurses can't even give an intravenous on their own. That takes a different kind of license. We would just explain to our workers how you had to fill the syringe, and how to be certain there was no air in it, and why that was important, and so on. We'd spend a lot of time explaining it. Then we would say to the patient, "Well this is the first time that Sue is giving anyone a shot. Maybe you can help her, and be patient with her." The patient was part of what was happening too. Part of the whole team.
>
> Sometimes in the middle of an abortion, we would switch positions to show that everyone in the service could do things, to show that the woman who was counseling could give a shot, and the one who was giving a shot could counsel too. We did it to make people see that they could do it too. They have the power to learn to counsel and give a shot. They have the power to change things and build alternatives.

We here come to the central analysis within the Jane tradition, as it is expressed in Jane's practice. The analysis operates in a very general way to criticize our society and to offer direction to move toward change. Let me state it first in terms of the social structure of the institution of medicine in the United States today.

In the United States, medical people operate within a hierarchical system of dominance and subordination. Those higher in the hierarchy have power which those lower do not have—and the power to order those lower ones around is the least of it. One key aspect of that power is what Howard Becker calls "the right to define the nature of reality." He uses the notion of a "hierarchy of credibility": "In any system of ranked groups, participants take it as given that members of the highest group have the right to define the way things really are."[24] I would argue that this "right of definition" means not only that the word of the higher has heavier weight than that of the lower (teacher over student, doctor over intern or aide) but that the very categories and concepts that are used, the "official" descriptions of reality, are descriptions from the point of view of the dominant persons in the hierarchy. What counts as knowledge itself is defined in terms of that viewpoint, and the definition further legitimates the power of the dominant person.

The power of those in dominant positions in the hierarchy is *legitimate authority*. This contrasts with the *natural authority* of a person who, regardless of position, happens to have a great deal of knowledge, experience, or wisdom about a subject. A doctor's authority is legitimated by the criteria, standards, and institutions which control access to his place in the hierarchy. These criteria and requirements for training on the one hand are aimed at insuring that those with legitimate authority in the hierarchy also have the natural authority required to do the jobs they are doing. Although we all know there are incompetent doctors, these criteria do operate to screen out incompetence *as defined from the top of the hierarchy*. Do they insure that those at the top have natural authority? I think not, and that is because *legitimate authority* carries with it a definition of what counts as knowledge: the definition from the top of the hierarchy, the "official" point of view.

This outlook on knowledge is sometimes called "objective" or "the scientific outlook" of experts. In fact, it is absolutist, and when the definition of reality is given solely in terms of the tradition of the dominant in a dominant-subordinate structure, the outlook is, in fact, biased.

In part, Jane members were operating from the viewpoint of a subordinate group in our society: women. They were using this viewpoint to try to create new social structures which were not based on dominance and subordination and in which authority was natural authority—knowledge which suits the situation to the best degree that we know at the moment. When the woman I interviewed said that the members of Jane tried to show other women that they "have the power to learn to counsel and give a shot" and that they "have the power to change things and build alternatives," she is talking not only about the natural authority of knowledge but what we might call natural *moral* power, or *moral* authority.

In structuring the abortion service as they did, the members of Jane were developing an alternative to hierarchy, but they were also overcoming the vices of dependency and feelings of ignorance and impotence by showing women that they did have the power to learn and do things themselves. The Jane organization itself was built on nonauthoritarian, nonhierarchical principles, and Jane members tried to run it as a collective.

> We tried to make it as nonauthoritarian as we could. We had rotating chairs. There wasn't a high value placed on one kind of work and a low value on another. Every position was so important to what we were doing, and it was treated as equally important, to the highest degree possible. This meant every one of us could do what she was best at. You didn't have people competing to do what was important, or feeling what they were doing wasn't valuable.

In April of 1973, the women of Jane asked themselves, "What next?" Whether abortion had been a good issue to move on or not, there was no place for an illegal abortion service now that abortions were legal. Some of the women went on to found a "well woman clinic," the Emma Goldman Clinic. They hoped to run the clinic on the nonauthoritarian, nonhierarchical model used by Jane.[25] The clinic was organized around the concept of self-help, in which the "patients" are trained too in the kind of medical knowledge they need to understand and care for their own bodies for a large range of normal functions and slight disorders.

Part IV: Bias in the World View

In my discussion here, both the Judith Thomson tradition and the Jane tradition were dealing with the problem of abortion. Neither would take it to be *the* problem. Abortion is a subsidiary problem chosen because of its connection with more central concerns. For Judith Thomson, it is a question of rights—we might even say a question of equal rights.[26] But it cannot be described that way for the Jane tradition without begging questions.

Within the Jane tradition, the problem was taken to be one of meaningful lives for women, or of free choice among genuine alternatives for meaningful lives. Some phrasing of the general problem in these terms seems appropriate to both traditions. Let me quote Betty Friedan, an activist who stands within traditions associated with Judith Thomson's:

> It is my thesis that the core of the problem for women today is not sexual but a problem of identity—a stunting or evasion of growth that is perpetuated by the feminine mystique. It is my thesis that as the Victorian culture did not permit women to accept or gratify their basic sexual needs, our culture does not permit women to accept or gratify their basic need to grow and fulfill their potentialities as human beings, a need which is not solely defined by their sexual roles.[27]

The statement of purpose of the liberal feminist National Organization for Women (NOW) also concerns opportunities for a meaningful life and moral development as a human being: NOW pledges to "take action to bring women into full participation in the mainstream of American society now, exercising all the privileges and responsibilities thereof, in truly equal partnership with men."[28] This makes it appear that for both traditions, the problem may be stated as one of equality, particularly equality so far as it relates to the moral questions of being a full human being and of having a meaningful (or good) life. I believe that this is a central concern of those within the Judith Thomson tradition. But it may be that the problem cannot be resolved under that tradition or its associated world view.

Concealing Data

In Part III, I presented the moral activity of the organization Jane under one tradition. If we look at the Jane organization under the Judith Thomson tradition, we get a different selection of data. Here's a quotation from the newspaper article:

> From the beginning, we discussed the moral implications of abortion from all angles. We listened to right-to-lifers, Catholic clergy, population-control freaks and women's liberationists.
>
> We heard legislators and lobbyists and political commentators arguing fine points of "fetal viability." When does a fetus become a person? When it can survive outside the womb (after six months)? When it begins to move (after four months)? Or from the moment of conception?
>
> Many opponents of abortion called it "murder." We argued the logical counterarguments: If a fetus is a person, then why aren't abortionists and women who have abortions charged with murder?
>
> Or, if the fetus has the rights of a person, then does the woman who carries it become subject to its rights? What happens when the rights of the woman and those of the fetus come into conflict?
>
> All philosophical and legalistic positions lost relevance when we began doing and viewing abortions . . . we knew that we were grappling with matters of life and death and no philosophical arguments could alter that belief.[29]

Judith Thomson, or someone from her tradition, would have been a great help to the Jane women in these early discussions on abortion. On the other hand, these early discussions had no clear relevance to the central moral activity the women of Jane were engaging in—*by their own judgment.* The terms in which they saw the problem were different. Their perception and their moral activity constitute data which are important to solving the problem of equality, but the Judith Thomson tradition not only ignores those data: it makes them invisible. Let's look at some of the mechanisms by which the data are concealed.

One way a tradition conceals data is through the concepts and categories it uses. The Judith Thomson tradition would focus on the Jane discussions of rights. It would ignore the discussions of hierarchy, dominance, and subordination; and perhaps some within the tradition would not take these as morally relevant discussions at all. Any theory must use concepts. Through their very use, some data are selected and some ignored. Yet the question of whether the concepts properly capture the data, or of whether they are *appropriate,* is a central, critical question about the adequacy of any tradition.

In a similar way, the categories a tradition uses to organize data reveal some and conceal others. For example, the Judith Thomson tradition uses the categories of moral agent and of groups of moral agents as aggregates. The tradition also uses a division of moral phenomena into questions of individual conscience and those of public policy, where the latter is a matter of *official* public policy, made by those with legitimate authority. I don't want to argue that the tradition *rules out* other sorts of moral phenomena. But using those categories, it cannot capture the sort of moral phenomena Jane members took to be central: people in a subordinate position acting to create a set of social relations which are not structured by dominance and subordination, through the subordinates' coming to know their own power (as opposed to legitimate authority) through acting in collectives (not aggregates).

But am I being fair to the Judith Thomson tradition? After all, people within it don't claim to cover *all* moral phenomena. Few theories claim to cover everything within their purview, and even within chemistry there are divisions into organic and inorganic. Mightn't there be divisions within the field of moral phenomena so that another part of the tradition might deal with Jane's moral activity and thus reveal it?

Perhaps any new moral tradition we develop will have to have something to do with the concept of rights (and associated concepts), and deal in some way with groups as aggregates and with public policy as officially handed down. But that new tradition could not be the Judith Thomson tradition, for a revolutionary change in the methodology of her tradition is necessary to uncover data like Jane's.

The Judith Thomson tradition supposes that there exists a set of moral concepts embedded in moral principles which "we" all know and understand. In her paper, Judith Thomson herself is clarifying concepts "we" grasp by the standard method of the tradition: the use of hypothetical cases. This method presupposes a very mentalistic view of concepts and word meanings—mentalistic in the way philosophical empiricists are mentalistic in their views on meanings as "ideas." The concepts exist in the speaker's understanding. If someone understands the concept, he or she knows whether it applies in any given case.[30] Considering hypothetical cases (in this view) points out cases the speaker might have overlooked; but once they are brought to his or her attention, the speaker allegedly knows whether the concepts apply or not, and so his or her explicit understanding of the concept is clarified. Similarly, one's explicit understanding of "our" moral principles is supposed to be clarified by considering hypothetical cases.

The most obvious thing to say about this method is that although bringing up hypothetical cases may clarify our understanding of concepts and principles, everyone knows that the selection of hypothetical cases also biases understanding. This bias may be (unintentionally) systematic. For example, Judith Thomson gives a case where Jones faces a frosty death because Smith owns the coat. Why not, instead, use a case where men, women, and children face poor diets, poor housing, and loss of dignity because the owner of a mill decides to move it out of one region into another having cheaper labor and lower tax rates? Philosophers may say the second example is too complicated, but the selection is not a trivial matter of simplicity. The coat example ignores an essential distinction in kinds of property ownership which the mill example reveals.

The method rules out empirical investigation to see what sorts of hypothetical cases might capture what is morally important to persons in a variety of circumstances in the United States. There seems to be no way whatsoever to insure that a fair consideration of hypothetical cases is made to reduce the bias. One can't develop a sampling procedure for hypothetical cases.

Worst of all, the method rules out empirical investigation to discover whether the moral concepts and principles the philosophers are dealing with are really the moral concepts which people use in the United States. It rules out empirical investigation to discover whether those concepts and those moral principles are relevant to the lives of people in different walks of life, investigation to discover whether they are relevant to solving those people's problems of human dignity and a meaningful life *as those people perceive* those problems.

The method itself has the mere appearance of being plausible only for ancient systems of concepts which are well worked out. It has not even the appearance of plausibility for a case like Jane's, in which people are in the process of creating new concepts through creating new social forms. The fundamental theory of meaning, of understanding, and of concept formation on which the method is based is not only inadequate: it is false.

All of this means that to encompass the Jane data, a revolutionary change is necessary in the methodology of the Judith Thomson tradition. Without it, the data remain concealed.

The data being concealed concern human moral activity and the possibilities of changing society. This constitutes a direct and very important value consequence. The Judith Thomson tradition dominates philosophy departments in the prestigious American universities, and even teachers in nonprestigious colleges are trained within it. This means that students are taught to see moral activity within that tradition. Activity requiring patterns of thinking and concepts and categories like Jane's is made invisible to them.

Official Points of View

From its beginnings, the tradition Judith Thomson works within has been centrally concerned with equality. People in this tradition have particularly been concerned that all human beings be equal under the moral law and under the positive law of the state. Equality before the moral or positive law means that the same laws and principles apply to all. Whether or not this is enlightened depends on which laws and principles one chooses and the society in which they apply.

The question of equality which those in the Jane tradition raise is one which takes dominant-subordinate structures in the society as *creators* of inequality. Their solution to the problem of equality is the use of the perception and power of the subordinate to eliminate dominant-subordinate structures through the creation of new social forms which do not have that structure. Those in the Judith Thomson tradition do not raise questions of dominance and subordination except in the moral, legal, and political spheres, where they are seen in terms of moral, legal, and political equality. Particularly, they do not raise the question of whether equality before the moral or positive law may not be rendered empty because of the dominant-subordinate structures in the economic or social (e.g., family) spheres.

It appears that there is a bias in our world view. It is a bias that allows moral problems to be defined from the top of various hierarchies of authority in such a way that the existence of the authority is concealed, and so the existence of alternative definitions that might challenge that authority and radically change our social organization is also concealed. But having acknowledged that, we must return to the question I asked at the beginning of the paper.

Part V: The Intellectual Pursuits

In this paper, I believe I uncovered a bias that requires a revolutionary change in ethics to remedy. But in the process of considering two approaches to the moral problem of abortion, it has become clear that there are serious questions to ask about the question with which I began the paper:

> Has a covert bias been introduced into our world view by the near exclusion of women from the domain of intellectual pursuits? If we ask about a bias in "our" world view, mustn't we ask who that "we" refers to? In fact, doesn't the question presuppose that "our" world view is constructed by people in the "intellectual pursuits"? That is, doesn't it presuppose a hierarchy of authority in which people in some occupations (academic humanists and scientists, professional writers, etc.) define a world view for everyone else? If so, then there is something further that the Jane case shows.

Judith Jarvis Thomson is a woman working in an established intellectual pursuit, and at the time she wrote her paper, she took a stand that amounted to criticizing certain ethical arguments for sex bias. She took her stand as an authority, she criticized other authorities, and her paper has been widely used by still other authorities who are certified to teach ethics classes. I have criticized her work in this paper, but I too write as an authority. This leads us to a certain conundrum—if I may call it that.

The women of Jane were certainly challenging the way men in important positions are certified to define the way we do things and, in fact, their authority to define "our" world view and say how things "really are." But some of the Jane members, at least, were not saying that we should remedy the problem by having women in important positions define the way we do things. They were saying that we should change the way we do things so that we do not have some important people giving the official world view for everyone else. That change cannot be accomplished merely by hiring more women to work in the intellectual pursuits. It requires changing the intellectual pursuits themselves. If Jane shows that we need a revolutionary change from the old moral theory, it is a change in the status of the authorities as well as a change in what has been taken to be moral theory. Unless we strive to find ways to do that, we violate the central moral and scientific injunction for respecting other human beings:

> . . . look upon human group life as chiefly a vast interpretive process in which people, singly and collectively *guide themselves* by *defining* the objects, events and situations they encounter.[31]

Notes

1. Judith Jarvis Thomson, "A Defense of Abortion," *Philosophy and Public Affairs* 1 (September 1971): 47–66.
2. Arlene Kaplan Daniels, "Feminist Perspectives in Sociological Research," in *Another Voice*, ed. Marcia Millman and Rosabeth Moss Kanter (Garden City, New York, 1975), p. 345.
3. Lyn Lofland, "The 'Thereness' of Women: A Selective Review of Urban Sociology," in Millman and Kanter, *Another Voice*, pp. 145–46, citing Herbert Blumer, *Symbolic Interactionism* (Englewood Cliffs, N.J., 1969), p. 132.
4. Lofland, "The 'Thereness' of Women," p. 162.
5. Thomas Kuhn, *The Structure of Scientific Revolutions*, 2nd ed. (Chicago, 1970).
6. Joel Feinberg, ed., *The Problem of Abortion* (Belmont, Calif., 1973), p. 1. All subsequent quotations from Judith Thomson's essay are from this edition.
7. John Locke's work forms an important foundation to this tradition, and the centrality of the concept of property to the concept of rights is explicit in his *Second Treatise of Government*.

8. Both the Marxists and the Freudians among us will raise their eyebrows at the use of this hypothetical case to explain the concept of justice. Plato, of course, would turn over in his grave.

9. Some repercussions for constitutional law are discussed in Betty Sarvis and Hyman Rodman, *The Abortion Controversy* (New York, 1974).

10. For their help in this part of the paper, I thank Howard Becker for his assistance with references on abortion and Shawn Pyne for her zeal and imagination in searching the library. I am much indebted to Shawn Pyne for very helpful conversations and to her unpublished paper "Alternatives to the Health System" (May 1977).

11. For a discussion of abortion laws see Sarvis and Rodman, *The Abortion Controversy*. An excellent and more detailed discussion is given by Kristin Booth Glen in "Abortion in the Courts: A Laywoman's Historical Guide to the New Disaster Area," *Feminist Studies* (January 1978): 1–26. Glen traces the political implications of the fact that the decision turned on the right of physicians to make medical decisions, not on the rights of women.
    The Supreme Court declared state laws restricting abortion unconstitutional on 22 January 1973.

12. See Willard Cates and R. W. Rochat, "Illegal Abortion in the United States: 1972–74," *Family Planning Perspectives* 8 (March/April 1976): 86–92.

13. Pauline B. Bart, Abraham Lincoln School of Medicine, University of Illinois, Chicago, "Seizing the Means of Reproduction," in *Qualitative Sociology*, based on interviews with forty-two members of the Jane collective. I did not know of this study in time to incorporate it into my discussion in this section. I am grateful to Pauline Bart for reading this paper and suggesting two places where my informant's perceptions differed from the majority perception so that I might delete them.

14. Jane, "The Most Remarkable Abortion Story Ever Told," *Hyde Park-Kenwood Voices,* June 1973, p. 2.

15. Ibid.

16. At this time, most abortionists refused to handle women more than twelve weeks pregnant. Nancy Howell Lee, *Search for an Abortionist* (Chicago, 1969), p. 6.

17. Op. Cit., Part VI, November 1973, p. 3.

18. The arrest was in the third year of the service. It appears to have been a renegade action by a few policemen, not a planned political arrest.

19. Jane members had to take on other duties too. Each week during its peak, the service used fifty ampules of ergotrate, ten bottles of xylocaine, a hundred disposable syringes, and six hundred tablets each of tetracycline and ergotrate. For a while, Dr. C's nurse had obtained the drugs. Eventually, Jane members had to devise ways of getting illegal supplies.

20. Lee, *Search for an Abortionist*, p. 161. In New York in the early 1960s, 93 percent of legal, therapeutic abortions were performed on white, private patients. During that period in the United States as a whole, the rate of legal abortions per 1,000 live births was 3.17 for private patients and 0.87 for clinic patients (those entering the hospital without a private physician). In Georgia in 1970, twenty-four times as many legal abortions were performed on unmarried white women as on unmarried black women. Sarvis and Rodman, *The Abortion Controversy*, p. 159.

21. Lee, *Search for an Abortionist*, pp. 169–70.

22. Information about illegal abortionists is spread through informal networks of acquaintances. More affluent women have more access to information about illegal abortionists of quality because they have acquaintances (some of them physicians) who have this information. Jane overcame this by publishing the telephone number of the service in underground newspapers and otherwise publicly spreading word about the service, through brochures, the Chicago Women's Liberation Union, and so on. See Lee, *Search for an Abortionist*, for extensive discussions on this.

23. I spoke with two women who worked with Jane, although only one interview is used in this paper. Both said that patients waited in the *living room*. They never called it the waiting room—although professionals using a house or apartment as an office, e.g., psychotherapists, call the living room the waiting room. Both said that abortions were done in the *bedroom*. They never used the term *operating room* or anything similar. This was part of the attempt to demystify medicine. Some other abortionists made great efforts to cloak themselves in medical mystique—Dr. C is an example, since he called himself "Doctor" when he was not. For a description of one service which smothered the patient in medical mystique (and for a glaring contrast with Jane), see Donald W. Ball, "An Abortion Clinic Ethnography," *Social Problems* 14 (Winter 1967): 293–301.

24. Howard Becker, "Whose Side Are We On?" *Sociological Work* (New Brunswick, N.J., 1977), p. 126.

25. From what I had learned from other sources, it seemed to me that Emma Goldman had been less successful as a nonauthoritarian, nonhierarchical collective activity offering first-quality service. I asked Jane about this. She said that because the abortion service was illegal, it was free of many authoritarian and hierarchal pressures from the medical profession. Because Emma Goldman was a legal clinic, it had to accommodate itself to the medical profession—by maintaining relations with physicians, for example, who would let the clinic use their licenses. This introduced factors of authority because of the licensing procedure, and

with it, hierarchy. For a discussion of self-help, see Boston Women's Health Book Collective, *Our Bodies, Ourselves.* 3rd ed. (New York, 1976), pp. 361–68.

26. For example, her interpreting women's remark, ''This body is *my* body'' by analogy with rights involved in property ownership parallels the great initial step toward equality made by John Locke when he interpreted a man's relation to his body and labor power by analogy with rights involved in property ownership.
27. Betty Friedan, *The Feminine Mystique* (New York, 1974), p. 69. The work originally published in 1963, was a major force in initiating the ''second wave'' in feminism.
28. Ibid., p. 270. Betty Friedan was one of the founders of NOW. Liberal feminists share important parts of a world view with those in the Judith Thomson tradition. They are much more radical than the philosophers, however, in part because they are feminists, in part because they are activists.
29. Jane, ''The Most Remarkable Abortion Story,'' Part VI, *Voices*, November 1973, p. 3.
30. Unless the concept is vague, in which case no one knows whether it applies in certain cases until some sort of definitional decision is made on whether it applies.
31. Blumer, *Symbolic Interactionism*, p. 132.

Study Questions

1. What is Addelson trying to show by using Judith Thomson's article on abortion?
2. What was ''Jane''? What did it do, and what were the reasons for its activities?
3. What is the difference in the way the problem of abortion is viewed in the Thomson tradition and in the Jane tradition? How does the Thomson tradition ''conceal data'' about Jane's activities?
4. What, according to Addelson, are the drawbacks of the method of considering hypothetical cases (a method she associates with the Judith Thomson tradition).
5. How does the Jane tradition view the problem of inequality? Why does Addelson think that Judith Thomson incorporates a dominant-subordinate structure?

In a Different Voice: Women's Conceptions of Self and of Morality

Carol Gilligan

The arc of developmental theory leads from infantile dependence to adult autonomy, tracing a path characterized by an increasing differentiation of self from other and a progressive freeing of thought from contextual constraints. The vision of Luther, journeying from the rejection of a self defined by others to the assertive boldness of ''Here I stand'' and the image of Plato's allegorical man in the cave, separating at last the shadows from the sun, have taken powerful hold on the psychological understanding of what constitutes development. Thus, the individual, meeting fully the developmental challenges of adolescence as set for him by Piaget, Erikson, and Kohlberg, thinks formally, proceeding from theory to fact, and defines

Carol Gilligan, ''Concepts of the Self and of Morality,'' *Harvard Educational Review*, November 1977, 47:4, pp. 481–517. Copyright © 1977 by President and Fellows of Harvard College.

both the self and the moral autonomously, that is, apart from the identification and conventions that had comprised the particulars of his childhood world. So equipped, he is presumed ready to live as an adult, to love and work in a way that is both intimate and generative, to develop an ethical sense of caring and a genital mode of relating in which giving and taking fuse in the ultimate reconciliation of the tension between self and other.

Yet the men whose theories have largely informed this understanding of development have all been plagued by the same problem, the problem of women, whose sexuality remains more diffuse, whose perception of self is so much more tenaciously embedded in relationships with others and whose moral dilemmas hold them in a mode of judgment that is insistently contextual. The solution has been to consider women as either deviant or deficient in their development.

That there is a discrepancy between concepts of womanhood and adulthood is nowhere more clearly evident than in the series of studies on sex-role stereotypes reported by Broverman, Vogel, Broverman, Clarkson, and Rosenkrantz (1972). The repeated finding of these studies is that the qualities deemed necessary for adulthood—the capacity for autonomous thinking, clear decision making, and responsible action—are those associated with masculinity but considered undesirable as attributes of the feminine self. The stereotypes suggest a splitting of love and work that relegates the expressive capacities requisite for the former to women while the instrumental abilities necessary for the latter reside in the masculine domain. Yet, looked at from a different perspective, these stereotypes reflect a conception of adulthood that is itself out of balance, favoring the separateness of the individual self over its connection to others and leaning more toward an autonomous life of work than toward the interdependence of love and care.

This difference in point of view is the subject of this essay, which seeks to identify in the feminine experience and construction of social reality a distinctive voice, recognizable in the different perspective it brings to bear on the construction and resolution of moral problems. The first section begins with the repeated observation of difference in women's concepts of self and of morality. This difference is identified in previous psychological descriptions of women's moral judgments and described as it again appears in current research data. Examples drawn from interviews with women in and around a university community are used to illustrate the characteristics of the feminine voice. The relational bias in women's thinking that has, in the past, been seen to compromise their moral judgment and impede their development now begins to emerge in a new developmental light. Instead of being seen as a developmental deficiency, this bias appears to reflect a different social and moral understanding.

This alternative conception is enlarged in the second section through consideration of research interviews with women facing the moral dilemma of whether to continue or abort a pregnancy. Since the research design allowed women to define as well as resolve the moral problem, developmental distinctions could be derived directly from the categories of women's thought. The responses of women to structured interview questions regarding the pregnancy decision formed the basis for describing a developmental sequence that traces progressive differentiations in their understanding and judgment of conflicts between self and other. While the sequence of women's moral development follows the three-level progression of all social developmental theory, from an egocentric through a societal to a universal perspective, this progression takes place within a distinct moral conception. This conception differs from that derived by Kohlberg from his all-male longitudinal research data.

This difference then becomes the basis in the third section for challenging the current assessment of women's moral judgment at the same time that it brings to bear a new perspective on developmental assessment in general. The inclusion in the overall conception of development of those categories derived from the study of women's moral judgment enlarges developmental understanding, enabling it to encompass better the thinking of both sexes. This is particularly true with respect to the construction and resolution of the dilemmas of adult life. Since the conception of adulthood retrospectively shapes the theoretical understanding of the development that precedes it, the changes in that conception that follow from the more central inclusion of women's judgments recast developmental understanding and lead to a reconsideration of the substance of social and moral development.

Characteristics of the Feminine Voice

The revolutionary contribution of Piaget's work is the experimental confirmation and refinement of Kant's assertion that knowledge is actively constructed rather than passively received. Time, space, self, and other, as well as the categories of developmental theory, all arise out of the active interchange between the individual and the physical and social world in which he lives and of which he strives to make sense. The development of cognition is the process of reappropriating reality at progressively more complex levels of apprehension, as the structures of thinking expand to encompass the increasing richness and intricacy of experience.

Moral development, in the work of Piaget and Kohlberg, refers specifically to the expanding conception of the social world as it is reflected in the understanding and resolution of the inevitable conflicts that arise in the relations between self and others. The moral judgment is a statement of priority, an attempt at rational resolution in a situation where, from a different point of view, the choice itself seems to do violence to justice.

Kohlberg (1969), in his extension of the early work of Piaget, discovered six stages of moral judgment, which he claimed formed an invariant sequence, each successive stage representing a more adequate construction of the moral problem, which in turn provides the basis for its more just resolution. The stages divide into three levels, each of which denotes a significant expansion of the moral point of view from an egocentric through a societal to a universal ethical conception. With this expansion in perspective comes the capacity to free moral judgment from the individual needs and social conventions with which it had earlier been confused and anchor it instead in principles of justice that are universal in application. These principles provide criteria upon which both individual and societal claims can be impartially assessed. In Kohlberg's view, at the highest stages of development morality is freed from both psychological and historical constraints, and the individual can judge independently of his own particular needs and of the values of those around him.

That the moral sensibility of women differs from that of men was noted by Freud (1925/1961) in the following by now well-quoted statement:

> I cannot evade the notion (though I hesitate to give it expression) that for women the level of what is ethically normal is different from what it is in man. Their superego is never so inexorable, so impersonal, so independent of its emotional origins as we require it to be in men. Character-traits which critics of every epoch have brought up against women—that they show less sense of justice than men, that they are less ready to submit to the great exigencies of life, that they are more often influenced in their judgments by feelings of affection or hostility— all these would be amply accounted for by the modification in the formation of their super-ego which we have inferred above.

While Freud's explanation lies in the deviation of female from male development around the construction and resolution of the Oedipal problem, the same observations about the nature of morality in women emerge from the work of Piaget and Kohlberg. Piaget (1932/1965), in his study of the rules of children's games, observed that, in the games they played, girls were "less explicit about agreement [than boys] and less concerned with legal elaboration."

In contrast to the boys' interest in the codification of rules, the girls adopted a more pragmatic attitude, regarding "a rule as good so long as the game repays it." As a result, in comparison to boys, girls were found to be "more tolerant and more easily reconciled to innovations."

Kohlberg (1971) also identifies a strong interpersonal bias in the moral judgments of women, which leads them to be considered as typically at the third of his six-stage developmental sequence. At that stage, the good is identified with "what pleases or helps others and is approved of by them." This mode of judgment is conventional in its conformity to generally held notions of the good but also psychological in its concern with intention and consequence as the basis for judging the morality of action.

That women fall largely into this level of moral judgment is hardly surprising when we read from the Broverman et al. (1972) list that prominent among the twelve attributes considered to be desirable for women are tact, gentleness, awareness of the feelings of others, strong need for security, and easy expression of tender feelings. And yet, herein lies the paradox, for the very traits that have traditionally defined the "goodness" of women, their care for and sensitivity to the needs of others, are those that mark them as deficient in moral development. The infusion of feeling into their judgments keeps them from developing a more independent and abstract ethical conception in which concern for others derives from principles of justice rather than from compassion and care. Kohlberg, however, is less pessimistic than Freud in his assessment, for he sees the development of women as extending beyond the interpersonal level, following the same path toward independent, principled judgment that he discovered in the research on men from which his stages were derived. In Kohlberg's view, women's development will proceed beyond Stage Three when they are challenged to solve moral problems that require them to see beyond the relationships that have in the past generally bound their moral experience.

What then do women say when asked to construct the moral domain; how do we identify the characteristically "feminine" voice? A Radcliffe undergraduate, responding to the question, "If you had to say what morality meant to you, how would you sum it up?" replies:

> When I think of the word morality, I think of obligations. I usually think of it as conflicts between personal desires and social things, social considerations, or personal desires of yourself versus personal desires of another person or people or whatever. Morality is that whole realm of how you decide these conflicts. A moral person is one who would decide, like by placing themselves more often than not as equals, a truly moral person would always consider another person as their equal . . . in a situation of social interaction, something is morally wrong where the individual ends up screwing a lot of people. And it is morally right when everyone comes out better off.*

Yet when asked if she can think of someone whom she would consider a genuinely moral person, she replies, "Well, immediately I think of Albert Schweitzer because he has obviously given his life to help others." Obligation and sacrifice override the ideal of equality, setting up a basic contradiction in her thinking.

Another undergraduate responds to the question, "What does it mean to say something is morally right or wrong?," by also speaking first of responsibilities and obligations:

> Just that it has to do with responsibilities and obligations and values, mainly values. . . . In my life situation I relate morality with interpersonal relationships

---

* The Radcliffe women whose responses are cited were interviewed as part of a pilot study on undergraduate moral development conducted by the author in 1970.

that have to do with respect for the other person and myself. [Why respect other people?] Because they have a consciousness or feelings that can be hurt, an awareness that can be hurt.

The concern about hurting others persists as a major theme in the responses of two other Radcliffe students:

[Why be moral?] Millions of people have to live together peacefully. I personally don't want to hurt other people. That's a real criterion, a main criterion for me. It underlies my sense of justice. It isn't nice to inflict pain. I empathize with anyone in pain. Not hurting others is important in my own private morals. Years ago, I would have jumped out of a window not to hurt my boyfriend. That was pathological. Even today though, I want approval and love and I don't want enemies. Maybe that's why there is morality—so people can win approval, love and friendship.

My main moral principle is not hurting other people as long as you aren't going against your own conscience and as long as you remain true to yourself. . . . There are many moral issues such as abortion, the draft, killing, stealing, monogamy, etc. If something is a controversial issue like these, then I always say it is up to the individual. The individual has to decide and then follow his own conscience. There are no moral absolutes. . . . Laws are pragmatic instruments, but they are not absolutes. A viable society can't make exceptions all the time, but I would personally. . . . I'm afraid I'm heading for some big crisis with my boyfriend someday, and someone will get hurt, and he'll get more hurt than I will. I feel an obligation to not hurt him, but also an obligation to not lie. I don't know if it is possible to not lie and not hurt.

The common thread that runs through these statements, the wish not to hurt others and the hope that in morality lies a way of solving conflicts so that no one will get hurt, is striking in that it is independently introduced by each of the four women as the most specific item in their response to a most general question. The moral person is one who helps others; goodness is service, meeting one's obligations and responsibilities to others, if possible, without sacrificing oneself. While the first of the four women ends by denying the conflict she initially introduced, the last woman anticipates a conflict between remaining true to herself and adhering to her principle of not hurting others. The dilemma that would test the limits of this judgment would be one where helping others is seen to be at the price of hurting the self.

The reticence about taking stands on "controversial issues," the willingness to "make exceptions all the time" expressed in the final example above, is echoed repeatedly by other Radcliffe students, as in the following two examples:

I never feel that I can condemn anyone else. I have a very relativistic position. The basic idea that I cling to is the sanctity of human life. I am inhibited about impressing my beliefs on others.

I could never argue that my belief on a moral question is anything that another person should accept. I don't believe in absolutes. . . . If there is an absolute for moral decisions, it is human life.

Or as a thirty-one-year-old Wellesley graduate says, in explaining why she would find it difficult to steal a drug to save her own life despite her belief that it would be right to steal for another: "It's just very hard to defend yourself against the rules. I mean, we live by consensus, and you take an action simply for yourself, by yourself, there's no consensus there, and that is relatively indefensible in this society now.''

What begins to emerge is a sense of vulnerability that impedes these women from taking a stand, what George Eliot (1860/1965) regards as the girl's ''susceptibility'' to adverse judgments of others, which stems from her lack of power and consequent inability to do something in the world. While relativism in men, the unwillingness to make moral judgments that Kohlberg and Kramer (1969) and Kohlberg and Gilligan (1971) have associated with the adolescent crisis of identity and belief, takes the form of calling into question the concept of morality itself, the women's reluctance to judge stems rather from their uncertainty about their right to make moral statements or, perhaps, the price for them that such judgment seems to entail. This contrast echoes that made by Matina Horner (1972), who differentiated the ideological fear of success expressed by men from the personal conflicts about succeeding that riddled the women's responses to stories of competitive achievement.

> Most of the men who responded with the expectation of negative consequences because of success were not concerned about their masculinity but were instead likely to have expressed existential concerns about finding a ''non-materialistic happiness and satisfaction in life.'' These concerns, which reflect changing attitudes toward traditional kinds of success or achievement in our society, played little, if any, part in the female stories. Most of the women who were high in fear of success imagery continued to be concerned about the discrepancy between success in the situation described and feminine identity.

When women feel excluded from direct participation in society, they see themselves as subject to a consensus or judgment made and enforced by the men on whose protection and support they depend and by whose names they are known. A divorced middle-aged woman, mother of adolescent daughters, resident of a sophisticated university community, tells the story as follows:

> As a woman, I feel I never understood that I was a person, that I can make decisions and I have a right to make decisions. I always felt that that belonged to my father or my husband in some way or church which was always represented by a male clergyman. They were the three men in my life; father, husband, and clergyman, and they had much more to say about what I should or shouldn't do. They were really authority figures which I accepted. I didn't rebel against that. It only has lately occurred to me that I never even rebelled against it, and my girls are much more conscious of this, not in the militant sense, but just in the recognizing sense. . . . I still let things happen to me rather than make them happen, than to make choices, although I know all about choices. I know the procedures and the steps and all. [Do you have any clues about why this might be true?] Well, I think in one sense, there is less responsibility involved. Because if you make a dumb decision, you have to take the rap. If it happens to you, well, you can complain about it. I think that if you don't grow up feeling that you ever had any choices, you don't either have the sense that you have emotional responsibility. With this sense of choice comes this sense of responsibility.

The essence of the moral decision is the exercise of choice and the willingness to accept responsibility for that choice. To the extent that women perceive themselves as having no choice, they correspondingly excuse themselves from the responsibility that decision entails. Childlike in the vulnerability of their dependence and consequent fear of abandonment, they claim to wish only to please but in return for their goodness they expect to be loved and cared for. This, then, is an "altruism" always at risk, for it presupposes an innocence constantly in danger of being compromised by an awareness of the trade-off that has been made. Asked to describe herself, a Radcliffe senior responds:

> I have heard of the onion skin theory. I see myself as an onion, as a block of different layers, the external layers for people that I don't know that well, the agreeable, the social, and as you go inward there are more sides for people I know that I show. I am not sure about the innermost, whether there is a core, or whether I have just picked up everything as I was growing up, these different influences. I think I have a neutral attitude towards myself, but I do think in terms of good and bad. . . . Good—I try to be considerate and thoughtful of other people and I try to be fair in situations and be tolerant. I use the words but I try and work them out practically. . . . Bad things—I am not sure if they are bad, if they are altruistic or I am doing them basically for approval of other people. [Which things are these?] The values I have when I try to act them out. They deal mostly with interpersonal type relations. . . . If I were doing it for approval, it would be a very tenuous thing. If I didn't get the right feedback, there might go all my values.

Ibsen's play, *A Doll House* (1879/1965), depicts the explosion of just such a world through the eruption of a moral dilemma that calls into question the notion of goodness that lies at its center. Nora, the "squirrel wife," living with her husband as she had lived with her father, puts into action this conception of goodness as sacrifice and, with the best of intentions, takes the law into her own hands. The crisis that ensues, most painfully for her in the repudiation of that goodness by the very person who was its recipient and beneficiary, causes her to reject the suicide that she had initially seen as its ultimate expression and chose instead to seek new and firmer answers to the adolescent questions of identity and belief.

The availability of choice and with it the onus of responsibility has now invaded the most private sector of the woman's domain and threatens a similar explosion. For centuries, women's sexuality anchored them in passivity, in a receptive rather than active stance, where the events of conception and childbirth could be controlled only by a withholding in which their own sexual needs were either denied or sacrificed. That such a sacrifice entailed a cost to their intelligence as well was seen by Freud (1908/1959) when he tied the "undoubted intellectual inferiority of so many women" to "the inhibition of thought necessitated by sexual suppression." The strategies of withholding and denial that women have employed in the politics of sexual relations appear similar to their evasion or withholding of judgment in the moral realm. The hesitance expressed in the previous examples to impose even a belief in the value of human life on others, like the reluctance to claim one's sexuality, bespeaks a self uncertain of its strength, unwilling to deal with consequence, and thus avoiding confrontation.

Thus women have traditionally deferred to the judgment of men, although often while intimating a sensibility of their own which is at variance with that judgment. Maggie Tulliver, in *The Mill on the Floss* (Eliot, 1860/1965) responds to the accusations that ensue from the discovery of her secretly continued relationship with Philip Wakeham by acceding to her brother's moral judgment while at the same time asserting a different set of standards by which she attests her own superiority:

> I don't want to defend myself. . . . I know I've been wrong—often continually. But yet, sometimes when I have done wrong, it has been because I have feelings that you would be the better for if you had them. If *you* were in fault ever, if

you had done anything very wrong, I should be sorry for the pain it brought you; I should not want punishment to be heaped on you.

An eloquent defense, Kohlberg would argue, of a Stage Three moral position, an assertion of the age-old split between thinking and feeling, justice and mercy, that underlies many of the clichés and stereotypes concerning the difference between the sexes. But considered from another point of view, it is a moment of confrontation, replacing a former evasion, between two modes of judging, two differing constructions of the moral domain—one traditionally associated with masculinity and the public world of social power, the other with femininity and the privacy of domestic interchange. While the developmental ordering of these two points of view has been to consider the masculine as the more adequate and thus as replacing the feminine as the individual moves toward higher stages, their reconciliation remains unclear.

The Development of Women's Moral Judgment

Recent evidence for a divergence in moral development between men and women comes from the research of Haan (Note 1) and Holstein (1976) whose findings lead them to question the possibility of a "sex-related bias" in Kohlberg's scoring system. This system is based on Kohlberg's six-stage description of moral development. Kohlberg's stages divide into three levels, which he designates as preconventional, conventional, and postconventional, thus denoting the major shifts in moral perspective around a center of moral understanding that equates justice with the maintenance of existing social systems. While the preconventional conception of justice is based on the needs of the self, the conventional judgment derives from an understanding of society. This understanding is in turn superseded by a postconventional or principled conception of justice where the good is formulated in universal terms. The quarrel with Kohlberg's stage scoring does not pertain to the structural differentiation of his levels but rather to questions of stage and sequence. Kohlberg's stages begin with an obedience and punishment orientation (Stage One), and go from there in invariant order to instrumental hedonism (Stage Two), interpersonal concordance (Stage Three), law and order (Stage Four), social contract (Stage Five), and universal ethical principles (Stage Six).

The bias that Haan and Holstein question in this scoring system has to do with the subordination of the interpersonal to the societal definition of the good in the transition from Stage Three to Stage Four. This is the transition that has repeatedly been found to be problematic for women. In 1969, Kohlberg and Kramer identified Stage Three as the characteristic mode of women's moral judgments, claiming that, since women's lives were interpersonally based, this stage was not only "functional" for them but also adequate for resolving the moral conflicts that they faced. Turiel (1973) reported that while girls reached Stage Three sooner than did boys, their judgments tended to remain at that stage while the boys' development continued further along Kohlberg's scale. Gilligan, Kohlberg, Lerner, and Belenky (1971) found a similar association between sex and moral-judgment stage in a study of high-school students, with the girls' responses being scored predominantly at Stage Three while the boys' responses were more often scored at Stage Four.

This repeated finding of developmental inferiority in women may, however, have more to do with the standard by which development has been measured than with the quality of women's thinking per se. Haan's data (Note 1) on the Berkeley Free Speech Movement and Holstein's (1976) three-year longitudinal study of adolescents and their parents indicate that the moral judgments of women differ from those of men in the greater extent to which women's judgments are tied to feelings of empathy and compassion and are concerned more with the resolution of "real-life" as opposed to hypothetical dilemmas (Note 1, p. 34). However, as long as the categories by which development is assessed are derived within a male perspective from male research data, divergence from the masculine standard can be seen only as a failure of development. As a result, the thinking of women is often classified with that of children. The systematic exclusion from consideration of alternative criteria that might better encompass the development of women indicates not only the limitations of a theory framed by men and validated by research samples disproportionately male and adolescent but also the effects of the diffidence prevalent among women, their reluctance to speak publicly in their own voice, given the constraints imposed on them by the politics of differential power between the sexes.

In order to go beyond the question, "How much like men do women think, how capable are they of engaging in the abstract and hypothetical construction of reality?" it is necessary to identify and define in formal terms developmental criteria that encompass the categories of women's thinking. Such criteria would include the progressive differentiations, comprehensiveness, and adequacy that characterize higher-stage resolution of the "more frequently occurring, real-life moral dilemmas of interpersonal, empathic, fellow-feeling concerns" (Haan, Note 1, p. 34), which have long been the center of women's moral judgments and experience. To ascertain whether the feminine construction of the moral domain relies on a language different from that of men, but one which deserves equal credence in the definition of what constitutes development, it is necessary first to find the places where women have the power to choose and thus are willing to speak in their own voice.

When birth control and abortion provide women with effective means for controlling their fertility, the dilemma of choice enters the center of women's lives. Then the relationships that have traditionally defined women's identities and framed their moral judgments no longer flow inevitably from their reproductive capacity but become matters of decision over which they have control. Released from the passivity and reticence of a sexuality that binds them in dependence, it becomes possible for women to question with Freud what it is that they want and to assert their own answers to that question. However, while society may affirm publicly the woman's right to choose for herself, the exercise of such choice brings her privately into conflict with the conventions of femininity, particularly the moral equation of goodness with self-sacrifice. While independent assertion in judgment and action is considered the hallmark of adulthood and constitutes as well the standard of masculine development, it is rather in their care and concern for others that women have both judged themselves and been judged.

The conflict between self and other thus constitutes the central moral problem for women, posing a dilemma whose resolution requires a reconciliation between femininity and adulthood. In the absence of such a reconciliation, the moral problem cannot be resolved. The "good woman" masks assertion in evasion, denying responsibility by claiming only to meet the needs of others, while the "bad woman" forgoes or renounces the commitments that bind her in self-deception and betrayal. It is precisely this dilemma—the conflict between compassion and autonomy, between virtue and power—which the feminine voice struggles to resolve in its effort to reclaim the self and to solve the moral problem in such a way that no one is hurt.

When a woman considers whether to continue or abort a pregnancy, she contemplates a decision that affects both self and others and engages directly the critical moral issue of hurting. Since the choice is ultimately hers and therefore one for which she is responsible, it raises precisely those questions of judgment that have been most problematic for women. Now she is asked whether she wishes to interrupt that stream of life which has for centuries immersed her in the passivity of dependence while at the same time imposing on her the responsibility for care. Thus the abortion decision brings to the core of feminine apprehension, to what Joan Didion (1972) calls "the irreconcilable difference of it—that sense of living one's deepest life underwater, that dark involvement with blood and birth and death," the adult questions of responsibility and choice.

How women deal with such choices has been the subject of my research, designed to clarify, through considering the ways in which women construct and resolve the abortion decision, the nature and development of women's moral judgment. Twenty-nine women, diverse in age, race, and social class, were referred by abortion and pregnancy counseling services and participated in the study for a variety of reasons. Some came to gain further clarification with respect to a decision about which they were in conflict, some in response to a counselor's concern about repeated abortions, and others out of an interest in and/or willingness to contribute to ongoing research. Although the pregnancies occurred under a variety of circumstances in the lives of these women, certain commonalities could be discerned. The adolescents often failed to use birth control because they denied or discredited their capacity to bear children. Some of the older women attributed the pregnancy to the omission of contraceptive measures in circumstances where intercourse had not been anticipated. Since the pregnancies often coincided with efforts on the part of the women to end a relationship, they may be seen as a manifestation of ambivalence or as a way of putting the relationship to the ultimate test of commitment. For these women, the pregnancy appeared to be a way of testing truth, making the baby an ally in the search for male support and protection or, that failing, a companion victim of his rejection. There were, finally, some women who became pregnant either as a result of a failure of birth control or intentionally as part of a joint decision that later was reconsidered. Of the twenty-nine women, four decided to have the baby, one miscarried, twenty-one chose abortion, and three remained in doubt about the decision.

In the initial part of the interview, the women were asked to discuss the decision that confronted them, how they were dealing with it, the alternatives they were considering, their reasons for and against each option, the people involved, the conflicts entailed, and the ways in which making this decision affected their self-concepts and their relationships with others. Then, in the second part of the interview, moral judgment was assessed in the hypothetical mode by presenting for resolution three of Kohlberg's standard research dilemmas.

While the structural progression from a preconventional through a conventional to a postconventional moral perspective can readily be discerned in the women's responses to both actual and hypothetical dilemmas, the conventions that shape women's moral judgments differ from those that apply to men. The construction of the abortion dilemma, in particular, reveals the existence of a distinct moral language whose evolution informs the sequence of women's development. This is the language of selfishness and responsibility, which defines the moral problem as one of obligation to exercise care and avoid hurt. The infliction of hurt is considered selfish and immoral in its reflection of unconcern, while the expression of care is seen as the fulfillment of moral responsibility. The reiterative use of the language of selfishness and responsibility and the underlying moral orientation it reflects sets the women apart from the men whom Kohlberg studied and may be seen as the critical reason for their failure to develop within the constraints of his system.

In the developmental sequence that follows, women's moral judgments proceed from an initial focus on the self at the *first level* to the discovery, in the transition to the *second level*, of the concept of responsibility as the basis for a new equilibrium between self and others. The elaboration of this concept of responsibility and its fusion with a maternal concept of morality, which seeks to ensure protection for the dependent and unequal, characterizes the *second level* of judgment. At this level the good is equated with caring for others. However, when the conventions of feminine goodness legitimize only others as the recipients of moral care, the logical inequality between self and other and the psychological violence that it engenders create the disequilibrium that initiates the *second* transition. The relationship between self and others is then reconsidered in an effort to sort out the confusion between conformity and care inherent in the conventional definition of feminine goodness and to establish a new equilibrium, which dissipates the tension between selfishness and responsibility. At the *third level*, the self becomes the arbiter of an independent judgment that now subsumes both conventions and individual needs under the moral principle of nonviolence. Judgment remains psychological in its concern with the intention and consequences of action, but it now becomes universal in its condemnation of exploitation and hurt.

Level I: Orientation to Individual Survival

In its initial and simplest construction, the abortion decision centers on the self. The concern is pragmatic, and the issue is individual survival. At this level, "should" is undifferentiated from "would," and others influence the decision only through their power to affect its consequences. An eighteen-year-old, asked what she thought when she found herself pregnant, replies: "I really didn't think anything except that I didn't want it. [Why was that?] I didn't want it, I wasn't ready for it, and next year will be my last year and I want to go to school."

Asked if there was a right decision, she says, "There is no right decision. [Why?] I didn't want it." For her the question of right decision would emerge only if her own needs were in conflict; then she would have to decide which needs should take precedence. This was the dilemma of another eighteen-year-old, who saw having a baby as a way of increasing her freedom by providing "the perfect chance to get married and move away from home," but also as restricting her freedom "to do a lot of things."

At this first level, the self, which is the sole object of concern, is constrained by lack of power; the wish "to do a lot of things" is constantly belied by the limitations of what, in fact, is being done. Relationships are, for the most part, disappointing: "The only thing you are ever going to get out of going with a guy is to get hurt." As a result, women may in some instances deliberately choose isolation to protect themselves against hurt. When asked how she would describe herself to herself, a nineteen-year-old, who held herself responsible for the accidental death of a younger brother, answers as follows:

> I really don't know. I never thought about it. I don't know. I know basically the outline of a character. I am very independent. I don't really want to have to ask anybody for anything and I am a loner in life. I prefer to be by myself than around anybody else. I manage to keep my friends at a limited number with the point that I have very few friends. I don't know what else there is. I am a loner and I enjoy it. Here today and gone tomorrow.

The primacy of the concern with survival is explicitly acknowledged by a sixteen-year-old delinquent in response to Kohlberg's Heinz dilemma, which asks if it is right for a desperate husband to steal an outrageously overpriced drug to save the life of his dying wife:

> I think survival is one of the first things in life and that people fight for. I think it is the most important thing, more important than stealing. Stealing might be wrong, but if you have to steal to survive yourself or even kill, that is what you should do. . . . Preservation of oneself, I think, is the most important thing; it comes before anything in life.

The First Transition: From Selfishness to Responsibility

In the transition which follows and criticizes this level of judgment, the words selfishness and responsibility first appear. Their reference initially is to the self in a redefinition of the self-interest which has thus far served as the basis for judgment. The transitional issue is one of attachment or connection to others. The pregnancy catches up the issue not only by representing an immediate, literal connection, but also by affirming, in the most concrete and physical way, the capacity to assume adult feminine roles. However, while having a baby seems at first to offer respite from the loneliness of adolescence and to solve conflicts over dependence and independence, in reality the continuation of an adolescent pregnancy generally compounds these problems, increasing social isolation and precluding further steps toward independence.

To be a mother in the societal as well as the physical sense requires the assumption of parental responsibility for the care and protection of a child. However, in order to be able to care for another, one must first be able to care responsibly for oneself. The growth from childhood to adulthood, conceived as a move from selfishness to responsibility, is articulated explicitly in these terms by a seventeen-year-old who describes her response to her pregnancy as follows:

> I started feeling really good about being pregnant instead of feeling really bad, because I wasn't looking at the situation realistically. I was looking at it from my own sort of selfish needs because I was lonely and felt lonely and stuff. . . . Things weren't really going good for me, so I was looking at it that I could have a baby that I could take care of or something that was part of me, and that made me feel good . . . but I wasn't looking at the realistic side . . . about the responsibility I would have to take on . . . I came to this decision that I was going to have an abortion [because] I realized how much responsibility goes with having a child. Like you have to be there, you can't be out of the house all the time which is one thing I like to do . . . and I decided that I have to take on responsibility for myself and I have to work out a lot of things.

Stating her former mode of judgment, the wish to have a baby as a way of combating loneliness and feeling connected, she now criticizes that judgment as both "selfish" and "unrealistic." The contradiction between wishes for a baby and for the freedom to be "out of the house all the time"—that is, for connection and also for independence—is resolved in terms of a new priority, as the criterion for judgment changes. The dilemma now assumes moral definition as the emergent conflict between wish and necessity is seen as a disparity between "would" and "should." In this construction the "selfishness" of willful decision is counterposed to the "responsibility" of moral choice:

> What I want to do is to have the baby, but what I feel I should do which is what I need to do, is have an abortion right now, because sometimes what you want isn't right. Sometimes what is necessary comes before what you want, because it might not always lead to the right thing.

While the pregnancy itself confirms femininity—"I started feeling really good; it sort of made me feel, like being pregnant, I started feeling like a woman"—the abortion decision becomes an opportunity for the adult exercise of responsible choice.

> [How would you describe yourself to yourself?] I am looking at myself differently in the way that I have had a really heavy decision put upon me, and I have never really had too many hard decisions in my life, and I have made it. It has taken some responsibility to do this. I have changed in that way, that I have made a hard decision. And that has been good. Because before, I would not have looked at it realistically, in my opinion. I would have gone by what I wanted to do, and I wanted it, and even if it wasn't right. So I see myself as I'm becoming

more mature in ways of making decisions and taking care of myself, doing something for myself. I think it is going to help me in other ways, if I have other decisions to make put upon me, which would take some responsibility. And I would know that I could make them.

In the epiphany of this cognitive reconstruction, the old becomes transformed in terms of the new. The wish to "do something for myself" remains, but the terms of its fulfillment change as the decision affirms both femininity and adulthood in its integration of responsibility and care. Morality, says another adolescent, "is the way you think about yourself . . . sooner or later you have to make up your mind to start taking care of yourself. Abortion, if you do it for the right reasons, is helping yourself to start over and do different things."

Since this transition signals an enhancement in self-worth, it requires a conception of self which includes the possibility for doing "the right thing," the ability to see in oneself the potential for social acceptance. When such confidence is seriously in doubt, the transitional questions may be raised but development is impeded. The failure to make this first transition, despite an understanding of the issues involved, is illustrated by a woman in her late twenties. Her struggle with the conflict between selfishness and responsibility pervades but fails to resolve her dilemma of whether or not to have a third abortion.

I think you have to think about the people who are involved, including yourself. You have responsibilities to yourself . . . and to make a right, whatever that is, decision in this depends on your knowledge and awareness of the responsibilities that you have and whether you can survive with a child and what it will do to your relationship with the father or how it will affect him emotionally.

Rejecting the idea of selling the baby and making "a lot of money in a black market kind of thing . . . because mostly I operate on principles and it would just rub me the wrong way to think I would be selling my own child," she struggles with a concept of responsibility which repeatedly turns back on the question of her own survival. Transition seems blocked by a self-image which is insistently contradictory:

[How would you describe yourself to yourself?] I see myself as impulsive, practical—that is a contradiction—and moral and amoral, a contradiction. Actually the only thing that is consistent and not contradictory is the fact that I am very lazy which everyone has always told me is really a symptom of something else which I have never been able to put my finger on exactly. It has taken me a long time to like myself. In fact there are times when I don't, which I think is healthy to a point and sometimes I think I like myself too much and I probably evade myself too much, which avoids responsibility to myself and to other people who like me. I am pretty unfaithful to myself . . . I have a hard time even thinking that I am a human being, simply because so much rotten stuff goes on and people are so crummy and insensitive.

Seeing herself as avoiding responsibility, she can find no basis upon which to resolve the pregnancy dilemma. Instead, her inability to arrive at any clear sense of decision only contributes further to her overall sense of failure. Criticizing her parents for having betrayed her during adolescence by coercing her to have an abortion she did not want, she now betrays herself and criticizes that as well. In this light, it is less surprising that she considered selling her child, since she felt herself to have, in effect, been sold by her parents for the sake of maintaining their social status.

The Second Level: Goodness as Self-Sacrifice

The transition from selfishness to responsibility is a move toward social participation. Whereas at the first level, morality is seen as a matter of sanctions imposed by a society of which one is more subject than citizen, at the second level, moral judgment comes to rely on shared norms and expectations. The woman at this level validates her claim to social membership through the adoption of societal values. Consensual judgment becomes paramount and goodness the overriding concern as survival is now seen to depend on acceptance by others.

Here the conventional feminine voice emerges with great clarity, defining the self and proclaiming its worth on the basis of the ability to care for and protect others. The woman now constructs the world perfused with the assumptions about feminine goodness reflected in the stereotypes of the Broverman et al. (1972) studies. There the attributes considered desirable for women all presume an other, a recipient of the "tact, gentleness and easy expression of feeling" which allow the woman to respond sensitively while evoking in return the care which meets her own "very strong need for security." The strength of this position lies in its capacity for caring; its limitation is the restriction it imposes on direct expression. Both qualities are elucidated by a nineteen-year-old who contrasts her reluctance to criticize with her boyfriend's straightforwardness:

> I never want to hurt anyone, and I tell them in a very nice way, and I have respect for their own opinions, and they can do the things the way that they want, and he usually tells people right off the bat. . . . He does a lot of things out in public which I do in private. . . . it is better, the other [his way], but I just could never do it.

While her judgment clearly exists, it is not expressed, at least not in public. Concern for the feelings of others imposes a deference which she nevertheless criticizes in an awareness that, under the name of consideration, a vulnerability and a duplicity are concealed.

At the second level of judgment, it is specifically over the issue of hurting that conflict arises with respect to the abortion decision. When no option exists that can be construed as being in the best interest of everyone, when responsibilities conflict and decision entails the sacrifice of somebody's needs, then the woman confronts the seemingly impossible task of choosing the victim. A nineteen-year-old, fearing the consequences for herself of a second abortion but facing the opposition of both her family and her lover to the continuation of the pregnancy, describes the dilemma as follows:

> I don't know what choices are open to me; it is either to have it or the abortion; these are the choices open to me. It is just that either way I don't . . . I think what confuses me is it is a choice of either hurting myself or hurting other people around me. What is more important? If there could be a happy medium, it would be fine, but there isn't. It is either hurting someone on this side or hurting myself.

While the feminine identification of goodness with self-sacrifice seems clearly to dictate the "right" resolution of this dilemma, the stakes may be high for the woman herself, and the sacrifice of the fetus, in any event, compromises the altruism of an abortion motivated by a concern for others. Since femininity itself is in conflict in an abortion intended as an expression of love and care, this is a resolution which readily explodes in its own contradiction.

"I don't think anyone should have to choose between two things that they love," says a twenty-five-year-old woman who assumed responsibility not only for her lover but also for his wife and children in having an abortion she did not want:

I just wanted the child and I really don't believe in abortions. Who can say when life begins. I think that life begins at conception and . . . I felt like there were changes happening in my body and I felt very protective . . . [but] I felt a responsibility, my responsibility if anything ever happened to her [his wife]. He made me feel that I had to make a choice and there was only one choice to make and that was to have an abortion and I could always have children another time and he made me feel if I didn't have it that it would drive us apart.

The abortion decision was, in her mind, a choice not to choose with respect to the pregnancy—"That was my choice, I had to do it." Instead, it was a decision to subordinate the pregnancy to the continuation of a relationship that she saw as encompassing her life—"Since I met him, he has been my life. I do everything for him; my life sort of revolves around him." Since she wanted to have the baby and also to continue the relationship, either choice could be construed as selfish. Furthermore, since both alternatives entailed hurting someone, neither could be considered moral. Faced with a decision which, in her own terms, was untenable, she sought to avoid responsibility for the choice she made, construing the decision as a sacrifice of her own needs to those of her lover. However, this public sacrifice in the name of responsibility engendered a private resentment that erupted in anger, compromising the very relationship that it had been intended to sustain.

Afterwards we went through a bad time because I hate to say it and I was wrong, but I blamed him. I gave in to him. But when it came down to it, I made the decision, I could have said, "I am going to have this child whether you want me to or not," and I just didn't do it.

Pregnant again by the same man, she recognizes in retrospect that the choice in fact had been hers, as she returns once again to what now appears to have been missed opportunity for growth. Seeking, this time, to make rather than abdicate the decision, she sees the issue as one of "strength" as she struggles to free herself from the powerlessness of her own dependence:

I think that right now I think of myself as someone who can become a lot stronger. Because of the circumstances, I just go along like with the tide. I never really had anything of my own before . . . [this time] I hope to come on strong and make a big decision, whether it is right or wrong.

Because the morality of self-sacrifice had justified the previous abortion, she now must suspend that judgment if she is to claim her own voice and accept responsibility for choice.

She thereby calls into question the underlying assumption of Level Two, which leads the woman to consider herself responsible for the actions of others, while holding others responsible for the choices she makes. This notion of reciprocity, backwards in its assumptions about control, disguises assertion as response. By reversing responsibility, it generates a series of indirect actions, which leave everyone feeling manipulated and betrayed. The logic of this position is confused in that the morality of mutual care is embedded in the psychology of dependence. Assertion becomes personally dangerous in its risk of criticism and abandonment as well as potentially immoral in its power to hurt. This confusion is captured by Kohlberg's (1969) definition of Stage Three moral judgment, which joins the need for approval with the wish to care for and help others.

When thus caught between the passivity of dependence and the activity of care, the woman becomes suspended in an immobility of both judgment and action. "If I were drowning, I couldn't reach out a hand to save myself, so unwilling am I to set myself up against fate," begins the central character of Margaret Drabble's novel, *The Waterfall* (1971), in an effort to absolve herself of responsibility as she at the same time relinquishes control. Facing the same moral conflict which George Eliot depicted in *The Mill on the Floss*, Drabble's heroine proceeds to relive Maggie Tulliver's dilemma but turns inward in her search for the way in which to retell that story. What is initially suspended and then called into question is the judgment which ''had in the past made it seem better to renounce myself than them.''

The Second Transition: From Goodness to Truth

The second transition begins with the reconsideration of the relationship between self and other, as the woman starts to scrutinize the logic of self-sacrifice in the service of a morality of care. In the interview data, this transition is announced by the reappearance of the word selfish. Retrieving the judgmental initiative, the woman begins to ask whether it is selfish or responsible, moral or immoral, to include her own needs within the compass of her care and concern. This question leads her to reexamine the concept of responsibility, juxtaposing the outward concern with what other people think with a new inner judgment.

In separating the voice of the self from those of others, the woman asks if it is possible to be responsible to herself as well as to others and thus to reconcile the disparity between hurt and care. The exercise of such responsibility, however, requires a new kind of judgment whose first demand is for honesty. To be responsible, it is necessary first to acknowledge what it is that one is doing. The criterion for judgment thus shifts from ''goodness'' to ''truth'' as the morality of action comes to be assessed not on the basis of its appearance in the eyes of others, but in terms of the realities of its intention and consequence.

A twenty-four-year-old married Catholic woman, pregnant again two months following the birth of her first child, identifies her dilemma as one of choice: ''You have to now decide; because it is now available, you have to make a decision. And if it wasn't available, there was no choice open; you just do what you have to do.'' In the absence of legal abortion, a morality of self-sacrifice was necessary in order to insure protection and care for the dependent child. However, when such sacrifice becomes optional, the entire problem is recast.

The abortion decision is framed by this woman first in terms of her responsibilities to others: having a second child at this time would be contrary to medical advice and would strain both the emotional and financial resources of the family. However, there is, she says, a third reason for having an abortion, ''sort of an emotional reason. I don't know if it is selfish or not, but it would really be tying myself down and right now I am not ready to be tied down with two.''

Against this combination of selfish and responsible reasons for abortion is her Catholic belief that

> . . . it is taking a life, and it is. Even though it is not formed, it is the potential, and to me it is still taking a life. But I have to think of mine, my son's and my husband's, to think about, and at first I think that I thought it was for selfish reasons, but it is not. I believe that too, some of it is selfish. I don't want another one right now; I am not ready for it.

The dilemma arises over the issue of justification for taking a life: ''I can't cover it over, because I believe this and if I do try to cover it over, I know that I am going to be in a mess. It will be denying what I am really doing.'' Asking ''Am I doing the right thing; is it moral?,'' she counterposes to her belief against abortion her concern with the consequences of continuing the pregnancy. While concluding that ''I can't be so morally strict as to hurt three other people with a decision just because of my moral beliefs,'' the issue of goodness still remains critical to her resolution of the dilemma:

The moral factor is there. To me it is taking a life, and I am going to take that upon myself, that decision upon myself and I have feelings about it, and talked to a priest . . . but he said it is there and it will be from now on, and it is up to the person if they can live with the idea and still believe they are good.

The criteria for goodness, however, move inward as the ability to have an abortion and still consider herself good comes to hinge on the issue of selfishness with which she struggles to come to terms. Asked if acting morally is acting according to what is best for the self or whether it is a matter of self-sacrifice, she replies:

I don't know if I really understand the question. . . . Like in my situation where I want to have the abortion and if I didn't it would be self-sacrificing, I am really in the middle of both those ways . . . but I think that my morality is strong and if these reasons—financial, physical reality and also for the whole family involved—were not here, that I wouldn't have to do it, and then it would be a self-sacrifice.

The importance of clarifying her own participation in the decision is evident in her attempt to ascertain her feelings in order to determine whether or not she was "putting them under" in deciding to end the pregnancy. Whereas in the first transition, from selfishness to responsibility, women made lists in order to bring to their consideration needs other than their own, now, in the second transition, it is the needs of the self which have to be deliberately uncovered. Confronting the reality of her own wish for an abortion, she now must deal with the problem of selfishness and the qualification that she feels it imposes on the "goodness" of her decision. The primacy of this concern is apparent in her description of herself:

I think in a way I am selfish for one thing, and very emotional, very . . . and I think that I am a very real person and an understanding person and I can handle life situations fairly well, so I am basing a lot of it on my ability to do the things that I feel are right and best for me and whoever I am involved with. I think I was very fair to myself about the decision, and I really think that I have been truthful, not hiding anything, bringing out all the feelings involved. I feel it is a good decision and an honest one, a real decision.

Thus she strives to encompass the needs of both self and others, to be responsible to others and thus to be "good" but also to be responsible to herself and thus to be "honest" and "real."

While from one point of view, attention to one's own needs is considered selfish, when looked at from a different perspective, it is a matter of honesty and fairness. This is the essence of the transitional shift toward a new conception of goodness which turns inward in an acknowledgement of the self and an acceptance of responsibility for decision. While outward justification, the concern with "good reasons," remains critical for this particular woman: "I still think abortion is wrong, and it will be unless the situation can justify what you are doing." But the search for justification has produced a change in her thinking, "not drastically, but a little bit." She realizes that in continuing the pregnancy she would punish not only herself but also her husband, toward whom she had begun to feel "turned off and irritated." This leads her to consider the consequences self-sacrifice can have both for the self and for others. "God," she says, "can punish, but He can also forgive." What remains in question is whether her claim to forgiveness is compromised by a decision that not only meets the needs of others but that also is "right and best for me."

The concern with selfishness and its equation with immorality recur in an interview with another Catholic woman whose arrival for an abortion was punctuated by the statement,

"I have always thought abortion was a fancy word for murder." Initially explaining this murder as one of lesser degree—"I am doing it because I have to do it. I am not doing it the least bit because I want to," she judges it "not quite as bad. You can rationalize that it is not quite the same." Since "keeping the child for lots and lots of reasons was just sort of impractical and out," she considers her options to be either abortion or adoption. However, having previously given up one child for adoption, she says: "I knew that psychologically there was no way that I could hack another adoption. It took me about four-and-a-half years to get my head on straight; there was just no way I was going to go through it again." The decision thus reduces in her eyes to a choice between murdering the fetus or damaging herself. The choice is further complicated by the fact that by continuing the pregnancy she would hurt not only herself but also her parents, with whom she lived. In the face of these manifold moral contradictions, the psychological demand for honesty that arises in counseling finally allows decision:

> On my own, I was doing it not so much for myself; I was doing it for my parents. I was doing it because the doctor told me to do it, but I had never resolved in my mind that I was doing it for me. Because it goes back to the fact that I never believed in abortions. . . . Actually, I had to sit down and admit, no, I really don't want to go the mother route now. I honestly don't feel that I want to be a mother, and that is not really such a bad thing to say after all. But that is not how I felt up until talking to Maureen [her counselor]. It was just a horrible way to feel, so I just wasn't going to feel it, and I just blocked it right out.

As long as her consideration remains "moral," abortion can be justified only as an act of sacrifice, a submission to necessity where the absence of choice precludes responsibility. In this way, she can avoid self-condemnation, since, "When you get into moral stuff then you are getting into self-respect and that stuff, and at least if I do something that I feel is morally wrong, then I tend to lose some of my self-respect as a person." Her evasion of responsibility, critical to maintaining the innocence necessary for self-respect, contradicts the reality of her own participation in the abortion decision. The dishonesty in her plea of victimization creates the conflict that generates the need for a more inclusive understanding. She must now resolve the emerging contradiction in her thinking between two uses of the term right: "I am saying that abortion is morally wrong, but the situation is right, and I am going to do it." But the thing is that eventually they are going to have to go together, and I am going to have to put them together somehow." Asked how this could be done, she replies:

> I would have to change morally wrong to morally right. [How?] I have no idea. I don't think you can take something that you feel is morally wrong because the situation makes it right and put the two together. They are not together, they are opposite. They don't go together. Something is wrong, but all of a sudden because you are doing it, it is right.

This discrepancy recalls a similar conflict she faced over the question of euthanasia, also considered by her to be morally wrong until she "took care of a couple of patients who had flat EEGs and saw the job that it was doing on their families." Recalling that experience, she says:

> You really don't know your black and whites until you really get into them and are being confronted with it. If you stop and think about my feelings on euthanasia until I got into it, and then my feelings about abortion until I got into it, I thought both of them were murder. Right and wrong and no middle but there is a gray.

In discovering the gray and questioning the moral judgments which formerly she considered to be absolute, she confronts the moral crisis of the second transition. Now the conventions which in the past had guided her moral judgment become subject to a new criticism, as she questions not only the justification for hurting others in the name of morality but also the "rightness" of hurting herself. However, to sustain such criticism in the face of conventions that equate goodness with self-sacrifice, the woman must verify her capacity for independent judgment and the legitimacy of her own point of view.

Once again transition hinges on self-concept. When uncertainty about her own worth prevents a woman from claiming equality, self-assertion falls prey to the old criticism of selfishness. Then the morality that condones self-destruction in the name of responsible care is not repudiated as inadequate but rather is abandoned in the face of its threat to survival. Moral obligation, rather than expanding to include the self, is rejected completely as the failure of conventional reciprocity leaves the woman unwilling any longer to protect others at what is now seen to be her own expense. In the absence of morality, survival, however "selfish" or "immoral," returns as the paramount concern.

A musician in her late twenties illustrates this transitional impasse. Having led an independent life which centered on her work, she considered herself "fairly strong-willed, fairly in control, fairly rational and objective" until she became involved in an intense love affair and discovered in her capacity to love "an entirely new dimension" in herself. Admitting in retrospect to "tremendous naiveté and idealism," she had entertained "some vague ideas that some day I would like a child to concretize our relationship . . . having always associated having a child with all the creative aspects of my life." Abjuring, with her lover, the use of contraceptives because, "as the relationship was sort of an ideal relationship in our minds, we liked the idea of not using foreign objects or anything artificial," she saw herself as having relinquished control, becoming instead "just simply vague and allowing events to just carry me along." Just as she began in her own thinking to confront "the realities of that situation"—the possibility of pregnancy and the fact that her lover was married—she found herself pregnant. "Caught" between her wish to end a relationship that "seemed more and more defeating" and her wish for a baby, which "would be a connection that would last a long time," she is paralyzed by her inability to resolve the dilemma which her ambivalence creates.

The pregnancy poses a conflict between her "moral" belief that "once a certain life has begun, it shouldn't be stopped artificially" and her "amazing" discovery that to have the baby she would "need much more [support] than I thought." Despite her moral conviction that she "should" have the child, she doubts that she could psychologically deal with "having the child alone and taking the responsibility for it." Thus a conflict erupts between what she considers to be her moral obligation to protect life and her inability to do so under the circumstances of this pregnancy. Seeing it as "my decision and my responsibility for making the decision whether to have or have not the child," she struggles to find a viable basis on which to resolve the dilemma.

Capable of arguing either for or against abortion "with a philosophical logic," she says, on the one hand, that in an overpopulated world one should have children only under ideal conditions for care but, on the other, that one should end a life only when it is impossible to sustain it. She describes her impasse in response to the question of whether there is a difference between what she wants to do and what she thinks she should do:

> Yes, and there always has. I have always been confronted with that precise situation in a lot of my choices, and I have been trying to figure out what are the things that make me believe that these are things I should do as opposed to what I feel I want to do. [In this situation?] It is not that clear cut. I both want the child and feel I should have it, and I also think I should have the abortion and want it, but I would say it is my stronger feeling, and that I don't have enough

confidence in my work yet and that is really where it is all hinged, I think . . . [the abortion] would solve the problem and I know I can't handle the pregnancy.

Characterizing this solution as "emotional and pragmatic" and attributing it to her lack of confidence in her work, she contrasts it with the "better thought out and more logical and more correct" resolution of her lover who thinks that she should have the child and raise it without either his presence or financial support. Confronted with this reflected image of herself as ultimately giving and good, as self-sustaining in her own creativity and thus able to meet the needs of others while imposing no demands of her own in return, she questions not the image itself but her own adequacy in filling it. Concluding that she is not yet capable of doing so, she is reduced in her own eyes to what she sees as a selfish and highly compromised fight

for my survival. But in one way or another, I am going to suffer. Maybe I am going to suffer mentally and emotionally having the abortion, or I would suffer what I think is possibly something worse. So I suppose it is the lesser of two evils. I think it is a matter of choosing which one I know that I can survive through. It is really. I think it is selfish, I suppose, because it does have to do with that. I just realized that. I guess it does have to do with whether I would survive or not. [Why is this selfish?] Well, you know, it is. Because I am concerned with my survival first, as opposed to the survival of the relationship or the survival of the child, another human being . . . I guess I am setting priorities, and I guess I am setting my needs to survive first. . . . I guess I see it in negative terms a lot . . . but I do think of other positive things; that I am still going to have some life left, maybe. I don't know.

In the face of this failure of reciprocity of care, in the disappointment of abandonment where connection was sought, survival is seen to hinge on her work which is "where I derive the meaning of what I am. That's the known factor." While uncertainty about her work makes this survival precarious, the choice for abortion is also distressing in that she considers it to be "highly introverted—that in this one respect, having an abortion would be going a step backward; going outside to love someone else and having a child would be a step forward." The sense of retrenchment that the severing of connection signifies is apparent in her anticipation of the cost which abortion would entail:

Probably what I will do is I will cut off my feelings, and when they will return or what would happen to them after that, I don't know. So that I don't feel anything at all, and I would probably just be very cold and go through it very coldly. . . . The more you do that to yourself, the more difficult it becomes to love again or to trust again or to feel again. . . . Each time I move away from that, it becomes easier, not more difficult, but easier to avoid committing myself to a relationship. And I am really concerned about cutting off that whole feeling aspect.

Caught between selfishness and responsibility, unable to find in the circumstances of this choice a way of caring which does not at the same time destroy, she confronts a dilemma which reduces to a conflict between morality and survival. Adulthood and femininity fly apart in the failure of this attempt at integration as the choice to work becomes a decision not only to renounce this particular relationship and child but also to obliterate the vulnerability that love and care engender.

The Third Level: The Morality of Nonviolence

In contrast, a twenty-five-year-old woman, facing a similar disappointment, finds a way to reconcile the initially disparate concepts of selfishness and responsibility through a transformed understanding of self and a corresponding redefinition of morality. Examining the assumptions underlying the conventions of feminine self-abnegation and moral self-sacrifice, she comes to reject these conventions as immoral in their power to hurt. By elevating nonviolence—the injuction against hurting—to a principle governing all moral judgment and action, she is able to assert a moral equality between self and other. Care then becomes a universal obligation, the self-chosen ethic of a postconventional judgment that reconstructs the dilemma in a way that allows the assumption of responsibility for choice.

In this woman's life, the current pregnancy brings to the surface the unfinished business of an earlier pregnancy and of the relationship in which both pregnancies occurred. The first pregnancy was discovered after her lover had left and was terminated by an abortion experienced as a purging expression of her anger at having been rejected. Remembering the abortion only as a relief, she nevertheless describes that time in her life as one in which she "hit rock bottom." Having hoped then to "take control of my life," she instead resumed the relationship when the man reappeared. Now, two years later, having once again "left my diaphragm in the drawer," she again becomes pregnant. Although initially "ecstatic" at the news, her elation dissipates when her lover tells her that he will leave if she chooses to have the child. Under these circumstances, she considers a second abortion but is unable to keep the repeated appointments she makes because of her reluctance to accept the reponsibility for that choice. While the first abortion seemed an "honest mistake," she says that a second would make her feel "like a walking slaughter-house." Since she would need financial support to raise the child, her initial strategy was to take the matter to "the welfare people" in the hope that they would refuse to provide the necessary funds and thus resolve her dilemma:

> In that way, you know, the responsibility would be off my shoulders, and I could say, it's not my fault, you know, the state denied me the money that I would need to do it. But it turned out that it was possible to do it, and so I was, you know, right back where I started. And I had an appointment for an abortion, and I kept calling and cancelling it and then remaking the appointment and cancelling it, and I just couldn't make up my mind.

Confronting the need to choose between the two evils of hurting herself or ending the incipient life of the child, she finds, in a reconstruction of the dilemma itself, a basis for a new priority that allows decision. In doing so, she comes to see the conflict as arising from a faulty construction of reality. Her thinking recapitulates the developmental sequence, as she considers but rejects as inadequate the components of earlier-stage resolutions. An expanded conception of responsibility now reshapes moral judgment and guides resolution of the dilemma, whose pros and cons she considers as follows:

> Well, the pros for having the baby are all the admiration that you would get from, you know, being a single woman, alone, martyr, struggling, having the adoring love of this beautiful Gerber baby . . . just more of a home life than I have had in a long time, and that basically was it, which is pretty fantasyland; it is not very realistic. . . . Cons against having the baby: it was going to hasten what is looking to be the inevitable end of the relationship with the man I am presently with. . . . I was going to have to go on welfare, my parents were going to hate me for the rest of my life, I was going to lose a really good job that

I have, I would lose a lot of independence . . . solitude . . . and I would have to be put in a position of asking help from a lot of people a lot of the time. Cons against having the abortion is having to face up to the guilt . . . and pros for having the abortion are I would be able to handle my deteriorating relation with S. with a lot more capability and a lot more responsibility for him and for myself . . . and I would not have to go through the realization that for the next twenty-five years of my life I would be punishing myself for being foolish enough to get pregnant again and forcing myself to bring up a kid just because I did this. Having to face the guilt of a second abortion seemed like, not exactly, well, exactly the lesser of the two evils but also the one that would pay off for me personally in the long run because by looking at why I am pregnant again and subsequently have decided to have a second abortion, I have to face up to some things about myself.

Although she doesn't "feel good about having a second abortion," she nevertheless concludes,

I would not be doing myself or the child or the world any kind of favor having this child. . . . I don't need to pay off my imaginary debts to the world through this child, and I don't think that it is right to bring a child into the world and use it for that purpose.

Asked to describe herself, she indicates how closely her transformed moral understanding is tied to a changing self-concept:

I have been thinking about that a lot lately, and it comes up different than what my usual subconscious perception of myself is. Usually paying off some sort of debt, going around serving people who are not really worthy of my attentions because somewhere in my life I think I got the impression that my needs are really secondary to other people's, and that if I feel, if I make any demands on other people to fulfill my needs, I'd feel guilty for it and submerge my own in favor of other people's, which later backfires on me, and I feel a great deal of resentment for other people that I am doing things for, which causes friction and the eventual deterioration of the relationship. And then I start all over again. How would I describe myself to myself? Pretty frustrated and a lot angrier than I admit, a lot more aggressive than I admit.

Reflecting on the virtues which comprise the conventional definition of the feminine self, a definition which she hears articulated in her mother's voice, she says, "I am beginning to think that all these virtues are really not getting me anywhere. I have begun to notice." Tied to this recognition is an acknowledgement of her power and worth, both previously excluded from the image she projected:

I am suddenly beginning to realize that the things that I like to do, the things I am interested in, and the things that I believe and the kind of person I am is not so bad that I have to constantly be sitting on the shelf and letting it gather dust. I am a lot more worthwhile than what my past actions have led other people to believe.

Her notion of a "good person," which previously was limited to her mother's example of hard work, patience and self-sacrifice, now changes to include the value that she herself places on directness and honesty. Although she believes that this new self-assertion will lead her "to feel a lot better about myself" she recognizes that it will also expose her to criticism:

> Other people may say, 'Boy, she's aggressive, and I don't like that,' but at least, you know, they will know that they don't like that. They are not going to say, 'I like the way she manipulates herself to fit right around me.' . . . What I want to do is just be a more self-determined person and a more singular person.

While within her old framework abortion had seemed a way of "copping out" instead of being a "responsible person [who] pays for his mistakes and pays and pays and is always there when she says she will be there and even when she doesn't say she will be there is there," now, her "conception of what I think is right for myself and my conception of self-worth is changing." She can consider this emergent self "also a good person," as her concept of goodness expands to encompass "the feeling of self-worth; you are not going to sell yourself short and you are not going to make yourself do things that, you know, are really stupid and that you don't want to do." This reorientation centers on the awareness that:

> I have a responsibility to myself, and you know, for once I am beginning to realize that that really matters to me . . . instead of doing what I want for myself and feeling guilty over how selfish I am, you realize that that is a very usual way for people to live . . . doing what you want to do because you feel that your wants and your needs are important, if to no one else, then to you, and that's reason enough to do something that you want to do.

Once obligation extends to include the self as well as others, the disparity between selfishness and responsibility is reconciled. Although the conflict between self and other remains, the moral problem is restructured in an awareness that the occurrence of the dilemma itself precludes non-violent resolution. The abortion decision is now seen to be a "serious" choice affecting both self and others: "This is a life that I have taken, a conscious decision to terminate, and that is just very heavy, a very heavy thing." While accepting the necessity of abortion as a highly compromised resolution, she turns her attention to the pregnancy itself, which she now considers to denote a failure of responsibility, a failure to care for and protect both self and other.

As in the first transition, although now in different terms, the conflict precipitated by the pregnancy catches up the issues critical to development. These issues now concern the worth of the self in relation to others, the claiming of the power to choose, and the acceptance of responsibility for choice. By provoking a confrontation with these issues, the crisis can become "a very auspicious time; you can use the pregnancy as sort of a learning, teeing-off point, which makes it useful in a way." This possibility for growth inherent in a crisis which allows confrontation with a construction of reality whose acceptance previously had impeded development was first identified by Coles (1964) in his study of the children of Little Rock. This same sense of possibility is expressed by the women who see, in their resolution of the abortion dilemma, a reconstructed understanding which creates the opportunity for "a new beginning," a chance "to take control of my life."

For this woman, the first step in taking control was to end the relationship in which she had considered herself "reduced to a nonentity," but to do so in a responsible way. Recognizing hurt as the inevitable concomitant of rejection, she strives to minimize that hurt "by dealing with [his] needs as best I can without compromising my own . . . that's a big point for me, because the thing in my life to this point has been always compromising, and I am not willing to do that any more." Instead, she seeks to act in a "decent, human kind of way . . . one that leaves maybe a slightly shook but not totally destroyed person." Thus the "nonentity" confronts her power to destroy which formerly had impeded any assertion, as she considers the possibility for a new kind of action that leaves both self and other intact.

The moral concern remains a concern with hurting as she considers Kohlberg's Heinz dilemma in terms of the question, "who is going to be hurt more, the druggist who loses some money or the person who loses their life?" The right to property and right to life are weighed not in the abstract, in terms of their logical priority, but rather in the particular, in terms of the actual consequences that the violation of these rights would have in the lives of the people involved. Thinking remains contextual and admixed with feelings of care, as the moral imperative to avoid hurt begins to be informed by a psychological understanding of the meaning of non-violence.

Thus, release from the intimidation of inequality finally allows the expression of a judgment that previously had been withheld. What women then enunciate is not a new morality, but a moral conception disentangled from the constraints that formerly had confused its perception and impeded its articulation. The willingness to express and take responsibility for judgment stems from the recognition of the psychological and moral necessity for an equation of worth between self and other. Responsibility for care then includes both self and other, and the obligation not to hurt, freed from conventional constraints, is reconstructed as a universal guide to moral choice.

The reality of hurt centers the judgment of a twenty-nine-year-old woman, married and the mother of a preschool child, as she struggles with the dilemma posed by a second pregnancy whose timing conflicts with her completion of an advanced degree. Saying that "I cannot deliberately do something that is bad or would hurt another person because I can't live with having done that," she nevertheless confronts a situation in which hurt has become inevitable. Seeking that solution which would best protect both herself and others, she indicates, in her definition of morality, the ineluctable sense of connection which infuses and colors all of her thinking:

> [Morality is] doing what is appropriate and what is just within your circumstances, but ideally it is not going to affect—I was going to say, ideally it wouldn't negatively affect another person, but that is ridiculous, because decisions are always going to affect another person. But you see, what I am trying to say is that it is the person that is the center of the decision making, of that decision making about what's right and what's wrong.

The person who is the center of this decision making begins by denying, but then goes on to acknowledge, the conflicting nature both of her own needs and of her various responsibilities. Seeing the pregnancy as a manifestation of the inner conflict between her wish, on the one hand, "to be a college president" and, on the other, "to be making pottery and flowers and having kids and staying at home," she struggles with contradiction between femininity and adulthood. Considering abortion as the "better" choice—because "in the end, meaning this time next year or this time two weeks from now, it will be less of a personal strain on us individually and on us as a family for me not to be pregnant at this time," she concludes that the decision has

> got to be, first of all, something that the woman can live with—a decision that the woman can live with, one way or another, or at least try to live with, and that it be based on where she is at and other people, significant people in her life, are at.

At the beginning of the interview she had presented the dilemma in its conventional feminine construction, as a conflict between her own wish to have a baby and the wish of others for her to complete her education. On the basis of this construction she deemed it "selfish" to continue the pregnancy because it was something "I want to do." However, as she begins to examine her thinking, she comes to abandon as false this conceptualization of the problem, acknowledging the truth of her own internal conflict and elaborating the tension which she feels between her femininity and the adulthood of her work life. She describes herself as "going in two directions" and values that part of herself which is "incredibly passionate and sensitive"—her capacity to recognize and meet, often with anticipation, the needs of others. Seeing her "compassion" as "something I don't want to lose" she regards it as endangered by her pursuit of professional advancement. Thus the self-deception of her initial presentation, its attempt to sustain the fiction of her own innocence, stems from her fear that to say that *she* does not want to have another baby at this time would be

> an acknowledgement to me that I am an ambitious person and that I want to have power and responsibility for others and that I want to live a life that extends from 9 to 5 every day and into the evenings and on weekends, because that is what the power and responsibility means. It means that my family would necessarily come second . . . there would be such an incredible conflict about which is tops, and I don't want that for myself.

Asked about her concept of "an ambitious person" she says that to be ambitious means to be

> power hungry [and] insensitive. [Why insensitive?] Because people are stomped on in the process. A person on the way up stomps on people, whether it is family or other colleagues or clientele, on the way up. [Inevitably?] Not always, but I have seen it so often in my limited years of working that it is scary to me. It is scary because I don't want to change like that.

Because the acquisition of adult power is seen to entail the loss of feminine sensitivity and compassion, the conflict between femininity and adulthood becomes construed as a moral problem. The discovery of the principle of nonviolence begins to direct attention to the moral dilemma itself and initiates the search for a resolution that can encompass both femininity and adulthood.

Developmental Theory Reconsidered

The developmental conception delineated at the outset, which has so consistently found the development of women to be either aberrant or incomplete, has been limited insofar as it has been predominantly a male conception, giving lip-service, a place on the chart, to the interdependence of intimacy and care but constantly stressing, at their expense, the importance and value of autonomous judgment and action. To admit to this conception the truth of the feminine perspective is to recognize for both sexes the central importance in adult life of the connection between self and other, the universality of the need for compassion and care. The concept of the separate self and of the moral principle uncompromised by the constraints of reality is an adolescent ideal, the elaborately wrought philosophy of a Stephen Daedalus, whose flight we know to be in jeopardy. Erikson (1964), in contrasting the ideological morality of the adolescent with the ethics of adult care, attempts to grapple with this problem of integration, but is impeded by the limitations of his own previous developmental conception.

When his developmental stages chart a path where the sole precursor to the intimacy of adult relationships is the trust established in infancy and all intervening experience is marked only as steps toward greater independence, then separation itself becomes the model and the measure of growth. The observation that for women, identity has as much to do with connection as with separation led Erikson into trouble largely because of his failure to integrate this insight into the mainstream of his developmental theory (Erikson, 1968).

The morality of responsibility which women describe stands apart from the morality of rights which underlies Kohlberg's conception of the highest stages of moral judgment. Kohlberg (Note 3) sees the progression toward these stages as resulting from the generalization of the self-centered adolescent rejection of societal morality into a principled conception of individual natural rights. To illustrate this progression, he cites as an example of integrated Stage Five judgment, "possibly moving to Stage Six," the following response of a twenty-five-year-old subject from his male longitudinal sample:

> [What does the word morality mean to you?] Nobody in the world knows the answer. I think it is recognizing the right of the individual, the rights of other individuals, not interfering with those rights. Act as fairly as you would have them treat you. I think it is basically to preserve the human being's right to existence. I think that is the most important. Secondly, the human being's right to do as he pleases, again without interfering with somebody else's rights. (p. 29)

Another version of the same conception is evident in the following interview response of a male college senior whose moral judgment also was scored by Kohlberg (Note 4) as at Stage Five or Six:

> [Morality] is a prescription, it is a thing to follow, and the idea of having a concept of morality is to try to figure out what it is that people can do in order to make life with each other livable, make for a kind of balance, a kind of equilibrium, a harmony in which everybody feels he has a place and an equal share in things, and it's doing that—doing that is kind of contributing to a state of affairs that go beyond the individual in the absence of which, the individual has no chance for self-fulfillment of any kind. Fairness; morality is kind of essential, it seems to me, for creating the kind of environment, interaction between people, that is prerequisite to this fulfillment of most individual goals and so on. If you want other people to not interfere with your pursuit of whatever you are into, you have to play the game.

In contrast, a woman in her late twenties responds to a similar question by defining a morality not of rights but of responsibility:

> [What makes something a moral issue?] Some sense of trying to uncover a right path in which to live, and always in my mind is that the world is full of real and recognizable trouble, and is it heading for some sort of doom and is it right to bring children into this world when we currently have an overpopulation problem, and is it right to spend money on a pair of shoes when I have a pair of shoes and other people are shoeless. . . . It is part of a self-critical view, part of saying, how am I spending my time and in what sense am I working? I think I have a real drive to, I have a real maternal drive to take care of someone. To take care of my mother, to take care of children, to take care of other people's children, to take care of my own children, to take care of the world. I think that

goes back to your other question, and when I am dealing with moral issues, I am sort of saying to myself constantly, are you taking care of all the things that you think are important and in what ways are you wasting yourself and wasting those issues?

While the postconventional nature of this woman's perspective seems clear, her judgments of Kohlberg's hypothetical moral dilemmas do not meet his criteria for scoring at the principled level. Kohlberg regards this as a disparity between normative and metaethical judgments which he sees as indicative of the transition between conventional and principled thinking. From another perspective, however, this judgment represents a different moral conception, disentangled from societal conventions and raised to the principled level. In this conception, moral judgment is oriented toward issues of responsibility. The way in which the responsibility orientation guides moral decision at the postconventional level is described by the following woman in her thirties:

[Is there a right way to make moral decisions?] The only way I know is to try to be as awake as possible, to try to know the range of what you feel, to try to consider all that's involved, to be as aware as you can be to what's going on, as conscious as you can of where you're walking. [Are there principles that guide you?] The principle would have something to do with responsibility, responsibility and caring about yourself and others. . . . But it's not that on the one hand you choose to be responsible and on the other hand you choose to be irresponsible—both ways you can be responsible. That's why there's not just a principle that once you take hold of you settle—the principle put into practice here is still going to leave you with conflict.

The moral imperative that emerges repeatedly in the women's interviews is an injunction to care, a responsibility to discern and alleviate the "real and recognizable trouble" of this world. For the men Kohlberg studied, the moral imperative appeared rather as an injunction to respect the rights of others and thus to protect from interference the right to life and self-fulfillment. Women's insistence on care is at first self-critical rather than self-protective, while men initially conceive obligation to others negatively in terms of noninterference. Development for both sexes then would seem to entail an integration of rights and responsibilities through the discovery of the complementarity of these disparate views. For the women I have studied, this integration between rights and responsibilities appears to take place through a principled understanding of equity and reciprocity. This understanding tempers the self-destructive potential of a self-critical morality by asserting the equal right of all persons to care. For the men in Kohlberg's sample as well as for those in a longitudinal study of Harvard undergraduates (Gilligan & Murphy, Note 5) it appears to be the recognition through experience of the need for a more active responsibility in taking care that corrects the potential indifference of a morality of noninterference and turns attention from the logic to the consequences of choice. In the development of a postconventional ethic understanding, women come to see the violence generated by inequitable relationships, while men come to realize the limitations of a conception of justice blinded to the real inequities of human life.

Kohlberg's dilemmas, in the hypothetical abstraction of their presentation, divest the moral actors from the history and psychology of their individual lives and separate the moral problem from the social contingencies of its possible occurrence. In doing so, the dilemmas are useful for the distillation and refinement of the "objective principles of justice" toward which Kohlberg's stages strive. However, the reconstruction of the dilemma in its contextual particularity allows the understanding of cause and consequence which engages the compassion and tolerance considered by previous theorists to qualify the feminine sense of justice. Only when substance is given to the skeletal lives of hypothetical people is it possible to consider the social injustices which their moral problems may reflect and to imagine the individual suffering their occurrence may signify or their resolution engender.

The proclivity of women to reconstruct hypothetical dilemmas in terms of the real, to request or supply the information missing about the nature of the people and the places where they live, shifts their judgment away from the hierarchical ordering of principles and the formal procedures of decision making that are critical for scoring at Kohlberg's highest stages. This insistence on the particular signifies an orientation to the dilemma and to moral problems in general that differs from any of Kohlberg's stage descriptions. Given the constraints of Kohlberg's system and the biases in his research sample, this different orientation can only be construed as a failure in development. While several of the women in the research sample clearly articulated what Kohlberg regarded as a postconventional metaethical position, none of them were considered by Kohlberg to be principled in their normative moral judgments of his hypothetical moral dilemmas (Note 4). Instead, the women's judgments pointed toward an identification of the violence inherent in the dilemma itself which was seen to compromise the justice of any of its possible resolutions. This construction of the dilemma led the women to recast the moral judgment from a consideration of the good to a choice between evils.

The woman whose judgment of the abortion dilemma concluded the developmental sequence presented in the preceding section saw Kohlberg's Heinz dilemma in these terms and judged Heinz's action in terms of a choice between selfishness and sacrifice. For Heinz to steal the drug, given the circumstances of his life (which she inferred from his inability to pay two thousand dollars), he would have "to do something which is not in his best interest, in that he is going to get sent away, and that is a supreme sacrifice, a sacrifice which I would say a person truly in love might be willing to make." However, not to steal the drug "would be selfish on his part . . . he would just have to feel guilty about not allowing her a chance to live longer." Heinz's decision to steal is considered not in terms of the logical priority of life over property which justifies its rightness, but rather in terms of the actual consequences that stealing would have for a man of limited means and little social power.

Considered in the light of its probable outcomes—his wife dead, or Heinz in jail, brutalized by the violence of that experience and his life compromised by a record of felony—the dilemma itself changes. Its resolution has less to do with the relative weights of life and property in an abstract moral conception than with the collision it has produced between two lives, formerly conjoined but now in opposition, where the continuation of one life can now occur only at the expense of the other. Given this construction, it becomes clear why consideration revolves around the issue of sacrifice and why guilt becomes the inevitable concomitant of either resolution.

Demonstrating the reticence noted in the first section about making moral judgments, this woman explains her reluctance to judge in terms of her belief

> that everybody's existence is so different that I kind of say to myself, that might be something I wouldn't do, but I can't say that it is right or wrong for that person. I can only deal with what is appropriate for me to do when I am faced with specific problems.

Asked if she would apply to others her own injunction against hurting, she says:

> See, I can't say that it is wrong. I can't say that it is right or that it's wrong because I don't know what the person did that the other person did something

to hurt him . . . so it is not right that the person got hurt, but it is right that the person who just lost the job has got to get that anger up and out. It doesn't put any bread on his table, but it is released. I don't mean to be copping out. I really am trying to see how to answer these questions for you.

Her difficulty in answering Kohlberg's questions, her sense of strain with the construction which they impose on the dilemma, stems from their divergence from her own frame of reference:

> I don't even think I use the words right and wrong anymore, and I know I don't use the word moral, because I am not sure I know what it means. . . . We are talking about an unjust society, we are talking about a whole lot of things that are not right, that are truly wrong, to use the word that I don't use very often, and I have no control to change that. If I could change it, I certainly would, but I can only make my small contribution from day to day, and if I don't intentionally hurt somebody, that is my contribution to a better society. And so a chunk of that contribution is also not to pass judgment on other people, particularly when I don't know the circumstances of why they are doing certain things.

The reluctance to judge remains a reluctance to hurt, but one that stems now not from a sense of personal vulnerability but rather from a recognition of the limitations of judgment itself. The deference of the conventional feminine perspective can thus be seen to continue at the postconventional level, not as moral relativism but rather as part of a reconstructed moral understanding. Moral judgment is renounced in an awareness of the psychological and social determinism of all human behavior at the same time as moral concern is reaffirmed in recognition of the reality of human pain and suffering.

> I have a real thing about hurting people and always have, and that gets a little complicated at times, because, for example, you don't want to hurt your child. I don't want to hurt my child but if I don't hurt her sometimes, then that's hurting her more, you see, and so that was a terrible dilemma for me.

Moral dilemmas are terrible in that they entail hurt; she sees Heinz's decision as "the result of anguish, who am I hurting, why do I have to hurt them." While the morality of Heinz's theft is not in question, given the circumstances which necessitated it, what is at issue is his willingness to substitute himself for his wife and become, in her stead, the victim of exploitation by a society which breeds and legitimizes the druggist's irresponsibility and whose injustice is thus manifest in the very occurrence of the dilemma.

The same sense that the wrong questions are being asked is evident in the response of another woman who justified Heinz's action on a similar basis, saying "I don't think that exploitation should really be a right." When women begin to make direct moral statements, the issues they repeatedly address are those of exploitation and hurt. In doing so, they raise the issue of nonviolence in precisely the same psychological context that brought Erikson (1969) to pause in his consideration of the truth of Gandhi's life.

In the pivotal letter, around which the judgment of his book turns, Erikson confronts the contradiction between the philosophy of nonviolence that informed Gandhi's dealing with the British and the psychology of violence that marred his relationships with his family and with the children of the ashram. It was this contradiction, Erikson confesses,

> which almost brought *me* to the point where I felt unable to continue writing *this* book because I seemed to sense the presence of a kind of untruth in the very

protestation of truth; of something unclean when all the words spelled out an unreal purity; and, above all, of displaced violence where nonviolence was the professed issue.

In an effort to untangle the relationship between the spiritual truth of Satyagraha and the truth of his own psychoanalytic understanding, Erikson reminds Gandhi that "truth, you once said, 'excludes the use of violence because man is not capable of knowing the absolute truth and therefore is not competent to punish.' " The affinity between Satyagraha and psychoanalysis lies in their shared commitment to seeing life as an "experiment in truth," in their being

> somehow joined in a universal "therapeutics," committed to the Hippocratic prin- ciple that one can test truth (or the healing power inherent in a sick situation) only by action which avoids harm—or better, by action which maximizes mutuality and minimizes the violence caused by unilateral coercion or threat.

Erikson takes Gandhi to task for his failure to acknowledge the relativity of truth. This failure is manifest in the coercion of Gandhi's claim to exclusive possession of the truth, his "unwill- ingness to learn from *anybody anything* except what was approved by the 'inner voice.' " This claim led Gandhi, in the guise of love, to impose his truth on others without awareness or regard for the extent to which he thereby did violence to their integrity.

The moral dilemma, arising inevitably out of a conflict of truths, is by definition a "sick situation" in that its either/or formulation leaves no room for an outcome that does not do violence. The resolution of such dilemmas, however, lies not in the self-deception of rationalized violence—"I was" said Gandhi, "a cruelly kind husband. I regarded myself as her teacher and so harassed her out of my blind love for her"— but rather in the replacement of the underlying antagonism with a mutuality of respect and care.

Gandhi, whom Kohlberg has mentioned as exemplifying Stage Six moral judgment and whom Erikson sought as a model of an adult ethical sensibility, instead is criticized by a judg- ment that refuses to look away from or condone the infliction of harm. In denying the valid- ity of his wife's reluctance to open her home to strangers and in his blindness to the different reality of adolescent sexuality and temptation, Gandhi compromised in his everyday life the ethic of nonviolence to which in principle and in public he was so steadfastly committed.

The blind willingness to sacrifice people to truth, however, has always been the danger of an ethics abstracted from life. This willingness links Gandhi to the biblical Abraham, who prepared to sacrifice the life of his son in order to demonstrate the integrity and supremacy of his faith. Both men, in the limitations of their fatherhood, stand in implicit contrast to the woman who comes before Solomon and verifies her motherhood by relinquishing truth in order to save the life of her child. It is the ethics of an adulthood that has become prin- cipled at the expense of care that Erikson comes to criticize in his assessment of Gandhi's life.

This same criticism is dramatized explicitly as a contrast between the sexes in *The Mer- chant of Venice* (1598/1912), where Shakespeare goes through an extraordinary complication of sexual identity (dressing a male actor as a female character who in turn poses as a male judge) in order to bring into the masculine citadel of justice the feminine plea for mercy. The limitation of the contractual conception of justice is illustrated through the absurdity of its literal execution, while the "need to make exceptions all the time" is demonstrated contrapuntally in the matter of the rings. Portia, in calling for mercy, argues for that resolu- tion in which no one is hurt, and as the men are forgiven for their failure to keep both their rings and their word, Antonio in turns foregoes his "right" to ruin Shylock.

The research findings that have been reported in this essay suggest that women impose a distinctive construction on moral problems, seeing moral dilemmas in terms of conflicting responsibilities. This construction was found to develop through a sequence of three levels and two transitions, each level representing a more complex understanding of the relationship between self and other and each transition involving a critical reinterpretation of the moral conflict between selfishness and responsibility. The development of women's moral judgment appears to proceed from an initial concern with survival, to focus on goodness, and finally to a principled understanding of nonviolence as the most adequate guide to the just resolution of moral conflicts.

In counterposing to Kohlberg's longitudinal research on the development of hypothetical moral judgment in men a cross-sectional study of women's responses to actual dilemmas of moral conflict and choice, this essay precludes the possibility of generalization in either direction and leaves to further research the task of sorting out the different variables of occasion and sex. Longitudinal studies of women's moral judgments are necessary in order to validate the claims of stage and sequence presented here. Similarly, the contrast drawn between the moral judgments of men and women awaits for its confirmation a more systematic comparison of the responses of both sexes. Kohlberg's research on moral development has confounded the variables of age, sex, type of decision, and type of dilemma by presenting a single configuration (the responses of adolescent males to hypothetical dilemmas of conflicting rights) as the basis for a universal stage sequence. This paper underscores the need for systematic treatment of these variables and points toward their study as a critical task for future moral development research.

For the present, my aim has been to demonstrate the centrality of the concepts of responsibility and care in women's constructions of the moral domain, to indicate the close tie in women's thinking between conceptions of the self and conceptions of morality, and, finally, to argue the need for an expanded developmental theory that would include, rather than rule out from developmental consideration, the difference in the feminine voice. Such an inclusion seems essential, not only for explaining the development of women but also for understanding in both sexes the characteristics and precursors of an adult moral conception.

Notes

1. Haan, N. *Activism as moral protest: Moral judgments of hypothetical dilemmas and an actual situation of civil disobedience.* Unpublished manuscript, University of California at Berkeley, 1971.
2. Turiel, E. *A comparative analysis of moral knowledge and moral judgment in males and females.* Unpublished manuscript, Harvard University, 1973.
3. Kohlberg, L. *Continuities and discontinuities in childhood and adult moral development revisited.* Unpublished paper, Harvard University, 1973.
4. Kohlberg, L. Personal communication, August, 1976.
5. Gilligan, C., & Murphy, M. *The philosopher and the "dilemma of the fact": Moral development in late adolescence and adulthood.* Unpublished manuscript, Harvard University, 1977.

Study Questions

1. What theme runs through the essays cited by Gilligan?
2. What does Gilligan think this recurring theme indicates about women's taking moral stands? Does the trait revealed indicate that women are like children?
3. What do women's constructions of the abortion dilemma reveal?
4. Kohlberg distinguishes three perspectives on moral conflict and choice. How does Gilligan view these three stages, or perspectives, in relation to women?
5. How does the first perspective show up in the abortion decisions? The second?
6. How does the third perspective differ from these in regard to abortion decisions?

7. Of the cases discussed of women explaining why they chose abortion, with which (if any) do you have the most sympathy? The least?
8. According to Gilligan, what moral imperative emerges from her interviews with women? How does it differ from the moral imperative that men hold?

Maternal Thinking

Sara Ruddick

We are familiar with Victorian renditions of Ideal Maternal Love. My own favorite, like so many of these poems, was written by a son.

> There was a young man loved a maid
> Who taunted him, "Are you afraid,"
> She asked, "to bring me today
> Your mother's head upon a tray?"

> He went and slew his mother dead,
> Tore from her breast her heart so red,
> Then towards his lady love he raced,
> But tripped and fell in all his haste.

> As the heart rolled on the ground
> It gave forth a plaintive sound.
> And it spoke, in accents mild:
> "Did you hurt yourself, my child?"[1]

Though many of the story's wishes and fantasies are familiar, there is an unfamiliar twist to the poem. The maid asked for the mother's head, the son brought her heart. The maid feared and respected thoughts; the son believed only feelings are powerful. Again we are not surprised. The passions of maternity are so sudden, intense, and confusing that we often remain ignorant of the perspective, the *thought* that has developed from mothering. Lacking pride, we have failed to deepen or articulate that thought. This is a paper about the head of the mother.

I speak about a mother's *thought*—the intellectual capacities she develops, the judgments she makes, the metaphysical attitudes she assumes, the values she affirms. A mother engages in a discipline. That is, she asks certain questions rather than others; she establishes criteria for the truth, adequacy, and relevance of proposed answers; and she cares about the findings she makes and can act on. Like any discipline, hers has *characteristic* errors, temptations, and

Condensed from *Feminist Studies*, Vol. 6, No. 2 (Summer 1980), pp. 342–67. Reprinted by permission of the publisher, Feminist Studies, Inc., c/o Women's Studies Program, University of Maryland, College Park, MD 20742. (Notes deleted.)

goals. The discipline of maternal thought consists in establishing criteria for determining failure and success, in setting the priorities, and in identifying the virtues and liabilities the criteria presume. To describe the capacities, judgments, metaphysical attitudes, and values of maternal thought does not presume maternal achievement. It is to describe a *conception* of achievement, the end to which maternal efforts are directed, conceptions and ends that are different from dominant public ones.

In stating my claims about maternal thinking, I use a vocabulary developed in formulating theories about the general nature of thought. According to these theories, *all* thought arises out of social practice. In their practices, people respond to a reality that appears to them as given, as presenting certain *demands*. The response to demands is shaped by *interests* that are generally interests in preserving, reproducing, directing, and understanding individual and group life.

These four interests are general in the sense that they arise out of the conditions of humans-in-nature and characterize us as a species. In addition, particular practices are characterized by specific interests in meeting the demands that some reality imposes on its participants. Religious, scientific, historical, mathematical, or any other thinking constitutes a disciplined response to a reality that appears to be "given." Socially organized thinkers name, elaborate, and test the particular realities to which they respond.

Maternal practice responds to the historical reality of a biological child in a particular social world. The agents of maternal practice, acting in response to the demands of their children, acquire a conceptual scheme—a vocabulary and logic of connections—through which they order and express the facts and values of their practice. In judgments and self-reflection, they refine and concretize this scheme. Intellectual activities are distinguishable but not separable from disciplines of feeling. There is a unity of reflection, judgment, and emotion. This unity I call "maternal thinking." Although I will not digress to argue the point here, it is important that maternal thinking is no more interest-governed, no more emotional, and no more relative to a particular reality (the growing child) than the thinking that arises from scientific, religious, or any other practice.

The demands of children and the interests in meeting those demands are always and only expressed by people in particular cultures and classes of their culture, living in specific geographical, technological, and historical settings. Some features of the mothering experience are invariant and nearly unchangeable; others, though changeable, are nearly universal. It is therefore possible to identify interests that seem to govern maternal practice throughout the species. Yet it is impossible even to begin to specify these interests without importing features specific to the class, ethnic group, and particular sex-gender system in which the interests are realized. In this essay I draw upon my knowledge of the institutions of motherhood in middle-class, white, Protestant, capitalist, patriarchal America, for these have expressed themselves in the heterosexual nuclear family in which I mother and was mothered. Although I have tried to compensate for the limits of my particular social and sexual history, I principally depend on others to correct my interpretations and translate across cultures.

Interests Governing Maternal Practice

Children "demand" their lives be preserved and their growth fostered. Their social group "demands" that growth be shaped in a way acceptable to the next generation. Maternal practice is governed by (at least) three interests in satisfying these demands for preservation, growth, and acceptability. Preservation is the most invariant and primary of the three. Because a caretaking mother typically bears her own children, preservation begins when conception is recognized and accepted. Although the form of preservation depends on widely variant beliefs about the fragility and care of the fetus, women have always had a lore in which they recorded their concerns for the baby they "carried." Once born, a child is physically vulnerable for many years. Even when she lives with the father of her child or other female adults, even when she has money to purchase or finds available supportive health and welfare services, a mother typically considers herself, and is considered by others, to be responsible for the maintenance of the life of her child.

Interest in fostering the physical, emotional, and intellectual growth of her child soon supplements a mother's interest in its preservation. The human child is typically capable of complicated emotional and intellectual development; the human adult is radically different in kind from the child it once was. A woman who mothers may be aided or assaulted by the help and advice of fathers, teachers, doctors, moralists, therapists, and others who have an interest in fostering and shaping the growth of her child. Although rarely given primary credit, a mother typically holds herself, and is held by others, responsible for the *malfunction* of the growth process. From early on, certainly by the middle years of childhood, a mother is governed by a third interest: she must shape natural growth in such a way that her child becomes the sort of adult that she can appreciate and others can accept. Mothers will vary enormously, individually and socially, in the traits and lives they will appreciate in their children. Nevertheless, a mother typically takes as the criterion of her success the production of a young adult acceptable to her group.

The three interests in preservation, growth, and acceptability of the child govern maternal practices in general. Not all mothers are, as individuals, governed by these interests, however. Some mothers are incapable of interested participation in the practices of mothering because of emotional, intellectual, or physical disability. Severe poverty may make interested maternal practice and therefore maternal thinking nearly impossible. Then, of course, mothers engage in practices other than, and often conflicting with, mothering. Some mothers, aware of the derogation and confinement of women in maternal practice, may be disaffected. In short, actual mothers have the same relation to maternal practice as actual scientists have to scientific practice, or actual believers have to religious practices. As mothers, they are governed by the interests of their respective practices. But the style, skill, commitment, and integrity with which they engage in these practices differ widely from individual to individual.

Interests in the preservation, growth, and acceptability of the child are frequently and unavoidably in conflict. A mother who watches a child eagerly push a friend aside as she or he climbs a tree is torn between preserving the child from danger, encouraging the child's physical skills and courage, and shaping a child according to moral restraints, which might, for example, inhibit the child's joy in competitive climbing. Although some mothers deny or are insensitive to the conflict, and others are clear about which interest should take precedence, mothers typically know that they cannot secure each interest, they know that goods conflict, and they know that unqualified success in realizing interests is an illusion. This unavoidable conflict of basic interests is one objective basis for the maternal humility I will shortly describe.

The Interest in Preserving the Life of the Child

A mother, acting in the interest of preserving and maintaining life, is in a peculiar relation to "nature." As childbearer, she often takes herself, and is taken by others, to be an especially "natural" member of her culture. As child tender, she must respect nature's limits and court its favor with foresightful actions that range from immunizations, to caps on household poisons, to magical imprecation, warnings, and prayers. "Nature" with its unpredictable varieties of dirt and disease is her enemy as much as her ally. Her children are natural creatures, often unable to understand or abet her efforts to protect them. Because they frequently find her necessary direction constraining, a mother can experience her children's own liveliness as another enemy of the life she is preserving.

No wonder, then, that as she engages in preservation, a mother is liable to the temptations of fearfulness and excessive control. If she is alone with and responsible for two or more young children, then control of herself, her children, and her physical environment is her only option, however rigid or excessive she appears to outsiders. Though necessarily controlling their acts, *reflecting* mothers themselves identify rigid or excessive control as the likely defects of the virtues they are required to practice. The identification of liability as such, with its implication of the will to overcome, characterizes this aspect of maternal thought. The epithet "controlling mother" is often unsympathetic, even matriphobic. On the other hand, it may, in line with the insights of maternal thought, remind us of what maternal thinking *counts as* failure.

To a mother, "life" may well seem "terrible, hostile, and quick to pounce on you if you give it a chance."[2] In response, she develops a metaphysical attitude toward "Being as such," an attitude I call "holding," an attitude governed by the priority of keeping over acquiring, of conserving the fragile, of maintaining whatever is at hand and necessary to the child's life. It is an attitude elicited by the work of "world-*protection*, world-*preservation*, world-*repair* . . . the invisible weaving of a frayed and threadbare family life."[3]

The priority of holding over acquiring distinguishes maternal thinking from scientific thinking and from the instrumentalism of technocracy. To be sure, under the pressures of consumerism, holding may become frantic accumulating and storing. More seriously, a parent may feel compelled to preserve her *own* children, whatever befalls other children. The more competitive and hierarchical the society, the more thwarted a mother's individual, autonomous pursuits, the more likely that preservation will become egocentric, frantic, and cruel. Mothers recognize these dangers and fight them.

Holding, preserving mothers have distinctive ways of seeing and being in the world that are worth considering. For example, faced with the fragility of the lives it seeks to preserve, maternal thinking recognizes humility and resilient cheerfulness as virtues of its practice. In so doing it takes issue with popular moralities of assertiveness and much contemporary moral theory.

Humility is a metaphysical attitude one takes toward a world beyond one's control. One might conceive of the world as governed by necessity and change (as I do) or by supernatural forces that cannot be comprehended. In either case, humility implies a profound sense of the limits of one's actions and of the unpredictability of the consequences of one's work. As the philosopher Iris Murdoch puts it: "Every natural thing, including one's own mind, is subject to chance. . . . One might say that chance is a subdivision of death. . . . We cannot dominate the world."[4] Humility that emerges from maternal practices accepts not only the facts of damage and death, but also the facts of the independent and uncontrollable, developing and increasingly separate existences of the lives it seeks to preserve. "Humility is not a peculiar habit of self-effacement, rather like having an inaudible voice, it is selfless respect for reality and one of the most difficult and central of virtues."[5]

If, in the face of danger, disappointment, and unpredictability, mothers are liable to melancholy, they are also aware that a kind, resilient good humor is a virtue. This good humor must not be confused with the cheery denial that is both a liability and, unfortunately, a characteristic of maternal practice. Mothers are tempted to denial simply by the insupportable difficulty of passionately loving a fragile creature in a physically threatening, socially violent, pervasively uncaring and competitive world. Defensive denial is exacerbated as it is officially encouraged, when we must defend against perceptions of our own subordination. Our cheery denials are cruel to our children and demoralizing to ourselves.

Clear-sighted cheerfulness is the virtue of which denial is the degenerative form. It is clear-sighted cheerfulness that Spinoza must have had in mind when he said: "Cheerfulness is always a good thing and never excessive"; it "increases and assists the power of action."[6]

Denying cheeriness drains intellectual energy and befuddles the will; the cheerfulness honored in maternal thought increases and assists the power of maternal action.

In a daily way, cheerfulness is a matter-of-fact willingness to continue, to give birth and to accept having given birth, to welcome life despite its conditions. Resilient good humor is a style of mothering "in the deepest sense of 'style' in which to discover the right style is to discover what you are really trying to do."[7]

Because in the dominant society "humility" and "cheerfulness" name virtues of subordinates, and because these virtues have in fact developed in conditions of subordination, it is difficult to credit them and easy to confuse them with the self-effacement and cheery denial that are their degenerative forms. Again and again, in attempting to articulate maternal thought, language is sicklied o'er by the pale cast of sentimentality and thought itself takes on a greeting-card quality. Yet literature shows us many mothers who in their "holding" actions value the humility and resilient good humor I have described. One can meet such mothers, recognize their thought, any day one learns to listen. One can appreciate the effects of their disciplined perseverance in the unnecessarily beautiful artifacts of the culture they created. "I made my quilt to keep my family warm. I made it beautiful so my heart would not break."[8]

The Interest in Fostering the Child's Growth

Mothers must not only preserve fragile life. They must also foster growth and welcome change. If the "being" preserved seems always to be endangered, undone, slipping away, the "being" that changes is always developing, building, purposively moving away. The "holding," preserving mother must, in response to change, be simultaneously a changing mother. Her conceptual scheme in terms of which she makes sense of herself, her child, and their common world will be more the Aristotelian biologist's than the Platonic mathematician's. Innovation takes precedence over permanence, disclosure and responsiveness over clarity and certainty. The idea of "objective reality" itself "undergoes important modification when it is to be understood, not in relation to the world described by science, but in relation to the progressing life of a person."[9]

Women are said to value open over closed structure, to eschew the clear-cut and unambiguous, to refuse a sharp division between inner and outer or self and other. They also are said to depend on and prize the private inner lives of the mind. If these facets of the "female mind" are elicited by maternal practices, they may well be interwoven responses to the changeability of a growing child. A child is itself an "open structure" whose acts are irregular, unpredictable, often mysterious. A mother, in order to understand her child, must assume the existence of a conscious continuing person whose acts make sense in terms of perceptions and responses to a meaning-filled world. She knows that her child's fantasies and thoughts are connected not only to the child's power to act, but often are the only basis for her understanding of the child and for the child's self-understanding.

A mother, in short, is committed to two philosophical positions: she is a mentalist rather than a behaviorist, and she assumes the priority of personhood over action. Moreover, if her "mentalism" is to enable her to understand and love, she must be realistic about the psyche whose growth she fosters. *All* psyches are moved by fear, lust, anger, pride, and defenses against them; by what Simone Weil called "*natural* movements of the soul" and likened to laws of physical gravity.[10] This is not to deny that the soul is also blessed by "grace," "light," and erotic hungering for goodness.[11] Mothers cannot take grace for granted, however, nor can they force or deny the less flattering aggrandizing and consolatory operations of childhood psychic life.

Her realistic appreciation of a person's continuous mental life allows a mother to expect change, to change with change. As psychologist Jean Baker Miller puts it: "In a very immediate and day-to-day way women *live* for change."[12] Change requires a kind of learning in which what one learns cannot be applied exactly, often not even by analogy, to a new situation. If science agrees to take as real the reliable results of *repeatable* experiments, its learning will be different in kind from maternal learning. Miller is hopeful that if we attend to maternal practices, we can develop new ways of studying learning that are appropriate to the changing natures of all people and communities, for it is not only children who change, grow, and need help in growing; those who care for children must also change in response to changing reality. And we all might grow—as opposed to aging—if we could learn how. For everyone's benefit, "women must now face the task of putting their vast unrecognized experience with change into a new and broader level of operation."[13]

Miller writes of achievement, of women who have learned to change and respond to change. But she admits: "Tragically in our society, women are prevented from fully enjoying these pleasures [of growth] themselves by being made to feel that fostering them in others is the only valid role for all women and by the loneliness, drudgery and isolated non-cooperative household setting in which they work."[14]

In delineating maternal thought, I do not claim that mothers realize, in themselves, the capacities and virtues we learn to value as we care for others. Rather, mothers develop *conceptions* of abilities and virtues, according to which they measure themselves and interpret their actions. It is no great sorrow that some mothers never acquire humility, resilient good humor, realism, respect for persons, and responsiveness to growth—that all of us fail often in many ways. What is a great sorrow is to find the task itself misdescribed, sentimentalized, and devalued.

The Interest in Shaping an Acceptable Child

The third demand that governs maternal practice is the demand, at once social and personal, that the child's growth be shaped in a manner that makes life acceptable. "Acceptability" is defined in terms of the values of the mother's social group—whatever of its values she has internalized as her own plus values of group members whom she feels she must please or is fearful of displeasing. Society demands that a mother produce an adult acceptable to the next generation. Mothers, roughly half of society, have an interest in meeting that demand. They are also governed by a more stringent form of acceptability. They want the child they produce to be a person whom they themselves, and those closest to them, can appreciate. The demand of appreciability gives an urgency—sometimes exhilarating, sometimes anguishing—to maternal practice.

The task of producing an appreciable child gives a mother a unique opportunity to explore, create, and insist on her own values; to train her children for strength and virtue; and ultimately to develop openness and reciprocity in regard to her child's most threatening differences from her, namely, moral ones. As a mother thinks upon the appreciability of her child, her maternal work becomes a self-conscious, reflective expression of a disciplined conscience.

In response to the demand of acceptability, maternal thinking becomes contradictory—that is, it betrays its own interest in the growth of children. Almost everywhere, the practices of mothering take place in societies in which women of all classes are less powerful than men of their class to determine the conditions under which their children grow. Throughout history, most women have mothered in conditions of military and social violence and often of extreme poverty. They have been governed by men, and increasingly by managers and experts of both sexes, whose policies mothers neither shape nor control. Out of maternal powerlessness, in response to a society whose values it does not determine, maternal thinking has often and largely opted for inauthenticity and the "good" of others.

By "inauthenticity" I designate a double willingness—first, a willingness to *travailler pour l'armée*,[15] to accept the uses to which others put one's children; and second, a willingness to remain blind to the implications of those uses for the actual lives of women and children.

Maternal thought embodies inauthenticity by taking on the values of the dominant culture. Like the "holding" of preservation, "inauthenticity" is a mostly nonconscious response to Being as Such. Only this attitude is not a caretaker's response to the natural exigencies of child tending, but a subordinate's reaction to a social reality essentially characterized by the domination and subordination of persons. Inauthenticity constructs and then assumes a world in which one's own values do not count. It is allied to fatalism and to some religious thought—some versions of Christianity, for example. As inauthenticity is lived out in maternal practice, it gives rise to the values of obedience and "being good"; that is, to fulfill the values of the dominant culture is taken as an achievement. Obedience is related to humility in the face of the limits of one's powers. But unlike humility, which respects indifferent nature, the incomprehensible supernatural, and human fallibility, obedience respects the actual control and preferences of dominant people.

Individual mothers, living out maternal thought, take on the values of the subcultures to which they belong and the men with whom they are allied. Because some groups and many men are vibrantly moral, these values are not necessarily inadequate. Nevertheless, even moral groups and men almost always accept the relative subordination of women, whatever other ideals of equality and autonomy they may hold. A "good" mother may well be praised for colluding in her own subordination, with destructive consequences to herself and her children. Moreover, most groups and men impose at least some values that are psychologically and physically damaging to children. Yet, to be "good," a mother may be expected to endorse these inimical values. She is the person principally responsible for training her children in the ways and desires of obedience. This may mean training her daughters for powerlessness, her sons for war, and both for crippling work in dehumanizing factories, businesses, and professions. It may mean training both daughters and sons for defensive or arrogant power over others in sexual, economic, or political life. A mother who trains either for powerlessness or abusive power over others betrays the life she has preserved, whose growth she has fostered. She denies her children even the possibility of being strong and good.

The strain of colluding in one's own powerlessness, coupled with the frequent and much greater strain of betraying the children one has tended, would be insupportable if conscious. A mother under strain may internalize as her own some values that are clearly inimical to her children. She has, after all, usually been rewarded for such protective albeit destructive internalization. In addition, she may blind herself to the implications of her obedience, a blindness excused and exacerbated by the cheeriness of denial. For precariously but deeply protected mothers, feminist accounts of power relations and their cost call into question the worthiness of maternal work and the genuineness of maternal love. It is understandable that such women fight insight as others fight bodily assault, revealing in their struggles a commitment to their own sufferings that may look "neurotic" but is in fact, given their options, realistic.

When I described maternal thought arising out of the interests in growth and preservation, I was not speaking of the actual achievement of mothers, but of a conception of achievement. Similarly, in describing the thought arising out of the interest in acceptability, I am not speaking of actual mothers' adherence to dominant values, but of a conception of their relations to those values in which obedience and "being good" is considered an achievement. Many individual mothers "fail," that is, they insist on their own values and will not remain blind to the implications of dominant values for the lives of their children. Moreover, given the damaging effects of prevailing sexual arrangements and social hierarchies on maternal lives, it is clearly outrageous to blame mothers for their (our) obedience.

Obedience is largely a function of social powerlessness. Maternal work is done according to the Law of the Symbolic Father and under His Watchful Eye, as well as, typically, according to the desires, even whims, of the father's house. "This is my Father's world/Oh let me ne'er forget/that though the wrong be oft so strong,/He is the ruler yet." In these conditions of work, inauthentic obedience to dominant patriarchal values is as plausible a maternal response as respect for the results of experiment is in scientific work.

As I have said, the work of mothering can become a rewarding, disciplined expression of conscience. In order for this opportunity to be realized, either collectively or by individual mothers, maternal thought will have to be transformed by feminist consciousness.

> Coming to have a feminist consciousness is the experience of coming to know the truth about oneself and one's society. . . . The very *meaning* of what the feminist apprehends is illuminated by the light of what ought to be. . . . The feminist apprehends certain features of social reality *as* intolerable, as to be rejected in behalf of a transforming project for the future. . . . Social reality is revealed as deceptive. . . . What is really happening is quite different from what appears to be happening.[16]

Feminist consciousness will first transform inauthentic obedience into wariness, uncertain reflection, and at times, anguished confusion. The feminist becomes "marked by the experience of moral ambiguity" as she learns new ways of living without betraying her women's past, without denying her obligations to others. "She no longer knows what sort of person she ought to be, and therefore, she does not know what she ought to do. One moral paradigm is called into question by the laborious and often obscure emergence of another."[17]

Out of confusion will arise new voices, recognized not so much by the content of the truths they enunciate as by the honesty and courage of enunciation. They will be at once familiar and original, these voices arising out of maternal practice, affirming its own criteria of acceptability, insisting that the dominant values are unacceptable and need not be accepted.

The Capacity for Attentive Love

Finally, I would like to discuss a capacity—attention—and a virtue—love—that are central to the conception of achievement that maternal thought as a whole articulates. This capacity and virtue, when realized, invigorate preservation and enable growth. Attention and love again and again undermine a mother's inauthentic obedience as she perceives and endorses a child's experience though society finds it intolerable. The identification of the capacity of attention and the virtue of love is at once the foundation and the corrective of maternal thought.

The notion of "attention" is central to the philosophy of Simone Weil and is developed, along with the related notion of "love," by Iris Murdoch, who was profoundly influenced by Weil. Attention and love are fundamental to the construction of "objective reality" understood "in relation to the progressing life of a person," a "reality which is revealed to the patient eye of love."[18] Attention is an *intellectual* capacity connected even by definition with love, a special "knowledge of the individual."[19] "The name of this intense, pure, disinterested, gratuitous, generous attention is love."[20] Weil thinks that the capacity for attention is a "miracle." Murdoch ties it more closely to familiar achievement: "The task of attention goes on all the time and at apparently empty and everyday moments we are 'looking,' making those little peering efforts of imagination which have such important cumulative results."[21]

For Weil and Murdoch, the enemy of attention is what they call "fantasy," defined not as rich imaginative play, which does have a central role in maternal thinking, but as the "proliferation of blinding self-centered aims and images."[22] Fantasy, according to their original conception, is intellectual and imaginative activity in the service of consolation, domination, anxiety, and aggrandizement. It is reverie designed to protect the psyche from pain, self-induced blindness designed to protect it from insight. Fantasy, so defined, works in the service of inauthenticity. "The difficulty is to keep the attention fixed on the real situation"[23]—or, as I would say, on the real children. Attention to real children, children seen by the "patient eye of love, . . . teaches us how real things [real children] can be looked at and loved without being seized and used, without being appropriated into the greedy organism of the self."[24]

Much in maternal practices works against attentive love: intensity of identification, vicarious living through a child, daily wear of maternal work, harassment and indignities of an indifferent social order, and the clamor of children themselves. Although attention is elicited by the very reality it reveals—the reality of a growing person—it is a discipline that requires effort and self-training. The love of children is not only the most intense of attachments, but it is also a detachment, a giving up, a letting grow. To love a child without seizing or using it, to see the child's reality with the patient, loving eye of attention—such loving and attending might well describe the separation of mother and child from the mother's point of view. Of course, many mothers fail much of the time in attentive love and loving attention. Many mothers also train themselves in the looking, self-restraining, and empathy that is loving attention. They can be heard doing so in any playground or coffee klatch.

I am not saying that mothers, individually or collectively, are (or are not) especially wonderful people. My point is that out of maternal practices distinctive ways of conceptualizing, ordering, and valuing arise. We *think* differently about what it *means* and what it takes to be "wonderful," to be a person, to be real.

Murdoch and Weil, neither mothers themselves nor especially concerned with mothers, are clear about the absolute value of attentive love and the reality it reveals. Weil writes:

> In the first legend of the Grail . . . it is said that the Grail . . . belongs to the first comer who asks the guardian of the vessel, a king three-quarters paralyzed by the most painful wound, "What are you going through?"
> The love of our neighbor in all its fullness simply means being able to say to him: "What are you going through?" . . . Only he who is capable of attention can do this.[25]

I do not claim absolute value, but only that attentive love, the training to ask "What are you going through?" is central to maternal practices. If I am right about its place in maternal thought, and if Weil and Murdoch are right about its absolute value, the self-conscious inclusion of maternal thought in the dominant culture will be of general intellectual and moral benefit.

Some Social and Political Implications

I have described a "thought" arising out of maternal practices organized by the interests of preservation, growth, and acceptability. Although in some respects the thought is "contradictory" (i.e., it betrays its own values and must be transformed by feminist consciousness), the thought as a whole, with its fulcrum and correction in attentive love, is worthy of being expressed and respected. This thought has emerged out of maternal practices that are oppressive to women and children. I believe that it has emerged largely in response to the relatively invariable requirements of children and despite oppressive circumstances. As in all women's thought, some worthy aspects of maternal thought may arise out of identification with the powerless and excluded. Nevertheless, oppression is largely responsible for the defects rather than the strengths of maternal thought, as in the obedient goodness to which mothers find themselves "naturally" subscribing. When the oppressiveness of gender arrangements is combined with the oppression of race, poverty, or the multiple injuries of class, it is a miracle that maternal thought can arise at all. On the other hand, that it does indeed arise, miraculously, is clear both from literature (Alice Walker, Tillie Olsen, Maya Angelou, Agnes Smedley, Lucille Clifton, Louisa May Alcott, Audre Lorde, Marilyn French, Grace Paley, and countless others) and from daily experience. Maternal thought *identifies* priorities, attitudes, and virtues; it *conceives* of achievement. The more oppressive the institutions of motherhood, the greater the pain and struggle in living out the worthy and transforming the damaging aspects of thought.

Maternal thinking is only one aspect of "womanly" thinking. In articulating and respecting the maternal, I do not underwrite the still current, false, and pernicious identification of womanhood with biological or adoptive mothering of particular children in families. For me, "maternal" is a social category. Although maternal thinking arises out of actual childcaring practices, biological parenting is neither necessary nor sufficient. Many women and some men express maternal thinking in various kinds of working and caring with others. And some biological mothers, especially in misogynistic societies, take a fearful, defensive distance from their own mothering and the maternal lives of any women.

Maternal thought does, I believe, exist for all women in a radically different way than for men. It is because we are *daughters*, nurtured and trained by women, that we early receive maternal love with special attention to its implications for our bodies, our passions, and our ambitions. We are alert to the values and costs of maternal practices whether we are determined to engage in them or avoid them.

It is now argued that the most revolutionary change we can make in the institution of motherhood is to include men equally in every aspect of childcare. When men and women live together with children, it seems not only fair but deeply moral that they share in every aspect of childcare. To prevent or excuse men from maternal practice is to encourage them to separate public action from private affection, the privilege of parenthood from its cares. Moreover, even when men are absent from the nursery, their dominance in every other public and private room shapes a child's earliest conceptions of power. To familiarize children with "natural" domination at their earliest age in a context of primitive love, assertion, and sexual passion is to prepare them to find equally "natural" and exhaustive the division between exploiter and exploited that pervades the larger world. Although daughter and son alike may internalize "natural" domination, neither typically can live with it easily. Identifying with and imitating exploiters, we are overcome with self-hate; aligning ourselves with the exploited, we are fearful and manipulative. Again and again, family power dramas are repeated in psychic, interpersonal, and professional dramas, while they are institutionalized in economic, political, and international life. Radically recasting the power-gender roles in those dramas just might revolutionize social conscience.

Assimilating men into childcare both inside and outside the home would also be conducive to serious social reform. Responsible, equal childcaring would require men to relinquish power and their own favorable position in the division between intellectual/professional and service labor as that division expresses itself domestically. Loss of preferred status at home might make socially privileged men more suspicious of unnecessary divisions of labor and damaging hierarchies in the public world. Moreover, if men were emotionally and practically committed to childcare, they would reform the work world in parents' interests. Once no one "else" was minding the child, good day-care centers with flexible hours would be established to which parents could trust their children from infancy on. These day-care centers, like the workweek itself, would be managed flexibly in response to human needs as well as to the demands of productivity, with an eye to growth rather than measurable profit. Such moral reforms of economic life would probably begin with professions and managers servicing themselves. Even in nonsocialist countries, however, their benefits could be unpredictably extensive.

I would not argue that the assimilation of men into childcare is the primary social goal for mothers. Rather, we must work to bring a *transformed* maternal thought in the public realm, to make the preservation and growth of *all* children a work of public conscience and legislation. This will not be easy. Mothers are no less corrupted than anyone else by concerns of status and class. Often our misguided efforts on behalf of the success and purity of our children frighten them and everyone else around them. As we increase and enjoy our public effectiveness, we will have less reason to live vicariously through our children. We may then begin to learn to sustain a creative tension between our inevitable and fierce desire to foster our own children and the less compulsive desire that all children grow and flourish.

Nonetheless, it would be foolish to believe that mothers, just because they are mothers, can transcend class interest and implement principles of justice. All feminists must join in articulating a theory of justice shaped by and incorporating maternal thinking. Moreover, the generalization of attentive love to *all* children requires politics. The most enlightened thought is not enough.

Closer to home again, we must refashion our domestic life in the hope that the personal will in fact betoken the political. We must begin by resisting the temptation to construe "home" simplemindedly, as a matter of justice between mothers and fathers. Single parents, lesbian mothers, and coparenting women remind us that many ways to provide children with examples of caring do not incorporate sexual inequalities of power and privilege. Those of us who live with the fathers of our children will eagerly welcome shared parenthood—for overwhelming practical as well as ideological reasons. But in our eagerness, we must not forget that as long as a mother is not effective publicly and self-respecting privately, male presence can be harmful as well as beneficial. It does a woman no good to have the power of the Symbolic Father brought right into the nursery, often despite the deep, affectionate egalitarianism of an individual man. It takes a strong mother and father to resist temptations to domination and subordination for which they have been trained and are socially rewarded. And whatever the hard-won equality and mutual respect an individual couple may achieve, as long as a mother—even if she is no more parent than father—is derogated and subordinate outside the home, children will feel angry, confused, and "wildly unmothered."[26]

Despite these reservations, I look forward to the day when men are willing and able to share equally and actively in transformed maternal practices. When that day comes, will we still identify some thought as maternal rather than merely parental? Might we echo the cry of some feminists—there shall be no more "women"—with our own—there shall be no more "mothers," only people engaging in childcare? To keep matters clear I would put the point differently. On that day there will be no more "fathers," no more people of either sex who have power over their children's lives and moral authority in their children's world, though they do not do the work of attentive love. There will be mothers of both sexes who live out a transformed maternal thought in communities that share parental care—practically, emotionally, economically, and socially. Such communities will have learned from their mothers how to value children's lives.

Notes

1. From J. Echegaray, "Severed Heart," quoted by Jessie Bernard in *The Future of Motherhood* (New York: Dial, 1974), p. 4.
2. The words are Mrs. Ramsay's in Virginia Woolf's *To the Lighthouse* (New York: Harcourt, Brace and World, 1927), p. 92.
3. Adrienne Rich, "Conditions for Work: The Common World of Women," in *Working It Out*, edited by Sara Ruddick and Pamela Daniels (New York: Pantheon, 1977), p. xvi (italics mine).
4. Iris Murdoch, *The Sovereignty of Good* (New York: Shocken Books, 1971), p. 99.
5. Ibid., p. 95.
6. Spinoza, *Ethics*, Book 3, Proposition 42, demonstration. See also Proposition 40, Note, and Proposition 45, both in Book 3.
7. Bernard Williams, *Morality* (New York: Harper Torchbooks, 1972), p. 11.
8. The words are those of a Texas farmwoman who quilted as she huddled with her family in a shelter as, above them, a tornado destroyed their home. The story was told to me by Miriam Schapiro.

9. Murdoch, *Sovereignty of Good*, p. 26.
10. Simone Weil, "Gravity and Grace," in *Gravity and Grace* (London: Routledge & Kegan Paul, 1952; first French ed., 1947), passim.
11. Ibid., and other essays in *Gravity and Grace*. Both the language and concepts are indebted to Plato.
12. Jean Baker Miller, *Toward a New Psychology for Women* (Boston: Beacon Press, 1973), p. 54.
13. Miller, *Toward a New Psychology*, p. 56.
14. Ibid., p. 40.
15. I am indebted to Adrienne Rich, *Of Woman Born* (New York: W. W. Norton, 1976), especially chapter 8, both for this phrase and for the working out of the idea of inauthenticity. My debt to this book as a whole is pervasive.
16. Sandra Lee Bartky, "Toward a Phenomenology of Feminist Consciousness," in *Feminism and Philosophy*, edited by Mary Vetterling-Braggin, Frederick A. Elliston, and Jane English (Totowa, N.J.: Littlefield, Adams, 1977), pp. 22–37. Quotes from pp. 33, 25, 28, 29.
17. Ibid., p. 31. On the riskiness of authenticity, the courage it requires of women, see also Miller, *Toward a New Psychology*, chapter 9.
18. Murdoch, *Sovereignty of Good*, p. 40.
19. Ibid., p. 28.
20. Simone Weil, "Human Personality," in *Collected Essays*, chosen and translated by Richard Rees (London: Oxford University Press, 1962). Also *Simone Weil Reader*, edited by George A. Panichas (New York: McKay, 1977), p. 333.
21. Murdoch, *Sovereignty of Good*, p. 43.
22. Ibid., p. 67.
23. Ibid., p. 91.
24. Ibid., p. 65.
25. Simone Weil, "Reflections of the Right Use of School Studies with a View to the Love of God," in *Waiting for God* (New York: G. Putnam's, 1951), p. 115.
26. Rich, *Of Woman Born*, p. 225.

Study Questions

1. What does Ruddick mean by "maternal thinking"? Do men have or can they acquire maternal thinking? Does such thinking grow out of biology?
2. Ruddick takes the view that thinking arises from practice. What is "maternal practice"? What three interests govern maternal practice?
3. Discuss how the maternal attitude Ruddick calls "holding" grows out of maternal practice? Why does this attitude manifest itself (among other ways) as humility?
4. A second aspect of maternal thinking that Ruddick discusses is the avoidance of the "clear-cut and unambiguous," that is, fluidity of conceptual outlook. How might such a form of thought grow out of maternal practice?
5. What are some of the "degenerate forms" of the maternal perspective?
6. In Ruddick's opinion, how should feminism transform maternal thought?
7. Ruddick says, "The identification of the capacity of attention and the virtue of love is at once the foundation and the corrective of maternal thought." Explain.
8. How does Ruddick feel about men becoming involved in childcare?

Women and Honor:
Some Notes on Lying

Adrienne Rich

These notes were first read at the Hartwick Women Writers' Workshop, founded and directed by Beverly Tanenhaus, at Hartwick College, Oneonta, New York, in June 1975. They were published as a pamphlet by Motheroot Press in Pittsburgh, 1977; in Heresies: A Feminist Magazine of Art and Politics, vol. 1, no. 1; and in a French translation by the Québecois feminist press, Les Editions du Remue-Ménage, 1979.

It is clear that among women we need a new ethics; as women, a new morality. The problem of speech, of language, continues to be primary. For if in our speaking we are breaking silences long established, "liberating ourselves from our secrets" in the words of Beverly Tanenhaus, this is in itself a first kind of action. I wrote Women and Honor *in an effort to make myself more honest, and to understand the terrible negative power of the lie in relationships between women. Since it was published, other women have spoken and written of things I did not include: Michelle Cliff's "Notes on Speechlessness" in* Sinister Wisdom *no. 5 led Catherine Nicolson (in the same issue) to write of the power of "deafness," the frustration of our speech by those who do not want to hear what we have to say. Nelle Morton has written of the act of "hearing each other into speech."* How do we listen? How do we make it possible for another to break her silence? These are some of the questions which follow on the ones I have raised here.*

(These notes are concerned with relationships between and among women. When "personal relationship" is referred to, I mean a relationship between two women. It will be clear in what follows when I am talking about women's relationships with men.)

The old, male idea of honor. A man's "word" sufficed—to other men—without   1
guarantee.

"Our Land Free, Our Men Honest, Our Women Fruitful"—a popular colonial toast   2
in America.

Male honor also having something to do with killing: *I could not love thee, Dear, so*   3
much/Lov'd I not Honour more. ("To Lucasta, On Going to the Wars"). Male honor as something needing to be avenged: hence, the duel.

Women's honor, something altogether else: virginity, chastity, fidelity to a husband.   4
Honesty in women has not been considered important. We have been depicted as generically whimsical, deceitful, subtle, vacillating. And we have been rewarded for lying.

Men have been expected to tell the truth about facts, not about feelings. They have   5
not been expected to talk about feelings at all.

*Nelle Morton, "Beloved Image!", paper delivered at the National Conference of the American Academy of Religion, San Francisco, California, December 28, 1977.

Yet even about facts they have continually lied.   6

We assume that politicians are without honor. We read their statements trying to crack   7
the code. The scandals of their politics: not that men in high places lie, only that they do
so with such indifference, so endlessly, still expecting to be believed. We are accustomed to
the contempt inherent in the political lie.

To discover that one has been lied to in a personal relationship, however, leads one to   8
feel a little crazy.

Lying is done with words, and also with silence.   9

The woman who tells lies in her personal relationships may or may not plan or invent   10
her lying. She may not even think of what she is doing in a calculated way.

A subject is raised which the liar wishes buried. She has to go downstairs, her parking   11
meter will have run out. Or, there is a telephone call she ought to have made an hour ago.

She is asked, point-blank, a question which may lead into painful talk: "How do you   12
feel about what is happening between us?" Instead of trying to describe her feelings in their
ambiguity and confusion, she asks, "How do *you* feel?" The other, because she is trying
to establish a ground of openness and trust, begins describing her own feelings. Thus the
liar learns more than she tells.

And she may also tell herself a lie: that she is concerned with the other's feelings, not   13
with her own.

But the liar is concerned with her own feelings.   14

The liar lives in fear of losing control. She cannot even desire a relationship without   15
manipulation, since to be vulnerable to another person means for her the loss of control.

The liar has many friends, and leads an existence of great loneliness.   16

The liar often suffers from amnesia. Amnesia is the silence of the unconscious.   17

To lie habitually, as a way of life, is to lose contact with the unconscious. It is like   18
taking sleeping pills, which confer sleep but blot out dreaming. The unconscious wants truth.
It ceases to speak to those who want something else more than truth.

In speaking of lies, we come inevitably to the subject of truth. There is nothing simple   19
or easy about this idea. There is no "the truth," "a truth'—truth is not one thing, or even
a system. It is an increasing complexity. The pattern of the carpet is a surface. When we
look closely, or when we become weavers, we learn of the tiny multiple threads unseen in
the overall pattern, the knots on the underside of the carpet.

This is why the effort to speak honestly is so important. Lies are usually attempts to   20
make everything simpler—for the liar—than it really is, or ought to be.

In lying to others we end up lying to ourselves. We deny the importance of an event,   21
or a person, and thus deprive ourselves of a part of our lives. Or we use one piece of the
past or present to screen out another. Thus we lose faith with our own lives.

The unconscious wants truth, as the body does. The complexity and fecundity of dreams   22
come from the complexity and fecundity of the unconscious struggling to fulfill that desire.
The complexity and fecundity of poetry come from the same struggle.

An honorable human relationship—that is, one in which two people have the right   23
to use the word "love"—is a process, delicate, violent, often terrifying to both persons involved,
a process of refining the truths they can tell each other.

It is important to do this because it breaks down human self-delusion and isolation.   24

It is important to do this because in so doing we do justice to our own complexity.   25

It is important to do this because we can count on so few people to go that hard way   26
with us.

I come back to the questions of women's honor. Truthfulness has not been considered   27
important for women, as long as we have remained physically faithful to a man, or chaste.

We have been expected to lie with our bodies: to bleach, redden, unkink or curl our   28
hair, pluck eyebrows, shave armpits, wear padding in various places or lace ourselves, take
little steps, glaze finger and toe nails, wear clothes that emphasized our helplessness.

We have been required to tell different lies at different times, depending on what the   29
men of the time needed to hear. The Victorian wife or the white southern lady, who were
expected to have no sensuality, to "lie still"; the twentieth-century "free" woman who is
expected to fake orgasms.

We have had the truth of our bodies withheld from us or distorted; we have been kept   30
in ignorance of our most intimate places. Our instincts have been punished; clitoridectomies
for "lustful" nuns or for "difficult" wives. It has been difficult, too, to know the lies of
our complicity from the lies we believed.

The lie of the "happy marriage," of domesticity—we have been complicit, have acted   31
out the fiction of a well-lived life, until the day we testify in court of rapes, beatings, psychic
cruelties, public and private humiliations.

Patriarchal lying has manipulated women both through falsehood and through silence.   32
Facts we needed have been withheld from us. False witness has been borne against us.

And so we must take seriously the question of truthfulness between women, truthful-   33
ness among women. As we cease to lie with our bodies, as we cease to take on faith what
men have said about us, is a truly womanly idea of honor in the making?

Women have been forced to lie, for survival, to men. How to unlearn this among other   34
women?

"Women have always lied to each other."   35

"Women have always whispered the truth to each other."   36

Both of these axioms are true.   37

"Women have always been divided against each other."   38

"Women have always been in secret collusion."   39

Both of these axioms are true.   40

In the struggle for survival we tell lies. To bosses, to prison guards, the police, men   41
who have power over us, who legally own us and our children, lovers who need us as proof
of their manhood.

There is a danger run by all powerless people: that we forget we are lying, or that lying   42
becomes a weapon we carry over into relationships with people who do not have power over us.

I want to reiterate that when we talk about women and honor, or women and lying, 43
we speak within the context of male lying, the lies of the powerful, the lie as false source of power.

Women have to think whether we want, in our relationships with each other, the kind 44
of power that can be obtained through lying.

Women have been driven mad, "gaslighted," for centuries by the refutation of our ex- 45
perience and our instincts in a culture which validates only male experience. The truth of
our bodies and our minds has been mystified to us. We therefore have a primary obligation
to each other: not to undermine each other's sense of reality for the sake of expediency; not
to gaslight each other.

Women have often felt insane when cleaving to the truth of our experience. Our future 46
depends on the sanity of each of us, and we have a profound stake, beyond the personal, in
the project of describing our reality as candidly and fully as we can to each other.

There are phrases which help us not to admit we are lying: "my privacy," "nobody's 47
business but my own." The choices that underlie these phrases may indeed be justified; but
we ought to think about the full meaning and consequences of such language.

Women's love for women has been represented almost entirely through silence and lies. 48
The institution of heterosexuality has forced the lesbian to dissemble, or be labeled a pervert,
a criminal, a sick or dangerous woman, etc. etc. The lesbian, then, has often been forced
to lie, like the prostitute or the married women.

Does a life "in the closet"—lying, perhaps of necessity, about ourselves to bosses, landlords, 49
clients, colleagues, family, because the law and public opinion are founded on a lie—does this,
can it, spread into private life, so that lying (described as *discretion*) becomes an easy way to
avoid conflict or complication? Can it become a strategy so ingrained that it is used even
with close friends and lovers?

Heterosexuality as an institution has also drowned in silence the erotic feelings between 50
women. I myself lived half a lifetime in the lie of that denial. That silence makes us all, to
some degree, into liars.

When a woman tells the truth she is creating the possibility for more truth around her. 51

The liar leads an existence of unutterable loneliness. 52

The liar is afraid. 53

But we are all afraid: without fear we become manic, hubristic, self-destructive. What 54
is this particular fear that possesses the liar?

She is afraid that her own truths are not good enough. 55

She is afraid, not so much of prison guards or bosses, but of something unnamed within 56
her.

The liar fears the void. 57

The void is not something created by patriarchy, or racism, or capitalism. It will not 58
fade way with any of them. It is part of every woman.

"The dark core," Virginia Woolf named it, writing of her mother. The dark core. It 59
is beyond personality; beyond who loves us or hates us.

We begin out of the void, out of darkness and emptiness. It is part of the cycle under- 60
stood by the old pagan religions, that materialism denies. Out of death, rebirth; out of nothing,
something.

The void is the creatrix, the matrix. It is not mere hollowness and anarchy. But in 61
women it has been identified with lovelessness, barrenness, sterility. We have been urged to
fill our "emptiness" with children. We are not supposed to go down into the darkness of
the core.

Yet, if we can risk it, the something born of that nothing is the beginning of our truth. 62

The liar in her terror wants to fill up the void, with anything. Her lies are a denial 63
of her fear; a way of maintaining control.

Why do we feel slightly crazy when we realize we have been lied to in a relationship? 64

We take so much of the universe on trust. You tell me: "In 1950 I lived on the north 65
side of Beacon Street in Somerville." You tell me: "She and I were lovers, but for months
now we have only been good friends." You tell me: "It is seventy degrees outside and the
sun is shining." Because I love you, because there is not even a question of lying between
us, I take these accounts of the universe on trust: your address twenty-five years ago, your
relationship with someone I know only by sight, this morning's weather. I fling unconscious
tendrils of belief, like slender green threads, across statements such as these, statements made
so unequivocally, which have no tone or shadow of tentativeness. I build them into the mosaic
of my world. I allow my universe to change in minute, significant ways, on the basis of things
you have said to me, of my trust in you.

I also have faith that you are telling me things it is important I should know; that 66
you do not conceal facts from me in an effort to spare me, or yourself, pain.

Or, at the very least, that you will say, "There are things I am not telling you." 67

When we discover that someone we trusted can be trusted no longer, it forces us to 68
reexamine the universe, to question the whole instinct and concept of trust. For awhile, we
are thrust back onto some bleak, jutting ledge, in a dark pierced by sheets of fire, swept by
sheets of rain, in a world before kinship, or naming, or tenderness exist; we are brought close
to formlessness.

The liar may resist confrontation, denying that she lied. Or she may use other language: 69
forgetfulness, privacy, the protection of someone else. Or, she may bravely declare herself a
coward. This allows her to go on lying, since that is what cowards do. She does not say,
I was afraid, since this would open the question of other ways of handling her fear. It would
open the question of what is actually feared.

She may say, *I didn't want to cause pain*. What she really did not want is to have to deal 70
with the other's pain. The lie is a short-cut through another's personality.

Truthfulness, honor, is not something which springs ablaze of itself; it has to be created 71
between people.

This is true in political situations. The quality and depth of the politics evolving from 72
a group depends in very large part on their understanding of honor.

Much of what is narrowly termed "politics" seems to rest on a longing for certainty 73
even at the cost of honesty, for an analysis which, once given, need not be reexamined. Such
is the deadendedness—for women—of Marxism in our time.

Truthfulness anywhere means a heightened complexity. But it is a movement into evolu- 74
tion. Women are only beginning to uncover our own truths; many of us would be grateful

for some rest in that struggle, would be glad just to lie down with the shreds we have painfully unearthed, and be satisfied with those. Often I feel this like an exhaustion in my own body.

The politics worth having, the relationships worth having, demand that we delve still   75
deeper.

The possibilities that exist between two people, or among a group of people, are a kind   76
of alchemy. They are the most interesting thing in life. The liar is someone who keeps losing
sight of these possibilities.

When relationships are determined by manipulation, by the need for control, they may   77
possess a dreary, bickering kind of drama, but they cease to be interesting. They are repetitious; the shock of human possibilities has ceased to reverberate through them.

When someone tells me a piece of the truth which has been withheld from me, and   78
which I needed in order to see my life more clearly, it may bring acute pain, but it can also
flood me with a cold, sea-sharp wash of relief. Often such truths come by accident, or from
strangers.

It isn't that to have an honorable relationship with you, I have to understand every   79
thing, or tell you everything at once, or that I can know, beforehand, everything I need to tell you.

It means that most of the time I am eager, longing for the possibility of telling you.   80
That these possibilities may seem frightening, but not destructive, to me. That I feel strong
enough to hear your tentative and groping words. That we both know we are trying, all
the time, to extend the possibilities of truth between us.

The possibility of life between us.   81

Study Questions

1. How does Rich view the relationship between lying and the unconscious?
2. In what ways have women been traditionally expected to lie? Have lesbians been less pressured to lie than nonlesbian women?
3. According to Rich, what is the liar afraid of?
4. What possibility does the liar lose sight of?

Conceiving Women:
Notes on the Logic of Feminism

Joyce Trebilcot

Feminism is not just a matter of reordering what exists, of, say, moving women from one "place" to another; feminism involves, rather, changes in the very nature of things. In this paper I want first to explicate one reason why feminism requires ontological change and then to give some examples of ways in which these changes are taking place in our redefinings of women.

If we begin with the assumption that women should not be mutilated, violated, locked up, exploited, restricted—dominated, because we are women, we have the basis for feminism in a narrow sense, a feminism that would concern itself only with the mistreatments of women which arise out of perceptions of us as female. But to be a feminist is to care about women, and it is arbitrary to limit our concern to just those aspects of our sufferings and limitations which arise from a particular cause; so feminism, it seems to me, must be concerned with all of the harm done to women, regardless of its source. This means that because women are oppressed not only because we are women but also because we are Black or Hispanic or Jewish, because we are Lesbian, because we are poor or paraplegic or fat or young or old or (fill in the blanks), we must, as feminists, seek to identify, understand, and eliminate all these oppressions.

They all have something in common. Their form is that a distinction is made, which is a division into two; and one part or half is held to be superior to the other; and it is claimed that the "superior" is justified in having power over the "inferior." This, of course, is dualism. It is a dualism that is essentially evaluative and that functions primarily as an excuse for power over.

The dualistic pair is the unit of hierarchy—that is, a hierarchy consists of overlapping dualistic pairs. A classical rendering is the pyramid with God at the apex, then angels, then man, then beasts, then the rest of the natural world. On this scheme, God is distinct from and better than man, and entitled to exercise control over him; man is distinct from and better than beasts, and entitled to exercise control over them; etc. The pyramid, of course, represents quantity: one on top, then a few, then more and more. While this particular version of the pyramid is perhaps antiquated, the form itself permeates dominant Western cultures.

It permeates received reality. At the epistemological level, it determines perception: we see—sight rather than, for example, touch, is primary—it is objects that are seen, and they are seen as having sharp boundaries. More obviously, dualism/hierarchy is the form of social organizations—governments, businesses, schools, families. It structures the person—self/other, mind/body, conscious and unconscious. There is even a dualism of right and left—the right hand, the right side, take precedence over the left. And so on.

In feminism, there is movement toward the elimination of all dualism, not just of those manifestations of it that oppress women as women or as members of other groups. One reason for this movement is the belief that only by getting rid of dualism in all of its manifestations

From *Sinister Wisdom* 11 (Fall 1979). © 1978 by Joyce Trebilcot. Reprinted by permission of Joyce Trebilcot.

can oppressions such as sexism, racism, and classism be permanently and thoroughly eradicated. Another reason is the sense that dualism as a form is discordant with women's values; even if no "inferior" category included women, dualism would block the flowering of women's modes.

The elimination of dualism—of either a specific manifestation of it or all of it—requires change in the nature of entities that are related to one another in dualistic/hierarchical orderings. This is because the nature of the entities is determined at least in part by their participation in the orderings. In academic terms, the relations among them are internal rather than external. An example of an external relation is the distance between two cups on a table; a change in the distance does not alter the nature of the cups. A change in an internal relation, however, does alter the nature of the things related. A nurse, for instance, cares for the sick by assisting and following the orders of doctors; if we eliminate her subordinate relationship to doctors, we change the meaning of the word "nurse." Similarly, what it is to be a worker, a deaf person, an Asian American, a wife—or, of course, a woman—is determined in part by relations between these and other concepts in hierarchical orderings. Because the relationships among items in dualistic/hierarchical orderings are internal, then, feminism, insofar as it is committed to the elimination of dualism/hierarchy, is committed to changing the nature of things.

Here I want to give examples of just some of the ways in which internal connections among items in hierarchies are broken by feminist reconceivings. I focus on reconceivings of women because they are starting points and centers of feminist theorizings. These reconceivings are, I take it, political strategies that weave bridges from patriarchy to women's spaces.

I use the distinction from academic philosophy between the descriptive and evaluative meanings of a term. The descriptive meaning is characterized as value neutral; it is supposed to imply only some facts about the thing in question. The evaluative meaning commends or condemns the facts described. To call someone forceful, for example, is to ascribe a certain style of behavior; this is the descriptive meaning of "forceful." But in addition, in most contexts, to say that someone is forceful commends if the subject is male and condemns if she is female; commending or condemning is the evaluative meaning of "forceful."

Because we engage in feminist theorizings in order to re-experience, to reconceive, that is, to bring forth new meanings, when we use a conventional word as central in our theorizings, the descriptive meaning of that word shifts. Sometimes the evaluative meaning shifts as well. Here I discuss three patterns of shift in evaluative and descriptive meaning. The words used to exemplify these shifts are "strong," "nurturant," and "lesbian." As these words, which are used by feminists to describe women, are given new meanings, the meaning of "woman" changes too—and the conceptual bonds which hold us in our traditional places in dualistic/hierarchical orderings are frayed.

1. *Descriptive meaning changes, evaluative meaning remains the same: Strength:* In patriarchy, a strong man is one who deals with difficulty calmly, quietly, unobtrusively. According to the cliché, he is the strong silent type—paradigmatically, the John Wayne character.

The patriarchal strong woman, like the strong man, handles or endures difficulties quietly, without disturbing others. But in other respects she differs from him. In particular, in accordance with the patriarchal practice of defining women in terms of our relationships to men and of our sexuality, the strong woman is typically one who both lacks a heterosexual partner and is thought to be sexually unattractive to men. She has no husband or mate (or, if she has, he is absent from the situation in which she is called strong) because if an appropriate male is present it is presumed that he takes care of and protects her, not that she does this for herself, and so the term "strong" is reserved for him. But even if she has no man, she can't be strong unless she is heterosexually unattractive—usually she is imaged as old—because if she is attractive she should or might have a man, and again the term "strong" is reserved, this time not for an actual but for a possible man. In patriarchy, then, we generally must be both unattached to a man and unattractive to men in order to qualify for strength.

The feminist concept of the strong woman preserves the notion of strength as dealing well with adversity—this is the common thread by virtue of which the same term, "strength," is used in both contexts. But of course the heterosexist limitations of women's strength drop out. A feminist strong woman may have a man—in many cases her strength is manifested primarily in her struggle against a husband or lover. And she need not be unattractive to men—we know that there are many young and conventionally beautiful women who are strong indeed.

Further, in feminism the idea of strength as quietly, privately, unobtrusively dealing with difficulty drops out. The feminist strong woman is likely to be noisy, even loud; she is inclined to protest, to complain, to call attention to her difficulty. This difference of course is based on the political difference between partriarchy's interest in preserving present systems and feminism's interest in changing them.

Thus, while the evaluative meaning of the expression "a strong woman" is the same in patriarchy and in feminism—it is positive in both contexts—the descriptive meaning shifts: *what* is valued changes. This change is the basis for a partial redefinition of the concept of women. Whereas in patriarchy, strength in women is an anomaly, in feminism there is a tendency to understand it as essential, as an element in the definition of woman: all women are potentially strong. But this move breaks one link in the internal connection between the concepts of woman and man. In partriarchy, women are weak as compared to men; therefore women are inferior; therefore women may justifiably be dominated by men. But if women are by nature strong, the syllogism fails.

2. *Descriptive meaning changes, evaluative meaning changes: Nurturance.* The term "nurturance," whose root idea, of course, is that of a mother nursing her child, is being given both new descriptive and new evaluative meaning by feminists. For example, Barbara Love and Elizabeth Shanklin, in their article, "The Answer is Matriarchy," provide an account of a feminist definition of nurturance which clearly differs from patriarchal ones.[1] To nurture a child, they say, is to support "the unique will of the child to grow into its full potential as a self-regulating individual": again, to nurture is to strengthen "the unique will of each individual to form open, trusting, creative bonds with others" (184).

This concept of nurturing retains the connection with mother-child relationships, but otherwise contrasts sharply with patriarchal views of nurturance. In patriarchy, the aim of childrearing is not to strengthen the child's will, but to direct and control it, to dominate it. In patriarchy, the aim of the "training" of children is not to enable them to think for themselves, but rather to prepare them to take their places in existing institutions. Barbara and Elizabeth note that "in capitalism the child's will is directed toward serving the interests of corporations; in socialism it is directed toward serving the state" (184). Their concept of nurturing as supporting the unique will of each individual to develop as self-regulating and self-realizing constitutes, then, a clear shift in the descriptive meaning of "nurturance."

Evaluatively, nurturance is viewed positively in patriarchy, but as second-rate. Nurturing is a good thing for women to do, but not good enough for men. In matriarchal theory, however, the value of nurturing is expanded. The nurturant mother-child relationship is to serve as the model of all relationships, and all social institutions are to be designed so as to support nurturing. Here, nurturing, a women's value, becomes a primary value.

But from a feminist perspective it is probably a mistake to say that matriarchal theories make nurturing primary, for feminists tend not to be concerned to order values hierarchically. We may say, then, that what matriarchal theory does is to horizontally expand the range of nurturance. Traditionally, only women are supposed to be nurturant, and we are expected to nurture men and children but not one another or ourselves. But a matriarchal society is one in which nurturing is valued for everyone, in all contexts. Thus, matriarchal theory not only gives nurturing a new descriptive meaning, it also radically expands its sphere as a value. And if nurturing is not second-rate, then women are not in this respect inferior to men, and one of the struts holding up the patriarchal hierarchy is toppled.

    3. *Descriptive meaning changes, evaluative meaning is reversed: Lesbian.* Another way in which patriarchal evaluative meanings are altered in feminism is by simply reversing them. The patriarchal intention to keep us in line by calling us dykes or witches or hags is blocked when we describe ourselves in these terms with pride and pleasure. We break out of secondary status, out of hierarchy, by flipping their evaluations over, by gladly acknowledging that we are what they condemn.

    This reversal of value is based on a reconceptualizing of the descriptive meaning of the term in question. While patriarchal concepts of lesbianism focus on women "having sex" with women—and on men (lesbians are women who can't get men, who need men, who hate men, etc.)—feminist conceivings retain only the emphasis on women, and transform it. Here are some samples. From the Radicalesbians: "A lesbian is the rage of all women condensed to the point of explosion."[2] From Ti-Grace Atkinson: Lesbianism is the "commitment, by choice, full-time, of one woman to others of her class."[3] From Sally Miller Gearhart: "A lesbian is a woman who seeks her own self-nurturance."[4] Such ways of understanding lesbianism depart from the patriarchal concept in description and reverse it in evaluation. And they not only move lesbians out of our patriarchal places as inferior to heterosexuals and to men, they also have implications for the concept of woman: if some women—lesbians—are not dependent on and inferior to men, then no women need be.

    I have so far talked about ways feminists re-create ourselves by giving new meanings to words that are used in both patriarchy and feminism to describe women. But not everything we need to say about ourselves can be expressed in this way. So feminists also describe women in terms not conventionally used to describe women at all. I have chosen three examples here. One is "together," an adverb in standard English, an adjective in slang, and a feminist adjective in the work of Inez Smith Reid. A different sort of example is a new combination of ordinary words: "woman-identified." The third case is a materially new word, a word formed by combining parts of standard words—"gynergy." These are terms we have appropriated or invented for ourselves. One might say that, unlike the words I discussed earlier, they are not old words given new meanings, but rather new words; they are, anyway, new descriptions of women. So to understand them as contributing to feminist conceivings of ourselves is not to trace shifts in their meanings from patriarchy to feminism—"gynergy," for example, has no meaning in patriarchy at all; it is, rather, just to understand why we need these new words, what they mean.

    "Together" is used by Inez Smith Reid in her book *"Together" Black Women* to describe politically conscious Black women.[5] Many of these women do not define themselves as feminists, but in their struggle against racism as a hierarchy of power they are clearly sisters of feminists. Inez's account of how she came to use the word "together" in thinking about these women helps to illuminate one sort of politically-based conceptual shift.

    Inez began her project with the intention of studying militant Black women and so she selected her subjects on the basis of their "reputation in the community for militancy." One of the questions the women were asked was to define militancy. Among the responses: "To be militant you have to be aware . . ."; "Militancy is when you can actually analyze . . ."; "a militant person is, for Black people, anybody who decides it's time for White folks to stop kicking my ass. It's just anybody who's tired of being messed over" (17, 18).

    But most importantly, many of the responses carry a sense of dissatisfaction with the term "militant" itself. This sense is perhaps best expressed by the woman who says: "I really feel it's just a name that the White people gave to the Black people. They call them that name because they speak the right things for the race. . . . I don't think there's such a word as that'' (20). *There is no such word as that.* This woman not merely refuses to accept a characterization imposed on her by the dominant group, she denies the very existence of the word.

As Inez listened to the women she was studying and began to appreciate their tendency to reject the standard concept of militancy, she herself moved away from this notion and came to think of these women not as militant, but as ''together.'' She cites the definition of ''together'' from the *Dictionary of Afro-American Slang:* ''to have one's mind free of confusion; to be positive; functional; to emerge as a whole person.'' Inez adds that in her work, ''together'' has ''a more collective connotation,'' it is ''characterized by a spiritual closeness in a common endeavor— that of a singular or peculiar commitment to erase oppression.'' Further, the term ''denotes a refusal to take on, uncritically, the total value structure of the White community'' (29). So here we have the discovery of the negative evaluative meaning of a term and its replacement with a new word, that is, with a word which in the standard language of the dominant culture is not used to describe persons at all.

The description of some women as ''together'' has, of course, implications for the concept of woman. Inez Smith Reid's work suggests that all women can be ''together''—that is, free of confusion, whole, and sharing commitment; insofar as this conception of women is inconsistent with patriarchal ideas of women as scattered, incomplete, and at odds with one another, it tends toward transforming the concept of woman and so breaking the bonds which hold us in our traditional places in hierarchical orderings.

Another approach to reconceiving ourselves is to make up terms. The expression ''woman-identified woman,'' introduced in the Radicalesbians' 1970 paper, names a woman who creates her identity in relation to women rather than in relation to men and who makes women her primary commitment: ''. . . we must be available and supportive to one another, give our commitment and our love, give the emotional support necessary to sustain this movement. Our energies must flow toward our sisters, not backward toward our oppressors'' (215). The paper provides a new, positive description of the lesbian feminist, along with a new name for her: woman-identified.

The meaning of the expression ''woman-identified woman'' has shifted somewhat within feminism. The expression has been used widely since its introduction, with the understanding that while not all lesbians are woman-identified, all women-identified women are perceived by patriarchy as lesbians. But then at the 1978 founding convention of the National Lesbian Feminist Organization, a resolution was adopted which specified that membership in the new organization is open to ''all lesbians and/or woman-identified women who agree with the purpose of this organization.'' ''Woman-identified woman'' was included partly to make space for lesbians who cannot publicly say they are lesbians. But it was understood also that this provision would admit to membership women who in patriarchal terms are not lesbians.

So the concept of the woman-identified woman has taken on a life of its own. Arising out of the rejection of the male practice of defining women in narrowly sexual terms, and specifically out of the rejection of the narrowly sexual patriarchal definition of lesbianism, the new concept at first simply added to the sexual: a woman-identified woman was a lesbian who lived primarily with and for women. But then the term was used in such a way that the sexual criterion dropped out entirely. Thus our reconceivings of women change.

Another new word invented by feminists is ''gynergy.'' Like ''woman-identified woman,'' it has become a regular part of the vocabulary of many feminists. (The women I know pronounce it with a soft ''g.'') Janice Raymond describes gynergy as ''the woman power/spirit/strength that is building up in 'woman-identified women' '' and as both individual and social: ''. . . it proceeds not only from an individual woman's realization of her own power of being but from a collective consciousness, i.e., a feminist collective consciousness.''[6]

Unlike the other concepts discussed here, gynergy is not an attribute of individual women; we do not speak of a "gynergetic woman." Gynergy is something we as individuals feel ourselves participating in. I can think of no patriarchal concept which works in the same way—that is, which expresses something personal (not merely an atmosphere) which is at the same time not an attribute of persons. It may happen, of course, that we will come to say things like "Sybil has great gynergy." Then the term "gynergy" would be rather like "spirit." But for now, it appears that gynergy is not only a new concept, but a new kind of concept. And it too is part of our redefinings of "woman."

These are just some of the ways in which we are reconceiving ourselves: taking on conventionally positive characteristics like strength, and changing them; redescribing and reevaluating aspects of ourselves like nurturance and lesbianism; and using words not conventionally used to describe women to express our becoming. These shifts all break internal definitional connections that exist in patriarchal systems between concepts of women and other concepts, particularly between concepts of women and of men. By breaking away from definitional connections that determine women's place in patriarchal conceptual systems and so in "the world," we move out of traditional dualistic/hierarchical orderings.

From a patriarchal perspective, all the concepts of women discussed here would be said to carry positive evaluative force, or to establish new ideals for women. But this account misrepresents the spirit in which these ideas are set forth. It is men who have invented the concepts of good and bad and for whom the making of value judgments is a major occupation. Feminists make vigorous value judgments about the patriarchy, but in our own worlds our concern tends to be more one of understanding and making space for processes than of evaluating persons and acts. Feminists are highly sensitive to the needs of women to create ourselves out of our own experiences, to our needs not to be told what we should do or be. The concepts of women I have discussed here then are not ideals or models, but gifts from some women to others, to be modified, transformed, abandoned, as each woman feels.

These conceivings of women are exercises of power: the power of naming ourselves, and the power in our new names. This is not different from "real" power. Although I have written here of words and concepts, the shifts I have sketched are also ontological; they are shifts from being women in patriarchy to becoming women in our own times and spaces. What patriarchy might see as logic, feminism understands as political strategy.

Notes

1. In *Our Right to Love: A Lesbian Resource Book,* edited by Ginny Vida (Englewood Cliffs, N.J.: Prentice-Hall, 1978).
2. "The Woman-Identified Woman" in *Radical Feminism,* edited by Ellen Levine and Anita Rapone (New York: Quadrangle/The New York Times Book Co., 1973), p. 240.
3. *Amazon Odyssey* (New York: Links Books, 1974), p. 132.
4. "The Spiritual Dimension: Death and Resurrection of a Hallelujah Dyke," in *Our Right to Love,* p. 187.
5. *"Together" Black Women* (New York: Emerson Hall Publishers, 1972).
6. "The Illusion of Androgyny" in *Quest: A Feminist Quarterly,* Vol. II, No. 1 (Summer 1975), pp. 64, 65.

Study Questions

1. What "dualism" does Trebilcot speak of, and how does it permeate our view of the world?
2. Why are feminists committed to eliminating dualism? What does this commit them to changing, and why?

3. What patterns of meaning change does Trebilcot discuss? Devise other examples besides the ones she gives.
4. What examples of term-formation (i.e., the creation—by feminists—of new words or phrases) does she discuss? Try to cite other examples.